# COMMENTARIES

ON

# THE FIRST BOOK OF MOSES

CALLED

# GENESIS

BY JOHN CALVIN

TRANSLATED FROM THE ORIGINAL LATIN, AND COMPARED
WITH THE FRENCH EDITION

BY THE REV. JOHN KING, M.A.,
OF QUEEN'S COLLEGE, CAMBRIDGE, INCUMBENT OF CHRIST'S CHURCH, HULL

VOLUME SECOND

WIPF & STOCK · Eugene, Oregon

Wipf and Stock Publishers
199 W 8th Ave, Suite 3
Eugene, OR 97401

Commentaries on the First Book of Moses Called Genesis,
Volume 2
Translated from the Original Latin, and Compared with the French Edition
By Calvin, John and King, John
Softcover ISBN-13: 979-8-3852-0978-1
Hardcover ISBN-13: 979-8-3852-0979-8
eBook ISBN-13: 979-8-3852-0980-4
Publication date 12/11/2023
Previously published by Baker Book House, 1847

This edition is a scanned facsimile of the original edition published in 1847.

# COMMENTARY

ON

# THE BOOK OF GENESIS.

## CHAPTER XXIV.

1. And Abraham was old, *and* well stricken in age: and the Lord had blessed Abraham in all things.

2. And Abraham said unto his eldest servant of his house, that ruled over all that he had, Put, I pray thee, thy hand under my thigh;

3. And I will make thee swear by the Lord, the God of heaven, and the God of the earth, that thou shalt not take a wife unto my son of the daughters of the Canaanites, among whom I dwell:

4. But thou shalt go unto my country, and to my kindred, and take a wife unto my son Isaac.

5. And the servant said unto him, Peradventure the woman will not be willing to follow me unto this land: must I needs bring thy son again unto the land from whence thou camest?

6. And Abraham said unto him, Beware thou that thou bring not my son thither again.

7. The Lord God of heaven, which took me from my father's house, and from the land of my kindred, and which spake unto me, and that sware unto me, saying, Unto thy seed will

1. Abraham autem senex venit in dies, et Iehova benedixerat Abraham in omnibus.

2. Et dixit Abraham ad servum suum seniorem domus suæ, qui præerat omnibus qui erant ei, Pone nunc manum tuam sub femore meo:

3. Et adjurabo te per Iehovam Deum cœli, et Deum terræ, quod non capies uxorem filio meo de filiabus Chenaanæi, in cujus medio ego habito:

4. Sed ad terram meam, et ad cognationem meam perges, et capies uxorem filio meo Ishac.

5. Et dixit ad eum servus, Si forsitan noluerit mulier venire post me ad terram hanc, numquid reducendo reducam filium tuum ad terram unde egressus es?

6. Et dixit ad eum Abraham Cave tibi ne forte reducas filium meum illuc.

7. Iehova Deus cœli, qui tulit me e domo patris mei, et e terra cognationis meæ, et qui loquutus est mihi, et qui juravit mihi, dicendo, Semini tuo dabo terram

I give this land; he shall send his angel before thee, and thou shalt take a wife unto my son from thence.

8. And if the woman will not be willing to follow thee, then thou shalt be clear from this my oath: only bring not my son thither again.

9. And the servant put his hand under the thigh of Abraham his master, and sware to him concerning that matter.

10. And the servant took ten camels, of the camels of his master, and departed; for all the goods of his master *were* in his hand; and he arose, and went to Mesopotamia, unto the city of Nahor.

11. And he made his camels to kneel down without the city by a well of water at the time of the evening, *even* at the time that women go out to draw *water*.

12. And he said, O Lord God of my master Abraham, I pray thee, send me good speed this day, and shew kindness unto my master Abraham.

13. Behold, I stand *here* by the well of water; and the daughters of the men of the city come out to draw water:

14. And let it come to pass, that the damsel to whom I shall say, Let down thy pitcher, I pray thee, that I may drink; and she shall say, Drink; and I will give thy camels drink also: *let the same be* she *that* thou hast appointed for thy servant Isaac; and thereby shall I know that thou hast shewed kindness unto my master.

15. And it came to pass, before he had done speaking, that, behold, Rebekah came out, who was born to Bethuel, son of Milcah, the wife of Nahor, Abraham's brother, with her pitcher upon her shoulder.

16. And the damsel *was* very fair to look upon, a virgin; neither had any man known her: and she went down to the well, and filled her pitcher, and came up.

17. And the servant ran to meet

hanc: ipse mittet Angelum suum ante te, et capies uxorem filio meo inde.

8. Quodsi noluerit mulier pergere post te, mundus eris ab adjuratione mea ista: duntaxat filium meum ne reducas illuc.

9. Et posuit servus manum suam sub femore Abraham domini sui, et juravit ei super re hac.

10. Et accepit servus decem camelos e camelis domini sui, et perrexit: quia omne bonum domini sui erat in manu ejus: et surrexit, et profectus est in Aram-naharaim, ad civitatem Nachor.

11. Et genu flectere fecit camelos extra civitatem ad puteum aquæ, tempore vespertino, tempore quo egrediuntur *mulieres*, quæ hauriunt.

12. Et dixit, Iehova Deus domini mei Abraham, occurrere fac nunc coram me hodie, et fac misericordiam cum domino meo Abraham.

13. Ecce, ego sto juxta fontem aquæ, et filiæ virorum civitatis egrediuntur ad hauriendam aquam.

14. Sit ergo, puella ad quam dixero, Inclina nunc hydriam tuam, et bibam: et dixerit, Bibe, et etiam camelis tuis potum dabo: ipsam præparaveris servo tuo Ishac: et per hoc sciam quod feceris misericordiam cum domino meo.

15. Et fuit, antequam ipse complevisset loqui, ecce, Ribca egrediebatur, quæ nata erat Bethuel filio Milchah uxoris Nachor fratris Abraham, et hydria ejus erat super humerum ejus.

16. Puella autem erat pulchra aspectu valde, virgo, et vir non cognoverat eam: quæ descendit ad fontem, et implevit hydriam suam, et ascendit.

17. Itaque cucurrit servus in oc-

her, and said, Let me, I pray thee, drink a little water of thy pitcher.

18. And she said, Drink, my lord: and she hasted, and let down her pitcher upon her hand, and gave him drink.

19. And when she had done giving him drink, she said, I will draw *water* for thy camels also, until they have done drinking.

20. And she hasted, and emptied her pitcher into the trough, and ran again into the well to draw *water*, and drew for all his camels.

21. And the man, wondering at her, held his peace, to wit whether the Lord had made his journey prosperous or not.

22. And it came to pass, as the camels had done drinking, that the man took a golden ear-ring of half a shekel weight, and two bracelets for her hands of ten *shekels* weight of gold,

23. And said, Whose daughter *art* thou? tell me, I pray thee. Is there room *in* thy father's house for us to lodge in?

24. And she said unto him, I *am* the daughter of Bethuel the son of Milcah, which she bare unto Nahor.

25. She said, moreover, unto him, We have both straw and provender enough, and room to lodge in.

26. And the man bowed down his head, and worshipped the Lord.

27. And he said, Blessed *be* the Lord God of my master Abraham, who hath not left destitute my master of his mercy and his truth: I *being* in the way, the Lord led me to the house of my master's brethren.

28. And the damsel ran, and told *them of* her mother's house these things.

29. And Rebekah had a brother, and his name *was* Laban: and Laban ran out unto the man unto the well.

30. And it came to pass, when he saw the ear-ring, and bracelets upon his sister's hands, and when he heard the words of Rebekah his sister, saying, Thus spake the man unto me,

cursum ejus, et dixit, Potum da mihi nunc parum aquæ ex hydria tua.

18. Et dixit, Bibe, domine mi: et festinavit, et demisit hydriam suam super manum suam, et potum dedit ei.

19. Ubi complevit potum dare ei: tunc dixit, Etiam camelis tuis hauriam, donec compleverint bibere.

20. Et festinavit, et effudit hydriam suam in canale, et cucurrit adhuc ad puteum ut hauriret: et hausit omnibus camelis ejus.

21. Porro vir stupebat super ea tacens, ut sciret utrum secundasset Iehova viam suam, an non.

22. Et fuit, quum complevissent cameli bibere, protulit vir inaurem auream, semissis pondus ejus: et duas armillas, et *posuit* super manus ejus: decem aurei pondus earum.

23. Et jam dixerat, Filia, cujus es? indica nunc mihi, numquid est in domo patris tui locus nobis ad pernoctandum?

24. Et dixerat ad eum, Filia Bethuel sum, filii Milchah, quem peperit ipsa Nachor.

25. Et dixit ad eum, Etiam palea, etiam pabulum multum est apud nos, etiam locus ad pernoctandum.

26. Et inclinavit se vir, et incurvavit se Iehovæ.

27. Et dixit, Benedictus Iehova Deus domini mei Abraham, qui non dereliquit misericordiam suam et veritatem suam a domino meo. Ego in via, duxit me Iehova ad domum fratrum domini mei.

28. Et cucurrit puella, et nuntiavit domui matris suæ secundum verba hæc.

29. Et ipsi Ribca erat frater, et nomen ejus Laban: et cucurrit Laban ad virum foras ad fontem.

30. Fuit autem, quum vidisset inaurem et armillas in manibus sororis suæ, et quum audisset ipse verba Ribca sororis suæ, dicendo, Sic loquutus est ad me vir: venit a

that he came unto the man; and, behold, he stood by the camels at the well.

31. And he said, Come in, thou blessed of the Lord; wherefore standest thou without? for I have prepared the house, and room for the camels.

32. And the man came into the house: and he ungirded his camels, and gave straw and provender for the camels, and water to wash his feet, and the men's feet that *were* with him.

33. And there was set *meat* before him to eat: but he said, I will not eat, until I have told mine errand. And he said, Speak on.

34. And he said, I *am* Abraham's servant.

35. And the Lord hath blessed my master greatly, and he is become great; and he hath given him flocks, and herds, and silver, and gold, and men-servants, and maid-servants, and camels, and asses.

36. And Sarah, my master's wife, bare a son to my master when she was old; and unto him hath he given all that he hath.

37. And my master made me swear, saying, Thou shalt not take a wife to my son of the daughters of the Canaanites, in whose land I dwell:

38. But thou shalt go unto my father's house, and to my kindred, and take a wife unto my son.

39. And I said unto my master, Peradventure the woman will not follow me.

40. And he said unto me, The Lord, before whom I walk, will send his angel with thee, and prosper thy way; and thou shalt take a wife for my son of my kindred, and of my father's house.

41. Then shalt thou be clear from *this* my oath, when thou comest to my kindred; and if they give not thee *one*, thou shalt be clear from my oath.

42. And I came this day unto the well, and said, O Lord God of my

31. Et dixit, Ingredere benedicte Iehovæ, ut quid manes foris? et ego paravi domum, et locum camelis.

32. Et venit vir ad domum, et solvit camelos, et dedit paleam et pabulum camelis, et aquam ad lavandum pedes ejus, et pedes virorum qui erant cum eo.

33. Et positum est coram eo, ut comederet: et dixit, Non comedam, donec loquutus fuero verba mea. Et dixit, Loquere.

34. Dixit igitur, Servus Abraham sum.

35. Iehova autem benedixit domino meo valde, et magnificatus est, et dedit ei pecudes et boves, et argentum, et aurum, et servos, et ancillas, et camelos, et asinos.

36. Et peperit Sarah uxor domini mei filium domino meo post senectutem suam, et dedit ei omnia quæ sunt ei.

37. Et jurare fecit me dominus meus, dicendo, Non capies uxorem filio meo de filiabus Chenaanæi, in cujus terra ego habito:

38. Sed ad domum patris mei perges, et ad familiam meam, et capies uxorem filio meo.

39. Et dixi domino meo, Forsitan non perget mulier post me.

40. Et dixit ad me, Iehova, in cujus conspectu ambulavi, mittet Angelum suum tecum, et secundabit viam tuam: et capies uxorem filio meo de familia mea, et de domo patris mei.

41. Tunc mundus eris ab adjuratione mea, si veneris ad familiam meam: et si non dederint tibi, eris mundus ab adjuratione mea.

42. Veni igitur hodie ad fontem, et dixi, Iehova Deus domini mei

master Abraham, if now thou do prosper my way which I go:

43. Behold, I stand by the well of water; and it shall come to pass, that when the virgin cometh forth to draw *water*, and I say to her, Give me, I pray thee, a little water of thy pitcher to drink;

44. And she say to me, Both drink thou, and I will also draw for thy camels: *let* the same *be* the woman whom the Lord hath appointed out for my master's son.

45. And before I had done speaking in mine heart, behold, Rebekah came forth with her pitcher on her shoulder; and she went down unto the well, and drew *water:* and I said unto her, Let me drink, I pray thee.

46. And she made haste, and let down her pitcher from her *shoulder*, and said, Drink; and I will give thy camels drink also: so I drank, and she made the camels drink also.

47. And I asked her, and said, Whose daughter *art* thou? And she said, The daughter of Bethuel, Nahor's son, whom Milcah bare unto him: and I put the ear-ring upon her face, and the bracelets upon her hands.

48. And I bowed down my head, and worshipped the Lord, and blessed the Lord God of my master Abraham, which had led me in the right way, to take my master's brother's daughter unto his son.

49. And now, if ye will deal kindly and truly with my master, tell me: and if not, tell me; that I may turn to the right hand, or to the left.

50. Then Laban and Bethuel answered and said, The thing proceedeth from the Lord: we cannot speak unto thee bad or good.

51. Behold, Rebekah *is* before thee, take *her*, and go, and let her be thy master's son's wife, as the Lord hath spoken.

52. And it came to pass, that, when Abraham's servant heard their words, he worshipped the Lord, *bowing himself* to the earth.

Abraham, si tu nunc secundas viam meam, per quam ego ambulo:

43. Ecce, ego sto juxta fontem aquæ: itaque sit, virgo quæ egredietur ad hauriendum, et dixero ei, Da mihi potum nunc parum aquæ ex hydria tua:

44. Et dixerit mihi, Etiam tu bibe, et etiam camelis tuis hauriam: ipsa *sit* uxor, quam præparavit Iehova filio domini mei.

45. Ego antequam complerem loqui in corde meo, ecce, Ribca egrediebatur, et hydria ejus erat super humerum ejus, et descendit ad fontem, et hausit: et dixi ad eam, Da mihi potum nunc.

46. Et festinavit, et demisit hydriam suam desuper se, et dixit, Bibe, et etiam camelis tuis potum dabo. Et bibi, et etiam camelis dedit potum.

47. Et interrogavi eam, et dixi, Filia cujus es? Et dixit, Filia Bethuel filii Nachor, quem peperit ei Milchah. Et posui inaurem super nares ejus, et armillas super manus ejus.

48. Et inclinavi me, incurvavique me Iehovæ, et benedixi Iehovæ Deo domini mei Abraham, qui duxit me per viam veritatis, (*vel certam fidem,*) ut acciperem filiam fratris domini mei filio ejus.

49. Et nunc si facitis misericordiam et veritatem cum domino meo, indicate mihi: et si non, indicate mihi, et vertam me ad dexteram vel ad sinistram.

50. Et responderunt Laban et Bethuel, et dixerunt, A Iehova egressa est res: non possumus loqui ad te malum vel bonum.

51. Ecce, Ribca coram te, accipe, et vade: et sit uxor filio domini tui, quemadmodum loquutus est Iehova.

52. Et fuit, quando audivit servus Abraham verba eorum, incurvavit se super terram Iehovæ.

53. And the servant brought forth jewels of silver, and jewels of gold, and raiment, and gave *them* to Rebekah: he gave also to her brother and to her mother precious things.

54. And they did eat and drink, he and the men that *were* with him, and tarried all night: and they rose up in the morning; and he said, Send me away unto my master.

55. And her brother and her mother said, Let the damsel abide with us *a few* days, at the least ten; after that she shall go.

56. And he said unto them, Hinder me not, seeing the Lord hath prospered my way; send me away, that I may go to my master.

57. And they said, We will call the damsel, and enquire at her mouth.

58. And they called Rebekah, and said unto her, Wilt thou go with this man? And she said, I will go.

59. And they sent away Rebekah their sister, and her nurse, and Abraham's servant, and his men.

60. And they blessed Rebekah, and said unto her, Thou *art* our sister, be thou *the mother* of thousands of millions, and let thy seed possess the gate of those which hate them.

61. And Rebekah arose, and her damsels, and they rode upon the camels, and followed the man; and the servant took Rebekah, and went his way.

62. And Isaac came from the way of the well Lahai-roi: for he dwelt in the south country.

63. And Isaac went out to meditate in the field at the even-tide; and he lifted up his eyes, and saw, and, behold, the camels *were* coming.

64. And Rebekah lifted up her eyes; and when she saw Isaac, she lighted off the camel.

65. For she *had* said unto the servant, What man *is* this that walketh in the field to meet us? And the servant *had* said, It *is* my master: therefore she took a vail, and covered herself.

66. And the servant told Isaac all things that he had done.

53. Et protulit servus vasa argentea, et vasa aurea, et vestes, et dedit ipsi Ribcæ, et pretiosa dedit fratri ejus, et matri ejus.

54. Et comederunt, et biberunt, ipse et viri qui erant cum eo, et pernoctaverunt: et surrexerunt mane: et dixit, Dimitte me, *ut vadam* ad dominum meum.

55. Et dixit frater ejus et mater ejus, Maneat puella nobiscum per dies, vel decem: postea ibis, (*vel ibit.*)

56. Et dixit ad eos, Ne retardetis me, quando Iehova secundavit viam meam: dimittite me, et ibo ad dominum meum.

57. Et dixerunt, Vocemus puellam, et interrogemus os ejus.

58. Et vocaverunt Ribcam, et dixerunt ad eam, Numquid ibis cum viro isto? Et dixit, Ibo.

59. Et dimiserunt Ribcam sororem suam, et nutricem ejus, et servum Abraham, et viros ejus.

60. Et benedixerunt Ribcæ, et dixerunt ei, Soror nostra es, sis in millia decem millium, et hæreditet semen tuum portam odio habentium illud.

61. Et surrexit Ribca et puellæ ejus, et ascenderunt super camelos, et perrexerunt post virum: et tulit servus Ribcah, et abiit.

62. Ishac autem veniebat, qua venitur a Puteo viventis videntis me: et ipse habitabat in terra Meridiana.

63. Et egressus erat Ishac ad orandum in agro, dum declinaret vespera: et elevavit oculos suos, et vidit, et ecce, cameli veniebant.

64. Tunc elevavit Ribcah oculos suos, et vidit Ishac, et projecit se de camelo.

65. Iam autem dixerat ad servum, Quis est vir iste, qui ambulat per agrum in occursum nostrum? Et dixit servus, Ipse est dominus meus: et accepit velum, et operuit se.

66. Et narravit servus ipsi Ishac omnia quæ fecerat.

| | |
|---|---|
| 67. And Isaac brought her into his mother Sarah's tent, and took Rebekah, and she became his wife; and he loved her: and Isaac was comforted after his mother's *death*. | 67. Et introduxit eam Ishac in tabernaculum Sarah matris suæ, et accepit Ribcah, fuitque ei in uxorem, et dilexit eam: et consolatus est se Ishac post matrem suam. |

1. *And Abraham was old.*[1] Moses passes onward to the relation of Isaac's marriage, because indeed Abraham, perceiving himself to be worn down by old age, would take care that his son should not marry a wife in the land of Canaan. In this place Moses expressly describes Abraham as an old man, in order that we may learn that he had been admonished, by his very age, to seek a wife for his son: for old age itself, which, at the most, is not far distant from death, ought to induce us so to order the affairs of our family, that when we die, peace may be preserved among our posterity, the fear of the Lord may flourish, and rightly-constituted order may prevail. The old age of Abraham was indeed yet green, as we shall see hereafter; but when he reckoned up his own years he deemed it time to consult for the welfare of his son. Irreligious men, partly because they do not hold marriage sufficiently in honour, partly because they do not consider the importance attached especially to the marriage of Isaac, wonder that Moses, or rather the Spirit of God, should be employed in affairs so minute; but if we have that reverence which is due in reading the Sacred Scriptures, we shall easily understand that here is nothing superfluous: for inasmuch as men can scarcely persuade themselves that the Providence of God extends to marriages, so much the more does Moses insist on this point. He chiefly, however, wishes to teach that God honoured the family of Abraham with especial regard, because the Church was to spring from it. But it will be better to treat of everything in its proper order.

2. *And Abraham said unto his eldest servant.* Abraham here fulfils the common duty of parents, in labouring for and being solicitous about the choice of a wife for his son: but he looks somewhat further; for since God had separated

---

[1] Abraham was a hundred years old when Isaac was born, (xxi. 5,) and Isaac was forty years old when he was married, (xxv. 20.) This makes Abraham's age a hundred and forty years.—*Ed.*

him from the Canaanites by a sacred covenant, he justly fears lest Isaac, by joining himself in affinity with them, should shake off the yoke of God. Some suppose that the depraved morals of those nations were so displeasing to him, that he conceived the marriage of his son must prove unhappy if he should take a wife from among them. But the special reason was, as I have stated, that he would not allow his own race to be mingled with that of the Canaanites, whom he knew to be already divinely appointed to destruction; yea, since upon their overthrow he was to be put into possession of the land, he was commanded to treat them with distrust as perpetual enemies. And although he had dwelt in tranquillity among them for a time, yet he could not have a community of offspring with them without confounding things which, by the command of God, were to be kept distinct. Hence he wished both himself and his family to maintain this separation entire.

*Put, I pray thee, thy hand.* It is sufficiently obvious that this was a solemn form of swearing; but whether Abraham had first introduced it, or whether he had received it from his fathers, is unknown. The greater part of Jewish writers declare that Abraham was the author of it; because, in their opinion, this ceremony is of the same force as if his servant had sworn by the sanctity of the divine covenant, since circumcision was in that part of his person. But Christian writers conceive that the hand was placed under the thigh in honour of the blessed seed.[1] Yet it may be that these earliest fathers had something different in view; and there are those among the Jews who assert that it was a token of subjection, when the servant was sworn on the thigh of his master. The more plausible opinion is, that the ancients in this manner swore by Christ; but because I do not willingly follow uncertain conjectures, I leave the question undecided. Nevertheless the latter supposition appears to me the more simple; namely, that servants, when they swore fidelity to

---

[1] *Under my thigh.* "A sign which Jacob also required of his son Joseph, (Gen. xlvii. 29,) either to signify subjection, or for a further mystery of the covenant of circumcision, or rather of Christ the promised seed, who was to come out of Abraham's loins or thigh."—*Ainsworth.*

their lords, were accustomed to testify their subjection by this ceremony, especially since they say that this practice is still observed in certain parts of the East. That it was no profane rite, which would detract anything from the glory of God, we infer from the fact that the name of God is interposed. It is true that the servant placed his hand under the thigh of Abraham, but he is adjured by God, the Creator of heaven and earth; and this is the sacred method of adjuration, whereby God is invoked as the witness and the judge; for this honour cannot be transferred to another without casting a reproach upon God. Moreover, we are taught, by the example of Abraham, that they do not sin who demand an oath for a lawful cause; for this is not recited among the faults of Abraham, but is recorded to his peculiar praise. It has already been shown that the affair was of the utmost importance, since it was undertaken in order that the covenant of God might be ratified among his posterity. He was therefore impelled, by just reasons, most anxiously to provide for the accomplishment of his object, by taking an oath of his servant: and beyond doubt, the disposition, and even the virtue of Isaac, were so conspicuous, that in addition to his riches, he had such endowments of mind and person, that many would earnestly desire affinity with him. His father, therefore, fears lest, after his own death, the inhabitants of the land should captivate Isaac by their allurements. Now, though Isaac has hitherto steadfastly resisted those allurements, the snares of which few young men escape, Abraham still fears lest, by shame and the dread of giving offence, he may be overcome. The holy man wished to anticipate these and similar dangers, when he bound his servant to fidelity, by interposing an oath; and it may be that some secret necessity also impelled him to take this course.

3. *That thou shalt not take a wife.* The kind of discipline which prevailed in Abraham's house is here apparent. Although this man was but a servant, yet, because he was put in authority by the master of the family, his servile condition did not prevent him from being next in authority to his lord; so that Isaac himself, the heir and successor of Abraham, submitted to his direction. To such an extent

did the authority of Abraham and reverence for him prevail, that when he substituted a servant in his place, he caused this servant, by his mere will or word, to exercise a power which other masters of families find it difficult to retain for themselves. The modesty also of Isaac, who suffered himself to be governed by a servant, is obvious; for it would have been in vain for Abraham to enter into engagements with his servant, had he not been persuaded that his son would prove submissive and tractable. It here appears what great veneration he cherished towards his father; because Abraham, relying on Isaac's obedience, confidently calls his servant to him. Now this example should be taken by us as a common rule, to show that it is not lawful for the children of a family to contract marriage, except with the consent of parents; and certainly natural equity dictates that, in a matter of such importance, children should depend upon the will of their parents. How detestable, therefore, is the barbarity of the Pope, who has dared to burst this sacred bond asunder! Wherefore the wantonness of youths is to be restrained, that they may not rashly contract nuptials without consulting their fathers.

4. *But thou shalt go unto my country and to my kindred.* It seems that, in the choice of the place, Abraham was influenced by the thought, that a wife would more willingly come from thence to be married to his son, when she knew that she was to marry one of her own race and country. But because it afterwards follows that the servant came to Padan Aram, some hence infer that Mesopotamia was Abraham's country. The solution, however, of this difficulty is easy. We know that Mesopotamia was not only the region contained between the Tigris and the Euphrates, but that a part also of Chaldea was comprehended in it; for Babylon is often placed there by profane writers. The Hebrew name simply means, "Syria of the rivers." They give the name "Aram" to that part of Syria which, beginning near Judea, embraces Armenia and other extensive regions, and reaches almost to the Euxine Sea. But when they especially designate those lands which are washed or traversed by the Tigris and Euphrates, they add the name "Padan:"

for we know that Moses did not speak scientifically, but in a popular style. Since, however, he afterwards relates that Laban, the son of Nahor, dwelt at Charran, (chap. xxix. 4,) it seems to me probable that Nahor, who had remained in Chaldea, because it would be troublesome to leave his native soil, in process of time changed his mind; either because filial piety constrained him to attend to his decrepit and declining father, or because he had learned that he might have there a home as commodious as in his own country. It certainly appears from the eleventh chapter that he had not migrated at the same time with his father.[1]

5. *And the servant said unto him.* Since he raises no objection respecting Isaac, we may conjecture that he was so fully persuaded of his integrity as to have no doubt of his acquiescence in his father's will. We must also admire the religious scrupulosity of the man, seeing he does not rashly take an oath. What pertained to the faithful and diligent discharge of his own duty he might lawfully promise, under the sanction of an oath; but since the completion of the affair depended on the will of others, he properly and wisely adduces this exception, " Peradventure the woman will not be willing to follow me."

6. *Beware that thou bring not my son thither again.* If the woman should not be found willing, Abraham, commending the event to God, firmly adheres to the principal point, that his son Isaac should not return to his country, because in this manner he would have deprived himself of the promised inheritance. He therefore chooses rather to live by hope, as a stranger, in the land of Canaan, than to rest among his relatives in his native soil: and thus we see that, in perplexed and confused affairs, the mind of the holy man was not drawn aside from the command of God by any agitating cares; and we are taught, by his example, to follow God through every obstacle. However, he afterwards declares that he looks for better things. By such words he confirms the confidence of his servant, so that he, anticipating with greater alacrity a prosperous issue, might prepare for the journey.

[1] See Gen. xi. 31.

7. *The Lord God of heaven.* By a twofold argument Abraham infers, that what he is deliberating respecting the marriage of his son will, by the grace of God, have a prosperous issue. First, because God had not led him forth in vain from his own country into a foreign land; and secondly, because God had not falsely promised to give the land, in which he was dwelling as a stranger, to his seed. He might also with propriety be confident that his design should succeed, because he had undertaken it only by the authority, and, as it were, under the auspices of God; for it was his exclusive regard for God which turned away his mind from the daughters of Canaan. He may, however, be thought to have inferred without reason that God would give his son a wife from that country and kindred to which he himself had bidden farewell. But whereas he had left his relatives only at the divine command, he hopes that God will incline their minds to be propitious and favourable to him. Meanwhile he concludes, from the past kindnesses of God, that his hand would not fail him in the present business; as if he would say, " I, who at the command of God left my country, and have experienced his continued help in my pilgrimage, do not doubt that he will also be the guide of thy journey, because it is in reliance on his promise that I lay upon thee this injunction." He then describes the mode in which assistance would be granted; namely, that God would send his angel, for he knew that God helps his servants by the ministration of angels, of which he had already received many proofs. By calling God " the God of heaven," he celebrates that divine power which was the ground of his confidence.

10. *And the servant took ten camels.* He takes the camels with him, to prove that Abraham is a man of great wealth, in order that he may the more easily obtain what he desires. For even an open-hearted girl would not easily suffer herself to be drawn away to a distant region, unless on the proposed condition of being supplied with the conveniences of life. Exile itself is sad enough, without poverty as its attendant. Therefore, that the maid might not be deterred by the apprehension of want, but rather invited by the prospect of affluence, he ladens ten camels with presents, to give suffi-

cient proof to the inhabitants of Chaldea of the domestic opulence of Abraham. What follows, namely, " that all the substance of Abraham was in the hand of his servant," some of the Hebrews improperly explain as meaning that the servant took with him an account of all Abraham's wealth, described and attested in written documents. It is rather the assigning of the reason of the fact, which might appear improbable, that the servant assumed so much power to himself. Therefore Moses, having said that a man who was but a servant set out on a journey with such a sumptuous and splendid equipage, immediately adds, that he did this of his own accord, because he had all the substance of Abraham in his hand. In saying that he came to the city of Nahor, he neither mentions the name of the city nor the part of Chaldea, or of any other region, where he dwelt, but only says, in general terms, that he came to "Syria of the rivers," concerning which term I have said something above.

12. *O Lord God of my master Abraham.* The servant, being destitute of counsel, betakes himself to prayers. Yet he does not simply ask counsel of the Lord ; but he also prays that the maid appointed to be the wife of Isaac should be brought to him with a certain sign, from which he might gather that she was divinely presented to him. It is an evidence of his piety and faith, that in a matter of such perplexity he is not bewildered, as one astonished ; but breaks forth into prayer with a collected mind. But the method which he uses[1] seems scarcely consistent with the true rule of prayer. For, first, we know that no one prays aright unless he subjects his own wishes to God. Wherefore there is nothing more unsuitable than to prescribe anything, at our own will, to God. Where, then, it

[1] " Divinatio quâ utitur." The word *divinatio* seems to be too strong for the occasion. The servant certainly sought a sign from heaven; and may seem improperly to have prescribed to God in what way his prayer should be answered. He might, however, be acting under a divine impulse, and the context would lead to such an inference. But if it was a weakness in this good man to be thus minute in his stipulations, it was one which God neither reproved nor condemned ; and therefore it seems harsh to give it the name of *divination*. Calvin's object, however, is, in thus strongly stating the case, to meet it as an objection, by a conclusive answer. A method which, the reader will have observed, he frequently adopts.—*Ed.*

may be asked, is the religion of the servant, who, according to his own pleasure, imposes a law upon God? Secondly, there ought to be nothing ambiguous in our prayers; and absolute certainty is to be sought for only in the Word of God. Now, since the servant prescribes to God what answer shall be given, he appears culpably to depart from the suitable modesty of prayer; for although no promise had been given him, he nevertheless desires to be made fully certain respecting the whole affair. God, however,[1] in hearkening to his wish, proves, by the event, that it was acceptable to himself. Therefore we must know, that although a special promise had not been made at the moment, yet the servant was not praying rashly, nor according to the lust of the flesh, but by the secret impulse of the Spirit. Moreover, the general law, by which all the pious are bound, does not prevent the Lord, when he determines to give something extraordinary, from directing the minds of his servants towards it; not that he would lead them away from his word, but only that he makes some peculiar concession to them in their mode of praying. The sum of the prayer before us is this: "O Lord, if a damsel shall present herself who, being asked to give me drink, shall also kindly and courteously offer it to my camels, I will seek after her as a wife for my master Isaac, just as if she were delivered into my hand by thee." He seems, indeed, to be laying hold on some dubious conjecture; but since he reposes on the Providence of God, he is certainly persuaded that this token shall be to him equivalent to an oracle; because God, who is the guardian of his enterprise, will not suffer him to err. Meanwhile this is worthy of remark, that he does not fetch the sign of recognition from afar, but takes it from something present; for she who shall be thus humane to an unknown guest, will, by that very act, give proof of an excellent disposition. This observation may be of use to prevent inquisitive men from adducing this example as a precedent for vain prognostications. In the words themselves the following particulars are to be noticed: first, that he addresses himself to the God of his master Abraham; not as being himself a stranger

---

[1] Calvin's answer to the objection above stated begins here.—*Ed.*

to the worship of God, but because the affair in question depends upon the promise given to Abraham. And truly he had no confidence in prayer, from any other source than from the covenant into which God had entered with the house of Abraham. The expression "cause to meet me this day,"[1] Jerome renders, "meet me, I pray, this day." But the verb is transitive, and the servant of Abraham intimates by the use of it, that the affairs of men were so ordered by the counsel and the hand of God, that the issue of them was not fortuitous; as if he would say, "O Lord, in vain shall I look on this side and on that; in vain shall I catch at success by my own labour, industry and various contrivances, unless thou direct the work." And when he immediately afterwards subjoins, "show kindness to my master," he implies that in this undertaking he rests upon nothing but the grace which God had promised to Abraham.

15. *Before he had done speaking.* The sequel sufficiently demonstrates that his wish had not been foolishly conceived. For the quickness of the answer manifests the extraordinary indulgence of God, who does not suffer the man to be long harassed with anxiety. Rebekah had, indeed, left her house before he began to pray; but it must be maintained that the Lord, at whose disposal are both the moments of time and the ways of men, had so ordered it on both sides as to give clear manifestation of his Providence. For sometimes he keeps us the longer in suspense, till, wearied with praying, we may seem to have lost our labour; but in this affair, in order that his blessing might not seem doubtful, he suddenly interposed. The same thing also happened to Daniel, unto whom the angel appeared, before the conclusion of his prayer. (Dan. ix. 21.) Now, although it frequently happens

[1] "Et dixit Iehova Deus domini mei Abraham, occurrere fac nunc coram me hodie, et fac misericordiam cum domino meo Abraham." Dathe seems to have taken the same view of the passage with Calvin. "O Iova Deus domini mei Abrahami, fac pro tuo erga dominum meum Abrahamum amore, ut mihi jam *quam quæro*, occurrat." "O Lord God of my master Abraham, cause, according to thy love towards my master Abraham, that she whom I seek may meet me." The English version is simply, "I pray thee, send me good speed this day." But probably the more specific meaning attached by Calvin and Dathe to the passage is the true one. Calvin properly objects against the translation of the Vulgate as being *intransitive*, whereas הקרה (*hakreh*) is transitive.—*Ed.*

that, on account of our sloth, the Lord delays to grant our requests, it is, at such times, expedient for us, that what we ask should be delayed. In the meantime, he has openly and conspicuously proved, by unquestionable examples, that although the event may not immediately respond to our wishes, the prayers of his people are never in vain : yea, his own declaration, that before they cry he is mindful of their wants, is invariably fulfilled. (Is. lxv. 24.)

21. *And the man, wondering at her, held his peace.* This wondering of Abraham's servant, shows that he had some doubt in his mind. He is silently inquiring within himself, whether God would render his journey prosperous. Has he, then, no confidence concerning that divine direction, of which he had received the sign or pledge? I answer, that faith is never so absolutely perfect in the saints as to prevent the occurrence of many doubts. There is, therefore, no absurdity in supposing that the servant of Abraham, though committing himself generally to the providence of God, yet wavers, and is agitated, amidst a multiplicity of conflicting thoughts. Again, faith, although it pacifies and calms the minds of the pious, so that they patiently wait for God, still does not exonerate them from all care ; because it is necessary that patience itself should be exercised, by anxious expectation, until the Lord fulfil what he has promised. But though this hesitation of Abraham's servant was not free from fault, inasmuch as it flowed from infirmity of faith ; it is yet, on this account, excusable, because he did not turn his eyes in another direction, but only sought from the event a confirmation of his faith, that he might perceive God to be present with him.

22. *The man took a golden ear-ring.* His adorning the damsel with precious ornaments is a token of his confidence. For since it is evident by many proofs that he was an honest and careful servant, he would not throw away without discretion the treasures of his master. He knows, therefore, that these gifts will not be ill-bestowed; or, at least, relying on the goodness of God, he gives them, in faith, as an earnest of future marriage. But it may be asked, Whether God approves ornaments of this kind, which pertain not so

much to neatness as to pomp? I answer, that the things related in Scripture are not always proper to be imitated. Whatever the Lord commands in general terms is to be accounted as an inflexible rule of conduct; but to rely on particular examples is not only dangerous, but even foolish and absurd. Now we know how highly displeasing to God is not only pomp and ambition in adorning the body, but all kind of luxury. In order to free the heart from inward cupidity, he condemns that immoderate and superfluous splendour, which contains within itself many allurements to vice. Where, indeed, is pure sincerity of heart found under splendid ornaments? Certainly all acknowledge this virtue to be rare. It is not, however, for us expressly to forbid every kind of ornament; yet because whatever exceeds the frugal use of such things is tarnished with some degree of vanity; and more especially, because the cupidity of women is, on this point, insatiable; not only must moderation, but even abstinence, be cultivated as far as possible. Further, ambition silently creeps in, so that the somewhat excessive adorning of the person soon breaks out into disorder. With respect to the ear-rings and bracelets of Rebekah, as I do not doubt that they were those in use among the rich, so the uprightness of the age allowed them to be sparingly and frugally used; and yet I do not excuse the fault. This example, however, neither helps us, nor alleviates our guilt, if, by such means, we excite and continually inflame those depraved lusts which, even when all incentives are removed, it is excessively difficult to restrain. The women who desire to shine in gold, seek in Rebekah a pretext for their corruption. Why, therefore, do they not, in like manner, conform to the same austere kind of life and rustic labour to which she applied herself? But, as I have just said, they are deceived who imagine that the examples of the saints can sanction them in opposition to the common law of God. Should any one object that it is abhorrent to the modesty of a virtuous and chaste maiden to receive ear-rings and bracelets from a man who was a stranger, and whom she had never before seen. In the first place, it may be, that Moses passes over much conversation held on both sides, by which it is probable she was induced to venture on the reception of them. It may also be, that he relates first what was last in order. For it follows soon afterwards in the context, that the servant of Abraham inquired whose daughter she was. We must also take into account the simplicity of that age. Whence does it arise that it was not disreputable for a maid to go alone out of the city, unless that then the morals of mankind did not require so severe a guard for the preservation of modesty? Indeed, it appears from the context, that the ornaments were not given her for a dishonourable purpose;[1] but a portion is offered to the parents to facilitate the contract for marriage. Interpreters are not agreed respecting the value of the presents. Moses estimates the ear-rings at half a shekel, and the bracelets at ten shekels. Jerome, instead of half a shekel, reads two shekels. I conceive the genuine sense to be, that the bracelets were worth ten shekels, and the frontal ornament or ear-rings worth half that sum, or five shekels. For since nothing is added after the word בקע, (bekah,) it has reference to the greater number.[2] Otherwise there is no suitable proportion between the bracelets and the ornaments for the head. Moreover, if we take the shekel for four Attic drachms, the value is trifling; therefore I think the weight of gold is indicated, which makes the sum much greater than the piece of money called a shekel.

26. *And the man bowed down his head.* When the servant of Abraham hears that he had alighted upon the daughter of Bethuel, he is more and more elated with hope. Yet he

---

[1] "Non turpis lenocinii causâ datum esse."

[2] Some suppose that by the ear-rings is meant an ornament for the face or forehead, as appears in the margin of our version, and as Calvin here seems to intimate. But the increased knowledge of Eastern customs which recent times have furnished, has given weight to the opinion of older commentators, that a nose-jewel is here intended. This ornament was not suspended from the central cartilaginous substance of the nose, but from one side, which was bored for the purpose. Calvin's interpretation, that the weight of this ornament was the half of ten shekels, instead of half a shekel, cannot be admitted. Though, according to its weight, it might not be worth more than ten or twelve shillings; yet its workmanship might be costly; and if it contained some precious stone, which is not improbable, it might be of very great value. There can be no doubt that the presents generally were exceedingly valuable.—*Ed.*

does not exult, as profane men are wont to do, as if the occurrence were fortuitous; but he gives thanks to God, regarding it, as the result of Providence, that he had been thus opportunely led straight to the place he had wished. He does not, therefore, boast of his good fortune; but he declares that God had dealt kindly and faithfully with Abraham; or, in other words, that, for his own mercy's sake, God had been faithful in fulfilling his promises. It is true that the same form of speech is applied to the persons present; just as it follows soon after in the same chapter, (ver. 49,) "*If ye will deal kindly and truly with my master, tell me.*" The language is, however, peculiarly suitable to the character of God, both because he gratuitously confers favours upon men, and is specially inclined to beneficence: and also, by never frustrating their hope, he proves himself to be faithful and true. This thanksgiving, therefore, teaches us always to have the providence of God before our eyes, in order that we may ascribe to him whatever happens prosperously to us.

28. *And the damsel ran and told them of her mother's house.* It is possible, that the mother of Rebekah occupied a separate house; not that she had a family divided from that of her husband, but for the purpose of keeping her daughters and maidens under her own custody. The expression may, however, be more simply explained to mean, that she came directly to her mother's chamber; because she could more easily relate the matter to her than to her father. It is also probable, that when Bethuel was informed of the fact, by the relation of his wife, their son Laban was sent by both of them to introduce the stranger. Other explanations are needless.

33. *I will not eat until I have told my errand.*[1] Moses begins to show by what means the parents of Rebekah were

---

[1] It was the custom of the ancients on occasions of this kind first to take their meal together, and when the wants of nature had been supplied, and the spirit had been exhilarated, to open the subject of communication; but Abraham's servant purposely reverses this order, to show his earnestness in attending to his master's business; and perhaps also his confidence of success, in consequence of the favourable indications which God had given in answer to his prayers. See *Dathe* and *Le Clerc.—Ed.*

induced to give her in marriage to their nephew. That the
servant, when food was set before him, should refuse to eat
till he had completed his work is a proof of his diligence and
fidelity; and it may with propriety be regarded as one of
the benefits which God had vouchsafed to Abraham, that he
should have a servant so faithful, and so intent upon his
duty. Since, however, this was the reward of the holy discipline which Abraham maintained, we cannot wonder that
very few such servants are to be found, seeing that everywhere they are so ill-governed.

Moreover, although the servant seems to weave a superfluous story, yet there is nothing in it which is not available
to his immediate purpose. He knew that it was a feeling
naturally inherent in parents, not willingly to send away their
children to a distance. He therefore first commemorates Abraham's riches, that they might not hesitate to connect their
daughter with a husband so wealthy. He secondly explains
that Isaac was born of his mother in her old age; not merely
for the purpose of informing them that he had been miraculously given to his father, whence they might infer that he
had been divinely appointed to this greatness and eminence;
but that an additional commendation might be given on
account of Isaac's age. In the third place, he affirms that
Isaac would be the sole heir of his father. Fourthly, he relates that he had been bound by an oath to seek a wife for
his master Isaac, from among his own kindred; which
special choice on the part of Abraham was very effectual in
moving them to compliance. Fifthly, he states that Abraham, in full confidence that God would be the leader of his
journey, had committed the whole business to him. Sixthly,
he declares, that whatever he had asked in prayer he had
obtained from the Lord; whence it appeared that the marriage of which he was about to treat was according to the
will of God. We now see the design of his narration: First,
to persuade the parents of Rebekah that he had not been
sent for the purpose of deceiving them, that he had not in anything acted craftily, or by oblique methods, but in the fear
of the Lord, as the religious obligation of marriage requires.
Secondly, that he was desiring nothing which would not be

profitable and honourable for them. And lastly, that God had been the director of the whole affair.

Moreover, since the servant of Abraham, though persuaded that the angel of God would be the guide of his journey, yet neither directs his prayers nor his thanksgivings to him, we may hence learn that angels are not, in such a sense, constituted the ministers of God to us, as that they should be invoked by us, or should transfer to themselves the worship due to God; a superstition which prevails nearly over the whole world to such a degree, that men turn aside a portion of their faith from the only fountain of all good to the rivulets which flow from it. The clause, *the Lord, before whom I walk,* (ver. 40,) which some refer to the probity and good conscience of Abraham, I rather explain as applying to the faith, by which he set God before him, as the governor of his life, being confident that he was the object of God's care, and dependent upon his grace.

*If ye will deal kindly.*[1] I have lately related the force of this expression; namely, to act with humanity and good faith. He thus modestly and suppliantly asks them to consent to the marriage of Isaac and Rebekah: should he meet with a repulse from them, he says, he will go either to the right hand or to the left; that is, he will look around elsewhere. For he places the right hand and the left in contrast with the straight way in which he had been led to them. It is, however, with fertile ingenuity that some of the Hebrews explain the words as meaning, that he would go to Lot, or to Ishmael.

50. *The thing proceedeth from the Lord.* Whereas they are convinced by the discourse of the man, that God was the Author of this marriage, they avow that it would be unlawful for them to offer anything in the way of contradiction. They declare that the thing proceedeth from the Lord; because he had, by the clearest signs, made his will manifest. Hence we perceive, that although the true religion was in part observed among them, and in part infected with vicious errors, yet the fear of God was never so utterly extinguished, but this axiom remained firmly fixed in all their minds, that God must be obeyed. If, then, wretched idola-

[1] " Si facitis misericordiam."

ters, who had almost fallen away from religion, nevertheless so subjected themselves to God, as to acknowledge it to be unlawful for them to swerve from his will, how much more prompt ought our obedience to be? Therefore, as soon as the will of God is made known to us, not only let our tongues be silent, but let all our senses be still; because it is an audacious profanation to admit any thought which is opposed to that will.

52. *He worshipped.* Moses again repeats that Abraham's servant gave thanks to God; and it is not without reason that he so often inculcates this religious duty; because, since God requires nothing greater from us, the neglect of it betrays the most shameful indolence. The acknowledgment of God's kindness is a sacrifice of sweet-smelling savour; yea, it is a more acceptable service than all sacrifices. God is continually heaping innumerable benefits upon men. Their ingratitude, therefore, is intolerable, if they fail to exercise themselves in celebrating those benefits.

54. *And they rose up in the morning.* On this point Moses insists the more particularly; partly, for the purpose of commending the faithful industry of the servant in fulfilling his master's commands; partly, for that of teaching, that his mind was inflamed by the Spirit of God, for he is so ardent as to allow no truce to others, and no relaxation to himself. Thus, although he conducted himself as became an honest and prudent servant, it is still not to be doubted that the Lord impelled him, for Isaac's sake, to act as he did. So the Lord watches over his own people while they sleep, expedites and accomplishes their affairs in their absence, and influences the dispositions of all, so far as is expedient, to render them assistance. It is by a forced interpretation, that some would explain the ten days, during which Laban and his mother desire the departure of Rebekah to be deferred, as meaning years or months. For it was merely the tender wish of the mother, who could ill bear that her daughter should thus suddenly be torn away from her bosom.

57. *We will call the damsel.* Bethuel, who had before unreservedly given his daughter in marriage, now seems to adhere, with but little constancy, to his purpose. When, how-

ever, he had previously offered his daughter, without making any exception, he is to be understood as having done it, only so far as he was able. But now, Moses declares that he did not exercise tyranny over his daughter, so as to thrust her out reluctantly, or to compel her to marry against her will, but left her to her own free choice. Truly, in this matter, the authority of parents ought to be sacred : but a middle course is to be pursued, so that the parties concerned may make their contract spontaneously, and with mutual consent. It is not right to understand that Rebekah in answering so explicitly, showed contempt for the paternal roof, or too anxiously desired a husband ;[1] but since she saw that the affair was transacted by the authority of her father, and with the consent of her mother, she also herself acquiesced in it.

59. *And they sent away Rebekah.* Moses first relates, that Rebekah was honourably dismissed ; because her nurse was given unto her. Moreover, I doubt not that they had domestic nurses, who were their handmaidens ; not that mothers entirely neglected that duty, but that they committed the care of education to one particular maid. They therefore who assisted mothers with subsidiary service were called nurses. Moses afterwards adds, that Rebekah's relatives " blessed her," (verse 60,) by which expression he means, that they prayed that her condition might be a happy one. We know that it was a solemn custom, in all ages, and among all people, to accompany marriages with all good wishes. And although posterity has greatly degenerated from the pure and genuine method of celebrating marriages used by the fathers; yet it is God's will that some public testimony should stand forth, by which men may be admonished, that no nuptials are lawful, except those which are rightly consecrated. Now, the particular form of benediction which is here related, was probably in common use, because nature dictates that the propagation of offspring is the special end of marriage. Under the notion of victory (ver. 60) is comprehended a prosperous state of life. The Lord, however, directed their tongues to utter a prophecy of which they themselves were ignorant. " To possess the gates of ene-

[1] " Vel procax juvencula maritum nimis cupide appeteret."

mies," means to obtain dominion over them ; because judgment was administered in the gates, and the bulwarks of the city were placed there.

63. *And Isaac went out.* It appears that Isaac dwelt apart from his father; either because the family was too large, or because such was the custom. And perhaps Abraham had already married another wife ; so that, for the sake of avoiding contentions, it would seem more convenient for him to have a house of his own. Thus great wealth has its attendant troubles. Doubtless, of all earthly blessings granted by God, none would have been sweeter to Abraham than that of living with his son. However, I by no means think that he was deprived of his society and assistance. For such was the piety of Isaac, that he undoubtedly studied to discharge every duty towards his father: this alone was wanting, that they did not live in the same house. Moses also relates how it happened that Isaac met with his wife before she reached his home. For he says, that Isaac went out in the evening to *meditate* or to *pray*. For the Hebrew word שוח (*soach*) may mean either. It is probable that he did this according to his custom, and that he sought a place of retirement for prayer, in order that his mind, being released from all avocations, might be the more at liberty to serve God. Whether, however, he was giving his mind to meditation or to prayer, the Lord granted him a token of his own presence in that joyful meeting.

64. *And Rebekah lifted up her eyes.* We may easily conjecture that Isaac, when he saw the camels, turned his steps towards them, from the desire of seeing his bride ; this gave occasion to the inquiry of Rebekah. Having received the answer, she immediately, for the sake of doing honour to her husband, dismounted her camel to salute him. For that she fell, struck with fear, as some suppose, in no way agrees with the narrative. She had performed too long a journey, under the protection of many attendants, to be so greatly afraid at the sight of one man. But these interpreters are deceived, because they do not perceive, that in the words of Moses, the reason is afterwards given to this effect, that when Rebekah saw Isaac, she alighted from her camel ;

because she had inquired of the servant who he was, and had been told that he was the son of his master Abraham. It would not have entered into her mind to make such inquiry respecting any person whom she might accidentally meet: but seeing she had been informed that Abraham's house was not far distant, she supposes him at least to be one of the domestics. Moses also says that she took a veil: which was a token of shame and modesty. For hence also, the Latin word which signifies "to marry,"[1] is derived, because it was the custom to give brides veiled to their husbands. That the same rite was also observed by the fathers, I have no doubt.[2] So much the more shameful, and the less capable of excuse, is the licentiousness of our own age; in which the apparel of brides seems to be purposely contrived for the subversion of all modesty.

67. *And Isaac brought her into his mother Sarah's tent.* He first brought her into the tent, then took her as his wife. By the very arrangement of his words, Moses distinguishes between the legitimate mode of marriage and barbarism. And certainly the sanctity of marriage demands that man and woman should not live together like cattle; but that, having pledged their mutual faith, and invoked the name of God, they might dwell with each other. Besides, it is to be observed, that Isaac was not compelled, by the tyrannical command of his father, to marry; but after he had given his mind to her he took her freely, and cordially gave her the assurance of conjugal fidelity.

*And Isaac was comforted after his mother's death.* Since his grief for the death of his mother was now first assuaged, we infer how great had been its vehemence; for a period sufficiently long had already elapsed.[3] We may also hence infer, that the affection of Isaac was tender and gentle: and that his love to his mother was of no common kind, seeing

[1] "Verbum nubendi." The original meaning of the word *nubere* is to *veil*, or *cover*.

[2] "Isaac was walking, and it would therefore have been the highest breach of Oriental good manners, to have remained on the camel when presented to him. No doubt they all alighted and walked to meet him, conducting Rebekah as a bride to meet the bridegroom."—*Bush.*—*Ed.*

[3] The time from the death of Sarah to Isaac's marriage was three years. —*Ed.*

he had so long lamented her death. And the knowledge of this fact is useful to prevent us from imagining that the holy patriarchs were men of savage manners and of iron hardness of heart, and from becoming like those who conceive fortitude to consist in brutality. Only care must be taken that grief should be duly mitigated; lest it burst forth in impious murmurings, or subvert the hope of a future resurrection. I do not however entirely excuse the sorrow of Isaac; I only advise, that what belongs to humanity, ought not to be altogether condemned. And although it was culpable not to be able to efface grief from the mind, until the opposite joy of marriage prevailed over it; Moses still reckons it among the benefits conferred by God, that he applies a remedy of any kind to his servant.

## CHAPTER XXV.

1. Then again Abraham took a wife, and her name *was* Keturah.
2. And she bare him Zimran, and Jokshan, and Medan, and Midian, and Ishbak, and Shuah.
3. And Jokshan begat Sheba and Dedan. And the sons of Dedan were Asshurim, and Letushim, and Leummim.
4. And the sons of Midian; Ephah, and Epher, and Hanoch, and Abidah, and Eldaah. All these *were* the children of Keturah.
5. And Abraham gave all that he had unto Isaac.
6. But unto the sons of the concubines, which Abraham had, Abraham gave gifts, and sent them away from Isaac his son, (while he yet lived,) eastward, unto the east country.
7. And these *are* the days of the years of Abraham's life which he lived, an hundred threescore and fifteen years.
8. Then Abraham gave up the ghost, and died in a good old age, an old man, and full *of years;* and was gathered to his people.
9. And his sons Isaac and Ishmael

1. Et addidit Abraham, et accepit uxorem, cujus nomen erat Cetura.
2. Et peperit ei Zimram, et Iocsan, et Medan, et Midian, et Isbah, et Suah.
3. Et Iocsan genuit Seba, et Dedan. Filii autem Dedan fuerunt Assurim, et Letusim, et Leummin.
4. Filii vero Midian, Hephah, et Hepher, et Hanoch, et Abidah, et Eldaah: omnes isti, filii Ceturæ.
5. Porro dedit Abraham omnia, quæ sua erant, ipsi Ishac.
6. Et filiis concubinarum quas habebat Abraham, dedit Abraham dona; et emisit eos ab Ishac filio suo, quum adhuc viveret, ad Orientem, ad terram Orientalem.
7. Porro isti sunt dies annorum vitæ Abraham quos vixit, centum anni et septuaginta anni et quinque anni.
8. Et obiit, et mortuus est Abraham in senectute bona, senex et satur: et congregatus est ad populos suos.
9. Et sepelierunt eum Ishac et

buried him in the cave of Machpelah, in the field of Ephron the son of Zohar the Hittite, which *is* before Mamre;

10. The field which Abraham purchased of the sons of Heth: there was Abraham buried, and Sarah his wife.

11. And it came to pass after the death of Abraham, that God blessed his son Isaac: and Isaac dwelt by the well Lahai-roi.

12. Now these *are* the generations of Ishmael, Abraham's son, whom Hagar the Egyptian, Sarah's handmaid, bare unto Abraham.

13. And these *are* the names of the sons of Ishmael, by their names, according to their generations: The first-born of Ishmael, Nebajoth; and Kedar, and Adbeel, and Mibsam,

14. And Mishma, and Dumah, and Maasa,

15. Hadar, and Tema, Jetur, Naphish, and Kedemah.

16. These *are* the sons of Ishmael, and these *are* their names, by their towns, and by their castles; twelve princes according to their nations.

17. And these *are* the years of the life of Ishmael, an hundred and thirty and seven years: and he gave up the ghost, and died, and was gathered unto his people.

18. And they dwelt from Havilah unto Shur, that *is* before Egypt, as thou goest toward Assyria: *and* he died in the presence of all his brethren.

19. And these *are* the generations of Isaac, Abraham's son: Abraham begat Isaac.

20. And Isaac was forty years old when he took Rebekah to wife, the daughter of Bethuel the Syrian of Padan-aram, the sister to Laban the Syrian.

21. And Isaac entreated the Lord for his wife, because she *was* barren: and the Lord was entreated of him, and Rebekah his wife conceived.

22. And the children struggled together within her: and she said, If *it be* so, why *am* I thus? And she went to enquire of the Lord.

10. Ismael filii ejus in spelunca duplici, in agro Ephron filii Sohar Hittæi, quæ est ante Mamre,

10. In agro quem emit Abraham a filiis Heth: ibi sepultus est Abraham et Sarah uxor ejus.

11. Et fuit, postquam mortuus est Abraham, benedixit Deus Ishac filio ejus; et habitavit Ishac apud Puteum viventis videntis me.

12. Istæ autem generationes Ismael filii Abraham, quem peperit Hagar Ægyptia ancilla Sarah ipsi Abraham.

13. Et hæc nomina filiorum Ismael per nomina sua, per generationes suas: primogenitus Ismael, Nebajoth, et Cedar, et Abdeel, et Mibsam,

14. Et Mismah, et Dumah, et Masa,

15. Hadar, et Thema, Jetur, Naphis, et Cedmah.

16. Isti sunt filii Ismael, et ista nomina eorum per villas suas, et per castella sua, duodecim principes per familias suas.

17. Et isti sunt anni vitæ Ismael, centum anni, et triginta anni, et septem anni: et obiit, et mortuus est, et congregatus est ad populos suos.

18. Et habitaverunt ab Havilah usque ad Sur, quæ est ante Ægyptum, dum pergis in Assur: coram omnibus fratribus suis habitavit.

19. Istæ vero sunt generationes Ishac filii Abraham: Abraham genuit Ishac.

20. Et erat Ishac quadragenarius, quando accepit Ribcam filiam Bethuel Aramæi de Padan Aram, sororem Laban Aramæi, sibi in uxorem.

21. Et oravit Ishac Iehovam respectu uxoris suæ, quia sterilis erat: et exoratus est ab ipso Iehova, et concepit Ribca uxor ejus.

22. Et collidebant se filii in utero ejus, et dixit, Si ita, ut quid ego? et ivit ad interrogandum Iehovam.

23. And the Lord said unto her, Two nations *are* in thy womb, and two manner of people shall be separated from thy bowels; and *the one* people shall be stronger than *the other* people; and the elder shall serve the younger.

24. And when her days to be delivered were fulfilled, behold, *there were* twins in her womb.

25. And the first came out red, all over like an hairy garment; and they called his name Esau.

26. And after that came his brother out, and his hand took hold on Esau's heel; and his name was called Jacob: and Isaac *was* threescore years old when she bare them.

27. And the boys grew: and Esau was a cunning hunter, a man of the field; and Jacob *was* a plain man, dwelling in tents.

28. And Isaac loved Esau, because he did eat of *his* venison; but Rebekah loved Jacob.

29. And Jacob sod pottage: and Esau came from the field, and he *was* faint.

30. And Esau said to Jacob, Feed me, I pray thee, with that same red *pottage*; for I *am* faint: therefore was his name called Edom.

31. And Jacob said, Sell me this day thy birthright.

32. And Esau said, Behold, I *am* at the point to die; and what profit shall this birthright do to me?

33. And Jacob said, Swear to me this day; and he sware unto him: and he sold his birthright unto Jacob.

34. Then Jacob gave Esau bread and pottage of lentiles: and he did eat and drink, and rose up, and went his way. Thus Esau despised *his* birthright.

23. Tunc dixit Iehova ad eam, Duæ gentes sunt in utero tuo, et duo populi a visceribus tuis separabunt se: et populus populo robustior erit, et major serviet minori.

24. Et impleti sunt dies ejus ut pareret, et ecce gemini *erant* in utero ejus.

25. Egressus est autem prior rufus, totus ipse sicut pallium pilosum: et vocaverunt nomen ejus Esau.

26. Et postea egressus est frater ejus, et manus ejus tenebat calcaneum Esau, et vocarunt nomen Iahacob. Ishac autem erat sexagenarius, quando peperit eos.

27. Et creverunt pueri: et fuit Esau vir peritus venationis, vir agricola: sed Iahacob erat vir integer, manens in tabernaculis.

28. Et dilexit Ishac Esau, quia venatio *erat* in ore ejus, et Ribca diligebat Iahacob.

29. Coxit autem Iahacob coctionem: et venit Esau ex agro, et erat lassus.

30. Et dixit Esau ad Iahacob, Fac me comedere nunc de rufo, rufo isto: quia lassus sum: idcirco vocarunt nomen ejus Edom.

31. Tunc dixit Iahacob, Vende hoc tempore primogenituram tuam mihi.

32. Et dixit Esau, Ecce ego vado ut moriar, et utquid mihi primogenitura?

33. Dixit itaque Iahacob, Iura mihi hoc tempore. Et juravit ei: et vendidit primogenituram suam ipsi Iahacob.

34. Et Iahacob dedit Esau panem et coctionem lenticularum, et comedit, atque bibit: et surrexit, et abiit, contempsitque Esau primogenituram.

1. *Then again Abraham took a wife.*[1] It seems very ab-

[1] "Et addidit Abraham et accepit uxorem." The Geneva version of our own Bible has it: "Now Abraham had taken him another wife called Keturah;" and adds in the margin, "while Sarah was yet alive," which agrees, as will appear in what follows, with the opinion of Calvin, expressed in this Commentary.—*Ed.*

surd that Abraham, who is said to have been dead in his own body thirty-eight years before the decease of Sarah, should, after her death, marry another wife. Such an act was, certainly, unworthy of his gravity. Besides, when Paul commends his faith, (Rom. iv. 19,) he not only asserts that the womb of Sarah was dead, when Isaac was about to be born, but also that the body of the father himself was dead. Therefore Abraham acted most foolishly, if, after the loss of his wife, he, in the decrepitude of old age, contracted another marriage. Further, it is at variance with the language of Paul, that he, who in his hundredth year was cold and impotent,[1] should, forty years afterwards, have many sons. Many commentators, to avoid this absurdity, suppose Keturah to have been the same person as Hagar. But their conjecture is immediately refuted in the context; where Moses says, Abraham gave gifts to the sons of his concubines. The same point is clearly established from 1 Chron. i. 32. Others conjecture that, while Sarah was yet living, he took another wife. This, although worthy of grave censure, is however not altogether incredible. We know it to be not uncommon for men to be rendered bold by excessive license. Thus Abraham having once transgressed the law of marriage, perhaps, after the dispute respecting Hagar, did not desist from the practice of polygamy. It is also probable that his mind had been wounded, by the divorce which Sarah had compelled him to make with Hagar. Such conduct indeed was disgraceful, or, at least, unbecoming in the holy patriarch. Nevertheless no other, of all the conjectures which have been made, seems to me more probable. If it be admitted, the narrative belongs to another place; but Moses is frequently accustomed to place those things which have precedence in time, in a different order. And though this reason should not be deemed conclusive, yet the fact itself shows an inverted order in the history.[2] Sarah had passed

[1] " Frigidus, et ad generandum impotens."

[2] " Atque ut hæc ratio non urgeat, res tamen ipsa ostendit esse in hac historia, ὕστερον πρότερον." " Et encore que ceste raison ne presse point, toutefois le faict monstre, qu'en ceste histoire il y a des choses mises devant derriere."—*French Tr.* The old English translator has it: " And though this reason serve not; yet nevertheless the matter itself declareth, that

her ninetieth year, when she brought forth her son Isaac; she died in the hundred and twenty-seventh year of her age; and Isaac married when he was forty years old. Therefore, nearly four years intervened between the death of his mother and his nuptials. If Abraham took a wife after this, what was he thinking of, seeing that he had been during so many years accustomed to a single life? It is therefore lawful to conjecture that Moses, in writing the life of Abraham, when he approached the closing scene, inserted what he had before omitted. The difficulty, however, is not yet solved. For whence proceeded Abraham's renovated vigour,[1] since Paul testifies that his body had long ago been withered by age? Augustine supposes not only that strength was imparted to him for a short space of time, which might suffice for Isaac's birth; but that by a divine restoration, it flourished again during the remaining term of his life. Which opinion, both because it amplifies the glory of the miracle, and for other reasons, I willingly embrace.[2] And what I have before said, namely, that Isaac was miraculously born, as being a spiritual seed, is not opposed to this view; for it was especially on his account that the failing body of Abraham was restored to vigour. That others were afterwards born was, so to speak, adventitious. Thus the blessing of

there is in this history a *Hysteron proteron*, that is, a setting of the cart before the horse."—*Ed.*

[1] " Unde enim novus illi ad muliebrem concubitum vigor."

[2] On the question, whether Abraham married Keturah during Sarah's life, or not till after her death, authorities are much divided. Whichever side is taken the difficulties are great, yet perhaps on neither side insuperable. So far as merely human probabilities are concerned, the evidence would turn in favour of Calvin's hypothesis, which is supported by Dr. A. Clarke and Professor Bush; the arguments of the latter writer, which seem to be mainly drawn from Calvin, are very forcibly put. On the other hand, great consideration is due to the authority of such men as Patrick, Le Clerc, Kidder, and Scott, who would preserve the present order of the sacred narrative; and would account for the events related on the ground of a miraculous renewal and continuance of strength, which Calvin himself allows to have taken place. It is in favour of this latter mode of interpretation, that it certainly better accords with the general character of Abraham, and is more consistent with the testimony which the Scriptures bear to his faith, than the other hypothesis; besides which the order of the narrative remains undisturbed. See this question treated at length in *Exercitationes Andreæ Riveti in Genesin*, p. 548. Lugd. 1633.—*Ed.*

God pronounced in the words, "Increase and multiply," which was annexed expressly to marriage, is also extended to unlawful connexions. Certainly, if Abraham married a wife while Sarah was yet alive, (as I think most probable,) his adulterous connexion was unworthy of the divine benediction. But although we know not why this addition was made to the just measure of favour granted to Abraham, yet the wonderful providence of God appears in this, that while many nations of considerable importance descended from his other sons, the spiritual covenant, of which the rest also bore the sign in their flesh, remained in the exclusive possession of Isaac.

6. *But unto the sons of the concubines.* Moses relates, that when Abraham was about to die, he formed the design of removing all cause of strife among his sons after his death, by constituting Isaac his sole heir, and dismissing the rest with suitable gifts. This dismissal was, indeed, apparently harsh and cruel; but it was agreeable to the appointment and decree of God, in order that the entire possession of the land might remain for the posterity of Isaac. For it was not lawful for Abraham to divide, at his own pleasure, that inheritance which had been granted entire to Isaac. Wherefore, no course was left to him but to provide for the rest of his sons in the manner here described. If any person should now select one of his sons as his heir, to the exclusion of the others, he would do them an injury; and, by applying the torch of injustice, in disinheriting a part of his children, he would light up the flame of pernicious strifes in his family. Wherefore, we must note the special reason by which Abraham was not only induced, but compelled, to deprive his sons of the inheritance, and to remove them to a distance; namely, lest by their intervention, the grant which had been divinely made to Isaac should, of necessity, be disturbed. We have elsewhere said that, among the Hebrews, she who is a partaker of the bed, but not of all the goods, is styled a concubine. The same distinction has been adopted into the customs, and sanctioned by the laws of all nations. So, we shall afterwards see, that Leah and Rachel were principal wives, but that Bilhah and Zil-

pah were in the second rank; so that their condition remained servile, although they were admitted to the conjugal bed. Since Abraham had made Hagar and Keturah his wives on this condition, it seems that he might lawfully bestow on their sons, only a small portion of his goods; to have transferred, however, from his only heir to them, equal portions of his property, would have been neither just nor right. It is probable that no subsequent strife or contention took place respecting the succession; but by sending the sons of the concubines far away, he provides against the danger of which I have spoken, lest they should occupy a part of the land which God had assigned to the posterity of Isaac alone.

7. *And these are the days.* Moses now brings us down to the death of Abraham; and the first thing to be noticed concerning his age is the number of years during which he lived as a pilgrim; for he deserves the praise of wonderful and incomparable patience, for having wandered through the space of a hundred years, while God led him about in various directions, contented, both in life and death, with the bare promise of God. Let those be ashamed who find it difficult to bear the disquietude of one, or of a few years, since Abraham, the father of the faithful, was not merely a stranger during a hundred years, but was also often cast forth into exile. Meanwhile, however, Moses expressly shows that the Lord had fulfilled his promise, "Thou shalt die in a good old age:" for although he fought a hard and severe battle, yet his consolation was neither light nor small; because he knew that, amidst so many sufferings, his life was the object of Divine care. But if this sole looking unto God sustained him through his whole life, amidst the most boisterous waves, amidst many bitter griefs, amidst tormenting cares, and in short an accumulated mass of evils; let us also learn—that we may not become weary in our course—to rely on this support, that the Lord has promised us a happy issue of life, and one truly far more glorious than that of our father Abraham.

8. *Then Abraham gave up the ghost.*[1] They are mistaken

[1] "Et obiit Abraham." And Abraham died. The expression "gave up the ghost" is not a literal rendering of the original.—*Ed.*

who suppose that this expression denotes sudden death, as intimating that he had not been worn out by long disease, but expired without pain. Moses rather means to say that the father of the faithful was not exempt from the common lot of men, in order that our minds may not languish when the outward man is perishing ; but that, by meditating on that renovation which is laid up as the object of our hope, we may, with tranquil minds, suffer this frail tabernacle to be dissolved. There is therefore no reason why a feeble, emaciated body, failing eyes, tremulous hands, and the lost use of all our members, should so dishearten us, that we should not hasten, after the example of our father, with joy and alacrity to our death. But although Abraham had this in common with the human race, that he grew old and died; yet Moses, shortly afterwards, puts a difference between him and the promiscuous multitude of men as to manner of dying; namely, that he should " die in a good old age, and satisfied with life." Unbelievers, indeed, often seem to participate in the same blessing; yea, David complains that they excelled in this kind of privilege; and a similar complaint occurs in the book of Job, namely, that they fill up their time happily, till in a moment they descend into the grave.[1] But what I said before must be remembered, that the chief part of a good old age consists in a good conscience and in a serene and tranquil mind. Whence it follows, that what God promises to Abraham, can only apply to those who truly cultivate righteousness: for Plato says, with equal truth and wisdom, that a good hope is the nutriment of old age ; and therefore old men who have a guilty conscience are miserably tormented, and are inwardly racked as by a perpetual torture. But to this we must add, what Plato knew not, that it is godliness which causes a good old age to attend us even to the grave, because faith is the preserver of a tranquil mind. To the same point belongs what is immediately added, " he was full of days," so that he did not desire a prolongation of life. We see how many are in bondage to the desire of life; yea, nearly the whole

---

[1] See Psalm lxxiii. 4. " There are no bands in their death; but their strength is firm ;" and Job xxi. 13, " They spend their days in wealth, and in a moment go down to the grave."—*Ed.*

world languishes between a weariness of the present life and an inexplicable desire for its continuance. That satiety of life, therefore, which shall cause us to be ready to leave it, is a singular favour from God.

*And was gathered to his people.* I gladly embrace the opinion of those who believe the state of our future life to be pointed out in this form of expression; provided we do not restrict it, as these expositors do, to the faithful only; but understand by it that mankind are associated together in *death* as well as in life.[1] It may seem absurd to profane men, for David to say, that the reprobate are gathered together like sheep into the grave; but if we examine the expression more closely, this gathering together will have no existence if their souls are annihilated.[2] The mention of Abraham's burial will presently follow. Now he is said to be gathered to his fathers, which would be inconsistent with fact if human life vanished, and men were reduced to annihilation: wherefore the Scripture, in speaking thus, shows that another state of life remains after death, so that a departure out of the world is not the destruction of the whole man.

9. *And his sons Isaac and Ishmael buried him.* Hence it appears, that although Ishmael had long ago been dismissed, he was not utterly alienated from his father, because he performed the office of a son in celebrating the obsequies of his deceased parent. Ishmael, rather than the other sons, did this, as being nearer.

12. *Now these are the generations of Ishmael.* This narration is not superfluous. In the commencement of the chapter, Moses alludes to what was done for the sons of Keturah. Here he speaks designedly more at large, for the purpose of showing that the promise of God, given in the seventeenth chapter, was confirmed by its manifest accom-

---

[1] Rivetus speaks in similar language on this clause. "This is never said concerning beasts when they die; and, therefore, from this form of speech, it is to be observed, that men by death are not reduced to nothing, nor does the whole of man die. . . . . The Scripture, in speaking thus, points out some other state; so that departure out of the world is not the destruction of the whole man."—*Exercitatio* cxiii. p. 553.

[2] See Psalm xlix.

plishment. In the first place, it was no common gift of God that Ishmael should have twelve sons who should possess rank and authority over as many tribes; but inasmuch as the event corresponded with the promise, we must chiefly consider the veracity of God, as well as the singular benevolence and honour which he manifested towards his servant Abraham, when, even in those benefits which were merely adventitious, he dealt so kindly and liberally with him; for that may rightly be regarded as adventitious which was superadded to the spiritual covenant: therefore Moses, after he has enumerated the towns in which the posterity of Ishmael was distributed, buries that whole race in oblivion, that substantial perpetuity may remain only in the Church, according to the declaration in Psalm cxxii. 28, "The sons of sons shall inhabit."[1] Further, Moses, as with his finger, shows the wonderful counsel of God, because, in assigning a region distinct from the land of Canaan to the sons of Ishmael, he has both provided for them in future, and kept the inheritance vacant for the sons of Isaac.

18. *He died in the presence of all his brethren.*[2] The major part of commentators understand this of his *death;* as if Moses had said that the life of Ishmael was shorter than that of his brethren, who long survived him: but because the word נפל (*naphal*) is applied to a *violent* death, and Moses testifies that Ishmael died a *natural* death, this exposition cannot be approved. The Chaldean Paraphrast supposes the word "*lot*" to be understood, and elicits this sense, that the *lot fell* to him, so as to assign him a habitation not far from his brethren. Although I do not greatly differ in this matter, I yet think that the words are not to be thus distorted.[3] The word נפל sometimes signifies to

---

[1] "Filii filiorum habitabunt." In the English it is, "The children of thy servants shall continue."—*Ed.*

[2] "Coram omnibus fratribus suis habitavit." He *dwelt* in the presence of all his brethren.

[3] This is the interpretation of Vatablus, favoured by Professor Bush, who says, "As Ishmael's death has already been mentioned, and as the term 'fall' is seldom used in the Scriptures in reference to 'dying,' except in cases of sudden and violent death, as when one 'falls' in battle, the probability is, that it here signifies that his territory or possessions 'fell' to him in the presence of his brethren, or immediately contiguous to their borders."—*Bush.*

lie down, or to rest, and also to dwell. The simple assertion therefore of Moses is, that a habitation was given to Ishmael opposite his brethren, so that he should indeed be a neighbour to them, and yet should have his distinct boundaries:[1] for I do not doubt that he referred to the oracle contained in the sixteenth chapter, where, among other things, the angel said to his mother Hagar, " He shall remain, or pitch his tents *in the presence of his brethren."* Why does he rather speak thus of Ishmael than of the others, except for this reason, that whereas they migrated towards the eastern region, Ishmael, although the head of a nation, separated from the sons of Abraham, yet retained his dwelling in their neighbourhood? Meanwhile the intention of God is also to be observed, namely, that Ishmael, though living near his brethren, was yet placed apart in an abode of his own, that he might not become mingled with them, but might dwell in their presence, or opposite to them. Moreover, it is sufficiently obvious that the prediction is not to be restricted *personally* to Ishmael.

19. *These are the generations of Isaac.* Because what Moses has said concerning the Ishmaelites was incidental, he now returns to the principal subject of the history, for the purpose of describing the progress of the Church. And in the first place, he repeats that Isaac's wife was taken from Mesopotamia. He expressly calls her the sister of Laban the Syrian, who was hereafter to become the father-in-law of Jacob, and concerning whom he had many things to relate. But it is chiefly worthy of observation that he declares Rebekah to have been barren during the early years of her marriage. And we shall afterwards see that her barrenness continued, not for three or four, but for twenty years, in order that her very despair of offspring might give greater lustre to the sudden granting of the blessing. But nothing seems less accordant with reason, than that the propagation of the Church should be thus small and slow. Abraham, in his extreme old age, received (as it seems) a

---

[1] Calvin's interpretation, though opposed to the Vulgate and to our own version, is supported by the Septuagint, the Targum Onkelos, the Syriac, and the Arabic versions. See *Walton's Polyglott.—Ed.*

slender solace for his long privation of offspring, in having all his hope centred in one individual. Isaac also, already advanced in years, and bordering on old age, was not yet a father. Where, then, was the seed which should equal the stars of heaven in number? Who would not suppose that God was dealing deceitfully in leaving those houses empty and solitary, which, according to his own word, ought to be replenished with teeming population? But that which is recorded in the psalm must be accomplished in reference to the Church, that " he maketh her who had been barren to keep house, and to be a joyful mother of many children." (Psalm cxiii. 9.) For this small and contemptible origin, these slow and feeble advances, render more illustrious that increase, which afterwards follows, beyond all hope and expectation, to teach us that the Church was produced and increased by divine power and grace, and not by merely natural means. It is indeed possible, that God designed to correct or moderate any excess of attachment in Isaac. But this is to be observed as the chief reason for God's conduct, that as the holy seed was given from heaven, it must not be produced according to the common order of nature, to the end, that we learn that the Church did not originate in the industry of man, but flowed from the grace of God alone.

21. *And Isaac entreated the Lord for his wife.* Some translate the passage, " Isaac entreated the Lord *in the presence* of his wife ;" and understand this to have been done, that she also might add her prayers, and they might jointly supplicate God. But the version here given is more simple. Moreover, this resort to prayer testifies that Isaac knew that he was deprived of children, because God had not blessed him. He also knew that fruitfulness was a special gift of God. For although the favour of obtaining offspring was widely diffused over the whole human race, when God uttered the words " increase and multiply ;" yet to show that men are not born fortuitously, he distributes this power of production in various degrees. Isaac, therefore, acknowledges, that the blessing, which was not at man's disposal, must be sought for by prayer from God. It now truly appears, that he was endued with no ordinary constancy of

faith. Forasmuch as the covenant of God was known to him, he earnestly (if ever any did) desired seed. It, therefore, had not now, for the first time, entered into his mind to pray, seeing that for more than twenty years he had been disappointed of his hope. Hence, although Moses, only in a single word, says that he had obtained offspring by his prayers to God; yet reason dictates that these prayers had continued through many years. The patience of the holy man is herein conspicuous, that while he seems in vain to pour forth his wishes into the air, he still does not remit the ardour of his devotion. And as Isaac teaches us, by his example, to persevere in prayer; so God also shows that he never turns a deaf ear to the wishes of his faithful people, although he may long defer the answer.

22. *And the children struggled together.* Here a new temptation suddenly arises, namely, that the infants struggle together in their mother's womb. This conflict occasions the mother such grief that she wishes for death. And no wonder; for she thinks that it would be a hundred times better for her to die, than that she have within her the horrible prodigy of twin-brothers, shut up in her womb, carrying on intestine war. They, therefore, are mistaken, who attribute this complaint to female impatience, since it was not so much extorted by pain or torture, as by abhorrence of the prodigy. For she doubtless perceived that this conflict did not arise from natural causes, but was a prodigy portending some dreadful and tragic end. She also necessarily felt some fear of the divine anger stealing over her: as it is usual with the faithful not to confine their thoughts to the evil immediately present with them, but to trace it to its cause; and hence they tremble through the apprehension of divine judgment. But though in the beginning she was more grievously disturbed than she ought to have been, and, breaking out into murmurings, preserved neither moderation nor temper; yet she soon afterwards receives a remedy and solace to her grief. We are thus taught by her example to take care that we do not give excessive indulgence to sorrow in affairs of perplexity, nor inflame our minds by inwardly cherishing secret causes of distress. It is, indeed, difficult

to restrain the first emotions of our minds; but before they become ungovernable, we must bridle them, and bring them into subjection. And chiefly we must pray to the Lord for moderation; as Moses hére relates that Rebekah went to ask counsel from the Lord; because, indeed, she perceived that nothing would be more effectual in tranquillizing her mind, than to aim at obedience to the will of God, under the conviction that she was directed by him. For although the response given might be adverse, or, at least, not such as she would desire, she yet hoped for some alleviation from a gracious God, with which she might be satisfied. A question here arises respecting the way in which Rebekah asked counsel of God. It is the commonly received opinion that she inquired of some prophet what was the nature of this prodigy: and Moses seems to intimate that she had gone to some place to hear the oracle. But since that conjecture has no probability, I rather incline to a different interpretation; namely, that she, having sought retirement, prayed more earnestly that she might receive a revelation from heaven. For, at that time, what prophets, except her husband and her father-in-law, could she have found in the world, still less in that neighbourhood? Moreover, I perceive that God then commonly made known his will by oracles. Once more, if we consider the magnitude of the affair, it was more fitting that the secret should be revealed by the mouth of God, than manifested by the testimony of man. In our times a different method prevails. For God does not, at this day, reveal things future by such miracles; and the teaching of the Law, the Prophets, and the Gospel, which comprises the perfection of wisdom, is abundantly sufficient for the regulation of our course of life.

23. *Two nations.* In the first place, God answers that the contention between the twin-brothers had reference to something far beyond their own persons; for in this way he shows that there would be discord between their posterities. When he says, " there are two nations," the expression is emphatical; for since they were brothers and twins, and therefore of one blood, the mother did not suppose that they would be so far disjoined as to become the heads of distinct

nations; yet God declares that dissension should take place between those who were by nature joined together. Secondly, he describes their different conditions, namely, that victory would belong to one of these nations, forasmuch as this was the cause of the contest, that they could not be equal, but one was chosen and the other rejected. For since the reprobate give way reluctantly, it follows of necessity that the children of God have to undergo many troubles and contests on account of their adoption. Thirdly, the Lord affirms that the order of nature being inverted, the younger, who was inferior, should be the victor.

We must now see what this victory implies. They who restrict it to earthly riches and wealth coldly trifle. Undoubtedly by this oracle Isaac and Rebekah were taught that the covenant of salvation would not be common to the two people, but would be reserved only for the posterity of Jacob. In the beginning, the promise was apparently general, as comprehending the whole seed: now, it is restricted to one part of the seed. This is the reason of the conflict, that God divides the seed of Jacob (of which the condition appeared to be one and the same) in such a manner that he adopts one part and rejects the other: that one part obtains the name and privilege of the Church, the rest are reckoned strangers; with one part resides the blessing of which the other is deprived; as it afterwards actually occurred: for we know that the Idumæans were cut off from the body of the Church; but the covenant of grace was deposited in the family of Jacob. If we seek the cause of this distinction, it will not be found in nature; for the origin of both nations was the same. It will not be found in merit; because the heads of both nations were yet enclosed in their mother's womb when the contention began. Moreover God, in order to humble the pride of the flesh, determined to take away from men all occasion of confidence and of boasting. He might have brought forth Jacob first from the womb; but he made the other the first-born, who, at length, was to become the inferior. Why does he thus, designedly, invert the order appointed by himself, except to teach us that, without regard to dignity, Jacob, who was to be the heir of the promised benediction, was gratuitously elected? The sum of the whole, then, is, that the preference which God gave to Jacob over his brother Esau, by making him the father of the Church, was not granted as a reward for his merits, neither was obtained by his own industry, but proceeded from the mere grace of God himself. But when an entire people is the subject of discourse, reference is made not to the secret election, which is confirmed to few, but the common adoption, which spreads as widely as the external preaching of the word. Since this subject, thus briefly stated, may be somewhat obscure, the readers may recall to memory what I have said above in expounding the seventeenth chapter, namely, that God embraced, by the grace of his adoption, all the sons of Abraham, because he made a covenant with all; and that it was not in vain that he appointed the promise of salvation to be offered promiscuously to all, and to be attested by the sign of circumcision in their flesh; but that there was a special chosen seed from the whole people, and these should at length be accounted the legitimate sons of Abraham, who by the secret counsel of God are ordained unto salvation. Faith, indeed, is that which distinguishes the spiritual from the carnal seed; but the question now under consideration is the *principle* on which the distinction is made, not the symbol or mark by which it is attested. God, therefore, chose the whole seed of Jacob without exception, as the Scripture in many places testifies; because he has conferred on all alike the same testimonies of his grace, namely, in the word and sacraments. But another and peculiar election has always flourished, which comprehended a certain definite number of men, in order that, in the common destruction, God might save those whom he would.

A question is here suggested for our consideration. Whereas Moses here treats of the former kind of election,[1] Paul turns his words to the latter.[2] For while he attempts to prove, that not all who are Jews by natural descent are heirs of life; and not all who are descended from Jacob

---

[1] Namely, that which is general or national.—*Ed.*
[2] Namely, that which is particular or individual.—*Ed.*

according to the flesh are to be accounted true Israelites; but that God chooses whom he will, according to his own good pleasure, he adduces this testimony, "the elder shall serve the younger." (Rom. ix. 7, 8, 12.) They who endeavour to extinguish the doctrine of gratuitous election, desire to persuade their readers that the words of Paul also are to be understood only of external vocation; but his whole discourse is manifestly repugnant to their interpretation; and they prove themselves to be not only infatuated, but impudent in their attempt to bring darkness or smoke over this light which shines so clearly. They allege that the dignity of Esau is transferred to his younger brother, lest he should glory in the flesh; inasmuch as a new promise is here given to the latter. I confess there is some force in what they say; but I contend that they omit the principal point in the case, by explaining the difference here stated, of the external vocation. But unless they intend to make the covenant of God of none effect, they must concede that Esau and Jacob were alike partakers of the external calling; whence it appears, that they to whom a common vocation had been granted, were separated by the secret counsel of God. The nature and object of Paul's argument is well known. For when the Jews, inflated with the title of the Church, rejected the Gospel, the faith of the simple was shaken, by the consideration that it was improbable that Christ, and the salvation promised through him, could possibly be rejected by an elect people, a holy nation, and the genuine sons of God. Here, therefore, Paul contends that not all who descend from Jacob, according to the flesh, are true Israelites, because God, of his own good pleasure, may choose whom he will, as heirs of eternal salvation. Who does not see that Paul descends from a general to a particular adoption, in order to teach us, that not all who occupy a place in the Church are to be accounted as true members of the Church? It is certain that he openly excludes from the rank of children those to whom (he elsewhere says) "pertaineth the adoption;" whence it is assuredly gathered, that in proof of this position, he adduces the testimony of Moses, who declares that God chose certain from among the sons of Abraham to himself, in whom he might render the grace of adoption firm and efficacious. How, therefore, shall we reconcile Paul with Moses? I answer, although the Lord separates the whole seed of Jacob from the race of Esau, it was done with a view to the Church, which was included in the posterity of Jacob. And, doubtless, the general election of the people had reference to this end, that God might have a Church separated from the rest of the world. What absurdity, then, is there in supposing that Paul applies to special election the words of Moses, by which it is predicted that the Church shall spring from the seed of Jacob? And an instance in point was exhibited in the condition of the heads themselves of these two nations. For Jacob was not only called by the external voice of the Lord, but, while his brother was passed by, he was chosen an heir of life. That good pleasure of God, which Moses commends in the person of Jacob alone, Paul properly extends further: and lest any one should suppose, that after the two nations had been rendered distinct by this oracle, the election should pertain indiscriminately to all the sons of Jacob, Paul brings, on the opposite side, another oracle, "I will have mercy on whom I will have mercy;" where we see a certain number severed from the promiscuous race of Jacob's sons, in the salvation of whom the special election of God might triumph. Whence it appears that Paul wisely considered the counsel of God, which was, in truth, that he had transferred the honour of primogeniture from the elder to the younger, in order that he might choose to himself a Church, according to his own will, out of the seed of Jacob; not on account of the merits of men, but as a matter of mere grace. And although God designed that the means by which the Church was to be collected should be common to the whole people, yet the end which Paul had in view is chiefly to be regarded; namely, that there might always be a body of men in the world which should call upon God with a pure faith, and should be kept even to the end. Let it therefore remain as a settled point of doctrine, that among men some perish, some obtain salvation; but the cause of this depends on the secret will of God. For whence does it arise that they who are born of

Abraham are not all possessed of the same privilege? The disparity of condition certainly cannot be ascribed either to the virtue of the one, or to the vice of the other, seeing they were not yet born. Since the common feeling of mankind rejects this doctrine, there have been found, in all ages, acute men, who have fiercely disputed against the election of God. It is not my present purpose to refute or to weaken their calumnies: let it suffice us to hold fast what we gather from Paul's interpretation; that whereas the whole human race deserves the same destruction, and is bound under the same sentence of condemnation, some are delivered by gratuitous mercy, others are justly left in their own destruction: and that those whom God has chosen are not preferred to others, because God foresaw they *would be* holy, but in order that they *might be* holy. But if the first origin of holiness is the election of God, we seek in vain for that difference in men, which rests solely in the will of God. If any one desires a mystical interpretation of the subject,[1] we may give the following:[2] whereas many hypocrites, who are for a time enclosed in the womb of the Church, pride themselves upon an empty title, and, with insolent boastings, exult over the true sons of God; internal conflicts will hence arise, which will grievously torment the mother herself.

24. *And when her days to be delivered were fulfilled.* Moses shows that the intestine strife in her womb continued to the time of bringing forth; for it was not by mere accident that Jacob seized his brother by the heel and attempted to get out before him. The Lord testified by this sign that the effect of his election does not immediately appear; but rather that the intervening path was strewed with troubles and conflicts. Therefore Esau's name was allotted to him on account of his asperity; which even from earliest infancy assumed a manly form; but the name Jacob signifies that this giant, vainly striving in his boasted strength, had still been vanquished.[3]

[1] Si quis anagogen desideret.
[2] Nous pourrons dire.—*French Tr.* The original has no corresponding expression; but one to the same effect is obviously understood.—*Ed.*
[3] The names of the two brothers was significant of their character. Esau is called Edom, which signifies *red*, because he was of sanguinary

27. *And the boys grew.* Moses now briefly describes the manners of them both. He does not, indeed, commend Jacob on account of those rare and excellent qualities, which are especially worthy of praise and of remembrance, but only says that he was *simple.* The word תָּם, (*tam,*) although generally taken for *upright* and *sincere,* is here put antithetically. After the sacred writer has stated that Esau was robust, and addicted to hunting, he places on the opposite side the mild disposition of Jacob, who loved the quiet of home so much, that he might seem to be indolent; just as the Greeks call those persons οἰκόσιτους, who, dwelling at home, give no evidence of their industry. In short, the comparison implies that Moses praises Esau on account of his vigour, but speaks of Jacob as being addicted to domestic leisure; and that he describes the disposition of the former as giving promise that he would be a courageous man, while the disposition of the latter had nothing worthy of commendation. Seeing that, by a decree of heaven, the honour of primogeniture would be transferred to Jacob, why did God suffer him to lie down in his tent, and to slumber among ashes; unless it be, that he sometimes intends his election to be concealed for a time, lest men should attribute something to their own preparatory acts?

28. *And Isaac loved Esau.* That God might more clearly show his own election to be sufficiently firm, to need no assistance elsewhere, and even powerful enough to overcome any obstacle whatever, he permitted Esau to be so preferred to his brother, in the affection and good opinion of his father, that Jacob appeared in the light of a rejected person. Since, therefore, Moses clearly demonstrates, by so many circumstances, that the adoption of Jacob was founded on the sole good pleasure of God, it is an intolerable presumption to suppose it to depend upon the will of man; or to ascribe it, in part, to means, (as they are called,) and to human preparations.[1] But how was it possible for the father, who was

temperament. He is said to have been hairy or shaggy, שֵׂעָר, from which word the mountainous country he inhabited was called *Seir.* The name Jacob, יַעֲקֹב, means to supplant, or trip up the heels.—*Ed.*

[1] C'est une outrecuidance insupportable de la vouloir faire dependre de la volonté de l'homme, ou transporter une partie d'icelle aux moyens et preparatifs humain.—*French Tr.*

not ignorant of the oracle, to be thus pre-disposed in favour of the first-born, whom he knew to be divinely rejected? It would rather have been the part of piety and of modesty to subdue his own private affection, that he might yield obedience to God. The first-born prefers a natural claim to the chief place in the parent's affection; but the father was not at liberty to exalt *him* above his brother, who had been placed in subjection by the oracle of God. That also is still more shameful and more unworthy of the holy patriarch, which Moses adds; namely, that he had been induced to give this preference to Esau, by the taste of his venison. Was he so enslaved to the indulgence of the palate, that, forgetting the oracle, he despised the grace of God in Jacob, while he preposterously set his affection on him whom God had rejected? Let the Jews now go and glory in the flesh; since Isaac, preferring food to the inheritance destined for his son, would pervert (as far as he had the power) the gratuitous covenant of God! For there is no room here for excuse; since with a blind, or, at least, a most inconsiderate love to his first-born, he undervalued the younger. It is uncertain whether the mother was chargeable with a fault of the opposite kind. For we commonly find the affections of parents so divided, that if the wife sees any one of the sons preferred by her husband, she inclines, by a contrary spirit of emulation, more towards another. Rebekah loved her son Jacob more than Esau. If, in so doing, she was obeying the oracle, she acted rightly; but it is possible that her love was ill regulated. And on this point the corruption of nature too much betrays itself. There is no bond of mutual concord more sacred than that of marriage: children form still further links of connection; and yet they often prove the occasion of dissension. But since we soon after see Rebekah chiefly in earnest respecting the blessing of God, the conjecture is probable, that she had been induced, by divine authority, to prefer the younger to the first-born. Meanwhile, the foolish affection of the father only the more fully illustrates the grace of the divine adoption.

29. *And Jacob sod pottage.* This narration differs little from the sport of children. Jacob is cooking pottage; his

brother returns from hunting weary and famishing, and barters his birthright for food. What kind of bargain, I pray, was this? Jacob ought of his own accord to have satisfied the hunger of his brother. When being asked, he refuses to do so: who would not condemn him for his inhumanity? In compelling Esau to surrender his right of primogeniture, he seems to make an illicit and frivolous compact. God, however, put the disposition of Esau to the proof in a matter of small moment; and still farther, designed to present an instance of Jacob's piety, or, (to speak more properly,) he brought to light what lay hid in both. Many indeed are mistaken in suspending the cause of Jacob's election on the fact, that God foresaw some worthiness in him; and in thinking that Esau was reprobated, because his future impiety had rendered him unworthy of the divine adoption before he was born. Paul, however, having declared election to be gratuitous, denies that the distinction is to be looked for in the persons of men; and, indeed, first assumes it as an axiom, that since mankind is ruined from its origin, and devoted to destruction, whosoever are saved are in no other way freed from destruction than by the mere grace of God. And, therefore, that some are preferred to others, is not on account of their own merits; but seeing that all are alike unworthy of grace, they are saved whom God, of his own good pleasure, has chosen. He then ascends still higher, and reasons thus: " Since God is the Creator of the world, he is, by his own right, in such a sense, the arbiter of life and death, that he cannot be called to account; but his own will is (so to speak) the *cause of causes*. And yet Paul does not, by thus reasoning, impute tyranny to God, as the sophists triflingly allege in speaking of his absolute power. But whereas He dwells in inaccessible light, and his judgments are deeper than the lowest abyss, Paul prudently enjoins acquiescence in God's sole purpose; lest, if men seek to be too inquisitive, this immense chaos should absorb all their senses. It is therefore foolishly inferred by some, from this place, that whereas God chose one of the two brothers, and passed by the other, the merits of both had been foreseen. For it was necessary that God should have decreed

that Jacob should differ from Esau, otherwise he would not
have been unlike his brother. And we must always remember the doctrine of Paul, that no one excels another by means
of his own industry or virtue, but by the grace of God alone.
Although, however, both the brothers were by nature equal,
yet Moses represents to us, in the person of Esau, as in a mirror,
what kind of men all the reprobate are, who, being left to their
own disposition, are not governed by the Spirit of God. While,
in the person of Jacob, he shows that the grace of adoption
is not idle in the elect, because the Lord effectually attests
it by his vocation. Whence then does it arise that Esau
sets his birthright to sale, but from this cause, that he, being
deprived of the Spirit of God, relishes only the things of the
earth? And whence does it happen that his brother Jacob,
denying himself his own food, patiently endures hunger, except that under the guidance of the Holy Spirit, he raises
himself above the world and aspires to a heavenly life?
Hence, let us learn, that they to whom God does not vouchsafe the grace of his Spirit, are carnal and brutal; and are so
addicted to this fading life, that they think not of the spiritual kingdom of God; but they whom God has undertaken
to govern, are not so far entangled in the snares of the flesh
as to prevent them from being intent upon their high vocation. Whence it follows, that all the reprobate remain immersed in the corruptions of the flesh; but that the elect are
renewed by the Holy Spirit, that they may be the workmanship of God, created unto good works. If any one should
raise the objection, that part of the blame may be ascribed
to God, because he does not correct the stupor and the depraved desires inherent in the reprobate, the solution is
ready, that God is exonerated by the testimony of their own
conscience, which compels them to condemn themselves.
Wherefore, nothing remains but that all flesh should keep
silence before God, and that the whole world, confessing itself to be obnoxious to his judgment, should rather be
humbled than proudly contend.

30. *Feed me, I pray thee, with that same red pottage.*[1]

[1] Literally the passage would run, " Feed me, I pray thee, with that *red,* that red," the word pottage being understood. " The repetition of

Although Esau declares in these words that he by no means desires delicacies, but is content with food of any kind, (seeing that he contemptuously designates the pottage from its colour only, without regard to its taste,) we may yet lawfully conjecture that the affair was viewed in a serious light by his parents; for his own name had not been given him on account of any ludicrous matter. In desiring and asking food he commits nothing worthy of reprehension; but when he says, "Behold I am at the point to die, and what profit shall this birthright do to me?" he betrays a profane desire entirely addicted to the earth and to the flesh. It is not, indeed, to be doubted that he spake sincerely, when he declared that he was impelled by a sense of the approach of death. For they are under a misapprehension who understand him to use the words, "Behold I die," as if he meant merely to say, that his life would not be long, because, by hunting daily among wild beasts, his life was in constant danger. Therefore, in order to escape immediate death, he exchanges his birthright for food; notwithstanding, he grievously sins in so doing, because he regards his birthright as of no value, unless it may be made profitable in the present life. For, hence it happens, that he barters a spiritual for an earthly and fading good. On this account the Apostle calls him a "profane person," (Heb. xii. 16,) as one who settles in the present life, and will not aspire higher. But it would have been his true wisdom rather to undergo a thousand deaths than to renounce his birthright; which, so far from being confined within the narrow limits of one age alone, was capable of transmitting the perpetuity of a heavenly life to his posterity also.[1] Now, let each of us look well to himself; for since the disposition of us all is earthly,

the epithet, and the omission of the substantive, indicated the extreme haste and eagerness of the asker. His eye was caught by the colour of the dish; and being faint with hunger and fatigue, he gave way to the solicitations of appetite, regardless of consequences."—*Bush.*

[1] It is to be remembered that the birthright included not merely earthly advantages, but those also which were spiritual. Till the tribe of Levi was accepted by God, in lieu of all the first-born of Israel, the eldest son was the *priest* of the family as well as its natural head. And this was probably the part of the birthright which Esau treated with peculiar contempt, and for which the Apostle Paul styles him a "profane person."— *Ed.*

if we follow nature as our leader, we shall easily renounce the celestial inheritance. Therefore, we should frequently recall to mind the Apostle's exhortation, " Let us not be profane persons as Esau was."

33. *And Jacob said, Swear to me.* Jacob did not act cruelly towards his brother, for he took nothing from him, but only desired a confirmation of that right which had been divinely granted to him; and he does this with a pious intention, that he may hereby the more fully establish the certainty of his own election. Meanwhile the infatuation of Esau is to be observed, who, in the name and presence of God, does not hesitate to set his birthright to sale. Although he had before rushed inconsiderately upon the food under the maddening impulse of hunger; now, at least, when an oath is exacted from him, some sense of religion should have stolen over him to correct his brutal cupidity. But he is so addicted to gluttony that he makes God himself a witness of his ingratitude.

34. *Then Jacob gave.* Although, at first sight, this statement seems to be cold and superfluous, it is nevertheless of great weight. For, in the first place, Moses commends the piety of holy Jacob, who in aspiring to a heavenly life, was able to bridle the appetite for food. Certainly he was not a log of wood; in preparing the food for the satisfying of his hunger, he would the more sharpen his appetite. Wherefore he must of necessity do violence to himself in order to bear his hunger. But he would never have been able in this manner to subdue his flesh, unless a spiritual desire of a better life had flourished within him. On the other side, the remarkable indifference of his brother Esau is emphatically described in few words, " he did eat and drink, and rose up and went his way." For what reason are these four things stated? Truly, that we may know what is declared immediately after, that he accounted the incomparable benefit of which he was deprived as nothing. The complaint of the Lacedemonian captive is celebrated by the historians. The army, which had long sustained a siege, surrendered to the enemy for want of water. After they had drunk out of the river, O comrades, (he exclaimed,) for what a little pleasure

have we lost an incomparable good! He, miserable man, having quenched his thirst, returned to his senses, and mourned over his lost liberty. But Esau having satisfied his appetite, did not consider that he had sacrificed a blessing far more valuable than a hundred lives, to purchase a repast which would be ended in half an hour. Thus are all profane persons accustomed to act: alienated from the celestial life, they do not perceive that they have lost anything, till God thunders upon them out of heaven. As long as they enjoy their carnal wishes, they cast the anger of God behind them; and hence it happens that they go stupidly forward to their own destruction. Wherefore let us learn, if, at any time, we, being deceived by the allurements of the world, swerve from the right way, quickly to rouse ourselves from our slumber.

## CHAPTER XXVI.

1. AND there was a famine in the land, besides the first famine that was in the days of Abraham. And Isaac went unto Abimelech king of the Philistines unto Gerar.

2. And the Lord appeared unto him, and said, Go not down into Egypt; dwell in the land which I shall tell thee of.

3. Sojourn in this land, and I will be with thee, and will bless thee: for unto thee, and unto thy seed, I will give all these countries; and I will perform the oath which I sware unto Abraham thy father:

4. And I will make thy seed to multiply as the stars of heaven, and will give unto thy seed all these countries: and in thy seed shall all the nations of the earth be blessed;

5. Because that Abraham obeyed my voice, and kept my charge, my commandments, my statutes, and my laws.

6. And Isaac dwelt in Gerar.

7. And the men of the place asked *him* of his wife; and he said, She *is* my sister: for he feared to say, *She is* my wife; lest, *said he*, the men of

1. Deinde fuit fames in terra præter famem superiorem, quæ fuerat in diebus Abraham: et profectus est Ishac ad Abimelech regem Pelisthim in Gerar.

2. Nam visus est ei Iehova, et dixit, Ne descendas in Ægyptum: habita in terra quam dicam tibi.

3. Inhabita terram hanc, et ero tecum, et benedicam tibi: quia tibi et semini tuo dabo omnes terras istas: et statuam juramentum quod juravi ad Abraham patrem tuum.

4. Et multiplicare faciam semen tuum sicut stellas cœli, et dabo semini tuo omnes terras istas: benedicenturque in semine tuo omnes gentes terræ:

5. Eo quod obedierit Abraham voci meæ, et custodierit custodiam meam, præcepta mea, statuta mea, et leges meas.

6. Et habitavit Ishac in Gerar.

7. Et interrogaverunt incolæ regionis de uxore ejus; et dixit, Soror mea est: quia timuit dicere, uxor mea est: ne forte occiderent me in-

the place should kill me for Rebekah; because she *was* fair to look upon.

8. And it came to pass, when he had been there a long time, that Abimelech king of the Philistines looked out at a window, and saw, and, behold, Isaac *was* sporting with Rebekah his wife.

9. And Abimelech called Isaac, and said, Behold, of a surety she *is* thy wife; and how saidst thou, She *is* my sister? And Isaac said unto him, Because I said, Lest I die for her.

10. And Abimelech said, What *is* this thou hast done unto us? one of the people might lightly have lien with thy wife, and thou shouldest have brought guiltiness upon us.

11. And Abimelech charged all *his* people, saying, He that toucheth this man, or his wife, shall surely be put to death.

12. Then Isaac sowed in that land, and received in the same year an hundred-fold; and the Lord blessed him.

13. And the man waxed great, and went forward, and grew, until he became very great:

14. For he had possession of flocks, and possession of herds, and great store of servants: and the Philistines envied him.

15. For all the wells which his father's servants had digged in the days of Abraham his father, the Philistines had stopped them, and filled them with earth.

16. And Abimelech said unto Isaac, Go from us; for thou art much mightier than we.

17. And Isaac departed thence, and pitched his tent in the valley of Gerar, and dwelt there.

18. And Isaac digged again the wells of water which they had digged in the days of Abraham his father; for the Philistines had stopped them after the death of Abraham: and he called their names after the names by which his father had called them.

19. And Isaac's servants digged

colæ regionis propter Ribcam, quia pulchra aspectu erat.

8. Verum fuit, quum protracti essent ei ibi dies, aspexit Abimelech rex Pelisthim per fenestram, et vidit, et ecce Ishac ludebat cum Ribca uxore sua.

9. Tunc vocavit Abimelech Ishac, et dixit, Vere ecce uxor tua est; et quomodo dixisti, Soror mea est? Et dixit ad eum Ishac, Quia dixi, Ne forte moriar propter eam.

10. Et dixit Abimelech, Quid hoc fecisti nobis? paulum abfuit quin dormierit unus e populo cum uxore tua, et venire fecisses super nos delictum.

11. Præcepit itaque Abimelech omni populo, dicendo, Qui tetigerit virum hunc, et uxorem ejus, moriendo morietur.

12. Et sevit Ishac in terra ipsa, et reperit in anno ipso centum modios: et benedixit ei Iehova.

13. Et crevit vir, et perrexit pergendo et crescendo, donec cresceret valde.

14. Et fuit ei possessio pecudum, et possessio boum, et proventus multus: et inviderunt ei Pelisthim.

15. Itaque omnes puteos, quos foderant servi patris sui in diebus Abraham patris sui, obturaverunt Pelisthim, et impleverunt eos terra.

16. Et dixit Abimelech ad Ishac, Abi a nobis: quia longe fortior es nobis.

17. Abiit ergo inde Ishac, et mansit in valle Gerar, et habitavit ibi.

18. Postquam reversus est Ishac, fodit puteos aquæ, quos foderant in diebus Abraham patris sui: quia obturaverant eos Pelisthim mortuo Abraham: et vocavit eos nominibus secundum nomina, quibus vocaverat eos pater suus.

19. Et foderunt servi Ishac in

in the valley, and found there a well of springing water.

20. And the herdmen of Gerar did strive with Isaac's herdmen, saying, The water *is* ours: and he called the name of the well Esek; because they strove with him.

21. And they digged another well, and strove for that also: and he called the name of it Sitnah.

22. And he removed from thence, and digged another well; and for that they strove not: and he called the name of it Rehoboth; and he said, For now the Lord hath made room for us, and we shall be fruitful in the land.

23. And he went up from thence to Beer-sheba.

24. And the Lord appeared unto him the same night, and said, I *am* the God of Abraham thy father: fear not, for I *am* with thee, and will bless thee, and multiply thy seed, for my servant Abraham's sake.

25. And he builded an altar there, and called upon the name of the Lord, and pitched his tent there: and there Isaac's servants digged a well.

26. Then Abimelech went to him from Gerar, and Ahuzzath one of his friends, and Phichol the chief captain of his army.

27. And Isaac said unto them, Wherefore come ye to me, seeing ye hate me, and have sent me away from you?

28. And they said, We saw certainly that the Lord was with thee: and we said, Let there be now an oath betwixt us, *even* betwixt us and thee, and let us make a covenant with thee;

29. That thou wilt do us no hurt, as we have not touched thee, and as we have done unto thee nothing but good, and have sent thee away in peace: thou *art* now the blessed of the Lord.

30. And he made them a feast, and they did eat and drink.

31. And they rose up betimes in the morning, and sware one to another: and Isaac sent them away, and they departed from him in peace.

valle, et invenerunt ibi puteum aquæ vivæ.

20. Sed litigaverunt pastores Gerar cum pastoribus Ishac, dicendo, Nostra est aqua: et vocavit nomen putei Hesech, quia litigaverunt cum eo.

21. Et foderunt puteum alium, et litigaverunt etiam super eo: et vocavit nomen ejus Sitnah.

22. Et transtulit se inde, et fodit puteum alium, et non litigaverunt super eo: ideo vocavit nomen ejus Rehoboth: et dixit, Quia nunc dilatationem fecit Iehova nobis, et crevimus in terra.

23. Et ascendit inde in Beer-sebah.

24. Et visus est ei Iehova nocte ipsa, et dixit, Ego sum Deus Abraham patris tui: ne timeas, quia tecum sum, et benedicam tibi, et multiplicare faciam semen tuum propter Abraham servum meum.

25. Tunc ædificavit ibi altare, et invocavit nomen Iehovæ, et tetendit ibi tabernaculum suum: et foderunt ibi servi Ishac puteum.

26. Porro Abimelech profectus est ad eum ex Gerar, et Ahuzath *qui erat* ex amicis ejus, et Phichol princeps exercitus ejus.

27. Et dixit ad eos Ishac, Cur venistis ad me, et vos odio habuistis me, et emisistis me ne essem vobiscum?

28. Et dixerunt, Videndo vidimus quod esset Iehova tecum, et diximus, Sit nunc juramentum inter nos, inter nos et inter te, et percutiamus fœdus tecum.

29. Si feceris nobiscum malum: quemadmodum non tetigimus te, et quemadmodum fecimus tecum duntaxat bonum, et dimisimus te in pace: tu nunc es benedictus Iehovæ.

30. Instruxit autem eis convivium, et ederunt, atque biberunt.

31. Et surrexerunt mane: et juraverunt alter alteri: et deduxit eos Ishac, et abierunt ab eo in pace.

32. And it came to pass the same day, that Isaac's servants came, and told him concerning the well which they had digged, and said unto him, We have found water.

33. And he called it Shebah: therefore the name of the city *is* Beer-sheba unto this day.

34. And Esau was forty years old when he took to wife Judith the daughter of Beeri the Hittite, and Bashemath the daughter of Elon the Hittite;

35. Which were a grief of mind unto Isaac and to Rebekah.

32. Adhæc fuit, in die ipsa venerunt servi Ishac, et nuntiaverunt ei de puteo quem foderant, et dixerunt ei, Invenimus aquam.

33. Et vocavit eum Sibhah: idcirco nomen urbis est Beer-sebah usque ad diem hanc.

34. Erat autem Esau quadragenarius, et accepit uxorem Iehudith filiam Beeri Hittæi, et Bosmath filiam Elon Hittæi.

35. Et irritabant spiritum Ishac et Ribcæ.

1. *And there was a famine.* Moses relates that Isaac was tried by nearly the same kind of temptation as that through which his father Abraham had twice passed. I have before explained how severe and violent was this assault. The condition in which it was the will of God to place his servants, as strangers and pilgrims in the land which he had promised to give them, seemed sufficiently troublesome and hard ; but it appears still more intolerable, that he scarcely suffered them to exist (if we may so speak) in this wandering, uncertain, and changeable kind of life, but almost consumed them with hunger. Who would not say that God had forgotten himself, when he did not even supply his own children,—whom he had received into his especial care and trust,—however sparingly and scantily, with food ? But God thus tried the holy fathers, that we might be taught, by their example, not to be effeminate and cowardly under temptations. Respecting the terms here used, we may observe, that though there were two seasons of dearth in the time of Abraham, Moses alludes only to the one, of which the remembrance was most recent.[1]

2. *And the Lord appeared unto him.* I do not doubt but a reason is here given why Isaac rather went to the country of Gerar than to Egypt, which perhaps would have been

---

[1] Abimelech, king of the Philistines, mentioned in this verse, was not he who is spoken of in Gen. xxi., but perhaps his descendant. "It is probable the name was common to the kings of Gerar, as Pharaoh was to the kings of Egypt. The meaning of the word אבימלך is, *My father the king.* Kings ought to be the fathers of their country."—*Menochius in Poli Syn.*

more convenient for him; but Moses teaches that he was withheld by a heavenly oracle, so that a free choice was not left him. It may here be asked, why does the Lord prohibit Isaac from going to Egypt, whither he had suffered his father to go? Although Moses does not give the reason, yet we may be allowed to conjecture that the journey would have been more dangerous to the son. The Lord could indeed have endued the son also with the power of his Spirit, as he had done his father Abraham, so that the abundance and delicacies of Egypt should not have corrupted him by their allurements; but since he governs his faithful people with such moderation, that he does not correct all their faults at once, and render them entirely pure, he assists their infirmities, and anticipates, with suitable remedies, those evils by which they might be ensnared. Because, therefore, he knew that there was more infirmity in Isaac than there had been in Abraham, he was unwilling to expose him to danger; for he is faithful, and will not suffer his own people to be tempted beyond what they are able to bear. (1 Cor. x. 13.) Now, as we must be persuaded, that however arduous and burdensome may be the temptations which alight upon us, the Divine help will never fail to renew our strength; so, on the other hand, we must beware lest we rashly rush into dangers; but each should be admonished by his own infirmity to proceed cautiously and with fear.

*Dwell in the land.* God commands him to settle in the promised land, yet with the understanding that he should dwell there as a stranger. The intimation was thus given, that the time had not yet arrived in which he should exercise dominion over it. God sustains indeed his mind with the hope of the promised inheritance, but requires this honour to be given to his word, that Isaac should remain inwardly at rest, in the midst of outward agitations; and truly we never lean upon a better support than when, disregarding the appearance of things present, we depend entirely upon the word of the Lord, and apprehend by faith that blessing which is not yet apparent. Moreover, he again inculcates the promise previously made, in order to render Isaac more prompt to obey; for so is the Lord wont to awaken his servants from their indolence, that they may fight valiantly for him, while he constantly affirms that their labour shall not be in vain ; for although he requires from us a free and unreserved obedience, as a father does from his children, he yet so condescends to the weakness of our capacity, that he invites and encourages us by the prospect of reward.

5. *Because that Abraham obeyed my voice.* Moses does not mean that Abraham's obedience was the reason why the promise of God was confirmed and ratified to him ; but from what has been said before, (chap. xxii. 18,) where we have a similar expression, we learn, that what God freely bestows upon the faithful is sometimes, beyond their desert, ascribed to themselves; that they, knowing their intention to be approved by the Lord, may the more ardently addict and devote themselves entirely to his service: so he now commends the obedience of Abraham, in order that Isaac may be stimulated to an imitation of his example. And although laws, statutes, rites, precepts, and' ceremonies, had not yet been written, Moses used these terms, that he might the more clearly show how sedulously Abraham regulated his life according to the will of God alone—how carefully he abstained from all the impurities of the heathen—and how exactly he pursued the straight course of holiness, without turning aside to the right hand or to the left : for the Lord often honours his own law with these titles for the sake of restraining our excesses ; as if he should say that it wanted nothing to constitute it a perfect rule, but embraced everything pertaining to absolute holiness. The meaning therefore is, that Abraham, having formed his life in entire accordance with the will of God, walked in his pure service.

7. *And the men of the place asked him.* Moses relates that Isaac was tempted in the same manner as his father Abraham, in having his wife taken from him ; and without doubt he was so led by the example of his father, that he, being instructed by the similarity of the circumstances, might become associated with him in his faith. Nevertheless, on this point he ought rather to have avoided than imitated his father's fault ; for no doubt he well remembered that the chastity of his mother had twice been

put in great danger; and although she had been wonderfully rescued by the hand of God, yet both she and her husband paid the penalty of their distrust: therefore the negligence of Isaac is inexcusable, in that he now strikes against the same stone. He does not in express terms deny his wife; but he is to be blamed, first, because, for the sake of preserving his life, he resorts to an evasion not far removed from a lie; and secondly, because, in absolving his wife from conjugal fidelity, he exposes her to prostitution: but he aggravates his fault, principally (as I have said) in not taking warning from domestic examples, but voluntarily casting his wife into manifest danger. Whence it appears how great is the propensity of our nature to distrust, and how easy it is to be devoid of wisdom in affairs of perplexity. Since, therefore, we are surrounded on all sides with so many dangers, we must ask the Lord to confirm us by his Spirit, lest our minds should faint, and be dissolved in fear and trembling; otherwise we shall be frequently engaged in vain enterprises, of which we shall repent soon, and yet too late to remedy the evil.

8. *Abimelech, king of the Philistines, looked out at a window.* Truly admirable is the kind forbearance of God, in not only condescending to pardon the twofold fault of his servant, but in stretching forth his hand, and in wonderfully averting, by the application of a speedy remedy, the evil which he would have brought upon himself. God did not suffer—what twice had occurred to Abraham—that his wife should be torn from his bosom; but stirred up a heathen king, mildly, and without occasioning him any trouble, to correct his folly. But although God sets before us such an example of his kindness, that the faithful, if at any time they may have fallen, may confidently hope to find him gentle and propitious; yet we must beware of self-security, when we observe, that the holy woman who was, at that time, the only mother of the Church on earth, was exempted from dishonour, by a special privilege. Meanwhile, we may conjecture, from the judgment of Abimelech, how holy and pure had been the conduct of Isaac, on whom not even a suspicion of evil could fall; and further, how much greater integrity

flourished in that age than in our own. For why does he not condemn Isaac as one guilty of fornication, since it was probable that some crime was concealed, when he disingenuously obtruded the name of sister, and tacitly denied her to be his wife? and therefore I have no doubt that his religion, and the integrity of his life, availed to defend his character. By this example we are taught so to cultivate righteousness in our whole life, that men may not be able to suspect anything wicked or dishonourable respecting us; for there is nothing which will more completely vindicate us from every mark of infamy than a life passed in modesty and temperance. We must, however, add, what I have also before alluded to, that lusts were not, at that time, so commonly and so profusely indulged, as to cause an unfavourable suspicion to enter into the mind of the king concerning a sojourner of honest character. Wherefore, he easily persuades himself that Rebekah was a wife and not a harlot. The chastity of that age is further proved from this, that Abimelech takes the familiar sporting of Isaac with Rebekah as an evidence of their marriage.[1] But now licentiousness has so broken through all bounds, that husbands are compelled to hear in silence of the dissolute conduct of their wives with strangers.

10. *What is this thou hast done unto us?* The Lord does not chastise Isaac as he deserved, perhaps because he was not so fully endued with patience as his father was; and, therefore, lest the seizing of his wife should dishearten him, God mercifully prevents it. Yet, that the censure may produce the deeper shame, God constitutes a heathen his master and his reprover. We may add, that Abimelech chides his folly, not so much with the design of injuring him, as of upbraiding him. It ought, however, deeply to have wounded the mind of the holy man, when he perceived that his offence was obnoxious to the judgment even of the blind. Wherefore, let us remember that we must walk in the light which God has kindled for us, lest even unbelievers, who are

---

[1] The following passage is here omitted in the translation :—" Non enim de coitu loquitur Moses, sed de aliquo liberiore gestu, qui vel dissolutæ lasciviæ, vel conjugalis amoris testis esset."

wrapped in the darkness of ignorance, should reprove our stupor. And certainly when we neglect to obey the voice of God, we deserve to be sent to oxen and asses for instruction.[1] Abimelech, truly, does not investigate nor prosecute the whole offence of Isaac, but only alludes to one part of it. Yet Isaac, when thus gently admonished by a single word, ought to have condemned himself, seeing that, instead of committing himself and his wife to God, who had promised to be the guardian of them both, he had resorted, through his own unbelief, to an illicit remedy. For faith has this property, that it confines us within divinely prescribed bounds, so that we attempt nothing except with God's authority or permission. Whence it follows that Isaac's faith wavered when he swerved from his duty as a husband. We gather, besides, from the words of Abimelech, that all nations have the sentiment impressed upon their minds, that the violation of holy wedlock is a crime worthy of divine vengeance, and have consequently a dread of the judgment of God. For although the minds of men are darkened with dense clouds, so that they are frequently deceived; yet God has caused some power of discrimination between right and wrong to remain, so that each should bear about with him his own condemnation, and that all should be without excuse. If, then, God cites even unbelievers to his tribunal, and does not suffer them to escape just condemnation, how horrible is that punishment which awaits us, if we endeavour to obliterate, by our own wickedness, that knowledge which God has engraven on our consciences?

11. *And Abimelech charged all his people.* In denouncing capital punishment against any who should do injury to this stranger, we may suppose him to have issued this edict as a special privilege; for it is not customary thus rigidly to avenge every kind of injury. Whence, then, arose this disposition on the part of the king to prefer Isaac to all the native inhabitants of the country, and almost to treat him as an equal, except that some portion of the divine majesty

---

[1] The allusion is obviously to Isaiah i. 3: "The ox knoweth his owner, and the ass his master's crib; but Israel doth not know, my people doth not consider."—*Ed.*

shone forth in him, which secured to him this degree of reverence? God, also, to assist the infirmity of his servant, inclined the mind of the heathen king, in every way, to show him favour. And there is no doubt that his general modesty induced the king thus carefully to protect him; for he, perceiving him to be a timid man, who had been on the point of purchasing his own life by the ruin of his wife, was the more disposed to assist him in his dangers, in order that he might live in security under his own government.

12. *Then Isaac sowed.* Here Moses proceeds to relate in what manner Isaac reaped the manifest fruit of the blessing promised to him by God; for he says, that when he had sowed, the increase was a hundredfold: which was an extraordinary fertility, even in that land. He also adds, that he was rich in cattle, and had a very great household. Moreover, he ascribes the praise of all these things to the blessing of God; as it is also declared in the psalm, that the Lord abundantly supplies what will satisfy his people while they sleep. (Ps. cxxvii. 2.) It may, however, be asked, how could Isaac sow when God had commanded him to be a stranger all his life? Some suppose that he had bought a field, and so translate the word קנה (*kanah*) a possession; but the context corrects their error: for we find soon afterwards, that the holy man was not delayed, by having land to sell, from removing his effects elsewhere: besides, since the purchasing of land was contrary to his peculiar vocation and to the command of God, Moses undoubtedly would not have passed over such a notable offence. To this may be added, that since express mention is immediately made of a tent, we may hence infer, that wherever he might come, he would have to dwell in the precarious condition of a stranger. We must, therefore, maintain, that he sowed in a hired field. For although he had not a foot of land in his own possession, yet, that he might discharge the duty of a good householder, it behoved him to prepare food for his family; and perhaps hunger quickened his care and industry, that he might with the greater diligence make provision for himself against the future. Nevertheless, it is right to keep in mind, what I

have lately alluded to, that he received as a divine favour the abundance which he had acquired by his own labour.

14. *And the Philistines envied him.* We are taught by this history that the blessings of God which pertain to the present earthly life are never pure and perfect, but are mixed with some troubles, lest quiet and indulgence should render us negligent. Wherefore, let us all learn not too ardently to desire great wealth. If the rich are harassed by any cause of disquietude, let them know that they are roused by the Lord, lest they should fall fast asleep in the midst of their pleasures; and let the poor enjoy this consolation, that their poverty is not without its advantages. For it is no light good to live free from envy, tumults, and strifes. Should any one raise the objection, that it can by no means be regarded as a favour, that God, in causing Isaac to abound in wealth, exposed him to envy, to contentions, and to many troubles; there is a ready answer, that not all the troubles with which God exercises his people, in any degree prevent the benefits which he bestows upon them from retaining the taste of his paternal love. Finally, he so attempers the favour which he manifests towards his children in this world, that he stirs them up, as with sharp goads, to the consideration of a celestial life. It was not, however, a slight trial, that the simple element of water, which is the common property of all animals, was denied to the holy patriarch; with how much greater patience ought we to bear our less grievous sufferings! If, however, at any time we are angry at being unworthily injured; let us remember that, at least, we are not so cruelly treated as holy Isaac was, when he had to contend for water. Besides, not only was he deprived of the element of water, but the wells which his father Abraham had dug for himself and his posterity were filled up. This, therefore, was the extreme of cruelty, not only to defraud a stranger of every service due to him, but even to take from him what had been obtained by the labour of his own father, and what he possessed without inconvenience to any one.

16. *And Abimelech said unto Isaac.* It is uncertain whether the king of Gerar expelled Isaac of his own accord

from his kingdom, or whether he commanded him to settle elsewhere, because he perceived him to be envied by the people. He possibly might, in this manner, advise him as a friend; although it is more probable that his mind had become alienated from Isaac; for at the close of the chapter Moses relates, that the holy man complains strongly of the king as well as of others. But since we can assert nothing with certainty respecting the real feelings of the king, let it suffice to maintain, what is of more importance, that in consequence of the common wickedness of mankind, they who are the most eminent fall under the suspicion of the common people. Satiety, indeed, produces ferocity. Wherefore there is nothing to which the rich are more prone than proudly to boast, to carry themselves more insolently than they ought, and to stretch every nerve of their power to oppress others. No such suspicion, indeed, could fall upon Isaac; but he had to bear that envy which was the attendant on a common vice. Whence we infer, how much more useful and desirable it often is, for us to be placed in a moderate condition; which is, at least, more peaceful, and which is neither exposed to the storms of envy, nor obnoxious to unjust suspicions. Moreover, how rare and unwonted was the blessing of God in rendering Isaac prosperous, may be inferred from the fact, that his wealth had become formidable both to the king and to the people. A large inheritance truly had descended to him from his father; but Moses shows, that from his first entrance into the land, he had so greatly prospered in a very short time, that it seemed no longer possible for the inhabitants to endure him.

18. *And Isaac digged again the wells of water.* First, we see that the holy man was so hated by his neighbours, as to be under the necessity of seeking a retreat for himself which was destitute of water; and no habitation is so troublesome and inconvenient for the ordinary purposes of life as that which suffers from scarcity of water. Besides, the abundance of his cattle and the multitude of his servants—who were like a little army—rendered a supply of water very necessary; whence we learn that he was brought into severe straits. But that this last necessity did not instigate him to seek

revenge, is a proof of singular forbearance; for we know that lighter injuries will often rack the patience even of humane and moderate men. If any one should object to this view, that he was deficient in strength; I grant, indeed, that he was not able to undertake a regular war; but as his father Abraham had armed four hundred servants, he also certainly had a large troop of domestics, who could easily have repelled any force brought against him by his neighbours. But the hope which he had entertained when he settled in the valley of Gerar, was again suddenly cut off. He knew that his father Abraham had there used wells which were his own, and which he had himself discovered; and although they had been stopped up, yet they were well known to have sufficient springs of water to prevent the labour of digging them again from being mispent. Moreover, the fact that the wells had been obstructed ever since the departure of Abraham, shows how little respect the inhabitants had for their guest; for although their own country would have been benefited by these wells, they chose rather to deprive themselves of this advantage than to have Abraham for a neighbour; for, in order that such a convenience might not attract him to the place, they, by stopping up the wells, did, in a certain sense, intercept his way. It was a custom among the ancients, if they wished to involve any one in ruin, and to cut him off from the society of men, to interdict him from water, and from fire: thus the Philistines, for the purpose of removing Abraham from their vicinity, deprive him of the element of water.

*He called their names.* He did not give new names to the wells, but restored those which had been assigned them by his father Abraham, that, by this memorial, the ancient possession of them might be renewed. But subsequent violence compelled him to change their names, that at least he might, by some monument, make manifest the injury which had been done by the Philistines, and reprove them on account of it: for whereas he calls one well *strife,* or *contention,* another *hostility,* he denies that the inhabitants possessed that by right, or by any honest title, which they had seized upon as enemies or robbers. Meanwhile, it is right to consider, that in the midst of these strifes he had a contest not less severe with thirst and deficiency of water, whereby the Philistines attempted to destroy him; such is the scope of the history. First, Moses, according to his manner, briefly runs through the summary of the affair: namely, that Isaac intended to apply again to his own purpose the wells which his father had previously found, and to acquire, in the way of recovery, the lost possession of them. He then prosecutes the subject more diffusely, stating that, when he attempted the work, he was unjustly defrauded of his labour; and whereas, in digging the third well, he gives thanks to God, and calls it *Room*,[1] because, by the favour of God, a more copious supply is now afforded him, he furnishes an example of invincible patience. Therefore, however severely he may have been harassed, yet when, after he had been freed from these troubles, he so placidly returns thanks to God, and celebrates his goodness, he shows that in the midst of trials he has retained a composed and tranquil mind.

23. *And he went up from thence to Beer-sheba.* Next follows a more abundant consolation, and one affording effectual refreshment to the mind of the holy man. In the tranquil enjoyment of the well, he acknowledges the favour which God had showed him: but forasmuch as one word of God weighs more with the faithful than the accumulated mass of all good things, we cannot doubt that Isaac received this oracle more joyfully than if a thousand rivers of nectar had flowed unto him: and truly Moses designedly commemorates in lofty terms this act of favour, that the Lord encouraged him by his own word, (verse 24;) whence we may learn, in ascribing proper honour to each of the other gifts of God, still always to give the palm to that proof of his paternal love which he grants us in his word. Food, clothing, health, peace, and other advantages, afford us a taste of the Divine goodness; but when he addresses us familiarly, and expressly declares himself to be our Father, then indeed it is that he thoroughly refreshes us to satiety. Moses does not explain

---

[1] Latitudines, a literal Latin translation of the Hebrew word רחבת, (*Rehoboth*,) a plural form, expressing the notion of abundant enlargement and room. — *Ed.*

what had been the cause of Isaac's removal to Beer-sheba, the ancient dwelling-place of his fathers. It might be that the Philistines ceased not occasionally to annoy him; and thus the holy man, worn out with their implacable malice, removed to a greater distance. It is indeed probable, taking the circumstance of the time into account, that he was sorrowful and anxious; for as soon as he had arrived at that place, God appeared unto him on the very first night. Here, then, something very opportune is noticed. Moreover, as often as Moses before related that God had appeared unto Abraham, he, at the same time, showed that the holy man was either tormented with grievous cares, or was held in suspense under some apprehension, or was plunged in sadness, or, after many distresses, was nearly borne down by fatigue, so as to render it apparent that the hand of God was seasonably stretched out to him as his necessity required, lest he should sink under the evils which surrounded him. So now, as I explain it, he came to Isaac, for the purpose of restoring him, already wearied and broken down by various miseries.

24. *And the Lord appeared unto him.* This vision (as I have elsewhere said) was to prepare him to listen more attentively to God, and to convince him that it was God with whom he had to deal; for a voice *alone* would have had less energy. Therefore God *appears*, in order to produce confidence in and reverence towards his word. In short, visions were a kind of symbols of the Divine presence, designed to remove all doubt from the minds of the holy fathers respecting him who was about to speak. Should it be objected, that such evidence was not sufficiently sure, since Satan often deceives men by similar manifestations, being, as it were, the ape of God;—we must keep in mind what has been said before, that a clear and unambiguous mark was engraven on the visions of God, by which the faithful might certainly distinguish them from those which were fallacious, so that their faith should not be kept in suspense: and certainly, since Satan can only delude us in the dark, God exempts his children from this danger, by illuminating their eyes with the brightness of his countenance. Yet God did not fully

manifest his glory to the holy fathers, but assumed a form
by means of which they might apprehend him according to
the measure of their capacities; for, as the majesty of God
is infinite, it cannot be comprehended by the human mind,
and by its magnitude it absorbs the whole world. Besides,
it follows of necessity that men, on account of their infirmity,
must not only faint, but be altogether annihilated in the
presence of God. Wherefore, Moses does not mean that God
was seen in his true nature and greatness, but in such a
manner as Isaac was able to bear the sight. But what we
have said, namely, that the vision was a testimony of Deity,
for the purpose of giving credibility to the oracle, will more
fully appear from the context; for this appearance was not
a mute spectre; but the word immediately followed, which
confirmed, in the mind of Isaac, faith in gratuitous adoption
and salvation.

*I am the God of Abraham.* This preface is intended to
renew the memory of all the promises before given, and to
direct the mind of Isaac to the perpetual covenant which had
been made with Abraham, and which was to be transmitted,
as by tradition, to his posterity. The Lord therefore begins
by declaring himself to be the God who had spoken at the
first to Abraham, in order that Isaac might not sever the
present from the former oracles: for as often as he repeated
the testimony of his grace to the faithful, he sustained their
faith with fresh supports. Yet he would have that very faith
to remain based upon the first covenant by which he had
adopted them to himself: and we must always keep this
method in mind, in order that we may learn to gather together the promises of God, as they are combined in an inseparable bond. Let this also ever occur to us, as a first
principle, that God thus kindly promises us his grace because
he has freely adopted us.

*Fear not.* Since these words are elsewhere expounded, I
shall now be the more brief. In the first place, we must observe, that God thus addresses the faithful for the purpose
of tranquillizing their minds; for, if his word be withdrawn,
they necessarily become torpid through stupidity, or are
tormented with disquietude. Whence it follows, that we can

receive peace from no other source than from the mouth of the Lord, when he declares himself the author of our salvation; not that we are then free from all fear, but because the confidence of faith is sufficiently efficacious to assuage our perturbations. Afterwards the Lord gives proofs of his love, by its effect, when he promises that he will bless Isaac.

25. *And he builded an altar there.* From other passages we are well aware that Moses here speaks of public worship; for inward invocation of God neither requires an altar, nor has any special choice of place; and it is certain that the saints, wherever they lived, worshipped. But because religion ought to maintain a testimony before men, Isaac, having erected and consecrated an altar, professes himself a worshipper of the true and only God, and by this method separates himself from the polluted rites of heathens. He also built the altar, not for himself alone, but for his whole family; that there, with all his household, he might offer sacrifices. Moreover, since the altar was built for the external exercises of faith, the expression, he called upon God, implies as much as if Moses had said that Isaac celebrated the name of God, and gave testimony of his own faith. The visible worship of God had also another use; namely, that men, according to their infirmity, may stimulate and exercise themselves in the fear of God. Besides, since we know that sacrifices were then commanded, we must observe that Isaac did not rashly trifle in worshipping God, but adhered to the rule of faith, that he might undertake nothing without the word of God. Whence also we infer how preposterous and erroneous a thing it is to imitate the fathers, unless the Lord join us with them by means of a similar command. Meanwhile, the words of Moses clearly signify, that whatever exercises of piety the faithful undertake are to be directed to this end, namely, that God may be worshipped and invoked. To this point, therefore, all rites and ceremonies ought to have reference. But although it was the custom of the holy fathers to build an altar in whatever place they pitched their tent, we yet gather, from the connexion of the words, that after God appeared to his servant Isaac, this altar was built by him in token of his gratitude.

*And there Isaac's servants digged a well.* It is remarkable that whereas this place had already received its name from the well which had been dug in it, Isaac should there again have to seek water, especially since Abraham had purchased, for himself and his posterity, the right to the well from the king. Moreover, the digging itself was difficult and laborious; for Moses had a design in saying, that afterwards the servants came and said to him, "We have found water." I have, therefore, no doubt, that throughout the whole of that region a conspiracy had been entered into by the inhabitants, for the purpose of expelling the holy man, through want of water; so that this well of Sheba also had been fraudulently stopped up. The context also shows, that the first care of the holy patriarch concerned the worship of God, because Moses relates that an altar was erected, before he speaks of the well. Now it is of importance to observe with what great troubles these holy fathers continually had to contend; which they never would have been able to overcome or to endure, unless they had been far removed from our delicate course of living. For how severely should we feel the loss of water, seeing that we often rage against God if we have not abundance of wine? Therefore, by such examples, let the faithful learn to accustom themselves to patient endurance: and if at any time food and other necessaries of life fail them, let them turn their eyes to Isaac, who wandered, parched with thirst, in the inheritance which had been divinely promised him.[1]

26. *Then Abimelech went to him.* We have had an exactly similar narrative in the twenty-first chapter and the twenty-second verse. The Lord, therefore, followed Isaac with the same favour which he had before shown to his father Abraham. For it was no common blessing, that Abimelech should voluntarily seek his friendship. Besides, he would be relieved from no little care and anxiety, when his neighbours, who had harassed him in so many ways, being now themselves afraid of him, desire to secure his friendship.

[1] Qui siticulosus in hæreditate sibi divinitus promissa erravit. Qui est errant en l'heritage qui Dieu lui avoit promis, et tarrissant de soif.— *Fr. Tr.*

Therefore the Lord both confers signal honour upon his servant, and provides at the same time for his tranquillity. There is not the least doubt that the king was led to this measure, by a secret divine impulse. For, if he was afraid, why did he not resort to some other remedy? why did he humble himself to supplicate a private man? why, at least, did he not rather send for him, or command him with authority to do what he wished? But God had so forcibly impressed his mind, that he, forgetting his regal pride, sought for peace and alliance with a man who was neither covetous, nor warlike, nor furnished with a great army. Thus we may learn, that the minds of men are in the hand of God, so that he not only can incline those to gentleness who before were swelling with fury, but can humble them by terror, as often as he pleases.

27. *And Isaac said unto them, Wherefore come ye to me?* Isaac not only expostulates concerning injuries received, but protests that in future he can have no confidence in them, since he had found in them a disposition so hostile to himself. This passage teaches us, that it is lawful for the faithful to complain of their enemies, in order, if possible, to recall them from their purpose of doing injury, and to restrain their force, frauds, and acts of injustice. For liberty is not inconsistent with patience: nor does God require of his own people, that they should silently digest every injury which may be inflicted upon them, but only that they should restrain their minds and hands from revenge.[1] Now, if their minds are pure and well regulated, their tongues will not be virulent in reproaching the faults of others; but their sole purpose will be to restrain the wicked by a sense of shame from iniquity. For where there is no hope of profiting by complaints, it is better to cherish peace by silence; unless, perhaps, for the purpose of rendering those who delight themselves in wickedness inexcusable. We must, indeed, always beware, lest, from a desire of vengeance, our tongues

---

[1] Neque hoc à suis requirit Deus, ut quicquid noxæ illatum fuerit, taciti devorent; sed tantum ut animos et manus contineant à vindicta.

Dieu ne requiert point des siens, qu'ils avallent sans mot dire toutes les nuisances qu'on leur fera, mais seulement qu'ils gardent leurs cœurs et leurs mains de vengence.—*Fr. Tr.*

break out in reproaches; and, as Solomon says, " hatred stirreth up strifes." (Prov. x. 12.)

28. *We saw certainly that the Lord was with thee.* By this argument they prove that they desired a compact with Isaac, not insidiously, but in good faith, because they acknowledge the favour of God towards him. For it was necessary to purge themselves from this suspicion, seeing that they now presented themselves so courteously to one against whom they had before been unreasonably opposed. This confession of theirs, however, contains very useful instruction. Profane men in calling one, whose affairs all succeed well and prosperously, the blessed of the Lord, bear testimony that God is the author of all good things, and that from him alone flows all prosperity. Exceedingly base, therefore, is our ingratitude, if, when God acts kindly towards us, we pass by his benefits with closed eyes. Again, profane men regard the friendship of one whom God favours, as desirable for themselves; considering that there is no better or holier commendation than the love of God. Perversely blind, therefore, are they, who not only neglect those whom God declares to be dear unto him, but also iniquitously vex them. The Lord proclaims himself ready to execute vengeance on any one who may injure those whom he takes under his protection; but the greater part, unmoved by this most terrible denunciation, still wickedly afflict the good and the simple. We here, however, see that the sense of nature dictated to unbelievers, what we scarcely credit when spoken by the mouth of God himself. Still it is surprising that they should be afraid of an inoffensive man; and should require from him an oath that he would do them no injury. They ought to have concluded, from the favour which God had showed him, that he was a just man, and therefore there could be no danger from him; yet because they form their estimate of him from their own disposition and conduct, they also distrust his probity. Such perturbation commonly agitates unbelievers, so that they are inconsistent with themselves; or at least waver and are tossed between conflicting sentiments, and have nothing fixed and equable. For those principles of right judgment, which

spring up in their breasts, are soon smothered by depraved affections. Hence it happens, that what is justly conceived by them vanishes; or is at least corrupted, and does not bring forth good fruit.

29. *As we have not touched thee.* An accusing conscience urges them to desire to hold him closely bound unto them; and therefore they require an oath from him that he will not hurt them. For they knew that he might rightfully avenge himself on them for the sufferings he had endured: but they dissemble on this point, and even make a wonderful boast of their own acts of kindness. At first, indeed, the humanity of the king was remarkable, for he not only entertained Isaac with hospitality, but treated him with peculiar honour; yet he by no means continued to act thus to the end. It accords, however, with the common custom of men, to disguise their own faults by whatever artifice or colour they can invent. But if we have committed any offence, it rather becomes us ingenuously to confess our fault, than by denying it, to wound still more deeply the minds of those whom we have injured. Nevertheless Isaac, since he had already sufficiently pierced their consciences, does not press them any further. For strangers are not to be treated by us as domestics; but if they do not receive profit, they are to be left to the judgment of God. Therefore, although Isaac does not extort from them a just confession; yet, that he may not be thought inwardly to cherish any hostility towards them, he does not refuse to strike a covenant with them. Thus we learn from his example, that if any have estranged themselves from us, they are not to be repelled when they again offer themselves to us. For if we are commanded to follow after peace, even when it seems to fly from us, it behoves us far less to be repulsive, when our enemies voluntarily seek reconciliation; especially if there be any hope of amendment in future, although true repentance may not yet appear. And he receives them to a feast, not only for the sake of promoting peace, but also for the sake of showing that he, having laid aside all offence, has become their friend.

*Thou art now the blessed of the Lord.* This is commonly explained to mean that they court his favour by flatteries, just as persons are accustomed to flatter when they ask a favour; but I rather think this expression to have been added in a different sense. Isaac had complained of their injuries in having expelled him through envy: they answer, that there was no reason why any particle of grief should remain in his mind, since the Lord had treated him so kindly and so exactly according to his own wish; as if they had said, What dost thou want? Art thou not content with thy present success? Let us grant that we have not discharged the duty of hospitality towards thee; yet the blessing of God abundantly suffices to obliterate the memory of that time. Perhaps, however, by these words, they again assert that they are acting towards him with good faith, because he is under the guardianship of God.

31. *And sware one to another.* Isaac does not hesitate to swear; partly, that the Philistines may be the more easily appeased; partly, that he may not be suspected by them. And this is the legitimate method of swearing, when men mutually bind themselves to the cultivation of peace. A simple promise, indeed, ought to have sufficed; but since dissimulation or inconstancy causes men to be distrustful of each other, the Lord grants them the use of his name, that this more holy confirmation may be added to our covenants; and he does not only permit, he even commands us to swear as often as necessity requires it. (Deut. vi. 13.) Meanwhile we must beware, lest his name be profaned by rashly swearing.

32. *And it came to pass the same day.* Hence it appears, (as I have said a little before,) that the waters were not found in a moment of time. If it be asked, whence a supply of water had been obtained for his cattle and his household during the intervening days, I doubt not, indeed, that he either bought it, or was compelled to go to a distance to see if any one would be found from whom he might obtain it by entreaty. With respect to the name, [Sheba,] they are mistaken, in my judgment, who deem it to be any other than that which Abraham had first given to the well. For since the Hebrew word is ambiguous, Abraham alluded to the covenant which he had struck with the king of Gerar; but

now Isaac recalling this ancient memorial to mind, joins with it the covenant in which he had himself engaged.

34. *And Esau was forty years old.* For many reasons Moses relates the marriages of Esau. Inasmuch as he mingled himself with the inhabitants of the land, from whom the holy race of Abraham was separated, and contracted affinities by which he became entangled; this was a kind of prelude of his rejection. It happened also, by the wonderful counsel of God, that these daughters-in-law were grievous and troublesome to the holy patriarch (Isaac) and his wife, in order that they might not by degrees become favourable to that reprobate people. If the manners of the people had been pleasing, and they had had good and obedient daughters, perhaps also, with their consent, Isaac might have taken a wife from among them. But it was not lawful for those to be bound together in marriage, whom God designed to be perpetual enemies. For how would the inheritance of the land be secured to the posterity of Abraham, but by the destruction of those among whom he sojourned for a time? Therefore God cuts off all inducements to these inauspicious marriages, that the disunion which he had established might remain. It appears hence, with what perpetual affection Esau was loved by Isaac; for although the holy man justly regarded his son's wives with aversion, and his mind was exasperated against them, he never failed to act with the greatest kindness towards his son, as we shall afterwards see. We have elsewhere spoken concerning polygamy. This corruption had so far prevailed in every direction among many people, that the custom, though vicious, had acquired the force of law. It is not, therefore, surprising that a man addicted to the flesh indulged his appetite by taking two wives.

## CHAPTER XXVII.

| | |
|---|---|
| 1. AND it came to pass, that when Isaac was old, and his eyes were dim, so that he could not see, he called Esau his eldest son, and said | 1. Fuit autem quum senuisset Ishac, et caligassent oculi ejus ita ut non videret, vocavit Esau filium suum majorem, et dixit ad eum, |

unto him, My son. And he said unto him, Behold, *here am* I.

2. And he said, Behold now, I am old, I know not the day of my death.

3. Now therefore take, I pray thee, thy weapons, thy quiver and thy bow, and go out to the field, and take me *some* venison;

4. And make me savoury meat, such as I love, and bring *it* to me, that I may eat; that my soul may bless thee before I die.

5. And Rebekah heard when Isaac spake to Esau his son. And Esau went to the field to hunt *for* venison, *and* to bring *it*.

6. And Rebekah spake unto Jacob her son, saying, Behold, I heard thy father speak unto Esau thy brother, saying,

7. Bring me venison, and make me savoury meat, that I may eat, and bless thee before the Lord before my death.

8. Now therefore, my son, obey my voice, according to that which I command thee.

9. Go now to the flock, and fetch me from thence two good kids of the goats; and I will make them savoury meat for thy father, such as he loveth.

10. And thou shalt bring *it* to thy father, that he may eat, and that he may bless thee before his death.

11. And Jacob said to Rebekah his mother, Behold, Esau my brother *is* a hairy man, and I *am* a smooth man:

12. My father peradventure will feel me, and I shall seem to him as a deceiver; and I shall bring a curse upon me, and not a blessing.

13. And his mother said unto him, Upon me *be* thy curse, my son; only obey my voice, and go fetch me *them*.

14. And he went, and fetched, and brought *them* to his mother: and his mother made savoury meat, such as his father loved.

15. And Rebekah took goodly raiment of her eldest son Esau, which *were* with her in the house,

Fili mi. Et dixit ad eum, Ecce adsum.

2. Et dixit, Ecce nunc senui: non novi diem quo moriar.

3. Nunc igitur cape quæso instrumenta tua, pharetram tuam, et arcum tuum, et egredere in agrum, et venare mihi venationem.

4. Et fac mihi cibos sapidos, quemadmodum diligo, et affer mihi, et comedam: ut benedicat tibi anima mea antequam moriar.

5. Ribca autem audiebat, dum loqueretur Isbac ad Esau filium suum: et perrexit Esau in agrum, ut venaretur venationem, ut afferret.

6. Tunc Ribca dixit ad Iahacob filium suum, dicendo, Ecce, audivi patrem tuum loquentem ad Esau fratrem tuum, dicendo,

7. Affer mihi venationem, et fac mihi cibos, et comedam, et benedicam tibi coram Domino antequam moriar.

8. Nunc igitur, fili mi, obedi voci meæ in eo quod præcipio tibi.

9. Vade nunc ad pecudes, et cape mihi inde duos hœdos caprarum bonos, et faciam ex eis escas sapidas patri tuo, quemadmodum diligit.

10. Et afferes patri tuo, et comedet, ut benedicat tibi antequam moriatur.

11. Et dixit Iahacob ad Ribcam matrem suam, Ecce Esau frater meus est vir pilosus, et ego vir lævis:

12. Si forte palpaverit me pater meus, ero in oculis ejus tanquam illusor: et venire faciam super me maledictionem et non benedictionem.

13. Tunc dixit ei mater ejus, Super me *sit* maledictio tua, fili mi: veruntamen obedi voci meæ et vade, cape mihi.

14. Profectus est itaque, et accepit, et attulit matri suæ, et fecit mater ejus cibos sapidos, quemadmodum diligebat pater ejus.

15. Et accepit Ribca vestes Esau filii sui majoris delectabiles, quæ *erant* apud se in domo, et induit

and put them upon Jacob her younger son.

16. And she put the skins of the kids of the goats upon his hands, and upon the smooth of his neck.

17. And she gave the savoury meat and the bread, which she had prepared, into the hand of her son Jacob.

18. And he came unto his father, and said, My father. And he said, Here *am* I; who *art* thou, my son?

19. And Jacob said unto his father, I *am* Esau thȳ first-born; I have done according as thou badest me: arise, I pray thee, sit and eat of my venison, that thy soul may bless me.

20. And Isaac said unto his son, How *is it* that thou hast found *it* so quickly, my son? And he said, Because the Lord thy God brought *it* to me.

21. And Isaac said unto Jacob, Come near, I pray thee, that I may feel thee, my son, whether thou *be* my very son Esau or not.

22. And Jacob went near unto Isaac his father; and he felt him, and said, The voice *is* Jacob's voice, but the hands *are* the hands of Esau.

23. And he discerned him not, because his hands were hairy, as his brother Esau's hands. So he blessed him.

24. And he said, *Art* thou my very son Esau? And he said, I *am*.

25. And he said, Bring *it* near to me, and I will eat of my son's venison, that my soul may bless thee. And he brought *it* near to him, and he did eat: and he brought him wine, and he drank.

26. And his father Isaac said unto him, Come near now, and kiss me, my son.

27. And he came near, and kissed him: and he smelled the smell of his raiment, and blessed him, and said, See, the smell of my son *is* as the smell of a field which the Lord hath blessed:

28. Therefore God give thee of the dew of heaven, and the fatness

Iahacob filium suum minorem.

16. Et pelles hœdorum caprarum circumdedit manibus ejus, et lævitati colli ejus.

17. Deditque cibos sapidos et panem, quos paraverat, in manu Iahacob filii sui.

18. Venit ergo ad patrem suum, et dixit, Pater mi. Ille autem respondit, Ecce adsum: qui es, fili mi?

19. Et dixit Iahacob ad patrem suum, Ego sum Esau primogenitus tuus, feci quemadmodum loquutus es ad me: surge nunc, sede, et comede de venatione mea, ut benedicat mihi anima tua.

20. Et dixit Ishac ad filium suum, Quid hoc *quod* festinasti ad inveniendum, fili mi? Cui respondit, Quia occurrere fecit Iehova Deus tuus coram me.

21. Tunc dixit Ishac ad Iacob, Appropinqua nunc, et palpabo te, fili mi, utrum sis ipse filius meus Esau, an non.

22. Et appropinquavit Iahacob Ishac patri suo: qui palpavit eum, et dixit, Vox vox Iahacob est: at manus, manus Esau.

23. Et non agnovit eum: quia erant manus ejus sicut manus Esau fratris sui pilosæ: et benedixit ei:

24. Et dixit, Tu es ipse filius meus Esau? Respondit, Sum.

25. Tunc dixit, Admove mihi, et comedam de venatione filii mei, ut benedicat tibi anima mea. Et admovit ei, et comedit: attulitque ei vinum, et bibit.

26. Et dixit ad eum Ishac pater ejus, Appropinqua nunc, et osculare me, fili mi.

27. Et appropinquavit, et osculatus est eum: et odoratus est odorem vestimentorum ejus: et benedixit ei, et dixit, Vide, odorem filii mei sicut odorem agri, cui benedixit Iehova.

28. Et det tibi Deus de rore cœli, et *de* pinguedinibus terræ, et

of the earth, and plenty of corn and wine:

29. Let people serve thee, and nations bow down to thee: be lord over thy brethren, and let thy mother's sons bow down to thee: cursed *be* every one that curseth thee, and blessed *be* he that blesseth thee.

30. And it came to pass, as soon as Isaac had made an end of blessing Jacob, and Jacob was yet scarce gone out from the presence of Isaac his father, that Esau his brother came in from his hunting.

31. And he also had made savoury meat, and brought it unto his father, and said unto his father, Let my father arise, and eat of his son's venison, that thy soul may bless me.

32. And Isaac his father said unto him, Who *art* thou? And he said, I *am* thy son, thy first-born, Esau.

33. And Isaac trembled very exceedingly, and said, Who? where *is* he that hath taken venison, and brought *it* me, and I have eaten of all before thou camest, and have blessed him? yea, *and* he shall be blessed.

34. And when Esau heard the words of his father, he cried with a great and exceeding bitter cry, and said unto his father, Bless me, *even* me also, O my father!

35. And he said, Thy brother came with subtilty, and hath taken away thy blessing.

36. And he said, Is not he rightly named Jacob? for he hath supplanted me these two times: he took away my birthright; and, behold, now he hath taken away my blessing. And he said, Hast thou not reserved a blessing for me?

37. And Isaac answered and said unto Esau, Behold, I have made him thy lord, and all his brethren have I given to him for servants; and with corn and wine have I sustained him: and what shall I do now unto thee, my son?

38. And Esau said unto his father, Hast thou but one blessing, my

multitudinem frumenti et musti novi.

29. Serviant tibi populi, et incurvent se tibi populi: esto dominus fratribus tuis, et incurvent se tibi filii matris tuæ: maledicentes tibi, maledicti erunt, et benedicentes tibi, benedicti.

30. Et fuit, quando complevit Ishac benedicere Iahacob: fuit, inquam, tantum egrediendo egressus erat Iahacob a facie Ishac patris sui, tunc Esau frater ejus venit a venatione sua.

31. Et fecit etiam ipse cibos sapidos, et attulit patri suo: dixitque patri suo, Surgat pater meus, et comedat de venatione filii sui, ut benedicat mihi anima tua.

32. Et dixit ei Ishac pater ejus, Quis es? Ille respondit, Ego sum filius tuus, primogenitus tuus Esau.

33. Et expavit Ishac pavore magno vehementissime, et dixit, Quis *est*, et ubi est qui venatus est venationem, et attulit mihi, et comedi ex omnibus antequam venires? et benedixi ei, etiam benedictus erit.

34. Quum audisset Esau verba patris sui, clamavit clamore magno, et amaro valde valde, dixitque patri suo, Benedic mihi: etiam ego *filius tuus sum*, pater mi.

35. Et dixit, Venit frater tuus dolose et accepit benedictionem tuam.

36. Dixit ergo, Vere vocatum est nomen ejus Iahacob, quia supplantavit me jam duabus vicibus: primogenituram meam accepit, et ecce nunc accepit benedictionem meam. Et dixit, Annon reservasti mihi *apud te* benedictionem?

37. Et respondit Ishac, et dixit ad Esau, Ecce, dominum posui eum tibi, et omnes fratres ejus dedi ei in servos, frumentumque et vinum addixi ei: et tibi nunc quid faciam, fili mi?

38. Tunc dixit Esau ad patrem suum, Numquid benedictio una est

father? bless me, *even* me also, O my father! And Esau lifted up his voice, and wept.

39. And Isaac his father answered and said unto him, Behold, thy dwelling shall be the fatness of the earth, and of the dew of heaven from above;

40. And by thy sword shalt thou live, and shalt serve thy brother: and it shall come to pass, when thou shalt have the dominion, that thou shalt break his yoke from off thy neck.

41. And Esau hated Jacob, because of the blessing wherewith his father blessed him: and Esau said in his heart, The days of mourning for my father are at hand; then will I slay my brother Jacob.

42. And these words of Esau her elder son were told to Rebekah. And she sent and called Jacob her younger son, and said unto him, Behold, thy brother Esau, as touching thee, doth comfort himself, *purposing* to kill thee.

43. Now therefore, my son, obey my voice; and arise, flee thou to Laban my brother, to Haran;

44. And tarry with him a few days, until thy brother's fury turn away;

45. Until thy brother's anger turn away from thee, and he forget *that* which thou hast done to him: then I will send and fetch thee from thence: why should I be deprived also of you both in one day?

46. And Rebekah said to Isaac, I am weary of my life because of the daughters of Heth: if Jacob take a wife of the daughters of Heth, such as these *which are* of the daughters of the land, what good shall my life do me?

tibi, pater mi? benedic. mihi, et etiam ego *filius tuus*, pater mi: et elevavit Esau vocem suam et flevit.

39. Tunc respondit Ishac pater ejus, et dixit ad eum, Ecce, de pinguedinibus terræ erit habitatio tua et de rore cœli desuper.

40. Et in gladio tuo vives, et fratri tuo servies: et erit, quando dominaberis, franges jugum ejus a collo tuo.

41. Itaque odio habuit Esau Iahacob propter benedictionem, qua benedixerat ei pater ejus: et cogitavit Esau in corde suo, Appropinquabunt dies luctus patris mei, et occidam Iahacob fratrem meum.

42. Et nuntiata sunt Ribcæ verba Esau filii sui majoris: et misit, et vocavit Iahacob filium suum minorem, et dixit ad eum, Ecce, Esau frater tuus consolatur se super te, ut occidat te.

43. Et nunc fili mi, obedi voci meæ, et surge, et fuge ad Laban fratrem meum in Charan.

44. Et habita cum eo dies aliquot, donec avertatur furor fratris tui a te.

45. Donec avertatur ira fratris tui a te, et obliviscatur eorum quæ fecisti ei: et mittam, et accipiam te inde: utquid orbabor etiam ambobus vobis die una?

46. Et dixit Ribca ad Ishac, Angustiis affecta sum in vita mea propter filias Heth: si acceperit Iahacob uxorem de filiabus Heth, sicut istas de filiabus terræ, utquid est mihi vita?

1. *And it came to pass that when Isaac was old.* In this chapter Moses prosecutes, in many words, a history which does not appear to be of great utility. It amounts to this; Esau having gone out, at his father's command, to hunt; Jacob, in his brother's clothing, was, by the artifice of his mother, induced to obtain by stealth the blessing due by the right of nature to the first-born. It seems even like child's

play to present to his father a kid instead of venison, to feign himself to be hairy by putting on skins, and, under the name of his brother, to get the blessing by a lie. But in order to learn that Moses does not in vain pause over this narrative as a most serious matter, we must first observe, that when Jacob received the blessing from his father, this token confirmed to him the oracle by which the Lord had preferred him to his brother. For the benediction here spoken of was not a mere prayer but a legitimate sanction, divinely interposed, to make manifest the grace of election. God had promised to the holy fathers that he would be a God to their seed for ever. They, when at the point of death, in order that the succession might be secured to their posterity, put them in possession, as if they would deliver, from hand to hand, the favour which they had received from God. So Abraham, in blessing his son Isaac, constituted him the heir of spiritual life with a solemn rite. With the same design, Isaac now, being worn down with age, imagines himself to be shortly about to depart this life, and wishes to bless his first-born son, in order that the everlasting covenant of God may remain in his own family. The Patriarchs did not take this upon themselves rashly, or on their own private account, but were public and divinely ordained witnesses. To this point belongs the declaration of the Apostle, "the less is blessed of the better." (Heb. vii. 7.) For even the faithful were accustomed to bless each other by mutual offices of charity; but the Lord enjoined this peculiar service upon the patriarchs, that they should transmit, as a deposit to posterity, the covenant which he had struck with them, and which they kept during the whole course of their life. The same command was afterwards given to the priests, as appears in Num. vi. 24, and other similar places. Therefore Isaac, in blessing his son, sustained another character than that of a father or of a private person, for he was a prophet and an interpreter of God, who constituted his son an heir of the same grace which he had received. Hence appears what I have already said, that Moses, in treating of this matter, is not without reason thus prolix. But let us weigh each of the circumstances of the case in its proper order; of which this is the first, that God transferred the blessing of Esau to Jacob, by a mistake on the part of the father; whose eyes, Moses tells us, were dim. The vision also of Jacob was dull when he blessed his grandchildren Ephraim and Manasseh; yet his want of sight did not prevent him from cautiously placing his hands in a transverse direction. But God suffered Isaac to be deceived, in order to show that it was not by the will of man that Jacob was raised, contrary to the course of nature, to the right and honour of primogeniture.

2. *Behold, now I am old, I know not the day of my death.* There is not the least doubt that Isaac implored daily blessings on his sons all his life: this, therefore, appears to have been an extraordinary kind of benediction. Moreover, the declaration that he knew not the day of his death, is as much as if he had said, that death was every moment pressing so closely upon him, a decrepid and failing man, that he dared not promise himself any longer life. Just as a woman with child when the time of parturition draws near, might say, that she had now no day certain. Every one, even in the full vigour of age, carries with him a thousand deaths. Death claims as its own the fœtus in the mother's womb, and accompanies it through every stage of life. But as it urges the old more closely, so they ought to place it more constantly before their eyes, and should pass as pilgrims through the world, or as those who have already one foot in the grave. In short, Isaac, as one near death, wishes to leave the Church surviving him in the person of his son.

4. *That my soul may bless thee.* Wonderfully was the faith of the holy man blended with a foolish and inconsiderate carnal affection. The general principle of faith flourishes in his mind, when, in blessing his son, he consigns to him, under the direction of the Holy Spirit, the right of the inheritance which had been divinely promised to himself. Meanwhile, he is blindly carried away by the love of his first-born son, to prefer him to the other; and in this way he contends against the oracle of God. For he could not be ignorant of that which God had pronounced before the children were born. If any one would excuse

him, inasmuch as he had received no command from God to
change the accustomed order of nature by preferring the
younger to the elder; this is easily refuted: because when
he knew that the first-born was rejected, he still persisted in
his excessive attachment. Again, in neglecting to inquire
respecting his duty, when he had been informed of the heavenly oracle by his wife, his indolence was by no means excusable. For he was not altogether ignorant of his calling;
therefore, his obstinate attachment to his son was a kind of
blindness, which proved a greater obstacle to him than the
external dimness of his eyes. Yet this fault, although deserving of reprehension, did not deprive the holy man of the
right of pronouncing a blessing; but plenary authority remained with him, and the force and efficacy of his testimony
stood entire, just as if God himself had spoken from heaven; to which subject I shall soon again allude.

5. *And Rebekah heard.* Moses now explains more fully
the artifice by which Jacob attained the blessing. It truly
appears ridiculous, that an old man, deceived by the cunning
of his wife, should, through ignorance and error, have given
utterance to what was contrary to his wish. And surely the
stratagem of Rebekah was not without fault; for although
she could not guide her husband by salutary counsel, yet it
was not a legitimate method of acting, to circumvent him by
such deceit. For, as a lie is in itself culpable, she sinned
more grievously still in this, that she desired to sport in a
sacred matter with such wiles. She knew that the decree
by which Jacob had been elected and adopted was immutable; why then does she not patiently wait till God shall
confirm it in fact, and shall show that what he had once
pronounced from heaven is certain? Therefore, she darkens
the celestial oracle by her lie, and abolishes, as far as
she was able, the grace promised to her son. Now, if we
consider farther, whence arose this great desire to bestir
herself; her extraordinary faith will on the other hand appear. For, as she did not hesitate to provoke her husband
against herself, to light up implacable enmity between the
brothers, to expose her beloved son Jacob to the danger of
immediate death, and to disturb the whole family; this cer-

tainly flowed from no other source than her faith.¹ The inheritance promised by God was firmly fixed in her mind; she knew that it was decreed to her son Jacob. And therefore, relying upon the covenant of God, and keeping in mind the oracle received, she forgets the world. Thus, we see, that her faith was mixed with an unjust and immoderate zeal. This is to be carefully observed, in order that we may understand that a pure and distinct knowledge does not always so illuminate the minds of the pious as to cause them to be governed, in all their actions, by the Holy Spirit, but that the little light which shows them their path is enveloped in various clouds of ignorance and error; so that while they hold a right course, and are tending towards the goal, they yet occasionally slide. Finally, both in Isaac and in his wife the principle of faith was pre-eminent. But each, by ignorance in certain particulars, and by other faults, either diverged a little from the way, or, at least, stumbled in the way. But seeing that, nevertheless, the election of God stood firm; nay, that he even executed his design through the deceit of a woman, he vindicates, in this manner, the whole praise of his benediction to his own gratuitous goodness.

11. *And Jacob said to Rebekah.* That Jacob does not voluntarily present himself to his father, but rather fears lest, his imposture being detected, he should bring a curse upon himself, is very contrary to faith.² For when the Apostle teaches, that " whatsoever is not of faith is sin," (Rom. xiv. 23,) he trains the sons of God to this sobriety, that they may not permit themselves to undertake anything

¹ This is a dangerous position, however it may be modified or explained. True faith never leads to sin. It was the mixture, not to say the predominance of unbelief, which caused Rebekah, instead of waiting for the fulfilment of God's promises in his own way, to plot and to execute a scheme of imposture, which involved herself and her family in perpetual disquietude. What Calvin calls zeal, he ought to have called rashness and something worse.—*Ed.*

² There is a great want of Calvin's accustomed caution and soundness in all this reasoning. It certainly was right that Jacob should feel and express the fear, lest the deception which his mother required him to practise should be detected, and should bring a curse upon him and not a blessing. It would indeed have been a still higher proof of integrity, and a still stronger exercise of faith, had he repelled the importunities of his mother, saying, " How shall I do this wickedness, and sin against God?" —*Ed.*

with a doubtful and perplexed conscience. This firm persuasion is the only rule of right conduct, when we, relying on the command of God, go intrepidly wheresoever he calls us. Jacob, therefore, by debating with himself, shows that he was deficient in faith; and certainly, although he was not entirely without it, yet, in this point, he is convicted of failure. But by this example we are again taught, that faith is not always extinguished by a given fault; yet, if God sometimes bears with his servants thus far, that he turns, what they have done perversely, to their salvation, we must not hence take a license to sin. It happened by the wonderful mercy of God, that Jacob was not cut off from the grace of adoption. Who would not rather fear than become presumptuous? And whereas we see that his faith was obscured by doubting, let us learn to ask of the Lord the spirit of prudence to govern all our steps. There was added another error of no light kind: for why does he not rather reverence God than dread his father's anger? why does it not rather occur to his mind, that a foul blot would stain the hallowed adoption of God, when it seemed to owe its accomplishment to a lie? For although it tended to a right end, it was not lawful to attain that end, through this oblique course. Meanwhile, there is no doubt that faith prevailed over these impediments. For what was the cause why he preferred the bare and apparently empty benediction of his father,[1] to the quiet which he then enjoyed, to the conveniences of home, and finally to life itself? According to the flesh, the father's benediction, of which he was so desirous, that he knowingly and willingly plunged himself into great difficulties, was but an imaginary thing. Why did he act thus, but because in the exercise of simple faith in the

---

[1] Quid enim fuit causæ cur nuda et in speciem inania patris *vota* . . . præferret? Tymme translates *vota* " wishes," and either for the sake of making sense of the passage, or because the edition from which he made his version had a different reading, he puts the word "mother" in the place of "father." But as the Amsterdam and Berlin editions both have the word *patris* and not *matris*, the translation above given seems to be required. It agrees substantially with the French version, which is as follows: Car qui a este cause qu'il a preferé la benediction de son pere, laquelle sembloit nue et vaine en apparence, au repos duquel il jouissoit lors, &c.—*Ed.*

word of God, he more highly valued the hope which was hidden from him, than the desirable condition which he actually enjoyed? Besides, his fear of his father's anger had its origin in the true fear of God. He says that he feared lest he should bring upon himself a curse. But he would not so greatly have dreaded a verbal censure, if he had not deemed the grace deposited in the hands of his father worth more than a thousand lives. It was therefore under an impulse of God that he feared his father, who was really God's minister. For when the Lord sees us creeping on the earth, he draws us to himself by the hand of man.[1]

13. *Upon me be thy curse, my son.* Here Rebekah sins again, because she burns with such hasty zeal that she does not consider how highly God disapproves of her evil course. She presumptuously subjects herself to the curse. But whence this unheeding confidence? Being unfurnished with any divine command, she took her own counsel. Yet no one will deny that this zeal, although preposterous, proceeds from special reverence for the word of God. For since she was informed by the oracle of God, that Jacob was preferred in the sight of God, she disregarded whatever was visible in the world, and whatever the sense of nature dictated, in comparison with God's secret election. Therefore we are taught by this example, that every one should walk modestly and cautiously according to the rule of his vocation; and should not dare to proceed beyond what the Lord allows in his word.

14. *And he went and fetched.* Although it is probable that Jacob was not only influenced by a desire to yield obedience to the authority of his mother, but was also persuaded by her reasonings, he yet sinned by overstepping the bounds of his vocation. When Rebekah had taken the blame upon herself, she told him, doubtless, that injury was done to no one: because Jacob was not stealing away another's right,

[1] It is much more probable that Jacob was influenced by a precipitate and ambitious desire to snatch the blessing from the hand of his brother; and though he paused for a moment at the apprehension of consequences, should his mother's scheme fail, yet he too readily acquiesced, and exposed himself to subsequent dangers, not from a supreme regard to the will of God, but from that self-love which so often overshoots its mark.—*Ed.*

but only seeking the blessing which was decreed to him by the celestial oracle. It seemed a fair and probable excuse for the fraud, that Isaac, unless he should be imposed upon, was prepared to invalidate the election of God. Therefore Jacob, instead of simply declining from what was right in submission to his mother, was rather obeying the word of God. In the meantime (as I have said) this particular error was not free from blame: because the truth of God was not to be aided by such falsehoods. The paternal benediction was a seal of God's grace, I confess it; but she ought rather to have waited till God should bring relief from heaven, by changing the mind and guiding the tongue of Isaac, than have attempted what was unlawful. For if Balaam, who prostituted his venal tongue, was constrained by the Spirit, contrary to his own wish, to bless the elect people, whom he would rather have devoted to destruction, (Num. xxii. 12,) how much more powerfully would the same spirit have influenced the tongue of holy Isaac, who was not a mercenary man, but one who desired faithfully to obey God, and was only hurried by an error in a contrary direction? Therefore, although in the main, faith shone pre-eminently in holy Jacob, yet in this respect he bears the blame of rashness, in that he was distrustful of the providence of God, and fraudulently gained possession of his father's blessing.

19. *And Jacob said unto his father, I am Esau.*[1] At first Jacob was timid and anxious; now, having dismissed his fear, he confidently and audaciously lies. By which example we are taught, that when any one has transgressed the proper bounds of duty, he soon allows himself unmeasured license. Wherefore there is nothing better than for each to keep himself within the limits divinely prescribed to him, lest by attempting more than is lawful, he should open the door to Satan. I have before shown how far his seeking the blessing by fraud, and insinuating himself into the possession of it by falsehood, was contrary to faith. Yet this par-

---

[1] " In this speech of Jacob's there are three direct falsehoods. 1st, ' I am *Esau;*' 2d, ' I have done according as thou *badest* me;' 3d, ' Eat of my *venison.*' We ought not to be extremely solicitous to find excuses for all the actions of holy men."—*Cornelius a Lapide in Poli Syn.*

ticular fault and divergence from the right path, did not prevent the faith which had been produced by the oracle from holding on, in some way, its course. In excusing the quickness of his return by saying that the venison was brought to him by God, he speaks in accordance with the rule of piety: he sins, however, in mixing the sacred name of God with his own falsehoods. Thus, when there is a departure from truth, the reverence which is apparently shown to God is nothing else than a profanation of his glory. It was right that the prosperous issue of his hunting should be ascribed to the providence of God, lest we should imagine that any good thing was the result of chance; but when Jacob pretended that God was the author of a benefit which had not been granted to himself, and that, too, as a cloak for his deception, his fault was not free from perjury.

21. *Come near, I pray thee, that I may feel thee.* It hence appears that the holy man was suspicious of fraud, and therefore hesitated. Whence it may seem that the benediction was vain, seeing it had no support of faith. But it thus pleased God so to perform his work by the hand of Isaac, as not to make him, who was the instrument, a willing furtherer of his design. Nor is it absurd that Isaac, like a blind man, should ignorantly transfer the blessing to a different person from him whom he intended. The ordinary function of pastors has something of a similar kind; for since by the command of God, they reconcile men to him, yet they do not discern to whom this reconciliation comes; thus they cast abroad the seed, but are uncertain respecting the fruit. Wherefore God does not place the office and power with which he has invested them, under the control of their own judgment. In this way the ignorance of Isaac does not nullify the heavenly oracles; and God himself, although the senses of his servant fail, does not desist from the accomplishment of his purpose. Here we have a clear refutation of the figment of the Papists, that the whole force of the sacrament depends upon the intention of the man who consecrates; as if, truly, it were left to the will of man to frustrate the design of God. Nevertheless, what I have already so often said must be remembered, that however Isaac

might be deceived in the person of his son, he yet did not pronounce the blessing in vain : because a general faith remained in his mind, and in part governed his conduct. In forming his judgment from the touch, disregarding the voice, he did not act according to the nature of faith. And, therefore, with respect to the person, he was plainly in error. This, however, did not happen in consequence of negligence ; since he diligently and even anxiously turned every way, that he might not deprive the first-born of his right. But it pleased the Lord thus to render his senses dull, partly for the purpose of showing how vain it is for men to strive to change what he has once decreed, (because it is impossible but that his counsel should remain firm and stable though the whole world should oppose it,) and partly, for the purpose of correcting, by this kind of chastisement, the absurd attachment by which Isaac was too closely bound to his first-born. For whence arose this minute investigation, except from the fact that an inordinate love of Esau, which had taken entire possession of his mind, turned him aside from the divine oracle ? Therefore, since he yielded an excessive indulgence to natural feeling, he deserved in every way to be blinded. So much the greater care ought we to take that, in carrying on God's work, we should not give the reins to our human affections.

26. *Come near now, and kiss me.* We know that the practice of kissing was then in use, which many nations retain to this day. Profane men, however, may say, that it is ludicrous for an old man, whose mind was already obtuse, and who moreover had eaten and drunk heartily, should pour forth his benedictions upon a person who was only acting a part.[1] But whereas Moses has previously recorded the oracle of God, by which the adoption was destined for the younger son, it behoves us reverently to contemplate the secret providence of God, towards which profane men pay no respect. Truly Isaac was not so in bondage to the attractions of meat and drink as to be unable, with sobriety of mind, to

---

[1] Vota sua in comicam personam effundit. Espande ses vœus et benedictions sur une personne disguisee et masquee. Should bestow his vows and benedictions upon a person masked and disguised.—*Fr. Tr.*

reflect upon the divine command given unto him, and to undertake in seriousness, and with a certain faith in his own vocation, the very work in which, on account of the infirmity of his flesh, he vacillated and halted. Therefore, we must not form our estimate of this blessing from the external appearance, but from the celestial decree; even as it appeared at length, by the issue, that God neither vainly sported, nor that man rashly proceeded in this affair: and, truly, if the same religion dwells in us which flourished in the patriarch's heart, nothing will hinder the divine power from shining forth the more clearly in the weakness of man.

27. *See, the smell of my son is as the smell of a field.* The allegory of Ambrose on this passage is not displeasing to me. Jacob, the younger brother, is blessed under the person of the elder; the garments which were borrowed from his brother breathe an odour grateful and pleasant to his father. In the same manner we are blessed, as Ambrose teaches, when, in the name of Christ, we enter the presence of our Heavenly Father: we receive from him the robe of righteousness, which, by its odour, procures his favour; in short, we are thus blessed when we are put in his place. But Isaac seems here to desire and implore nothing for his son but what is earthly; for this is the substance of his words, that it might be well with his son in the world, that he might gather together the abundant produce of the earth, that he might enjoy great peace, and shine in honour above others. There is no mention of the heavenly kingdom; and hence it has arisen, that men without learning, and but little exercised in true piety, have imagined that these holy fathers were blessed by the Lord only in respect to this frail and transitory life. But it appears from many passages to have been far otherwise: and as to the fact that Isaac here confines himself to the earthly favours of God, the explanation is easy; for the Lord did not formerly set the hope of the future inheritance plainly before the eyes of the fathers, (as he now calls and raises us directly towards heaven,) but he led them as by a circuitous course. Thus he appointed the land of Canaan as a mirror and pledge to them of the celestial inheritance. In all his acts of kindness he gave them tokens

of his paternal favour, not indeed for the purpose of making them content with present good, so that they should neglect heaven, or should follow a merely empty shadow, as some foolishly suppose; but that, being aided by such helps, according to the time in which they lived, they might by degrees rise towards heaven; for since Christ, the first-fruits of those who rise again, and the author of the eternal and incorruptible life, had not yet been manifested, his spiritual kingdom was, in this way, shadowed forth under figures only, until the fulness of the time should come; and as all the promises of God were involved, and in a sense clothed in these symbols, so the faith of the holy fathers observed the same measure, and made its advances heavenward by means of these earthly rudiments. Therefore, although Isaac makes the temporal favours of God prominent, nothing is further from his mind than to confine the hope of his son to this world; he would raise him to the same elevation to which he himself aspired. Some proof of this may be drawn from his own words; for this is the principal point, that he assigns him the dominion over the nations. But whence the hope of such a dignity, unless he had been persuaded that his race had been elected by the Lord, and, indeed, with this stipulation, that the right of the kingdom should remain with one son only? Meanwhile, let it suffice to adhere to this principle, that the holy man, when he implores a prosperous course of life for his son, wishes that God, in whose paternal favour stands our solid and eternal happiness, may be propitious to him.

29. *Cursed be every one that curseth thee.* What I have before said must be remembered, namely, that these are not bare wishes, such as fathers are wont to utter on behalf of their children, but that promises of God are included in them; for Isaac is the authorized interpreter of God, and the instrument employed by the Holy Spirit; and therefore, as in the person of God, he efficaciously pronounces those accursed who shall oppose the welfare of his son. This then is the confirmation of the promise, by which God, when he receives the faithful under his protection, declares that he will be an enemy to their enemies. The whole force of the

benediction turns to this point, that God will prove himself to be a kind father to his servant Jacob in all things, so that he will constitute him the chief and the head of a holy and elect people, will preserve and defend him by his power, and will secure his salvation in the face of enemies of every kind.

30. *Jacob was yet scarce gone out.* Here is added the manner in which Esau was repulsed, which circumstance availed not a little to confirm the benediction to Jacob: for if Esau had not been rejected, it might seem that he was not deprived of that honour which nature had given him: but now Isaac declares, that what he had done, in virtue of his patriarchal office, could not but be ratified. Here, truly, it again appears, that the primogeniture which Jacob obtained, at the expense of his brother, was made his by a free gift; for if we compare the works of both together, Esau obeys his father, brings him the produce of his hunting, prepares for his father the food obtained by his own labour, and speaks nothing but the truth: in short, we find nothing in him which is not worthy of praise. Jacob never leaves his home, substitutes a kid for venison, insinuates himself by many lies, brings nothing which would properly commend him, but in many things deserves reprehension. Hence it must be acknowledged, that the cause of this event is not to be traced to works, but that it lies hid in the eternal counsel of God. Yet Esau is not unjustly reprobated, because they who are not governed by the Spirit of God can receive nothing with a right mind; only let it be firmly maintained, that since the condition of all is equal, if any one is preferred to another, it is not because of his own merit, but because the Lord hath gratuitously elected him.

33. *And Isaac trembled very exceedingly.*[1] Here now again the faith which had been smothered in the breast of the holy man shines forth and emits fresh sparks; for there is no doubt that his fear springs from faith. Besides, it is no common fear which Moses describes, but that which utterly

---

[1] The original is very forcible, and cannot be fully expressed in a translation. " Isaac trembled with a great trembling exceedingly." The Septuagint represents him as in an ecstasy of astonishment.—*Ed.*

confounds the holy man : for, whereas he was perfectly conscious of his own vocation, and therefore was persuaded that the duty of naming the heir with whom he should deposit the covenant of eternal life was divinely enjoined upon him, he no sooner discovered his error than he was filled with fear, that in an affair so great and so serious God had suffered him to err; for unless he had thought that God was the director of this act, what should have hindered him from alleging his ignorance as an excuse, and from becoming enraged against Jacob, who had stolen in upon him by fraud and by unjustifiable arts? But although covered with shame on account of the error he had committed, he nevertheless, with a collected mind, ratifies the benediction which he had pronounced; and I do not doubt that he then, as one awaking, began to recall to memory the oracle to which he had not been sufficiently attentive. Wherefore, the holy man was not impelled by ambition to be thus tenacious of his purpose, as obstinate men are wont to be, who prosecute to the last what they have once, though foolishly, begun; but the declaration, "I have blessed him, yea, and he shall be blessed," was the effect of a rare and precious faith; for he, renouncing the affections of the flesh, now yields himself entirely to God, and, acknowledging God as the Author of the benediction which he had uttered, ascribes due glory to him in not daring to retract it. The benefit of this doctrine pertains to the whole Church, in order that we may certainly know, that whatever the heralds of the gospel promise to us by the command of God, will be efficacious and stable, because they do not speak as private men, but as by the command of God himself; and the infirmity of the minister does not destroy the faithfulness, power, and efficacy of God's word. He who presents himself to us charged with the offer of eternal happiness and life, is subject to our common miseries and to death; yet, notwithstanding, the promise is efficacious. He who absolves us from sins is himself a sinner; but because his office is divinely assigned him, the stability of this grace, having its foundation in God, shall never fail.

34. *He cried with a great and exceeding bitter cry.* Though Esau persists in imploring the blessing, he yet gives a sign

of desperation, which is the reason why he obtains no benefit, because he enters not by the gate of faith. True piety, indeed, draws forth tears and great cries from the children of God; but Esau, trembling and full of fears, breaks out in wailings; afterwards he casts, at a venture, his wish into the air, that he also may receive a blessing. But his blind incredulity is reproved by his own words; for whereas one blessing only had been deposited with his father, he asks that another should be given to him, as if it were in his father's power indiscriminately to breathe out blessings, independently of the command of God. Here the admonition of the Apostle may suggest itself to our minds, " that Esau, when he sought again the forfeited blessing with tears and loud lamentations, found no place for repentance," (Heb. xii. 17;) for they who neglect to follow God when he calls on them, afterwards call upon him in vain, when he has turned his back. So long as God addresses and invites us, the gate of the kingdom of heaven is in a certain sense open : this opportunity we must use, if we desire to enter, according to the instruction of the Prophet, "Seek ye the Lord while he may be found; call ye upon him while he is near." (Isa. lv. 6.) Of which passage Paul is the interpreter, in defining that to be the acceptable time of the day of salvation in which grace is brought unto us by the gospel. (2 Cor. v. 17.) They who suffer that time to pass by, may, at length, knock too late, and without profit, because God avenges himself of their idleness. We must therefore fear lest if, with deafened ears, we suffer the voice of God now to pass unheeded by, he should, in turn, become deaf to our cry. But it may be asked, how is this repulse consistent with the promise, " If the wicked will turn from all his sins that he hath committed, and keep all my statutes, and do that which is lawful and right, he shall surely live?" (Ezekiel xxiii. 21.) Moreover, it may seem at variance with the clemency of God to reject the sighings of those who, being crushed by misery, fly for refuge to his mercy. I answer, that repentance, if it be true and sincere, will never be too late; and the sinner who, from his soul, is displeased with himself, will obtain pardon: but God in this manner punishes the contempt of his grace, because they who obstinately reject it, do not seriously purpose in their mind to return to him. Thus it is that they who are given up to a reprobate mind are never touched with genuine penitence. Hypocrites truly break out into tears, like Esau, but their heart within them will remain closed as with iron bars. Therefore, since Esau rushes forward, destitute of faith and repentance, to ask a blessing, there is no wonder that he should be rejected.

36. *Is he not rightly named Jacob?* That the mind of Esau was affected with no sense of penitence appears hence; he accused his brother and took no blame to himself. But the very beginning of repentance is grief felt on account of sin, together with self-condemnation. Esau ought to have descended into himself, and to have become his own judge. Having sold his birthright, he had darted, like a famished dog, upon the meat and the pottage; and now, as if he had done no wrong, he vents all his anger on his brother. Further, if the blessing is deemed of any value, why does he not consider that he had been repelled from it, not simply by the fraud of man, but by the providence of God? We see, therefore, that like a blind man feeling in the dark, he cannot find his way.

37. *Behold, I have made him thy Lord.* Isaac now more openly confirms what I have before said, that since God was the author of the blessing, it could neither be vain nor evanescent. For he does not here magnificently boast of his dignity, but keeps himself within the bounds and measure of a servant, and denies that he is at liberty to alter anything. For he always considers, (which is the truth,) that when he sustains the character of God's representative, it is not lawful for him to proceed further than the command will bear him. Hence, indeed, Esau ought to have learned from whence he had fallen by his own fault, in order that he might have humbled himself, and might rather have joined himself with his brother, in order to become a partaker of his blessing, as his inferior, than have desired anything separately for himself. But a depraved cupidity carries him away, so that he, forgetful of the kingdom of God, pursues and cares for nothing except his own private advantage.

Again, we must notice Isaac's manner of speaking, by which he claims a certain force and efficacy for his benediction, as if his word carried with it dominion, abundance of corn and wine, and whatever else God had promised to Abraham. For God, in requiring the faithful to depend on himself alone, would nevertheless have them to rest securely upon the word, which, at his command, is declared to them by the tongue of men. In this way *they* are said to remit sins, who are only the messengers and interpreters of free forgiveness.

38. *Hast thou but one blessing?* Esau seems to take courage; but he neglects the care of his soul, and turns, like a swine, to the pampering of his flesh. He had heard that his father had nothing left to grant; because, truly, the full and entire grace of God so rested upon Jacob, that out of his family there was no happiness. Wherefore, if Esau sought his own welfare, he ought to have drawn from that fountain, and rather to have subjected himself to his brother, than to have cut himself off from a happy connexion with him. He chose, however, rather to be deprived of spiritual grace, provided he might but possess something of his own, and apart from his brother, than to be his inferior at home. He could not be ignorant, that there was one sole benediction by which his brother Jacob had been constituted the heir of the divine covenant: for Isaac would be daily discoursing with them concerning the singular privilege which God had vouchsafed to Abraham and his seed. Esau would not previously have complained so bitterly, unless he had felt that he had been deprived of an incomparable benefit. Therefore, by departing from this one source of blessing, he indirectly renounces God, and cuts himself off from the body of the Church, caring for nothing but this transitory life. But it would have been better for him, miserably to perish through the want of all things in this world, and with difficulty to draw his languishing breath, than to slumber amidst temporal delights. What afterwards follows;—namely, that he wept with loud lamentations,—is a sign of fierce and proud indignation, rather than of penitence; for he remitted nothing of his ferocity, but raged like a cruel beast of prey.

So the wicked, when punishment overtakes them, bewail the salvation they have lost; but, meanwhile, do not cease to delight themselves in their vices; and instead of heartily seeking after the righteousness of God, they rather desire that his deity should be extinct. Of a similar character is that gnashing of teeth and weeping in hell which, instead of stimulating the reprobate to seek after God, only consumes them with unknown torments.

39. *Behold, thy dwelling shall be the fatness of the earth.* At length Esau obtains what he had asked. For, perceiving himself to be cast down from the rank and honour of primogeniture, he chooses rather to have prosperity in the world, separated from the holy people, than to submit to the yoke of his younger brother. But it may be thought that Isaac contradicts himself, in offering a new benediction, when he had before declared, that he had given to his son Jacob all that was placed at his disposal. I answer, that what has been before said concerning Ishmael must be noted in this place. For God, though he hearkened to Abraham's prayer for Ishmael, so far as concerned the present life, yet immediately restricts his promise, by adding the exception implied in the declaration, that in Isaac only should the seed be called. I do not, however, doubt, that the holy man, when he perceived that his younger son Jacob was the divinely ordained heir of a happy life, would endeavour to retain his first-born, Esau, in the bond of fraternal connection, in order that he might not depart from the holy and elect flock of the Church. But now, when he sees him obstinately tending in another direction, he declares what will be his future condition. Meanwhile the spiritual blessing remains in its integrity with Jacob alone, to whom Esau refusing to attach himself, voluntarily becomes an exile from the kingdom of God. The prophecy uttered by Malachi, (i. 3,) may seem to be contradictory to this statement. For, comparing the two brothers, Esau and Jacob, with each other, he teaches that Esau was hated, inasmuch as a possession was given to him in the deserts; and yet Isaac promises him a fertile land. There is a twofold solution: either that the Prophet, speaking comparatively, may with truth call Idumea a desert in com-

parison with the land of Canaan, which was far more fruitful; or else that he was referring to his own times. For although the devastation of both lands had been terrible, yet the land of Canaan in a short time flourished again, while the territory of Edom was condemned to perpetual sterility, and given up to dragons. Therefore, although God, with respect to his own people, banished Esau to desert mountains, he yet gave to him a land sufficiently fertile in itself to render the promise by no means nugatory. For that mountainous region both had its own natural fruitfulness, and was so watered by the dew of heaven, that it would yield sustenance to its inhabitants.

40. *By thy sword shalt thou live, and shalt serve thy brother.* It is to be observed that events are here predicted which were never fulfilled in the person of Esau; and therefore, that the prophecy is concerning things at that time far distant. For Jacob was so far from having obtained dominion over his brother, that on his return from Padan-aram, he suppliantly tendered him his obedience; and the breaking off of the yoke which Isaac here mentions, is referred to a very remote period. He is therefore relating the future condition of Esau's posterity. And he says first, that they shall live by their sword: which words admit a twofold sense, either that, being surrounded by enemies, they shall pass a warlike and unquiet life; or that they shall be free, and their own masters. For there is no power to use the sword where there is no liberty. The former meaning seems the more suitable; namely, that God would limit his promise, lest Esau should be too much exalted: for nothing is more desirable than peace. The holy people also are warned that there will always be some enemies to infest them. This, however, is a very different thing from living by his own sword; which is as if he had said, that the sons of Esau, like robbers, should maintain their security by arms and violence, rather than by legitimate authority. A second limitation of the promise is, that though armed with the sword, he should still not escape subjection to his brother. For the Idumeans were, at length, made tributary to the chosen people;[1] but

[1] That is, under King David.—*Ed.*

the servitude was not long continued; because when the kingdoms were divided, the power by which they had held all their neighbours in subjection and fear, was cut off; yet the Lord would have the Idumeans brought into subjection for a short time, that he might furnish a visible demonstration of this prophecy. As to the rest of the time, the restless and unbridled liberty of Esau was more wretched than any state of subjection.

41. *And Esau hated Jacob.* It hence appears more clearly, that the tears of Esau were so far from being the effect of true repentance, that they were rather evidences of furious anger. For he is not content with secretly cherishing enmity against his brother, but openly breaks out in wicked threats. And it is evident how deeply malice had struck its roots, when he could indulge himself in the desperate purpose of murdering his brother. Even a profane and sacrilegious contumacy betrays itself in him, seeing that he prepares himself to abolish the decree of God by the sword. I will take care, he says, that Jacob shall not enjoy the inheritance promised to him. What is this but to annihilate the force of the benediction, of which he knew that his father was the herald and the minister? Moreover, a lively picture of a hypocrite is here set before us. He pretends that the death of his father would be to him a mournful event: and doubtless it is a religious duty to mourn over a deceased father. But it was a mere pretence on his part, to speak of the day of mourning, when in his haste to execute the impious murder of his brother, the death of his father seemed to come too slowly, and he rejoiced at the prospect of its approach.[1] With what face could he ever pretend to any human affection, when he gasps for his brother's death, and at the same time attempts to subvert all the laws of nature? It is even possible, that an impulse of nature itself, extorted from him the avowal, by which he would the more grievously condemn himself; as God often censures the wicked out of their

---

[1] " The Greek translateth, ' Let the days of my father's mourning be nigh, that I may kill Jacob my brother;' so making it a wish for his father's speedy death; and the Hebrew also will bear that translation."—*Ainsworth.*

own mouth, and renders them more inexcusable. But if a sense of shame alone restrains a cruel mind, this is not to be deemed worthy of great praise; nay, it even betrays a stupid and brutal contempt of God. Sometimes, indeed, the fear of man influences even the pious, as we have seen, in the preceding chapter, respecting Jacob: but they soon rise above it, so that with them the fear of God predominates; while forgetfulness of God so pervades the hearts of the wicked, that they rest their hopes in men alone. Therefore, he who abstains from wickedness merely through the fear of man, and from a sense of shame, has hitherto made but little progress. Yet the confession of the Papists is chiefly honoured by them with this praise, that it deters many from sin, through the fear lest they should be compelled to proclaim their own disgrace. But the rule of piety is altogether different, since it teaches our conscience to set God before us as our witness and our judge.

42. *And these words of Esau . . . . were told to Rebekah.* Moses now makes a transition to a new subject of history, showing how Jacob, as a wanderer from his father's house, went into Mesopotamia. Without doubt, it was an exceedingly troublesome and severe temptation to the holy matron, to see that, by her own deed, her son was placed in imminent danger of death. But by faith she wrestled to retain the possession of the grace once received. For, if she had been impelled by a merely womanly attachment to her younger son, it certainly would have been her best and shortest method, to cause the birthright to be restored to Esau: for thus the cause of emulation would have been removed; and he who was burning with grief at the loss of his right, would have had his fury appeased. It is therefore an evidence of extraordinary faith, that Rebekah does not come to any agreement, but persuades her son to become a voluntary exile, and chooses rather to be deprived of his presence, than that he should give up the blessing he had once received. The benediction of the father might now seem illusory; so as to make it appear wonderful that so much should be made of it by Rebekah and Jacob: nevertheless, they were so far from repenting of what they had done, that they do not re-

fuse the bitter punishment of exile, if only Jacob may carry with him the benediction uttered by his father. Moreover, we are taught by this example, that we must bear it patiently, if the cross attends the hope of a better life, as its companion; or even if the Lord adopts us into his family, with this condition, that we should wander as pilgrims without any certain dwelling-place in the world. For, on this account, Jacob is thrust out from his paternal home, where he might quietly have passed his life, and is compelled to migrate to a strange land; because the blessing of God is promised unto him. And as he did not attempt to purchase temporal peace with his brother by the loss of the grace received; so must we beware lest any carnal advantage or any allurements of the world should draw us aside from the course of our vocation: let us rather bear with magnanimity losses of all kinds, so that the anchor of our hope may remain fixed in heaven. When Rebekah says that Esau consoled himself with the thought, that he would slay his brother; the meaning is, that he could not be pacified by any other means, than by this wicked murder.

44. *And tarry with him a few days.* This circumstance mitigates the severity of banishment. For the shortness of the time of suffering avails not a little to support us in adversity. And it was probable that the enmity of Esau would not prove so obstinate as to be unassuaged by his brother's absence. In the Hebrew expression which is translated "a few days," the word few is literally "one" put in the plural number.[1] Rebekah means, that as soon as Jacob should have gone away of his own accord, the memory of the offence would be obliterated from the mind of Esau; as if she had said, Only depart hence for a little while, and we shall soon assuage his anger.

45. *Why should I be deprived of you both in one day?* Why does Rebekah fear a double privation? for there was no danger that Jacob, endued with a disposition so mild and placid, should rise up against his brother. We see, therefore, that

---

[1] Hebraice ad verbum habetur, Unis diebus. ימים אחדים (*yamim achedim*). There is no mode of giving a literal rendering of the expression in the English language.—*Ed.*

Rebekah concluded that God would be the avenger of the iniquitous murder. Moreover, although God, for a time, might seem to overlook the deed, and to suspend his judgment, it would yet be necessary for him to withdraw from the parricide. Therefore, by this law of nature, Rebekah declares that she should be entirely bereaved; because she would be compelled to dread and to detest him who survived But if Rebekah anticipated in her mind what the judgment of God would be, and devoted the murderer to destruction, because she was persuaded that wickedness so great would not be unpunished; much less ought we to close our eyes against the manifest chastisements of God.[1]

46. *And Rebekah said to Isaac.* When Jacob might have fled secretly, his mother, nevertheless, obtains leave for his departure from his father; for so a well-ordered domestic government and discipline required. In giving another cause than the true one to her husband, she may be excused from the charge of falsehood; inasmuch as she neither said the whole truth nor left the whole unsaid. No doubt, she truly affirms that she was tormented, even to weariness of life, on account of her Hittite daughters-in-law: but she prudently conceals the more inward evil, lest she should inflict a mortal wound on her husband: and also, lest she should the more influence the rage of Esau; for the wicked, often, when their crime is detected, are the more carried away with desperation. Now, although in consequence of the evil manners of her daughters-in-law, affinity with the whole race became hateful to Rebekah, yet in this again the wonderful providence of God is conspicuous, that Jacob neither blended, nor entangled himself, with the future enemies of the Church.

---

[1] The French is more diffuse: "Tant plus nous faut-il appercevoir les fleaux de Dieu qui sont manifestes, et ne faut point ciller les yeux en ne faisant semblant de les voir." So much the more ought we to perceive the scourges of God, which are manifest; and we ought not to wink as pretending not to see them.—*Fr. Tr.*

## CHAPTER XXVIII.

1. And Isaac called Jacob, and blessed him, and charged him, and said unto him, Thou shalt not take a wife of the daughters of Canaan.
2. Arise, go to Padan-aram, to the house of Bethuel thy mother's father, and take thee a wife from thence of the daughters of Laban thy mother's brother.
3. And God Almighty bless thee, and make thee fruitful, and multiply thee, that thou mayest be a multitude of people;
4. And give thee the blessing of Abraham, to thee, and to thy seed with thee; that thou mayest inherit the land wherein thou art a stranger, which God gave unto Abraham.
5. And Isaac sent away Jacob: and he went to Padan-aram unto Laban, son of Bethuel the Syrian, the brother of Rebekah, Jacob's and Esau's mother.
6. When Esau saw that Isaac had blessed Jacob, and sent him away to Padan-aram, to take him a wife from thence; and that, as he blessed him, he gave him a charge, saying, Thou shalt not take a wife of the daughters of Canaan;
7. And that Jacob obeyed his father and his mother, and was gone to Padan-aram;
8. And Esau seeing that the daughters of Canaan pleased not Isaac his father;
9. Then went Esau unto Ishmael, and took unto the wives which he had Mahalath the daughter of Ishmael, Abraham's son, the sister of Nebajoth, to be his wife.
10. And Jacob went out from Beer-sheba, and went toward Haran.
11. And he lighted upon a certain place, and tarried there all night, because the sun was set; and he took of the stones of that place, and put *them for* his pillows, and lay down in that place to sleep.
12. And he dreamed, and behold

1. Vocavit ergo Ishac Iahacob, et benedixit ei: præcepitque, et dixit ei, Non capies uxorem de filiabus Chenaan.
2. Surge, vade in Padan Aram, ad domum Bethuel patris matris tuæ, et cape tibi inde uxorem de filiabus Laban fratris matris tuæ.
3. Deus autem omnipotens benedicat tibi, et crescere faciat te, et multiplicare faciat te, et sis in cœtum populorum.
4. Et det tibi benedictionem Abraham, tibi et semini tuo tecum, ut hæreditate accipias terram peregrinationum tuarum, quam dedit Deus ipsi Abraham.
5. Et misit Ishac Iahacob, et profectus est in Padan Aram ad Laban filium Bethuel Aramæi fratris Ribcæ, matris Iahacob et Esau.
6. Et vidit Esau quod benedixisset Ishac Iahacob, et misisset eum in Padan Aram, ut caperet sibi inde uxorem: et benedicendo ei, præcepisset ei, dicendo, Non accipies uxorem de filiabus Chenaan:
7. Et obedivisset Iahacob patri suo et matri suæ, et ivisset in Padan Aram.
8. Videns præterea Esau quod malæ filiæ Chenaan in oculis Ishac patris sui:
9. Tunc abiit Esau ad Ismael, et accepit Mahalath filiam Ismael filii Abraham sororem Nebajoth, super uxores suas, sibi in uxorem.
10. Iahacob vero egressus est e Beer-sebah, et perrexit in Aram:
11. Et occurrit in locum, et pernoctavit ibi, quia occubuerat sol: et tulit de lapidibus loci, et posuit sub capite suo, et dormivit in loco eodem.
12. Et somniavit, et ecce scala

a ladder set up on the earth, and the top of it reached to heaven; and behold the angels of God ascending and descending on it.

13. And, behold, the Lord stood above it, and said, I *am* the Lord God of Abraham thy father, and the God of Isaac: the land whereon thou liest, to thee will I give it, and to thy seed;

14. And thy seed shall be as the dust of the earth; and thou shalt spread abroad to the west, and to the east, and to the north, and to the south: and in thee, and in thy seed, shall all the families of the earth be blessed.

15. And, behold, I *am* with thee, and will keep thee in all *places* whither thou goest, and will bring thee again into this land; for I will not leave thee, until I have done *that* which I have spoken to thee of.

16. And Jacob awaked out of his sleep, and he said, Surely the Lord is in this place, and I knew *it* not.

17. And he was afraid, and said, How dreadful *is* this place! this *is* none other but the house of God, and this *is* the gate of heaven.

18. And Jacob rose up early in the morning, and took the stone that he had put *for* his pillows, and set it up *for* a pillar, and poured oil upon the top of it.

19. And he called the name of that place Beth-el: but the name of that city *was called* Luz at the first.

20. And Jacob vowed a vow, saying, If God will be with me, and will keep me in this way that I go, and will give me bread to eat, and raiment to put on,

21. So that I come again to my father's house in peace, then shall the Lord be my God:

22. And this stone, which I have set *for* a pillar, shall be God's house: and of all that thou shalt give me, I will surely give the tenth unto thee.

erecta erat super terram, et caput ejus tangebat cœlum; et ecce, Angeli Dei ascendebant et descendebant per eam.

13. Et ecce, Iehova stabat super eam, et dixit, Ego Iehova Deus Abraham patris tui, et Deus Ishac: terram, super quam tu dormis, tibi dabo et semini tuo.

14. Et erit semen tuum sicut pulvis terræ, et multiplicaberis ad Occidentem, et ad Orientem, et ad Aquilonem, et ad Meridiem: et benedicentur in te omnes familiæ terræ, et in semine tuo.

15. Et ecce sum tecum, et custodiam te quocunque profectus fueris, et redire faciam te ad terram hanc: quia non derelinquam te, donec faciam quod loquutus sum tibi.

16. Deinde expergefactus est Iahacob a somno suo, et dixit, Vere est Iehova in loco isto, et ego nesciebam.

17. Timuit ergo, et dixit, Quam terribilis est locus iste! non est hic nisi domus Dei, et hic est porta cœli.

18. Surrexit autem Iahacob mane, et tulit lapidem, quem posuerat sub capite suo, et posuit eum in statuam, et effudit oleum supra summitatem ejus.

19. Et vocavit nomen loci ipsius Beth-el, et quidem Luz erat nomen urbis prius.

20. Adhæc vovit Iahacob votum, dicendo, Si fuerit Iehova Deus mecum, et custodierit me in via ista, quam ego ingredior, et dederit mihi panem ad vescendum, et vestimentum ad operiendum:

21. Et reversus fuero in pace ad domum patris mei, erit Iehova mihi in Deum.

22. Et lapis iste, quem posui in statuam, erit domus Dei: et omne quod dederis mihi, decimando decimabo illud tibi.

1. *And Isaac called Jacob, and blessed him.* It may be asked, whether the reason why Isaac repeats anew the bene-

diction which he had before pronounced, was that the former one had been of no force; whereas, if he was a prophet and interpreter of the will of God, what had once proceeded from his mouth ought to have been firm and perpetual. I answer, although the benediction was in itself efficacious, yet the faith of Jacob required support of this kind: just as the Lord, in reiterating frequently the same promises, derogates nothing either from himself or from his word, but rather confirms the certainty of that word to his servants, lest, at any time, their confidence should be shaken through the infirmity of the flesh. What I have said must also be kept in mind, that Isaac prayed, not as a private person, but as one furnished with a special command of God, to transmit the covenant deposited with himself to his son Jacob. It was also of the greatest importance that now, at length, Jacob should be blessed by his father, knowingly and willingly; lest at a future time a doubt, arising from the recollection of his father's mistake and of his own fraud, might steal over his mind. Therefore Isaac, now purposely directing his words to his son Jacob, pronounces the blessing to be due to him by right, lest it should be thought that, having been before deceived, he had uttered words in vain, under a false character.

2. *Arise, go to Padan-aram.* In the first place, he commands him to take a wife from his maternal race. He might have sent for her by some one of his servants, as Rebekah had been brought to him; but perhaps he took this course to avoid the envy of Esau, who might regard it as a reproach if more solicitude were manifested about his brother's marriage than about his own.

3. *And God Almighty bless thee.* Here follows the form of benediction, which slightly differs in words from the former, but nevertheless tends to the same end. First, he desires that Jacob should be blessed by God; that is, that he should be so increased and amplified in his own offspring, as to grow into a multitude of nations; or, in other words, that he should produce many people who might combine into one body under the same head; as if he had said, "Let there arise from thee many tribes, who shall constitute one people." And this truly was, in some measure, fulfilled when

Moses distributed the people into thirteen divisions. Nevertheless, Isaac looked for a further result, namely, that many were at length to be gathered together out of various nations, to the family of his son, that, in this manner, from a vast and previously scattered multitude, might be formed one assembly. For it is not to be doubted, that he wished to hand down what he had received; seeing that he immediately afterwards celebrates the memory of the original covenant, deriving his present benediction from thence as its source: as if he had said, that he transferred whatever right he had from his father, to his son Jacob, in order that the inheritance of life might remain with him, according to the covenant of God made with Abraham. They who expound this as being said in the way of comparison, as if Isaac[1] wished those benefits which God had before conferred on Abraham to be in the same manner granted to his son, attenuate the meaning of the words. For since God, in making his covenant with Abraham, had annexed this condition, that it should descend to his posterity, it was necessary to trace its commencement to his person as its root. Therefore, Isaac constitutes his son Jacob the heir of Abraham, as successor to the benediction deposited with him, and promised to his seed. This also appears more clearly from the context following, where he assigns to him the dominion over the land, because it had been given to Abraham. Moreover, we perceive, in this member of the sentence, with what consistency of faith the holy fathers rested on the word of the Lord; for otherwise, they would have found it no small temptation to be driven about as strangers and pilgrims in the very land, the possession of which had been divinely assigned them a hundred years before. But we see, that in their wanderings and their unsettled mode of life, they no less highly estimated what God had promised them, than if they had already been in the full enjoyment of it. And this is the true trial of faith; when relying on the word of God alone, although tossed on the waves of the world, we stand as firmly as if

---

[1] In the editions of Amsterdam and Berlin, the name *Jacob* is here inserted; and the old English version has it too. The mistake is obvious, and stands corrected in the French translation.—*Ed.*

our abode were already fixed in heaven. Isaac expressly fortifies his son against this temptation, when he calls the land of which he constitutes him lord, "the land of his wanderings." For by these words he teaches him that it was possible he might be a wanderer all the days of his life: but this did not hinder the promise of God from being so ratified, that he, contented with that alone, might patiently wait for the time of revelation. Even the plural number[1] seems to express something significant, namely, that Jacob would be a wanderer not once only, but in various ways and perpetually. Since, however, the Hebrew plural has not always such emphasis, I do not insist on this interpretation. It is more worthy of notice, that the faith of Jacob was proved by a severe and rigid trial, seeing, that for this very reason, the land is promised to him in *word* only, while in *fact*, he is cast far away from it. For he seems to be the object of ridicule, when he is commanded to possess the dominion of the land, and yet to leave it and to bid it farewell, and to depart into distant exile.

6. *When Esau saw.* A brief narration concerning Esau is here inserted, which it is useful to know; because we learn from it that the wicked, though they exalt themselves against God, and though, in contempt of his grace, they please themselves in obtaining their desires, are yet not able to despise that grace altogether. So now, Esau is penetrated with a desire of the blessing; not that he aspires to it sincerely and from his heart; but perceiving it to be something valuable, he is impelled to seek after it, though with reluctance. A further fault is, that he does not seek it as he ought: for he devises a new and strange method of reconciling God and his father to himself; and therefore all his diligence is without profit. At the same time he does not seem to be careful about pleasing God, so that he may but propitiate his father. Before all things, it was his duty to cast aside his profane disposition, his perverse manners, and his corrupt affections of the flesh, and then to bear with meekness the chastisement inflicted upon him: for genuine repentance would have dictated to him this sentiment, "Seeing I have hitherto ren-

---

[1] Terram peregrinationum—the land of *wanderings*.

dered myself unworthy of the birthright, my brother is deservedly preferred before me. Nothing, therefore, remains for me but to humble myself; and since I am deprived of the honour of being the head, let it suffice me to be at least one of the members of the Church." And, certainly, it would have been more desirable for him to remain in some obscure corner of the Church, than, as one cut off and torn away from the elect people, to shine with a proud pre-eminence on earth. He aims, however, at nothing of this kind, but attempts, by I know not what prevarications, to appease his father in whatever way he may be able. Moses, in this example, depicts all hypocrites to the life. For as often as the judgment of God urges them, though they are wounded with the pain of their punishment, they yet do not seek a true remedy; for having aimed at offering one kind of satisfaction only, they entirely neglect a simple and real conversion: and even in the satisfaction offered, they only make a pretence. Whereas Esau ought thoroughly to have repented, he only tried to correct the single fault of his marriage; and this too in a most absurd manner. Yet another defect follows: for while he retains the wives who were so hateful to his parents, he supposes he has discharged his duty by marrying a third. But by this method, neither was the trouble of his parents alleviated, nor his house cleansed from guilt. And now truly, whence does he marry his third wife? From the race of Ishmael, whom we know to have been himself degenerate, and whose posterity had departed from the pure worship of God. A remarkable proof of this is discernible at the present day, in the pretended and perfidious intermeddlers, who imagine they can admirably adjust religious differences by simply adorning their too gross corruptions with attractive colours.[1] The actual state of things compels them to confess that the vile errors and abuses of Popery have so far pre-

---

[1] The Council of Trent is here obviously referred to, which held its sessions from the year 1545 to the year 1563. This council was the Romanist reaction upon the Protestant reformation. Father Paul gives a singular and graphic description of the persons, the characters, and the arguments, by which this last council of the Church of Rome was distinguished. It will be remembered that Calvin's Commentary on Genesis was published about the middle of this protracted period.—*Ed.*

vailed as to render a Reformation absolutely necessary: but they are unwilling that the filth of this Camarine marsh be stirred;[1] they only desire to conceal its impurities, and even that they do by compulsion. For they had previously called their abominations the sacred worship of God; but since these are now dragged to light by the word of God, they therefore descend to novel artifices. They flatter themselves, however, in vain, seeing they are here condemned by Moses, in the person of Esau. Away, then, with their impure pretended reformation, which has nothing simple nor sincere. Moreover, since it is a disease inherent in the human race, willingly to attempt to deceive God by some fictitious pretext, let us know that we do nothing effectually, until we tear up our sins by the roots, and thoroughly devote ourselves to God.

10. *And Jacob went out.* In the course of this history we must especially observe, how the Lord preserved his own Church in the person of one man. For Isaac, on account of his age, lay like a dry trunk; and although the living root of piety was concealed within his breast, yet no hope of further offspring remained in his exhausted and barren old age. Esau, like a green and flourishing branch, had much of show and splendour, but his vigour was only momentary. Jacob, as a severed twig, was removed into a far distant land; not that, being ingrafted or planted there, he should acquire strength and greatness, but that, being moistened with the dew of heaven, he might put forth his shoots as into the air itself. For the Lord wonderfully nourishes him, and supplies him with strength, until he shall bring him back again to his father's house. Meanwhile, let the reader diligently observe, that while he who was blessed by God is cast into exile; occasion of glorying was given to the reprobate Esau, who was left in the possession of

---

[1] Camarina was a city on the south of Sicily, placed near the mouths of two rivers, close to which was a marsh or lake, called the Camarine lake, injurious to health, and often producing pestilence. It is reported that the inhabitants consulted Apollo whether or not they should drain it. The answer was, that it would be better undrained. This answer they disregarded, and in consequence the enemy found it easy to attack and plunder the city. Hence the proverb, "Ne moveas Camarinam;" that is, "Do not get rid of one evil to bring on you a greater."—*Ed.*

everything, so that he might securely reign without a rival. Let us not, then, be disturbed, if at any time the wicked sound their triumphs, as having gained their wishes, while we are oppressed. Moses mentions the name of Beersheba, because, as it formed one of the boundaries of the land of Canaan, and lay towards the great desert and the south, it was the more remote from the eastern region towards which Jacob was going. He afterwards adds Charran, (chap. xxix.,) where Abraham, when he left his own country, dwelt for some time. Now, it appears that not only the pious old man Terah, when he followed his son, or accompanied him on his journey, came to Charran where he died; but that his other son Nahor, with his family, also came to the same place. For we read in the eleventh chapter, that Terah took his son Abraham, and Lot his grandson, and Sarai his daughter-in-law. Whence we infer that Nahor, at that time, remained in Chaldea, his native country. But now, since Moses says, that Laban dwelt at Charran, we may hence conjecture, that Nahor, in order that he might not appear guilty of the inhumanity of deserting his father, afterwards gathered together his goods and came to him.

Moses here, in a few words, declares what a severe and arduous journey the holy man (Jacob) had, on account of its great length: to which also another circumstance is added; namely, that he lay on the ground, under the open sky, without a companion, and without a habitation. But as Moses only briefly alludes to these facts, so will I also avoid prolixity, as the thing speaks for itself. Wherefore, if, at any time, we think ourselves to be roughly treated, let us remember the example of the holy man, as a reproof to our fastidiousness.

12. *And he dreamed.* Moses here teaches how opportunely, and (as we may say) in the critical moment, the Lord succoured his servant. For who would not have said that holy Jacob was neglected by God, since he was exposed to the incursion of wild beasts, and obnoxious to every kind of injury from earth and heaven, and found nowhere any help or solace? But when he was thus reduced to the last necessity, the Lord suddenly stretches out his

hand to him, and wonderfully alleviates his trouble by a remarkable oracle. As, therefore, Jacob's invincible perseverance had before shone forth, so now the Lord gives a memorable example of his paternal care towards the faithful. Three things are here to be noticed in their order; first, that the Lord appeared unto Jacob in a dream; secondly, the nature of the vision as described by Moses; thirdly, the words of the oracle. When mention is made of a dream, no doubt that mode of revelation is signified, which the Lord formerly was wont to adopt towards his servants. (Numb. xii. 6.) Jacob, therefore, knew that this dream was divinely sent to him, as one differing from common dreams; and this is intimated in the words of Moses, when he says that God appeared to him in a dream. For Jacob could not see God, nor perceive him present, unless his majesty had been distinguishable by certain marks.

*And behold a ladder.* Here the *form* of the vision is related, which is very pertinent to the subject of it; namely, that God manifested himself as seated upon a ladder, the extreme parts of which touched heaven and earth, and which was the vehicle of angels, who descended from heaven upon earth. The interpretation of some of the Hebrews, that the ladder is a figure of the Divine Providence, cannot be admitted: for the Lord has given another sign more suitable.[1] But to us, who hold to this principle, that the covenant of God was founded in Christ, and that Christ himself was the eternal image of the Father, in which he manifested himself to the holy patriarchs, there is nothing in this vision intricate or ambiguous. For since men are alienated from God by sin, though he fills and sustains all things by his

---

[1] Whatever force and truth, as well as beauty, there may be in the exposition of Calvin which follows, he appears to have dismissed too hastily the opinion of the Jews, that the vision was symbolical of *Divine Providence.* The circumstances of Jacob seemed to require some such intimations of Divine protection and care during his journey, as this interpretation of the vision presents. And in every way the passage thus understood is both useful and encouraging. There is, however, no need to question, that the higher mystical interpretation, on which Calvin exclusively insists, is legitimately applicable, as conveying the ultimate and, in short, the most important meaning of the vision. The reader may consult the 123d Exercitation of Rivetus on this subject.—*Rivetus in Gen.,* p. 602.

power, yet that communication by which he would draw us to himself is not perceived by us; but, on the other hand, so greatly are we at variance with him, that, regarding him as adverse to us, we, in our turn, flee from his presence. Moreover the angels, to whom is committed the guardianship of the human race, while strenuously applying themselves to their office, yet do not communicate with us in such a way that we become conscious of their presence. It is Christ alone, therefore, who connects heaven and earth: he is the only Mediator who reaches from heaven down to earth: he is the medium through which the fulness of all celestial blessings flows down to us, and through which we, in turn, ascend to God. He it is who, being the head over angels, causes them to minister to his earthly members. Therefore, (as we read in John i. 51,) he properly claims for himself this honour, that after he shall have been manifested in the world, angels shall ascend and descend. If, then, we say that the ladder is a figure of Christ, the exposition will not be forced. For the similitude of a ladder well suits the Mediator, through whom ministering angels, righteousness and life, with all the graces of the Holy Spirit, descend to us step by step. We also, who were not only fixed to the earth, but plunged into the depths of the curse, and into hell itself, ascend even unto God. Also, the God of hosts is seated on the ladder; because the fulness of the Deity dwells in Christ; and hence also it is, that it reaches unto heaven. For although all power is committed even to his human nature by the Father, he still would not truly sustain our faith, unless he were God manifested in the flesh. And the fact that the body of Christ is finite, does not prevent him from filling heaven and earth, because his grace and power are everywhere diffused. Whence also, Paul being witness, he ascended into heaven that he might fill all things. They who translate the particle עַל by the word "near," entirely destroy the sense of the passage. For Moses wishes to state that the fulness of the Godhead dwelt in the person of the Mediator. Christ not only approached unto us, but clothed himself in our nature, that he might make us one with himself. That the ladder was a symbol of Christ, is also confirmed by this consideration, that nothing was more suitable than that God should ratify his covenant of eternal salvation in his Son to his servant Jacob. And hence we feel unspeakable joy, when we hear that Christ, who so far excels all creatures, is nevertheless joined with us. The majesty, indeed, of God, which here presents itself conspicuously to view, ought to inspire terror; so that every knee should bow to Christ, that all creatures should look up to him and adore him, and that all flesh should keep silence in his presence. But his friendly and lovely image is at the same time depicted; that we may know by his descent, that heaven is opened to us, and the angels of God are rendered familiar to us. For hence we have fraternal society with them, since the common Head both of them and us has his station on earth.

13. *I am the Lord God of Abraham.* This is the third point which, I said, was to be noticed: for mute visions are cold; therefore the word of the Lord is as the soul which quickens them. The figure, therefore, of the ladder was the inferior appendage of this promise; just as God illustrates and adorns his word by external symbols, that both greater clearness and authority may be added to it. Whence also we prove that sacraments in the Papacy are frivolous, because no voice is heard in them which may edify the soul. We may therefore observe, that whenever God manifested himself to the fathers, he also *spoke*, lest a mute vision should have held them in suspense. Under the name יהוה (*Jehovah*) God teaches that he is the only Creator of the world, that Jacob might not seek after other gods. But since his majesty is in itself incomprehensible, he accommodates himself to the capacity of his servant, by immediately adding, that he is the God of Abraham and Isaac. For though it is necessary to maintain that the God whom we worship is the only God; yet because when our senses would aspire to the comprehension of his greatness, they fail at the first attempt; we must diligently cultivate that sobriety which teaches us not to desire to know more concerning him than he reveals unto us; and then he, accommodating himself to our weakness, according to his infinite goodness, will omit nothing

which tends to promote our salvation. And whereas he made a special covenant with Abraham and Isaac, proclaiming himself their God, he recalls his servant Jacob to the true source of faith, and retains him also in his perpetual covenant. This is the sacred bond of religion, by which all the sons of God are united among themselves, when from the first to the last they hear the same promise of salvation, and agree together in one common hope. And this is the effect of that benediction which Jacob had lately received from his father; because God with his own mouth pronounces him to be the heir of the covenant, lest the mere testimony of man should be thought illusive.

*The land whereon thou liest.* We read that the land was given to his posterity; yet he himself was not only a stranger in it to the last, but was not permitted even to die there. Whence we infer, that under the pledge or earnest of the land, something better and more excellent was given, seeing that Abraham was a spiritual possessor of the land, and contented with the mere beholding of it, fixed his chief regard on heaven. We may observe, however, that the seed of Jacob is here placed in opposition to the other sons of Abraham, who, according to the flesh, traced their origin to him, but were cut off from the holy people: yet, from the time when the sons of Jacob entered the land of Canaan, they had the perpetual inheritance unto the coming of Christ, by whose advent the world was renewed.

14. *And thy seed shall be as the dust of the earth.* The sum of the whole is this, Whatever the Lord had promised to Abraham, Jacob transmitted to his sons. Meanwhile it behoved the holy man, in reliance on this divine testimony, to hope against hope; for though the promise was vast and magnificent, yet, wherever Jacob turned himself, no ray of good hope shone upon him. He saw himself a solitary man; no condition better than that of exile presented itself; his return was uncertain and full of danger; but it was profitable for him to be thus left destitute of all means of help, that he might learn to depend on the word of God alone. Thus, at the present time, if God freely promises to give us all things, and yet seems to approach us empty-handed, it is still

proper that we should pay such honour and reverence to his word, that we may be enriched and filled with faith. At length, indeed, after the death of Jacob, the event declared how efficacious had been this promise : by which example we are taught that the Lord by no means disappoints his people, even when he defers the granting of those good things which he has promised, till after their death.

*And in thee, and in thy seed, shall all the families of the earth be blessed.*[1] This clause has the greater weight, because in Jacob and in his seed the blessing is to be restored from which the whole human race had been cut off in their first parent. But what this expression means, I have explained above; namely, that Jacob will not only be an exemplar, or *formula* of blessing, but its fountain, cause, or foundation; for though a certain exquisite degree of happiness is often signified by an expression of this kind; yet, in many passages of Scripture, it means the same as to desire from any one his blessing, and to acknowledge it as his gift. Thus men are said to bless themselves in God, when they acknowledge him as the author of all good. So here God promises that in Jacob and his seed all nations shall bless themselves, because no happiness will ever be found except what proceeds from this source. That, however, which is peculiar to Christ, is without impropriety transferred to Jacob, in whose loins Christ then was. Therefore, inasmuch as Jacob, at that time, represented the person of Christ, it is said that all nations are to be blessed in him; but, seeing that the manifestation of a benefit so great depended on another, the expression *in thy seed* is immediately added in the way of explanation. That the word seed is a collective noun, forms no objection to this interpretation, (as I have elsewhere said,) for since all unbelievers deprive themselves of honour and of grace, and are thus accounted strangers; it is necessary to refer to the Head, in order that the unity of the seed may appear. Whoever will reverently ponder this, will easily

---

[1] Et benedicent se in te omnes fines terræ. "And all the ends of the earth shall bless themselves in thee." The reader will perceive that Calvin's remarks turn chiefly on the expression "bless themselves," which does not appear in our version.—*Ed.*

see that, in this interpretation, which is that of Paul, there is nothing tortuous or constrained.

15. *I am with thee, and will keep thee.* God now promptly anticipates the temptation which might steal over the mind of holy Jacob; for though he is, for a time, thrust out into a foreign land, God declares that he will be his keeper until he shall have brought him back again. He then extends his promise still further; saying, that he will never desert him till all things are fulfilled. There was a twofold use of this promise: first, it retained his mind in the faith of the divine covenant; and, secondly, it taught him that it could not be well with him unless he were a partaker of the-promised inheritance.

16. *And Jacob awaked.* Moses again affirms that this was no common dream; for when any one awakes he immediately perceives that he had been under a delusion in dreaming. But God impressed a sign on the mind of his servant, by which, when he awoke, he might recognise the heavenly oracle which he had heard in his sleep. Moreover, Jacob, in express terms, accuses himself, and extols the goodness of God, who deigned to present himself to one who sought him not; for Jacob thought that he was there alone: but now, after the Lord appeared, he wonders, and exclaims that he had obtained more than he could have dared to hope for. It is not, however, to be doubted that Jacob had called upon God, and had trusted that he would be the guide of his journey; but, because his faith had not availed to persuade him that God was thus near unto him, he justly extols this act of grace. So, whenever God anticipates our wishes, and grants us more than our minds have conceived; let us learn, after the example of this patriarch, to wonder that God should have been present with us. Now, if each of us would reflect how feeble his faith is, this mode of speaking would appear always proper for us all; for who can comprehend, in his scanty measure, the immense multitude of gifts which God is perpetually heaping upon us?

17. *And he was afraid, and said.* It seems surprising that Jacob should fear, when God spoke so graciously to him; or that he should call that place " dreadful," where he had been

filled with incredible joy. I answer, although God exhilarates his servants, he at the same time inspires them with fear, in order that they may learn, with true humility and self-denial, to embrace his mercy. We are not therefore to understand that Jacob was struck with terror, as reprobates are, as soon as God shows himself; but he was inspired with a fear which produces pious submission. He also properly calls that place the *gate of heaven,* on account of the manifestation of God: for, because God is placed in heaven as on his royal throne, Jacob truly declares that, in seeing God, he had penetrated into heaven. In this sense the preaching of the gospel is called the kingdom of heaven, and the sacraments may be called the gate of heaven, because they admit us into the presence of God. The Papists, however, foolishly misapply this passage to their temples, as if God dwelt in filthy places.[1] But if we concede, that the places which they designate by this title, are not polluted with impious superstitions, yet this honour belongs to no peculiar place, since Christ has filled the whole world with the presence of his Deity. Those helps to faith only, (as I have before taught,) by which God raises us to himself, can be called the gates of heaven.

18. *And Jacob rose up early.* Moses relates that the holy father was not satisfied with merely giving thanks at the time, but would also transmit a memorial of his gratitude to posterity. Therefore he raised a monument, and gave a name to the place, which implied that he thought such a signal benefit of God worthy to be celebrated in all ages. For this reason, the Scripture not only commands the faithful to sing the praises of God among their brethren; but also enjoins them to train their children to religious duties, and to propagate the worship of God among their descendants.

*And set it up for a pillar.* Moses does not mean that the stone was made an idol, but that it should be a special memorial. God indeed uses this word מצבה, (*matsbah,*) when he forbids statues to be erected to himself, (Lev. xxvi. 1,) because almost all statues were objects of veneration, as if they were likenesses of God. But the design of

---

[1] In fœtidis lupanaribus.

Jacob was different; namely, that he might leave a testimony of the vision which had appeared unto him, not that he might represent God by that symbol or figure. Therefore the stone was not there placed by him, for the purpose of depressing the minds of men into any gross superstition, but rather of raising them upward. He used oil as a sign of consecration, and not without reason; for as, in the world, everything is profane which is destitute of the Spirit of God, so there is no pure religion except that which the heavenly unction sanctifies. And to this point the solemn right of consecration, which God commanded in his law, tends, in order that the faithful may learn to bring in nothing of their own, lest they should pollute the temple and worship of God. And though, in the times of Jacob, no teaching had yet been committed to writing; it is, nevertheless, certain that he had been imbued with that principle of piety which God from the beginning had infused into the hearts of the devout: wherefore, it is not to be ascribed to superstition that he poured oil upon the stone; but he rather testified, as I have said, that no worship can be acceptable to God, or pure, without the sanctification of the Spirit. Other commentators argue, with more subtlety, that the stone was a symbol of Christ, on whom all the graces of the Spirit were poured out, that all might draw out of his fulness; but I do not know that any such thing entered the mind of Moses or of Jacob. I am satisfied with what I have before stated, that a stone was erected to be a witness or a memorial (so to speak) of a vision, the benefit of which reaches to all ages. It may be asked, Whence did the holy man obtain oil in the desert? They who answer that it had been brought from a neighbouring city are, in my opinion, greatly deceived; for this place was then void of inhabitants, as I shall soon show. I therefore rather conjecture, that on account of the necessity of the times, seeing that suitable accommodations could not always be had, he had taken some portion of food for his journey along with him; and as we know that great use was made of oil in those parts, it is no wonder if he carried a flaggon of oil with his bread.

19. *And he called the name of that place Beth-el.* It may

appear absurd that Moses should speak of that place as a city, respecting which he had a little while before said that Jacob had slept there in the open air; for why did not he seek an abode, or hide himself in some corner of a house? But the difficulty is easily solved, because the city was not yet built; neither did the place immediately take the name which Jacob had assigned, but lay long concealed. Even when a town was afterwards built on the spot, no mention is made of Beth-el, as if Jacob had never passed that way; for the inhabitants did not know what had been done there, and therefore they called the city Luz,[1] according to their own imagination; which name it retained until the Israelites, having taken possession of the land, recalled into common use, as by an act of restoration, the former name which had been abolished. And it is to be observed, that when posterity, by a foolish emulation, worshipped God in Beth-el, seeing that it was done without a divine command, the prophets severely inveighed against that worship, calling the name of the place Bethaven, that is, the house of iniquity: whence we infer how unsafe it is to rely upon the examples of the fathers without the word of God. The greatest care, therefore, must be taken, in treating of the worship of God, that what has been once done by men, should not be drawn into a precedent; but that what God himself has prescribed in his word should remain an inflexible rule.

20. *And Jacob vowed a vow.* The design of this vow was, that Jacob would manifest his gratitude, if God should prove favourable unto him. Thus they offered peace-offerings under the law, to testify their gratitude; and since thanksgiving is a sacrifice of a sweet odour, the Lord declares vows of this nature to be acceptable to him; and therefore we must also have respect to this point, when we are asked *what* and *how* it is lawful to vow to God;

---

[1] The word לוז (*Luz*) signifies an almond-tree, and the town may have derived this name from the fact that almond-trees abounded in the neighbourhood. Yet the verb from which it is taken means "to turn away, to depart, to go back;" also "to be perverse, or wicked;" and it is not impossible that this name may have been assigned to it on account of the wickedness of its inhabitants. See the Lexicons of Schindler, Gesenius, &c.—*Ed.*

for some are too fastidious, who would utterly condemn all vows rather than open the door to superstitions. But if the rashness of those persons is perverse, who indiscriminately pour forth their vows, we must also beware lest we become like those on the opposite side, who disallow all vows without exception. Now, in order that a vow may be lawful and pleasing to God, it is first necessary that it should tend to a right end; and next, that men should devote nothing by a vow but what is in itself approved by God, and what he has placed within their own power. When the separate parts of this vow are examined, we shall see holy Jacob so regulating his conduct as to omit none of these things which I have mentioned. In the first place, he has nothing else in his mind than to testify his gratitude. Secondly, he confines whatever he is about to do, to the lawful worship of God. In the third place, he does not proudly promise what he had not the power to perform, but devotes the tithe of his goods as a sacred oblation. Wherefore, the folly of the Papists is easily refuted; who, in order to justify their own confused farrago of vows, catch at one or another vow, soberly conceived, as a precedent, when in the meantime their own license exceeds all bounds. Whatever comes uppermost they are not ashamed to obtrude upon God. One man makes his worship to consist in abstinence from flesh, another in pilgrimages, a third in sanctifying certain days by the use of sackcloth, or by other things of the same kind; and not to God only do they make their vows, but also admit any dead person they please into a participation of this honour. They arrogate to themselves the choice of perpetual celibacy. What do they find in the example of Jacob which has any similitude or affinity to such rashness, that they should hence catch at such a covering for themselves? But, for the purpose of bringing all these things clearly to light, we must first enter upon an explanation of the words. It may seem absurd that Jacob here makes a covenant with God, to be his worshipper, if he will give him what he desires; as if truly he did not intend to worship God for nothing. I answer, that, by interposing this condition, Jacob did not by any means act from distrust, as if he doubted of

God's continual protection; but that in this manner he made provision against his own infirmity, in preparing himself to celebrate the divine goodness by a vow previously made.[1] The superstitious deal with God just as they do with mortal man; they try to soothe him with their allurements. The design of Jacob was far different; namely, that he might the more effectually stimulate himself to the duties of religion. He had often heard from the mouth of God, "I will be always with thee;" and he annexes his vow as an appendage to that promise. He seems indeed, at first sight, like a mercenary, acting in a servile manner; but since he depends entirely upon the promises given unto him, and forms both his language and his affections in accordance with them, he aims at nothing but the confirmation of his faith, and gathers together those aids which he knows to be suitable to his infirmity. When, therefore, he speaks of food and clothing, we must not, on that account, accuse him of solicitude respecting this earthly life alone; whereas he rather contends, like a valiant champion, against violent temptations. He found himself in want of all things; hunger and nakedness were continually threatening him with death, not to mention his other innumerable dangers: therefore he arms himself with confidence, that he might proceed through all difficulties and obstacles, being fully assured that every kind of assistance was laid up for him in the grace of God: for he confesses himself to be in extreme destitution, when he says, "If the Lord will supply me with food and raiment." It may nevertheless be asked, since his grandfather Abraham had sent his servant with a splendid retinue, with camels and precious ornaments; why does Isaac now send away his son without a single companion, and almost without provisions? It is possible that he was thus dismissed, that the mind of cruel Esau might be moved to tenderness by a spectacle so miserable. Yet, in my judgment, another reason was of greater weight; for Abraham, fearing lest his son Isaac should remain with his relatives, took an oath from his

---

[1] Se desposant à celebrer la bonté de Dieu, en se vouant expressement à luy. Preparing himself to celebrate the goodness of God, in devoting himself expressly to him.—*Fr. Tr.*

servant that he would not suffer his son to go into Mesopotamia. But now, since necessity compels holy Isaac to determine differently for his son Jacob; he, at least, takes care not to do anything which might retard his return. He therefore supplies him with no wealth, and with no delicacies which might ensnare his mind, but purposely sends him away poor and empty, that he might be the more ready to return. Thus we see that Jacob preferred his father's house to all kingdoms, and had no desire of settled repose elsewhere.

21. *Then shall the Lord be my God.* In these words Jacob binds himself never to apostatize from the pure worship of the One God; for there is no doubt that he here comprises the sum of piety. But he may seem to promise what far exceeds his strength; for newness of life, spiritual righteousness, integrity of heart, and a holy regulation of the whole life, were not in his own power. I answer, when holy men vow those things which God requires of them, and which are due from them as acts of piety; they, at the same time, embrace what God promises concerning the remission of sins by the help of his Holy Spirit. Hence it follows that they ascribe nothing to their own strength; and also, that whatever falls short of entire perfection does not vitiate their worship, because God, mercifully and with paternal indulgence, pardons them.

22. *And this stone which I have set for a pillar.* This ceremony was an appendage to divine worship; for external rites do not make men true worshippers of God, but are only aids to piety. But because the holy fathers were then at liberty to erect altars wherever they pleased, Jacob poured a libation upon the stone, because he had then no other sacrifice to offer; not that he worshipped God according to his own will, (for the direction of the Spirit was instead of the written law,) but he erected in that place a stone—as he was permitted to do by the kindness and permission of God—which should be a testimony of the vision. Moreover, this form of speech, that " the stone shall be Beth-el," is *metonymical;* as we are sanctioned, by common usage, to transfer to external signs what properly belongs to the things represented. I have lately shown how ignorantly posterity has

abused this holy exercise of piety. What next follows respecting the offering of tithes, is not a simple ceremony, but has a duty of charity annexed; for Jacob enumerates, in a threefold order, first, the spiritual worship of God; then the external rite, by which he both assists his own piety, and makes profession of it before men; in the third place, an oblation, by which he exercises himself in giving friendly aid to his brethren; for there is no doubt that tithes were applied to that use.

## CHAPTER XXIX.

1. THEN Jacob went on his journey, and came into the land of the people of the east.
2. And he looked, and behold a well in the field, and, lo, there *were* three flocks of sheep lying by it; for out of that well they watered the flocks: and a great stone *was* upon the well's mouth.
3. And thither were all the flocks gathered: and they rolled the stone from the well's mouth, and watered the sheep, and put the stone again upon the well's mouth in his place.
4. And Jacob said unto them, My brethren, whence *be* ye? And they said, Of Haran *are* we.
5. And he said unto them, Know ye Laban the son of Nahor? And they said, We know *him*.
6. And he said unto them, *Is* he well? And they said, *He is* well; and, behold, Rachel his daughter cometh with the sheep.
7. And he said, Lo, *it is* yet high day, neither *is it* time that the cattle should be gathered together: water ye the sheep, and go *and* feed *them*.
8. And they said, We cannot, until all the flocks be gathered together, and *till* they roll the stone from the well's mouth; then we water the sheep.
9. And while he yet spake with them, Rachel came with her father's sheep; for she kept them.
10. And it came to pass, when Jacob saw Rachel, the daughter of

1. Et levavit Iahacob pedes suos, et perrexit ad terram filiorum Orientalium.
2. Et vidit, et ecce puteus erat in agro, ecce quoque ibi tres greges pecudum, qui cubabant juxta illum: quia e puteo ipso potum dabant gregibus, et lapis magnus erat super os putei.
3. Et congregabant se illuc omnes greges, et revolvebant lapidem ab ore putei potumque dabant pecudibus: et restituebant lapidem super os putei in locum suum.
4. Dixit ergo ad eos Iahacob, Fratres mei unde estis? Et dixerunt, De Charan sumus.
5. Tunc dixit ad eos, Numquid nostis Laban filium Nachor? Et dixerunt, Novimus.
6. Et dixit ad eos, Numquid est pax ei? Et dixerunt, Pax: et ecce Rachel filia ejus veniens cum pecudibus.
7. Tunc dixit, Ecce, adhuc dies magnus: non est tempus ut congregetur pecus: potum date pecudibus, et ite, pascite.
8. Qui dixerunt, Non possumus, donec congregentur omnes greges, et revolvant lapidem ab ore putei, et potum demus pecudibus.
9. Adhuc eo loquente cum eis, Rachel venit cum pecudibus quæ erant patris sui: quia ipsa pascebat.
10. Fuit autem quando vidit Iahacob Rachel filiam Laban fratris

| | |
|---|---|
| Laban his mother's brother, and the sheep of Laban his mother's brother, that Jacob went near, and rolled the stone from the well's mouth, and watered the flock of Laban his mother's brother. | matris suæ, et pecudes Laban fratris matris suæ, accessit Iahacob, et revolvit lapidem ab ore putei, et potum dedit pecudibus Laban fratris matris suæ. |
| 11. And Jacob kissed Rachel, and lifted up his voice, and wept. | 11. Et osculatus est Iahacob Rachel, qui elevavit vocem suam, et flevit. |
| 12. And Jacob told Rachel that he *was* her father's brother, and that he *was* Rebekah's son: and she ran and told her father. | 12. Et nuntiavit Iahacob ipsi Rachel quod frater patris sui esset, et quod filius Ribcæ esset: cucurrit itaque, et nuntiavit patri suo. |
| 13. And it came to pass, when Laban heard the tidings of Jacob his sister's son, that he ran to meet him, and embraced him, and kissed him, and brought him to his house. And he told Laban all these things. | 13. Et fuit, quum audisset Laban sermonem (*vel, nuntium*) Iahacob filii sororis suæ, cucurrit in occursum ejus, et amplexatus est eum, osculatusque est eum, et deduxit eum ad domum suam, et narravit ipsi Laban omnia hæc. |
| 14. And Laban said to him, Surely thou *art* my bone and my flesh. And he abode with him the space of a month. | 14. Tunc dixit ei Laban, Profecto os meum et caro mea es. Et habitavit cum eo mensem integrum. |
| 15. And Laban said unto Jacob, Because thou *art* my brother, shouldest thou therefore serve me for nought? tell me, what *shall* thy wages *be?* | 15. Dixit autem Laban ad Iahacob, Num quoniam frater meus es, servies mihi gratis? indica mihi quæ sit merces tua. |
| 16. And Laban had two daughters: the name of the elder *was* Leah, and the name of the younger *was* Rachel. | 16. Et Laban *erant* duæ filiæ: nomen majoris, Leah, et nomen minoris Rachel. |
| 17. Leah *was* tender-eyed; but Rachel was beautiful and well-favoured. | 17. Oculi autem Leah erant teneri: at Rachel erat pulchra forma, et pulchra aspectu. |
| 18. And Jacob loved Rachel; and said, I will serve thee seven years for Rachel thy younger daughter. | 18. Dilexit itaque Iahacob Rachel: et dixit, Serviam tibi septem annos pro Rachel filia tua minore. |
| 19. And Laban said, *It is* better that I give her to thee, than that I should give her to another man: abide with me. | 19. Tunc dixit Laban, Melius est ut dem eam tibi, quam dem eam viro alteri: mane mecum. |
| 20. And Jacob served seven years for Rachel; and they seemed unto him *but* a few days, for the love he had to her. | 20. Servivit itaque Iahacob pro Rachel septem annos; et fuerunt in oculis ejus sicut dies pauci, eo quod diligeret eam. |
| 21. And Jacob said unto Laban, Give *me* my wife, for my days are fulfilled, that I may go in unto her. | 21. Postea dixit Iahacob ad Laban, Da uxorem meam: quia completi sunt dies mei, ut ingrediar ad eam. |
| 22. And Laban gathered together all the men of the place, and made a feast. | 22. Et congregavit Laban omnes viros loci, et fecit convivium. |
| 23. And it came to pass in the | 23. Fuit autem vesperi, in vespera |

evening, that he took Leah his daughter, and brought her to him; and he went in unto her.

24. And Laban gave unto his daughter Leah Zilpah his maid *for* an handmaid.

25. And it came to pass, that, in the morning, behold, it *was* Leah: and he said to Laban, What *is* this thou hast done unto me? did not I serve with thee for Rachel? wherefore then hast thou beguiled me?

26. And Laban said, It must not be so done in our country, to give the younger before the first-born.

27. Fulfil her week, and we will give thee this also, for the service which thou shalt serve with me yet seven other years.

28. And Jacob did so, and fulfilled her week; and he gave him Rachel his daughter to wife also.

29. And Laban gave to Rachel his daughter Bilhah his handmaid to be her maid.

30. And he went in also unto Rachel, and he loved also Rachel more than Leah, and served with him yet seven other years.

31. And when the Lord saw that Leah *was* hated, he opened her womb; but Rachel *was* barren.

32. And Leah conceived, and bare a son; and she called his name Reuben: for she said, Surely the Lord hath looked upon my affliction; now therefore my husband will love me.

33. And she conceived again, and bare a son; and said, Because the Lord hath heard that I *was* hated, he hath therefore given me this *son* also: and she called his name Simeon.

34. And she conceived again, and bare a son; and said, Now this time will my husband be joined unto me, because I have born him three sons: therefore was his name called Levi.

35. And she conceived again, and bare a son; and she said, Now will I praise the Lord: therefore she called his name Judah; and left bearing.

accepit Leah filiam suam, et adduxit eam ad illum, et ingressus est ad eam.

24. Et dedit Laban ei Zilpah ancillam suam, Leah filiæ suæ ancillam.

25. Et fuit mane, et ecce erat Leah, et dixit ad Laban, Quid hoc fecisti mihi? numquid non pro Rachel servivi tibi? et utquid decepisti me?

26. Tunc dixit Laban, Non fit ita in loco nostro, ut detur minor ante primogenitam.

27. Comple hebdomadem hujus, et dabimus tibi etiam hanc pro servitute, quam servies mihi adhuc septem annos alios.

28. Fecit ergo Iahacob sic, et complevit hebdomadem illius, et dedit ei Rachel filiam suam in uxorem.

29. Et dedit Laban Rachel filiæ suæ Bilhah ancillam suam in ancillam.

30. Et ingressus est etiam ad Rachel: et dilexit etiam Rachel magis quam Leah: servivitque ei adhuc septem annos alios.

31. Vidit autem Iehova quod exosa esset Leah, et aperuit vulvam ejus, et Rachel erat sterilis.

32. Et concepit Leah, et peperit filium, vocavitque nomen ejus Reuben: quia dixit, Nempe vidit Iehova afflictionem meam: nunc enim diliget me vir meus.

33. Et concepit adhuc, et peperit filium, et dixit, Quia audivit Iehova quod exosa essem, dedit mihi etiam hunc. Et vocavit nomen ejus Simeon.

34. Et concepit adhuc, et peperit filium, et dixit, Nunc vice hac copulabitur vir meus mihi, quia peperi ei tres filios. Idcirco vocavit nomen ejus Levi.

35. Et concepit adhuc, et peperit filium, et dixit, Vice hac confitebor Iehovæ. Idcirco vocavit nomen ejus Iehudah: et destitit a pariendo.

1. *Then Jacob went on his journey.*¹ Moses now relates the arrival of Jacob in Mesopotamia, and the manner in which he was received by his uncle; and although the narration may seem superfluous, it yet contains nothing but what is useful to be known; for he commends the extraordinary strength of Jacob's faith, when he says, that "he lifted up his feet" to come into an unknown land. Again, he would have us to consider the providence of God, which caused Jacob to fall in with the shepherds, by whom he was conducted to the home he sought; for this did not happen accidentally, but he was guided by the hidden hand of God to that place; and the shepherds, who were to instruct and confirm him respecting all things, were brought thither at the same time. Therefore, whenever we may wander in uncertainty through intricate windings, we must contemplate, with eyes of faith, the secret providence of God which governs us and our affairs, and leads us to unexpected results.

4. *My brethren, whence be ye?* The great frankness of that age appears in this manner of meeting together; for, though the fraternal name is often abused by dishonest and wicked men, it is yet not to be doubted that friendly intercourse was then more faithfully cultivated than it is now. This was the reason why Jacob salutes unknown men as brethren, undoubtedly according to received custom. Frugality also is apparent, in that Rachel sometimes pays attention to the flock; for, since Laban abounds with servants, how does it happen that he employs his own daughter in a vile and sordid service, except that it was deemed disgraceful to educate children in idleness, softness, and indulgence? Whereas, on the contrary, at this day, since ambition, pride, and refinement, have rendered manners effeminate, the care of domestic concerns is held in such contempt, that women, for the most part, are ashamed of their proper office. It followed, from the same purity of manners which has been mentioned,

¹ Et levavit Iahacob pedes suos. And Jacob lifted up his feet. See margin of English Bible. This is a correct translation of the Hebrew ישא רגליו, (*yissa reglav.*) "The phrase is emphatic, and implies that he travelled on briskly and cheerfully, notwithstanding his age, being refreshed in his spirit by the recent manifestation of the Divine favour."— Bush.—*Ed.*

that Jacob ventured so unceremoniously to kiss his cousin; for much greater liberty was allowed in their chaste and modest mode of living.[1] In our times, impurity and ungovernable lusts are the cause why not only kisses are suspected, but even looks are dreaded; and not unjustly, since the world is filled with every kind of corruption, and such perfidy prevails, that the intercourse between men and women is seldom conducted with modesty: [2]wherefore, that ancient simplicity ought to cause us deeply to mourn; so that this vile corruption into which the world has fallen may be distasteful to us, and that the contagion of it may not affect us and our families. The order of events, however, is inverted in the narration of Moses; for Jacob did not kiss Rachel till he had informed her that he was her relative. Hence also his weeping; for, partly through joy, partly through the memory of his father's house, and through natural affection, he burst into tears.

13. *And he told Laban all these things.* Since Laban had previously seen one of Abraham's servants replenished with great wealth, an unfavourable opinion of his nephew might instantly enter into his mind: it was therefore necessary for holy Jacob to explain the causes of his own departure, and the reason why he had been sent away so contemptibly clothed. It is also probable that he had been instructed by his mother respecting the signs and marks by which he might convince them of his relationship: therefore Laban exclaims, "Surely thou art my bone and my flesh;" intimating that he was fully satisfied, and that he was induced by indubitable tokens to acknowledge Jacob as his nephew. This knowledge inclines him to humanity; for the sense of nature dictates that they who are united by ties of blood should endeavour to assist each other; but though the bond between relatives is closer, yet our kindness ought to extend more widely, so that it may diffuse itself through the

---

[1] Nam in vita casta et modesta multo major erat libertas. Car la liberté estoit beaucoup plus grande en leur facon de vivre, chaste et modeste.—*Fr. Tr.*

[2] It is scarcely to be doubted that, notwithstanding Calvin's sweeping charge, there were many exceptions to this general dissoluteness of manners in his days, as we must thankfully acknowledge there are in our own times, however extensively the evil he reprobates may have prevailed.— *Ed.*

whole human race. If, however, all the sons of Adam are thus joined together, that spiritual relationship which God produces between the faithful, and than which there is no holier bond of mutual benevolence, ought to be much more effectual.

14. *And he abode with him the space of a month.* Though Laban did not doubt that Jacob was his nephew by his sister, he nevertheless puts his character to trial during a month, and then treats with him respecting wages. Hence may be inferred the uprightness of the holy man; because he was not idle while with his uncle, but employed himself in honest labours, that he might not in idleness eat another's bread for nothing; hence Laban is compelled to acknowledge that some reward beyond his mere food was due to him. When he says, " Because thou art my brother, shouldest thou therefore serve me for nought ?" his meaning may be two-fold; either that it would be excessively absurd and unjust to defraud a relation of his due reward, for whom he ought to have greater consideration than for any stranger; or that he was unwilling to exact gratuitous service under the colour of relationship. This second exposition is the more suitable, and is received nearly by the consent of all. For they read in one connected sentence, " Because thou art my brother, shalt thou therefore serve me for nought ?" Moreover, we must note the end for which Moses relates these things. In the first place, a great principle of equity is set before us in Laban; inasmuch as this sentiment is inherent in almost all minds, " that justice ought to be mutually cultivated," till blind cupidity draws them away in another direction. And God has engraven in man's nature a law of equity; so that whoever declines from that rule, through an immoderate desire of private advantage, is left utterly without excuse. But a little while after, when it came to a matter of practice, Laban, forgetful of this equity, thinks only of what may be profitable to himself. Such an example is certainly worthy of notice, for men seldom err in general principles, and therefore, with one mouth, confess that every man ought to receive what is his due; but as soon as they descend to their own affairs, perverse self-love blinds them, or at least envelopes them in such clouds that they are carried in an oppo-

site course. Wherefore, let us learn to restrain ourselves, that a desire of our own advantage may not prevail to the sacrifice of justice. And hence has arisen the proverb, that no one is a fit judge in his own cause, because each, being unduly favourable to himself, becomes forgetful of what is right. Wherefore, we must ask God to govern and restrain our affections by a spirit of sound judgment. Laban, in wishing to enter into a covenant, does what tends to avoid contentions and complaints. The ancient saying is known, " We should deal lawfully with our friends, that we may not afterwards be obliged to go to law with them." For, whence arise so many legal broils, except that every one is more liberal towards himself, and more niggardly towards others than he ought to be? Therefore, for the purpose of cherishing concord, firm compacts are necessary, which may prevent injustice on one side or the other.

18. *I will serve thee seven years.* The iniquity of Laban betrays itself in a moment; for it is a shameful barbarity to give his daughter, by way of reward, in exchange for Jacob's services, making her the subject of a kind of barter. He ought, on the other hand, not only to have assigned a portion to his daughter, but also to have acted more liberally towards his future son-in-law. But under the pretext of affinity, he defrauds him of the reward of his labour, the very thing which he had before acknowledged to be unjust.[1] We therefore perceive still more clearly what I have previously alluded to, that although from their mother's womb men have a general notion of justice, yet as soon as their own advantage presents itself to view, they become actually unjust, unless the Lord reforms them by his Spirit. Moses does not

---

[1] Perhaps undue severity of language is here used respecting Laban; for we find it not unusual for the father to demand something for his daughter, instead of giving a dowry with her. See the history of Shechem, who says concerning Dinah, " Ask me never so much dowry and gift, and I will give it." Chap. xxxiv. 12. David also had to purchase Saul's daughter by the slaughter of the Philistines. The Prophet Hosea bought his wife " for fifteen pieces of silver and a homer and a half of barley." Still it was by no means generous on the part of Laban to make such terms with a near relative; and, at all events, he ought to have given to his daughters and their children any profit that he might have obtained by his hard bargain with Jacob.—*Ed.*

here relate something rare or unusual, but what is of most common occurrence. For though men do not set their daughters to sale, yet the desire of gain hurries the greater part so far away, that they prostitute their honour and sell their souls. Further, it is not altogether to be deemed a fault that Jacob was rather inclined to love Rachel; whether it was that Leah, on account of her tender eyes, was less beautiful, or that she was pleasing only by the comeliness of her eyes,[1] while Rachel excelled her altogether in elegance of form. For we see how naturally a secret kind of affection produces mutual love. Only excess is to be guarded against, and so much the more diligently, because it is difficult so to restrain affections of this kind, that they do not prevail to the stifling of reason. Therefore he who shall be induced to choose a wife, because of the elegance of her form, will not necessarily sin, provided reason always maintains the ascendency, and holds the wantonness of passion in subjection. Yet perhaps Jacob sinned in being too self-indulgent, when he desired Rachel the younger sister to be given to him, to the injury of the elder; and also, while yielding to the desire of his own eyes, he undervalued the virtues of Leah: for this is a very culpable want of self-government, when any one chooses a wife only for the sake of her beauty, whereas excellence of disposition ought to be deemed of the first importance. But the strength and ardour of his attachment manifests itself in this, that he felt no weariness in the labour of seven years: but chastity was also joined with it, so that he persevered, during this long period, with a patient and quiet mind in the midst of so many labours. And here again the integrity and continence of that age is apparent, because, though dwelling under the same roof, and accustomed to familiar intercourse, Jacob yet conducted himself with modesty, and abstained from all impropriety. Therefore, at the close of the appointed time he said, "Give me my wife, that I may go in unto her," by which he implies that she had been hitherto a pure virgin.

[1] This latter opinion is adopted by Dr. A. Clarke, who says, "The chief recommendation of Leah was her *soft* and *beautiful* eyes; but Rachel was beautiful in her *shape, person, mien,* and *gait,* and beautiful in her countenance." The greater part of commentators, however, take the same view of the case as our translators.—*Ed.*

22. *And Laban gathered together.* Moses does not mean that a supper was prepared for the whole people, but that many guests were invited, as is customary in splendid nuptials; and there is no doubt that he applied himself with the greater earnestness to adorn that feast, for the purpose of holding Jacob bound by a sense of shame, so that he should not dare to depreciate the marriage into which he had been deceived. We hence gather what, at that time, was the religious observance connected with the marriage bed. For this was the occasion of Jacob's deception, that, out of regard for the modesty of brides, they were led veiled into the chamber; but now, the ancient discipline being rejected, men become almost brutal.

25. *And he said to Laban.* Jacob rightly expostulates respecting the fraud practised upon him. And the answer of Laban, though it is not without a pretext, yet forms no excuse for the fraud. It was not the custom to give the younger daughters in marriage before the elder: and injustice would have been done to the first-born by disturbing this accustomed order. But he ought not, on that account, craftily to have betrothed Rachel to Jacob, and then to have substituted Leah in her place. He should rather have cautioned Jacob himself, in time, to turn his thoughts to Leah, or else to refrain from marriage with either of them. But we may learn from this, that wicked and deceitful men, when once they have turned aside from truth, make no end of transgressing: meanwhile, they always put forward some pretext for the purpose of freeing themselves from blame. He had before acted unjustly toward his nephew in demanding seven years' labour for his daughter; he had also unjustly set his daughter to sale, without dowry, for the sake of gain; but the most unworthy deed of all was perfidiously to deprive his nephew of his betrothed wife, to pervert the sacred laws of marriage, and to leave nothing safe or sound. Yet we see him pretending that he has an honourable defence for his conduct, because it was not the custom of the country to prefer the younger to the elder.

27. *Fulfil her week.* Laban now is become callous in wickedness, for he extorts other seven years from his nephew to allow him to marry his other daughter. If he had

had ten more daughters, he would have been ready thus to dispose of them all: yea, of his own accord, he obtrudes his daughter as an object of merchandise, thinking nothing of the disgrace of this illicit sale, if only he may make it a source of gain. In this truly he grievously sins, that he not only involves his nephew in polygamy, but pollutes both him and his own daughters by incestuous nuptials. If by any means a wife is not loved by her husband, it is better to repudiate her than that she should be retained as a captive, and consumed with grief by the introduction of a second wife. Therefore the Lord, by Malachi, pronounces divorce to be more tolerable than polygamy. (Mal. ii. 14.) Laban, blinded by avarice, so sets his daughters together, that they spend their whole lives in mutual hostility. He also perverts all the laws of nature by casting two sisters into one marriage-bed.[1] Since Moses sets these crimes before the Israelites in the very commencement of their history, it is not for them to be inflated by the sense of their nobility, so that they should boast of their descent from holy fathers. For, however excellent Jacob might be, he had no other offspring than that which sprung from an impure source; since, contrary to nature, two sisters are mixed together in one bed;[2] and two concubines are afterwards added to the mass. We have seen indeed, above, that this license was too common among oriental nations; but it was not allowable for men, at their own pleasure, to subvert, by a depraved custom, the law of marriage divinely sanctioned from the beginning. Therefore, Laban is, in every way, inexcusable. And although necessity may, in some degree, excuse the fault of Jacob, it cannot altogether absolve him from blame. For he might have dismissed Leah, because she had not been his lawful wife: because the mutual consent of the man and the woman, respecting which mistake is impossible, constitutes marriage. But Jacob reluctantly retains her as his wife, from whom he was released and free, and thus doubles his fault by polygamy, and trebles it by an incestuous marriage. Thus we see that the inordinate love of Rachel, which had been once

[1] It is here added, " ut altera sit alterius pellex."
[2] Quasi belluino more.

excited in his mind, was inflamed to such a degree, that he possessed neither moderation nor judgment. With respect to the words made use of, interpreters ascribe to them different meanings. Some refer the demonstrative pronoun to the week ;[1] others to Leah, as if it had been said, that he should not have Rachel until he had lived with her sister one week. But I rather explain it of Rachel, that he should purchase a marriage with her by another seven years' service; not that Laban deferred the nuptials to the end of that time, but that Jacob was compelled to engage himself in a new servitude.

30. *And he loved also Rachel more than Leah.* No doubt Moses intended to exhibit the sins of Jacob, that we might learn to fear, and to conform all our actions to the sole rule of God's word. For if the holy patriarch fell so grievously, who among us is secure from a similar fall, unless kept by the guardian care of God? At the same time, it appears how dangerous it is to imitate the fathers while we neglect the law of the Lord. And yet the foolish Papists so greatly delight themselves in this imitation, that they do not scruple to observe, as a law, whatever they find to have been practised by the fathers. Besides which, they own as fathers those who are worthy of such sons, so that any raving monk is of more account with them than all the patriarchs. It was not without fault on Leah's part that she was despised by her husband; and the Lord justly chastised her, because she, being aware of her father's fraud, dishonourably obtained possession of her sister's husband; but her fault forms no excuse for Jacob's lust.

31. *And when the Lord saw.* Moses here shows that Jacob's extravagant love was corrected by the Lord; as the affections of the faithful, when they become inordinate, are wont to be tamed by the rod. Rachel is loved, not without wrong to her sister, to whom due honour is not given. The

---

[1] מלא שבע זאת, (*Malai shebuah zot.*) The demonstrative pronoun זאת, if applied to *week*, would require the translation to be, " Fulfil *this* week;" that is, the week of Leah; meaning the festive week in which the marriage was commemorated, and, as soon as that week was over, he would also give Jacob his remaining daughter to wife. This opinion is supported by eminent critics.—*Ed.*

Lord, therefore, interposes as her vindicator, and, by a suitable remedy, turns the mind of Jacob into that direction, to which it had been most averse. This passage teaches us, that offspring is a special gift of God; since the power of rendering one fertile, and of cursing the womb of the other with barrenness, is expressly ascribed to him. We must observe further, that the bringing forth of offspring tends to conciliate husbands to their wives. Whence also the ancients have called children by the name of *pledges ;* because they avail, in no slight degree, to increase and to cherish mutual love. When Moses asserts that Leah was hated, his meaning is, that she was not loved so much as she ought to have been. For she was not intolerable to Jacob, neither did he pursue her with hatred ; but Moses, by the use of this word, amplifies his fault, in not having discharged the duty of a husband, and in not having treated her who was his first wife with adequate kindness and honour. It is of importance carefully to notice this, because many think they fulfil their duty if they do not break out into mortal hatred. But we see that the Holy Spirit pronounces those as hated who are not sufficiently loved ; and we know, that men were created for this end, that they should love one another. Therefore, none will be counted guiltless of the crime of hatred before God, but he who embraces his neighbours with love. For not only will a secret displeasure be accounted as hatred, but even that neglect of brethren, and that cold charity which ever reigns in the world. But in proportion as any one is more closely connected with another, must be the endeavour to adhere to each other in a more sacred bond of affection. Moreover, with respect to married persons, though they may not openly disagree, yet if they are cold in their affection towards each other, this disgust is not far removed from hatred.

32. *She called his name Reuben.* Moses relates that Leah was not ungrateful to God. And truly, I do not doubt, that the benefits of God were then commonly more appreciated than they are now. For a profane stupor so occupies the mind of nearly all men, that, like cattle, they swallow up whatever benefits God, in his kindness, bestows upon them.

Further, Leah not only acknowledges God as the author of her fruitfulness; but also assigns as a reason, that her affliction had been looked upon by the Lord, and a son had been given her who should draw the affection of her husband to herself. Whence it appears probable, that when she saw herself despised, she had recourse to prayer, in order that she might receive more succour from heaven. For thanksgiving is a proof that persons have previously exercised themselves in prayer; since they who hope for nothing from God do, by their indolence, bury in oblivion all the favours he has conferred upon them. Therefore, Leah inscribed on the person of her son[1] a memorial whereby she might stir herself up to offer praise to God. This passage also teaches, that they who are unjustly despised by men are regarded by the Lord. Hence it affords a singularly profitable consolation to the faithful; who, as experience shows, are for the most part despised in the world. Whenever, therefore, they are treated harshly and contumeliously by men, let them take refuge in this thought, that God will be the more propitious to them. Leah followed the same course in reference to her second son; for she gave him a name which is derived from "hearing,"[2] to recall to her memory that her sighs had been heard by the Lord. Whence we conjecture (as I have just before said) that when affliction was pressing upon her, she cast her griefs into the bosom of God. Her third son she names from "joining;"[3] as if she would say, now a new link is interposed, so that she should be more loved by her husband. In her fourth son, she again declares her piety towards God, for she gives to him the name of "praise,"[4] as having been granted to her by the special kindness of God. She had, indeed, previously given thanks to the Lord; but

---

[1] ראובן. "See a son."
[2] שמעון, from שמע, (*shamah*,) to hear.
[3] לוי, from לוה, (*lavah*,) to join.
[4] יהודה, from ידה, (*yadah*,) to praise. There is something, as Calvin intimates, in the series of names given by Leah to her children, which seems to show the pious feelings of her heart. In her first-born, *Reuben*, she acknowledged that God had *looked* upon her affliction; in *Simeon*, that he had *heard* her prayer; in *Levi*, that he had *joined* her husband to her; and in *Judah*, she commemorates all these mercies with gratitude and *praise*.—*Ed.*

whereas more abundant material for praise is supplied, she acknowledges not once only, nor by one single method, but frequently, that she has been assisted by the favour of God.

## CHAPTER XXX.

1. AND when Rachel saw that she bare Jacob no children, Rachel envied her sister; and said unto Jacob, Give me children, or else I die.

2. And Jacob's anger was kindled against Rachel; and he said, *Am* I in God's stead, who hath withheld from thee the fruit of the womb?

3. And she said, Behold my maid Bilhah, go in unto her; and she shall bear upon my knees, that I may also have children by her.

4. And she gave him Bilhah her handmaid to wife; and Jacob went in unto her.

5. And Bilhah conceived, and bare Jacob a son.

6. And Rachel said, God hath judged me, and hath also heard my voice, and hath given me a son: therefore called she his name Dan.

7. And Bilhah, Rachel's maid, conceived again, and bare Jacob a second son.

8. And Rachel said, With great wrestlings have I wrestled with my sister, and I have prevailed: and she called his name Naphtali.

9. When Leah saw that she had left bearing, she took Zilpah her maid, and gave her Jacob to wife.

10. And Zilpah, Leah's maid, bare Jacob a son.

11. And Leah said, A troop cometh: and she called his name Gad.

12. And Zilpah, Leah's maid, bare Jacob a second son.

13. And Leah said, Happy am I, for the daughters will call me blessed: and she called his name Asher.

14. And Reuben went, in the days of wheat-harvest, and found man-

1. Porro vidit Rachel, quod non pareret ipsi Iahacob: et invidit Rachel sorori suæ, et dixit ad Iahacob, Da mihi filios: sin minus, mortua sum.

2. Et iratus est furor Iahacob in Rachel, et dixit, Numquid pro Deo sum, qui prohibuit a te fructum ventris?

3. Et dixit, Ecce ancilla mea Bilhah, ingredere ad eam, et pariet super genua mea: et erit etiam mihi filius ex ea.

4. Dedit ergo ei Bilhah ancillam suam in uxorem, et ingressus est ad eam Iahacob.

5. Et concepit Bilhah, et peperit ipsi Iahacob filium.

6. Et dixit Rachel, Iudicavit me Deus, et etiam audivit vocem meam, et dedit mihi filium. Idcirco vocavit nomen ejus Dan.

7. Et concepit adhuc, et peperit Bilhah ancilla Rachel filium secundum ipsi Iahacob.

8. Tunc dixit Rachel, Luctationibus divinis luctata sum cum sorore mea, etiam prævalui. Et vocavit nomen ejus Nephthali.

9. Vidit autem Leah, quod cessasset parere, et accepit Zilpah ancillam suam, et dedit eam Iahacob in uxorem.

10. Et peperit Zilpah ancilla Leah ipsi Iahacob filium.

11. Et dixit Leah, Venit turba: et vocavit nomen ejus Gad.

12. Et peperit Zilpah ancilla Leah filium secundum ipsi Iahacob.

13. Et dixit Leah, Ut beata dicar, quia beatam me dicent filiæ. Et vocavit nomen illius Aser.

14. Ivit autem Reuben in diebus messis triticeæ, et reperit mandra-

drakes in the field, and brought them unto his mother Leah. Then Rachel said to Leah, Give me, I pray thee, of thy son's mandrakes.

15. And she said unto her, *Is it* a small matter that thou hast taken my husband? and wouldest thou take away my son's mandrakes also? And Rachel said, Therefore he shall lie with thee to-night for thy son's mandrakes.

16. And Jacob came out of the field in the evening, and Leah went out to meet him, and said, Thou must come in unto me; for surely I have hired thee with my son's mandrakes. And he lay with her that night.

17. And God hearkened unto Leah, and she conceived, and bare Jacob the fifth son.

18. And Leah said, God hath given me my hire, because I have given my maiden to my husband: and she called his name Issachar.

19. And Leah conceived again, and bare Jacob the sixth son.

20. And Leah said, God hath endued me *with* a good dowry; now will my husband dwell with me, because I have born him six sons: and she called his name Zebulun.

21. And afterwards she bare a daughter, and called her name Dinah.

22. And God remembered Rachel, and God hearkened to her, and opened her womb.

23. And she conceived, and bare a son; and said, God hath taken away my reproach:

24. And she called his name Joseph; and said, The Lord shall add to me another son.

25. And it came to pass, when Rachel had born Joseph, that Jacob said unto Laban, Send me away, that I may go unto mine own place, and to my country.

26. Give *me* my wives and my children, for whom I have served thee, and let me go: for thou knowest my service which I have done thee.

15. Et dixit ei, Numquid parum est quod abstuleris virum meum, ut auferas etiam mandragoras filii mei? Et dixit Rachel, Idcirco dormiat tecum hac nocte, pro mandragoris filii tui.

16. Venit autem Iahacob ex agro vesperi, et egressa est Leah in occursum ejus, et dixit, Ad me ingredieris: quia mercando mercata sum te mandragoris filii mei. Et dormivit cum ea nocte illa.

17. Exaudivit Deus Leah, et concepit, et peperit ipsi Iahacob filium quintum.

18. Tunc dixit Leah, Dedit Deus mercedem meam: quia dedi ancillam meum viro meo. Et vocavit nomen ejus Issachar.

19. Et concepit adhuc Leah, et peperit filium sextum ipsi Iahacob.

20. Dixit ergo Leah, Dotavit me Deus dote bona: vice hac habitavit mecum vir meus: quia peperi ei sex filios. Et vocavit nomen ejus Zebulon.

21. Et postea peperit filiam: et vocavit nomen ejus Dinah.

22. Porro recordatus est Deus Rachel, et exaudivit eam Deus, et aperuit vulvam illius.

23. Et concepit, et peperit filium, et dixit, Amovit Deus probrum meum.

24. Et vocavit nomen ejus Ioseph, dicendo, Addat Ichova mihi filium alium.

25. Fuit autem quum peperisset Rachel Ioseph, dixit Iahacob ab Laban, Dimitte me, et ibo ad locum meum, et ad terram meam.

26. Da uxores meas, et liberos meos, propter quas servivi tibi, et ibo: tu enim nosti servitium meum, quo servivi tibi.

27. And Laban said unto him, I pray thee, if I have found favour in thine eyes, *tarry: for* I have learned by experience that the Lord hath blessed me for thy sake.

28. And he said, Appoint me thy wages, and I will give *it*.

29. And he said unto him, Thou knowest how I have served thee, and how thy cattle was with me.

30. For *it was* little which thou hadst before I *came*, and it is *now* increased unto a multitude; and the Lord hath blessed thee since my coming: and now, when shall I provide for mine own house also?

31. And he said, What shall I give thee? And Jacob said, Thou shalt not give me any thing. If thou wilt do this thing for me, I will again feed *and* keep thy flock.

32. I will pass through all thy flock to-day, removing from thence all the speckled and spotted cattle, and all the brown cattle among the sheep, and the spotted and speckled among the goats; and *of such* shall be my hire.

33. So shall my righteousness answer for me in time to come, when it shall come for my hire before thy face: every one that *is* not speckled and spotted among the goats, and brown among the sheep, that shall be counted stolen with me.

34. And Laban said, Behold, I would it might be according to thy word.

35. And he removed that day the he-goats that were ring-straked and spotted, and all the she-goats that were speckled and spotted, *and* every one that had *some* white in it, and all the brown among the sheep, and gave *them* into the hand of his sons.

36. And he set three days' journey betwixt himself and Jacob: and Jacob fed the rest of Laban's flocks.

37. And Jacob took him rods of green poplar, and of the hazel and chestnut-tree, and pilled white strakes in them, and made the white appear which *was* in the rods.

27. Et dixit ad cum Laban, Si, quæso, inveni gratiam in oculis tui, (expertus sum quod benedixit mihi Iehova propter te.)

28. Dixit ergo, Indica mercedem tuam mihi, et dabo.

29. Et dixit ad eum, Tu nosti qualiter servierim tibi, et quale fuit pecus tuum mecum:

30. Quia pusillum, quod fuit tibi ante me, crevit in multitudinem, et benedixit Dominus tibi ad *ingressum* pedis mei: et nunc quando faciam etiam ego domui meæ?

31. Et dixit, Quid dabo tibi? Respondit Iahacob, Non dabis mihi quicquam, si feceris mihi hoc, revertar, pascam, pecudes tuas custodiam.

32. Transibo per omnes pecudes tuas hodie, removendo inde omne pecus parvum punctis parvis respersum, et respersum maculis latis: et omnem agnum rufum in ovibus et respersum maculis latis, et respersum punctis parvis in capris: et erit merces mea.

33. Et testificabitur mihi justitia mea die crastino, quum venerit ad mercedem meam coram te: quicquid non erit punctis parvis respersum, et maculis latis respersum in capris, et rufum in ovibus, furto ablatum erat a me.

34. Tunc dixit Laban, Ecce utinam sit secundum verbum tuum.

35. Removit itaque in die illa hircos minores variegatos, et maculis latis respersos, et omnes capras punctis parvis respersas, et maculis latis respersas, omne in quo erat candor, et omne rufum in ovibus, et dedit in manus filiorum suorum.

36. Et posuit viam trium dierum inter se et inter Iahacob: et Iahacob pascebat pecudes Laban residuas.

37. Tulit autem sibi Iahacob virgam populeam viridem, et amygdalinam, et castaneam, et decorticavit in eis cortices albos, denudationem candoris, qui erat in virgis.

38. And he set the rods which he had pilled before the flocks in the gutters in the watering-troughs, when the flocks came to drink, that they should conceive when they came to drink.

39. And the flocks conceived before the rods, and brought forth cattle ring-straked, speckled, and spotted.

40. And Jacob did separate the lambs, and set the faces of the flocks toward the ring-straked and all the brown in the flock of Laban; and he put his own flocks by themselves, and put them not unto Laban's cattle.

41. And it came to pass, whensoever the stronger cattle did conceive, that Jacob laid the rods before the eyes of the cattle in the gutters, that they might conceive among the rods.

42. But when the cattle were feeble, he put *them* not in: so the feebler were Laban's, and the stronger Jacob's.

43. And the man increased exceedingly, and had much cattle, and maid-servants, and men-servants, and camels, and asses.

38. Et statuit virgas, quas decorticavit, in fluentis, in canalibus aquarum (ad quos veniebant pecudes ad bibendum) e regione pecudum, ut coirent dum venirent ad bibendum.

39. Et coibant pecudes prope virgas, et pariebant pecudes *fœtus* lineis distinctos, et punctis parvis respersos, et maculis latis respersos.

40. Et oves separavit Iahacob, et posuit facies pecudum ad *fœtus* lineis distinctos: et omne rufum in pecudibus *erat* Laban: et posuit sibi greges seorsum, et non posuit eos juxta pecudes Laban.

41. Fuit autem, in omni coitu pecudum primitivarum, ponebat Iahacob virgas in oculis pecudum in canalibus, ut coirent ad virgas.

42. Ad serotinos vero coitus pecudum non ponebat: et erant serotina ipsius Laban: primitiva autem ipsius Iahacob.

43. Crevit vir ergo supra modum: fueruntque ei pecudes multæ, et ancillæ, et servi, et cameli, et asini.

1. *And when Rachel saw.* Here Moses begins to relate that Jacob was distracted with domestic strifes. But although the Lord was punishing him, because he had been guilty of no light sin in marrying two wives, and especially sisters; yet the chastisement was paternal; and God himself, seeing that he is wont mercifully to pardon his own people, restrained in some degree his hand. Whence also it happened, that Jacob did not immediately repent, but added new offences to the former. But first we must speak of Rachel. Whereas she rejoiced to see her sister subjected to contempt and grief, the Lord represses this sinful joy, by giving his blessing to Leah, in order to make the condition of both of them equal. She hears the grateful acknowledgment of her sister, and learns from the names given to the four sons, that God had pitied, and had sustained by his favour, her who had been unjustly despised by man. Nevertheless envy inflames her, and will not suffer anything of the

dignity becoming a wife to appear in her. We see what ambition can do. For Rachel, in seeking pre-eminence, does not spare even her own sister; and scarcely refrains from venting her anger against God, for having honoured that sister with the gift of fruitfulness. Her emulation did not proceed from any injuries that she had received, but because she could not bear to have a partner and an equal, though she herself was really the younger. What would she have done had she been provoked, seeing that she envies her sister who was contented with her lot ? Now Moses, by exhibiting this evil in Rachel, would teach us that it is inherent in all; in order that each of us, tearing it up by the roots, may vigilantly purify himself from it. That we may be cured of envy, it behoves us to put away pride and self-love; as Paul prescribes this single remedy against contentions, " Let nothing be done through vain-glory." (Phil. ii. 3.)

2. *And Jacob's anger was kindled.* The tenderness of Jacob's affection rendered him unwilling to offend his wife; yet her unworthy conduct compelled him to do so, when he saw her petulantly exalt herself, not only against her sister, who piously, holily, and thankfully was enjoying the gifts of God; but even against God himself, of whom it is said that " the fruit of the womb is his reward." (Ps. cxxvii. 3.) On this account, therefore, Jacob is angry, because his wife ascribes nothing to the providence of God, and, by imagining that children are the offspring of chance, would deprive God of the care and government of mankind. It is probable that Jacob had been already sorrowful on account of his wife's barrenness. He now, therefore, fears lest her folly should still farther provoke God's anger to inflict more severe strokes. This was a holy indignation, by which Jacob maintained the honour due to God, while he corrected his wife, and taught her that it was not without sufficient cause that she had been hitherto barren. For when he affirms that the Lord had shut her womb, he obliquely intimates that she ought the more deeply to humble herself.

3. *Behold my maid Bilhah.* Here the vanity of the female disposition appears. For Rachel is not induced to flee unto the Lord, but strives to gain a triumph by illicit arts.

Therefore she hurries Jacob into a third marriage. Whence we infer, that there is no end of sinning, when once the Divine institution is treated with neglect. And this is what I have said, that Jacob was not immediately brought back to a right state of mind by Divine chastisements. He acts, indeed, in this instance, at the instigation of his wife: but is his wife in the place of God, from whom alone the law of marriage proceeds? But to please his wife, or to yield to her importunity, he does not scruple to depart from the command of God. *To bear upon the knees,* is nothing more than to commit the child when born to another to be brought up. Bilhah was a maid-servant; and therefore did not bear for herself but for her mistress, who, claiming the child as her own, thus procured the honour of a mother. Therefore it is added, in the way of explanation, *I shall have children,* or *I shall be built up by her.* For the word which Moses here uses, is derived from בֵּן, *a son:* because children are as the support and stay of a house. But Rachel acted sinfully, because she attempted, by an unlawful method, and in opposition to the will of God, to become a mother.

5. *And Bilhah conceived.* It is wonderful that God should have deigned to honour an adulterous connexion with offspring: but he does sometimes thus strive to overcome by kindness the wickedness of men, and pursues the unworthy with his favour. Moreover, he does not always make the punishment equal to the offences of his people, nor does he always rouse them, alike quickly, from their torpor, but waits for the matured season of correction. Therefore it was his will that they who were born from this faulty connexion, should yet be reckoned among the legitimate children; just as Moses shortly before called Bilhah a wife, who yet might more properly have been called a harlot. And the common rule does not hold, that what had no force from the beginning can never acquire validity by succession of time; for although the compact, into which the husband and wife sinfully entered against the Divine command and the sacred order of nature, was void; it came to pass nevertheless, by special privilege, that the conjunction, which in itself was adulterous, obtained the honour of wedlock. At length Rachel begins

to ascribe to God what is his own; but this confession of hers is so mixed up with ambition, that it breathes nothing of sincerity or rectitude. She pompously announces, that her cause has been undertaken by the Lord. As if truly, she had been so injured by her sister, that she deserved to be raised by the favour of God; and as if she had not attempted to deprive herself of his help. We see, then, that under the pretext of praising God, she rather does him wrong, by rendering him subservient to her desires. Add to this, that she imitates hypocrites, who, while in adversity, rush against God with closed eyes; yet when more prosperous fortune favours them, indulge in vain boastings, as if God smiled upon all their deeds and sayings. Rachel, therefore, does not so much celebrate the goodness of God, as she applauds herself. Wherefore let the faithful, instructed by her example, abstain from polluting the sacred name of God by hypocrisy.

8. *With great wrestlings.*[1] Others translate it, "I am joined with the joinings of God;"[2] as if she exulted in having recovered what she had lost; or, certainly, in having obtained an equal degree of honour with her sister. Others render it, "I am doubled with the duplications of God." But both derive the noun and the verb from the root פתל, (*patal,*) which signifies a twisted thread. The former of these senses comes to this; that since Rachel has attained a condition equal to that of her sister, there is no reason why her sister should claim any superiority over her. But the latter sense expresses more confident boasting, since she proclaims herself a conqueror, and doubly superior. But a more simple meaning is (in my opinion) adduced by others, namely, that she "wrestled with divine or excellent wrestlings." For the Hebrews indicate all excellence by adding the name of God; because the more excellent anything is, the more does the glory of God shine in it. But perverse is that boasting with which she glories over her sister, when she ought rather suppliantly to have implored forgiveness. In

---

[1] Luctationibus divinis. Margin of English Bible, " with wrestlings of God."

[2] Conjunctionibus Dei conjuncta sum.

Rachel the pride of the human mind is depicted; because they whom God has endowed with his benefits, for the most part are so elated, that they rage contumeliously against their neighbours. Besides, she foolishly prefers herself to her sister in fruitfulness, in which she is still manifestly inferior. But they who are puffed up with pride have also the habit of malignantly depreciating those gifts which the Lord has bestowed on others, in comparison with their own smaller gifts. Perhaps, also, she expected a numerous progeny, as if God were under obligation to her. She did not, as pious persons are wont to do, conceive hope from benefits received; but, by a confident presumption of the flesh, made herself sure of everything she wished. Hitherto, then, she gave no sign of pious modesty. Whence is this, but because her temporary barrenness had not yet thoroughly subdued her? Therefore we ought the more to beware, lest if God relaxes our punishments, we, being inflated by his kindness, should perish.

9. *When Leah saw that she had left bearing.* Moses returns to Leah, who, not content with four sons, devised a method whereby she might always retain her superior rank: and therefore she also, in turn, substitutes her maid in her place. And truly Rachel deserved such a reward of her perverse design; since she, desiring to snatch the palm from her sister, does not consider that the same contrivance to which she had resorted, might speedily be employed against herself. Yet Leah sins still more grievously, by using wicked and unjust arts in the contest. Within a short period, she had experienced the wonderful blessing of God; and now, because she ceased from bearing, for a little while, she despairs concerning the future, as if she had never participated in the Divine favour. What, if her desire was strong; why did she not resort to the fountain of blessing? In obtruding, therefore, her maid, she gave proof not only of impatience, but also of distrust; because with the remembrance of Divine mercy, faith also is extinguished in her heart. And we know that all who rely upon the Lord are so tranquil and sedate in their mind, that they patiently wait for what he is about to give. And it is the just punishment of

unbelief when any one stumbles through excessive haste. So much the more ought we to beware of the assaults of the flesh, if we desire to maintain a right course.

As to the name *Gad*, this passage is variously expounded by commentators. In this point they agree, that בגד (*Bagad*) means the same as if Leah had said "the time of bearing is come."[1] But some suppose גד (*Gad*) to be the prosperous star of Jupiter; others, Mercury; others, *good fortune*. They adduce Isaiah lxv. 11, where it is written, "they offer a libation to Gad."[2] But the context of the Prophet shows that this ought rather to be understood of the host of heaven, or of the number of false gods; because it immediately follows that they offer sacrifices to the stars, and furnish tables for a multitude of gods: the punishment is then added, that as they had fabricated an immense number of deities, so God will "number" them "to the sword." As it respects the present passage, nothing is less probable than that Leah should extol the planet Jupiter instead of God, seeing that she, at least, maintained the principle that the propagation of the human race flows from God alone. I wonder also that interpreters understand this of prosperous fortune, when Moses afterwards, chap. xlix. 19, leads us to an opposite meaning. For the allusion he there makes would be inappropriate, "Gad, a troop shall overcome him," &c., unless it had been the design of Leah to congratulate herself on the *troop* of her children. For since she had so far surpassed her sister,[3] she declares that she has children in great abundance. When she proclaims herself *happy*[4] in her sixth son,

---

[1] *Venit felicitas.* In the French translation, "Mon heur est venu." My hour is come. The word בגד is explained in the margin of the Hebrew Bible by בא גד. *Venit turma, ceu exercitus*—a troop or army cometh. See Schindler.—*Ed.*

[2] "Ye are they that forsake the Lord, that forget my holy mountain, that prepare a table for that *troop* (margin, ·Gad), and that furnish a drink-offering to that number" (margin, Meni).—English Translation. Calvin has quoted from memory, and not accurately, having put libation instead of table.—*Ed.*

[3] *Nam quum sesquialtera parte superior esset, prædicat se habere in magna copia liberos.*

[4] "And Leah said, Happy am I, for the daughters shall call me blessed; and she called his name Asher."—English Translation.
It may be observed that the names given to these children of the hand-

it again appears in what great esteem fecundity was then held. And certainly it is a great honour, when God confers on mortals the sacred title of parents, and through them propagates the human race formed after his own image.

14. *And Reuben went in the days of wheat harvest.* This narration of the fact that a boy brought home I know not what kind of fruit out of the fields, and presented it to his mother, by which she purchased of her sister one night with her husband, has the appearance of being light and puerile. Yet it contains a useful instruction. For we know how foolishly the Jews glory in extolling the origin of their own nation: for they scarcely deign to acknowledge that they have sprung from Adam and Noah, with the rest of mankind. And certainly they do excel in the dignity of their ancestors, as Paul testifies, (Rom. ix. 5,) but they do not acknowledge this as coming from God. Wherefore the Spirit purposely aimed at beating down this arrogance, when he described their race as sprung from a beginning so mean and abject. For he does not here erect a splendid stage on which they may exhibit themselves; but he humbles them and exalts the grace of God, seeing that he had brought forth his Church out of nothing. Respecting the kind of fruit mentioned, I have nothing certain to adduce.[1] That it was fragrant is gathered from Canticles vii. 13.[2] And whereas all translate it *mandrakes,* I do not contend on that point.

15. *Is it a small matter that thou hast taken my husband?* Moses leaves more for his readers to reflect upon than he ex-

maidens were far less indicative of a pious state of mind, than those which Leah had previously given to her own sons. A fact which confirms the remarks of Calvin on the impiety of the course pursued by the rival wives. Rachel seems to make no reference to God in the names of the children of her handmaid; Leah, in imitating the example of her sister, seems to lose her own previous devotional feeling; and both sink in our esteem, as they proceed in their unseemly contentions.—*Ed.*

[1] Mandrakes—Heb. דוּדָאִים, (*dudaim,*) from דּוּד, (*dud,*) beloved; supposed to be a species of melon with purple flowers. It grows abundantly in Palestine, and is held in high respect for its prolific virtues. Gesenius describes mandrakes as "Love apples (Liebes äpfel), the apples of the Mandragora, an herb resembling the belladonna, with a root like a carrot, having white and reddish blossoms of a sweet smell, and with yellow odoriferous apples."—*Ed.*

[2] "The mandrakes give a smell, and at our gates are all manner of pleasant fruits."

presses in words; namely, that Jacob's house had been filled with contentions and strifes. For Leah speaks haughtily, because her mind had been long so exasperated that she could not address herself mildly and courteously to her sister. Perhaps the sisters were not thus contentious by nature; but God suffered them to contend with each other, that the punishment of polygamy might be exhibited to posterity. And it is not to be doubted that this domestic private quarrel, yea, hostile dissension, brought great grief and torment to the holy man. But the reason why he found himself thus distracted by opposite parties was, that against all right, he had broken the unity of the conjugal bond.

17. *And God hearkened unto Leah.* Moses expressly declares this, in order that we may know how indulgently God dealt with that family. For who would have thought, that, while Leah was hatefully denying to her sister the fruits gathered by her boy, and was purchasing, by the price of those fruits, a night with her husband, there would be any place for prayers? Moses, therefore, teaches us, that pardon was granted for these faults, to prove that the Lord would not fail to complete his work notwithstanding such great infirmity. But Leah ignorantly boasts that her son was given to her as a reward of her sin; for she had violated the fidelity of holy wedlock, when she introduced a fresh concubine to oppose her sister. Truly, she is so far from the confession of her fault, that she proclaims her own merit. I grant there was some excuse for her conduct; for she intimates that she was not so much excited by lust, as by modest love, because she desired to increase her family and to fulfil the duty of an honourable mother of a family. But though this pretext is specious in the eyes of men, yet the profanation of holy marriage cannot be pleasing to God. She errs, therefore, in taking what was *no cause* for *the cause*. And this is the more to be observed; because it is a fault which too much prevails in the world, for men to reckon the free gifts of God as their own reward; yea, even to boast of their deserts, when they are condemned by the word of God. In her sixth son, she more purely and rightly estimates the divine goodness, when she gives thanks to God, that, by his kind-

ness, her husband would hereafter be more closely united to her, (ver. 20). For although he had lived with her before, yet, being too much attached to Rachel, he was almost entirely alienated from Leah. It has before been said, that children born in lawful wedlock are bonds to unite the minds of their parents.

21. *And afterward she bare a daughter.* It is not known whether Jacob had any other daughter; for it is not uncommon in Scripture, when genealogies are recorded, to omit the women, since they do not bear their own name, but lie concealed under the shadow of their husbands. Meanwhile, if anything worthy of commemoration occurs to any women, especial mention is then made of them. This was the case with Dinah, on account of the violence done to her; of which more will be said hereafter. But whereas the sons of Jacob subsequently regarded it as an indignity that their sister should marry one of another nation; and as Moses records nothing of any other daughters, either as being settled in the land of Canaan, or married in Egypt, it is probable that Dinah was the only one born to him.

22. *And God remembered Rachel.* Since with God nothing is either *before* or *after*, but all things are present, he is subject to no forgetfulness, so that, in the lapse of time, he should need to be reminded of what is past. But the Scripture describes the presence and memory of God from the effect produced upon ourselves, because we conceive him to be such as he appears to be by his acts. Moreover, whether Rachel's child was born the last of all, cannot with certainty be gathered from the words of Moses. They who, in this place, affirm that the figure *hysteron proteron*, which puts the last first, is used, are moved by the consideration, that if Joseph had been born after the last of his brethren, the age which Moses records in chapter xli. 46, would not accord with the fact. But they are deceived in this, that they reckon the nuptials of Rachel from the end of the second seven years; whereas it is certainly proved from the context, that although Jacob agreed to give his service for Rachel, yet he obtained her immediately; because from the beginning, the strife between the two sisters broke forth. Moses clearly intimates, in this

place, that the blessing of God was bestowed late, when Rachel had despaired of issue, and had long been subject to reproach because of her barrenness. On account of this prosperous omen she gave the name Joseph[1] to her son, deriving the hope of two sons from the prospect of *one*.[2]

25. *Send me away, that I may go.* Seeing that Jacob had been retained by a proposed reward for his services, it might appear that he was acting craftily in desiring his dismissal from his father-in-law. I cannot, however, doubt that the desire to return had already entered his mind, and that he ingenuously avowed his intention. First; having experienced, in many ways, how unjust, how perfidious, and even cruel, Laban had been, there is no wonder that he should wish to depart from him, as soon as ever the opportunity was afforded. Secondly; since, from the long space of time which had elapsed, he hoped that his brother's mind would be appeased, he could not but earnestly wish to return to his parents; especially as he had been oppressed by so many troubles, that he could scarcely fear a worse condition in any other place. But the promise of God was the most powerful stimulant of all to excite his desire to return. For he had not rejected the benediction which was dearer to him than his own life. To this point his declaration refers, "I will go to my own place and to my country;" for he does not use this language concerning Canaan, only because he was born there, but because he knew that it had been divinely granted to him. For if he had said that he desired to return, merely because it was his native soil, he might have been exposed to ridicule; since his father had passed a wandering and unsettled life, continually changing his abode. I therefore conclude, that although he might have dwelt commodiously elsewhere, the oracle of God, by which the land of Canaan had been destined for him, was ever fresh in his memory. And although, for a time, he submits to detention, this does not alter his purpose to depart: for necessity, in part, extorted it from

---

[1] יוסף, (*Yoseph,*) he will add.
[2] "The Lord shall add to me another son." This may be regarded either as a prophecy respecting Benjamin, or as a prayer which was fulfilled when Benjamin was born.—*Ed.*

him, since he was unable to extricate himself from the snares of his uncle; in part also, he voluntarily gave way, in order that he might acquire something for himself and his family, lest he should return poor and naked to his own country. But here the insane wickedness of Laban is discovered. After he had almost worn out his nephew and son-in-law, by hard and constant toil for fourteen years, he yet offers him no wages for the future. The equity, of which at first he had made such pretensions, had already vanished. For the greater had been the forbearance of Jacob, the more tyrannical license did he usurp over him. So the world abuses the gentleness of the pious; and the more meekly they conduct themselves, the more ferociously does the world assail them. But though, like sheep, we are exposed, in this world, to the violence and injuries of wolves; we must not fear lest they should hurt or devour us, since the Heavenly Shepherd keeps us under his protection.

27. *I pray thee, if I have found favour in thine eyes.* We perceive hence, that Jacob had not been a burdensome guest, seeing that Laban soothes him with bland address, in order to procure from him a longer continuance in his service. For, sordid and grasping as he was, he would not have suffered Jacob to remain a moment in his house, unless he had found his presence to be a certain source of gain. Inasmuch therefore, as he not only did not thrust him out, but anxiously sought to retain him, we hence infer that the holy man had undergone incredible labours, which had not only sufficed for the sustenance of a large family, but had also brought great profit to his father-in-law. Wherefore, he complains afterwards, not unjustly, that he had endured the heat of the day, and the cold of the night. Nevertheless, there is no doubt, that the blessing of God availed more than any labours whatever, so that Laban perceived Jacob to be a kind of horn of plenty, as he himself confesses. For he not only commends his fidelity and diligence, but expressly declares that he himself had been blessed by the Lord, for Jacob's sake. It appears, then, that the wealth of Laban had so increased, from the time of Jacob's coming, that it was as if his gains had visibly distilled from heaven. Moreover, as

the word נחש (*nachash*), among the Hebrews, means to know by auguries or by divination, some interpreters imagine that Laban, having been instructed in magic arts, found that the presence of Jacob was useful and profitable to him. Others, however, expound the words more simply, as meaning that he had proved it to be so by experiment. To me the true interpretation seems to be, as if he had said, that the blessing of God was as perceptible to him, as if it had been attested by prophecy, or found out by augury.

29. *Thou knowest how I have served thee.* This answer of Jacob is not intended to increase the amount of his wages; but he would expostulate with Laban, and would charge him with acting unjustly and unkindly in requiring a prolongation of the time of service. There is also no doubt that he is carried forth, with every desire of his mind, towards the land of Canaan. Therefore a return thither was, in his view, preferable to any kind of riches whatever. Yet, in the meantime, he indirectly accuses his father-in-law, both of cunning and of inhumanity, in order that he may extort something from him, if he must remain longer. For he could not hope that the perfidious old fox would, of himself, perform an act of justice; neither does Jacob simply commend his own industry, but shows that he had to deal with an unjust and cruel man. Meanwhile, it is to be observed, that although he had laboured strenuously, he yet ascribes nothing to his own labour, but imputes it entirely to the blessing of God that Laban had been enriched. For though when men faithfully devote themselves to their duty, they do not lose their labour; yet their success depends entirely upon the favour of God. What Paul asserts concerning the efficacy of teaching, extends still further, "that he who plants and he who waters is nothing," (1 Cor. iii. 7,) for the similitude is taken from general experience. The use of this doctrine is twofold. First, whatever I attempt, or to whatever work I apply my hands, it is my duty to desire God to bless my labour, that it may not be vain and fruitless. Then, if I have obtained anything, my second duty is to ascribe the praise to God; without whose blessing, men in vain rise up early, fatigue themselves the whole day, late take rest, eat the bread of

carefulness, and taste even a little water with sorrow. With respect to the meaning of the *words,* when Jacob says, "It was little that thou hadst *in my sight*,"[1] Jerome has well and skilfully translated them "before I came." For Moses puts the *face* of Jacob for his actual *coming* and dwelling with Laban.

30. *And now, when shall I provide for mine own house also?* He reasons, that when he had so long expended his labours for another, it would be unjust that his own family should be neglected. For nature prescribes this order, that every one should take care of the family committed to him. To which point the saying of Solomon is applicable, "Drink water from thy own fountains, and let rivers flow to thy neighbours."[2] Had Jacob been alone, he might have devoted himself more freely to the interests of another; but now, since he is the husband of four wives, and the father of a numerous offspring, he ought not to be forgetful of those whom he has received at the hand of God to bring up.

31. *Thou shalt not give me anything.* The antithesis between this and the preceding clause is to be noticed. For Jacob does not demand for himself certain and definite wages; but he treats with Laban, on this condition, that he shall receive whatever offspring may be brought forth by the sheep and goats of a pure and uniform colour, which shall prove to be party-coloured and spotted. There is indeed some obscurity in the words. For, at first, Jacob seems to require for himself the spotted sheep as a present reward. But from the thirty-third verse another sense may be gathered: namely, that Jacob would suffer whatever was variegated in the flock to be separated and delivered to the sons of Laban to be fed; but that he himself would retain the unspotted sheep and goats. And certainly it would be absurd that Jacob should now claim part of the flock for himself, when he had just confessed, that hitherto he had made no gain. Moreover, the gain thus acquired would have been more than was just; and there was no hope that this could be obtained from Laban.

---

[1] In conspectu meo. לְפָנַי. Ver. 30.

[2] Et defluant rivi ad vicinos. The English version is different: "Drink waters out of thine own cistern; and running waters out of thine own well."

A question however arises, by what hope, or by what counsel had Jacob been induced to propose this condition? A little afterwards, Moses will relate that he had used cunning, in order that party-coloured and spotted lambs might be brought forth by the pure flock; but in the following chapter he more fully declares that Jacob had been divinely instructed thus to act. Therefore, although it was improbable in itself that this agreement should prove useful to the holy man, he yet obeys the celestial oracle, and wishes to be enriched in no other manner than according to the will of God. But Laban was dealt with according to his own disposition; for he eagerly caught at what seemed advantageous to himself, but God disappointed his shameful cupidity.

33. *So shall my righteousness answer for me.* Literally it is, "My righteousness shall answer in me." But the particle בִּי (*bi*) signifies *to me* or *for me.*[1] The sense, however, is clear, that Jacob does not expect success, except through his faith and integrity.[2] Respecting the next clause, interpreters differ. For some read, "When thou shalt come to my reward."[3] But others, translating in the third person, explain it of righteousness, which shall come to the reward, or to the remunerating of Jacob. Although either sense will suit the passage, I rather refer it to righteousness; because it is immediately added, "before thee."[4] For it would be an improper form of expression, "Thou wilt come before thine own eyes to my reward." It now sufficiently appears what Jacob meant. For he declares that he hoped for a testimony of his faith and uprightness from the Lord, in the happy result of his labours, as if he had said, "The Lord who is the best judge and vindicator of my righteousness, will indeed

---

[1] In the Amsterdam edition the particle is בִּי, evidently the printer's mistake. In Hengstenberg's edition, it is לִי, which looks as if the editor, instead of turning to the original, had, at a venture, translated Calvin's Latin words *mihi,* or *pro me,* into Hebrew.—*Ed.*

[2] *Vide* Vatablus in Poli Syn.

[3] That is, to see that I receive my reward or wages, at the time when the flock is divided according to our compact.—*Ed.*

[4] This seems to be the sense in which the English translators understood the passage. " So shall my righteousness answer for me in time to come, when it (my righteousness) shall come for my hire (or reward) before thy face." *Coram te.*—*Ed.*

show with what sincerity and faithfulness I have hitherto conducted myself." And though the Lord often permits sinners to be enriched by wicked arts, and suffers them to acquire abundant gain by seizing the goods of others as their own: this proves no exception to the rule, that his blessing is the ordinary attendant on good faith and equity. Wherefore, Jacob justly gave this token of his fidelity, that he committed the success of his labours to the Lord, in order that his integrity might hence be made manifest. The sense of the words is now clear, " My righteousness shall openly testify for me, because it will voluntarily come to remunerate me ; and that so obviously, that it shall not be hidden even from thee." A tacit reproof is couched in this language, intimating that Laban should feel how unjustly he had withheld the wages of the holy man, and that God would shortly show, by the result, how wickedly he had dissembled respecting his own obligation to him. For there is an antithesis to be understood between the future and the past time, when he says, " *To-morrow* [or in time to come] it will answer for me," since indeed, *yesterday* and the *day before*, he could extort no justice from Laban.

*Every one that is not speckled and spotted.* Jacob binds himself to the crime and punishment of theft, if he should take away any unspotted sheep from the flock: as if he would say, " Shouldst thou find with me anything unspotted, I am willing to be charged as a thief; because I require nothing to be given to me but the spotted lambs." Some expound the words otherwise, " Whatsoever thou shalt find deficient in thy flock, require of me, as if I had stolen it;" but this appears to me a forced interpretation.

35. *And he removed that day.* From this verse the form of the compact is more certainly known. Laban separates the sheep and goats marked with spots from the pure flock, that is, from the white or black, and commits these to his sons to be fed; interposing a three days' journey between them and the rest; lest,. by promiscuous intercourse, a party-coloured offspring should be produced. It follows, therefore, that, in the flock which Jacob fed, nothing remained but cattle of one colour: thus but faint hope of gain remained

to the holy man, while every provision was made for Laban's advantage. It also appears, from the distance of the places, in which Laban kept his flocks apart, that he was not less suspicious than covetous; for dishonest men are wont to measure others by their own standard; whence it happens that they are always distrustful and alarmed.

37. *And Jacob took him rods of green poplar.* The narration of Moses, at first sight, may seem absurd: for he either intends to censure holy Jacob as guilty of fraud, or to praise his industry. But from the context it will appear that this adroitness was not culpable. Let us then see how it is to be excused. Should any one contend that he was impelled to act as he did, by the numerous injuries of his father-in-law, and that he sought nothing but the reparation of former losses; the defence would perhaps be plausible: yet in the sight of God it is neither firm nor probable; for although we may be unjustly treated, we must not enter the contest with equal injustice. And were it permitted to avenge our own injuries, or to repair our own wrongs, there would be no place for legal judgments, and thence would arise horrible confusion. Therefore Jacob ought not to have resorted to this stratagem, for the purpose of producing degenerate cattle, but rather to have followed the rule which the Lord delivers by the mouth of Paul, that the faithful should study to overcome evil with good, (Rom. xii. 21.) This simplicity, I confess, ought to have been cultivated by Jacob, unless the Lord from heaven had commanded otherwise. But in this narrative there is a *hysteron proteron,* (a putting of the last first,) for Moses first relates the fact, and then subjoins that Jacob had attempted nothing but by the command of God. Wherefore, it is not for those persons to claim him as their advocate, who oppose malignant and fraudulent men with fallacies like their own; because Jacob did not, of his own will, take license craftily to circumvent his father-in-law, by whom he had been unworthily deceived; but, pursuing the course prescribed to him by the Lord, kept himself within due bounds. In vain, also, according to my judgment, do some dispute whence Jacob learnt this; whether by long practice or by the teaching of his fathers; for it is possible, that he had been suddenly

instructed respecting a matter previously unknown. If any one object, the absurdity of supposing, that this act of deceit was suggested by God; the answer is easy, that God is the author of no fraud, when he stretches out his hand to protect his servant. Nothing is more appropriate to him, and more in accordance with his justice, than that he should interpose as an avenger, when any injury is inflicted. But it is not our part to prescribe to him his method of acting. He suffered Laban to retain what he unjustly possessed; but in six years he withdrew his blessing from Laban, and transferred it to his servant Jacob. If an earthly judge condemns a thief to restore twofold or fourfold, no one complains: and why should we concede less to God, than to a mortal and perishing man? He had other methods in his power; but he purposed to connect his grace with the labour and diligence of Jacob, that he might openly repay to him those wages of which he had been long defrauded. For Laban was constrained to open his eyes, which being before shut, he had been accustomed to consume the sweat and even the blood of another. Moreover, as it respects physical causes, it is well known, that the sight of objects by the female has great effect on the form of the fœtus.[1] Now Jacob did three things. For first, he stripped the bark from twigs that he might make bare some white places by the incisions in the bark, and thus a varying and manifold colour was produced. Secondly, he chose the times when the males and females were assembled. Thirdly, he put the twigs in the waters.[2] By the *stronger* cattle Moses may be understood to speak of those who bore in spring—by the feeble, those who bore in autumn.

43. *And the man increased exceedingly.* Moses added this for the purpose of showing that he was not made thus sud-

---

[1] The whole passage is this:—Porro quantum ad physicam rationem spectat, satis notum est, aspectum in coitu ad formam fœtus multum valere. Id quum mulieribus accidat, præcipue in brutis pecudibus locum habet, ubi nulla viget ratio, sed violentus libidinis impetus grassatur.

[2] Tertio, posuit in aquis virgas: quia sicut potus animalia vegetat, sic incitat etiam ad coitum. Hoc modo accidit ut virgæ in conspectu essent, quum incalescebant. Quod de robustis ac debilibus dicit Moses, sic intellige, in priore admissura, quæ sit sub initium veris, Jacob posuisse virgas in canalibus, ut sibi vernos fœtus acquireret, qui meliores erant: in serotina vero admissura circa autumnum, tali artificio usum non esse.

denly rich without a miracle. We shall see hereafter how great his wealth was. For being entirely destitute, he yet gathered out of nothing, greater riches than any man of moderate wealth could do in twenty or thirty years. And that no one may deem this fabulous, as not being in accordance with the usual method, Moses meets the objection by saying, that the holy man was enriched in an extraordinary manner.

## CHAPTER XXXI.

1. AND he heard the words of Laban's sons, saying, Jacob hath taken away all that *was* our father's; and of *that* which *was* our father's hath he gotten all this glory.

2. And Jacob beheld the countenance of Laban, and, behold, it *was* not toward him as before.

3. And the Lord said unto Jacob, Return unto the land of thy fathers, and to thy kindred; and I will be with thee.

4. And Jacob sent and called Rachel and Leah to the field unto his flock,

5. And said unto them, I see your father's countenance, that it *is* not toward me as before; but the God of my father hath been with me.

6. And ye know, that with all my power I have served your father.

7. And your father hath deceived me, and changed my wages ten times: but God suffered him not to hurt me.

8. If he said thus, The speckled shall be thy wages; then all the cattle bare speckled: and if he said thus, The ring-straked shall be thy hire; then bare all the cattle ring-straked.

9. Thus God hath taken away the cattle of your father, and given *them* to me.

10. And it came to pass at the time that the cattle conceived, that I lifted up mine eyes, and saw in a dream, and, behold, the rams which

1. Postea audivit verba filiorum Laban dicentium, Tulit Iahacob omnia quæ erant patris nostri: et de his quæ erant patris nostri, acquisivit omnem gloriam hanc.

2. Et vidit Iahacob faciem Laban, et ecce non erat cum eo sicut heri et nudiustertius.

3. Dixit autem Iehova ad Iahacob, Revertere ad terram patrum tuorum, et ad cognationem tuam, et ero tecum.

4. Et misit Iahacob, et vocavit Rachel et Leah in agrum ad pecudes suas.

5. Qui dixit ad eas, Video faciem patris vestri, quod non sit erga me sicut heri et nudiustertius: Deus autem patris mei fuit mecum.

6. Et vos nostis, quod omnibus viribus meis servierim patri vestro:

7. At pater vester mentitus est mihi, et mutavit mercedem meam decem vicibus: sed non permisit ei Deus, ut malefaceret mihi.

8. Si ita dicebat, Punctis parvis respersa erunt merces tua: pariebant omnes pecudes punctis parvis respersa: et si ita dicebat, Lineis distincta erunt merces tua: tunc pariebant omnes pecudes lineis distincta.

9. Et abstulit Deus pecus patris vestri, et dedit mihi.

10. Et fuit, in tempore quo coibant pecudes, levavi oculos meos, et vidi in somnio, et ecce hirci majores ascendebant super capras variegatas,

leaped upon the cattle *were* ringstraked, speckled, and grisled.

11. And the angel of God spake unto me in a dream, *saying*, Jacob. And I said, Here *am* I.

12. And he said, Lift up now thine eyes and see, all the rams which leap upon the cattle *are* ring-straked, speckled, and grisled: for I have seen all that Laban doeth unto thee.

13. I *am* the God of Beth-el, where thou anointedst the pillar, *and* where thou vowedst a vow unto me: now arise, get thee out from this land, and return unto the land of thy kindred.

14. And Rachel and Leah answered and said unto him, *Is there* yet any portion or inheritance for us in our father's house?

15. Are we not counted of him strangers? for he hath sold us, and hath quite devoured also our money.

16. For all the riches which God hath taken from our father, that *is* ours, and our children's: now then, whatsoever God hath said unto thee, do.

17. Then Jacob rose up, and set his sons and his wives upon camels:

18. And he carried away all his cattle, and all his goods which he had gotten, the cattle of his getting, which he had gotten in Padan-aram, for to go to Isaac his father in the land of Canaan.

19. And Laban went to shear his sheep: and Rachel had stolen the images that *were* her father's.

20. And Jacob stole away unawares to Laban the Syrian, in that he told him not that he fled.

21. So he fled with all that he had; and he rose up, and passed over the river, and set his face *toward* the mount Gilead.

22. And it was told Laban on the third day, that Jacob was fled.

23. And he took his brethren with him, and pursued after him seven days' journey; and they overtook him in the mount Gilead.

punctis parvis respersas, et maculis latis respersas.

11. Et dixit ad me Angelus Dei in somnio, Iahacob. Et dixi, Ecce adsum.

12. Et dixit, Leva nunc oculos tuos, et vide omnes hircos majores ascendentes super capras lineis distinctas, punctis parvis respersas, et maculis latis respersas: vidi enim omnia, quæ Laban facit tibi.

13. Ego Deus Bethel, ubi unxisti statuam, ubi vovisti mihi votum: nunc surge, egredere de terra hac, et revertere ad terram cognationis tuæ.

14. Et respondit Rachel et Leah, et dixerunt ei, Numquid adhuc est nobis pars et hæreditas in domo patris nostri?

15. Nonne extraneæ reputatæ sumus ab eo, quod vendidit nos, et consumpsit etiam consumendo argentum nostrum?

16. Quia omnes divitiæ, quas abstulit Deus a patre nostro, nostræ sunt, ac filiorum nostrorum: nunc igitur omnia, quæ dixit Deus ad te, fac.

17. Et surrexit Iahacob, et sustulit filios suos et uxores suas super camelos.

18. Et abduxit omnes pecudes suas, et omnem substantiam suam, quam acquisierat, pecudes acquisitionis suæ, quas acquisierat in Padan Aram, ut veniret ad Ishac patrem suum in terram Chenaan.

19. Laban autem profectus erat ad tondendum oves suas, et furata est Rachel idola, quæ erant patri suo.

20. Furatus itaque est Iahacob cor Laban Aramæi, quia non indicavit ei quod fugeret.

21. Et fugit ipse, et omnia quæ erant ei: et surrexit, et transivit flumen, posuitque faciem suam ad montem Gilhad.

22. Et nuntiatum fuit ipsi Laban die tertia, quod fugeret Iahacob.

23. Tunc sumpsit fratres suos secum, secutusque est eum itinere septem dierum, et assecutus est eum in monte Gilhad.

24. And God came to Laban the Syrian in a dream by night, and said unto him, Take heed that thou speak not to Jacob either good or bad.

25. Then Laban overtook Jacob. Now Jacob had pitched his tent in the mount: and Laban with his brethren pitched in the mount of Gilead.

26. And Laban said to Jacob, What hast thou done, that thou hast stolen away unawares to me, and carried away my daughters, as captives *taken* with the sword?

27. Wherefore didst thou flee away secretly, and steal away from me, and didst not tell me, that I might have sent thee away with mirth, and with songs, with tabret, and with harp?

28. And hast not suffered me to kiss my sons and my daughters? Thou hast now done foolishly in *so* doing.

29. It is in the power of my hand to do you hurt: but the God of your father spake unto me yesternight, saying, Take thou heed that thou speak not to Jacob either good or bad.

30. And now, *though* thou wouldest needs be gone, because thou sore longedst after thy father's house, *yet* wherefore hast thou stolen my gods?

31. And Jacob answered and said to Laban, Because I was afraid: for I said, Peradventure thou wouldest take by force thy daughters from me.

32. With whomsoever thou findest thy gods, let him not live: before our brethren discern thou what *is* thine with me, and take *it* to thee. For Jacob knew not that Rachel had stolen them.

33. And Laban went into Jacob's tent, and into Leah's tent, and into the two maid-servants' tents; but he found *them* not. Then went he out of Leah's tent, and entered into Rachel's tent.

34. Now Rachel had taken the images, and put them in the camel's furniture, and sat upon them. And Laban searched all the tent, but found *them* not.

35. And she said to her father,

24. Porro venit Deus ad Laban Aramæum in somnio noctis, et dixit ei, Cave tibi ne forte loquaris cum Iahacob a bono usque ad malum.

25. Assecutus autem est Laban ipsum Iahacob: et Iahacob fixerat tabernaculum suum in monte, et Laban fixit cum fratribus suis in monte Gilhad.

26. Et dixit Laban ad Iahacob, Quid fecisti, et furatus es cor meum, et abduxisti filias meas sicut captivas gladio?

27. Utquid abscondisti te ut fugeres? et furatus es me, et non indicasti mihi, et dimisissem te cum lætitia et canticis, cum tympano et cithara.

28. Et non permisisti mihi, ut oscularer filios meos et filias meas: nunc stulte egisti *sic* faciendo.

29. Est fortitudo in manu mea ad inferendum vobis malum: sed Deus patris vestri nocte præterita dixit ad me, dicendo, Cave tibi ne loquaris cum Iahacob a bono usque ad malum.

30. Et nunc eundo ivisti: si desiderando desirabas ire ad domum patris tui, utquid furatus es deos meos?

31. Et respondit Iahacob, et dixit ad Laban, Quia timui, si dixissem, ne forte raperes filias tuas a me.

32. Is, cum quo inveneris deos tuos non vivat. coram fratribus nostris, agnosce si quid est apud me *de tuo*, et cape tibi: nesciebat autem Iahacob, quod Rachel furata esset eos.

33. Et venit Laban in tabernaculum Iahacob, et in tabernaculum Leah, et in tabernaculum ambarum ancillarum, et non invenit: et egressus de tabernaculo Lea, venit in tabernaculum Rachel.

34. Rachel autem acceperat idola, et posuerat ea in clitellis cameli, et sedebat super ea: et contrectavit Laban totum tabernaculum, et non invenit.

35. Et dixit ad patrem suum, Ne

Let it not displease my lord that I cannot rise up before thee; for the custom of women *is* upon me. And he searched, but found not the images.

36. And Jacob was wroth, and chode with Laban: and Jacob answered and said to Laban, What *is* my trespass? what *is* my sin, that thou hast so hotly pursued after me?

37. Whereas thou hast searched all my stuff, what hast thou found of all thy household stuff? set *it* here before my brethren and thy brethren, that they may judge betwixt us both.

38. This twenty years *have* I *been* with thee; thy ewes and thy she-goats have not cast their young, and the rams of thy flock have I not eaten.

39. That which was torn *of beasts* I brought not unto thee; I bare the loss of it: of my hand didst thou require it, *whether* stolen by day, or stolen by night.

40. *Thus* I was; in the day the drought consumed me, and the frost by night; and my sleep departed from mine eyes.

41. Thus have I been twenty years in thy house: I served thee fourteen years for thy two daughters, and six years for thy cattle; and thou hast changed my wages ten times.

42. Except the God of my father, the God of Abraham, and the Fear of Isaac, had been with me, surely thou hadst sent me away now empty. God hath seen mine affliction, and the labour of my hands, and rebuked *thee* yesternight.

43. And Laban answered and said unto Jacob, *These* daughters *are* my daughters, and *these* children *are* my children, and *these* cattle *are* my cattle, and all that thou seest *is* mine: and what can I do this day unto these my daughters, or unto their children which they have born?

44. Now therefore come thou, let us make a covenant, I and thou; and let it be for a witness between me and thee.

45. And Jacob took a stone, and set it up *for* a pillar.

sit ira in oculis domini mei, quod non possim surgere a facie tua: quia consuetudo mulierum est mihi: et scrutatus est, et non invenit idola.

36. Tunc iratus est Iahacob, et jurgatus est cum Laban: et respondit Iahacob, et dixit ad Laban, Quæ est prævaricatio mea, quod peccatum meum, quod persecutus es me?

37. Quando contrectasti omnem supellectilem meam, quid invenisti ex omni supellectili domus tuæ? pone hic coram fratribus meis et fratribus tuis, et declarent inter nos ambos.

38. Iam viginti annos *fui* tecum; oves tuæ et capræ non abortiverunt: et arietes pecudum tuarum non comedi.

39. Raptum non attuli tibi, ego pœnas luebam pro eo: de manu mea requirebas illud, quod furto ablatum erat tam die quam nocte.

40. *Ita* fui ut interdiu consumeret me æstus, et gelu in nocte, et recedebat somnus meus ab oculis meis.

41. Iam mihi *sunt* viginti anni in domo tua: servivi tibi quatuordecim annos pro duabus filiabus tuis, et sex annos pro pecudibus tuis, et mutasti mercedem meam decem vicibus.

42. Nisi Deus patris mei, Deus Abraham, et pavor Ishac fuisset pro me, certe nunc vacuum dimisisses me: afflictionem meam et laborem manuum mearum vidit Deus, et increpavit *te* nocte præterita.

43. Tunc respondit Laban, et dixit ad Iahacob, Filiæ, filiæ meæ sunt: et filii, filii mei sunt: et pecudes meæ sunt: et quicquid vides, meum est: et filiabus meis quid faciam istis hodie, vel filiis earum quos pepererunt?

44. Et nunc, veni, percutiamus fœdus ego et tu, et erit in testimonium inter me et inter te.

45. Tulit itaque Iahacob lapidem, et erexit illum in statuam.

46. And Jacob said unto his brethren, Gather stones; and they took stones, and made an heap: and they did eat there upon the heap.
47. And Laban called it Jegar-sahadutha: but Jacob called it Galeed.
48. And Laban said, This heap *is* a witness between me and thee this day. Therefore was the name of it called Galeed;
49. And Mizpah: for he said, The Lord watch between me and thee, when we are absent one from another.
50. If thou shalt afflict my daughters, or if thou shalt take *other* wives besides my daughters, no man *is* with us; see, God *is* witness betwixt me and thee.
51. And Laban said to Jacob, Behold this heap, and behold *this* pillar, which I have cast betwixt me and thee;
52. This heap *be* witness, and *this* pillar *be* witness, that I will not pass over this heap to thee, and that thou shalt not pass over this heap and this pillar unto me, for harm.
53. The God of Abraham, and the God of Nahor, the God of their father, judge betwixt us. And Jacob sware by the fear of his father Isaac.
54. Then Jacob offered sacrifice upon the mount, and called his brethren to eat bread: and they did eat bread, and tarried all night in the mount.
55. And early in the morning Laban rose up, and kissed his sons and his daughters, and blessed them: and Laban departed, and returned unto his place.

46. Et dixit Iahacob fratribus suis, Colligite lapides : et tulerunt lapides, et fecerunt cumulum, et comederunt ibi super cumulum.
47. Et vocavit eum Laban Jegar Sahadutha: Iahacob autem vocavit eum Galhed.
48. Et dixit Laban, Cumulus iste sit testis inter me et te hodie. Idcirco vocavit nomen ejus Galhed,
49. Et Mispah: quia dixit, Speculetur Iehova inter me et te, quando latebimus alter alterum.
50. Si afflixeris filias meas, et si acceperis uxores super filias meas, non est quisquam nobiscum, vide, Deus est testis inter me et te.
51. Dixit ergo Laban ad Iahacob, Ecce, cumulus iste, et ecce statua, quam jeci inter me et te.
52. Testis cumulus iste, et testis statua, quod ego non transibo *veniens* ad te cumulum istum, et quod tu non transibis *veniens* ad me cumulum istum, et statuam istam, ad malum.
53. Deus Abraham et Deus Nachor judicet inter nos, Deus patris eorum: et juravit Iahacob per pavorem patris sui Ishac.
54. Et mactavit Iahacob victimam in monte, et vocavit fratres suos, ut comederent panem: et comederunt panem, et pernoctaverunt in monte.
55. Et surrexit Laban mane, et osculatus est filios suos ac filias suas, benedixitque eis, et abiit: et reversus est Laban ad locum suum.

1. *And he heard the words.* Although Jacob ardently desired his own country, and was continually thinking of his return to it; yet his admirable patience appears in this, that he suspends his purpose till a new occasion presents itself. I do not, however, deny, that some imperfection was mixed with this virtue, in that he did not make more haste to return; but that the promise of God was always retained in his mind will shortly appear. In this respect, however, he

showed something of human nature, that for the sake of obtaining wealth he postponed his return for six years: for when Laban was perpetually changing his terms, he might justly have bidden him farewell. But that he was detained by force and fear together, we infer from his clandestine flight. Now, at least, he had a sufficient cause for asking his dismissal; because his riches had become grievous and hateful to the sons of Laban: nevertheless he does not dare openly to withdraw himself from their enmity, but is compelled to flee secretly. Yet though his tardiness is in some degree excusable, it was probably connected with indolence; even as the faithful, when they direct their course towards God, often do not pursue it with becoming fervour. Wherefore, whenever the indolence of the flesh retards us, let us learn to fan the ardour of our spirits into a flame. There is no doubt that the Lord corrected the infirmity of his servant, and gently spurred him on as he proceeded in his course. For if Laban had treated him kindly and pleasantly, his mind would have been lulled to sleep; but now he is driven away by adverse looks. So the Lord often better secures the salvation of his people, by subjecting them to the hatred, the envy, and the malevolence of the wicked, than by suffering them to be soothed with bland address. It was far more useful to holy Jacob to have his father-in-law and his sons opposed, than to have them courteously obsequious to his wishes; because their favour might have deprived him of the blessing of God. We also have more than sufficient experience of the power of earthly attractions, and of the ease with which, when they abound, the oblivion of celestial blessings steals over us. Wherefore let us not think it hard to be awakened by the Lord, when we fall into adversity, or receive but little favour from the world; for hatred, threats, disgrace, and slanders, are often more advantageous to us than the applause of all men on every side. Moreover, we must notice the inhumanity of Laban's sons, who complain throughout as if they had been plundered by Jacob. But sordid and avaricious men labour under the disease of thinking that they are robbed of everything with which they do not gorge themselves. For since their avarice is insatiable, it follows of necessity that the prosperity of others torments them, as if they themselves would be thereby reduced to want. They do not consider whether Jacob acquired this great wealth justly or unjustly; but they are enraged and envious, because they conceive that so much has been abstracted from them. Laban had before confessed, that he had been enriched by the coming of Jacob, and even that he had been blessed by the Lord for Jacob's sake; but now his sons murmur, and he himself is tortured with grief, to find that Jacob also is made a partaker of the same blessing. Hence we perceive the blindness of avarice which can never be satisfied. Whence also it is called by Paul "the root of all evil;" because they who desire to swallow up everything must be perfidious, and cruel, and ungrateful, and in every way unjust. Besides, it is to be observed that the sons of Laban, in the impetuosity of their younger years, give vent to their vexation; but the father, like a cunning old fox, is silent, yet betrays his wickedness by his countenance.

3. *And the Lord said unto Jacob.* The timidity of the holy man is here more plainly seen; for he, perceiving that evil was designed against him by his father-in-law, still dared not to move a foot, unless encouraged by a new oracle. But the Lord, who, by facts, had shown him already that no longer delay was to be made, now also urges him by words. Let us learn from this example, that although the Lord may incite us to duty by adversity, yet we shall thereby profit little, unless the stimulus of the word be added. And we see what will happen to the reprobate; for either they become stupified in their wickedness, or they break out into fury. Wherefore, that the instruction conveyed by outward things may profit us, we must ask the Lord to shine upon us in his own word. The design, however, of Moses chiefly refers to this point, that we may know that Jacob returned to his own country, under the special guidance of God. Now the land of Canaan is called the land of Abraham and Isaac, not because they had sprung from it; but because it had been divinely promised to them as their inheritance. Wherefore, by this voice the holy man was admonished, that although Isaac had been a stranger, yet,

in the sight of God, he was the heir and lord of that land, in which he possessed nothing but a sepulchre.

4. *And Jacob sent.* He sends for his wives, in order to explain to them his intention, and to exhort them to accompany him in his flight; for it was his duty as a good husband to take them away with him; and therefore it was necessary to inform them of his design. And he was not so blind as to be unmindful of the many dangers of his plan. It was difficult to convey women, who had never left their father's house, to a remote region, by an unknown journey. Moreover, there was ground to fear lest they, in seeking protection for themselves, might betray their husband to his enemies. The courage of many would so far have failed them, in such a state of perturbation, that they would have disregarded conjugal fidelity, to provide for their own safety. Jacob, therefore, acted with great constancy in choosing rather to expose himself to danger than to fail in the duty of a good husband and master of a family. If his wives had refused to accompany him, the call of God would have compelled him to depart. But God granted him what was far more desirable, that his whole family, with one consent, were prepared to follow him: moreover, his wives, with whose mutual strifes his house before had rung, now freely consent to go with him into exile. So the Lord, when in good faith we discharge our duty, and shun nothing which he commands, enables us to succeed, even in the most doubtful affairs. Further, from the fact that Jacob calls his wives to him into the field, we infer what an anxious life he led. Certainly it would have been a primary convenience of his life, to dwell at home with his wives. He was already advanced in age, and worn down with many toils; and therefore he had the greater need of their service. Yet satisfied with a cottage in which he might watch over his flock, he lived apart from them. If, then, there had been a particle of equity in Laban and his sons, they would have found no cause for envy.

5. *I see your father's countenance.* This address consists of two parts. For first, he speaks of his own integrity, and expostulates concerning the perfidy of his father-in-law. He

next testifies that God is the author of his prosperity, in order that Rachel and Leah may the more willingly accompany him. And whereas he had become very rich in a short space of time, he purges himself from all suspicion; and even appeals to them as witnesses of his diligence. And though Moses does not minutely relate everything; yet there is no doubt that the honesty of their husband had been made clear to them by many proofs, and that, on the other hand, the injuries, frauds, and rapacity of their father, were well known. When he complains that his wages had been changed ten times, it is probable that the number *ten* is simply put for *many* times. Nevertheless it may be, that within six years Laban might thus frequently have broken his agreements; since there would be twice as many seasons of breeding lambs, namely, at spring and autumn, as we have said. But this narration of the dream, although it follows in a subsequent part of the history, shows that holy Jacob had undertaken nothing but by the Divine command. Moses had before related the transaction simply, saying nothing respecting the counsel from which it had proceeded; but now, in the person of Jacob himself, he removes all doubt respecting it; for he does not intimate that Jacob was lying, in order, by this artifice, to deceive his wives; but he introduces the holy servant of God, avowing truly, and without pretence, the case as it really was. For otherwise he would have abused the name of God, not without abominable impiety, by connecting this vision with that former one, in which we see that the gate of heaven was opened unto him.

13. *I am the God of Beth-el.* It is not wonderful that the angel should assume the person of God: either because God the Father appeared to the holy patriarchs in his own Word, as in a lively mirror, and that under the form of an angel; or because angels, speaking by the command of God, rightly utter their words, as from his mouth. For the prophets are accustomed to this form of speaking; not that they may exalt themselves into the place of God; but only that the majesty of God, whose ministers they are, may shine forth in his message. Now, it is proper that we should more carefully consider the force of this form of expression. He does

not call himself the God of Beth-el, because he is confined within the limits of a given place, but for the purpose of renewing to his servant the remembrance of his own promise; for holy Jacob had not yet attained to that degree of perfection which rendered the more simple rudiments unnecessary for him. But little light of true doctrine at that time prevailed; and even that was wrapped in many shadows. Nearly the whole world had apostatized to false gods; and that region, nay, even the house of his father-in-law, was filled with unholy superstitions. Therefore, amid so many hinderances, nothing was more difficult for him than to hold his faith in the one true God firm and invincible. Wherefore, in the first place, pure religion is commended to him, in order that, among the various errors of the world, he may adhere to the obedience and worship of that God whom he had once known. Secondly; the promise which he had before received is anew confirmed to him, in order that he may always keep his mind fixed on the special covenant which God had made with Abraham and his posterity. Thus he is directed to the land of Canaan, which was his own inheritance; lest the temporal blessing of God, which he was soon to enjoy, should detain his heart in Mesopotamia. For since this oracle was only an appendix of the previous one, whatever benefits God afterwards bestowed ought to be referred to that first design. We may also conjecture from this passage, that Jacob had before preached to his household concerning the true God and the true religion, as became a pious father of his family. For he would have acted absurdly in uttering this discourse, unless his wives had been previously instructed respecting that wonderful vision. To the same point belongs what he had said before, "that the God of his father had brought him assistance." For it is just as if he would openly distinguish the God whom he worshipped from the god of Laban. And now, because he holds familiar discourse with his wives, as on subjects which they know, the conjecture is probable, that it was not Jacob's fault if they were not imbued with the knowledge of the one God, and with sincere piety. Further, by this oracle the Lord declared that he is always mindful of the godly, even when they seem to be cast down and deserted. For who would not have said that the outcast Jacob was now deprived of all celestial help? And truly the Lord appears to him late; but beyond all expectation shows, that he had never been forgetful of him. Let the faithful, also, at this day, feel that he is the same towards them; and if, in any way, the wicked tyrannically oppress them by unjust violence, let them bear it patiently, until at length, in due time, he shall avenge them.

14. *And Rachel and Leah answered.* Here we perceive that to be fulfilled which Paul teaches, that all things work together for good to the children of God. (Rom. viii. 28.) For since the wives of Jacob had been unjustly treated by their father, they so far act in opposition to the natural tenderness of their sex, that at the desire of their husband, they become willing to follow him into a distant and unknown region. Therefore, if Jacob is compelled to take many and very bitter draughts of grief, he is now cheered by the most satisfying compensation, that his wives are not separated from him by their attachment to their father's house: but rather, being overcome by the irksome nature of their sufferings, they earnestly undertake to join him in his flight. "There is nothing," they say, "which should cause us to remain with our father; for daughters adhere to their fathers, because they are esteemed members of his family; but what a cruel rejection is this, not only that he has passed us off[1] without dowry, but that he has set us to sale, and has devoured the price for which he sold us?" By the word *money* (ver. 15), I understand the price of sale. For they complain that, at least, they had not received, instead of dowry, the profit which had been unjustly extorted from their husband, but this gain also had been unjustly suppressed by their covetous father. Therefore the particle גם (*gam*) is inserted, which is used for the purpose of amplification among the Hebrews. For this increased not a little the meanness of Laban, that, as an insatiable whirlpool, he had absorbed the gain acquired by this most dishonourable traffic. And it is to be noted, that they were then devoted to their

---

[1] The word in the original is harsh, "prostituit."

husband, and were therefore free to depart from their father; especially since they knew that the hand of God was stretched out to them. There is also no doubt, seeing they were persuaded that Jacob was a faithful prophet of God, but that they freely embraced the heavenly oracle from his mouth; for at the close of their reply, they show that they did not so much yield to his wish as to the command of God.

16. *For all the riches which God hath taken from our father.* Rachel and Leah confirm the speech of Jacob; but yet in a profane and common manner, not with a lively and pure sense of religion. For they only make a passing allusion to the fact, that God, in pity to his servant, had deigned to honour him with peculiar favour; and in the meantime, insist upon a reason of little solidity, that what they were carrying away was justly their due, because a part of the inheritance pertained to them. They do not argue that the riches they possessed were theirs, because they had been justly acquired by the labour of their husband; but because they themselves ought not to have been defrauded of their dowry, and now deprived of their lawful inheritance. For this reason they mention also their children with themselves, as having sprung from the blood of Laban. By this method they not only obscure the blessing of God, but indulge themselves in greater license than is right. They also form a mean estimate of their husband's labours, in boasting that the fruit of those labours proceeded from themselves. Wherefore we are, by no means, to seek hence a precedent for the way in which each is to defend his own right, or to attempt the recovery of it, when it has been unjustly wrested from him.

17. *Then Jacob rose up.* The departure of Jacob Moses afterwards more fully relates, he now only briefly says that " he rose up;" by which he means, that as soon as he could obtain the consent of his wives to go with him, he yielded to no other obstacles. Herein appears the manly strength and constancy of his mind. For Moses leaves many things to be reflected upon by his readers; and especially that intermediate period, during which the holy man was doubtless agitated with a multiplicity of cares. He had believed that his exile from home would be only for a short time: but, deprived of

the sight of his parents and of his native soil during twenty years, he suffered many things so severe and bitter, that the endurance of them might have rendered him callous, or, at least, might have so oppressed him as to have consumed the remnant of his life. He was now verging towards old age, and the coldness of old age produces tardiness. Yet the flight for which he was preparing was not free from danger. Therefore it was necessary that he should be armed with the spirit of fortitude, in order that the vigour and alacrity of which Moses speaks, might cause him to hasten his steps. And since we read that the departure of the holy man was effected by stealth, and was attended with discredit; let us learn, whenever God abases us, to turn our minds to such examples as this.

19. *And Rachel had stolen.* Although the Hebrews sometimes call those images תרפים, (*teraphim,*) which are not set forth as objects of worship: yet since this term is commonly used in an ill sense, I do not doubt that they were the household gods of Laban.[1] Even he himself, shortly afterwards, expressly calls them his gods. It appears hence how great is the propensity of the human mind to idolatry: since in all ages this evil has prevailed; namely, that men seek out for themselves visible representations of God. From the death of Noah not yet two hundred years had elapsed; Shem had departed but a little while before; his teaching, handed down by tradition, ought most of all to have flourished among the posterity of Terah; because the Lord had chosen this family to himself, as the only sanctuary on earth in which he was to be worshipped in purity. The voice of Shem himself was sounding in their ears until the death of Abraham; yet now, from Terah himself, the common filth of superstition inundated this place, while the patriarch Shem was still living and speaking. And though there is no doubt that he endeavoured, with all his power, to bring back his descendants to a right mind, we see what was his success. It is not indeed to be believed, that Bethuel had

---

[1] See the subject of Teraphim discussed at length in Rivetus, who confirms the opinion of Calvin by arguments and illustrations drawn from learned writers. Exercitatio cxxxii.—*Ed.*

been entirely ignorant of the call of Abraham; yet neither he, with his family, was, on that account, withdrawn from this vanity. Holy Jacob also had not been silent during twenty years, but had endeavoured, by counsel and admonition, to correct these gross vices, but in vain; because superstition, in its violent course, prevailed. Therefore, that idolatry is almost innate in the human mind, the very antiquity of its origin bears witness. And that it is so firmly fixed there as scarcely to be capable of being uprooted, shows its obstinacy. But it is still more absurd, that not even Rachel could be healed of this contagion, in so great a length of time. She had often heard her husband speaking of the true and genuine worship of God: yet she is so addicted to the corruptions which she had imbibed from her childhood, that she is ready to infect the land chosen by God with them. She imagines that, with her husband, she is following God as her leader, and at the same time takes with her the idols by which she would subvert his worship. It is even possible that by the excessive indulgence of his beloved wife, Jacob might give too much encouragement to such superstitions. Wherefore, let pious fathers of families learn to use their utmost diligence that no stain of evil may remain in their wives or children. Some inconsiderately excuse Rachel, on the ground that, by a pious theft, she wished to purge her father's house from idols. But if this had been her design, why, in crossing the Euphrates, did she not cast away these abominations? why did she not, after her departure, explain to her husband what she had done? But there is no need of conjecture, since, from the sequel of the history, it is manifest that the house of Jacob was polluted with idols, even to the time of the violation of Dinah. It was not, then, the piety of Rachel, but her insane hankering after superstition which impelled her to the theft: because she thought that God could not be worshipped but through idols; for this is the source of the disease, that since men are carnal, they imagine God to be carnal too.

20. *And Jacob stole away unawares to Laban.*[1] By the

---

[1] Et furatus est Jahacob cor Laban. The margin of the English translation renders the passage in the same way, " And Jacob stole away the

Hebrew form of expression, "stole away the heart of Laban," Moses shows that Jacob departed privately, or by stealth, unknown to his father-in-law. Meanwhile, he wishes to point out to what straits Jacob was reduced, so that he had no hope of deliverance but in flight. For Laban had determined to hold him all his life as a captive, as if he had been a slave bound to the soil, or sentenced to the mines. Therefore let us also learn, by his example, when the Lord calls us, courageously to strive against every kind of obstacle, and not to be surprised if many arduous difficulties oppose themselves against us.

22. *And it was told Laban.* The Lord gave to his servant the interval of a three days' journey, so that having passed the Euphrates, he might enter the boundaries of the promised land. And perhaps, in the mean time, he cooled the rage of Laban, the assault of which, in its first heat, might have been intolerably severe.[1] By afterwards permitting Jacob to be intercepted in the midst of his journey, God intended to render his own interposition the more illustrious. It seemed desirable that Jacob's course should not be interrupted, and that he should not be filled with alarm by the hostile approach of his father-in-law; but when Laban, like a savage wild beast, breathing nothing but slaughter, is suddenly restrained by the Lord, this was far more likely to confirm the faith of the holy man, and therefore far more useful to him. For, as in the very act of giving assistance, the power of God shone forth more clearly; so, relying on Divine help, he passed more courageously through remaining trials. Whence we learn, that those perturbations which, at the time, are troublesome to us, yet tend to our salvation, if only we obediently submit to the will of God; who purposely thus tries us, that he may indeed show more fully the care which he takes of us. It was a sad and miserable sight, that

heart of Laban." To this translation the remarks of Calvin apply. He understands the passage, however, in the sense which the English version of the text gives.—*Ed.*

[1] "Doubtless this pursuit, undertaken with such vehemence by Laban, was for the purpose of bringing back Jacob with all his family and all his wealth, and under the pretext that he had taken flight and had been guilty of theft, to retain him henceforth as a captive, and to subject him to perpetual slavery."—*Rivetus in Gen.*, p. 655.

Jacob, taking so large a family with him, should flee as if his conscience had accused him of evil: but it was far more bitter and more formidable, that Laban, intent on his destruction, should threaten his life. Yet the method of his deliverance, which is described by Moses, was more illustrious than any victory. For God, descending from heaven to bring assistance to his servant, places himself between the parties, and in a moment assuages the indomitable fury with which Laban was inflamed.

23. *And pursued him seven days' journey.* Since the cruelty of Laban was now appeased, or at least bridled, he did not dare severely to threaten; but laying aside his ferocity, he descended to feigned and hypocritical blandishments He complains that injury had been done him, because he had been kept in ignorance of Jacob's departure, whom he would rather have sent forth with customary tokens of joy, in token of his paternal affection. Thus hypocrites, when the power of inflicting injury is taken away from them, heap false complaints upon the good and simple, as if the blame rested with them. Wherefore, if at any time wicked and perfidious men, when they have unjustly harassed us, put forward some pretext of equity on their own part, we must bear with the iniquity; not because a just defence is to be entirely omitted; but because we find it inevitable that perverse men, ever ready to speak evil, will shamelessly cast upon us the blame of crimes of which we are innocent. Meanwhile, we must prudently guard against giving them the occasion against us which they seek.

29. *It is in the power of my hand.* The Hebrew phrase is different, "my hand is to power;" yet the meaning is clear, that Laban declares he is ready to take vengeance. Some expound the words thus: "my hand is to God;" but from other places it appears that the word אל is taken for *power.* But Laban, inflated with foolish boasting, contradicts himself; for whereas he had been forbidden by God to attempt anything against Jacob, where was the *power* of which he boasted? We see, therefore, he precipitates himself by a blind impulse, as if, at his own pleasure, he could do anything against the purpose of God. For when he per-

ceives that God is opposed to him, he yet does not hesitate to glory in his own strength; and why is this, unless he aimed at being superior to God? Finally; pride is always the companion of unbelief; so that unbelievers, although vanquished, yet cease not impetuously to rise up against God. To this they add another sin, that they complain of being unjustly oppressed by God.

*But the God of your father.* Why does he not also acknowledge God as his own God, unless because Satan had so fascinated his mind already, that he chose rather to wander in darkness than to turn to the light presented before him? Willingly or unwillingly, he is compelled to yield to the God of Abraham; and yet he defrauds him of the glory which is due, by retaining those fictitious deities by which he had been deceived. We see then that the ungodly, even when they have had proof of the power of God, yet do not entirely submit themselves to his authority. Wherefore, when God manifests himself to us, we must also seek from heaven the spirit of meekness, which shall bend and subdue us to obedience unto himself.

30. *Wherefore hast thou stolen my gods?*[1] The second head of accusation which is alleged against Jacob is, that he had not departed through love to his country, nor for any just and probable cause; but that, in fact, he was implicated in an act of robbery. Heavy and disgraceful charge, of which Jacob was far from being guilty! But we learn hence, that no one can live so innocently in the world, but he must sometimes bear undeserved reproach and marks of infamy. Whenever this may happen to us, let that precious promise sustain us, that the Lord, in his own time, will bring forth our innocence as the morning light. (Ps. xxxvii. 6.) For by this artifice Satan attempts to seduce us from the practice of well-doing, when, without any fault of ours, we are traduced by false calumnies. And since the world is ungrateful, it often makes the very worst return for acts of

[1] " Wonderful is the madness of idolatry. He confesses that those whom he calls his *gods*, might yet be carried off by theft. It was the part of impiety that he worshipped idols; but it was the part of folly that he declared those to be gods, who were unable to preserve themselves from being stolen."—*Rivetus in Gen.*, p. 656.

kindness. Some, indeed, are found, who, with heroic magnanimity, despise unfavourable reports, because they esteem the testimony of a good conscience more highly than depraved popular opinion. But it behoves the faithful to look to God, that their conscience may never fail them. We see that Laban calls his gods תרפים, (*teraphim,*) not because he thought the Deity was enclosed within them; but because he worshipped these images in honour of the gods. Or rather, because, when he was about to pay homage to God, he turned himself to those images. At this day, by the sole difference of a word, the Papists think they skilfully effect their escape, because they do not attribute to idols the name of gods. But the subterfuge is frivolous, since in reality they are altogether alike; for they pour forth before pictures or statues whatever honour they acknowledge to be due to the one God. To the ancient idolaters the pretext was not wanting, that by a metonymy they styled those images gods, which were formed for the sake of representing God.

31. *And Jacob answered.* He briefly refutes each head of the accusation: with respect to his secret departure, he modestly excuses himself, as having been afraid that he might be deprived of his wives. And in this way he takes part of the blame to himself, deeming it sufficient to exonerate himself from the malice of which he was thought to be guilty. He does not dispute, as a casuist, whether it was lawful to depart by stealth; but leaves it undetermined whether or not his fear was culpable. Let all the children of God learn to imitate this modesty, lest through an immoderate desire to vindicate their own reputation, they should rush into contentions: just as we have seen many raise tragic scenes out of nothing, because they will not endure that any censure, however trifling, should be cast upon them. Jacob, therefore, was content with this excuse, that he had done nothing wickedly. His defence on the other charge follows, in which Jacob shows his confidence, by adjudicating the person to death, with whom the things stolen should be found.[1] He speaks, indeed, from his heart;

---

[1] "Jacob might cover himself with the shield of his own innocence; but

but if the truth had then been discovered, he must, of necessity, have been ashamed of his rashness. Therefore, though he was not conscious of guilt, he yet sinned through excessive haste, in not having diligently inquired before he pronounced concerning a doubtful matter. He ought to have called both his wives and his children, and to have inquired of each how the affair stood. He was, indeed, persuaded, that his family was so well conducted, that no suspicion of the theft had ever entered into his mind; but he ought not so to have relied upon his own discipline, as to be free from fear when a crime is alleged against his family. Wherefore, let us learn to suspend our judgment in matters of which we are ignorant, lest we should repent too late of our temerity. We may add, that hence it happened, that the pollution which he might have exterminated immediately, continued still longer in the family of Jacob.

32. *That Rachel had stolen them.* Moses relates the manner in which Rachel had concealed her theft; namely, by sitting on the idols, and pretending the custom of women as her excuse. It is a question, whether she did this through shame or pertinacity. It was disgraceful to be caught in the act of theft; she also dreaded the severe sentence of her husband. Yet to me it appears probable, that fear did not so much influence her as the obstinate love of idolatry. For we know how greatly superstition infatuates the mind. Therefore, as if she had obtained an incomparable treasure, she thinks that she must attempt anything rather than allow herself to be deprived of it. Moreover, she chooses rather to incur the displeasure of her father and her husband, than to relinquish the object of her superstition. To her stratagem she also adds lying words, so that she deserves manifold censure.

36. *And Jacob was wroth, and chode with Laban.* Jacob again acts amiss, in contending with Laban about a matter not sufficiently known, and in wrongfully fastening on him the charge of calumny. For although he supposed all his

it was not large enough to cover all others, not even his most beloved wife, whom he, in ignorance, adjudicates to death, and incautiously gives sentence against her."—*Rivetus in Gen.*, p. 657.

family to be free from blame, yet he was deceived by his own negligence. He acts, indeed, with moderation, because in expostulating with Laban he does not use reproaches; but in this he is not to be excused, that he undertakes the cause of his whole family, when they were not exempt from blame. If any one should make the objection to this statement, that Jacob was constrained by fear, because Laban had brought with him a great band of companions: the circumstances themselves show, that his mind was thus influenced by moderation rather than by fear. For he boldly resists, and shows no sign of fear; only he abstains from the insolence of evil speaking. He then adds that he had just cause of accusation against Laban; not because he wished to rise in a spirit of recrimination against his father-in-law; but because it was right that the kindred and associates of Laban should be made witnesses of all that had passed, in order that, by the protracted patient endurance of Jacob, his integrity might be the more manifest. Jacob also calls to mind, not only that he had been a faithful keeper of the flock, but also that his labour had been rendered prosperous by the blessing of God; he adds, besides, that he had been held accountable for all losses. In this he insinuates against Laban the charge of great injustice: for it was not the duty of Jacob voluntarily to inflame the avarice and rapacity of his father-in-law, by attempting to soothe him; but he yielded, by constraint, to his injuries. When he says that "sleep departed from his eyes," he not only intimates that he passed sleepless nights, but that he had so contended against nature itself, as to defraud himself of necessary repose.

42. *Except the God of my father.* Jacob here ascribes it to the favour of God, that he was not about to return home entirely empty; whereby he not only aggravates the sin of Laban, but meets an objection which might seem at variance with his complaints. He therefore denies that he has been made rich by the kindness of his father-in-law; but testifies that he has been favourably regarded by the Lord: as if he had said, "I owe it not to thee, that thou hast not further injured me; but God, who is propitious to me, has withstood thee." Now, since God is not the defender of unfaithfulness,

nor is wont to help the wicked, the integrity of Jacob may be ascertained from the fact that God interposed as his vindicator. It is also to be observed, that by expressly distinguishing the God of Abraham from all fictitious gods, he declares that there is no other true God: by which he, at the same time, proves himself to be a truly pious worshipper. The expression " the fear of Isaac," is to be taken passively for the God whom Isaac revered ; just as, on account of the reverence due to him, he is called " the fear and the dread" of his people.[1] A similar expression occurs immediately after, in the same chapter. Now the pious, while they fear God, are by no means horror-struck at his presence, like the reprobates ; but trembling at his judgment, they walk circumspectly before him.

*God hath seen my affliction, and the labour of my hands.* This was spoken from a pious feeling that God would bring help to him when afflicted, if he should conduct himself with fidelity and honesty. Therefore, in order that the Lord may sustain us with his favour, let us learn to discharge our duty rightly ; let us not flee from our proper work ; and let us not refuse to purchase peace by submitting to many inconveniences. Further, if they from whom we have deserved well treat us severely and unjustly, let us bear our cross in hope and in silence, until the Lord shall succour us : for he will never forsake us, as the whole Scripture testifies. But Jacob distinctly presses his father-in-law with his own confession. For why had God rebuked him, unless because he was persecuting an innocent man in defiance of justice and equity ; for as I have lately intimated, it is abhorrent to the nature of God to favour evil and unjust causes.

43. *These daughters are my daughters.* Laban begins now to speak in a manner very different from before : he sees that he has no farther ground of contention. Therefore, being convinced, he buries all strife, and glides into placid and amicable discourse. " Why," he asks, " should I be hostile to thee, when all things between us are common ? Shall I rage against my own bowels ? for both thy wives

---

[1] Isaiah viii. 13. " Sanctify the Lord of hosts himself; and let him be your fear, and let him be your dread."

and thy children are my own blood; wherefore I ought to be affected towards you, as if you all were part of myself."[1] He now answers like an honourable man. Whence, then, has this humanity so suddenly sprung up in the breast of him who lately had been hurried onward, without any respect to right or wrong, to ruin Jacob; unless it were, that he knew Jacob to have acted towards him with fidelity, and to have been at length compelled by necessity to adopt the design of departing by stealth? And this was an indication that he was not absolutely desperate: for we may find many persons of such abandoned impudence, that though overcome and silenced by arguments, they yet do not cease to rush headlong in insane rebellion. From this passage we infer, that although avarice and other sinful affections take away judgment and soundness of mind; there yet remains a knowledge of truth engraven on the souls of men, which being stirred up emits scintillations, to prevent the universal triumph of depravity. If any one before had said, "What doest thou, Laban? what brutality is this to rage against thine own bowels?" the remonstrance would not have been heard, for he burned with headstrong fury. But now he voluntarily suggests this to himself, and proclaims what he would have been unwilling to hear from another. It appears, then, that the light of justice which now breaks forth, had been smothered in his mind. In short, it is self-love alone which blinds us; because we all judge aright where personal interests are not concerned. If, however, it should so happen that we are for a time in perplexity, we must still seek to obey the dictates of reason and justice. But if any one hardens himself in wickedness, the interior and hidden knowledge, of which I have spoken, will yet remain engraven in his mind, and will suffice for his condemnation.

44. *Let us make a covenant, I and thou.* Laban here acts as men conscious of guilt are wont to do, when they wish to guard themselves against revenge: and this kind of trepida-

---

[1] Acsi gererem omnium personam. "As if I bore the person or character of all," perhaps, "as your representative—the one who personates you." Yet, in the translation, the sense is given which will, perhaps, on the whole, be most intelligible to the reader.—*Ed.*

tion and anxiety is the just reward of evil deeds. Besides, wicked men always judge of others from their own disposition: whence it happens that they have fears on all sides. Moses before relates a somewhat similar example, when Abimelech made a covenant with Isaac. Wherefore we must take the greater care, if we desire to possess tranquil minds, that we act sincerely and without injury towards our neighbours. Meanwhile Moses shows how placable Jacob was, and how easily he permitted himself to be conciliated. He had endured very many and grievous wrongs; but now, forgetting all, he freely stretches out the hand of kindness: and so far is he from being pertinacious in defending his own right, that he, in a manner, anticipates Laban himself, being the first to take a stone, and set it up for a pillar. And truly it becomes the children of God, not only with alacrity to embrace peace, but even ardently to search for it, as we are commanded in Psalm xxxiv. 14.[1] As to the heap of stones, it was always the practice to use some ceremony which might confirm the compact on both sides; on this occasion a heap of stones is raised, in order that the memory of the covenant might be transmitted to posterity. That Jacob took part in this was a proof, as we have said, of a mind disposed to peace. He freely complained, indeed, when it was right to do so; but when the season of pacification arrived, he showed that he cherished no rancour. Moses, in relating afterwards that ".they did eat there, upon the heap," does not observe the order of the history. For, on both sides, the conditions of the covenant were agreed upon and declared, before the feast was celebrated: but this figure of speech (as we have before seen) was sufficiently in use.

47. *And Laban called it.* Each, in his own language, gives a name, of the same signification, to the heap. Whence it appears, that Laban used the Syrian tongue, though born of the race of Heber. But it is not wonderful that he, dwelling among Syrians, should have accustomed himself to the language as well as to the manners of the Syrians. And a little before, he is twice called a Syrian; as if Moses would describe him as degenerate, and alienated from the Hebrews.

[1] " Depart from evil and do good; seek peace and pursue it."

But this seems by no means accordant with the previous history, where we read that the daughters of Laban gave Hebrew names to their sons. Yet the solution is not difficult; for since the affinity between these languages was great, the inflection of one word into another was easy: besides, if the wives of Jacob were tractable, it is not surprising that they should have learned his language. And beyond doubt, he would himself make a point of this matter: seeing he knew that his family was separated from the rest of the nations. Moses, in using the name of Galeed, does it proleptically; for since he was writing for his own times, he does not scruple to give it the generally received name. Moreover we hence infer, that ceremonies and rites ought to refer to that which those who use them mutually agree upon. Which rule also ought to be applied to the sacraments; because if the word by which God enters into covenant with us be taken away, useless and dead figures will alone remain.

49. *The Lord watch between me and thee.* Laban commits to the judgment of God, for vengeance, whatever offence either of them should be guilty of against the other in his absence; as if he would say, " Though the knowledge of the injury should not reach me, because I shall be far distant, yet the Lord, who is everywhere present, will behold it." Which sentiment he more clearly expresses afterwards, when he says, " No one is with us; God will be witness between me and thee." By which words he means, that God will be a severe avenger of every wickedness, though there should be no judge upon earth to decide the cause. And certainly if there were any religion flourishing within us, the presence of God would influence us far more than the observation of men. But it arises from the brutal stupidity of our flesh, that we reverence men only; as if we might mock God with impunity, when we are not convicted by the testimony of men. If, then, this common feeling of nature dictated to Laban, that the frauds which were hidden from men would come into judgment before God; we who enjoy the light of the gospel should indeed be ashamed to seek a covert for our fallacies. Hence also, we gather the legitimate use of an oath,

which the Apostle declares in his epistle to the Hebrews; namely, that men, in order to put an end to their controversies, resort to the judgment of God.

50. *If thou shalt take other wives besides my daughters.* Laban declares that it would be a species of perfidy, if Jacob should take to himself any other wives. But he had himself compelled Jacob to the act of polygamy: for whence was it that the holy man had more wives than one, except that Leah had been craftily substituted in the place of Rachel? But he now, from a pure sentiment of nature, condemns the fault, of which, blinded by avarice, he had wickedly been the author. And certainly, when the bond of marriage is broken, than which none among men is more sacred, the whole of human society sinks into decay. Wherefore, those fanatical men, who, at this day, delight to defend polygamy, have no need of any other judge than Laban.

53. *The God of Abraham.* It is indeed rightly and properly done, that Laban should adjure Jacob by the name of God. For this is the confirmation of covenants; to appeal to God on both sides, that he may not suffer perfidy to pass unpunished. But he sinfully blends idols with the true God, between whom there is nothing in common. Thus, truly, men involved in superstitions, are accustomed to confound promiscuously sacred things with profane, and the figments of men with the true God. He is compelled to give some honour to the God of Abraham, yet he lies plunged in his own idolatrous pollution; and, that his religion may not appear the worse, he gives it the colour of antiquity. For in calling him the God of his father, he boasts that this God was handed down to him from his ancestors. Meanwhile Jacob does not swear superstitiously. For Moses expressly declares, that he sware only by the " fear of Isaac;" whence we learn that he did not assent to the preposterous form of oath dictated by his father-in-law; as too many do, who, in order to gain the favour of the wicked, pretend to be of the same religion with them. But when once the only God is made known to us, we wickedly suppress his truth, unless by its light all the clouds of error are dispersed.

54. *And called his brethren to eat bread.* In courteously

receiving his kindred, by whom he had been ill-treated, as his guests, Jacob showed his kindness. Moses also intimates that it was by the special favour of God that, after the most dreadful storm which threatened the holy man with destruction, a placid serenity suddenly shone forth. To the same cause is to be assigned what immediately follows, that Laban departed in a friendly manner: for by this method the Lord openly manifested himself as the guardian of his servant, seeing that he wonderfully delivered him as a lost sheep out of the jaws of the wolf. And truly, not only was the fury of Laban appeased; but he put on paternal affection, as if he had been changed into a new man.

55. *And blessed them.* The character of the person is here to be noticed, because Laban, who had lapsed from true piety, and was a man of unholy and wicked manners, yet retained the habit of giving his blessing. For we are hereby taught, that certain principles of divine knowledge remain in the hearts of the wicked, so that no excuse may be left to them on the ground of ignorance; for the custom of pronouncing a blessing arises hence, that men are certainly persuaded that God alone is the author of all good things. For although they may proudly arrogate what they please to themselves; yet when they return to their right mind, they are compelled, whether they will or no, to acknowledge that all good proceeds from God alone.

## CHAPTER XXXII.

1. AND Jacob went on his way, and the angels of God met him.
2. And when Jacob saw them, he said, This *is* God's host: and he called the name of that place Mahanaim.
3. And Jacob sent messengers before him to Esau his brother, unto the land of Seir, the country of Edom.
4. And he commanded them, saying, Thus shall ye speak unto my lord Esau; Thy servant Jacob saith thus, I have sojourned with Laban, and stayed there until now:

1. Postea Iahacob abiit in viam suam, et occurrerunt ei Angeli Dei.
2. Et dixit Iahacob, quando vidit eos, Castra Dei sunt hæc: et vocavit nomen loci illius Mahanaim.
3. Misit autem Iahacob nuntios ante se ad Esau fratrem suum ad terram Sehir in regionem Edom.
4. Et præcepit eis dicendo, Sic dicetis domino meo Esau, Sic dixit servus tuus Iahacob, Cum Laban habitavi et moratus sum huc usque.

5. And I have oxen, and asses, flocks, and men-servants, and women-servants: and I have sent to tell my lord, that I may find grace in thy sight.

6. And the messengers returned to Jacob, saying, We came to thy brother Esau, and also he cometh to meet thee, and four hundred men with him.

7. Then Jacob was greatly afraid and distressed: and he divided the people that *was* with him, and the flocks, and herds, and the camels, into two bands;

8. And said, If Esau come to the one company, and smite it, then the other company which is left shall escape.

9. And Jacob said, O God of my father Abraham, and God of my father Isaac, the Lord which saidst unto me, Return unto thy country, and to thy kindred, and I will deal well with thee:

10. I am not worthy of the least of all the mercies, and of all the truth, which thou hast showed unto thy servant; for with my staff I passed over this Jordan, and now I am become two bands.

11. Deliver me, I pray thee, from the hand of my brother, from the hand of Esau: for I fear him, lest he will come and smite me, *and* the mother with the children.

12. And thou saidst, I will surely do thee good, and make thy seed as the sand of the sea, which cannot be numbered for multitude.

13. And he lodged there that same night; and took of that which came to his hand a present for Esau his brother;

14. Two hundred she-goats and twenty he-goats, two hundred ewes and twenty rams,

15. Thirty milch camels with their colts, forty kine and ten bulls, twenty she-asses and ten foals.

16. And he delivered *them* into the hand of his servants, every drove by themselves; and said unto his ser-

5. Et sunt mihi boves et asini, pecudes et servi, et ancillæ, et misi ut nuntiarem domino meo, ut invenirem gratiam in oculis tuis.

6. Reversi autem sunt nuntii ad Iahacob, dicendo, Venimus ad fratrem tuum, ad Esau, et etiam pergit in occursum tuum, et quadringenti viri cum eo.

7. Et timuit Iahacob valde, et angustiis affectus est; et divisit populum, qui erat secum, et pecudes, et boves, et camelos in duas turmas.

8. Dixit enim, Si veniret Esau ad turmam unam, et percusserit eam, turma, quæ remanserit, evadet.

9. Et dixit Iahacob, Deus patris mei Abraham, et Deus patris mei Ishac, Domine, qui dixisti ad me, Revertere ad terram tuam et cognationem tuam, et benefaciam tibi.

10. Minor sum cunctis misericordiis, et omni veritate, quam fecisti cum servo tuo: quia in baculo meo transivi Iordanem hunc, et nunc factus sum in duas turmas.

11. Erue me nunc de manu fratris mei, de manu Esau: timeo enim eum, ne forte veniat, et percutiat me, matremque cum filiis.

12. Et tu dixisti, Benefaciendo benefaciam tibi, et ponam semen tuum sicut arenam maris, quæ non numeratur præ multitudine.

13. Et pernoctavit ibi nocte ipsa, et accepit ex iis, quæ occurrebant ad manum suam, munus *mittendum* ad Esau fratrem suum.

14. Capras ducentas et hircos viginti, oves ducentas et arietes viginti:

15. Camelos lactantes, et pullos earum triginta: vaccas quadraginta, et juvencos decem: asinas viginti, et pullos decem.

16. Et dedit in manum servorum suorum, singulos greges seorsum: dixitque ad servos suos, Transite

vants, Pass over before me, and put a space betwixt drove and drove.

17. And he commanded the foremost, saying, When Esau my brother meeteth thee, and asketh thee, saying, Whose *art* thou? and whither goest thou? and whose *are* these before thee?

18. Then thou shalt say, *They be* thy servant Jacob's; it *is* a present sent unto my lord Esau: and, behold, also he *is* behind us.

19. And so commanded he the second, and the third, and all that followed the droves, saying, On this manner shall ye speak unto Esau, when ye find him.

20. And say ye moreover, Behold, thy servant Jacob *is* behind us. For he said, I will appease him with the present that goeth before me, and afterward I will see his face; peradventure he will accept of me.

21. So went the present over before him; and himself lodged that night in the company.

22. And he rose up that night, and took his two wives, and his two women-servants, and his eleven sons, and passed over the ford Jabbok.

23. And he took them, and sent them over the brook, and sent over that he had.

24. And Jacob was left alone; and there wrestled a man with him until the breaking of the day.

25. And when he saw that he prevailed not against him, he touched the hollow of his thigh; and the hollow of Jacob's thigh was out of joint as he wrestled with him.

26. And he said, Let me go, for the day breaketh. And he said, I will not let thee go, except thou bless me.

27. And he said unto him, What *is* thy name? And he said, Jacob.

28. And he said, Thy name shall be called no more Jacob, but Israel: for as a prince hast thou power with God and with men, and hast prevailed.

29. And Jacob asked *him*, and said, Tell *me*, I pray thee, thy name.

ante me, et interstitium ponetis inter gregem et gregem.

17. Et præcepit primo, dicendo, Si occurrerit tibi Esau frater meus, et interrogaverit te, dicendo, Cujus es, et quo pergis, et cujus sunt ista ante te?

18. Dices, Servi tui Iahacob munus est, missum ad dominum meum Esau: et ecce etiam ipse est post nos.

19. Præcepit etiam secundo, etiam tertio, etiam cunctis pergentibus post greges, dicendo, Secundum verbum hoc loquemini ad Esau, quando invenietis eum.

20. Et dicetis etiam, Ecce servus tuus Iahacob est post nos: dixit enim, Placabo faciem ejus munere, quod vadit ante me, et postea videbo faciem ejus, si forte suscipiat faciem meam.

21. Transivit itaque munus ante eum: et ipse pernoctavit nocte ipsa cum turma.

22. Et surrexit nocte ipsa, et accepit duas uxores suas, et duas ancillas suas, et undecim liberos suos, et transivit vadum Jaboc.

23. Et accepit eos, et transire fecit eos torrentem, transire, inquam, fecit *omnia* quæ erant sibi.

24. Porro remansit Iahacob solus ipse: et luctatus est vir cum eo, donec ascendit aurora.

25. Et vidit quod non prævaleret ei, et tetigit palam femoris ejus, et movit se pala femoris Iahacob, luctante illo cum eo.

26. Tunc dixit, Dimitte me, quia ascendit aurora. Cui respondit, Non dimittam te, nisi benedixeris mihi.

27. Et dixit ad eum, Quod est nomen tuum? Et ait, Iahacob.

28. Tunc dixit, Non Iahacob dicetur ultra nomen tuum, sed Israel: quia princeps fuisti cum Deo, et hominibus prævalebis.

29. Et interrogavit Iahacob, et dixit, Indica, quæso, nomen tuum.

| | |
|---|---|
| And he said, Wherefore *is* it *that* thou dost ask after my name? And he blessed him there. | Et dixit, Utquid interrogas de nomine meo? et benedixit ei illic. |
| 30. And Jacob called the name of the place Peniel: for I have seen God face to face, and my life is preserved. | 30. Vocavit ergo Iahacob nomen loci, Peniel: quia vidi Deum facie ad faciem, et evasit anima mea. |
| 31. And as he passed over Penuel, the sun rose upon him, and he halted upon his thigh. | 31. Et ortus est ei sol, quando transivit Penuel, et claudicabat in femore suo. |
| 32. Therefore the children of Israel eat not *of* the sinew which shrank, which *is* upon the hollow of the thigh, unto this day: because he touched the hollow of Jacob's thigh in the sinew that shrank. | 32. Idcirco non comedunt filii Israel nervum contractionis, qui est in pala femoris, usque ad diem hanc: quia tetigit palam femoris Iahacob in nervo contractionis. |

1. *And Jacob went on his way.* After Jacob has escaped from the hands of his father-in-law, that is, from present death, he meets with his brother, whose cruelty was as much, or still more, to be dreaded; for by the threats of this brother he had been driven from his country; and now no better prospect lies before him. He therefore proceeds with trepidation, as one who goes to the slaughter. Seeing, however, it was scarcely possible but that he should sink oppressed by grief, the Lord affords him timely succour; and prepares him for this conflict, as well as for others, in such a manner that he should stand forth a brave and invincible champion in them all. Therefore, that he may know himself to be defended by the guardianship of God, angels go forth to meet him, arranged in ranks on both sides. Hebrew interpreters think that the camp of the enemy had been placed on one side; and that the angels, or rather God, stood on the other. But it is much more probable, that angels were distributed in two camps on different sides of Jacob, that he might perceive himself to be everywhere surrounded and fortified by celestial troops; as in Psalm xxxiv. 7, it is declared that angels, to preserve the worshippers of God, pitch their tents around them. Yet I am not dissatisfied with the opinion of those who take the dual number simply for the plural; understanding that Jacob was entirely surrounded with an army of angels. Now the use of this vision was twofold; for, first, since the holy man was very anxious about the future, the Lord designed early to

remove this cause of terror from him; or, at least, to afford him some alleviation, lest he should sink under temptation. Secondly, God designed, when Jacob should have been delivered from his brother, so to fix the memory of the past benefit in his mind, that it should never be lost. We know how prone men are to forget the benefits of God. Even while God is stretching out his hand to help them, scarcely one out of a hundred raises his eyes towards heaven. Therefore it was necessary that the visible protection of God should be placed before the eyes of the holy man ; so that, as in a splendid theatre, he might perceive that he had been lately delivered, not by chance, out of the hand of Laban ; but that he had the angels of God fighting for him ; and might certainly hope, that their help would be ready for him against the attempts of his brother ; and finally, that, when the danger was surmounted, he might remember the protection he had received from them. This doctrine is of use to us all, that we may learn to mark the invisible presence of God in his manifested favours. Chiefly, however, it was necessary that the holy man should be furnished with new weapons to endure the approaching contest. He did not know whether his brother Esau had been changed for the better or the worse. But he would rather incline to the suspicion that the sanguinary man would devise nothing but what was hostile. Therefore the angels appear for the purpose of confirming his faith in future, not less than for that of calling past favours to his remembrance. The number of these angels also encourages him not a little : for although a single angel would suffice as a guardian for us, yet the Lord acts more liberally towards us. Therefore they who think that each of us is defended by one angel only, wickedly depreciate the kindness of God. And there is no doubt that the devil, by this crafty device, has endeavoured, in some measure, to diminish our faith. The gratitude of the holy man is noted by Moses, in the fact that he assigns to the place a name, (Galeed,) as a token of perpetual remembrance.

3. *And Jacob sent messengers.* It now happened, by the providence of God, that Esau, having left his father, had gone to Mount Seir of his own accord ; and had thus de-

parted from the land of promise, by which means the possession of it would remain void for the posterity of Jacob, without slaughter among brethren. For it was not to be believed that he had changed his habitation, either because he was compelled by his father's command, or because he was willing to be accounted inferior to his brother. I rather conjecture that he had become greatly enriched, and that this induced him to leave his father's house. For we know that profane persons and men of this world so vehemently pant for present advantages, that when anything offers itself in accordance with their desire, they are hurried towards it with a brutish impetuosity. Esau was imperious and ferocious; he was incensed against his mother; had shaken off all reverence for his father, and knew that he was himself also obnoxious to them both: his wives were engaged in incessant contentions; it seemed to him hard and troublesome, to be in the condition of a child in the family, when he was now advancing to old age; for proud men do not regard themselves as free, so long as any one has the pre-eminence over them. Therefore, in order to pass his life free from the authority of others, he chose to live in a state of separation from his father; and, allured by this attraction, he disregarded the promised inheritance, and left the place for his brother. I have said that this was done by the divine will: for God himself declares by Malachi, that it was by a species of banishment that Esau was led to Mount Seir. (Mal. i. 3.)[1] For although he departed voluntarily; yet, by the secret counsel of God was he deprived of that land which he had earnestly desired. But, attracted by the present lust of dominion, he was blinded in his choice; since the land of Seir was mountainous and rugged, destitute of fertility and pleasantness. Moreover, he would appear to himself a great man, in giving his own name to the country. Nevertheless, it is probable that Moses called that country the land of Edom by the figure *prolepsis*, because it afterwards began to be so called. The question now occurs, Whence did Jacob know that his brother dwelt in that region? Though I assert nothing as

[1] " I hated Esau, and laid his mountains and his heritage waste for the dragons of the wilderness."—*English Translation*.

certain; yet the conjecture is probable, that he had been informed of it by his mother; for, in the great number of her servants, a faithful messenger would not be wanting. And it is easily gathered from the words of Moses, that Jacob, before he had entered the land, knew the fact respecting the new residence of his brother. And we know that many things of this kind were omitted by Moses, which may easily suggest themselves to the mind of the reader.

4. *Thus shall ye speak unto my lord Esau.* Moses here relates the anxiety of Jacob to appease his brother. For this suppliant deprecation was extorted only by great and severe torture of mind. It seems, however, to be an absurd submission, whereby he cedes to his brother that dominion for which he had contended at the hazard of his life. For if Esau has the primogeniture, what does Jacob reserve for himself? For what end did he bring upon himself such hatred, expose himself to such dangers, and at length endure twenty years of banishment,'if he does not refuse to be in subjection to his brother? I answer, that though he gives up the temporal dominion, he yields nothing of his right to the secret benediction. He knows that the effect of the divine promise is still suspended: and therefore, being content with the hope of the future inheritance, he does not hesitate, at present, to prefer his brother in honour to himself, and to profess himself his brother's servant. Nor was there anything feigned in these words; because he was willing to bear his brother on his shoulders; so that he might not lose his own future right, which was as yet concealed.

5. *I have oxen.* Jacob does not proclaim his riches for the sake of boasting, but that by this method Esau might be inclined to humanity. For it would have been exceedingly disgraceful, cruelly to drive away one who had been enriched, by the favour of God, in a distant land. Besides, he cuts off occasion of future emulation: for if he had come empty and famishing, Esau might conceive fresh indignation against him, through fear of the expense which might be entailed on himself. Therefore Jacob declares, that he does not come for the purpose of consuming his father's substance, nor of being made rich by his brother's ruin: as

if he had said, " Let thy earthly inheritance be secure; thy claim shall not be injured by me; only suffer me to live." By this example we are taught in what way we are to cultivate peace with the wicked. The Lord does not indeed forbid us to defend our own right, so far as our adversaries allow; but we must rather recede from that right, than originate contention by our own fault.

6. *And the messengers returned.* Esau advances to meet his brother with a feeling of benevolence: but Jacob, reflecting on his cruel ferocity, inflated spirits, and savage threats, expects no humanity from him. And the Lord willed that the mind of his servant should be oppressed by this anxiety for a time, although without any real cause, in order the more to excite the fervour of his prayer. For we know what coldness, on this point, security engenders. Therefore, lest our faith, being stirred up by no stimulants, should become torpid, God often suffers us to fear things which are not terrible in themselves. For although he anticipates our wishes, and opposes our evils, he yet conceals his remedies until he has exercised our faith. Meanwhile it is to be noted, that the sons of God are never endued with a constancy so steadfast, that the infirmity of the flesh does not betray itself in them. For they who fancy that faith is exempt from all fear, have had no experience of the true nature of faith. For God does not promise that he will be present with us, for the purpose of removing the sense of our dangers, but in order that fear may not prevail, and overwhelm us in despair. Moreover our faith is never so firm at every point, as to repel wicked doubts and sinful fears, in the way that might be wished.

7. *And he divided the people.* Moses relates that Jacob formed his plans according to the existing state of affairs. He divides his family into two parts,[1] and puts his maids in the foremost place, that they may bear the first assault, if necessary; but he places his free wives further

---

[1] " Into two bands," more literally, " into two camps or encampments;" לשני מחנות, (*leshenai machanoth*). The word here used is the same in which the host of God is described in the second verse, and from which the name of the city Mahanaim is derived.—*Ed.*

from the danger. Hence indeed we gather, that Jacob was not so overcome with fear as to be unable to arrange his plans. We know that when a panic seizes the mind, it is deprived of discretion; and they who ought to look after their own concerns, become stupid and inanimate. Therefore it proceeded from the spirit of faith that Jacob interposed a certain space between the two parts of his family, in order that if any destruction approached, the whole seed of the Church might not perish. For by this scheme, he offered the half of his family to the slaughter, that, at length, the promised inheritance might come to the remainder who survived.

9. *O God of my father Abraham.* Having arranged his affairs as the necessity of the occasion suggested, he now betakes himself to prayer. And this prayer is evidence that the holy man was not so oppressed with fear as to prevent faith from proving victorious. For he does not, in a hesitating manner, commend himself and his family to God; but trusting both to God's promises and to the benefits already received, he casts his cares and his troubles into his heavenly Father's bosom. We have declared before, what is the point aimed at in assigning these titles to God; in calling God the God of his fathers Abraham and Isaac, and what the terms mean; namely, that since men are so far removed from God, that they cannot, by their own power, ascend to his throne, he himself comes down to the faithful. God in thus calling himself the God of Abraham and Isaac, graciously invites their son Jacob to himself: for, access to the God of his fathers was not difficult to the holy man. Again, since the whole world had sunk under superstition, God would have himself to be distinguished from all idols, in order that he might retain an elect people in his own covenant. Jacob, therefore, in expressly addressing God as the God of his fathers, places fully before himself the promises given to him in their person, that he may not pray with a doubtful mind, but may securely rely on this stay, that the heir of the promised blessing will have God propitious towards him. And indeed we must seek the true rule of prayer in the word of God, that we may not rashly break

through to Him, but may approach him in the manner in which he has revealed himself to us. This appears more clearly from the adjoining context, where Jacob, recalling the command and promise of God to memory, is supported as by two pillars. Certainly the legitimate method of praying is, that the faithful should answer to God who calls them; and thus there is such a mutual agreement between his word and their vows, that no sweeter and more harmonious symphony can be imagined. " O Lord," he says, " I return at thy command: thou also didst promise protection to me returning; it is therefore right that thou shouldest become the guide of my journey." This is a holy boldness, when, having discharged our duty according to God's calling, we familiarly ask of him whatsoever he has promised; since he, by binding himself gratuitously to us, becomes in a sense voluntarily our debtor. But whoever, relying on no command or promise of God, offers his prayers, does nothing but cast vain and empty words into the air. This passage gives stronger confirmation to what has been said before, that Jacob did not falsely pretend to his wives, that God had commanded him to return. For if he had then spoken falsely, no ground of hope would now be left to him. But he does not scruple to approach the heavenly tribunal with this confidence, that he shall be protected by the hand of God, under whose auspices he had ventured to return to the land of Canaan.

10. *I am not worthy of the least of all the mercies.*[1] Although this expression sounds harsh to Latin ears, the sense is not obscure. Jacob confesses, that greater mercies of God had been heaped upon him than he had dared to hope for: and therefore, far be it from him that he should plead anything of dignity or merit, for the purpose of obtaining what he asks. He therefore says, that he is less than God's favours; because he felt himself to be unworthy of those excellent gifts which the Lord had so liberally bestowed upon him. Moreover, that the design of the holy patriarch may more clearly appear, the craft of Satan is to be observed:

[1] Minor sum cunctis misericordiis: " I am less than all the mercies."— *Margin of English Translation.*

for, in order to deter us from praying, through a sense of our unworthiness, he would suggest to us this thought, "Who art thou that thou shouldst dare to enter into the presence of God?" Jacob early anticipates this objection, in declaring beforehand that he is unworthy of God's former gifts, and at the same time acknowledges that God is not like men, in ever becoming weary to continue and increase his acts of kindness. Meanwhile, Jacob collects materials for confidence from the fact, that he has so often found God benignant towards him. Therefore, he had a double end in view; first, because he wished to counteract the distrust which might steal upon him in consequence of the magnitude of God's gifts; and then, he turns those gifts to a different purpose, to assure himself that God would be the same to him that he had hitherto been. He uses two words, *mercies* and *truth*, to show that God is inclined by his mere goodness to benefit us; and in this way proves his own faithfulness. This combination of mercy with truth frequently occurs in the Scriptures, to teach us that all good things flow to us through the gratuitous favour of God; but that we are made capable of receiving them, when by faith we embrace his promises.

*For with my staff.*[1] Jacob does not enumerate separately the mercies of God, but under one species comprises the rest; namely, that whereas he had passed over Jordan, a poor and solitary traveller, he now returns rich, and replenished with abundance. The antithesis between a *staff* and *two troops* is to be noticed; in which he compares his former solitude and poverty with his present affluence.

11. *Deliver me.* After he has declared himself to be bound by so many of God's benefits that he cannot boast of his own merits, and thus raised his mind to higher expectation, he now mentions his own necessity, as if he would say, "O Lord, unless thou choosest to reduce so many excellent gifts to nothing, now is the time for thee to succour me, and to avert the destruction which, through my brother, is suspended over me." But having thus expressed his fear, he adds a clause concerning the blessing promised him,

[1] That is, "*poor, naked,* and *weak.*"—*Rivet. in Gen.*, p. 676.

that he may confirm himself in the promises made to him. *To slay the mother with the children,* I suppose to have been a proverbial saying among the Jews, which means to leave nothing remaining. It is a metaphor taken from birds, when hawks seize the young with their dams, and empty the whole nest.¹

13. *And took of that which came to his hand.* In endeavouring to appease his brother by presents, he does not act distrustfully, as if he doubted whether he should be safe under the protection of God. This, indeed, is a fault too common among men, that when they have prayed to God, they turn themselves hither and thither, and contrive vain subterfuges for themselves: whereas the principal advantage of prayer is, to wait for the Lord in silence and quietness. But the design of the holy man was not to busy and to vex himself, as one discontented with the solé help of God. For although he was certainly persuaded that to have God propitious to him would alone be sufficient, yet he did not omit the use of the means which were in his power, while leaving success in the hand of God. For though by prayer we cast our cares upon God, that we may have peaceful and tranquil minds; yet this security ought not to render us indolent. For the Lord will have all the aids which he affords us applied to use. But the diligence of the pious differs greatly from the restless activity of the world; because the world, relying on its own industry, independently of the blessing of God, does not consider what is right or lawful; moreover it is always in trepidation, and by its bustling, increases more and more its own disquietude. The pious, however, hoping for the success of their labour, only from the mercy of God, apply their minds in seeking out means, for this sole reason, that they may not bury the gifts of God by their own torpor. When they have discharged their duty, they still depend on the same grace of God; and when nothing remains which they can attempt, they nevertheless are at rest.

¹ Perhaps Calvin's interpretation would appear more striking, had the original been more literally rendered, "the mother *upon* the children," (עַל בָּנִים,) which would represent the hawk as pouncing upon the parent bird when seated on her young, or protecting them beneath her feathers. —*Ed.*

14. *Two hundred she-goats.* Hence we perceive the value which Jacob set upon the promise given to him, seeing he does not refuse to make so great a sacrifice of his property. We know that those things which are obtained with great toil and trouble are the more highly esteemed. So that generally they who are enriched by their own labour are proportionably sparing and tenacious. It was, however, no trivial diminution even of great wealth, to give forty cows, thirty camels with their young, twenty bulls, and as many asses with their foals, two hundred she-goats, and as many sheep, with twenty rams, and the same number of he-goats. But Jacob freely lays upon himself this tax, that he may obtain a safe return to his own country. Certainly it would not have been difficult to find some nook where he might live with his property entire: and an equally commodious habitation might have been found elsewhere. But, that he might not lose the benefit of the promise, he purchases, at so great a price, from his brother, a peaceable abode in the land of Canaan. Therefore should we be ashamed of our effeminacy and tardiness, who wickedly turn aside from the duty of our calling, as soon as any loss is to be sustained. With a clear and loud voice the Lord commands us to do what he pleases; but some, because they find it troublesome to take up their burdens, lie in idleness; pleasures also keep back some; riches or honours impede others; finally, few follow God, because scarcely one in a hundred will bear to be losers. In putting a space between the messengers, and in sending them at different times from each other, he does it to mitigate by degrees the ferocity of his brother: whence we infer again, that he was not so seized with fear, as to be unable prudently to order his affairs.

22. *And he rose up that night.* After he has prayed to the Lord, and arranged his plans, he now takes confidence and meets the danger. By which example the faithful are taught, that whenever any danger approaches, this order of proceeding is to be observed; first, to resort directly to the Lord; secondly, to apply to immediate use whatever means of help may offer themselves; and thirdly, as persons prepared for any event, to proceed with intrepidity whitherso-

ever the Lord commands. So Jacob, that he might not fail in this particular, does not dread the passage which he perceives to be full of hazard, but, as with closed eyes, pursues his course. Therefore, after his example, we must overcome anxiety in intricate affairs, lest we should be hindered or retarded in our duty. He remains alone,—having sent forward his wives and children,[1]—not that he might himself escape if he heard of their destruction, but because solitude was more suitable for prayer. And there is no doubt that, fearing the extremity of his peril, he was completely carried away with the ardour of supplication to God.

24. *There wrestled a man with him*.[2] Although this vision was particularly useful to Jacob himself, to teach him beforehand that many conflicts awaited him, and that he might certainly conclude that he should be the conqueror in them all; there is yet not the least doubt that the Lord exhibited, in his person, a specimen of the temptations—common to all his people—which await them, and must be constantly submitted to, in this transitory life. Wherefore it is right to keep in view this design of the vision, which is to represent all the servants of God in this world as wrestlers; because the Lord exercises them with various kinds of conflicts. Moreover, it is not said that Satan, or any mortal man, wrestled with Jacob, but God himself: to teach us that our faith is tried by him; and whenever we are tempted, our business is truly with him, not only because we fight under his auspices, but because he, as an antagonist, descends into the arena to try our strength. This, though at first sight it seems absurd, experience and reason teaches us to be true. For as all prosperity flows from his goodness, so adversity is either the rod with which he corrects our sins, or the test of our faith and patience. And since there is no kind of temptation by which God does not try his faithful people,

[1] " Over the brook Jabbok." יבֹק is the proper name of a stream near Mount Gilead, on the northern border of the Ammonites, flowing into Jordan on the east, now called *Wady Zurka, i.e.*, blue river. The name is alluded to in verse 25, as if it were from the root אבק, (*Abak*,) which in Niphal means *to wrestle*.—See *Gesenius' Lexicon.* The name is, therefore, here given proleptically.—*Ed.*

[2] יאבק, *yebek*, from אבק, *dust*, because in wrestling the dust is raised.— *Gesenius.*

the similitude is very suitable, which represents him as
coming, hand to hand, to combat with them. Therefore,
what was once exhibited under a visible form to our father
Jacob, is daily fulfilled in the individual members of the
Church; namely, that, in their temptations, it is necessary
for them to wrestle with God. He is said, indeed, to tempt us
in a different manner from Satan; but because he alone is the
Author of our crosses and afflictions, and he alone creates
light and darkness, (as is declared in Isaiah,) he is said to
tempt us when he makes a trial of our faith. But the question now occurs, Who is able to stand against an Antagonist,
at whose breath alone all flesh perishes and vanishes away,
at whose look the mountains melt, at whose word or beck
the whole world is shaken to pieces, and therefore to attempt
the least contest with him would be insane temerity? But it
is easy to untie the knot. For we do not fight against him,
except by his own power, and with his own weapons; for he,
having challenged us to this contest, at the same time furnishes us with means of resistance, so that he both fights
*against* us and *for* us. In short, such is his apportioning of this
conflict, that, while he assails us with one hand, he defends
us with the other; yea, inasmuch as he supplies us with
more strength to resist than he employs in opposing us, we
may truly and properly say, that he fights *against* us with
his *left* hand, and *for* us with his *right* hand. For while he
lightly opposes us, he supplies invincible strength whereby
we overcome. It is true he remains at perfect unity with himself: but the double method in which he deals with us cannot
be otherwise expressed, than that in striking us with a
human rod, he does not put forth his full strength in the
temptation; but that in granting the victory to our faith, he
becomes in us stronger than the power by which he opposes us.
And although these forms of expression are harsh, yet their
harshness will be easily mitigated in practice. For if temptations are contests, (and we know that they are not accidental,
but are divinely appointed for us,) it follows hence, that
God acts in the character of an antagonist, and on this the
rest depends; namely, that in the temptation itself he appears to be weak *against* us, that he may conquer *in* us.

Some restrict this to one kind of temptation only, where God openly and avowedly manifests himself as our adversary, as if armed for our destruction. And truly, I confess, that this differs from common conflicts, and requires, beyond all others, a rare, and even heroic strength. Yet I include willingly every kind of conflict in which God exercises the faithful: since in all they have God for an antagonist, although he may not openly proclaim himself hostile unto them. That Moses here calls *him* a man whom a little after he declares to have been God, is a sufficiently usual form of speech. For since God appeared under the form of a man, the name is thence assumed; just as, because of the visible symbol, the Spirit is called a dove; and, in turn, the name of the Spirit is transferred to the dove. That this disclosure was not sooner made to the holy man, I understand to be for this reason, because God had resolved to call him, as a soldier, robust and skilful in war, to more severe contests. For as raw recruits are spared, and young oxen are not immediately yoked to the plough; so the Lord more gently exercises his own people, until, having gathered strength, they become more inured to toil. Jacob, therefore, having been accustomed to bear sufferings, is now led forth to real war. Perhaps also, the Lord had reference to the conflict which was then approaching. But I think Jacob was admonished, at his very entrance on the promised land, that he was not there to expect a tranquil life for himself. For his return to his own country might seem to be a kind of release; and thus Jacob, like a soldier who had kept his term of service, would have given himself up to repose. Wherefore it was highly necessary for him to be taught what his future condition should be. We, also, are to learn from him, that we must fight during the whole course of our life; lest any one, promising himself rest, should wilfully deceive himself. And this admonition is very needful for us; for we see how prone we are to sloth. Whence it arises, that we shall not only be thinking of a truce in perpetual war; but also of peace in the heat of the conflict, unless the Lord rouse us.

25. *And when he saw that he prevailed not against him.* Here is described to us the victory of Jacob, which, however,

was not gained without a wound. In saying that the wrestling angel, or God, wished to retire from the contest, because he saw he should not prevail, Moses speaks after the manner of men. For we know that God, when he descends from his majesty to us, is wont to transfer the properties of human nature to himself. The Lord knew with certainty the event of the contest, before he came down to engage in it; he had even already determined what he would do: but his knowledge is here put for the experience of the thing itself.

*He touched the hollow of his thigh.* Though Jacob gains the victory; yet the angel strikes him on the thigh, from which cause he was lame even to the end of his life. And although the vision was by night, yet the Lord designed this mark of it to continue through all his days, that it might thence appear not to have been a vain dream. Moreover, by this sign it is made manifest to all the faithful, that they can come forth conquerors in their temptations, only by being injured and wounded in the conflict. For we know that the strength of God is made perfect in our weakness, in order that our exaltation may be joined with humility; for if our own strength remained entire, and there were no injury or dislocation produced, immediately the flesh would become haughty, and we should forget that we had conquered by the help of God. But the wound received, and the weakness which follows it, compel us to be modest.

26. *Let me go.* God concedes the praise of victory to his servant, and is ready to depart, as if unequal to him in strength: not because a truce was needed by him, to whom it belongs to grant a truce or peace whenever he pleases; but that Jacob might rejoice over the grace afforded to him. A wonderful method of triumphing; where the Lord, to whose power all praise is entirely due, yet chooses that feeble man shall excel as a conqueror, and thus raises him on high with special eulogy. At the same time he commends the invincible perseverance of Jacob, who, having endured a long and severe conflict, still strenuously maintains his ground. And certainly we adopt a proper mode of contending, when we never grow weary, till the Lord recedes of his own accord. We are, indeed, permitted to ask him to consider our infir-

mity, and, according to his paternal indulgence, to spare the tender and the weak : we may even groan under our burden, and desire the termination of our contests ; nevertheless, in the meantime, we must beware lest our minds should become relaxed or faint ; and rather endeavour, with collected mind and strength, to persist unwearied in the conflict. The reason which the angel assigns, namely, that *the day breaketh*, is to this effect, that Jacob may know that he has been divinely taught by the nocturnal vision.[1]

*I will not let thee go, except.* Hence it appears, that at length the holy man knew his antagonist ; for this prayer, in which he asks to be blessed, is no common prayer. The inferior is blessed by the greater ; and therefore it is the property of God alone to bless us. Truly the father of Jacob did not otherwise bless him, than by divine command, as one who represented the person of God. A similar office also was imposed on the priests under the law, that, as ministers and expositors of divine grace, they might bless the people. Jacob knew, then, that the combatant with whom he had wrestled was God ; because he desires a blessing from him, which it was not lawful simply to ask from mortal man. So, in my judgment, ought the place in Hosea (chap. xii. 3) to be understood, " Jacob prevailed over the angel, and was strengthened ; he wept, and made supplication to him." For the Prophet means, that after Jacob had come off conqueror, he was yet a suppliant before God, and prayed with tears. Moreover, this passage teaches us always to expect the blessing of God, although we may have experienced his presence to be harsh and grievous, even to the disjointing of our members. For it is far better for the sons of God to be blessed, though mutilated and half destroyed, than to desire that peace in which they shall fall asleep, or than they should withdraw themselves from the presence of God, so as to

---

[1] There might be other reasons why the angel should say, " Let me go, for the day breaketh." The vision was intended for Jacob *alone;* had the struggle been continued till daylight, others would have witnessed it, and a vain curiosity would have been excited, which God did not design to gratify. The break of day, also, would be the time when Jacob himself must set about the work of conducting his family ; and, therefore, on his account, it was important that no farther delay should take place.—*Ed.*

turn away from his command, that they may riot with the wicked.

28. *Thy name shall be called no more Jacob.* Jacob, as we have seen, received his name from his mother's womb, because he had seized the heel of his brother's foot, and had attempted to hold him back. God now gives him a new and more honourable name; not that he may entirely abolish the other, which was a token of memorable grace, but that he may testify a still higher progress of his grace. Therefore, of the two names the second is preferred to the former, as being more honourable. The name is derived from שרה, or שור, which signifies to rule, as if he were called a Prince of God: for I have said, a little before, that God had transferred the praise of his own strength to Jacob, for the purpose of triumphing in his person. The explanation of the name which is immediately annexed, is thus given literally by Moses, " Because thou hast ruled with, or, towards God and towards man, and shalt prevail." Yet the sense seems to be faithfully rendered by Jerome:[1] but if Jacob acted thus heroically with God, much more should he prove superior to men; for certainly it was the purpose of God to send forth his servant to various combats, inspired with the confidence resulting from so great a victory, lest he should afterwards become vacillating. For he does not merely impose a name, as men are accustomed to do, but with the name he gives the thing itself which the name implies, that the event may correspond with it.

29. *Tell me, I pray thee, thy name.* This seems opposed to what is declared above; for I have lately said, that when Jacob sought a blessing, it was a token of his submission. Why, therefore, as if he were of doubtful mind, does he now inquire the name of him whom he had before acknowledged to be God? But the solution of the question is easy; for, though Jacob does acknowledge God, yet, not content with an obscure and slight knowledge, he wishes to ascend higher. And it is not to be wondered at, that the holy man, to whom God had manifested himself under so many veils and coverings, that he had not yet obtained any clear knowledge

[1] Quoniam si contra Deum fortis fuisti, quanto magis contra homines prævalebis? If thou hast been so strong against God, how much more shalt thou prevail against men?—*Vulgate.*

of him, should break forth in this wish; nay, it is certain that all the saints, under the law, were inflamed with this desire. Such a prayer also of Manoah, is read in the book of Judges, (xiii. 18,) to which the answer from God is added, except that there, the Lord pronounces his name to be wonderful and secret, in order that Manoah may not proceed further. The sum therefore is this, that though Jacob's wish was pious, the Lord does not grant it, because the time of full revelation was not yet completed: for the fathers, in the beginning, were required to walk in the twilight of morning; and the Lord manifested himself to them, by degrees, until, at length, Christ the Sun of Righteousness arose, in whom perfect brightness shines forth. This is the reason why he rendered himself more conspicuous to Moses, who nevertheless was only permitted to behold his glory from behind: yet because he occupied an intermediate place between patriarchs and apostles, he is said, in comparison with them, to have seen, face to face, the God who had been hidden from the fathers. But now, since God has approached more nearly unto us, our ingratitude is most impious and detestable, if we do not run to meet him with ardent desire to obtain such great grace; as also Peter admonishes us in the first chapter of his first epistle. (Ver. 12, 13.) It is to be observed, that although Jacob piously desires to know God more fully, yet, because he is carried beyond the bounds prescribed to the age in which he lived, he suffers a repulse: for the Lord, cutting short his wish, commands him to rest contented with his own blessing. But if that measure of illumination which we have received, was denied to the holy man, how intolerable will be our curiosity, if it breaks forth beyond the extended limit now prescribed by God.

30. *And Jacob called the name of the place.*[1] The gratitude of our father Jacob is again commended, because he took diligent care that the memory of God's grace should never perish. He therefore leaves a monument to posterity, from which they might know that God had appeared there; for this was not a private vision, but had reference to the whole Church. Moreover, Jacob not only declares that he

[1] פניאל, (*Peniel,*) the face of God.

has seen the face of God, but also gives thanks that he has been snatched from death. This language frequently occurs in the Scriptures, and was common among the ancient people; and not without reason; for, if the earth trembles at the presence of God, if the mountains melt, if darkness overspreads the heavens, what must happen to miserable men! Nay, since the immense majesty of God cannot be comprehended even by angels, but rather absorbs them; were his glory to shine on us it would destroy us, and reduce us to nothing, unless he sustained and protected us. So long as we do not perceive God to be present, we proudly please ourselves; and this is the imaginary life which the flesh foolishly arrogates to itself when it inclines towards the earth. But the faithful, when God reveals himself to them, feel themselves to be more evanescent than any smoke. Finally; would we bring down the pride of the flesh, we must draw near to God. So Jacob confesses that, by the special indulgence of God, he had been rescued from destruction when he saw God. It may however be asked, " Why, when he had obtained so slight a taste only of God's glory, he should boast that he had seen him, face to face?" I answer, it is in no way absurd that Jacob highly celebrates this vision above all others, in which the Lord had not so plainly appeared unto him; and yet, if it be compared with the splendour of the gospel, or even of the law, it will appear like sparks, or obscure rays. The simple meaning then is, that he saw God in an unwonted and extraordinary manner. Now, if Jacob so greatly exults and congratulates himself in that slender measure of knowledge; what ought we to do at this day, to whom Christ, the living image of God, is evidently set before our eyes in the mirror of the gospel! Let us therefore learn to open our eyes, lest we be blind at noonday, as Paul exhorts us in the second epistle to the Corinthians, the third and fourth chapters.

31. *And he halted upon his thigh.* It is probable, and it may be gathered even from the words of Moses, that this halting was without the sense of pain, in order that the miracle might be the more evident. For God, in the flesh of his servant, has exhibited a spectacle to all ages, from

which the faithful may perceive that no one is such a powerful combatant as not to carry away some wound after a spiritual conflict, for infirmity ever cleaves to all, that no one may be pleased with himself above measure. Whereas Moses relates that the Jews abstained from the shrunken sinew, or that part of the thigh in which it was placed: this was not done out of superstition.[1] For that age, as we know, was the infancy of the Church; wherefore the Lord retained the faithful, who then lived, under the teaching of the schoolmaster. And now, though, since the coming of Christ, our condition is more free; the memory of the fact ought to be retained among us, that God disciplined his people of old by external ceremonies.

## CHAPTER XXXIII.

1. AND Jacob lifted up his eyes, and looked, and, behold, Esau came, and with him four hundred men. And he divided the children unto Leah, and unto Rachel, and unto the two handmaids.

2. And he put the handmaids and their children foremost, and Leah and her children after, and Rachel and Joseph hindermost.

3. And he passed over before them, and bowed himself to the ground seven times, until he came near to his brother.

4. And Esau ran to meet him, and embraced him, and fell on his neck, and kissed him: and they wept.

5. And he lifted up his eyes, and saw the women and the children, and said, Who *are* those with thee? And he said, The children which God hath graciously given thy servant.

1. Levavit autem Iahacob oculos suos, et vidit, et ecce Esau veniebat, et cum eo erant quadringenti viri: et divisit liberos cum Leah et cum Rachel, et cum ambabus ancillis.

2. Tunc posuit ancillas et liberos earum prius, et Leah et liberos ejus posteriores, Rachel autem et Ioseph postremos.

3. Et ipse transivit ante eos, et incurvavit se super terram septem vicibus, donec appropinquaret fratri suo.

4. Cucurrit vero Esau in occursum ejus, et complexus est eum, et jactavit se super collum ejus, et osculatus est eum; et fleverunt.

5. Postea levavit oculos suos, et vidit uxores et liberos, et dixit, Qui isti tibi? Et dixit, Liberi *sunt*, quos donavit Deus servo tuo.

[1] The sinew which shrank; "that sinew or tendon which fastens the hip-bone in its socket, which comprehends the flesh of that muscle which is connected to it. He that ate of this was to be beaten, as the Jewish masters tell us."—*Patrick.* See also Ainsworth on this passage. Professor Bush says, "At present the Jews do not know what sinew this was, nor even which thigh it was in; and the effect of this uncertainty is, that they judge it necessary to abstain from both the hind quarters, lest they should inadvertently eat the interdicted sinew. They sell those parts to Christians."—*Ed.*

6. Then the handmaidens came near, they and their children, and they bowed themselves:

7. And Leah also with her children came near, and bowed themselves: and after came Joseph near and Rachel, and they bowed themselves.

8. And he said, What *meanest* thou by all this drove which I met? And he said, *These are* to find grace in the sight of my lord.

9. And Esau said, I have enough, my brother; keep that thou hast unto thyself.

10. And Jacob said, Nay, I pray thee, if now I have found grace in thy sight, then receive my present at my hand; for therefore I have seen thy face, as though I had seen the face of God, and thou wast pleased with me.

11. Take, I pray thee, my blessing that is brought to thee; because God hath dealt graciously with me, and because I have enough. And he urged him, and he took *it*.

12. And he said, Let us take our journey, and let us go, and I will go before thee.

13. And he said unto him, My lord knoweth that the children *are* tender, and the flocks and herds with young *are* with me; and if men should overdrive them one day, all the flock will die.

14. Let my lord, I pray thee, pass over before his servant; and I will lead on softly, according as the cattle that goeth before me and the children be able to endure, until I come unto my lord unto Seir.

15. And Esau said, Let me now leave with thee *some* of the folk that *are* with me. And he said, What needeth it? let me find grace in the sight of my lord.

16. So Esau returned that day on his way unto Seir.

17. And Jacob journeyed to Succoth, and built him an house, and made booths for his cattle: therefore the name of the place is called Succoth.

18. And Jacob came to Shalem, a

6. Et appropinquaverunt ancillæ ipsæ, et liberi earum, et incurvaverunt se.

7. Et appropinquavit etiam Leah, et liberi ejus, et incurvaverunt se: et subinde appropinquavit Ioseph et Rachel, et incurvaverunt se.

8. Et dixit, Qui isti? tuane omnis turma illa, quam obviam habui? Et dixit, Ut invenirem gratiam in oculis domini mei.

9. Et dixit Esau, Est mihi multum, frater mi, sit tuum quod tuum est.

10. Ait autem Iahacob, Ne quæso: si nunc inveni gratiam in oculis tuis, accipe munus meum e manu mea: quia idcirco vidi faciem tuam, acsi viderem faciem Angeli: et propitius eris erga me.

11. Cape quæso benedictionem meam, quæ allata est tibi: quia donavit mihi Deus, et quia sunt mihi omnia. Et coegit eum, et accepit.

12. Tunc dixit, Proficiscamur, et ambulemus, et ambulabo ante te.

13. Sed dixit ad eum, Dominus meus scit, quod pueri teneri sunt: et pecudes, et boves fœtæ sunt mihi: et *si* pulsaverint eas die una, morientur omnes pecudes.

14. Transeat quæso dominus meus ante servum suum, et ego ducam me pedetentim ad pedem gregis, qui est ante me, et ad pedem puerorum, donec veniam ad dominum meum in Sehir.

15. Et dixit Esau, Stare faciam nunc tecum de populo, qui est mecum. Et dixit, Utquid hoc? inveniam gratiam in oculis domini mei.

16. Reversus est itaque in die ipsa Esau per viam suam in Sehir.

17. Iahacob autem profectus est in Suchoth, et ædificavit sibi domum, et pecudibus suis fecit tabernacula: idcirco vocavit nomen loci Suchoth.

18. Et venit Iahacob incolumis in

city of Shechem, which *is* in the land of Canaan, when he came from Padan-aram, and pitched his tent before the city.

19. And he bought a parcel of a field, where he had spread his tent, at the hand of the children of Hamor, Shechem's father, for an hundred pieces of money.

20. And he erected there an altar, and called it El-elohe-Israel.

19. Et emit partem agri, in quo tetendit tabernaculum suum, de manu filiorum Hamor patris Sechem, centum nummis.

20. Et statuit ibi altare: et vocavit illud, Fortis Deus Israel.

1. *And Jacob lifted up his eyes.* We have said how greatly Jacob feared for himself from his brother; but now when Esau himself approaches, his terror is not only renewed, but increased. For although he goes forth like a courageous and spirited combatant to this contest, he is still not exempt from a sense of danger; whence it follows, that he is not free, either from anxiety or fear. For his cruel brother had still the same cause of hatred against him as before. And it was not probable, that, after he had left his father's house, and had been living as he pleased, he had become more mild. Therefore, as in a doubtful affair, and one of great danger, Jacob placed his wives and children in the order described; that, if Esau should attempt anything hostile, the whole seed might not perish, but part might have time for flight. The only thing which appears to be done by him out of order is, that he prefers Rachel and her son Joseph to all the rest; whereas the substance of the benediction is really in Judah. But his excuse in reference to Judah is, that the oracle had not yet been revealed; nor, in fact, was made known till shortly before his death, in order that he might become at once its witness and its herald. Meanwhile, it is not to be denied, that he was excessively indulgent to Rachel. It is, indeed, a proof of distinguished courage, that, from a desire to preserve a part of his seed, he precedes his companies, and offers himself as a victim, if necessity demanded it. For there is no doubt that the promise of God was his authority and his guide in this design; nor would he have been able, unless sustained by the confident expectation of celestial life, thus bravely to meet death. It happens, indeed, sometimes, that a father, regardless of himself, will expose his life to danger for his

children: but holy Jacob's reason was different; for the promise of God was so deeply fixed in his mind, that he, disregarding the earth, looked up towards heaven. But while he follows the word of God, yet by the affection of the flesh, he is slightly drawn aside from the right way. For the faith of the holy fathers was not so pure, in all respects, but that they were liable to swerve to one side or the other. Nevertheless, the Spirit always so far prevailed, that the infirmity of the flesh might not divert them from their aim, but that they might hold on their course. So much the more ought every one of us to be suspicious of himself, lest he should deem himself perfectly pure, because he intends to act rightly; for the flesh ever mingles itself with our holy purpose, and many faults and corruptions steal in upon us. But God deals kindly with us, and does not impute faults of this kind to us.

3. *And bowed himself to the ground seven times.* This, indeed, he might do for the sake of giving honour: for we know that the people of the east are addicted to far more ceremonies than are in use with us. To me, however, it seems more probable, that Jacob did not pay this honour simply to his brother, but that he worshipped God, partly to give him thanks, and partly to implore him to render his brother propitious; for he is said to have bowed down seven times before he approached his brother. Therefore, before he came in sight of his brother, he had already given the token of reverence or worship. Hence we may conjecture, as I have said, that this homage was paid to God and not to man: yet this is not at variance with the fact, that he also approached as a suppliant, for the purpose of assuaging his brother's ferocity by his humiliation.[1] If any one object, that in this

[1] Rivetus judiciously observes on this passage: "There are those who think that by this ceremony Jacob worshipped God; but by what argument they prove this I do not see; for whatever precedes or follows indicates that he wished to show reverence to his brother; and for this reason, he went before his family; so also the handmaidens and their sons bowed themselves; likewise Leah and her sons, and lastly, Rachel with Joseph; in each case the same word is used, which the Vulgate renders 'adored.' This verse also proves the same thing; for after he saw his brother approaching, he bowed seven times, till his brother drew near. .... This, therefore, was civil reverence, (reverentia civilis,) which did not derogate

manner he depreciated his right of primogeniture; the answer is easy, that the holy man, by the eyes of faith, was looking higher; for he knew that the effect of the benediction was deferred to its proper season, and was, therefore, now like the decaying seed under the earth. Therefore, although he was despoiled of his patrimony, and lay contemptible at his brother's feet; yet since he knew that his birthright was secured to him, he was contented with this latent right, counted honours and riches as nothing, and did not shrink from being regarded as an inferior in the presence of his brother.

4. *And Esau ran to meet him.* That Esau meets his brother with unexpected benevolence and kindness, is the effect of the special favour of God. Therefore, by this method, God proved that he has the hearts of men in his hand, to soften their hardness, and to mitigate their cruelty as often as he pleases: in short, that he tames them as wild beasts are wont to be tamed; and then, that he hearkened to the prayers of his servant Jacob. Wherefore, if at any time the threats of enemies alarm us, let us learn to resort to this sacred anchor. God, indeed, works in various ways, and does not always incline cruel minds to humanity; but, while they rage, he restrains them from doing harm by his own power: but if it is right, he can as easily render them placable towards us; and we here see that Esau became so towards his brother Jacob. It is also possible, that even while cruelty was pent up within, the feeling of humanity may have had a temporary ascendency. And as we see that the Egyptians were constrained, for a moment, to the exercise of humanity, although they were rendered nothing better than before, as their madness, which soon afterwards broke out, bears witness: so it is credible that the malice of Esau was now under constraint; and not only so, but that his mind was divinely moved to put on fraternal affection. For even in the reprobate, God's established order of nature prevails, not indeed in an even tenor, but as far as he restrains them, to the end that they may not mingle all

from the spiritual right and prerogative of the covenant entered into with Jehovah." This account seems much more probable than that given by Calvin.—*Ed.*

things in one common slaughter. And this is most necessary for the preservation of the human race. For few are so governed by the spirit of adoption, as sincerely to cultivate mutual charity among themselves, as brethren. Therefore, that men spare each other, and do not furiously rush on each other's destruction, arises from no other cause than the secret providence of God, which watches for the protection of mankind. But to God the life of his own faithful people is still more precious, so that he vouchsafes to them peculiar care. Wherefore it is no wonder, that for the sake of his servant Jacob, he should have composed the fierce mind of Esau to gentleness.

5. *And he lifted up his eyes.* Moses relates the conversation held between the brothers. And as Esau had testified his fraternal affection by tears and embraces, there is no doubt that he inquires after the children in a spirit of congratulation. The answer of Jacob breathes piety as well as modesty; for when he replies, that his numerous seed had been given him by God, he acknowledges and confesses that children are not so produced by nature as to subvert the truth of the declaration, that "the fruit of the womb is a reward and gift of God." And truly, since the fecundity of brute animals is the gift of God, how much more is this the case with men, who are created after his own image. Let parents then learn to consider, and to celebrate the singular kindness of God, in their offspring. It is the language of modesty, when Jacob calls himself the servant of his brother. Here again it is proper to recall to memory what I have lately touched upon, that the holy man caught at nothing either of earthly advantage or honour in the birthright; because the hidden grace of God was abundantly sufficient for him, until the appointed time of manifestation. And it becomes us also, according to his example, while we sojourn in this world, to depend upon the word of the Lord; that we may not deem it wearisome, to be held wrapped in the shadow of death, until our real life be manifested. For although apparently our condition is miserable and accursed, yet the Lord blesses us with his word; and, on this account only, pronounces us happy, because he owns us as sons.

6. *Then the handmaidens came near.* The wives of Jacob, having left their country, had come as exiles into a distant land. Now, at their first entrance, the terror of death meets them; and when they prostrate themselves in the presence of Esau, they do not know whether they are not doing homage to their executioner. This trial was very severe to them, and grievously tormented the mind of the holy man: but it was right that his obedience should be thus tried, that he might become an example to us all. Moreover, the Holy Spirit here places a mirror before us, in which we may contemplate the state of the Church as it appears in the world. For though many tokens of the divine favour are manifest in the family of Jacob; nevertheless we perceive no dignity in him while lying with unmerited contempt in the presence of a profane man. Jacob also himself thinks that he is well treated, if he may be permitted by his brother, as a matter of favour, to dwell in the land of which he was the heir and lord. Therefore let us bear it patiently, if, at this day also, the glory of the Church, being covered with a sordid veil, is an object of derision to the wicked.

8. *What meanest thou by all this drove?* He does not inquire as if he were altogether ignorant; seeing he had heard from the servants, that oxen and camels and asses and other cattle were sent him as a present; but for the purpose of refusing the gift offered to him: for when anything does not please us, we are wont to make inquiry as concerning a thing unknown to us. Jacob, however, is urgent; nor does he cease to ask, till he induces his brother to receive the gift: for this was as a pledge of reconciliation. Besides, for the purpose of persuading his brother, he declares, that it would be taken as a great kindness not to refuse what was given. For we do not willingly receive anything but what we certainly know to be offered to us freely and with a ready mind. And because it is not possible that we should willingly honour any but those we love, Jacob says that he rejoiced in the sight of his brother as if he had seen God or an angel: by which words he means, not only that he truly loved his brother, but also that he held him in esteem. But it may seem, that he does wrong to God, in comparing Him with a reprobate man; and

that he speaks falsely, because had the choice been given
him, he would have desired nothing more earnestly than to
avoid this meeting with his brother. Both these knots are
easily untied. It is an accustomed form of speaking among
the Hebrews, to call whatever is excellent, divine. And certainly Esau being thus changed, was no obscure figure of the
favour of God: so that Jacob might properly say, that he
had been exhilarated by that friendly and fraternal reception,
as if he had seen God or an angel; that is, as if God had
given some sign of his presence. And, indeed, he does not
speak feignedly, nor pretend something different from what
he has in his mind. For, being himself perfectly free from
all hatred, it was his chief wish, to discharge whatever duty
he could towards his brother; provided that Esau, in return,
would show himself a brother to him.

10. *Receive my present at my hand.* This noun may be
taken passively as well as actively. If understood actively,
the sense will be, "Accept the present by which I desire to
testify my goodwill towards thee." If understood passively,
it may be referred to God, as if Jacob had said, "Those
things which the Lord has bestowed upon me by his grace,
I liberally impart to thee, that thou mayest be, in some measure, a partaker with me of that divine blessing which I have
received." But not to insist upon a word, Jacob immediately
afterwards clearly avows that whatever he possesses, is not
the fruit of his labour or industry, but has been received by
him through the grace of God, and by this reasoning he attempts to induce his brother to accept the gift; as if he had
said, "The Lord has poured upon me an abundance, of which
some part, without any loss to me, may overflow to thee."
And though Jacob thus speaks under the impulse of present
circumstances, he yet makes an ingenuous confession by which
he celebrates the grace of God. Nearly the same words are
on the tongues of all; but there are few who truly ascribe
to God what they possess: the greater part sacrifice to their
own industry. Scarcely one in a hundred is convinced, that
whatever is good flows from the gratuitous favour of God;
and yet by nature this sense is engraven upon our minds,
but we obliterate it by our ingratitude. It has appeared

already, how laborious was the life of Jacob: nevertheless, though he had suffered the greatest annoyances, he celebrates only the mercy of God.

12. *Let us take our journey.* Although Esau was inclined to benevolence, Jacob still distrusts him: not that he fears to be ensnared, or that he suspects perfidy to lie hidden under the garb of friendship; but that he cautiously avoids new occasions of offence: for a proud and ferocious man might easily be exasperated again by light causes. Now, though just reason for fear was not wanting to the holy man, yet I dare not deny that his anxiety was excessive. He suspected the liberality of Esau; but did he not know that a God was standing between them, who, as he was convinced by clear and undoubted experience, watched for his salvation? For, whence such an incredible change of mind in Esau, unless he had been divinely transformed from a wolf into a lamb? Let us then learn, from this example, to restrain our anxieties, lest when God has provided for us, we tremble, as in an affair of doubt.

13. *My lord knoweth.* The things which Jacob alleges, as grounds of excuse, are true; nevertheless he introduces them under false pretexts; except, perhaps, as regards the statement, that he was unwilling to be burdensome and troublesome to his brother. But since he afterwards turns his journey in another direction, it appears that he feigned something foreign to what was really in his mind. He says that he brings with him many encumbrances, and therefore requests his brother to precede him. " *I will follow* (he says) *at the feet of the children;* that is, I will proceed gently as the pace of the children will bear; and thus I will follow at my leisure, until I come to thee in Mount Seir." In these words he promises what he was not intending to do; for, leaving his brother, he journeyed to a different place.[1] But

[1] Peter Martyr inclines to the opinion of Calvin, though he expresses himself with greater caution. There appears no reason to doubt that Jacob said what he meant. It is true he might have other reasons besides those he gave, for not accompanying his brother; reasons sufficient to deter a pious mind from too close and frequent intercourse with persons uninfluenced by true religion. But it is by no means certain that Jacob did not go to Seir; though he would probably go unaccompanied by his wives and children, his flocks and herds. The omission of the sacred writers to mention it, affords no proof that he did not take the journey.

truth is so precious to God, that he will not allow us to lie or deceive, even when no injury follows. Wherefore, we must take care, when any fear of danger occupies our minds, that we do not turn aside to these subterfuges.

17. *And Jacob journeyed to Succoth.* In the word Succoth, as Moses shortly afterwards shows, there is a *prolepsis.* It is probable that Jacob rested there for some days, that he might refresh his family and his flock after the toil of a long journey; for he had found no quiet resting-place till he came thither. And therefore he gave to that place the name of Succoth, or " Tents," because he had not dared firmly to plant his foot elsewhere. For though he had pitched tents in many other places; yet on this alone he fixes the memorial of divine grace, because now at length it was granted to him that he might remain in some abode. But since it was not commodious as a dwelling-place, Jacob proceeded farther till he came to Sichem. Now, whereas the city has its recent name from the son of Hamor, its former name is also mentioned, (ver. 18 ;) for I agree with the interpreters who think Salem to be a proper name. Although I do not contend, if any one prefers a different interpretation ; namely, that Jacob came *in safety* to Sichem.[1] But though this city may have been called Salem, we must nevertheless observe, that it was different from the city afterwards called Jerusalem; as there were also two cities which bore the name of Succoth. As respects the subject in hand, the purchase of land which Moses records in the nineteenth verse, may seem to have been absurd. For Abraham would buy nothing all his life but a sepulchre ; and Isaac his son, waiving all immediate possession of lands, was contented with that paternal inheritance ; for God had constituted them lords and heirs of the land, with this condition, that they should be strangers in it unto death. Jacob therefore

Still less, is there any proof that he did not *intend* to take it; which is all that a regard to truth and sincerity required of him.—*Ed.*

[1] To understand the above passage the English reader will require to be informed that the word שׁלם, (*Shalem,*) which our translators, with Calvin, regarded as a *proper name,* means also " peace," or " safety ;" and therefore the 18th verse may be read " Jacob came in safety to the city of Sichem." And this is the translation given in Calvin's own version, *Et venit Iahacob incolumis in civitatem Sechem.* Thus his own text is, singularly enough, at variance with his Commentary.—*Ed.*

may seem to have done wrong in buying a field for himself with money, instead of waiting the proper time. I answer, that Moses has not expressed all that ought to come freely into the mind of the reader. Certainly from the price we may readily gather that the holy man was not covetous. He pays a hundred pieces of money; could he acquire for himself large estates at so small a price, or anything more than some nook in which he might live without molestation? Besides, Moses expressly relates that he bought that part on which he had pitched his tent opposite the city. Therefore he possessed neither meadows, nor vineyards, nor arable land. But since the inhabitants did not grant him an abode near the city, he made an agreement with them, and purchased peace at a small price.[1] This necessity was his excuse; so that no one might say, that he had bought from man what he ought to have expected as the free gift of God: or that, when he ought to have embraced, by hope, the dominion of the promised land, he had been in too great haste to enjoy it.

20. *And he erected there an altar.* Jacob having obtained a place in which he might provide for his family, set up the solemn service of God; as Moses before testified concerning Abraham and Isaac. For although, in every place, they gave themselves up to the pure worship of God in prayers and other acts of devotion; nevertheless they did not neglect the external confession of piety, whenever the Lord granted them any fixed place in which they might remain. For (as I have elsewhere stated) whenever we read that an altar was built by them, we must consider its design and use: namely, that they might offer victims, and might invoke the name of God with a pure rite; so that, by this method, their religion and faith might be made known. I say this, lest any one should think that they rashly trifled with the worship of God; for it was their care to direct their actions accord-

[1] " For a hundred pieces of money." The word rendered pieces of money, קשיטה, (*Kisitah*,) means also *lambs;* and the price given might have been one hundred lambs; the probability, however, is, that the coin itself was called a *lamb*, as we have a coin called a *sovereign*. It is supposed that the coin bore the image of a *lamb*, perhaps because it was the conventional price at which lambs were generally valued. The testimony of St. Stephen (Acts vii. 16) is decisive as to the fact that money was in use.—*Ed.*

ing to the divinely prescribed rule which was handed down to them from Noah and Shem. Wherefore, under the word " altar," let the reader understand, by *synecdoche*, the external testimony of piety. Moreover, it may hence be clearly perceived how greatly the love of divine worship prevailed in the holy man; because though broken down by various troubles, he nevertheless was not forgetful of the altar. And not only does he privately worship God in the secret feeling of his mind; but he exercises himself in ceremonies which are useful and commanded by God. For he knew that men want helps, as long as they are in the flesh, and that sacrifices were not instituted without reason. He had also another purpose; namely, that his whole family should worship God with the same sense of piety. For it behoves a pious father of a family diligently to take care that he has no profane house, but rather that God should reign there as in a sanctuary. Besides, since the inhabitants of that region had fallen into many superstitions, and had corrupted the true worship of God, Jacob wished to make a distinction between himself and them. The Shechemites and other neighbouring nations had certainly altars of their own. Therefore Jacob, by establishing a different method of worship for his household, thus declares that he has a God peculiar to himself, and has not degenerated from the holy fathers, from whom the perfect and genuine religion had proceeded. This course could not but subject him to reproach, because the Shechemites and other inhabitants would feel that they were despised: but the holy man deemed anything preferable to mixing himself with idolaters.

21. *And he called it El-elohe-Israel.*[1] This name appears little suitable to the altar; for it sounds as if a heap of stones or turf formed a visible statue of God. But the meaning of the holy man was different. For, because the altar was a memorial and pledge of all the visions and promises of God, he honours it with this title, to the end that, as often as he beheld the altar, he should call God to

---

[1] Et vocavit illud, Fortis Deus Israel; " the strong God of Israel." The margin of the English translation is more literal, " God, the God of Israel."—*Ed.*

remembrance. That inscription of Moses, "The Lord is my help," has the same signification; and also that which Ezekiel inscribes on the New Jerusalem, " the Lord is there." And truly in these forms of speaking there is a want of strict propriety of metaphor; yet this is not without reason. For as superstitious men foolishly and wickedly attach God to symbols, and, as it were, draw him down from his heavenly throne to render him subject to their gross inventions: so the faithful, piously and rightly, ascend from earthly signs to heaven. The conclusion is this: Jacob wished to testify that he worshipped no other God than him who had been manifested by certain oracles, in order that he might distinguish Him from all idols. And we must observe it as a rule of modesty, not to speak carelessly concerning the mysteries and the glory of the Lord, but from a sense of faith, so far, indeed, as he is made known to us in his word. Moreover Jacob had respect to his posterity; for since the Lord had appeared to him, on the express condition, that he would make with him the covenant of salvation, Jacob leaves this monument, from which, after his death, his descendants might ascertain that his religion had not flowed from a dark or obscure well, or from a turbid pool, but from a clear and pure fountain; as if he had engraved the oracles and visions, by which he had been taught, upon the altar.

## CHAPTER XXXIV.

1. AND Dinah the daughter of Leah, which she bare unto Jacob, went out to see the daughters of the land.

2. And when Shechem the son of Hamor the Hivite, prince of the country, saw her, he took her, and lay with her, and defiled her.

3. And his soul clave unto Dinah the daughter of Jacob; and he loved the damsel, and spake kindly unto the damsel.

4. And Shechem spake unto his father Hamor, saying, Get me this damsel to wife.

1. Et egressa est Dinah filia Leah, quam pepererat ipsi Iahacob, ut videret filias regionis.

2. Et vidit eam Sechem filius Hamor Hivvæi principis terræ, et tulit eam, et concubuit cum ea, et humiliavit eam.

3. Et adhæsit anima ejus ipsi Dinah filiæ Iahacob, et dilexit puellam: et loquutus est ad cor puellæ.

4. Et dixit Sechem ad Hamor patrem suum, dicendo, Cape mihi puellam hanc in uxorem.

5. And Jacob heard that he had defiled Dinah his daughter; (now his sons were with his cattle in the field;) and Jacob held his peace until they were come.

6. And Hamor the father of Shechem went out unto Jacob to commune with him.

7. And the sons of Jacob came out of the field when they heard *it;* and the men were grieved; and they were very wroth, because he had wrought folly in Israel, in lying with Jacob's daughter; which thing ought not to be done.

8. And Hamor communed with them, saying, The soul of my son Shechem longeth for your daughter: I pray you give her him to wife.

9. And make ye marriages with us, *and* give your daughters unto us, and take our daughters unto you.

10. And ye shall dwell with us: and the land shall be before you; dwell and trade ye therein, and get you possessions therein.

11. And Shechem said unto her father, and unto her brethren, Let me find grace in your eyes, and what ye shall say unto me I will give.

12. Ask me never so much dowry and gift, and I will give according as ye shall say unto me: but give me the damsel to wife.

13. And the sons of Jacob answered Shechem and Hamor his father deceitfully, and said, (because he had defiled Dinah their sister:)

14. And they said unto them, We cannot do this thing, to give our sister to one that is uncircumcised; for that *were* a reproach unto us:

15. But in this will we consent unto you: If ye will be as we *be,* that every male of you be circumcised;

16. Then will we give our daughters unto you, and we will take your daughters to us, and we will dwell with you, and we will become one people.

17. But if ye will not hearken unto us, to be circumcised; then will we take our daughter, and we will be gone.

5. Audivit autem Iahacob, quod violasset Dinah filiam suam: et filii ejus erant cum pecudibus ejus in agro, et siluit Iahacob, donec venirent ipsi.

6. Egressus est autem Hamor pater Sechem ad Iahacob, ut loqueretur cum eo.

7. Porro filii Iahacob venerunt de agro: *qui* quum audierunt ipsi, dolore affecti sunt viri, iratique sunt valde: quia flagitium designasset in Israel, ut coiret cum filia Iahacob: et sic non fiet.

8. Et loquutus est Hamor cum eis, dicendo, Sechem filii mei complacuit anima in filia vestra: date quæso eam illi in uxorem.

9. Et affinitatem contrahite nobiscum: filias vestras dabitis nobis, et filias nostras accipietis vobis.

10. Et nobiscum habitabitis, et terra erit coram vobis, habitate, et negotiamini in ea, et possessiones acquirite in ea.

11. Adhæc dixit Sechem ad patrem ejus, et ad fratres ejus, Inveniam gratiam in oculis vestris: et quod dixeritis mihi, dabo.

12. Augete mihi valde dotem, et donum: et dabo quemadmodum dixeritis mihi, et date mihi puellam in uxorem.

13. Et responderunt filii Iahacob ad Sechem et Hamor patrem ejus in dolo, et loquuti sunt, (quia violaverat Dinah sororem suam,)

14. Et dixerunt ad eos, Non possumus facere hoc, ut demus sororem nostram viro, cui est præputium: quia opprobrium esset nobis.

15. Veruntamen in hoc acquiescemus vobis, si fueritis sicut nos, ut circumcidatur in vobis omnis masculus.

16. Et dabimus filias nostras vobis, et filias vestras capiemus nobis: et habitabimus vobiscum, et erimus in populum unum.

17. Quodsi non obedieritis nobis, ut circumcidamini: capiemus filiam nostram et recedemus.

18. And their words pleased Hamor, and Shechem, Hamor's son.

19. And the young man deferred not to do the thing, because he had delight in Jacob's daughter; and he *was* more honourable than all the house of his father.

20. And Hamor and Shechem his son came unto the gate of their city, and communed with the men of their city, saying,

21. These men *are* peaceable with us; therefore let them dwell in the land, and trade therein; for the land, behold, *it is* large enough for them; let us take their daughters to us for wives, and let us give them our daughters.

22. Only herein will the men consent unto us for to dwell with us, to be one people, if every male among us be circumcised, as they *are* circumcised.

23. *Shall* not their cattle, and their substance, and every beast of theirs, *be* ours? only let us consent unto them, and they will dwell with us.

24. And unto Hamor, and unto Shechem his son, hearkened all that went out of the gate of his city; and every male was circumcised, all that went out of the gate of his city.

25. And it came to pass on the third day, when they were sore, that two of the sons of Jacob, Simeon and Levi, Dinah's brethren, took each man his sword, and came upon the city boldly, and slew all the males.

26. And they slew Hamor and Shechem his son with the edge of the sword, and took Dinah out of Shechem's house, and went out.

27. The sons of Jacob came upon the slain, and spoiled the city, because they had defiled their sister.

28. They took their sheep, and their oxen, and their asses, and that which *was* in the city, and that which *was* in the field,

18. Et placuerunt verba eorum in oculis Hamor, et in oculis Sechem filii Hamor.

19. Nec tardavit juvenis ad perficiendum negotium, quia complacuerat ei in filia Iahacob: et ipse erat honorabilis præ tota domo patris sui.

20. Et venit Hamor et Sechem filius ejus ad portam civitatis suæ, et loquuti sunt ad viros civitatis suæ, dicendo,

21. Viri isti pacati sunt nobiscum, et habitabunt in terra, et negotiabuntur in ea (et terra ecce, lata est spatiis ante eos) filias eorum accipiemus nobis in uxores, et filias nostras dabimus eis.

22. Veruntamen in hoc acquiescent nobis viri, ut habitent nobiscum, ut sint populus unus, quando circumcisus erit in nobis omnis masculus, quemadmodum ipsi sunt circumcisi.

23. Greges eorum, et substantia eorum et omnia jumenta eorum, nonne nostra erunt? tantum acquiescamus eis, et habitabunt nobiscum.

24. Et assensi sunt Hamor et Sechem filio ejus, omnes qui egrediebantur per portam civitatis ejus: et circumciderunt se omnis masculus, omnes egredientes per portam civitatis ejus.

25. Et fuit in die tertia, quum essent ipsi dolore affecti, acceperunt duo filii Iahacob Simhon et Levi fratres Dinah, quisque gladium suum, et venerunt ad civitatem confidenter, et occiderunt omnem masculum.

26. Et Hamor et Sechem filium ejus occiderunt acie gladii, et tulerunt Dinah e domo Sechem et egressi sunt.

27. Filii Iahacob progressi sunt super occisos, et prædati sunt urbem, quia violaverant sororém suam.

28. Pecudes eorum, et boves eorum, et asinos eorum, et quæ erant in urbe, et quæ in agro, acceperunt.

29. And all their wealth, and all their little ones, and their wives took they captive, and spoiled even all that *was* in the house.

30. And Jacob said to Simeon and Levi, Ye have troubled me, to make me to stink among the inhabitants of the land, among the Canaanites and the Perizzites: and I *being* few in number, they shall gather themselves together against me, and slay me; and I shall be destroyed, I and my house.

31. And they said, Should he deal with our sister as with an harlot?

29. Et omnem substantiam eorum, et omnes parvulos eorum, et uxores eorum captivas duxerunt, et prædati sunt omnia, quæ erant in domo.

30. Et dixit Iahacob ad Simhon et ad Levi, Turbastis me, ut fœtere feceritis me habitatoribus terræ, Chenanæo, et Perizæo: et ego paucos mecum habeo, et congregabunt se adversum me, et percutient me, et disperdar ego, et domus mea.

31. At dixerunt, Numquid ut cum meretrice aget cum sorore nostra?

1. *And Dinah . . . . went out.* This chapter records a severe contest, with which God again exercised his servant. How precious the chastity of his daughter would be to him, we may readily conjecture from the probity of his whole life. When therefore he heard that she was violated, this disgrace would inflict the deepest wound of grief upon his mind: yet soon his grief is trebled, when he hears that his sons, from the desire of revenge, have committed a most dreadful crime. But let us examine everything in order. Dinah is ravished, because, having left her father's house, she wandered about more freely than was proper. She ought to have remained quietly at home, as both the Apostle teaches and nature itself dictates; for to girls the virtue is suitable, which the proverb applies to women, that they should be οἰκουροὶ, or keepers of the house. Therefore fathers of families are taught to keep their daughters under strict discipline, if they desire to preserve them free from all dishonour; for if a vain curiosity was so heavily punished in the daughter of holy Jacob, not less danger hangs over weak virgins at this day, if they go too boldly and eagerly into public assemblies, and excite the passions of youth towards themselves. For it is not to be doubted that Moses in part casts the blame of the offence upon Dinah herself, when he says, "she went out to see the daughters of the land;" whereas she ought to have remained under her mother's eyes in the tent.

3. *And his soul clave unto Dinah.* Moses intimates that she was not so forcibly violated, that Shechem having once

abused her, treated her with contempt, as is usual with harlots; for he loved her as a wife; and did not even object to be circumcised that he might have her; but the fervour of lust had so prevailed, that he first subjected her to disgrace. And therefore although he embraced Dinah with real and sincere attachment, yet, in this want of self-government, he grievously sinned. Shechem " spoke to the heart" of the maid, that is, he addressed her courteously, to allure her to himself by his bland speeches: whence it follows, that when she was unwilling and resisted, he used violence towards her.

4. *And Shechem said to his father Hamor.* In this place it is more clearly expressed, that Shechem desired to have Dinah for his wife; for his lust was not so unbridled, that when he had defiled, he despised her. Besides, a laudable modesty is shown, since he pays deference to the will of his father; for he does not attempt to form a contract of marriage of his own mind, but leaves this to his father's authority. For though he had basely fallen through the precipitate ardour of lust; yet now returning to himself, he follows the guidance of nature. So much the more ought young men to take heed to themselves, lest in the slippery period of their age, the lusts of the flesh should impel them to many crimes. For, at this day, greater license everywhere prevails, so that no moderation restrains youths from shameful conduct. Since, however, Shechem, under the rule and direction of nature, desired his father to be the procurer of his marriage, we hence infer that the right which parents have over their children is inviolable; so that they who attempt to overthrow it, confound heaven and earth. Wherefore, since the Pope, in honour of marriage, has dared to break this sacred bond of nature; this fornicator Shechem alone, will prove a judge sufficient, and more than sufficient, to condemn that barbarous conduct.

5. *And Jacob heard.* Moses inserts a single verse concerning the silent sorrow of Jacob. We know that they who have not been accustomed to reproaches, are the more grievously affected when any dishonour happens to them. Therefore the more this prudent man had endeavoured to keep his family pure from every stain, chaste and well-ordered, the

more deeply is he wounded. But since he is at home alone, he dissembles, and keeps his grief to himself, till his sons return from the field. Moreover, by this word, Moses does not mean that Jacob deferred vengeance till their return; but that, being alone and devoid of counsel and of consolation, he lay prostrate as one disheartened. The sense then is, that he was so oppressed with insupportable grief, that he held his peace.[1] By using the word "defiled," Moses teaches us what is the true purity of man; namely, when chastity is religiously cultivated, and every one possesses his vessel in honour. But whoever prostitutes his body to fornication, filthily defiles himself. If then Dinah is said to have been polluted, whom Shechem had forcibly violated, what must be said of voluntary adulterers and fornicators?

7. *And the sons of Jacob came out of the field.* Moses begins to relate the tragic issue of this history. Shechem, indeed, had acted wickedly and impiously; but it was far more atrocious and wicked that the sons of Jacob should murder a whole people, to avenge themselves of the private fault of one man. It was by no means fitting to seek a cruel compensation for the levity and rashness of one youth, by the slaughter of so many men. Again, who had constituted them judges, that they should dare, with their own hands, to execute vengeance for an injury inflicted upon them? Perfidy was also superadded, because they proceeded, under the pretext of a covenant, to perpetrate this enormous crime. In Jacob, moreover, we have an admirable example of patient endurance; who, though afflicted with so many evils, yet did not faint under them. But chiefly we must consider the mercy of God, by which it came to pass, that the covenant of grace remained with the posterity of Jacob. For what seemed less suitable, than that a few men in whom such furious rage and such implacable malice reigned, should be reckoned among the people and the sons of God, to the ex-

---

[1] Or, he might be restrained by prudence from imparting his feelings to others, lest by making them public, he should expose himself to danger, before he was prepared to meet it. At all events, it was wise to restrain the expression of his indignation, till he was surrounded by those who might help him with their counsel, or attempt the rescue of his daughter from the hands of her violator.—*Ed.*

clusion of all the world besides? We see certainly that it was not through any power of their own that they had not altogether declined from the kingdom of God. Whence it appears that the favour which God had vouchsafed unto them was gratuitous, and not founded upon their merits. We also require to be treated by Him with the same indulgence, seeing that we should utterly fall away, if God did not pardon our sins. The sons of Jacob have, indeed, a just cause of offence, because not only are they affected with their own private ignominy, but they are tormented with the indignity of the crime, because their sister had been dragged forth from the house of Jacob, as from a sanctuary, to be violated. For this they chiefly urge, that it would have been wickedness to allow such disgrace in the elect and holy people:[1] but they themselves, through the hatred of one sin, rush furiously forward to greater and more intolerable crimes. Therefore we must beware, lest, after we have become severe judges in condemning the faults of others, we hasten inconsiderately into evil. But chiefly we must abstain from violent remedies which surpass the evil we desire to correct.

*Which thing ought not to be done.*[2] Interpreters commonly explain the passage as meaning, " it is not becoming that such a thing should be done ;" but, in my judgment, it applies more properly to the sons of Jacob, who had determined with themselves that the injury was not to be borne. Yet they wrongfully appropriate to themselves the right of taking revenge : why do they not rather reflect thus ; " God, who has received us under his care and protection, will not suffer this injury to pass unavenged ; in the meantime, it is our part to be silent, and to leave the act of punishing, which

---

[1] " He had wrought folly in Israel." Ainsworth says, " Or against Israel." " Israel being put for the posterity of Israel." Professor Bush says, " Rather, ' Because folly had been wrought in Israel,' (the active for the passive)." But perhaps Ainsworth's translation is to be preferred. " This is the first instance on record where the family of Jacob is designated by the distinguished patronymic title of ' Israel,' which afterwards became the dominant appellation of his posterity."—*Bush in loc.*—*Ed.*

[2] Et sic non fiet. " And so it may not, or shall not be done." The sense given in the English translation is that which Calvin rejects, though he allows it to be the common meaning attached by commentators to the expression.—*Ed.*

is not placed in our hands, entirely to his sovereign will." Hence we may learn, when we are angry at the sins of other men, not to attempt anything which is beyond our own duty.

8. *And Hamor communed with them.* Though the sons of Jacob were justly incensed, yet their indignation ought to have been appeased, or at least somewhat mitigated, by the great courteousness of Hamor. And if the humanity of Hamor could not reconcile the sons of Jacob to Shechem, the old man himself was indeed worthy of a benignant reception. We see what equitable conditions he offers; he himself was the prince of the city, the sons of Jacob were strangers. Therefore their minds must have been savage beyond measure, not to be inclined to lenity. Besides, the suppliant entreaty of Shechem himself deserved this, that they should have granted forgiveness to his fervent love. Therefore, that they remained implacable, is a sign of most cruel pride. What would they have done to enemies who had purposely injured them, when they are not moved by the prayers of him, who, being deceived by blind love, and by the error of incontinency, has injured them without any malicious intention?

13. *And the sons of Jacob answered.* The commencement of their perfidious course is here related: for they, being outrageous rather than simply angry, wish to overthrow the whole city, and not being sufficiently strong to contend against so great a number of people, they contrive a new fraud, in order that they may suddenly rise upon the inhabitants weakened by wounds. Therefore, since the Shechemites had no strength to resist, it became a cruel butchery rather than a conquest, which increased the atrocity of wickedness in Jacob's sons, who cared for nothing so that they might but gratify their rage. They allege in excuse, that, whereas they were separated from other nations, it was not lawful for them to give wives of their own family to the uncircumcised. Which indeed was true if they said it sincerely; but they falsely use the sacred name of God as a pretext; yea, their double profanation of that name proves them to be doubly sacrilegious; for they cared nothing about circumcision, but were intent on this one thing, how they might crush the miserable men

in a state of weakness. Besides, they wickedly sever the sign from the truth which it represents; as if any one, by laying aside his uncircumcision, might suddenly pass over into the Church of God. And in this mode they pollute the spiritual symbol of life, by admitting foreigners, promiscuously and without discrimination, into its society. But since their pretence has some colour of probability, we must observe what they say, that it would be disgraceful to them to give their sister to a man uncircumcised. This also is true, if they who used the words were sincere; for since they bore the mark of God in their flesh, it was wicked in them to contract marriages with unbelievers. So also, at the present time, our baptism separates us from the profane, so that whoever mixes himself with them, fixes a mark of infamy upon himself.

18. *And their words pleased Hamor.* Moses prosecutes the history until he comes to the slaughter of the Shechemites. Hamor had, no doubt, been induced by the entreaties of his son, to show himself thus tractable. Whence appears the excessive indulgence of the kind old man. He ought, in the beginning, severely to have corrected the fault of his son; but he not only covers it as much as possible, but yields to all his wishes. This moderation and equity would have been commendable, if what his son had required was just; but that the old man, for the sake of his son, should adopt a new religion, and suffer a wound to be inflicted on his own flesh, cannot be deemed free from folly. The youth is said not to have delayed, because he vehemently loved the maid, and excelled in dignity among his own citizens; and on account of the honour of his rank he easily obtained what he wished: for the fervour of his love would have availed nothing, unless he had possessed the power of accomplishing his object.

21. *These men are peaceable.* Moses describes the mode of acting, whereby they persuaded the Shechemites to accept the conditions which the sons of Jacob had imposed. It was difficult to induce a whole people to submit in an affair of such magnitude to a few foreigners. For we know what displeasure a change of religion produces: but Hamor

and Shechem reason from utility; and this is natural rhetoric. For although honour has a more plausible appearance, it is yet for the most part cold in persuasion. But among the vulgar, utility carries almost every point; because the major part eagerly pursues what it deems expedient for itself. With this design, Hamor and Shechem extol the family of Jacob for their honesty and tranquil habits, in order that the Shechemites may deem it useful to themselves to receive such guests. They add that the land is sufficiently large, so that no loss is to be feared on the part of the original inhabitants. They then enumerate other advantages; meanwhile, they cunningly conceal the private and real cause of their request. Whence it follows that all these pretexts were fallacious. But it is a very common disease, that men of rank who have great authority, while making all things subservient to their own private ends, feign themselves to be considerate for the common good, and pretend to a desire for the public advantage. And, truly, it may be believed, that the persons here spoken of were the best among all the people, and were endowed with singular superiority; for the Shechemites had chosen Hamor for their prince, as one who was pre-eminent in excellent gifts. Yet we see how he and his son lie and deceive, under the appearance of rectitude. Whence also we perceive hypocrisy to be so deeply rooted in human minds, that it is a miracle to find any one entirely free from it; especially where private advantage is concerned. From this example let all who govern, learn to cultivate sincerity in public designs, without any sinister regard to their own interests. On the other hand; let the people exercise self-government, lest they too earnestly seek their own advantage; because it will often happen that they are caught by a specious appearance of good, as fishes by the hook. For as self-love is blind, we are drawn without judgment to the hope of gain. And the Lord also justly chastises this cupidity, to which he sees us to be unduly prone, when he suffers us to be deceived by it. Moses says that this discourse took place in the gate of the city, where public assemblies were then wont to be held and judgment administered.

24. *And unto Hamor and unto Shechem his son hearkened,* &c. Apparently this consent may be ascribed to modesty and humanity; for, by readily obeying their princes, and kindly admitting the strangers to an equality of rights in the city, they show themselves, in both respects, modest and humane. But if we reflect on the true import of circumcision, it will easily appear that they were too much addicted to their own selfish interests. They knew that, by a new sacrament, they would be committed to a different worship of God. They had not yet been taught that the ablutions and sacrifices, to which they had been all their life accustomed, were unprofitable trifles. Therefore, to change their religion so carelessly betrays, on their part, a gross contempt of God; for never do they who seriously worship God, so suddenly cast aside their superstitions, unless they are convinced by sound doctrine and arguments. But the Shechemites, blinded by an evil conscience, and by the hope of gain, pass over, like men half brutalized, to an unknown God. " Search the isles, (saith the Prophet,) is there any nation which deserts its gods, who yet are not gods?"[1] Yet this was done at Shechem, when no defect had been shown to exist in the received superstitions; wherefore none ought to wonder that a sad result followed this levity of mind. Nevertheless, Simeon and Levi were not, on that account, excusable for the indulgence of their own cruelty: yea, their impiety appears the more detestable, because they not only rush impetuously upon men, but, in a sense, trample upon the sacred covenant of God, of which alone they make their boast. Certainly, if they had no feeling for the men themselves, yet reverence for God ought to have restrained their ferocity, when they reflected from what cause the weakness of the Shechemites proceeded.

25. *Simeon and Levi, Dinah's brethren.* Because Moses says that the slaughter took place on the third day, the Hebrews think that, at that time, the pain of the wound was most severe. The proof, however, is not valid; nor is it of much moment. Although Moses names only two authors of the slaughter, it does not appear to me probable that they came alone, but that they were the leaders of the troop: for

---

[1] Jer. ii. 10, 11.

Jacob had a large family, and it might be that they called some of their brothers to join them; yet, because the affair was conducted by their counsel and direction, it is ascribed to them, as Carthage is said to have been destroyed by Scipio. Moses also calls them the brothers of Dinah, because they were by the same mother. We have seen that Dinah was the daughter of Leah; for which reason Simeon and Levi, whose own sister she was by both parents, were the more enraged at the violation of her chastity: they were therefore impelled, not so much by the common reproach brought upon the holy and elect race, (according to their recent boast,) as by a sense of the infamy brought upon themselves. However, there is no reader who does not readily perceive how dreadful and execrable was this crime. One man only had sinned, and he endeavoured to compensate for the injury, by many acts of kindness; but the cruelty of Simeon and Levi could only be satiated by the destruction of the whole city; and, under the pretext of a covenant, they form a design against friends and hospitable persons, in a time of peace, which would have been deemed intolerable against enemies in open war. Hence we perceive how mercifully God dealt with that people; seeing that, from the posterity of a sanguinary man, and even of a wicked robber, he raised up a priesthood for himself. Let the Jews now go and be proud of their noble origin. But the Lord declared his gratuitous mercy by too many proofs for the ingratitude of man to be able to obscure it. Moreover, we hence learn that Moses did not speak from carnal sense; but was the instrument of the Holy Spirit, and the herald of the celestial Judge; for though he was a Levite, he yet is so far from sparing his own race, that he does not hesitate to brand the father of his tribe with perpetual infamy. And it is not to be doubted that the Lord purposely intended to stop the mouths of impure and profane men, such as the Lucianists, who confess that Moses was a very great man, and of rare excellence; but that he procured for himself, by craft and subtlety, authority over a great people, as if, indeed, an acute and intelligent man would not have known that, by this single act of wickedness, the honour of his race would be greatly tarnished. He had, however, no other design than to extol the goodness of God towards his people; and truly there was nothing which he less desired than to exercise dominion, as appears clearly from the fact, that he transferred the office of priesthood to another family, and commanded his sons to be only ministers. With respect to the Shechemites, although in the sight of God they were not innocent; seeing they preferred their own advantage to a religion which they thought lawful, yet it was not the Lord's will that they should be so grievously punished for their fault; but he suffered this signal punishment to follow the violation of one maid, that he might testify to all ages his great abhorrence of lust. Besides, seeing that the iniquity had arisen from a prince of the city, the punishment is rightly extended to the whole body of the people: for since God never commits the government to evil and vicious princes, except in righteous judgment, there is no wonder that, when they sin, they involve their subjects with them in the same condemnation. Moreover, from this example let us learn, that if, at any time, fornications prevail with impunity, God will, at length, exact punishments so much the more severe: for if the violation of one maid was avenged by the horrible massacre of a whole city; he will not sleep nor be quiet, if a whole people indulge in a common license of fornication, and, on all sides, connive at each other's iniquity. The sons of Jacob acted indeed wickedly; but we must observe that fornication was, in this manner, divinely condemned.

27. *The sons of Jacob came.* Moses shows that, not content with simple revenge, they fly together to the spoil. As it respects the words, they are said to have "come upon the slain," either because they made themselves a way over the slaughtered bodies; or because, in addition to the slaughter, they rushed to the plunder. In whichever way it is taken, Moses teaches that, not satisfied with their former wickedness, they made this addition to it. Be it, that they were blinded with anger in shedding blood; yet by what right do they sack the city? This certainly cannot be ascribed to anger. But these are the ordinary fruits of human in-

temperance, that he who gives himself the rein in perpetrating one wickedness, soon breaks out into another. Thus the sons of Jacob, from being murderers, become also robbers, and the guilt of avarice is added to that of cruelty. The more anxious then should be our endeavours to bridle our desires; lest they should mutually fan each other, so that at length, by their combined action, a dreadful conflagration should arise; but especially, we must beware of using force of arms, which brings with it many perverse and brutal assaults. Moses says that the sons of Jacob did this, because the Shechemites had defiled their sister; but the whole city was not guilty. Moses, however, only states in what way the authors of the slaughter are affected: for although they wish to appear just avengers of the injury, yet they pay no respect to what it was lawful for them to do, and make no attempt to control their depraved affections, and consequently set no bounds to their wickedness. Should any one prefer taking the expression in a higher sense, it may be referred to the judgment of God, by which the whole city was involved in guilt, because no one had opposed the lust of the prince: perhaps many had consented to it, as not being very much concerned about the unjust dishonour done to their guests; but the former sense is what I most approve.

30. *And Jacob said.* Moses declares that the crime was condemned by the holy man, lest any one should think that he had participated in their counsel. He also expostulates with his sons, because they had caused him to stink among the inhabitants of the land; that is, they had rendered him so odious, that no one would be able to bear him. If then the neighbouring nations should conspire among themselves, he would be unable to resist them, seeing he had so small a band, in comparison with their great number. He also expressly names the Canaanites and Perizzites, who, though they had received no wrong, were yet by nature exceedingly prone to inflict injury. But Jacob may seem to act preposterously, in overlooking the offence committed against God, and in considering only his own danger. Why is he not rather angry at their cruelty? why is he not offended at their perfidy? why does he not reprove their rapaciousness? It is how-

ever probable, that when he saw them terror-stricken at their recent crime, he suited his words to their state of mind. For he acts as if he were complaining that he, rather than the Shechemites, was slain by them. We know that men are seldom if ever drawn to repentance, except by the fear of punishment: especially when they have any specious pretext as a covering for their fault. Besides, we know not whether Moses may not have selected this as a part out of a long expostulation, to cause his readers to understand that the fury of Simeon and Levi was so outrageous, that they were more insensible than brute beasts to their own destruction and that of their whole family. This is clear from their own answer, which not only breathes a barbarous ferocity, but shows that they had no feeling. It was barbarous, first, because they excuse themselves for having destroyed a whole people and plundered their city, on account of the injury done by one man; secondly, because they answer their father so shortly and contumaciously; thirdly, because they obstinately defend the revenge which they had rashly taken. Moreover, their insensibility was prodigious, because they were not affected by the thought of their own death, and that of their parents, wives, and children, which seemed just at hand Thus we are taught, how intemperate anger deprives men of their senses. We are also admonished, that it is not enough for us to be able to lay blame on our opponents; but we must always see how far it is lawful for us to proceed.

## CHAPTER XXXV.

1. AND God said unto Jacob, Arise, go up to Beth-el, and dwell there; and make there an altar unto God, that appeared unto thee when thou fleddest from the face of Esau thy brother.

2. Then Jacob said unto his household, and to all that *were* with him, Put away the strange gods that *are* among you, and be clean, and change your garments:

3. And let us arise, and go up to Beth-el; and I will make there an

1. Dixit autem Deus ad Iahacob, Surge, ascende in Beth-el, et mane ibi: et fac ibi altare Deo, qui visus est tibi, dum fugeres a facie Esau fratris tui.

2. Et dixit Iahacob familiæ suæ, et omnibus qui erant secum, Removete deos alienos, qui sunt in medio vestri, et mundate vos, vestimentaque vestra mundate.

3. Et surgamus, et ascendamus in Beth-el, et faciam illic altare Deo,

altar unto God, who answered me in the day of my distress, and was with me in the way which I went.

4. And they gave unto Jacob all the strange gods which *were* in their hand, and *all their* ear-rings which *were* in their ears; and Jacob hid them under the oak which *was* by Shechem.

5. And they journeyed: and the terror of God was upon the cities that *were* round about them, and they did not pursue after the sons of Jacob.

6. So Jacob came to Luz, which *is* in the land of Canaan, that *is*, Beth-el, he, and all the people that *were* with him.

7. And he built there an altar, and called the place El-beth-el; because there God appeared unto him, when he fled from the face of his brother.

8. But Deborah, Rebekah's nurse, died, and she was buried beneath Beth-el under an oak: and the name of it was called Allon-bachuth.

9. And God appeared unto Jacob again, when he came out of Padan-aram, and blessed him.

10. And God said unto him, Thy name *is* Jacob: thy name shall not be called any more Jacob, but Israel shall be thy name; and he called his name Israel.

11. And God said unto him, I *am* God Almighty; be fruitful and multiply: a nation, and a company of nations, shall be of thee, and kings shall come out of thy loins;

12. And the land which I gave Abraham and Isaac, to thee I will give it, and to thy seed after thee will I give the land.

13. And God went up from him in the place where he talked with him.

14. And Jacob set up a pillar in the place where he talked with him, *even* a pillar of stone; and he poured a drink-offering thereon, and he poured oil thereon.

15. And Jacob called the name of the place where God spake with him, Beth-el.

qui exaudivit me in die angustiæ meæ, et fuit mecum in via, qua ambulavi.

4. Dederunt ergo ipsi Iahacob omnes deos alienos, qui erant in manu sua, et inaures quæ erant in auribus suis, et abscondit eos Iahacob subter quercum, quæ erat apud Sechem.

5. Tunc profecti sunt, et fuit terror Dei super urbes, quæ erant in circuitibus eorum, et non persequuti sunt filios Iahacob.

6. Et venit Iahacob in Luz, quæ est in terra Chenaan, hæc est Beth-el, ipse et omnis populus qui erat cum eo.

7. Et ædificavit ibi altare, et vocavit locum El Beth-el: quia apparuerant ei Angeli, dum fugeret a facie fratris sui.

8. Mortua est autem Deborah nutrix Ribcah, et sepulta est subter Beth-el sub quercu: et vocavit nomen ejus Allon Bachuth.

9. Porro visus fuerat Deus ipsi Iahacob adhuc, dum veniret de Padan Aram, et benedixerat ei.

10. Atque dixerat ei ipse Deus, Nomen tuum est Iahacob: non vocabitur nomen tuum ultra Iahacob, sed Israel erit nomen tuum, et vocavit nomen ejus Israel.

11. Et dixit ei Deus, Ego sum Deus omnipotens, cresce, et multiplicare: gens, et cœtus Gentium erit ex te, et reges e lumbis tuis egredientur.

12. Et terram, quam dedi Abraham et Isaac, tibi dabo, et semini tuo post te dabo terram *istam*.

13. Et ascendit ab eo Deus e loco, in quo loquutus est cum eo.

14. Tunc statuit Iahacob statuam in loco, in quo loquutus est cum eo, statuam lapideam: et libavit super illam libamen, et effudit super illam oleum.

15. Et vocavit Iahacob nomen loci, in quo loquutus est cum ipso Deus, Beth-el.

16. And they journeyed from Beth-el; and there was but a little way to come to Ephrath: and Rachel travailed, and she had hard labour.

17. And it came to pass, when she was in hard labour, that the midwife said unto her, Fear not; thou shalt have this son also.

18. And it came to pass, as her soul was in departing, (for she died,) that she called his name Ben-oni: but his father called him Benjamin.

19. And Rachel died, and was buried in the way to Ephrath, which *is* Beth-lehem.

20. And Jacob set a pillar upon her grave: that *is* the pillar of Rachel's grave unto this day.

21. And Israel journeyed, and spread his tent beyond the tower of Edar.

22. And it came to pass, when Israel dwelt in that land, that Reuben went and lay with Bilhah his father's concubine: and Israel heard *it.* Now the sons of Jacob were twelve.

23. The sons of Leah; Reuben, Jacob's first-born, and Simeon, and Levi, and Judah, and Issachar, and Zebulun.

24. The sons of Rachel; Joseph and Benjamin.

25. And the sons of Bilhah, Rachel's handmaid; Dan and Naphtali.

26. And the sons of Zilpah, Leah's handmaid; Gad and Asher. These *are* the sons of Jacob, which were born to him in Padan-aram.

27. And Jacob came unto Isaac his father unto Mamre, unto the city of Arbah, which *is* Hebron, where Abraham and Isaac sojourned.

28. And the days of Isaac were an hundred and fourscore years.

29. And Isaac gave up the ghost, and died, and was gathered unto his people, *being* old and full of days: and his sons Esau and Jacob buried him.

16. Profecti vero sunt de Beth-el: erat autem adhuc ferme milliare terræ ad veniendum in Ephrath, et peperit Rachel, et difficultatem passa est, dum pareret.

17. Fuit autem, ea difficultatem patiente dum pareret, dixit ei obstetrix, Ne timeas, quia etiam iste tibi filius.

18. Et fuit, egrediente anima ejus dum moreretur, vocavit nomen ejus Benoni: at pater ejus vocavit eum Benjamin.

19. Mortua est itaque Rachel, et sepulta est in via Ephrath, hæc est Bethlehem.

20. Et statuit Iahacob titulum super sepulcrum ejus: hic est titulus sepulcri Rachel usque ad diem hanc.

21. Et profectus est Israel, et tetendit tabernaculum suum trans turrim Eder.

22. Et fuit quum habitaret Israel in terra ipsa, profectus est Reuben, et concubuit cum Bilhah concubina patris sui: et audivit Israel. Fuerunt autem filii Iahacob duodecim.

23. Filii Leah, primogenitus Iahacob, Reuben, et Simhon, et Levi, Iehudah, et Issachar, et Zebulun.

24. Filii Rachel, Ioseph et Benjamin.

25. Et filii Bilhah ancillæ Rachel, Dan et Nephthali.

26. Et filii Zilpah ancillæ Leah, Gad et Aser. Isti sunt filii Iahacob, qui nati sunt in Padan Aram.

27. Et venit Iahacob ad Ishac patrem suum in Mamre civitatem Arbah: hæc est Hebron, in qua habitavit Abraham et Ishac.

28. Et fuerunt dies Ishac, centum anni et octoginta anni.

29. Et obiit Ishac, et mortuus est, et collectus est ad populos suos, senex et satur dierum: et sepelierunt eum Esau et Iahacob filii ejus.

1. *And God said unto Jacob.* Moses relates that when Jacob had been reduced to the last extremity, God came to

his help in the right time, and as at the critical juncture. And thus he shows, in the person of one man, that God never deserts his Church which he has once embraced, but will procure its salvation. We must, however, observe the order of his procedure; for God did not immediately appear to his servant, but suffered him first to be tormented by grief and excessive cares, that he might learn patience, deferring his consolation to the time of extreme necessity. Certainly the condition of Jacob was then most miserable. For all, on every side, might be so incensed against him that he would be surrounded with as many deaths as there were neighbouring nations: and he was not so stupid as to be insensible of his danger. God suffered the holy man to be thus tossed with cares and tormented with troubles, until, by a kind of resurrection, he restored him, as one half-dead. Whenever we read this and similar passages, let us reflect that the providence of God watches for our salvation, even when it most seems to sleep. Moses does not say how long Jacob was kept in anxiety, but we may infer from the context, that he had been very greatly perplexed, when the Lord thus revived him. Moreover, we must observe that the principal medicine by which he was restored, was contained in the expression, "The Lord spake." Why did not God by a miracle translate him to some other place, and thus immediately remove him from all danger? Why did he not even, without a word, stretch out the hand over him, and repress the ferocity of all, so that no one should attempt to hurt him? But Moses does not insist upon this point in vain. For hereby we are taught whence our greatest consolation in our afflictions is to be sought; and also, that it is the principal business of our life, to depend upon the word of God, as those who are certainly persuaded that, when he has promised salvation, he will deal well with us, so that we need not hesitate to walk through the midst of deaths. Another reason for the vision was, that Jacob might not only truly perceive that God was his deliverer; but, being forewarned by his word, might learn to ascribe to God whatever afterwards followed. For seeing that we are slow and dull, bare experience by no means suffices to attest the favour of God towards us, unless faith arising from the word be added.

*Go up to Beth-el.* Though it is God's design to raise his servant from death to life, he may yet have appeared to hold him up to derision; for the objection was ready, " Thou indeed, O Lord, commandest me to go up, but all the ways are closed; for my sons have raised such a flame against me, that I cannot remain safe in any hiding-place. I dare scarcely move a finger : what therefore will become of me, if with a great multitude, I now begin to move my camp ? shall I not provoke new enmities against me by my movements ?" But by this mode the faith of Jacob was most fully proved ; because, knowing God to be the leader and guardian of his journey, he girded himself to it, relying on the divine favour. Moreover, the Lord does not simply command what it is his will to have done, but he encourages his servant, by adding the promise. For, in reminding him that he is the same God who had before appeared unto him as he was fleeing in alarm from his brother, a promise is included in these words. The altar also refers to the same point ; for since it is the divinely appointed token of thanksgiving, it follows that Jacob would come thither in safety, in order that he might duly celebrate the grace of God. God chooses and assigns Beth-el, rather than any other place, for his sanctuary; because the very sight of it would greatly avail to take away terror, when he should remember that there the glory of the Lord had been seen by him. Further, since God exhorts his servant to gratitude, he shows that he is kind to the faithful, in order that they, in return, may own themselves to be indebted for everything to his grace, and may exercise themselves in the celebration of it.

2. *Then Jacob said unto his household.* The prompt obedience of Jacob is here described. For when he heard the voice of God, he neither doubted nor disputed with himself respecting what was necessary to be done : but, as he was commanded, he quickly prepared himself for his journey. But to show that he obeyed God, he not only collected his goods, but also purified his house from idols. For if we desire that God should be propitious to us, all hinderances are

to be removed, which in any way separate him from us.
Hence also we perceive to what point the theft of Rachel
tended. For, (as we have said,) she neither wished to draw
her father away from superstition, but rather followed him
in his fault; nor did she keep this poison to herself, but
spread it through the whole family. Thus was that sacred
house infected with the worst contagion. Whence also it appears,
how great is the propensity of mankind to impious and
vicious worship; since the domestics of Jacob, to whom the
pure religion had been handed down, thus eagerly laid hold
on the idols offered to them. And Jacob was not entirely
ignorant of the evil: but it is probable that he was so far
under the influence of his wife, that, by connivance, he
silently cherished this plague of his family. And truly,
in one word, he convicts and condemns both himself and the
rest, by calling idols " strange gods." For whence arose
the distinction here made, unless from his knowing that he
ought to be devoted to one God only? For there is a tacit
comparison between the God of Abraham and all other gods
which the world had wickedly invented for itself: not because
it was in the power of Abraham to determine who should be
the true God: but because God had manifested himself to
Abraham, he also wished to assume His name. Jacob therefore
confesses his own negligence, in having admitted to his
house idols, against which the door had been closed by God.
For wherever the knowledge of the true God shines, it is necessary
to drive far away whatever men fabricate to themselves
which is contrary to the true knowledge of him. But whereas
Jacob had been lulled to sleep either by the blandishments
of his wife, or had neglected to do his duty, through the
carelessness of the flesh, he is now aroused by the fear of
danger, to become more earnest in the pure worship of God.
If this happened to the holy patriarch, how much more
ought carnal security to be dreaded by us, in the season of
prosperity? If, however, at any time such torpor and neglect
shall have stolen upon us, may the paternal chastisement of
God excite and stimulate us diligently to purge ourselves
from whatever faults we, by our negligence, may have contracted.
The infinite goodness of God is here conspicuous;

seeing that he still deigned to regard the house of Jacob, though polluted with idols, as his sanctuary. For although Jacob mingled with idolaters, and even his wife,—a patroness of idolatry,—slept in his bosom, his sacrifices were always acceptable to God. Yet this great benignity of God in granting pardon, neither lessens the fault of the holy man, nor ought to be used by us as an occasion for negligence. For though Jacob did not approve of these superstitions, yet it was not owing to him that the pure worship of God was not gradually subverted. For the corruption which originated with Rachel was now beginning to spread more widely. And the example of all ages teaches the same thing. For scarcely ever does the truth of God so prevail among men, however strenuously pious teachers may labour in maintaining it, but that some superstitions will remain among the common people. If dissimulation be added to them, the mischief soon creeps onward, until it takes possession of the whole body. By being thus cherished, the mass of superstitions which at this day pervades the Papacy, has gained its influence. Wherefore we must boldly resist those beginnings of evil, lest the true religion should be injured by the sloth and silence of the pastors.

*And be clean, and change your garments.* This is an exhortation to the external profession of penitence. For Jacob wishes that his domestics, who before had polluted themselves, should testify their renewed purification by a change of garments. With the same design and end, the people, after they had made the golden calves, were commanded by Moses to put off their ornaments. Only in that instance a different method was observed; namely, that the people having laid aside their ornaments, simply confessed their guilt by mournful and mean apparel: but in the house of Jacob the garments were changed, in order that they who had been defiled might come forth as new men: yet the end (as I have said) was the same, that by this external rite, idolaters might learn how great was the atrocity of their wickedness. For although repentance is an inward virtue, and has its seat in the heart, yet this ceremony was by no means superfluous; for we know how little disposed men are to be displeased with themselves on account of their sins, unless they are pierced with many goads. Again, the glory of God is also concerned in this, that men should not only inwardly reflect upon their guilt, but at the same time openly declare it. This then is the sum; although God had given no express command concerning the purifying of his house, yet because he had commanded an altar to be raised, Jacob, in order that he might yield pure obedience to God, took care that all impediments should be removed; and he did this when necessity compelled him to seek help from God.

4. *And they gave unto Jacob.* Though the holy man had his house in suitable subordination; yet as all yielded such prompt obedience to his command by casting away their idols, I doubt not that they were influenced by the fear of danger. Whence also we infer how important it is for us to be aroused from slumber by suffering. For we know how pertinacious and rebellious is superstition. If, in a peaceful and joyous state of affairs, Jacob had given any such command, the greater part of his family would have fraudulently concealed their idols: some, perhaps, would have obstinately refused to surrender them; but now the hand of God urges them, and with ready minds they quickly repent. It is also probable, that, according to the circumstances of the time, Jacob preached to them concerning the righteous judgment of God, to inspire them with fear. When he commands them to " cleanse themselves," it is as if he had said, " Hitherto ye have been defiled before the Lord; now, seeing that he has regarded us so mercifully, wash out this filth, lest he should again avert his face from us." It seems, however, absurd, that Jacob should have buried the idols under an oak, and not rather have broken them in pieces and consumed them in the fire, as we read that Moses did with the golden calves, (Exod. xxxii. 20,) and Hezekiah with the brazen serpent, (2 Kings xviii. 4.) The fact is not thus related without reason: but the infirmity of Jacob is touched upon, because he had not been sufficiently provident against the future. And perhaps the Lord punished his previous excessive connivance and want of firmness, by depriving him of prudence or courage. Yet God accepted his obedience,

although it had some remainder of defect, knowing that it was the design of the holy man to remove idols from his family, and, in token of his detestation, to bury them in the earth. The ear-rings were doubtless badges of superstition; as at this day innumerable trifles are seen in the Papacy, by which impiety displays itself.

5. *And the terror of God was upon the cities.* It now manifestly appears that deliverance was not in vain promised to the holy man by God; since, amidst so many hostile swords, he goes forth not only in safety but undisturbed. By the destruction of the Shechemites all the neighbouring people were inflamed with enmity against a single family; yet no one moves to take vengeance. The reason is explained by Moses, that the terror of God had fallen upon them, which repressed their violent assaults. Hence we may learn that the hearts of men are in the hands of God; that he can inspire those with fortitude who in themselves are weak; and, on the other hand, soften their iron-hardness whenever he pleases. Sometimes, indeed, he suffers many to cast up the foam of their pride, against whom he afterwards opposes his power: but he often weakens those with fear who were naturally bold as lions: thus we find these giants, who were able to devour Jacob a hundred times, so struck with terror that they faint away. Wherefore, whenever we see the wicked furiously bent on our destruction, lest our hearts should fail with fear and be broken by desperation, let us call to mind this terror of God, by which the rage, however furious, of the whole world may be easily subdued.

7. *And he built there an altar.* It has been already stated why it behoved the holy fathers, wherever they came, to have an altar of their own, distinct from those of other nations; namely, to make it manifest that they did not worship gods of various kinds, a practice to which the world was then everywhere addicted, but that they had a God peculiar to themselves. For although God is worshipped with the mind, yet an external confession is the inseparable companion of faith. Besides, all acknowledge how very useful it is to us to be stirred up by outward helps to the worship of God. If any one object that these altars differed nothing from other altars in

appearance; I answer, that whereas others rashly, and with inconsiderate zeal, built altars to unknown gods, Jacob always adhered to the word of God. And there is no lawful altar but that which is consecrated by the word; nor indeed did the worship of Jacob excel by any other mark than this, that he attempted nothing beyond the command of God. In calling the name of the place "The God of Beth-el,"[1] he is thought to be too familiar; and yet this very title commends the faith of the holy man, and that rightly, since he confines himself within the divinely prescribed bounds. The Papists act foolishly in affecting the praise of humility by a modesty which is most degrading. But the humility of faith is praiseworthy, seeing it does not desire to know more than God permits. And as when God descends to us, he, in a certain sense, abases himself, and stammers with us, so he allows us to stammer with him. And this is to be truly wise, when we embrace God in the manner in which he accommodates himself to our capacity. For in this way, Jacob does not keenly dispute concerning the essence of God, but renders God familiar to himself by the oracle which he has received. And because he applies his senses to the revelation, this stammering and simplicity (as I have said) is acceptable to God. Now, though at this day, the knowledge of God has shined more clearly, yet since God, in the gospel, takes upon him the character of a nursing father, let us learn to subject our minds to him; only let us remember that he descends to us in order to raise us up to himself. For he does not speak to us in this earthly manner, to keep us at a distance from heaven, but rather by this vehicle, to draw us up thither. Meanwhile this rule must be observed, that since the name of the altar was given by a celestial oracle, the building of it was a proof of faith. For where the living voice of God does not sound, whatever pomps may be introduced will be like shadowy spectres; as in the Papacy nothing can be seen except bladders filled with wind. It may be added that Jacob shows the constant tenor

[1] As the word *Beth-el* means the House of God, the farther addition of *El*, the name of God, seems to be a tautology; and this is made by Calvin the basis of an objection which he proceeds to answer.—*Ed*.

of his faith, from the time that God began to manifest himself to him; because he keeps in view the fact, that the angels had appeared unto him.[1] For since the word is in the plural number, I willingly interpret it of angels; and this is not contrary to the former doctrine; for although the majesty of God was then conspicuous, so far as he could comprehend it, yet Moses does not without reason mention the angels whom Jacob saw ascending and descending on the steps of the ladder. For he then beheld the glory of God in the angels, as we see the splendour of the sun flowing to us through his rays.

8. *But Deborah, Rebekah's nurse, died.* Here is inserted a short narration of the death of Deborah, whom we may conclude to have been a holy matron, and whom the family of Jacob venerated as a mother; for the name given in perpetuity to the place, testifies that she was buried with peculiar honour, and with no common mourning. Shortly afterwards the death and burial of Rachel are to be recorded: yet Moses does not say that any sign of mourning for Deborah was transmitted to posterity;[2] therefore it is probable that she was held by all in the place of a grandmother. But it may be asked, how she then happened to be in Jacob's company, seeing that he had not yet come to his father; and the age of a decrepid old woman rendered her unfit for so long a journey.[3] Some interpreters imagine that she had

---

[1] Quia apparuerunt ei Angeli dum fugeret a facie fratris sui. In the English translation the name of God is put instead of angels, and no doubt rightly. The reason given for Calvin's translation of the word אלהים, (*Elohim,*) by *angels* is, that, contrary to the usual custom, when the word means God, it is accompanied by a verb in the plural number. But this is not conclusive. See note 2, vol. i., p. 531, on chap. xx. ver. 13.

Yet there is some difficulty in the passage, arising from the apparent harshness of the repetition of *El*, the name of God, in this title. Bush thinks that the first El does not belong to the name of the place. Rivetus reads the first *El* as the genitive, supposing the word *place* to be understood. "And he called the place, 'the place of the God of Beth-el.' This Dathé thinks harsh, and he follows Michaelis in connecting למקום with the first אל. And he called the place of God, Beth-el."—*Ed.*

[2] The meaning, perhaps, is, that no monumental pillar was raised to Deborah, as was done to Rachel; the probable reason given for the fact, namely, that she was regarded as a grandmother, does not seem very intelligible.—*Ed.*

[3] It appears, from a calculation of the ages of Rebekah, of Jacob, and

been sent by Rebekah to meet her son Jacob; but I do not see what probability there is in the conjecture; nor yet have I anything certain to affirm, except that, perhaps, she had loved Jacob from a boy, because she had nursed him; and when she knew the cause of his exile, she followed him from her regard for religion. Certainly Moses does not in vain celebrate her death with an eulogy so remarkable.

9. *And God appeared unto Jacob.* Moses, having introduced a few words on the death of Deborah, recites a second vision, by which Jacob was confirmed, after his return to Beth-el. Once, in this place, God had appeared unto him, when he was on his way into Mesopotamia. In the meantime God had testified in various methods, as need required, that he would be present with him everywhere through his whole journey; but now he is brought back again to that very place where a more illustrious and memorable oracle had been given him, in order that he may receive again a new confirmation of his faith. The blessing of God here means nothing else than his promise; for though men pray for blessings on each other; God declares himself to be the sole Dispenser of perfect happiness. Now Jacob heard at this time nothing new; but the same promise is repeated to him, that he, as one who had returned from captivity to his own country, and had gathered new strength to his faith, might accomplish with greater courage the remaining course of his life.

10. *Thy name shall not be called any more Jacob.* We have before given the meaning of these words. The former name is not abolished, but the dignity of the other, which was afterwards put upon him, is preferred: for he was called Jacob from the womb, because he had strongly wrestled with

of Rachel, that Deborah must, at this time, have lived far beyond the common term of human life. "Jacob was then about one hundred and seven years of age. Isaac had been sixty years old when Jacob was born; he married Rebekah when he was at the age of forty, and she could not be less than twenty at the time of her marriage; it will follow that she bore twins in, or after, the fortieth year of her age. If these forty years be added to the one hundred and seven of Jacob's life, this will make one hundred and forty-seven. Supposing Deborah to have been twenty-five when she was given as a nurse to Rebekah, she could not now be less than one hundred and seventy years old."—See *Rivetus*, p. 701.—*Ed.*

his brother; but he was afterwards called Israel, because he entered into contest with God, and obtained the victory; not that he had prevailed by his own power, (for he had borrowed courage and strength and arms from God alone,) but because it was the Lord's will freely to confer upon him this honour. He therefore speaks comparatively, showing that the name Jacob is obscure and ignoble when compared with the name Israel. Some understand it thus, "Not only shalt thou be called Jacob, but the surname of Israel shall be added;" yet the former exposition seems to me the more simple; namely, that the old name, having in it less of splendour, should give place to the second. What Augustine adduces is specious rather than solid; namely, that he was called Jacob in reference to his present life, but Israel in reference to his future life. Let this, however, be regarded as settled, that a double name was given to the holy man, of which one was by far the most excellent; for we see that the prophets often combine them both, thus marking the constancy of God's grace from the beginning to the end.

11. *I am God Almighty.* God here, as elsewhere, proclaims his own might, in order that Jacob may the more certainly rely on his faithfulness. He then promises that he will cause Jacob to increase and multiply, not only into one nation, but into a multitude of nations. When he speaks of "a nation," he no doubt means that the offspring of Jacob should become sufficiently numerous to acquire the body and the name of one great people. But what follows concerning "nations" may appear absurd; for if we wish it to refer to the nations which, by gratuitous adoption, are inserted into the race of Abraham, the form of expression is improper: but if it be understood of sons by natural descent, then it would be a curse rather than a blessing, that the Church, the safety of which depends on its unity, should be divided into many distinct nations. But to me it appears that the Lord, in these words, comprehended both these benefits; for when, under Joshua, the people was apportioned into tribes, as if the seed of Abraham was propagated into so many distinct nations; yet the body was not thereby divided; it is called an assembly of nations, for this reason, because in

connection with that distinction a sacred unity yet flourished. The language also is not improperly extended to the Gentiles, who, having been before dispersed, are collected into one congregation by the bond of faith; and although they were not born of Jacob according to the flesh; yet, because faith was to them the commencement of a new birth, and the covenant of salvation, which is the seed of spiritual birth, flowed from Jacob, all believers are rightly reckoned among his sons, according to the declaration, " I have constituted thee a father of many nations."

*And kings shall come out of thy loins.* This, in my judgment, ought properly to be referred to David and his posterity; for God did not approve of the kingdom of Saul, and therefore it was not established; and the kingdom of Israel was but a corruption of the legitimate kingdom. I acknowledge truly that, sometimes, those things which have sprung from evil sources are numbered among God's benefits; but because here the simple and pure benediction of God is spoken of, I willingly understand it of David's successors only. Finally; Jacob is constituted the lord of the land, as the sole heir of his grandfather Abraham, and of his father Isaac; for the Lord manifestly excludes Esau from the holy family, when he transfers the dominion of the land, by hereditary right, to the posterity of Jacob alone.

13. *And God went up from him.* This ascent of God is analogous to his descent; for God, who fills heaven and earth, is yet said to descend to us, though he changes not his place, whenever he gives us any token of his presence; a mode of expression adopted in accommodation to our littleness. He went up, therefore, from Jacob, when he disappeared from his sight, or when the vision ended. By the use of such language, God shows us the value of his word, because, indeed, he is near to us in the testimony of his grace; for, seeing that there is a great distance between us and his heavenly glory, he descends to us by his word. This, at length, was fully accomplished in the person of Christ; who while, by his own ascension to heaven, he raised our faith thither; nevertheless dwells always with us by the power of his Spirit.

14. *And Jacob set up a pillar.* Though it is possible that he may again have erected a sacred monument, in memory of the second vision; yet I readily subscribe to the opinion of those who think that reference is made to what had been done before; as if Moses should say, that was the ancient temple of God, in which Jacob had poured forth his libation: for he had not been commanded to come thither for the sake of dwelling there; but in order that a fresh view of the place might renew his faith in the ancient oracle, and more fully confirm it. We read elsewhere that altars were built by the holy fathers, where they intended to remain longer; but their reason for doing so was different: for whereas Jacob had made a solemn vow in Beth-el, on condition that he should be brought back by the Lord in safety; thanksgiving is now required of him, after he has become bound by his vow,[1] that, being strengthened, he may pass onward on his journey.

16. *And they journeyed from Beth-el.* We have seen how severe a wound the defilement of his daughter inflicted on holy Jacob, and with what terror the cruel deed of his two sons had inspired him. Various trials are now blended together, by which he is heavily afflicted throughout his old age; until, on his departure into Egypt, he receives new joy at the sight of his son Joseph. But even this was a most grievous temptation, to be exiled from the promised land even to his death. The death of his beloved wife is next related; and soon after follows the incestuous intercourse of his firstborn with his wife Bilhah. A little later, Isaac his father dies; then his son Joseph is snatched away, whom he supposes to have been torn in pieces by wild beasts. While he is almost consumed with perpetual mourning, a famine arises, so that he is compelled to seek food from Egypt. There another of his sons is kept in chains; and, at length, he is deprived of his own most beloved Benjamin, whom he sends

---

[1] Nunc gratiarum actio ab eo exigitur, postquam reus voti factus est, ut confirmatus alio transeat. The French translation of "postquam reus voti factus est" is, "apres qu'il a eu jouissance de son souhait," "after he had obtained the enjoyment of his wish;" and this would read more smoothly than the translation given above; but is "reus voti" capable of such a version?—*Vide Lexicon Facciolati, sub voce reus.—Ed.*

away as if his own bowels were torn from him. We see, therefore, by what a severe conflict, and by what a continued succession of evils, he was trained to the hope of a better life. And whereas Rachel died in childbirth, through the fatigue of the journey, before they reached a resting-place; this would prove no small accession to his grief. But, as to his being bereaved of his most beloved wife, this was probably the cause, that the Lord intended to correct the exorbitance of his affection for her. The Holy Spirit fixes no mark of infamy upon Leah, seeing that she was a holy woman, and endowed with greater virtue; but Jacob more highly appreciated Rachel's beauty. This fault in the holy man was cured by a bitter medicine, when his wife was taken away from him: and the Lord often deprives the faithful of his own gifts, to correct their perverse abuse of them. The wicked, indeed, more audaciously profane the gifts of God; but if God connives longer at their misconduct, a more severe condemnation remains to them on account of his forbearance. But in taking away from his own people the occasion of sinning, he promotes their salvation. Whoever, therefore, desires the continued use of God's gifts, let him learn not to abuse them, but to enjoy them with purity and sobriety.

17. *The midwife said unto her.* We know that the ancients were very desirous of offspring, especially of male offspring. Since Rachel therefore does not accept this kind of consolation when offered, we infer that she was completely oppressed with pain. She therefore died in agonies, thinking of nothing but her sad childbirth and her own sorrows: from the feeling of which she gave a name to her son; but Jacob afterwards corrected the error. For the change of the name sufficiently shows, that, in his judgment, the excess of sorrow in his wife was wrong; seeing that she had branded his son with a sinister and opprobrious name;[1] for that sadness is not free from ingratitude, which so occupies our

---

[1] Rachel, in the act of dying, called her son Benoni, the son of my sorrow; Jacob called him Benjamin, the son of my right hand. It is worthy of remark that Benjamin was the only son of Jacob born in the land of Canaan.—*Ed.*

minds in adversity that the kindness of God does not exhilarate them; or, at least, does not infuse some portion of sweetness to mitigate our grief. Then her burial is mentioned; to which the holy fathers could not have attended with such religious care, except on account of their hope of the future resurrection. Whenever, therefore, we read concerning their burying the dead, as if they were anxious about the performance of some extraordinary duty, let us think of that end of which I have spoken; for it was no foolish ceremony, but a lively symbol of the future resurrection. I acknowledge, indeed, that profane and degenerate men at that time, in various places, vainly incurred much expense and toil in burying their dead, only as an empty solace of their grief. But although they had declined from the original institution into gross errors, yet the Lord caused that this rite should remain entire among his own people. Moreover, he designed that a testimony should exist among unbelievers, by which they might be rendered inexcusable. For since, independently of instruction, this sentiment was innate in all men, that to bury the dead was one of the offices of piety, nature has clearly dictated to them that the human body is formed for immortality; and, therefore, that, by sinking into death, it does not utterly perish. The statue or monument, erected by him, signifies the same thing. He reared no citadel which might stand as a token of his glory among his posterity: but he took care to raise the memorial of a sepulchre, which might be a witness to all ages that he was more devoted to the life to come; and, by the providence of God, this memorial remained standing, till the people returned out of Egypt.

22. *Reuben went and lay with Bilhah.* A sad and even tragic history is now related concerning the incestuous intercourse of Reuben with his mother-in-law. Moses, indeed, calls Bilhah Jacob's concubine: but though she had not come into the hands of her husband, as the mistress of the family and a partaker of his goods; yet, as it respected the bed, she was his lawful wife, as we have before seen. If even a stranger had defiled the wife of the holy man, it would have been a great disgrace; it was, however, far more atrocious

that he should suffer such an indignity from his own son. But how great and how detestable was the dishonour, that the mother of two tribes should not only contaminate herself with adultery, but even with incest; which crime is so abhorrent to nature, that, not even among the Gentiles, has it ever been held tolerable? And truly, by the wonderful artifice of Satan, this great obscenity penetrated into the holy house, in order that the election of God might seem to be of no effect. Satan endeavours, by whatever means he can, to pervert the grace of God in the elect; and since he cannot effect that, he either covers it with infamy, or at least obscures it. Hence it happens that disgraceful examples often steal into the Church. And the Lord, in this manner, suffers his own people to be humbled, that they may be more attentively careful of themselves, that they may more earnestly watch unto prayer, and may learn entirely to depend on his mercy. Moses only relates that Jacob was informed of this crime; but he conceals his grief, not because he was unfeeling, (for he was not so stupid as to be insensible to sorrow,) but because his grief was too great to be expressed. For here Moses seems to have acted as the painter did who, in representing the sacrifice of Iphigenia, put a veil over her father's face, because he could not sufficiently express the grief of his countenance. In addition to this eternal disgrace of the family, there were other causes of anxiety which transfixed the breast of the holy man. The sum of his happiness was in his offspring, from which the salvation of the whole world was to proceed. Whereas, already, two of his sons had been perfidious and sanguinary robbers; the first-born, now, exceeds them both in wickedness. But here the gratuitous election of God has appeared the more illustrious, because it was not on account of their worthiness that he preferred the sons of Jacob to all the world; and also because, when they had fallen so basely, this election nevertheless remained firm and efficacious. Warned by such examples, let us learn to fortify ourselves against those dreadful scandals by which Satan strives to disturb us. Let every one also privately apply this to the strengthening of his own faith. For sometimes even good men slide, as if they had fallen from grace. Desperation would necessarily be the consequence of such ruin, unless the Lord, on the other hand, held out the hope of pardon. A remarkable instance of this is set before us in Reuben; who, after this extreme act of iniquity, yet retained his rank of a patriarch in the Church. We must, however, remain under the custody of fear and watchfulness, lest temptation should seize upon us unawares, and thus the snares of Satan should envelop us. For the Holy Spirit did not design to set before us an example of vile lust, in order that every one might rush into incestuous connexions; but would rather expose to infamy the baseness of this crime, in an honourable person, that all, on that account, might more vehemently abhor it. This passage also refutes the error of Novatus. Reuben had been properly instructed; he bore in his flesh, from early infancy, the symbol of the divine covenant; he was even born again by the Spirit of God; we see, therefore, what was the deep abyss from which he was raised by the incredible mercy of God. The Novatians, therefore, and similar fanatics, have no right to cut off the hope of pardon from the lapsed: for it is no slight injury to Christ, if we suppose the grace of God to be more restricted by his advent.

*Now the sons of Jacob were twelve.* Moses again recounts the sons of Jacob in a regular series. Reuben is put the first among them, not for the sake of honour, but that he may be loaded with the greater opprobrium: for the greater the honour which any one receives from the Lord, the more severely is he to be blamed, if he afterwards makes himself the slave of Satan, and deserts his post. Moses seems to insert this catalogue before the account of the death of Isaac, for the purpose of discriminating between the progeny of Jacob and the Idumeans, of whom he is about to make mention in the following chapter. For on the death of Isaac the fountain of the holy race became divided, as into two streams; but since the adoption of God restrained itself to one branch only, it was necessary to distinguish it from the other.

28. *And the days of Isaac.* The death of Isaac is not related in its proper order, as will soon appear from the connection of the history: but, as we have elsewhere seen, the

figure *hysteron proteron* was familiar to Moses.[1] When it is said, *that he died old, and full of days,* the meaning is, that, having fulfilled the course of his life, he departed by a mature death; this, therefore, is ascribed to the blessing of God. Nevertheless, I refer these words not merely to the duration of his life, but also to the state of his feelings; implying that Isaac, being satisfied with life, willingly and placidly departed out of the world. For we may see certain decrepid old men, who are not less desirous of life than they were in the flower of their age; and with one foot in the grave, they still have a horror of death. Therefore, though long life is reckoned among the blessings of God; yet it is not enough for men to be able to count up a great number of years; unless they feel that they have lived long, and, being satisfied with the favour of God and with their own age, prepare themselves for their departure. Now, in order that old men may have their minds formed to this kind of moderation, it behoves them to have a good conscience, to the end, that they may not flee from the presence of God; for an evil conscience pursues and agitates the wicked with terror. Moses adds, that Isaac was buried by his two sons. For since, at that time, the resurrection was not clearly revealed, and its first fruits had not yet appeared, it behoved the holy fathers to be so much the more diligently trained in significant ceremonies, in order that they might correct the impression produced by the semblance of destruction which is presented in death. By the fact that Esau is put first, we are taught again, that the fruit of the paternal benediction was not received by Jacob in this life; for he who was the first-born by right, is still subjected to the other, after his father's death.

[1] The death of Isaac is mentioned here, out of place, to prevent the subsequent interruption of the history. The events of the thirty-seventh and thirty-eighth chapters preceded it; for Isaac lived about fifteen years after the removal of Joseph into Egypt.— *Ed.*

## CHAPTER XXXVI.

1. Now these *are* the generations of Esau, who *is* Edom.
2. Esau took his wives of the daughters of Canaan; Adah the daughter of Elon the Hittite, and Aholibamah the daughter of Anah, the daughter of Zibeon the Hivite;
3. And Bashemath, Ishmael's daughter, sister of Nebajoth.
4. And Adah bare to Esau Eliphaz; and Bashemath bare Reuel;
5. And Aholibamah bare Jeush, and Jaalam, and Korah. These *are* the sons of Esau, which were born unto him in the land of Canaan.
6. And Esau took his wives, and his sons, and his daughters, and all the persons of his house, and his cattle, and all his beasts, and all his substance, which he had got in the land of Canaan, and went into the country from the face of his brother Jacob.
7. For their riches were more than that they might dwell together; and the land wherein they were strangers could not bear them because of their cattle.
8. Thus dwelt Esau in Mount Seir. Esau *is* Edom.
9. And these *are* the generations of Esau, the father of the Edomites, in Mount Seir.
10. These *are* the names of Esau's sons; Eliphaz the son of Adah the wife of Esau; Reuel the son of Bashemath the wife of Esau.
11. And the sons of Eliphaz were Teman, Omar, Zepho, and Gatam, and Kenaz.
12. And Timna was concubine to Eliphaz, Esau's son; and she bare to Eliphaz Amalek: these *were* the sons of Adah, Esau's wife.
13. And these *are* the sons of Reuel; Nahath, and Zerah, Shammah, and Mizzah: these were the sons of Bashemath, Esau's wife.
14. And these were the sons of

1. Istæ vero sunt generationes Esau, hic est Edom.
2. Esau accepit uxores suas e filiabus Chenaan, Hadah filiam Elon Hittæi, et Aholibamah filiam Anah, filiam Sibhon Hivvæi,
3. Et Bosmath filiam Ismael sororem Nebajoth.
4. Et peperit Adah ipsi Esau Eliphaz: et Bosmath peperit Rehuel.
5. Et Aholibamah peperit Jehus, et Jahalam, et Corah: isti filii Esau, qui nati sunt ei in terra Chenaan.
6. Et accepit Esau uxores suas, et filios suos, et filias suas, et omnes animas domus suæ, et pecudes suas, et omnia jumenta sua, et omnem acquisitionem suam, quam acquisierat in terra Chenaan: et profectus est ad *aliam* terram a facie Iahacob fratris sui.
7. Erat enim substantia eorum multa, ita ut nequirent habitare pariter: nec poterat terra peregrinationum eorum ferre eos propter substantiam eorum.
8. Habitavit itaque Esau in monte Sehir: Esau est Edom.
9. Ac istæ sunt generationes Esau patris Edom in monte Sehir.
10. Ista sunt nomina filiorum Esau: Eliphaz filius Hadah uxoris Esau, Rehuel filius Bosmath uxoris Esau.
11. Et fuerunt filii Eliphaz, Theman, Omar, Sepho, et Gahatham, et Cenaz.
12. Timnah autem fuit concubina Eliphaz filii Esau, et peperit ipsi Eliphaz Hamalec. Isti sunt filii Hadah uxoris Esau.
13. Isti vero sunt filii Rehuel: Nahath, et Zerach, Sammah, et Mizza: isti sunt filii Bosmath uxoris Esau.
14. Et isti fuerunt filii Aholiba-

Aholibamah, the daughter of Anah, the daughter of Zibeon, Esau's wife; and she bare to Esau Jeush, and Jaalam, and Korah.

15. These *were* dukes of the sons of Esau: the sons of Eliphaz, the first-born *son* of Esau; duke Teman, duke Omar, duke Zepho, duke Kenaz,

16. Duke Korah, duke Gatam, *and* duke Amalek. These *are* the dukes *that came* of Eliphaz in the land of Edom: these *were* the sons of Adah.

17. And these *are* the sons of Reuel, Esau's son; duke Nahath, duke Zerah, duke Shammah, duke Mizzah. These *are* the dukes *that came* of Reuel in the land of Edom; these *are* the sons of Bashemath, Esau's wife.

18. And these *are* the sons of Aholibamah, Esau's wife; duke Jeush, duke Jaalam, duke Korah: these *were* the dukes *that came* of Aholibamah, the daughter of Anah, Esau's wife.

19. These *are* the sons of Esau, who *is* Edom, and these *are* their dukes.

20. These *are* the sons of Seir the Horite, who inhabited the land; Lotan, and Shobal, and Zibeon, and Anah,

21. And Dishon, and Ezer, and Dishan. These *are* the dukes of the Horites, the children of Seir in the land of Edom.

22. And the children of Lotan were Hori, and Heman: and Lotan's sister *was* Timna.

23. And the children of Shobal *were* these; Alvan, and Manahath, and Ebal, Shepho, and Onam.

24. And these *are* the children of Zibeon; both Ajah and Anah: this *was that* Anah that found the mules in the wilderness, as he fed the asses of Zibeon his father.

25. And the children of Anah *were* these; Dishon, and Aholibamah the daughter of Anah.

26. And these *are* the children of Dishon; Hemdan, and Eshban, and Ithran, and Cheran.

15. Isti duces filiorum Esau. Filii Eliphaz primogeniti Esau, dux Theman, dux Omar, dux Sepho, dux Chenaz,

16. Dux Corah, dux Gahatham, dux Hamalec: isti sunt duces Eliphaz in terra Edom: isti sunt filii Hadah.

17. Et isti sunt filii Rehuel filii Esau: dux Nahath, dux Zerach, dux Sammah, dux Mizzah: isti sunt duces Rehuel in terra Edom: isti sunt filii Bosmath uxoris Esau.

18. Isti autem sunt filii Aholibamah uxoris Esau, dux Jehus, dux Jahalam, dux Corah: isti sunt duces Aholibamah filiæ Hanah uxoris Esau.

19. Isti sunt filii Esau, et isti duces eorum: ipse est Edom.

20. Isti sunt filii Sehir Horæi, habitatores terræ: Lotan, et Sobal, et Sibhon, et Hanah,

21. Et Dison, et Eser, et Disan. Isti duces Horæorum filiorum Sehir in terra Edom.

22. Et fuerunt filii, Lotan, Hori, et Heman: et soror Lotan, Thimnah.

23. Isti sunt filii Sobal: Halvan, et Manahath, et Hebal, Sepho, et Onam.

24. Et isti sunt filii Sibhon: Ajah et Hanah: hic est Hanah, qui invenit mulos in deserto, quum pasceret asinos Sibhon patris sui.

25. Et isti sunt filii Hanah: Disan, et Aholibamah filia Hanah.

26. Et isti sunt filii Dison: Hemdan, et Esban, et Ithran, et Cheran.

27. The children of Ezer *are* these; Bilhan, and Zaavan, and Akan.
28. The children of Dishan *are* these; Uz, and Aran.
29. These *are* the dukes *that came* of the Horites; duke Lotan, duke Shobal, duke Zibeon, duke Anah,
30. Duke Dishon, duke Ezer, duke Dishan. These *are* the dukes *that came* of Hori, among their dukes in the land of Seir.
31. And these *are* the kings that reigned in the land of Edom, before there reigned any king over the children of Israel.
32. And Bela the son of Beor reigned in Edom: and the name of his city *was* Dinhabah.
33. And Bela died; and Jobab the son of Zerah of Bozrah reigned in his stead.
34. And Jobab died; and Husham of the land of Temani reigned in his stead.
35. And Husham died; and Hadad the son of Bedad, who smote Midian in the field of Moab, reigned in his stead: and the name of his city *was* Avith.
36. And Hadad died; and Samlah of Masrekah reigned in his stead.
37. And Samlah died; and Saul of Rehoboth *by* the river reigned in his stead.
38. And Saul died; and Baal-hanan the son of Achbor reigned in his stead.
39. And Baal-hanan the son of Achbor died; and Hadar reigned in his stead: and the name of his city *was* Pau; and his wife's name *was* Mehetabel, the daughter of Matred, the daughter of Mezahab.
40. And these *are* the names of the dukes *that came* of Esau, according to their families, after their places, by their names; duke Timnah, duke Alvah, duke Jetheth,
41. Duke Aholibamah, duke Elah, duke Pinon,
42. Duke Kenaz, duke Teman, duke Mibzar,
43. Duke Magdiel, duke Iram. These *be* the dukes of Edom, according to their habitations in the land

27. Isti sunt filii Eser: Bilhan, et Zaavan, et Acan.
28. Isti sunt filii Disan: Us et Aran.
29. Isti sunt duces Horæorum: dux Lotan, dux Sobal, dux Sibhon, dux Hanah.
30. Dux Dison, dux Eser, dux Disan: isti sunt duces Horæorum, in ducibus eorum, in terra Sehir.
31. Et isti sunt reges, qui regnaverunt in terra Edom, antequam regnaret rex super filios Israel.
32. Nempe regnavit in Edom, Belah filius Behor: et nomen urbis ejus Dinhabah.
33. Et mortuus est Belah, et regnavit pro eo Jobab, filius Zerah de Bosrah.
34. Et mortuus est Jobab, et regnavit pro eo Hussam e terra Australi.
35. Et mortuus est Hussam, et regnavit pro eo Hadad filius Bedad, qui percussit Midian in agro Moab: et nomen urbis ejus Avith.
36. Et mortuus est Hadad, et regnavit pro eo Samlah de Masrecah.
37. Et mortuus est Samlah, et regnavit pro eo Saul de Rehoboth fluminis.
38. Et mortuus est Saul et regnavit pro eo Bahal-hanan filius Hachbor.
39. Et mortuus est Bahal-hanan filius Hachbor, et regnavit pro eo Hadar: et nomen civitatis ejus Pahu: nomen autem uxoris ejus Mehetabel filia Matred filiæ Me-zahab.
40. Ista ergo sunt nomina ducum Esau, per familias suas, per loca sua, secundum nomina sua: dux Thimnah, dux Haluah, dux Jetheth,
41. Dux Aholibamah, dux Elah, dux Pinon,
42. Dux Cenaz, dux Theman, dux Mibsar,
43. Dux Magdiel, dux Hiram: isti sunt duces Edom per habitationes suas, in terra hæreditatis

of their possession: he *is* Esau, the ipsorum: ipse est Esau pater E-
father of the Edomites. dom.

1. *Now these are the generations of Esau.* Though Esau was an alien from the Church in the sight of God; yet since he also, as a son of Isaac, was favoured with a temporal blessing, Moses celebrates his race, and inscribes a sufficiently lengthened catalogue of the people born from him. This commemoration, however, resembles an honourable sepulture. For although Esau, with his posterity, took the precedence; yet this dignity was like a bubble, which is comprised under the figure of the world, and which quickly perishes. As, therefore, it has been before said of other profane nations, so now Esau is exalted as on a lofty theatre. But since there is no permanent condition out of the kingdom of God, the splendour attributed to him is evanescent, and the whole of his pomp departs like the passing scene of the stage. The Holy Spirit designed, indeed, to testify that the prophecy which Isaac uttered concerning Esau was not vain; but he has no sooner shown its effect, than he turns away our eyes, as if he had cast a veil over it, that we may confine our attention to the race of Jacob. Now, though Esau had children by three wives, in whom afterwards the blessing of God shone forth, yet polygamy is not, on that account, approved, nor the impure lust of man excused: but in this the goodness of God is rather to be admired, which, contrary to the order of nature, gave a good issue to evil beginnings.

6. *And went into the country from the face of his brother Jacob.* Moses does not mean that Esau departed purposely to give place to his brother; for he was so proud and ferocious, that he never would have allowed himself to seem his brother's inferior. But Moses, without regard to Esau's design, commends the secret providence of God, by which he was driven into exile, that the possession of the land might remain free for Jacob alone. Esau removed to Mount Seir, through the desire of present advantage, as is elsewhere stated. Nothing was less in his mind than to provide for his brother's welfare; but God directed the blind man by his own hand, that he might not occupy that place in the

land which he had appointed for his own servant. Thus it often happens that the wicked do good to the elect children of God, contrary to their own intention; and while their hasty cupidity pants for present advantages, they promote the eternal salvation of those whose destruction they have sometimes desired. Let us, then, learn from the passage before us, to see, by the eyes of faith, both in accidental circumstances (as they are called) and in the evil designs of men, that secret providence of God, which directs all events to a result predetermined by himself. For when Esau went forth, that he might live more commodiously apart from his father's family, he is said to have departed from the face of his brother, because the Lord had so determined it. It is stated indefinitely, that he departed "into the country;" because, being in uncertainty respecting his plan, he sought a home in various places, until Mount Seir presented itself; and as we say, he went out at a venture.[1]

9. *And these are the generations of Esau, the father of the Edomites.*[2] Though Esau had two names, yet in this place the second name refers to his posterity, who are called Idumeans. For, to make it appear what God had bestowed upon him for the sake of his father Isaac, Moses expressly calls him the father of a celebrated and famous people. And certainly, it served this purpose not a little, to trace the effect and fulfilment of the prophecy in the progeny of Esau. For if the promise of God so mightily flourished towards a stranger, how much more powerfully would it put itself forth towards the children, to whom pertaineth the adoption, and consequently the inheritance of grace? Esau was an obscure man, and a sojourner in that country: whence therefore is it, that suddenly rulers should spring from him, and a great body of people should flourish, unless because the benediction which proceeded from the mouth of Isaac, was confirmed by the result? For Esau did not reign in this desert without opposition; since a people of no ignoble name previously inhabited Mount Seir. On this account Moses relates that the men who had before inhabited that

[1] Quemadmodum Gallice dicitur, *Il s'en est allé à son aventure.*
[2] Patris Edom.

land were mighty: so that it would not have been easy for a stranger to acquire such power as Esau possessed, if he had not been divinely assisted.

24. *This was that Anah that found the mules.* Mules are the adulterous offspring of the horse and the ass. Moses says that Anah was the author of this connection.[1] But I do not consider this as said in praise of his industry; for the Lord has not in vain distinguished the different kinds of animals from the beginning. But since the vanity of the flesh often solicits the children of this world, so that they apply their minds to superfluous matters, Moses marks this unnatural pursuit in Anah, who did not think it sufficient to have a great number of animals; but he must add to them a degenerate race produced by unnatural intercourse. Moreover, we learn hence, that there is more moderation among brute animals in following the law of nature, than in men, who invent vicious admixtures.

31. *These are the kings that reigned, &c.* We must keep in memory what we have said a little before, that reprobates are suddenly exalted, that they may immediately fall, like the herb upon the roofs, which is destitute of root, and has a hasty growth, but withers the more quickly. To the two sons of Isaac had been promised the honour that kings should spring from them. The Idumeans first began to reign, and thus the condition of Israel seemed to be inferior. But at length, lapse of time taught how much better it is, by creeping on the ground, to strike the roots deep, than to acquire an extravagant pre-eminence for a moment, which speedily vanishes away. There is, therefore, no reason why the faithful, who slowly pursue their way, should envy the quick children of this world, their rapid succession of delights; since the felicity which the Lord promises them is far more stable, as it is expressed in the psalm, " The children's children shall dwell there, and their inheritance shall be perpetual." (Psalm cii. 28.)

[1] The word ימים, rendered mules by our translators, and by Calvin, is of doubtful signification; it occurs in this place only. It is by many commentators translated " waters," or " warm springs;" and probably this interpretation is to be preferred. The reader may see the question discussed in Professor Bush's note on this verse.—*Ed.*

## CHAPTER XXXVII.

1. AND Jacob dwelt in the land wherein his father was a stranger, in the land of Canaan.
2. These *are* the generations of Jacob. Joseph, *being* seventeen years old, was feeding the flock with his brethren; and the lad *was* with the sons of Bilhah, and with the sons of Zilpah, his father's wives: and Joseph brought unto his father their evil report.
3. Now Israel loved Joseph more than all his children, because he *was* the son of his old age: and he made him a coat of *many* colours.
4. And when his brethren saw that their father loved him more than all his brethren, they hated him, and could not speak peaceably unto him.
5. And Joseph dreamed a dream, and he told *it* his brethren: and they hated him yet the more.
6. And he said unto them, Hear, I pray you, this dream which I have dreamed:
7. For, behold, we *were* binding sheaves in the field, and, lo, my sheaf arose, and also stood upright; and, behold, your sheaves stood round about, and made obeisance to my sheaf.
8. And his brethren said to him, Shalt thou indeed reign over us? or shalt thou indeed have dominion over us? And they hated him yet the more for his dreams, and for his words.
9. And he dreamed yet another dream, and told it his brethren, and said, Behold, I have dreamed a dream more; and, behold, the sun, and the moon, and the eleven stars, made obeisance to me.
10. And he told *it* to his father, and to his brethren: and his father rebuked him, and said unto him, What *is* this dream that thou hast dreamed? Shall I, and thy mother,

1. Habitavit itaque Iahacob in terra peregrinationum patris sui, in terra Chenaan.
2. Istæ sunt generationes Iahacob. Joseph filius septendecim annorum pascebat cum fratribus suis pecudes, et erat puer cum filiis Bilhah et cum filiis Zilpah uxorum patris sui: et retulit Ioseph obloquutionem eorum malam patri eorum.
3. Porro Israel diligebat Joseph præ cunctis filiis suis, quia filius senectutis erat ei: et fecerat ei tunicam multicolorem.
4. Et viderunt fratres ejus, quod eum diligeret pater eorum præ cunctis fratribus ejus, et odio habebant eum, et non poterant alloqui eum pacifice.
5. Somniavit autem Joseph somnium, et nuntiavit fratribus suis: et addiderunt amplius odio habere eum.
6. Dixit enim ad eos, Audite quæso somnium hoc quod somniavi.
7. Ecce enim ligabamus manipulos in medio agri: et ecce surrexit manipulus meus, ac etiam stabat: et ecce circumdabant manipuli vestri, et incurvabant se manipulo meo.
8. Et dixerunt ei fratres ejus, Num regnando regnabis super nos? num dominando dominaberis nobis? Addiderunt ergo adhuc odio habere eum propter somnium ejus, et propter verba ejus.
9. Et somniavit adhuc somnium alterum, et narravit illud fratribus suis, et dixit, Ecce, somniavi somnium adhuc: et ecce, sol et luna et undecim stellæ incurvabant se mihi.
10. Et narravit patri suo et fratribus suis: et increpavit eum pater ejus, et dixit ei, Quid est hoc somnium quod somniasti? num veniendo veniemus ego et mater tua, et fra-

and thy brethren, indeed come to bow down ourselves to thee to the earth?

11. And his brethren envied him; but his father observed the saying.

12. And his brethren went to feed their father's flock in Shechem.

13. And Israel said unto Joseph, Do not thy brethren feed *the flock* in Shechem? come, and I will send thee unto them. And he said to him, Here *am I.*

14. And he said to him, Go, I pray thee, see whether it be well with thy brethren, and well with the flocks; and bring me word again. So he sent him out of the vale of Hebron, and he came to Shechem.

15. And a certain man found him, and, behold, *he was* wandering in the field: and the man asked him, saying, What seekest thou?

16. And he said, I seek my brethren: tell me, I pray thee, where they feed *their flocks.*

17. And the man said, They are departed hence; for I heard them say, Let us go to Dothan. And Joseph went after his brethren, and found them in Dothan.

18. And when they saw him afar off, even before he came near unto them, they conspired against him to slay him.

19. And they said one to another, Behold, this dreamer cometh.

20. Come now therefore, and let us slay him, and cast him into some pit; and we will say, Some evil beast hath devoured him: and we shall see what will become of his dreams.

21. And Reuben heard *it*, and he delivered him out of their hands; and said, Let us not kill him.

22. And Reuben said unto them, Shed no blood, *but* cast him into this pit that *is* in the wilderness, and lay no hand upon him; that he might rid him out of their hands, to deliver him to his father again.

23. And it came to pass, when Joseph was come unto his brethren,

tres tui, ut incurvemus nos tibi ad terram?

11. Et inviderunt ei fratres ejus: sed pater ejus observabat rem.

12. Profecti autem sunt fratres ejus, ut pascerent pecudes patris sui in Sechem.

13. Et dixit Israel ad Joseph, Nonne fratres tui pascunt in Sechem? veni, et mittam te ad eos. Et dixit ei, Ecce adsum.

14. Et ait ei, Vade nunc, vide incolumitatem fratrum tuorum, et incolumitatem pecorum, et refer mihi rem: et misit eum ex valle Hebron: et venit in Sechem.

15. Porro invenit eum vir, et ecce errabat in agro: interrogavit autem eum vir ille, dicendo, Quid quæris?

16. Et dixit, Fratres meos ego quæro, nuntia, obsecro, mihi, ubi ipsi pascant.

17. Et dixit vir ille, Profecti sunt hinc: audivi enim eos dicentes, Eamus in Dothan. Et perrexit Joseph post fratres suos, et invenit eos in Dothan.

18. Et viderunt eum e longinquo: et antequam appropinquaret eis, machinati sunt contra eum ut interimerent eum.

19. Ac dicebat alter alteri, Ecce, magister ille somniorum venit.

20. Nunc igitur venite, et occidamus illum, et projiciamus eum in unam e cisternis: et dicemus, Bestia mala devoravit eum: et videbimus quid erunt somnia ejus.

21. Et audivit Reuben, et eripuit eum e manu eorum, et dixit, Ne percutiamus eum *in* anima.

22. Dixit ergo ad eos Reuben, Ne effundatis sanguinem: projicite eum in cisternam hanc, quæ est in deserto, et manum ne mittatis in eum: ut erueret eum e manu eorum, ut reduceret eum ad patrem suum.

23. Et fuit, ut venit Joseph ad fratres suos, exuerunt Joseph tunica

CHAP. XXXVII.       THE BOOK OF GENESIS.       257

that they stripped Joseph out of his coat, *his* coat of *many* colours, that *was* on him;

24. And they took him, and cast him into a pit: and the pit *was* empty, *there was* no water in it.

25. And they sat down to eat bread: and they lifted up their eyes, and looked, and, behold, a company of Ishmeelites came from Gilead, with their camels bearing spicery, and balm, and myrrh, going to carry *it* down to Egypt.

26. And Judah said unto his brethren, What profit *is it* if we slay our brother, and conceal his blood?

27. Come, and let us sell him to the Ishmeelites, and let not our hand be upon him; for he *is* our brother, *and* our flesh: and his brethren were content.

28. Then there passed by Midianites, merchant-men; and they drew and lifted up Joseph out of the pit, and sold Joseph to the Ishmeelites for twenty *pieces* of silver: and they brought Joseph into Egypt.

29. And Reuben returned unto the pit; and, behold, Joseph *was* not in the pit: and he rent his clothes.

30. And he returned unto his brethren, and said, The child *is* not; and I, whither shall I go?

31. And they took Joseph's coat, and killed a kid of the goats, and dipped the coat in the blood:

32. And they sent the coat of *many* colours, and they brought *it* to their father; and said, This have we found: know now whether it *be* thy son's coat or no.

33. And he knew it, and said, *It is* my son's coat; an evil beast hath devoured him: Joseph is without doubt rent in pieces.

34. And Jacob rent his clothes, and put sackcloth upon his loins, and mourned for his son many days.

35. And all his sons, and all his daughters, rose up to comfort him; but he refused to be comforted: and

sua, tunica multicolore, quæ erat super eum.

24. Et tulerunt eum, et projecerunt eum in cisternam: et cisterna erat vacua, non erat in ea aqua.

25. Postea sederunt ut comederent panem, et levaverunt oculos suos, et viderunt, et ecce turba Ismaelitarum veniebat de Gilhad, et cameli eorum portabant aromata, et resinam, et stacten, iter facientes ut deferrent in Ægyptum.

26. Et dixit Jehudah fratribus suis, Quæ utilitas si occiderimus fratrem nostrum, et celaverimus sanguinem ejus?

27. Venite, et vendamus eum Ismaelitis, et manus nostra ne sit in eum, quia frater noster, caro nostra est: et paruerunt ei fratres ejus.

28. Et transierunt viri Madianitæ mercatores, et extraxerunt et sustulerunt Joseph e cisterna: et vendiderunt Joseph Ismaelitis viginti argenteis, qui abduxerunt Ioseph in Ægyptum.

29. Deinde reversus est Reuben ad cisternam, et ecce non erat Joseph in cisterna, et scidit vestimenta sua.

30. Et reversus est ad fratres suos, et dixit, Puer non est, et ego quo, ego *quo* ibo?

31. Et tulerunt tunicam Joseph, et jugulaverunt hircum caprarum, et tinxerunt tunicam in sanguine.

32. Et miserunt tunicam multicolorem, et deferri fecerunt ad patrem suum, et dixerunt, Hanc invenimus, agnosce nunc utrum tunica filii tui sit, annon.

33. Et agnovit eam, et dixit, Tunica filii mei est: bestia mala devoravit eum, rapiendo raptus est Ioseph.

34. Et scidit Iahacob vestimenta sua, et posuit saccum in lumbis suis, et luxit super filio suo diebus multis.

35. Et surrexerunt omnes filii ejus, et omnes filiæ ejus, ut consolarentur eum, sed noluit consolationem

he said, For I will go down into the grave unto my son mourning. Thus his father wept for him.

36. And the Midianites sold him into Egypt unto Potiphar, an officer of Pharaoh's, *and* captain of the guard.

admittere: et dixit, Certe descendam ad filium meum lugens ad sepulcrum: et luxit eum pater ejus.

36. Madianitæ autem vendiderunt eum in Ægypto Potiphar satrapæ Pharaonis, principi satellitum.

1. *And Jacob dwelt.* Moses confirms what he had before declared, that, by the departure of Esau, the land was left to holy Jacob as its sole possessor. Although in appearance he did not obtain a single clod; yet, contented with the bare sight of the land, he exercised his faith; and Moses expressly compares him with his father, who had been a stranger in that land all his life. Therefore, though by the removal of his brother to another abode, Jacob was no little gainer; yet it was the Lord's will that this advantage should be hidden from his eyes, in order that he might depend entirely upon the promise.

2. *These are the generations of Jacob.* By the word תולדות (*toledoth*) we are not so much to understand a genealogy, as a record of events, which appears more clearly from the context. For Moses having thus commenced, does not enumerate sons and grandsons, but explains the cause of the envy of Joseph's brethren, who formed a wicked conspiracy against him, and sold him as a slave: as if he had said, "Having briefly summed up the genealogy of Esau, I now revert to the series of my history, as to what happened to the family of Jacob."[1] Moreover, Moses being about to speak

[1] The second verse is rendered by Professor Bush in a manner different from that of any other commentator whom the Editor has had the opportunity of consulting. His view of the passage is, at least, worthy of consideration. "The correct translation," he says, "is doubtless the following: 'Joseph, being seventeen years old, was tending his brethren among the flocks, and he a (mere) lad, (even) the sons of Bilhah, &c.' The mention of his youth is brought in parenthetically, as something peculiarly worthy of notice; while the clause, 'the sons of Bilhah, &c.,' is designed to limit and specify the term 'brethren' going before." This interpretation he proceeds to vindicate by reference to passages of similar construction, which we have not room to quote. The point which it would establish is, that Jacob assigned to his boy, of seventeen years of age, the superintendence or oversight of the sons of Bilhah among the flocks; so that he was rather an overlooker of the *shepherds* than of the *sheep.* This would show more clearly the propriety of Joseph's conduct, in carrying an ill report of his brethren to their father; and would also account for the hostility they

of the abominable wickedness of Jacob's sons, begins with the statement, that Joseph was dear beyond the rest to his father, because he had begotten him in his old age: and as a token of tender love, had clothed him with a coat woven of many colours. But it was not surprising that the boy should be a great favourite with his aged father, for so it is wont to happen: and no just ground is here given for envy; seeing that sons of a more robust age, by the dictate of nature, might well concede such a point. Moses, however, states this as the cause of odium, that the mind of his father was more inclined to him than to the rest. The brethren conceive enmity against the boy, whom they see to be more tenderly loved by their father, as having been born in his old age.[1] If they did not choose to join in this love to their brother, why did they not excuse it in their father? Hence, then, we perceive their malignant and perverse disposition. But, that a many-coloured coat and similar trifles inflamed them to devise a scheme of slaughter, is a proof of their detestable cruelty. Moses also says that their hatred increased, because Joseph conveyed the evil speeches of his brethren to their father. Some expound the word *evil* as meaning some intolerable crime; but others more correctly suppose, that it was a complaint of the boy that his brothers vexed him with their reproaches; for, what follows in Moses, I take to have been added in explanation, that we may know the cause for which he had been treated so ill and with such hostility. It may be asked, why Moses here accuses only the sons of Bilhah and Zilpah, when, afterwards, he does not exempt the sons of Leah from the same charge? One, indeed, of her sons, Reuben, was milder than any of the rest; next to him was Judah, who was his uterine brother. But what is to be said of Simeon? what of Levi? Certainly since they were older, it is probable that they were leaders in the affair. The suspicion may, however, be entertained, that because these were

felt towards him. But it may be doubted whether this interpretation can stand.—*Ed.*

[1] "Son of his old age." The Chaldee renders it, "a wise son;" as if he were a man in intellect, while a boy in years. This would avoid a difficulty; for Benjamin was far more properly the son of Jacob's old age than Joseph.—*Ed.*

the sons of concubines and not of true wives, their minds would be more quickly moved with envy; as if their servile extraction, on the mother's side, subjected them to contempt.

6. *And Joseph dreamed a dream.* Moses having stated what were the first seeds of this enmity, now ascends higher, and shows that Joseph had been elected, by the wonderful purpose of God, to great things; that this had been declared to him in a dream; and that, therefore, the hatred of his brethren broke forth into madness. God, however, revealed in dreams what he would do, that afterwards it might be known that nothing had happened fortuitously: but that what had been fixed by a celestial decree, was at length, in its proper time, carried forward through circuitous windings to its completion. It had been predicted to Abraham that his seed should be wanderers from the land of Canaan. In order, then, that Jacob might pass over into Egypt, this method was divinely appointed; namely, that Joseph, being president over Egypt in a time of famine, might bring his father thither with his whole family, and supply them with food. Now, from the facts first related, no one could have conjectured such a result. The sons of Jacob conspire to put the very person to death, without whom they cannot be preserved; yea, he who was ordained to be the minister of salvation to them, is thrown into a well, and with difficulty rescued from the jaws of death. Driven about by various misfortunes, he seems to be an alien from his father's house. Afterwards, he is cast into prison, as into another sepulchre, where, for a long time, he languishes. Nothing, therefore, was less probable than that the family of Jacob should be preserved by his means, when he was cut off from it, and carried far away, and not even reckoned among the living. Nor did any hope of his liberation remain, especially from the time in which he was neglected by the chief butler; but being condemned to perpetual imprisonment, he was left there to rot. God, however, by such complicated methods, accomplishes what he had purposed. Wherefore, in this history, we have not only a most beautiful example of Divine Providence, but also two other points are added especially worthy of notice: first, that the Lord

performs his work by wonderful and unusual modes; and, secondly, that he brings forth the salvation of his Church, not from magnificent splendour, but from death and the grave. Besides, in the person of Joseph, a lively image of Christ is presented, as will more fully appear from the context. But since these subjects will be often repeated, let us follow the thread of Moses' discourse. God, of his mere grace, conferred peculiar honour on the boy, who was the last but one among twelve, in giving him the priority among his brethren. For, by what merit or virtue shall we say that he attained the lordship over his brethren? Afterwards he seemed, indeed, to acquire this by his own great beneficence: but from the dream we learn, that it was the free gift of God, which in no way depended upon Joseph's beneficence. Rather, he was ordained to be chief, by the mere good pleasure of God, in order that he might show kindness to his brethren. Now, since the Lord was, at that time, wont to reveal his secrets by two methods—by visions and by dreams—one of these kinds is here noted. For no doubt Joseph had often dreamed in the common manner: but Moses shows that a dream was now divinely sent to him, which might have the force and weight of an oracle. We know that dreams are often produced by our daily thoughts: sometimes they are indications of an unhealthy state of the body: but whenever God intends to make known his counsel by dreams, he engraves on them certain marks, which distinguish them from passing and frivolous imaginations, in order that their credibility and authority may stand firm. Thus Joseph, being certainly persuaded that he had not been deluded by an empty spectre, fearlessly announced his dream as a celestial oracle. Now, although the dominion is promised to him under a rural symbol, it is one which does not seem suitable for instruction to the sons of Jacob; for we know that they were herdsmen, not ploughmen. Since they had no harvest which they could gather in, it seems hardly congruous that homage should be paid to his *sheaf*. But perhaps God designedly chose this similitude, to show that this prophecy was not founded upon the present fortunes of Joseph, and that the material of his dominion would not consist in those things which were at hand, but that it should be a future benefit, the cause of which was to be sought for elsewhere than at home.

8. *Shalt thou indeed reign over us?* Here it is plainly shown to us that the paternal favour of God towards the elect, is like a fan to excite against them the enmity of the world. When the sons of Jacob heard that they were fighting in vain against God, their unjust hatred ought, by such means, to have been corrected. For it was as if God, setting himself in the midst, would repress their fury by these words, "Your impious conspiring will be fruitless; for although you boast, I have constituted as your chief, the man whose ruin your wicked envy hurries you to seek." Perhaps, also, by this consolatory dream, he intended to alleviate the trouble of the holy youth. Yet their obstinacy caused it to be the more increased. Let us then learn not to be grieved if, at any time, the shining of the grace of God upon us should cause us to be envied. The sons of Jacob, however, were but too acute interpreters of the dream: yet they deride it as a fable, because it was repugnant to their wishes. Thus it often happens that they who are ill-disposed, quickly perceive what is the will of God: but, because they feel no reverence, they despise it. To this contumacy, however, succeeds a stupor which destroys their former quick-sightedness.

9. *And he dreamed yet another dream.* The scope of this dream is the same. The only difference is, that God, to inspire greater confidence in the oracle, presents him with a figure from heaven. The brethren of Joseph had despised what was said concerning the sheaves; the Lord now calls upon them to look towards heaven, where his august Majesty shines forth. It may, however, be asked, how it can be reconciled with fact, that his mother, who was now dead, could come and bow down to him. The interpretation of certain Hebrews, who refer it to Bilhah, is frigid, and the sense appears plain without such subterfuges: for the sun and moon designate the head of the family on each side: thus, in this figure, Joseph sees himself reverenced by the whole house of his father.

10. *And his father rebuked him.* If Jacob suspected that the dream originated in vain ambition, he rightly rebuked

his son; but if he knew that God was the author of the dream, he ought not to have expostulated with him. But that he did know it, may be hence inferred, because he is afterwards said seriously to have considered it. For Moses, making a distinction between him and his sons, says that *they* breathed nothing but the *virus* of envy; while *he* revolved in his own mind what this might mean; which could not have happened, unless he had been affected with reverence. But seeing that a certain religious impression on the subject rested on his mind, how was it that he rebuked his son? This truly was not giving honour to God and to his word. For it ought to have occurred to the mind of Jacob that, although Joseph was under his authority, he yet sustained a prophetic character. It is probable, when he saw his sons so malevolent, that he wished to meet the danger by feigning what he did not feel: for he was not offended at the dream, but he was unwilling to exasperate the minds of those who, on account of their pride, would not bear to be in subjection. Therefore I do not doubt that he feignedly reproved his son, from a desire to appease contention. Nevertheless, this method of pretending to be adverse to the truth, when we are endeavouring to appease the anger of those who rage against it, is by no means approved by God. He ought rather ingenuously to have exhorted his sons not to " kick against the pricks." Or at least he should have used this moderate address, " If this is a common dream, let it be treated with ridicule rather than with anger; but if it has proceeded from God, it is wicked to speak against it." It is even possible that the unsuitableness of the dream had struck the mind of the old man. For we know how difficult it is entirely to throw off all sense of superiority. Certainly, though Jacob declines slightly from the right course, yet his piety appears to be of no common order; because his reverence for the oracle so easily prevailed over every other feeling. But the most wicked obstinacy betrays itself in his sons, seeing they break out into greater enmity. For though they despise the dream, yet they are not made angry about nothing. Gladly would they have had their brother as a laughing-stock; but a certain secret sense of the Deity constrains them, so that, with or against their will, they are compelled to feel that there is something authentic in the dream. Meanwhile, a blind ferocity impels them to an unintentional resistance against God. Therefore, that we may be held in obedience to God, let us learn to bring down our high spirits; because the beginning of docility is for men to submit to be brought into order. This obstinacy in the sons of Jacob was most censurable, because they not only rejected the oracle of God through their hatred of subjection, but were hostile to his messenger and herald. How much less excusable, then, will be our hardness, if we do not meekly submit our necks to the yoke of God; since the doctrine of humility, which subdues and even mortifies us, is not only more clearly revealed, but also confirmed by the precious blood of Christ? If, however, we see many refractory persons at this day, who refuse to embrace the gospel, and who perversely rise up against it, let us not be disturbed as by some new thing, seeing that the whole human race is infected with the disease of pride; for by the gospel all the glory of the flesh is reduced to nothing; rather let us know that all remain obstinate, except those who are rendered meek by the subduing influence of the Spirit.

12. *And his brethren went.* Before Moses treats of the horrible design of fratricide, he describes the journey of Joseph, and amplifies, by many circumstances, the atrocity of the crime. Their brother approaches them in the discharge of a duty, to make a fraternal inquiry after their state. He comes by the command of his father; and obeys it without reluctance, as appears from his answer. He searches them out anxiously; and though they had changed their place, he spares neither labour nor trouble till he finds them. Therefore their cruelty was something more than madness, seeing they did not shrink with horror from contriving the death of a brother so pious and humane. We now see that Moses does not relate, without a purpose, that a man met Joseph in his wanderings, and told him that his brethren had departed to Dothan. For the greater was his diligence in his indefatigable pursuit, so much the less excusable were they by whom such an unworthy recompense was repaid.

18. *And when they saw him afar off.* Here again Moses, so far from sparing the fame of his own family by adulation, brands its chiefs with a mark of eternal infamy, and exposes them to the hatred and execration of all nations. If, at any time, among heathens, a brother murdered his brother, such impiety was treated with the utmost severity in tragedies, that it might not pass into an example for imitation. But in profane history no such thing is found, as that nine brethren should conspire together for the destruction of an innocent youth, and, like wild beasts, should pounce upon him with bloody hands. Therefore a horrible, and even diabolical fury, took possession of the sons of Jacob, when, having cast aside the sense of nature, they were thus prepared cruelly to rage against their own blood.

But, in addition to this wickedness, Moses condemns their impious contempt of God, *Behold this master of dreams.* For why do they insult the unhappy youth, except because he had been called by the celestial oracle to an unexpected dignity? Besides, in this manner, they themselves proclaim their own baseness more publicly than any one could do, who should purposely undertake severely to chastise them. They confess that the cause why they persecuted their brother was his having dreamed; as if truly this was an inexpiable offence; but if they are indignant at his dreams, why do they not rather wage war with God? For Joseph deemed it necessary to receive, as a precious deposit, what had been divinely revealed unto him. But because they did not dare directly to assail God, they wrap themselves in clouds, that, losing sight of God, they may vent their fury against their brother. If such blindness seized upon the patriarchs, what shall become of the reprobates, whom obstinate malice drives along, so that they do not hesitate to resist God even to the last? And we see that they willingly disturb and excite themselves, as often as they are offended with the threatenings and chastisements of God, and rise up against his ministers for the sake of taking vengeance. The same thing, indeed, would at times happen to us all, unless God should put on his bridle to render us submissive. With respect to Joseph, the special favour of God was manifested to him, and he was raised to the highest dignity; but only in a dream, which is ridiculed by the wicked scorn of his brethren. To this is also added a conspiracy, so that he narrowly escaped death. Thus the promise of God, which had exalted him to honour, almost plunges him into the grave. We, also, who have received the gratuitous adoption of God amidst many sorrows, experience the same thing. For, from the time that Christ gathers us into his flock, God permits us to be cast down in various ways, so that we seem nearer hell than heaven. Therefore, let the example of Joseph be fixed in our minds, that we be not disquieted when many crosses spring forth to us from the root of God's favour. For I have before showed, and the thing itself clearly testifies, that in Joseph was adumbrated, what was afterwards more fully exhibited in Christ, the Head of the Church, in order that each member may form itself to the imitation of his example.

20. *And cast him into some pit.* Before they perpetrate the murder, they seek a pretext whereby they may conceal their crime from men. Meanwhile, it never enters into their mind, that what is hidden from men cannot escape the eyes of God. But so stupid is hypocrisy, that while it flees from the disgrace of the world, it is careless about the judgment of God. But it is a disease deeply rooted in the human mind, to put some specious colour on every extreme act of iniquity. For although an inward judge convicts the guilty, they yet confirm themselves in .impudence, that their disgrace may not appear unto others.

*And we shall see what will become of his dreams.* As if the truth of God could be subverted by the death of one man, they boast that they shall have attained their wish when they have killed their brother; namely, that his dreams will come to nothing. This is not, indeed, their avowed purpose, but turbulent envy drives them headlong to fight against God. But whatever they design in thus contending with God in the dark, their attempts will, at length, prove vain. For God will always find a way through the most profound abyss, to the accomplishment of what he has decreed. If, then, unbelievers provoke us by their reproaches, and proudly boast that our faith will profit us nothing; let not their insolence discourage or weaken us, but let us confidently proceed.

21. *And Reuben heard it.* It may be well to observe, while others were hastening to shed his blood, by whose care Joseph was preserved. Reuben doubtless, in one affair, was the most wicked of them all, when he defiled his father's couch ; and that unbridled lust, involving other vices, was the sign of a depraved nature : now suddenly, he alone, having a regard to piety, and being mindful of fraternal duty, dissolves the impious conspiracy. It is uncertain whether he was now seeking the means of making some compensation, for the sake of which he might be restored to his father's favour. Moses declares that it was his intention to restore the boy in safety to his father : whence the conjecture which I have stated is probable, that he thought the life of his brother would be a sufficient price by which he might reconcile his father's mind to himself. However this may be, yet the humanity which he showed in attempting to liberate his brother, is a proof that he was not abandoned to every kind of wickedness. And perhaps God, by this testimony of his penitence, designed in some degree to lessen his former disgrace. Whence we are taught that the characters of men are not to be estimated by a single act, however atrocious, so as to cause us to despair of their salvation.

22. *Cast him into this pit.* The pious fallacy to which Reuben descended, sufficiently proves with what vehemence the rage of his brethren was burning. For he neither dares openly to oppose them, nor to dissuade them from their crime ; because he saw that no reasons would avail to soften them. Nor does it extenuate their cruelty, that they consent to his proposal, as if they were disposed to clemency ; for if either one course or the other were necessary, it would have been better for him immediately to die by their hands, than to perish by slow hunger in the pit, which is the most cruel kind of punishment. Their gross hypocrisy is rather to be noticed ; because they think that they shall be free from crime, if only they do not stain their hands with their brother's blood. As if, indeed, it made any difference, whether

they ran their brother through with a sword, or put him to death by suffocation. For the Lord, when he accuses the Jews by Isaiah, of having hands full of blood, does not mean that they were assassins, but he calls them bloody, because they did not spare their suffering brethren. Therefore, the sons of Jacob are nothing better, in casting their brother alive under ground, that, as one buried, he might in vain contend with death, and perish after protracted torments; and in choosing a pit in the desert, from which no mortal could hear his dying cry, though his sighing would ascend even to heaven. It was a barbarous thought, that they should not touch his life, if they did not embrue their hands in his blood; since it was a kind of death, not less violent, which they wished to inflict by hunger. Reuben, however, accommodating his language to their brutal conceptions, deemed it sufficient to repress, by any kind of artifice, their impetuosity for the present.

23. *They stripped Joseph out of his coat.*[1] We see that these men are full of fictions and lies. They carelessly strip their brother; they feel no dread at casting him with their own hands into the pit, where hunger worse than ten swords might consume him; because they hope their crime will be concealed; and in taking home his clothes, no suspicion of his murder would be excited; because, truly, their father would believe that he had been torn by a wild beast. Thus Satan infatuates wicked minds, so that they entangle themselves by frivolous evasions. Conscience is indeed the fountain of modesty; but Satan so soothes by his allurements those whom he has entangled in his snares, that conscience itself, which ought to have cited them as guilty before the bar of God, only hardens them the more. For, having found out

---

[1] The coat of many colours was supposed by some to be the garment belonging of right to the first-born; consequently, Reuben would be entitled to it, till he forfeited it by his misconduct. Jacob, therefore, is understood to have transferred this coat, together with the rank of primogeniture, from Reuben to the eldest son of Rachel, his most beloved wife. If this were so, it would make the conduct of Reuben, on this occasion, still more generous than it appears on the ordinary supposition. There is, however, this objection to such an interpretation, that Jacob is said to have *made it* for Joseph, (see ver. 3,) and not merely to have *given it* to him.— *Ed.*

subterfuges, they break forth far more audaciously into sin, as if they might commit with impunity whatever escapes the eyes of men. Surely it is a reprobate sense, a spirit of frenzy and of stupor, which is withheld from any daring attempt, only by a fear of the shame of men; while the fear of divine judgment is trodden under foot. And although all are not carried thus far, yet the fault of paying more honour to men than to God, is too common. The repetition of the word *coat* in the sentence of Moses is emphatical, showing that this mark of the father's love could not mollify their minds.

25. *And they sat down to eat bread.* This was an astonishing barbarity, that they could quietly feast, while, in intention, they were guilty of their brother's death: for, had there been one drop of humanity in their souls, they would at least have felt some inward compunctions; yea, commonly, the very worst men are afraid after the commission of a crime. Since the patriarchs fell into such a state of insensibility, let us learn, from their example, to fear lest, by the righteous anger of God, the same lethargy should seize upon our senses. Meanwhile, it is proper to consider the admirable progress of God's counsel. Joseph had already passed through a double death: and now, as if by a third death, he is, beyond all expectation, rescued from the grave. For what was it less than death, to be sold as a slave to foreigners? Indeed his condition was rendered worse by the change; because Reuben, secretly drawing him out of the pit, would have brought him back to his father: whereas now he is dragged to a distant part of the earth, without hope of return. But this was a secret turn, by which God had determined to raise him on high. And at length, he shows by the event, how much better it was that Joseph should be led far away from his own family, than that he should remain in safety at home. Moreover, the speech of Judah, by which he persuades his brethren *to sell* Joseph, has somewhat more reason. For he ingenuously confesses that they would be guilty of homicide, if they suffered him to perish in the pit. What gain shall we make, he says, if his blood be covered; for our hands will nevertheless be polluted with blood. By this time their fury was in some degree abated, so that they listened to

more humane counsel; for though it was outrageous perfidy to sell their brother to strangers; yet it was something to send him away alive, that, at least, he might be nourished as a slave. We see, therefore, that the diabolical flame of madness, with which they had all burned, was abating, when they acknowledged that they could profit nothing by hiding their crime from the eyes of men; because homicide must of necessity come into view before God. For at first, they absolved themselves from guilt, as if no Judge sat in heaven. But now the sense of nature, which the cruelty of hatred had before benumbed, begins to exert its power. And certainly, even in the reprobate, who seem entirely to have cast off humanity, time shows that some residue of it remains. When wicked and violent affections rage, their tumultuous fervour hinders nature from acting its part. But no minds are so stupid, that a consideration of their own wickedness will not sometimes fill them with remorse: for, in order that men may come inexcusable to the judgment-seat of God, it is necessary that they should first be condemned by themselves. They who are capable of cure, and whom the Lord leads to repentance, differ from the reprobates in this, that while the latter obstinately conceal the knowledge of their crimes, the former gradually return from the indulgence of sin, to obey the voice of reason. Moreover, what Judah here declares concerning his brother, the Lord, by the prophet, extends to the whole human race. Whenever, therefore, depraved lust impels to unjust violence, or any other injury, let us remember this sacred bond by which the whole of society is bound together, in order that it may restrain us from evil doings. For man cannot injure man, but he becomes an enemy to his own flesh, and violates and perverts the whole order of nature.

28. *Then there passed by Midianites.* Some think that Joseph was twice sold in the same place. For it is certain, since Midian was the son of Abraham and Keturah, that his sons were distinct from the sons of Ishmael: and Moses has not thoughtlessly put down these different names.[1]

---

[1] Perhaps, however, the passage may be better explained by supposing the caravan which was passing, to be made up of Ishmaelites and Midianites. The Ishmaelites might form the larger and more conspicuous part of the

But I thus interpret the passage: that Joseph was exposed for sale to any one who chose, and seeing the purchase of him was declined by the Midianites, he was sold to the Ishmaelites. Moreover, though they might justly suspect the sellers of having stolen him, yet the desire of gain prevents them from making inquiry. We may also add, what is probable, that, on the journey, they inquired who Joseph was. But they did not set such a value on their common origin as to prevent them from eagerly making gain. This passage, however, teaches us how far the sons of Abraham, after the flesh, were preferred to the elect offspring, in which, nevertheless, the hope of the future Church was included. We see that, of the two sons of Abraham, a posterity so great was propagated, that from both proceeded merchants in various places : while that part of his seed which the Lord had chosen to himself was yet small. But so the children of this world, like premature fruit, quickly arrive at the greatest wealth and at the summit of happiness ; whereas the Church, slowly creeping through the greatest difficulties, scarcely attains, during a long period, to the condition of mediocrity.

30. *And he returned.* We may hence gather that Reuben, under pretence of some other business, stole away from his brethren, that, unknown to them all, he might restore his brother, drawn out of the pit, to his father ; and that therefore he was absent at the time when Joseph was sold. And there is no wonder that he was anticipated, when he had taken his course in a different direction from theirs, intending to reach the pit by a circuitous path. But now at length Reuben having lost all hope, unfolds to his brethren the intention which before he dared not confess, lest the boy should be immediately murdered.

31. *And they took Joseph's coat.* They now return to their first scheme. In order that their father may have no suspicion of their crime, they send the bloody coat, from which he might conjecture that Joseph had been torn by some wild beast. Although Moses alludes to this briefly, I yet think that they rather sent some of their servants, who

company, and thus give the name to the whole ; but the actual purchasers of Joseph might be the Midianitish merchants among them.—*Ed.*

were not accessary to the crime, than any of their number. For he says soon afterwards, that his sons and daughters came to offer some consolation to him in his grief. And although in the words they use, there lurks some appearance of insult, it seems to me more probable that they gave this command to avert suspicion from themselves. For they feign themselves to be of confused mind, as is usual in affairs of perplexity. Yet whatever they intend, their wickedness drives them to this point, that they inflict a deadly wound upon the mind of their father. This is the profit which hypocrites gain by their disguises, that in wishing to escape the consequences of one fault, they add sin to sin. With respect to Jacob, it is a wonder that after he had been tried in so many ways, and always come forth a conqueror, he should now sink under grief. Certainly it was very absurd that the death of his son should occasion him greater sorrow than the incestuous pollution of his wife, the slaughter of the Shechemites, and the defilement of his daughter. Where was that invincible strength, by which he had even prevailed over the angel? Where the many lessons of patience with which God had exercised him, in order that he might never fail? This disposition to mourn, teaches us that no one is endued with such heroic virtues, as to be exempt from that infirmity of the flesh, which betrays itself sometimes even in little things; whence also it happens, that they who have long been accustomed to the cross, and who like veteran soldiers ought bravely to bear up against every kind of attack, fall like young recruits in some slight skirmish. Who then among us may not fear for himself, when we see holy Jacob faint, after having given so many proofs of patience?

35. *And all his sons and daughters rose up.* The burden of his grief is more clearly expressed by the circumstance that all his sons and daughters meet together to comfort him. For by the term " rose up," is implied a common deliberation, they having agreed to come together, because necessity urged them. But hence it appears how vast is the innate dissimulation of men. The sons of Jacob assume a character by no means suitable to them; and perform an office of piety, from which their minds are most alien. If they had

had respect unto God, they would have acknowledged their fault, and though no remedy might have been found for their evil, yet repentance would have brought forth some fruit; but now they are satisfied with a vanity as empty as the wind. By this example we are taught how carefully we ought to avoid dissimulation, which continually implicates men in new snares.

*But he refused to be comforted.* It may be asked, whether Jacob had entirely cast off the virtue of patience: for so much the language seems to mean. Besides, he sins more grievously, because he, knowingly and voluntarily, indulges in grief: for this is as if he would purposely augment his sorrow, which is to rebel against God. But I suppose his refusal to be restricted to that alleviation of grief which man might offer. For nothing is more unreasonable than that a holy man, who, all his life had borne the yoke of God with such meekness of disposition, should now, like an unbroken horse, bite his bridle; in order that, by nourishing his grief, he might confirm himself in unsubdued impetuosity. I therefore do not doubt that he was willing now to submit himself unto the Lord, though he rejects human consolations. He seems also angrily to chide his sons, whose envy and malevolence towards Joseph he knew, as if he would upbraid them by declaring that he esteemed this one son more than all the rest: since he rather desires to be with him, dead in the grave, than to enjoy the society of ten living sons whom he had yet remaining; for I except little Benjamin. I do not, however, here excuse that excess of grief which I have lately condemned. And certainly he proves himself to be overwhelmed with sadness, in speaking of the grave, as if the sons of God did not pass through death to a better life. And hence we learn the blindness of immoderate grief, which almost quenches the light of faith in the saints; so much the more diligent, then, ought we to be in our endeavour to restrain it. Job greatly excelled in piety; yet we see, after he had been oppressed by the magnitude of his grief, in what a profane manner he mixes men with beasts in death. If the angelic minds of holy men were thus darkened by sadness, how much deeper gloom will rest upon us, unless God, by the shining of his word and Spirit, should scatter it, and we also, with suitable anxiety, meet the temptation, before it overwhelms us? The principal mitigation of sorrow is the consolation of the future life; to which whosoever applies himself, need not fear lest he should be absorbed by excess of grief. Now though the immoderate sorrow of Jacob is not to be approved; yet the special design of Moses was, to set a mark of infamy on that iron hardness which cruelly reigned in the hearts of his sons. They saw that, if their father should miserably perish, consumed with grief, they would be the cause of it; in short, they saw that he was already dying through their wickedness. If they are not able to heal the wound, why, at least, do they not attempt to alleviate his pain? Therefore they are exceedingly cruel, seeing that they have not sufficient care of their father's life, to cause them to drop a single word in mitigation of his sorrow, when it was in their power to do so.

36. *And the Midianites sold him into Egypt.* It was a sad spectacle, that Joseph should be thus driven from one hand to another. For it added no small indignity to his former suffering, that he is set to sale as a slave. The Lord, however, ceased not to care for him. He even suffered him to be transferred from hand to hand, in order that, at length, it might indeed appear, that he had come, by celestial guidance, to that very dominion which had been promised him in his dreams. Potiphar is called a eunuch, not because he was one really; but because, among the Orientals, it was usual to denote the satraps and princes of the court by that name. The Hebrews are not agreed respecting the dignity which Moses ascribes to him; for some explain it as the " chief of the slaughterers,"[1] whom the Greek interpreters follow. But I rather agree with others, who say that he was " the prefect of the soldiers;" not that he had the command of the whole army, but because he had the royal troops under his hand and authority: such are now the captains of the guard, if

---

[1] The term applies primarily to butchers, who slaughter animals for *food;* then to persons who slaughter animals for *sacrifice;* and then to executioners who put men to the slaughter under the authority of the monarch or the state.— *Ed.*

you join with it another office which the prefects of the prison exercise. For this may be gathered from the thirty-ninth chapter.[1]

## CHAPTER XXXVIII.

1. AND it came to pass at that time, that Judah went down from his brethren, and turned in to a certain Adullamite, whose name *was* Hirah.
2. And Judah saw there a daughter of a certain Canaanite, whose name *was* Shuah; and he took her, and went in unto her.
3. And she conceived, and bare a son; and he called his name Er.
4. And she conceived again, and bare a son; and she called his name Onan.
5. And she yet again conceived, and bare a son; and called his name Shelah: and he was at Chezib when she bare him.
6. And Judah took a wife for Er his first-born, whose name *was* Tamar.
7. And Er, Judah's first-born, was wicked in the sight of the Lord; and the Lord slew him.
8. And Judah said unto Onan, Go in unto thy brother's wife, and marry her, and raise up seed to thy brother.
9. And Onan knew that the seed should not be his: and it came to pass, when he went in unto his brother's wife, that he spilled *it* on the ground, lest that he should give seed to his brother.
10. And the thing which he did displeased the Lord; wherefore he slew him also.
11. Then said Judah to Tamar his daughter-in-law, Remain a widow

1. Fuit autem tempore illo descendit Jehudah a fratribus suis, et declinavit ad virum Hadullamitem, et nomen ejus Hirah.
2. Et vidit ibi Jehudah filiam viri Chenaanaei: et nomen ejus Suah: qui accepit eam, et ingressus est ad eam.
3. Quæ concepit, et peperit filium, et vocavit nomen ejus Her.
4. Et concepit adhuc, et peperit filium, et vocavit nomen ejus Onan.
5. Et addidit adhuc, et peperit filium, et vocavit nomen ejus Selah: erat autem in Chezib, quando hunc ipsa peperit.
6. Et accepit Jehudah uxorem ipsi Her primogenito suo, et nomen ejus Thamar.
7. Verum erat Her primogenitus Jehudah malus in oculis Jehovæ, ideo interemit eum Jehova.
8. Et dixit Jehudah ad Onan, Ingredere ad uxorem fratris tui, et affinitatem contrahe cum ea, et suscita semen fratri tuo.
9. Et cognovit Onan, quod non sibi futurum esset semen: et erat quando ingrediebatur ad uxorem fratris sui, corrumpebat *semen* super terram, ne poneret semen fratri suo.
10. Displicuit autem in oculis Jehovæ quod fecit, ideoque mori fecit etiam eum.
11. Et dixit Jehudah ad Thamar nurum suam, Mane vidua in domo

---

[1] See ver. 20. The words rendered " prefects of the prison," are præfecti hospitii—and in the French, Prevosts de l'hostel—perhaps, prefects of the town-house, or town-hall, would have been more correct. The expression in the original, שׂר־הטבחים, *sar-hatabachim*, means the captain of the executioners; that is, of the king's body guard, whose office it was to inflict capital punishments; as in the Turkish court at present.—*See Gesenius' Lexicon.—Ed.*

at thy father's house, till Shelah my son be grown: for he said, Lest peradventure he die also, as his brethren *did*. And Tamar went and dwelt in her father's house.

12. And, in process of time, the daughter of Shuah, Judah's wife, died: and Judah was comforted, and went up unto his sheep-shearers to Timnath, he and his friend Hirah the Adullamite.

13. And it was told Tamar, saying, Behold, thy father-in-law goeth up to Timnath to shear his sheep.

14. And she put her widow's garments off from her, and covered her with a vail, and wrapped herself, and sat in an open place, which *is* by the way to Timnath: for she saw that Shelah was grown, and she was not given unto him to wife.

15. When Judah saw her, he thought her *to be* an harlot; because she had covered her face.

16. And he turned unto her by the way, and said, Go to, I pray thee, let me come in unto thee; (for he knew not that she *was* his daughter-in-law.) And she said, What wilt thou give me, that thou mayest come in unto me?

17. And he said, I will send *thee* a kid from the flock. And she said, Wilt thou give *me* a pledge till thou send *it?*

18. And he said, What pledge shall I give thee? And she said, Thy signet, and thy bracelets, and thy staff that *is* in thine hand: and he gave *it* her, and came in unto her; and she conceived by him.

19. And she arose, and went away, and laid by her vail from her, and put on the garments of her widowhood.

20. And Judah sent the kid by the hand of his friend the Adullamite, to receive *his* pledge from the woman's hand; but he found her not.

21. Then he asked the men of that place, saying, Where *is* the harlot that *was* openly by the way-side? And they said, There was no harlot in this *place*.

patris tui, donec crescat Selah filius meus: dicebat enim, Ne forte moriatur etiam ipse, sicut et fratres ejus, et abiit Thamar, et mansit in domo patris sui.

12. Et multiplicati sunt dies, et mortua est filia Suah uxor Jehudah: et consolatus est se Jehudah, et ascendit ad tonsores ovium suarum, ipse, et Hirah amicus ejus, Hadullamita in Thimnath.

13. Et nuntiatum fuit ipsi Thamar, dicendo, Ecce, socer tuus ascendit in Thimnath ad tondendum oves suas.

14. Tunc removit vestes viduitatis suæ a se, et operuit *se* velamine, et celavit se, mansitque in ostio Henaim, quod erat juxta viam Thimnath: viderat enim quod creverat Selah, ipsa vero non fuerat data ei in uxorem.

15. Et vidit eam Jehudah, et putavit eam esse meretricem: operuerat enim faciem suam.

16. Et declinavit ad eam e via: et dixit, Age quæso, ingrediar ad te (non enim noverat quod nurus sua esset). Illa dixit, Quid dabis mihi, si ingrediaris ad me?

17. Et ait, Ego mittam hœdum caprarum de pecudibus. Et dixit, Num dabis pignus donec miseris?

18. Et dixit, Quod pignus vis ut dem tibi? Et dixit, Sigillum tuum, et pallium tuum, et virgam tuam, quæ est in manu tua. Et dedit ei: et ingressus est ad eam, et concepit ex eo.

19. Illa surrexit, et abiit, et removit velamen suum a se, et induit se vestibus viduitatis suæ.

20. Et misit Jehudah hœdum caprarum per manum amici sui Hadullamitæ, ut caperet pignus e manu mulieris; qui non invenit eam.

21. Et interrogavit viros loci illius, dicendo, Ubi est meretrix illa in Henaim juxta viam? Et dixerunt, Non fuit hic meretrix.

22. And he returned to Judah, and said, I cannot find her; and also the men of the place said, *that* there was no harlot in this *place*.

23. And Judah said, Let her take *it* to her, lest we be shamed: behold, I sent this kid, and thou hast not found her.

24. And it came to pass, about three months after, that it was told Judah, saying, Tamar thy daughter-in-law hath played the harlot; and also, behold, she *is* with child by whoredom. And Judah said, Bring her forth, and let her be burnt.

25. When *she* was brought forth, she sent to her father-in-law, saying, By the man whose these *are am* I with child: and she said, Discern, I pray thee, whose *are* these, the signet, and bracelets, and staff.

26. And Judah acknowledged *them*, and said, She hath been more righteous than I; because that I gave her not to Shelah my son: and he knew her again no more.

27. And it came to pass, in the time of her travail, that, behold, twins *were* in her womb.

28. And it came to pass, when she travailed, that *the one* put out *his* hand; and the midwife took and bound upon his hand a scarlet thread, saying, This came out first.

29. And it came to pass, as he drew back his hand, that, behold, his brother came out; and she said, How hast thou broken forth? *this* breach *be* upon thee: therefore his name was called Pharez.

30. And afterward came out his brother, that had the scarlet thread upon his hand; and his name was called Zarah.

22. Reversus est ergo ad Jehudah, et dixit, Non inveni eam: et etiam viri illius loci dixerunt, Non fuit hic meretrix.

23. Et dixit Jehudah, Capiat sibi, ne forte simus in probrum: ecce, misi hœdum hunc, et tu non invenisti eam.

24. Et fuit, circiter post tres menses, nuntiatum fuit ipsi Jehudah, dicendo, Fornicata est Thamar nurus tua, et etiam ecce, est gravida ex fornicationibus. Et dixit Jehudah, Educite eam, et comburatur.

25. Ipsa, quum educeretur, misit ad socerum suum, dicendo, De viro cujus hæc sunt, sum gravida. Et dixit, Agnosce quæso, cujus sint sigillum, et pallium, et virga isthæc.

26. Et agnovit Jehudah, et dixit, Justior me est: idcirco enim *hæc fecit*, quod non dedi eam Selah filio meo. Verum non addidit adhuc cognoscere eam.

27. Et fuit, in tempore quo parturiebat ipsa, ecce, gemini erant in utero ejus.

28. Fuit autem, ea pariente, *unus* dedit manum, et accepit obstetrix, et ligavit ad manum ejus coccinum, dicendo, Iste egressus est prior.

29. Et fuit, quum retraheret manum suam, ecce, egressus est frater ejus, et dixit, Cur rupisti super te interstitium? et vocavit nomen ejus Peres.

30. Et postea egressus est frater ejus, ad cujus manum erat coccinum: et vocavit nomen ejus Zerah.

1. *And it came to pass at that time, that Judah.* Before Moses proceeds in relating the history of Joseph, he inserts the genealogy of Judah, to which he devotes more labour, because the Redeemer was thence to derive his origin; for the continuous history of that tribe, from which salvation was to be sought, could not remain unknown, without loss. And yet its glorious nobility is not here celebrated, but the

greatest disgrace of the family is exposed. What is here related, so far from inflating the minds of the sons of Judah, ought rather to cover them with shame. Now although, at first sight, the dignity of Christ seems to be somewhat tarnished by such dishonour: yet since here also is seen that "emptying" of which St. Paul speaks,[1] it rather redounds to his glory, than, in the least degree, detracts from it. First, we wrong Christ, unless we deem him alone sufficient to blot out any ignominy arising from the misconduct of his progenitors, which offer to unbelievers occasion of offence. Secondly, we know that the riches of God's grace shines chiefly in this, that Christ clothed himself in our flesh, with the design of making himself of no reputation. Lastly, it was fitting that the race from which he sprang should be dishonoured by reproaches, that we, being content with him alone, might seek nothing besides him; yea, that we might not seek earthly splendour in him, seeing that carnal ambition is always too much inclined to such a course. These two things, then, we may notice; first, that peculiar honour was given to the tribe of Judah, which had been divinely elected as the source whence the salvation of the world should flow; and secondly, that the narration of Moses is by no means honourable to the persons of whom he speaks; so that the Jews have no right to arrogate anything to themselves or to their fathers. Meanwhile, let us remember that Christ derives no glory from his ancestors; and even, that he himself has no glory in the flesh, but that his chief and most illustrious triumph was on the cross. Moreover, that we may not be offended at the stains with which his ancestry was defiled, let us know that, by his infinite purity, they were all cleansed; just as the sun, by absorbing whatever impurities are in the earth and air, purges the world.

2. *And Judah saw there a daughter of a certain Canaanite.* I am not satisfied with the interpretation which some give of "merchant" to the word Canaanite. For Moses charges Judah with perverse lust, because he took a wife out of that nation with which the children of Abraham were divinely

---

[1] Phil. ii. 7. " But made himself of no reputation," literally, " emptied himself, ἑαυτὸν ἐκένωσι."—*Ed.*

commanded to be at perpetual strife. For neither he nor his other brethren were ignorant that they sojourned in the land of Canaan, under the stipulation, that afterwards their enemies were to be cut off and destroyed, in order that they might possess the promised dominion over it. Moses, therefore, justly regards it as a fault, that Judah should entangle himself in a forbidden alliance; and the Lord, at length, cursed the offspring thus accruing to Judah, that the prince and head of the tribe of Judah might not be born, nor Christ himself descend, from this connexion. This also ought to be numbered among the exercises of Jacob's patience, that a wicked grandson was born to him through Judah, of whose sin he was not ignorant. Moses says, that the youth was cut off by the vengeance of God. The same thing is not said of others whom a sudden death has swept away in the flower of their age. I doubt not, therefore, that the wickedness, of which death was the immediate punishment, was extraordinary, and known to all men. And although this trial was in itself severe to the holy patriarch; yet nothing tormented his mind more than the thought, that he could scarcely hope for the promise of God to be so ratified that the inheritance of grace should remain in the possession of wicked and abandoned men. It is true that a large family of children is regarded as a source of human happiness. But this was the peculiar condition of the holy patriarch, that, though God had promised him an elect and blessed seed, he now sees an accursed progeny increase and shoot forth together with his offspring, which might destroy the expected grace. It is said, that *Er was wicked in the sight of the Lord*, (verse 7.) Notwithstanding, his iniquity was not hidden from men. Moses, however, means that he was not merely infected with common vices, but rather was so addicted to crimes, that he was intolerable in the sight of God.

7. *And the Lord slew him.* We know that long life is reckoned among the gifts of God; and justly: for since it is by no means a despicable honour that we are created after the image of God, the longer any one lives in the world, and daily experiences God's care over him, it is certain that he is the more bountifully dealt with by the Lord. Even

amidst the many miseries with which life is filled, this divine goodness still shines forth, that God invites us to himself, and exercises us in the knowledge of himself; while at the same time he adorns us with such dignity, that he subjects to our authority whatever is in the world. Wherefore it is no wonder that God, as an act of kindness, prolongs the life of man. Whence it follows, that when the wicked are taken away by a premature death, a punishment for their wickedness is inflicted upon them: for it is as if the Lord should pronounce judgment from heaven, that they are unworthy to be sustained by the earth, unworthy to enjoy the common light of heaven. Let us therefore learn, as long as God keeps us in the world, to meditate on his benefits, to the end that every one may the more cheerfully endeavour to give praise to God for the life received from him. And although, at the present day also, sudden death is to be reckoned among the scourges of God; since that doctrine is always true, " Bloody and deceitful men shall not live out half their days," (Ps. lv. 23;) yet God executed this judgment more fully under the law, when the knowledge of a future life was comparatively obscure; for now, since the resurrection is clearly manifested to us in Christ, it is not right that death should be so greatly dreaded. And this difference between us and the ancient people of God is elsewhere noted. Nevertheless, it can never be laid down as a general rule, that they who had a long life were thereby proved to be pleasing and acceptable to the Lord, whereas God has sometimes lengthened the life of reprobates, in aggravation of their punishment. We know that Cain survived his brother Abel many centuries. But as God does not always, and to all persons, cause his temporal benefits manifestly to flow in a perpetual and equable course; so neither, on the other hand, does he always execute temporal punishments by the same rule. It is enough that, as far as the present life is concerned, certain examples of punishments and rewards are set before us. Moreover, as the miseries of the present life, which spring from the corruption of nature, do not extinguish the first and special grace of God; so, on the other hand, death, which is in itself the curse of God, is so far from doing any injury, that it tends, by a supernatural remedy, to the salvation of the elect. Especially now, from the time that the first-fruits of the resurrection in Christ have been offered, the condition of those who are quickly taken out of life is in no way deteriorated; because Christ himself is gain both for life and death. But the vengeance of God was so clear and remarkable in the death of Er, that the earth might plainly appear to have been purged as from its filthiness.

8. *Go in unto thy brother's wife.* Although no law had hitherto been prescribed concerning brother's marriages, that the surviving brother should raise up seed to one who was dead; it is, nevertheless, not wonderful that, by the mere instinct of nature, men should have been inclined to this course. For since each man is born for the preservation of the whole race, if any one dies without children, there seems to be here some defect of nature. It was deemed therefore an act of humanity to acquire some name for the dead, from which it might appear that they had lived. Now, the only reason why the children born to the surviving brother, should be reckoned to him who had died, was, that there might be no dry branch in the family; and in this manner they took away the reproach of barrenness. Besides, since the woman is given as a help to the man, when any woman married into a family, she was, in a certain sense, given up to the name of that family. According to this reasoning, Tamar was not altogether free, but was held under an obligation to the house of Judah, to procreate some seed. Now, though this does not proceed from any rule of piety, yet the Lord had impressed it upon the hearts of man as a duty of humanity; as he afterwards commanded it to the Jews in their polity. Hence we infer the malignity of Onan, who envied his brother this honour, and would not allow him, when dead, to obtain the title of father; and this redounds to the dishonour of the whole family. We see that many grant their own sons to their friends for adoption: it was, therefore, an outrageous act of barbarity to deny to his own brother what is given even to strangers. . . . .[1]

[1] A line or two is here omitted, as well as the comment on the tenth verse.—*Ed.*

11. *Then said Judah to Tamar.* Moses intimates that Tamar was not at liberty to marry into another family, so long as Judah wished to retain her under his own authority. It is possible that she voluntarily submitted herself to the will of her father-in-law, when she might have refused: but the language seems to mean, that it was according to a received practice, that Tamar should not pass over to another family, except at the will of her father-in-law, as long as there was a successor who might raise up seed by her. However this may be, Judah acted very unjustly in keeping one bound, whom he intended to defraud. For truly there was no cause why he should be unwilling to allow her to depart free from his house, unless he dreaded the charge of inconstancy. But he should not have allowed this ambitious sense of shame to render him perfidious and cruel to his daughter-in-law. Besides, this injury sprung from a wrong judgment: because, without considering the causes of the death of his sons, he falsely and unjustly transfers the blame to an innocent woman. He believes the marriage with Tamar to have been an unhappy one; why therefore does he not, for his own sake, permit her to seek a husband elsewhere? But in this also he does wrong, that whereas the cause of his sons' destruction was their own wickedness, he judges unfavourably of Tamar herself, to whom no evil could be imputed. Let us then learn from this example, whenever anything adverse happens to us, not to transfer the blame to another, nor to gather from all quarters doubtful suspicions, but to shake off our own sins. We must also beware lest a foolish shame should so prevail over us, that while we endeavour to preserve our reputation uninjured among men, we should not be equally careful to maintain a good conscience before God.

13. *And it was told Tamar.* Moses relates how Tamar avenged herself for the injury done her. She did not at first perceive the fraud, but discovered it after a long course of time. When Shelah had grown up, finding herself deceived, she turned her thoughts to revenge. And it is not to be doubted that she had long meditated, and, as it were, hatched this design. For the message respecting Judah's departure was not brought to her accidentally; but, because she

was intent upon her purpose, she had set spies who should bring her an account of all his doings. Now, although she formed a plan which was base, and unworthy of a modest woman, yet this circumstance is some alleviation of her crime, that she did not desire a connexion with Judah, except while in a state of celibacy. In the meantime, she is hurried, by a blind error of mind, into another crime, not less detestable than adultery. For, by adultery, conjugal fidelity would have been violated; but, by this incestuous intercourse, the whole dignity of nature is subverted. This ought carefully to be observed, that they who are injured should not hastily rush to unlawful remedies. It was not lust which impelled Tamar to prostitute herself. She grieved, indeed, that she had been forbidden to marry, that she might remain barren at home: but she had no other purpose than to reproach her father-in-law with the fraud by which he had deceived her: at the same time, we see that she committed an atrocious crime. This is wont to happen, even in good causes, when any one indulges his carnal affections more than is right. What Moses alludes to respecting garments of widowhood, pertains to the law of modesty. For elegant clothing which may attract the eyes of men, does not become widows. And therefore, Paul concedes more to wives than to them; as having husbands whom they should wish to please.

14. *And sat in an open place.*[1] Interpreters expound this passage variously. Literally, it is " in the door of fountains, or of eyes." Some suppose there was a fountain which branched into two streams; others think that a broad place is indicated, in which the eyes may look around in all directions. But a third exposition is more worthy of reception; namely, that by this expression is meant a way which is forked and divided into two; because then, as it were, a door is opened before the eyes, that they which are really in one way may diverge in two directions. Probably it was a place whence Tamar might be seen, to which some by-way was near, where Judah might turn, so that he should not be guilty of fornication, in a public way, under

---

[1] Mansitque in ostio Henaim, " in the door of eyes, or Enajim."—*Margin of English Version.*—*Ed.*

the eyes of all. When it is said she veiled her face, we hence infer that the license of fornication was not so unbridled as that which, at this day, prevails in many places. For she dressed herself after the manner of harlots, that Judah might suspect nothing. And the Lord has caused this sense of shame to remain engraven on the hearts of those who live wickedly, that they may be witnesses to themselves of their own vileness. For if men could wash out the stains from their sins, we know that they would do so most willingly. Whence it follows, that while they flee from the light, they are affected with horror against their will, that their conscience may anticipate the judgment of God. By degrees, indeed, the greater part have so far exceeded all measure in stupor and impudence, that they are less careful to hide their faults; yet God has never suffered the sense of nature to be so entirely extinguished, by the brutal intemperance of those who desire to sin with impunity, but that their own obscenity shall compel even the most wicked to be ashamed.[1] In short, the veil of Tamar shows that fornication was not only a base and filthy thing in the sight of God and the angels; but that it has always been condemned, even by those who have practised it.

15. *When Judah saw her.* It was a great disgrace to Judah that he hastily desired intercourse with an unknown woman. He was now old; and therefore age alone, even in a lascivious man, ought to have restrained the fervour of intemperance. He sees the woman at a distance, and it is not possible that he should have been captivated by her beauty.[2] . . . Hence we gather, that the fear of God, or a regard to justice and prosperity, cannot have flourished greatly in the heart of one who thus eagerly breaks forth to the indulgence of his passions. He is therefore set before us as an example, that we may learn how easily the lust of the flesh would break forth, unless the Lord should restrain it; and thus, conscious of our infirmity, let us desire from the Lord, a spirit

---

[1] The following sentence is omitted in the translation. " Putida igitur fuit Cynici illius protervia, qui in flagitio deprehensus, sine rubore jactavit se plantare hominem."

[2] The original here adds, " Pruritus tamen non secus in eo accenditur quam in equo, qui ad equarum odorem adhinnit."

of continence and moderation. But lest the same security should steal over us, which caused Judah to precipitate himself into fornication ; let us mark, that the dishonour which Judah sustained in consequence of his incest, was a punishment divinely inflicted upon him. Who then will indulge in a crime which he sees, by this dreadful kind of vengeance, to be so very hateful to God?

16. *What wilt thou give me,* &c. Tamar did not wish to make a gain by the prostitution of her person, but to have a certain pledge, in order that she might boast of the revenge taken for the injury she had received: and indeed there is no doubt that God blinded Judah, as he deserved ; for how did it happen that he did not know the voice of his daughter-in-law, with which he had been long familiar? Besides, if a pledge must be given for the promised kid, what folly to deliver up his ring to a harlot ? I pass over the absurdity of his giving a double pledge. It appears, therefore, that he was then bereft of all judgment ; and for no other cause are these things written by Moses, than to teach us that his miserable mind was darkened by the just judgment of God, because, by heaping sin upon sin, he had quenched the light of the Spirit.

20. *And Judah sent the kid.* He sends by the hand of a friend, that he may not reveal his ignominy to a stranger. This is also the reason why he does not dare to complain of the lost pledges, lest he should expose himself to ridicule. For I do not approve the sense given, by some, to the words, *Let her take it to her, lest we be shamed,* as if Judah would excuse himself, as having fulfilled the promise he had given. Another meaning is far more suitable ; namely, that Judah would rather lose the ring, than, by spreading the matter further, give occasion to the speeches of the vulgar ; because lighter is the loss of money than of character. He might also fear being exposed to ridicule for having been so credulous. But he was chiefly afraid of the disgrace arising from his fornication. Here we see that men who are not governed by the Spirit of God are always more solicitous about the opinion of the world than about the judgment of God. For why, when the lust of the flesh excited him, did

it not come into his mind, "Behold now I shall become vile in the sight of God and of angels?" Why, at least, after his lust has cooled, does he not blush at the secret knowledge of his sin? But he is secure, if only he can protect himself from public infamy. This passage, however, teaches, what I have said before, that fornication is condemned by the common sense of men, lest any one should seek to excuse himself on the ground of ignorance.

24. *And it came to pass about three months after.* Tamar might sooner have exposed the crime; but she waited till she should be demanded for capital punishment; for then she would have stronger ground for expostulation. The reason why Judah subjects his daughter-in-law to a punishment so severe, was, that he deemed her guilty of adultery: for what the Lord afterwards confirmed by his law, appears then to have prevailed by custom among men, that a maid, from the time of her espousals, should be strictly faithful to her husband. Tamar had married into the family of Judah; she was then espoused to his third son. It was not therefore simple and common fornication which was the question for judgment; but the crime of adultery, which Judah prosecuted in his own right, because he had been injured in the person of his son. Now this kind of punishment is a proof that adultery has been greatly abhorred in all ages. The law of God commands adulterers to be stoned. Before punishment was sanctioned by a written law, the adulterous woman was, by the consent of all, committed to the flames. This seems to have been done by a divine instinct, that, under the direction and authority of nature, the sanctity of marriage might be fortified, as by a firm guard: and although man is not the lord of his own body, but there is a mutual obligation between himself and his wife, yet husbands who have had illicit intercourse with unmarried women have not been subject to capital punishment; because that punishment was awarded to women, not only on account of their immodesty, but also, of the disgrace which the woman brings upon her husband, and of the confusion caused by the clandestine admixture of seeds. For what else will remain safe in human society, if license be given to bring in by stealth the off-

spring of a stranger? to steal a name which may be given to spurious offspring? and to transfer to them property taken away from the lawful heirs? It is no wonder, then, that formerly the fidelity of marriage was so sternly asserted on this point. How much more vile, and how much less excusable, is our negligence at this day, which cherishes adulteries, by allowing them to pass with impunity. Capital punishment, indeed, is deemed too severe for the measure of the offence. Why then do we punish lighter faults with greater rigour? Truly, the world was beguiled by the wiles of Satan, when it suffered the law, engraven on all by nature, to become obsolete. Meanwhile, a pretext has been found for this gross madness, in that Christ dismissed the adulteress in safety, (John viii. 11,) as if, truly, he had undertaken to inflict punishment upon thieves, homicides, liars, and sorcerers. In vain, therefore, is a rule sought to be established by an act of Christ, who purposely abstained from the office of an earthly judge. It may however be asked, since Judah, who thus boldly usurps the right of the sword, was a private person, and even a stranger in the land; whence had he this great liberty to be the arbiter of life and death? I answer, that the words ought not to be taken as if he would command, on his own authority, his daughter-in-law to be put to death, or as if executioners were ready at his nod; but because the offence was verified and made known, he, as her accuser, freely pronounces concerning the punishment, as if the sentence had already been passed by the judges. Indeed I do not doubt that assemblies were then wont to be held, in which judgments were passed; and therefore I simply explain, that Judah commanded Tamar to be brought forward in public; in order that, the cause being tried, she might be punished according to custom. But the specification of the punishment is to this effect, that the case is one which does not admit of dispute; because Tamar is convicted of the crime before she is cited to judgment.

26. *And Judah acknowledged them.* The open reproach of Tamar proceeded from the desire of revenge. She does not seek an interview with her father-in-law, for the purpose of appeasing his mind; but, with a deliberate contempt of

death, she demands him as the companion of her doom. That Judah immediately acknowledges his fault, is a proof of his honesty; for we see with how many fallacies nearly all are wont to cover their sins, until they are dragged to the light, and all means of denying their guilt have failed. Here, though no one is present who could extort a confession, by force or threats, Judah voluntarily stoops to make one, and takes the greater share of the blame to himself. Yet, seeing that, in confessing his fault, he is now silent respecting punishment; we hence infer, that they who are rigid in censuring others, are much more pliant in forgiving themselves. In this, therefore, we ought to imitate him; that, without rack or torture, truth should so far prevail with us, that we should not be ashamed to confess, before the whole world, those sins with which God charges us. But we must avoid his partiality; lest, while we are harsh towards others, we should spare ourselves. This narrative also teaches us the importance of not condemning any one unheard; not only because it is better that the innocent should be absolved than that a guilty person should perish, but also, because a defence brings many things to light, which sometimes render a change in the form of judgment necessary.

*She hath been more righteous than I.* The expression is not strictly proper; for he does not simply approve of Tamar's conduct; but speaks comparatively, as if he would say, that he had been, unjustly and without cause, angry against a woman, by whom he himself might rather have been accused. Moreover, by the result, it appears how tardily the world proceeds in exacting punishment for crimes, where no private person stands forward to avenge his own injury. An atrocious and horrible crime had been committed; as long as Judah thought himself aggrieved, he pressed on with vehemence, and the door of judgment was opened. But now, when the accusation is withdrawn, both escape; though certainly it was the duty of all to rise up against them. Moses however intimates that Judah was sincerely penitent; because " he knew" his daughter-in-law " again no more." He also confirms what I have said before, that by nature men are imbued with a great horror of such a crime. For whence did it arise, that he abstained from intercourse with Tamar, unless he judged naturally, that it was infamous for a father-in-law to be connected with his daughter-in-law? Whoever attempts to destroy the distinction which nature dictates, between what is base and what is honourable, engages, like the giants, in open war with God.

27. *Behold twins were in her womb.* Although both Judah obtained pardon for his error, and Tamar for her wicked contrivance; yet the Lord, in order to humble them, caused a prodigy to take place in the birth. Something similar had before happened in the case of Jacob and Esau, but for a different reason: as we know that prodigies sometimes portend good, sometimes evil. Here, however, there is no doubt that the twins, in their very birth, bring with them marks of their parents' infamy. For it was both profitable to themselves that the memory of their shame should be renewed, and it served as a public example, that such a crime should be branded with eternal disgrace. There is an ambiguity in the meaning of the midwife's words. Some suppose the " breaking forth" to apply to the membrane of the womb,[1] which is broken when the fœtus comes forth. Others more correctly suppose, that the midwife wondered how Pharez, having broken through the barrier interposed, should have come out first; for his brother, who had preceded him, was, as an intervening wall, opposed to him. To some the expression appears to be an imprecation; as if it had been said, " Let the blame of the rupture be upon thee." But Moses, so far as I can judge, intends to point out nothing more, than that a prodigy took place at the birth.

## CHAPTER XXXIX.

1. AND Joseph was brought down to Egypt; and Potiphar, an officer of Pharaoh, captain of the guard, an Egyptian, bought him of the hands of the Ishmeelites, which had brought him down thither.

1. Joseph autem ductus est in Ægyptum, et emit eum Potiphar princeps Pharaonis, princeps satellitum, vir Ægyptius, e manu Ismaelitarum, qui deduxerant eum illuc.

[1] " Secundinis,"—secundina is the membrane which incloses the fœtus during the period of gestation; and which, being rent at the protrusion of the child, comes away as part of the after-birth. The whole is called *secundine* in English, and in French " *arrière faix.*"—*Ed.*

2. And the Lord was with Joseph, and he was a prosperous man; and he was in the house of his master the Egyptian.

3. And his master saw that the Lord *was* with him, and that the Lord made all that he did to prosper in his hand.

4. And Joseph found grace in his sight, and he served him: and he made him overseer over his house, and all *that* he had put into his hand.

5. And it came to pass, from the time *that* he had made him overseer in his house, and over all that he had, that the Lord blessed the Egyptian's house for Joseph's sake; and the blessing of the Lord was upon all that he had in the house, and in the field.

6. And he left all that he had in Joseph's hand; and he knew not ought he had, save the bread which he did eat: and Joseph was *a* goodly *person*, and well-favoured.

7. And it came to pass after these things, that his master's wife cast her eyes upon Joseph; and she said, Lie with me.

8. But he refused; and said unto his master's wife, Behold, my master wotteth not what *is* with me in the house, and he hath committed all that he hath to my hand:

9. *There is* none greater in this house than I; neither hath he kept back anything from me but thee, because thou *art* his wife: how then can I do this great wickedness, and sin against God?

10. And it came to pass, as she spake to Joseph day by day, that he hearkened not unto her, to lie by her, *or* to be with her.

11. And it came to pass about this time, that *Joseph* went into the house to do his business; and *there was* none of the men of the house there within.

12. And she caught him by his garment, saying, Lie with me: and he left his garment in her hand, and fled, and got him out.

2. Et fuit Iehova cum Joseph: itaque fuit vir prospere agens, fuitque in domo domini sui Ægyptii.

3. Et vidit dominus ejus, quod Iehova esset cum eo: et omnia quæ ipse faciebat, Iehova prosperabat in manu ejus.

4. Et invenit Joseph gratiam in oculis ejus, et ministrabat ei: et præposuit eum domui suæ: et omnia quæ erant ei, dedit in manum ejus.

5. Fuit autem ex eo tempore, quo præposuit eum domui suæ, et omnibus quæ erant ei, benedixit Iehova domui Ægyptii propter Joseph: et fuit benedictio Iehovæ in omnibus, quæ erant ei in domo et in agro.

6. Reliquit ergo omnia sua in manu Joseph, et non cognovit cum eo quicquam, nisi panem quem ipse comedebat: erat autem Joseph pulcher forma, et pulcher aspectu.

7. Et fuit, post hæc levavit uxor domini ejus, oculos suos super Joseph, et dixit, Concumbe mecum.

8. Et renuit, et dixit ad uxorem domini sui, Ecce, dominus meus non cognovit mecum, quid sit in domo: et omnia quæ erant ei, dedit in manum meam.

9. Non est major me in domo hac: et non prohibuit a me quicquam nisi te, eo quod tu sis uxor ejus: et quomodo faciam malum grande hoc, ut peccem contra Deum?

10. Et fuit, quum loqueretur ipsa ad Joseph quotidie, nec ei morem gereret, ut cum ea concumberet, et ut esset cum ea.

11. Fuit inquam, secundum diem hanc ingressus est domum, ut faceret opus suum: et non erat quisquam ex viris domus illic in domo:

12. Tunc apprehendit eum per vestimentum ejus, dicendo, Concumbe mecum. Ergo reliquit vestimentum suum in manu ejus, et fugit, egressusque est foras.

| | |
|---|---|
| 13. And it came to pass, when she saw that he had left his garment in her hand, and was fled forth, | 13. Et fuit, quum vidisset ipsa, quod reliquisset vestimentum suum in manu sua, et fugisset foras: |
| 14. That she called unto the men of her house, and spake unto them, saying, See, he hath brought in an Hebrew unto us to mock us; he came in unto me to lie with me, and I cried with a loud voice: | 14. Vocavit viros domus suæ, et dixit ad eos, dicendo, Videte, adduxit nobis virum Hebræum, ut illuderet nobis: ingressus est ad me ut concumberet mecum, et clamavi voce magna. |
| 15. And it came to pass, when he heard that I lifted up my voice and cried, that he left his garment with me, and fled, and got him out. | 15. Et fuit, quum audisset ipse, quod elevassem vocem meam et clamassem, reliquit vestimentum suum apud me, et fugit, egressusque est foras. |
| 16. And she laid up his garment by her, until his lord came home. | 16. Retinuit autem vestimentum ejus apud se, donec veniret dominus ejus ad domum suam. |
| 17. And she spake unto him according to these words, saying, The Hebrew servant, which thou hast brought unto us, came in unto me to mock me: | 17. Et loquuta est ad eum secundum verba ista, dicendo, Ingressus est ad me servus Hebræus, ut illuderet mihi. |
| 18. And it came to pass, as I lifted up my voice and cried, that he left his garment with me, and fled out. | 18. Et fuit, quum elevassem vocem meam, et clamassem, reliquit vestimentum suum apud me, et fugit foras. |
| 19. And it came to pass, when his master heard the words of his wife, which she spake unto him, saying, After this manner did thy servant to me; that his wrath was kindled. | 19. Fuit autem, quum audisset dominus ejus verba uxoris suæ, quæ loquuta est ad eum, dicendo, Secundum hæc fecit mihi servus tuus: iratus est furor ejus. |
| 20. And Joseph's master took him, and put him into the prison, a place where the king's prisoners *were* bound: and he was there in the prison. | 20. Et accepit dominus ipsius Joseph eum, et posuit eum in domo carceris, in loco in quo vincti regis vinciebantur, fuitque illic in domo carceris. |
| 21. But the Lord was with Joseph, and showed him mercy, and gave him favour in the sight of the keeper of the prison. | 21. Fuit vero Iehova cum Joseph, et inclinavit ad eum misericordiam, et dedit gratiam ejus in oculis principis domus carceris. |
| 22. And the keeper of the prison committed to Joseph's hand all the prisoners that *were* in the prison; and whatsoever they did there, he was the doer *of it.* | 22. Et dedit princeps domus carceris in manu Joseph omnes vinctos, qui erant in domo carceris: et omnia quæ faciebant illic, ipse faciebat. |
| 23. The keeper of the prison looked not to any thing *that was* under his hand; because the Lord was with him, and *that* which he did, the Lord made *it* to prosper. | 23. Neque princeps domus carceris videbat quicquam *ex iis quæ erant* in manu ejus, eo quod Iehova erat cum eo: et quod ipse faciebat, Iehova secundabat. |

1. *And Joseph was brought down.* For the purpose of connecting it with the remaining part of the history, Moses

repeats what he had briefly touched upon, that Joseph had been sold to Potiphar the Egyptian: he then subjoins that God was with Joseph, so that he prospered in all things. For although it often happens that all things proceed with wicked men according to their wish, whom God nevertheless does not bless with his favour; still the sentiment is true and the expression of it proper, that it is never well with men, except so far as the Lord shows himself to be gracious to them. For he vouchsafes his blessing, for a time, even to reprobates, with whom he is justly angry, in order that he may gently invite and even allure them to repentance; and may render them more inexcusable, if they remain obstinate; meanwhile, he curses their felicity. Therefore, while they think they have reached the height of fortune, their prosperity, in which they delighted themselves, is turned into ruin. Now whensoever God deprives men of his blessing, whether they be strangers or of his own household, they must necessarily decline; because no good flows except from Him as the fountain. The world indeed forms for itself a goddess of fortune, who whirls round the affairs of men; or each man adores his own industry; but Scripture draws us away from this depraved imagination, and declares that adversity is a sign of God's absence, but prosperity, a sign of his presence. However, there is not the least doubt that the peculiar and extraordinary favour of God appeared towards Joseph, so that he was plainly known to be blessed by God. Moses immediately afterwards adds, that Joseph *was in the house of his master*, to teach us that he was not at once elevated to an honourable condition. There was nothing more desirable than liberty; but he is reckoned among the slaves, and lives precariously, holding his life itself subject to the will of his master. Let us then learn, even amidst our sufferings, to perceive the grace of God; and let it suffice us, when anything severe is to be endured, to have our cup mingled with some portion of sweetness, lest we should be ungrateful to God, who, in this manner, declares that he is present with us.

3. *And his master saw.* Here that which has been lately alluded to more clearly appears, that the grace of God shone

forth in Joseph, in no common or usual manner; since it became thus manifest to a man who was a heathen, and, in this respect, blind. How much more base is our ingratitude, if we do not refer all our prosperous events to God as their author; seeing that Scripture often teaches us, that nothing proceeding from men, whether counsels, or labours, or any means which they can devise, will profit them, except so far as God gives his blessing. And whereas Potiphar, on this account, conceived so much greater regard for Joseph, as to set him over his house; we hence gather, that heathens may be so affected by religion, as to be constrained to ascribe glory to God. However, his ingratitude again betrays itself, when he despises that God whose gifts he estimates so highly in the person of Joseph. He ought at least to have inquired who that God was, that he might conform himself to the worship due to him: but he deems it enough, insomuch as he thinks it will be for his private advantage, to acknowledge that Joseph was divinely directed, in order that he may use his labour with greater profit.

*The Lord made all that he did to prosper in his hand.* This was a wonderful method of procedure, that the entire blessing by which the Lord was pleased to testify his paternal love towards Joseph, should turn to the gain of the Egyptians. For since Joseph neither sowed nor reaped for himself, he was not at all enriched by his labour. But in this way it was brought about that a proud man, who otherwise might have abused him as a vile and sordid slave, should treat him humanely and liberally. And the Lord often soothes the wicked by such favours, lest when they have suffered any injury, they should turn the fury of their indignation against the pious. We here see how abundantly the grace of God is poured out upon the faithful, since a portion of his kindness flows from them even to the reprobate. We are also taught what an advantage it is to receive the elect children of God to our hospitality, or to join ourselves to those whom the divine favour thus accompanies, that it may diffuse its fragrance to those who are near them. But since it would not greatly profit us to be saturated with those temporal benefits of God, which suffocate and ruin the reprobate; we ought to centre all our wishes on this one point, that God may be propitious to us. Far better was it for Joseph that Potiphar's wealth should be increased for his sake; than it was for Potiphar to make great gain by Joseph.

6. *And he left all that he had.*[1] Joseph reaped this fruit of the divine love and kindness towards him, that he was cheered by some alleviation of his servitude, at least, for a short time. But a new temptation soon assailed him. For the favour which he had obtained was not only annihilated, but became the cause and origin of a harsher fortune. Joseph was governor over the whole house of Potiphar. From that post of honour he is hurried into prison, in order that he may be soon brought forth to the punishment of death. What then could enter into his mind, but that he was forsaken and abandoned by God, and was continually exposed to new dangers? He might even imagine that God had declared himself his enemy. This history, therefore, teaches us that the pious have need of peculiar discernment to enable them, with the eyes of faith, to consider those benefits of God by which he mitigates the severity of their crosses. For when he seems to stretch out his hand to them, for the sake of bringing them assistance, the light which had shone forth often vanishes in a moment, and denser darkness follows in its place. But here it is evident, that the Lord, though he often plunges his own people into the waves of adversity, yet does not deceive them; seeing that, by sometimes moderating their sufferings, he grants them time to breathe. So Joseph, though fallen from his office as governor of the house, was yet never deserted; nor had that relaxation of his sufferings proved in vain, by which his mind was raised, not to pride, but to the

---

[1] " Potiphar placed Joseph over his house and over all his substance, and the Lord blessed him for the sake of Joseph, in all which he had, in the house and in the field. Joseph had also, after his exaltation, a man who was over his house. A peculiar and characteristic Egyptian trait! ' Among the objects of tillage and husbandry,' says *Rosellini*, ' which are pourtrayed on the Egyptian tombs, we often see a steward who takes account and makes a registry of the harvest, before it is deposited in the storehouse.'"—*Hengstenberg's Egypt and the Books of Moses*, p. 24. Such incidental testimony to the truth of the sacred narrative, is invaluable, especially at a time when men, wise above what is written, are endeavouring to bring the sacred volume into contempt, by casting a doubt upon the veracity of Moses.—*Ed.*

patient endurance of a new cross. And truly for this end, God meets with us in our difficulties, that then, with collected strength, as men refreshed, we may be the better prepared for other conflicts.

*And Joseph was a goodly person, and well-favoured.* Whereas elegance of form was the occasion of great calamity to holy Joseph, let us learn not greatly to desire those graces of person which may conciliate the favour of the world ; but rather let each be content with his own lot. We see to how many dangers they are exposed, who excel in beauty ; for it is very difficult for such to restrain themselves from all lascivious desires. Although in Joseph religion so prevailed that he abhorred all impurity ; yet Satan contrived a means of destruction for him, from another quarter, just as he is accustomed to turn the gifts of God into snares whereby to catch souls. Wherefore we must earnestly ask of God, that amid so many dangers, he would govern us by his Spirit, and preserve those gifts with which he has adorned us, pure from every stain. When it is said that Potiphar's wife " cast her eyes upon Joseph," the Holy Spirit, by this form of speech, admonishes all women, that if they have chastity in their heart, they must guard it by modesty of demeanour. For, on this account also, they bear a veil upon their heads, that they may restrain themselves from every sinful allurement : not that it is wrong for a woman to look at men; but Moses here describes an impure and dissolute look. She had often before looked upon Joseph without sin : but now, for the first time, she casts her eyes upon him, and contemplates his beauty more boldly and wantonly than became a modest woman. Thus we see that the eyes were as torches to inflame the heart to lust. By which example we are taught that nothing is more easy, than for all our senses to infect our minds with depraved desires, unless we are very earnestly on our guard. For Satan never ceases diligently to suggest those things which may incite us to sin. The senses both readily embrace the occasion of sin which is presented to them, and also eagerly and quickly convey it to the mind. Wherefore let every one endeavour sedulously to govern his eyes, and his ears, and the other members of his body, unless he wishes to open so many doors to Satan, into the innermost affections of his heart : and especially as the sense of the eyes is the most tender, no common care must be used in putting them under restraint.

7. *Lie with me.*[1] Moses only briefly touches upon the chief points, and the sum of the things he relates. For there is no doubt that this impure woman endeavoured, by various arts, to allure the pious youth, and that she insinuated herself by indirect blandishments, before she broke forth to such a shameless kind of license. But Moses, omitting other things, shows that she had been pushed so far by base lust, as not to shrink from openly soliciting a connection with Joseph. Now as this filthiness is a signal proof that carnal lust acts from blind and furious impulses ; so, in the person of Joseph, an admirable example of fidelity and continence is set before us. His fidelity and integrity appear in this, that he acknowledges himself to be the more strictly bound, the greater the power with which he is entrusted. Ingenuous and courageous men have this property, that the more is confided to them, the less they can bear to deceive : but it is a rare virtue for those who have the power of doing injury to cultivate honesty gratuitously. Wherefore Joseph is not undeservedly commended by Moses, for regarding the authority with which he was invested by his master, as a bridle to restrain him from transgressing the bounds of duty. Besides, he gives also a proof of his gratitude, in bringing forward the benefits received from his master, as a reason why he should not subject him to any disgrace. And truly hence arises at this day such confusion everywhere, that men are half brutal, because this sacred bond of mutual society is broken. All, indeed, confess, that

---

[1] " How great the corruption of manners with reference to the marriage relation was among the Egyptians, appears from *Herodotus*, whose account *Larcher* has compared with the one under consideration. The wife of one of the oldest kings was untrue to him. It was long before a woman could be found who was faithful to her husband ; and when one was, at last, found, the king took her without hesitation to himself. From such a state of morals the Biblical narrative can easily be conceived to be natural. The evidence of the monuments is also not very favourable to the Egyptian women. Thus they are represented as addicted to excess in drinking wine, as even becoming so much intoxicated, as to be unable to stand or walk alone, or to carry their liquor discreetly."—*Egypt and the Books of Moses*, p. 25.—*Ed.*

if they have received any benefit from another, they are under obligation to him: one even reproaches another for his ingratitude; but there are few who sincerely follow the example of Joseph. Lest, however, he should seem to be restrained only by a regard to man, he also declares that the act would be offensive to God. And, indeed, nothing is more powerful to overcome temptation than the fear of God. But he designedly commends the generosity of his master, in order that the wicked woman may desist from her abandoned purpose. To the same point is the objection which he mentions, *Neither hath he kept anything back from me but thee, because thou art his wife.* Why does he say this, except that, by recalling the religious obligation of marriage, he may wound the corrupt mind of the woman, and may cure her of her insane passion? Therefore he not only strenuously strives to liberate himself from her wicked allurements; but, lest her lusts should prove indomitable, he proposes to her the best remedy. And we may know that the sanctity of marriage is here commended to us in the history of Joseph, whereby the Lord would declare himself to be the maintainer of matrimonial fidelity, so that none who violate another's bed should escape his vengeance. For he is a surety between the man and his wife, and requires mutual chastity from each. Whence it follows that, besides the injury inflicted upon man, God himself is grievously wronged.

10. *As she spake to Joseph day by day.* The constancy of Joseph is commended; from which it appears that a real fear of God reigned in his mind. Whence it came to pass that he not only repelled one attack, but stood forth, to the last, the conqueror of all temptations. We know how easy it is to fall when Satan tempts us through another: because we seem exempt from blame, if he who induces us to commit the crime, bears a part of it.[1] Holy Joseph, therefore,

[1] Scimus quam lubricus sit lapsus, dum aliunde nobis flabella suscitat Satan: quia videmur culpâ exempti, si ejus partem sustinet qui nos ad flagitium inducit. The French translation is, Nous savons combien il est aisé de tomber, quand Satan nous suscite des soufflets d'ailleurs: car il nous semble que nous sommes exempts de la faute, si celuy qui nous a induit à mal en soustient une partie. The sentiment of the passage seems loosely expressed, and certainly required some limitation. The old English translator omits it, as he does many others, entirely.—*Ed.*

must have been endowed with the extraordinary power of the Spirit, seeing that he stood invincible to the last, against all the allurements of the impious woman. So much the more detestable is the wickedness of her, who is neither corrected by time, nor restrained by many repulses. When she sees a stranger, and one who had been sold as a slave, so discreet and so faithful to his master, when she is also sacredly admonished by him not to provoke the anger of God, how indomitable is that lust which gives no place to shame. Now, because we here see into what evils persons will rush, when regard to propriety is extinguished by carnal intemperance, we must entreat the Lord that he will not suffer the light of his Spirit to be quenched within us.

11. *And it came to pass about this time.* That is, in the process of time, seeing she will not desist from soliciting holy Joseph, it happens at length, that she adds force to blandishments. Now, Moses here describes the crisis[1] of the combat. Joseph had already exhibited a noble and memorable example of constancy; because, as a youth, so often tempted, through a constant succession of many days, he had preserved the even tenor of his way; and at that age, to which pardon is wont to be granted, if it break forth into intemperance, he was more moderate than almost any old man. But now when the woman openly raves, and her love is turned into fury, the more arduous the contest has become, the more worthy of praise is his magnanimity, which remains inflexible against this assault. Joseph saw that he must incur the danger of losing both his character and his life: he chose to sacrifice his character, and was prepared to relinquish life itself, rather than to be guilty of such wickedness before God. Seeing the Spirit of God proposes to us such an example in a youth, what excuse does he leave for men and women of mature age, if they voluntarily precipitate themselves into crime, or fall into it by a light temptation? To this, therefore, we must bend all our efforts, that regard for God alone, may prevail to subdue all carnal affections, and even that we may more highly value a good and upright conscience than the plaudits of the whole world.

[1] *Epitasis,* Greek ἐπίτασις, the point in a play wherein the plot thickens.—*Ed.*

For no one will prove that he heartily loves virtue, but he who, being content with God as his only witness, does not hesitate to submit to any disgrace, rather than decline from the path of duty. And truly, since even among heathens such proverbs as these are current, "that conscience is a thousand witnesses," and that it is "a most beautiful theatre," we should be greatly ashamed of our stupor, unless the tribunal of God stands so conspicuously in our view, as to cast all the perverse judgments of the world into the shade. Therefore, away with those vain pretexts, "I wish to avoid offence," " I am afraid lest men should interpret amiss what I have done aright;" because God does not regard himself as being duly honoured, unless we, ceasing to be anxious about our own reputation, follow wheresoever he alone calls us; not that he wishes us simply to be indifferent to our own reputation, but because it is an indignity, as well as an absurdity, that he should not be preferred to men. Let, then, the faithful, as much as in them lies, endeavour to edify their neighbours by the example of an upright life; and for this end, let them prudently guard against every mark of evil; but if it be necessary to endure the infamy of the world, let them through this temptation also, proceed in the direction of their divine vocation.

*He hath brought in an Hebrew unto us.* Here we see what desperation can effect. For the wicked woman breaks forth from love into fury. Whence it clearly appears what brutal impulses lust brings with it, when its reins are loosened. Certainly when Satan has once gained the dominion over miserable men, he never ceases to hurry them hither and thither, until he drives them headlong by the spirit of giddiness and madness. We see, also, how he hardens to obstinacy the reprobate, whom he holds fast bound under his power. God, indeed, often inspires the wicked with terror, so that they commit their crimes with trembling. And it is possible that the signs of a guilty conscience appeared in the countenance and in the words of this impure woman: nevertheless, Satan confirms her in that degree of hardness, that she boldly adopts the design to ruin the holy youth; and, at the moment, contrives the fraud by which she may oppress him, though innocent, just as if she had long meditated, at leisure, on his destruction. She had before sought secrecy, that no witness might be present; now she calls her domestics, that, by this kind of prejudging of the case, she may condemn the youth before her husband. Besides, she involves her husband in the accusation, that she may compel him, by a sense of shame, to punish the guiltless. "It is by thy fault, (she says,) that this stranger has been mocking me." What other course does she leave open to her husband, than that he should hasten, with closed eyes, to avenge her, for the sake of purging himself from this charge? Therefore, though all wicked persons are fearful, yet they contract such hardness from their stupor, that no fear hinders them from rushing obstinately forward into every abyss of iniquity, and insolently trampling upon the good and simple. And we must observe this trial of the holy man, in order that we may take care to be clothed with that spirit of fortitude, which not even the iron-hardness of the wicked shall be able to break. Even this other trial was not a light one, that he receives so unworthy a reward of his humanity. He had covered the disgrace of the woman in silence, in order that she might have had opportunity to repent, if she had been curable; he now sees that, by his modesty, he has brought himself into danger of death. We learn, by his not sinking under the trial, that it was his sincere determination to yield himself freely to the service of God. And we must do the same, in order that the ingratitude of men may, by no means, cause us to swerve from our duty.

19. *When his master heard the words of his wife.* Seeing that a colour so probable was given to the transaction, there is no wonder that jealousy, the motions of which are exceedingly vehement and ardent, should so far have prevailed with Potiphar, as to cause him to credit the calumnies of his wife. Yet the levity with which he instantly thrust a servant, whom he had found prudent and honest, into prison, without examining the cause, cannot be excused. He ought certainly to have been less under the influence of his wife. And, therefore, he received the just reward of his too easy folly, by cherishing with honour, a harlot in the place of a wife, and

by almost performing the office of a pander. This example is useful to all; yet husbands especially are taught that they must use prudence, lest they should be carried rashly hither and thither, at the will of their wives. And, truly, since we everywhere see that they who are too obsequious to their wives are held up to ridicule; let us know that the folly of these men is condemned by the just judgment of God, so that we may learn to pray for the spirit of gravity and moderation. There is no doubt that Moses expressly condemns the rashness of Potiphar, in becoming inflamed against Joseph, as soon as he had heard his wife, and in giving the reins to his indignation, just as if the guilt of Joseph had been proved; for thus all equity is excluded, no just defence is allowed, and finally, the true and accurate investigation of the cause is utterly rejected. But it may be asked, How could the jealousy of Potiphar be excited, since Moses before has said that he was an eunuch?[1] The solution of the question is easy; they were accustomed to be called eunuchs in the East, not only who were so really, but who were satraps and nobles. Wherefore, this name is of the same force as if Moses had said that he was one of the chief men of the court.[2]

20. *And put him into the prison.* Though Moses does not state with what degree of severity Joseph was afflicted at the beginning of his imprisonment, yet we readily gather that he was not allowed any liberty, but was thrust into some obscure dungeon. The authority of Potiphar was paramount; he had the keeper of the prison under his power, and at his disposal. What clemency could be hoped for from a man who was jealous and carried away with the vehemence of his anger? There is no doubt that what is related of Joseph in

---

[1] See the comment on chap. xxxvii. 36.

[2] To the whole of this account the sceptical writers of the continent imagine that they have found an insuperable objection. *Tuch* remarks, " The narrator abandons the representation of a distinguished Egyptian, in whose house *the women live separately,*" &c. " The error," observes Hengstenberg, " however, lies here, not on the side of the author, but on that of his critics. They are guilty of inadvertently transferring that which universally prevails in the East to Egypt, which the author avoids, and thereby exhibits his knowledge of the condition of the Egyptians. According to the monuments, the women in Egypt lived under far less restraint than in the East, or even in *Greece.*"—*Egypt and the Books of Moses,* p. 26.—*Ed.*

Psalm cv. 18, " His feet were made fast in fetters, and the iron entered into his soul," had been handed down by tradition from the fathers. What a reward of innocence! for, according to the flesh, he might ascribe whatever he was suffering to his integrity. Truly, in this temptation he must have mourned in great perplexity and anxiety before God. And though Moses does not record his prayers, yet, since it is certain that he was not crushed beneath the cross, and did not murmur against it, it is also probable that he was reposing on the hope of Divine help. And to flee unto God is the only stay which can support us in our afflictions, the only armour which renders us invincible.

21. *But the Lord was with Joseph.* It appears, from the testimony of the Psalmist just cited, that Joseph's extreme sufferings were not immediately alleviated. The Lord purposely suffered him to be reduced to extremity, that he might bring him back as from the grave. We know that as the light of the sun is most clearly seen when we are looking from a dark place; so, in the darkness of our miseries, the grace of God shines more brightly when, beyond expectation, he succours us. Moreover, Moses says, *the Lord was with Joseph,* because he extended this grace or mercy towards him; whence we may learn, that God, even when he delivers us from unjust violence, or when he assists us in a good cause, is yet induced to do so by his own goodness. For since we are unworthy that he should grant us his help, the cause of its communication must be in himself; seeing that he is merciful. Certainly if merits, which should lay God under obligation, are to be sought for in men, they would have been found in Joseph; yet Moses declares that he was assisted by the gratuitous favour of God. This, however, is no obstacle to his having received the reward of his piety, which is perfectly consistent with the gratuitous kindness of God. The manner of exercising this kindness is also added; namely, that the Lord gave him favour with the keeper of the prison. There is, indeed, no doubt that Joseph was acceptable to the keeper for many reasons: for even virtue conciliates favour to itself; and Moses has before shown that the holy man was amiable in many ways; but because it often hap-

pens that the children of God are treated with as great inhumanity as if they were the worst of all men, Moses expressly states that the keeper of the prison, at length, became humane; because his mind, which was not spontaneously disposed to equity, had been divinely inclined to it. Therefore, that the keeper of the prison, having laid aside his cruelty, acted with kindness and gentleness, was a change which proceeded from God, who governs the hearts of men according to his own will. But it is a wonder that the keeper of the prison did not fear lest he should incur the displeasure of Potiphar: and even that Potiphar himself, who without difficulty could have interfered, should yet have suffered a man whom he mortally hated to be thus kindly and liberally treated. It may be answered with truth, that his cruelty had been divinely restrained: but it is also probable that he had suspected, and at length, been made acquainted with the subtle scheme of his wife. Although, however, he might be appeased towards holy Joseph, he was unwilling to acquit him to his own dishonour. Meanwhile the remarkable integrity of Joseph manifests itself in this, that when he is made the guard of the prison, and has the free administration of it, he nevertheless does not attempt to escape, but waits for the proper season of his liberation.

## CHAPTER XL.

1. AND it came to pass after these things, *that* the butler of the king of Egypt and *his* baker had offended their lord the king of Egypt.
2. And Pharaoh was wroth against two *of* his officers, against the chief of the butlers, and against the chief of the bakers.
3. And he put them in ward in the house of the captain of the guard, into the prison, the place where Joseph *was* bound.
4. And the captain of the guard charged Joseph with them, and he served them; and they continued a season in ward.
5. And they dreamed a dream both of them, each man his dream in

1. Fuit autem, posthæc peccaverunt pincerna regis Ægypti, et pistor contra dominum suum regem Ægypti.
2. Itaque iratus est Pharao contra utrumque satrapam suum, contra principem pincernarum et contra principem pistorum.
3. Et posuit illos in custodia domus principis satellitum, in domo carceris, in loco in quo Joseph vinctus erat.
4. Et præposuit princeps satellitum ipsum Joseph eis, et ministrabat eis: fuerunt autem per annum in custodia.
5. Porro somniaverunt somnium uterque ipsorum, quisque somnium

one night, each man according to the interpretation of his dream, the butler and the baker of the king of Egypt, which *were* bound in the prison.

6. And Joseph came in unto them in the morning, and looked upon them, and, behold, they *were* sad.

7. And he asked Pharaoh's officers, that *were* with him in the ward of his lord's house, saying, Wherefore look ye *so* sadly to-day?

8. And they said unto him, We have dreamed a dream, and *there is* no interpreter of it. And Joseph said unto them, *Do* not interpretations *belong* to God? tell me *them*, I pray you.

9. And the chief butler told his dream to Joseph, and said to him, In my dream, behold, a vine *was* before me;

10. And in the vine *were* three branches: and it *was* as though it budded, *and* her blossoms shot forth; and the clusters thereof brought forth ripe grapes:

11. And Pharaoh's cup *was* in my hand: and I took the grapes, and pressed them into Pharaoh's cup, and I gave the cup into Pharaoh's hand.

12. And Joseph said unto him, This *is* the interpretation of it: The three branches *are* three days.

13. Yet within three days shall Pharaoh lift up thine head, and restore thee unto thy place; and thou shalt deliver Pharaoh's cup into his hand, after the former manner when thou wast his butler.

14. But think on me when it shall be well with thee, and shew kindness, I pray thee, unto me; and make mention of me unto Pharaoh, and bring me out of this house:

15. For indeed I was stolen away out of the land of the Hebrews; and here also have I done nothing that they should put me into the dungeon.

16. When the chief baker saw that the interpretation was good, he said unto Joseph, I also *was* in my dream, and, behold, *I had* three white baskets on my head.

suum nocte eadem: singuli secundum interpretationem somnii sui, pincerna et pistor qui fuerant regi Ægypti, qui erant vincti in domo carceris.

6. Et venit ad eos Joseph mane, et vidit eos, et ecce, erant tristitia affecti.

7. Tunc interrogavit principes Pharaonis, qui erant secum in custodia domus domini sui, dicendo, Cur facies vestræ sunt afflictæ hodie?

8. Et dixerunt ad eum, Somnium somniavimus, et qui interpretetur illud, non est. Et dixit ad eos Joseph, Nonne Dei sunt interpretationes? narrate quæso mihi.

9. Et narravit princeps pincernarum somnium suum ipsi Joseph, et dixit ei, Me somniante, ecce, vitis *erat* coram me.

10. Et in vite erant tres rami, et dum floreret, ascendit flos ejus, et maturuerunt botri ejus in uvas.

11. Et calix Pharaonis erat in manu mea, et accipiebam uvas, et exprimebam eas in calicem Pharaonis, et dabam calicem in manu Pharaonis.

12. Et dixit ei Joseph, Hæc est interpretatio ejus, Tres rami, tres dies sunt.

13. In fine trium dierum elevabit Pharao caput tuum, et redire faciet te ad locum tuum, et dabis calicem Pharaoni in manu ejus secundum consuetudinem primam, quando eras pincerna ejus.

14. Sed memento mihi tecum, quum bene fuerit tibi: et fac quæso mecum misericordiam, et mentionem mei fac Pharaoni, et educere fac me e domo hac:

15. Quia furto auferendo, furto ablatus sum e terra Hebræorum: et etiam hic non feci quicquam, ut ponerent me in carcerem.

16. Et vidit princeps pistorum, quod bene interpretatus esset, et dixit ad Joseph, Etiam me somniante, ecce, tria canistra alba super caput meum.

17. And in the uppermost basket *there was* of all manner of bakemeats for Pharaoh; and the birds did eat them out of the basket upon my head.

18. And Joseph answered and said, This *is* the interpretation thereof: The three baskets *are* three days.

19. Yet within three days shall Pharaoh lift up thy head from off thee, and shall hang thee on a tree; and the birds shall eat thy flesh from off thee.

20. And it came to pass the third day, *which was* Pharaoh's birthday, that he made a feast unto all his servants: and he lifted up the head of the chief butler and of the chief baker among his servants.

21. And he restored the chief butler unto his butlership again; and he gave the cup into Pharaoh's hand:

22. But he hanged the chief baker, as Joseph had interpreted to them.

23. Yet did not the chief butler remember Joseph, but forgat him.

17. Et in canistro superiori erat ex omni cibo Pharaonis, opere pistorio: et aves comedebant illud e canistro, quod erat super caput meum.

18. Et respondit Joseph, et dixit, Hæc est interpretatio ejus, Tria canistra, tres dies sunt.

19. In fine trium dierum auferet Pharao caput tuum a te, et suspendet te in ligno, et comedent aves carnem tuam a te.

20. Et fuit in die tertia, die qua natus fuerat Pharao, fecit convivium omnibus servis suis, et elevavit caput principis pincernarum et caput principis pistorum in medio servorum suorum.

21. Ac redire fecit principem pincernarum ad propinationem suam, et dedit calicem in manu Pharaoni:

22. Principem autem pistorum suspendit, quemadmodum interpretatus fuerat eis Joseph.

23. Et non est recordatus princeps pincernarum ipsius Joseph, sed oblitus est ejus.

1. *And it came to pass after these things.* We have already seen, that when Joseph was in bonds, God cared for him. For whence arose the relaxation afforded him, but from the divine favour? Therefore, God, before he opened the door for his servant's deliverance, entered into the very prison to sustain him with his strength. But a far more illustrious benefit follows; for he is not only liberated from prison, but exalted to the highest degree of honour. In the meantime, the providence of God led the holy man through wonderful and most intricate paths. The butler and baker of the king are cast into the prison; Joseph expounds to them their dreams. Restoration to his office having been promised to the butler, some light of hope beams upon the holy captive; for the butler agreed, after he should have returned to his post, to become the advocate for Joseph's pardon. But, again, that hope was speedily cut off, when the butler failed to speak a word to the king on behalf of the miserable captive. Joseph, therefore, seemed to himself to be buried in perpetual

oblivion, until the Lord again suddenly rekindles the light which had been smothered, and almost extinguished. Thus, when he might have delivered the holy man directly from prison, he chose to lead him around by circuitous paths, the better to prove his patience, and to manifest, by the mode of his deliverance, that he has wonderful methods of working, hidden from our view. He does this that we may learn not to measure, by our own sense, the salvation which he has promised us; but that we may suffer ourselves to be turned hither or thither by his hand, until he shall have performed his work. By the butler and the baker we are not to understand any common person of each rank, but those who presided over the rest; for, soon afterwards, they are called eunuchs or nobles. Ridiculous is the fiction of the trifler Gerundensis, who, according to his manner, asserts that they were made eunuchs for the sake of infamy, because Pharaoh had been enraged against them. They were, in short, two of the chief men of the court. Moses now more clearly declares that the prison was under the authority of Potiphar. Whence we learn what I have before said, that his anger had been mitigated, since without his consent, the jailor could not have acted with such clemency towards Joseph. Even Moses ascribes such a measure of humanity to Potiphar, that he committed the butler and baker to the charge of Joseph. Unless, perhaps, a new successor had been then appointed in Potiphar's place; which, however, is easily refuted from the context, because a little afterwards Moses says that the master of Joseph was the captain of the guard, (ver. 3.) When Moses says they were kept in prison *a season,* some understand by the word, *a whole year;* but in my judgment they are mistaken; it rather denotes a long but uncertain time, as appears from other places.

5. *And they dreamed a dream.* What I have before alluded to respecting dreams must be recalled to memory; namely, that many frivolous things are presented to us, which pass away and are forgotten;[1] some, however, have the force

---

[1] Calvin's words are: "Quæ transeunt per portam corneam."—*Vide Virgil. Æneid. VI. in finem.* This is an obviously mistaken allusion, arising probably from a lapse of memory in Calvin, or in the transcriber

and significance of prophecy. Of this kind were these two dreams, by which God made known the hidden result of a future matter. For unless the mark of a celestial oracle had been engraven upon them, the butler and the baker would not have been in such consternation of mind. I acknowledge, indeed, that men are sometimes vehemently agitated by vain and rashly conceived dreams; yet their terror and anxiety gradually subsides; but God had fixed an arrow in the minds of the butler and the baker, which would not suffer them to rest; and by this means, each was rendered more attentive to the interpretation of his dream. Moses, therefore, expressly declares that it was a presage of something certain.

6. *And Joseph came in unto them in the morning.* As I have lately said, we ought here to behold, with the eyes of faith, the wonderful providence of God. For, although the butler and baker are certainly informed of their own fate; yet this was not done so much out of regard to them, as in favour of Joseph; whom God designed, by this method, to make known to the king. Therefore, by a secret instinct he had rendered them sad and astonished, as if he would lead them by the hand to his servant Joseph. It is, however, to be observed, that by a new inspiration of the Spirit, the gift of prophecy, which he had not before possessed, was imparted to him in the prison. When he had previously dreamed himself, he remained, for a while, in suspense and doubt respecting the divine revelation; but now he is a certain interpreter to others. And though, when he was inquiring into the cause of their sadness, he perhaps did not think of dreams; yet, from the next verse it appears that he was conscious to himself of having received the gift of the Spirit; and, in this confidence, he exhorts them to relate the dreams, of which he was about to be the interpreter. *Do not interpretations* (he says) *belong to God ?* Certainly he does not arrogantly transfer to himself what he acknowledges to be peculiar to God; but according to the means which his vocation

---

of his works. He should have said "portam eburnam." The ancient mythologists distinguished true dreams from false, by representing the former as passing through the "horny gate," (porta cornea,) the latter through the "ivory gate," (porta eburna.)—*Ed.*

supplied, he offers them his service. This must be noted, in order that no one may undesignedly usurp more to himself than he knows that God has granted him. For, on this account, Paul so diligently teaches that the gifts of the Spirit are variously distributed, (1 Cor. xii. 4,) and that God has assigned to each a certain post, in order that no one may act ambitiously, or intrude himself into another's office; but rather that each should keep himself within the bounds of his own calling. Unless this degree of moderation shall prevail, all things will necessarily be thrown into confusion; because the truth of God will be distorted by the foolish temerity of many; peace and concord will be disturbed, and, in short, no good order will be maintained. Let us learn, therefore, that Joseph confidently promised an interpretation of the dreams, because he knew that he was furnished and adorned with this gift by God. The same remark applies to his interrogation respecting the dreams. For he does not attempt to proceed beyond what his own power authorized him to do: he does not, therefore, divine what they had dreamed, but confesses it was hidden from him. The method pursued by Daniel was different, for he was enabled, by a direct revelation, to state and interpret the dream which had entirely escaped the memory of the king of Babylon. (Dan. ii. 28.) He, therefore, relying upon a larger measure of the Spirit, does not hesitate to profess that he can both divine and interpret dreams. But Joseph, to whom the half only of these gifts was imparted, keeps himself within legitimate bounds. Besides, he not only guards himself against presumption; but, by declaring that whatever he has received is from God, he ingenuously testifies that he has nothing from himself. He does not, therefore, boast of his own quickness or clear-sightedness, but wishes only to be known as the servant of God. Let those who excel, follow this rule; lest, by ascribing too much to themselves, (which commonly happens,) they obscure the grace of God. Moreover, this vanity is to be restrained, not only that God alone may be glorified, and may not be robbed of his right; but that prophets, and teachers, and all others who are indued with heavenly grace, may humbly submit themselves to the direction of the Spirit. What

Moses says is also to be observed, that Joseph was concerned at the sadness of those who were with him in prison. For thus men become softened by their own afflictions, so that they do not despise others who are in misery ; and, in this way, common sufferings generate sympathy. Wherefore it is not wonderful that God should exercise us with various sorrows ; since nothing is more becoming than humanity towards our brethren, who, being weighed down with trials, lie under contempt. This humanity, however, must be learned by experience ; because our innate ferocity is more and more inflated by prosperity.

12. *The three branches are three days.* Joseph does not here offer what he thought to be probable, like some ambiguous conjecturer ; but asserts, by the revelation of the Spirit, the meaning of the dream. For why does he say, that by the three branches, three *days* rather than *years* are signified, unless because the Spirit of God had suggested it ? Joseph, therefore, proceeds, by a special impulse above nature, to expound the dream ; and by immediately commending himself to the butler, as if he was already restored, shows how certain and indubitable was the truth of his interpretation : as if he had said, " Be convinced that what thou hast heard of me has come from God." Where also he shows how honourably he thinks of the oracles of God, seeing that he pronounces concerning the future effect with as much confidence as if it had already taken place. But it may be deemed absurd, that Joseph asks for a reward of his prophecy. I answer, that he did not speak as one who would set the gift of God to sale : but it came into his mind, that a method of deliverance was now set before him by God, which it was not lawful for him to reject. Indeed, I do not doubt that a hope of better fortune had been divinely imparted to him. For God, who, even from his childhood, had twice promised him dominion, did not leave him, amidst so many straits, entirely destitute of all consolation. Now this opportunity of seeking deliverance was offered to him by none but God. Wherefore, it is not surprising that Joseph should thus make use of it. With respect to the expression, *Lift up thine head ;* it signifies to raise any one from a low and contemptible condition,

to one of some reputation. Therefore, "*Pharaoh will lift up thine head,*" means, he will bring thee forth from the darkness of the prison, or he will raise thee who art fallen, and restore thee to thy former rank. For I take the word to mean simply *place* or *rank*, and not *basis*.[1]

14. *Show kindness I pray thee unto me.*[2] Although the expression "show kindness" is used among the Hebrews to describe the common exercise of humanity; there is yet no doubt that Joseph spoke simply as his own sad and afflicted condition suggested, for the purpose of inclining the mind of the butler to procure him help. He insists, however, chiefly on this, that he had been thrust into prison for no crime, in order that the butler might not refuse his assistance to an innocent man. For although they who are most wicked find patrons; yet commendation elicited by importunity, which rescues a wicked man from deserved punishment, is in itself an odious and infamous thing. It is, however, probable that Joseph explained his whole cause, so that he fully convinced the butler of his innocence.

16. *When the chief baker saw.*[3] He does not care respecting the skill and fidelity of Joseph as an interpreter; but because Joseph had brought good and useful tidings to his companion, he also desires an interpretation, which he hopes will prove according to his mind. So, many, with ardour and alacrity, desire the word of God, not because they simply wish to be governed by the Lord, and to know what is right, but because they dream of mere enjoyment. When, however, the

---

[1] Pro loco et ordine simpliciter accipio, non autem pro basi. The passage needs explanation. The word ראשך, rendered "thy head," might be rendered "thy *nail*," and some writers have supposed that it should be so translated in this place. The reason given for such a rendering arises from a supposed custom among eastern monarchs of having a large white tablet, on which the name of each officer of state was inscribed, and a *nail* was placed in a hole opposite the name. When the officer offended, the nail was removed from its place, that is, from its *basis* or foundation, and the man's distinction and character were lost.—*Junius in Poli Synopsin.*—*Ed.*

[2] Fac quæso mecum misericordiam.

[3] "The chief baker, in his dream, carries the wicker baskets with various choice baker's commodities on his head. Similar woven baskets, flat and open, for carrying grapes and other fruits, are found represented on the monuments. The art of baking was carried to a high degree of perfection among the Egyptians."—*Egypt and the Books of Moses*, p. 27.—*Ed.*

doctrine does not correspond with their wishes, they depart sorrowful and wounded. Now, although the explanation of the dream was about to prove unpleasant and severe; yet Joseph, by declaring, without ambiguity, what had been revealed unto him, executed with fidelity the office divinely committed to him. This freedom must be maintained by prophets and teachers, that they may not hesitate, by their teaching, to inflict a wound on those whom God has sentenced to death. All love to be flattered. Hence the majority of teachers, in desiring to yield to the corrupt wishes of the world, adulterate the word of God. Wherefore, no one is a sincere minister of God's word, but he, who despising reproach, and being ready, as often as it may be necessary, to attack various offences, will frame his method of teaching according to the command of God. Joseph would, indeed, have preferred to augur well concerning both; but since it is not in his power to give a prosperous fortune to any one, nothing remains for him but frankly to pronounce whatever he has received from the Lord. So, formerly, although the people chose for themselves prophets who would promise them abundance of wine and oil and corn, while they exclaimed loudly against the holy prophets, because they let fall nothing but threatenings, (for these complaints are related in Micah,) yet it was the duty of the servants of the Lord, who had been sent to denounce vengeance, to proceed with severity, although they brought upon themselves hatred and danger.

19. *Pharaoh shall lift up thy head from off thee.* This phrase (in the original) is ambiguous without some addition; and may be taken in a good or a bad sense; just as we say, "With *regard* to any one," or "With *respect* to him;" here the expression is added "from thee." Yet there seems to be an allusion of this kind, as if Joseph had said, "Pharaoh will lift up thy head, that he may take it off." Now, when Moses relates, that what Joseph had predicted happened to both of them, he proves by this sign that Joseph was a true prophet of God, as it is written in Jeremiah. (xxviii. 9.) For that the prophets sometimes threatened punishments, which God abstained from inflicting, was done for this reason, because to such prophecies a condition was annexed. But when

the Lord speaks positively by his servants, it is necessary that whatever he predicts should be confirmed by the result. Therefore, Moses expressly commends in Joseph, his confidence in the heavenly oracle. With regard to what Moses records, that Pharaoh celebrated his birth-day by a great feast, we know that this custom has always been in use, not only among kings, but also among plebeian men. Nor is the custom to be condemned, if only men would keep the right end in view; namely, that of giving thanks unto God by whom they were created and brought up, and whom they have found, in innumerable ways, to be a beneficent Father. But such is the depravity of the world, that it greatly distorts those things which formerly were honestly instituted by their fathers, into contrary corruptions. Thus, by a vicious practice, it has become common for nearly all to abandon themselves to luxury and wantonness on their birth-day. In short, they keep up the memory of God, as the Author of their life, in such a manner as if it were their set purpose to forget Him.

23. *Yet did not the chief butler remember.* This was the most severe trial of Joseph's patience, as we have before intimated. For since he had obtained an advocate who, without trouble, was able to extricate him from prison, especially as the opportunity of doing so had been granted to him by God, he felt a certain assurance of deliverance, and earnestly waited for it every hour. But when he had remained to the end of the second year in suspense, not only did this hope vanish, but greater despair than ever rested upon his mind. Therefore, we are all taught, in his person, that nothing is more improper, than to prescribe the time in which God shall help us; since he purposely, for a long season, keeps his own people in anxious suspense, that, by this very experiment, they may truly know what it is to trust in Him. Besides, in this manner he designed openly to claim for himself the glory of Joseph's liberation. For, if liberty had been granted to him through the entreaty of the butler, it would have been generally believed that this benefit was from man and not from God. Moreover, when Moses says, that the butler was forgetful of Joseph, let it be so understood, that

he did not dare to make any mention of him, lest he should be subjected to reproach, or should be troublesome to the king himself. For it is common with courtiers perfidiously to betray the innocent, and to deliver them to be slain, rather than to offend those of whom they themselves are afraid.

## CHAPTER XLI.

1. AND it came to pass at the end of two full years, that Pharaoh dreamed; and, behold, he stood by the river.
2. And, behold, there came up out of the river seven well-favoured kine, and fat-fleshed; and they fed in a meadow.
3. And, behold, seven other kine came up after them out of the river, ill-favoured, and lean-fleshed; and stood by the *other* kine upon the brink of the river.
4. And the ill-favoured and lean-fleshed kine did eat up the seven well-favoured and fat kine. So Pharaoh awoke.
5. And he slept, and dreamed the second time: and, behold, seven ears of corn came up upon one stalk, rank and good.
6. And, behold, seven thin ears, and blasted with the east wind, sprung up after them.
7. And the seven thin ears devoured the seven rank and full ears. And Pharaoh awoke, and, behold, *it was* a dream.
8. And it came to pass in the morning, that his spirit was troubled; and he sent and called for all the magicians of Egypt, and all the wise men thereof: and Pharaoh told them his dreams; but *there was* none that could interpret them unto Pharaoh.
9. Then spake the chief butler unto Pharaoh, saying, I do remember my faults this day.
10. Pharaoh was wroth with his servants, and put me in ward in the

1. Verum fuit in fine duorum annorum dierum, Pharao somniavit, et ecce, stabat juxta flumen.
2. Ecce autem e flumine ascendebant septem vaccæ pulchræ aspectu, et pingues carne, et pascebant in carecto.
3. Et ecce, septem vaccæ aliæ ascendebant post eas e flumine, turpes aspectu, et tenues carne, et stabant juxta vaccas, *quæ erant* juxta ripam fluminis.
4. Et comederunt vaccæ turpes aspectu, et tenues carne, septem vaccas pulchras aspectu et pingues: et expergefactus est Pharao.
5. Deinde dormivit, et somniavit secundo, et ecce, septem spicæ ascendebant in culmo uno pingues et pulchræ.
6. Et ecce, septem spicæ tenues, et arefactæ Euro, oriebantur post eas.
7. Et deglutiverunt spicæ tenues, septem spicas pingues et plenas: et expergefactus est Pharao, et ecce somnium.
8. Et fuit, mane consternatus est spiritus ejus: misit igitur, et vocavit omnes magos Ægypti, et omnes sapientes ejus, et narravit Pharao eis somnium suum, et non erat ex eis qui interpretaretur ipsi Pharaoni.
9. Et loquutus est princeps pincernarum ad Pharaonem, dicendo, Peccata mea ego reduco in memoriam hodie.
10. Pharao iratus est contra servos suos, et posuit me in custodiam

captain of the guard's house, *both* me and the chief baker:

11. And we dreamed a dream in one night, I and he: we dreamed each man according to the interpretation of his dream.

12. And *there was* there with us a young man, an Hebrew, servant to the captain of the guard; and we told him, and he interpreted to us our dreams: to each man according to his dream he did interpret.

13. And it came to pass, as he interpreted to us, so it was; me he restored unto mine office, and him he hanged.

14. Then Pharaoh sent and called Joseph, and they brought him hastily out of the dungeon: and he shaved *himself*, and changed his raiment, and came in unto Pharaoh.

15. And Pharaoh said unto Joseph, I have dreamed a dream, and *there is* none that can interpret it: and I have heard say of thee, *that* thou canst understand a dream to interpret it.

16. And Joseph answered Pharaoh, saying, *It is* not in me: God shall give Pharaoh an answer of peace.

17. And Pharaoh said unto Joseph, In my dream, behold, I stood upon the bank of the river:

18. And, behold, there came up out of the river seven kine, fat-fleshed, and well-favoured; and they fed in a meadow.

19. And, behold, seven other kine came up after them, poor, and very ill-favoured, and lean-fleshed, such as I never saw in all the land of Egypt for badness:

20. And the lean and the ill-favoured kine did eat up the first seven fat kine.

21. And when they had eaten them up, it could not be known that they had eaten them; but they *were* still ill-favoured, as at the beginning. So I awoke.

22. And I saw in my dream, and, behold, seven ears came up in one stalk, full and good:

23. And, behold, seven ears, with-

---

domus principis satellitum, me et principem pistorum.

11. Et somniavimus somnium nocte eadem, ego et ipse: uterque secundum interpretationem somnii sui somniavimus.

12. Ibi autem erat nobiscum puer Hebræus, servus principis satellitum, et narravimus ei, et interpretatus est nobis somnia nostra, utrique secundum somnium suum interpretatus est.

13. Et fuit, quemadmodum interpretatus est nobis, sic fuit: me redire fecit ad locum meum, et ipsum suspendit.

14. Tunc misit Pharao, et arcessivit Joseph, et celeriter eduxerunt eum e carcere, et totondit *se*, et mutavit vestes suas, et venit ad Pharaonem.

15. Et dixit Pharao ad Joseph, Somnium somniavi, et qui illud interpretetur non est: ego autem audivi de te dici, quod audias somnium ad interpretandum illud.

16. Et respondit Joseph ad Pharaonem, dicendo, Præter me, Deus respondebit in pacem Pharaonis.

17. Tunc loquutus est Pharao ad Joseph, Me somniante ecce, stabam juxta ripam fluminis.

18. Et ecce, e flumine ascendebant septem vaccæ pingues carne, et pulchræ forma, et pascebant in carecto.

19. Ecce vero septem vaccæ aliæ ascendebant post eas tenues, et turpes forma valde, et tenues carne: non vidi similes illis in tota terra Ægypti in turpitudine.

20. Et comederunt vaccæ tenues et turpes, septem vaccas priores pingues.

21. Et venerunt ad interiora earum, et non est cognitum quod venissent ad interiora earum: et aspectus earum turpis, quemadmodum in principio: et expergefactus sum.

22. Vidi præterea dum somniarem, et ecce, septem spicæ ascendebant in culmo uno plenæ et pulchræ.

23. Et ecce item septem spicæ

ered, thin, *and* blasted with the east wind, sprung up after them:

24. And the thin ears devoured the seven good ears. And I told *this* unto the magicians; but *there was* none that could declare *it* to me.

25. And Joseph said unto Pharaoh, The dream of Pharaoh *is* one : God hath shewed Pharaoh what he *is* about to do.

26. The seven good kine *are* seven years; and the seven good ears *are* seven years: the dream *is* one.

27. And the seven thin and ill-favoured kine that came up after them, *are* seven years: and the seven empty ears, blasted with the east wind, shall be seven years of famine.

28. This *is* the thing which I have spoken unto Pharaoh: What God *is* about to do he sheweth unto Pharaoh.

29. Behold, there come seven years of great plenty throughout all the land of Egypt:

30. And there shall arise after them seven years of famine; and all the plenty shall be forgotten in the land of Egypt; and the famine shall consume the land:

31. And the plenty shall not be known in the land by reason of that famine following; for it *shall be* very grievous.

32. And for that the dream was doubled unto Pharaoh twice; *it is* because the thing *is* established by God, and God will shortly bring it to pass.

33. Now therefore let Pharaoh look out a man discreet and wise, and set him over the land of Egypt.

34. Let Pharaoh do *this*, and let him appoint officers over the land, and take up the fifth part of the land of Egypt in the seven plenteous years.

35. And let them gather all the food of those good years that come, and lay up corn under the hand of Pharaoh, and let them keep food in the cities.

36. And that food shall be for store to the land against the seven

parvæ et tenues, percussæ Euro germinabant post eas.

24. Et deglutiverunt spicæ tenues, septem spicas pulchras. Et dixi ad magos, et non fuit qui indicaret mihi.

25. Et dixit Joseph ad Pharaonem, Somnium Pharaonis unum est: quæ Deus facit, indicavit Pharaoni.

26. Septem vaccæ pulchræ, septem anni sunt, et septem spicæ pulchræ, septem anni sunt: somnium idem est.

27. Et septem vaccæ vacuæ et turpes, ascendentes post eas, septem anni sunt: et septem spicæ vacuæ arefactæ Euro, erunt septem anni famis.

28. Hoc est verbum quod loquutus sum ad Pharaonem, quod Deus facit, videre fecit Pharaonem.

29. Ecce, septem anni veniunt abundantiæ magnæ in omni terra Ægypti.

30. Et surgent septem anni famis post eos: et erit in oblivione omnis abundantia in terra Ægypti, et consumet fames terram.

31. Nec cognoscetur abundantia in terra, propter famem ipsam sequentem, quia gravis erit valde.

32. Propterea vero iteratum est somnium ipsi Pharaoni duabus vicibus, quia firma est res a Deo, et festinat Deus facere eam.

33. Nunc igitur provideat Pharao virum prudentem, et sapientem, et constituat illum super terram Ægypti.

34. Faciat Pharao, et præficiat præfectos super terram, et quintam. partem sumat a terra Ægypti in septem annis abundantiæ.

35. Et congregent totam annonam horum annorum bonorum qui venient, congregent, inquam, frumentum sub manu Pharaonis, cibum in urbibus, et servent.

36. Et erit cibus in depositum pro terra, pro septem annis famis qui

years of famine, which shall be in the land of Egypt; that the land perish not through the famine.

37. And the thing was good in the eyes of Pharaoh, and in the eyes of all his servants.

38. And Pharaoh said unto his servants, Can we find *such a one* as this *is*, a man in whom the Spirit of God *is?*

39. And Pharaoh said unto Joseph, Forasmuch as God hath shewed thee all this, *there is* none so discreet and wise as thou *art:*

40. Thou shalt be over my house, and according unto thy word shall all my people be ruled: only in the throne will I be greater than thou.

41. And Pharaoh said unto Joseph, See, I have set thee over all the land of Egypt.

42. And Pharaoh took off his ring from his hand, and put it upon Joseph's hand, and arrayed him in vestures of fine linen, and put a gold chain about his neck:

43. And he made him to ride in the second chariot which he had; and they cried before him, Bow the knee: and he made him *ruler* over all the land of Egypt.

44. And Pharaoh said unto Joseph, I *am* Pharaoh, and without thee shall no man lift up his hand or foot in all the land of Egypt.

45. And Pharaoh called Joseph's name Zaphnath-paaneah; and he gave him to wife Asenath, the daughter of Poti-pherah priest of On. And Joseph went out over *all* the land of Egypt.

46. And Joseph *was* thirty years old when he stood before Pharaoh king of Egypt. And Joseph went out from the presence of Pharaoh, and went throughout all the land of Egypt.

47. And in the seven plenteous years the earth brought forth by handfuls.

48. And he gathered up all the food of the seven years, which were in the land of Egypt, and laid up

erunt in terra Ægypti: ita non succidetur terra propter famem.

37. Placuit sermo in oculis Pharaonis, et in oculis omnium servorum ejus.

38. Et dixit Pharao ad servos suos, Num inveniemus talem virum, in quo Spiritus Dei?

39. Dixit ergo Pharao ad Joseph, Postquam cognoscere fecit Deus te totum hoc, non est intelligens et sapiens sicut tu.

40. Tu eris super domum meam, et ad os tuum osculabitur omnis populus meus: tantum solio major ero te.

41. Itaque dixit Pharao ad Joseph, Vide, posui te super totam terram Ægypti.

42. Et removit Pharao annulum suum e manu sua, posuitque illum in manu Joseph: et indui fecit eum vestibus byssinis, et posuit torquem aureum in collo ejus.

43. Et equitare fecit eum in curru secundi, qui erat apud se, clamabantque ante eum, Abrech, (*id est, pater tener,*) et constituit eum super universam terram Ægypti.

44. Dixit ergo Pharao ad Joseph, Ego Pharao, et sine te non levabit quisquam manum suam et pedem suum in tota terra Ægypti.

45. Et vocavit Pharao nomen Joseph, Saphenath-Paneah, (*id est, vir cui abscondita revelata sunt, vel, absconditorum expositor,*) et dedit ci Asenath filiam Poti-pherah principis On in uxorem, et egressus est Joseph super terram Ægypti.

46. Joseph vero erat vir triginta annorum, quando stetit coram Pharaone rege Ægypti: et egressus est Joseph a facie Pharaonis, et transivit per totam terram Ægypti.

47. Et protulit terra septem annis saturitatis ad collectiones.

48. Et congregavit de universis cibis septem annorum, qui fuerunt in terra Ægypti, et posuit cibum in

the food in the cities: the food of the field, which *was* round about every city, laid he up in the same.

49. And Joseph gathered corn as the sand of the sea, very much, until he left numbering: for *it was* without number.

50. And unto Joseph were born two sons before the years of famine came, which Asenath, the daughter of Poti-pherah priest of On, bare unto him.

51. And Joseph called the name of the first-born Manasseh: For God, *said he,* hath made me forget all my toil, and all my father's house.

52. And the name of the second called he Ephraim: For God hath caused me to be fruitful in the land of my affliction.

53. And the seven years of plenteousness that was in the land of Egypt were ended.

54. And the seven years of dearth began to come, according as Joseph had said: and the dearth was in all lands; but in all the land of Egypt there was bread.

55. And when all the land of Egypt was famished, the people cried to Pharaoh for bread: and Pharaoh said unto all the Egyptians, Go unto Joseph; what he saith to you, do.

56. And the famine was over all the face of the earth. And Joseph opened all the storehouses, and sold unto the Egyptians; and the famine waxed sore in the land of Egypt.

57. And all countries came into Egypt to Joseph for to buy *corn;* because that the famine was *so* sore in all lands.

urbibus: cibum agri civitatis, qui erat in circuitu ejus, posuit in medio ejus.

49. Congregavit itaque Joseph frumentum, tanquam arenam maris multum valde, adeo ut cessaverit numerari, quia non erat numerus.

50. Porro ipsi Joseph nati sunt duo filii antequam veniret annus famis, quos peperit ei Asenath filia Poti-pherah principis On.

51. Et vocavit Joseph nomen primogeniti, Menasseh: quia *dixit,* Oblivisci fecit me Deus omnis laboris mei, et omnis domus patris mei.

52. Nomen autem secundi vocavit Ephraim: quia *dixit,* Crescere fecit me Deus in terra afflictionis meæ.

53. Et finiti sunt septem anni saturitatis, quæ fuit in terra Ægypti.

54. Inceperunt vero septem anni famis venire, quemadmodum dixerat Joseph, fuitque fames in omnibus terris: at in tota terra Ægypti erat panis.

55. Postea esuriit tota terra Ægypti, et clamavit populus ad Pharaonem pro pane: et dixit Pharao omnibus Ægyptiis, Ite ad Joseph, quod dixerit vobis, facietis.

56. Et fames erat in omni superficie terræ: et aperuit Joseph omnia horrea, in quibus erant *frumenta,* et vendidit Ægyptiis: et invaluit fames in terra Ægypti.

57. Et omnes habitatores terræ venerunt in Ægyptum, ut emerent a Joseph: quia invaluerat fames in omni terra.

1. *At the end of two full years.*[1] What anxiety oppressed

[1] In fine duorum annorum dierum. "In the account of Pharaoh's dream, we are first struck with the use of the word אחו, (*Achu,*) Nile grass, an Egyptian word for an Egyptian thing." A note on this passage adds, "Our translators have inaccurately rendered it *meadow,* (ver. 2,) the aquatic plants of the Nile, particularly those of the *litus* kind, were so valuable in Egypt, that they were reaped in as regular a harvest as the flax and corn." The writer proceeds, "In the next place, the seven poor and the seven fat kine attract our attention. The symbol of the cow is very peculiar and

the mind of the holy man during this time, each of us may
conjecture from his own feeling; for we are so tender and
effeminate, that we can scarcely bear to be put off for a short
time. The Lord exercised his servant not only by a delay of
long continuance, but also by another kind of temptation,
because he took all human grounds of hope away from him:
therefore Moses puts "years of days" for complete and full
years. That we may better understand the invincible nature of
his fortitude, we must also notice that winding course of divine
providence, of which I have spoken, and by which Joseph was
led about, till he rose into notice with the king. In the king's
dream, this is worthy to be observed in the first place, that God
sometimes deigns to present his oracles even to unbelieving
and profane men. It was certainly a singular honour to be
instructed concerning an event yet fourteen years future:
for truly the will of God was manifested to Pharaoh, just as
if he had been taught by the word, except that the interpretation of it was to be sought elsewhere. And although
God designs his word especially for the Church, yet it ought
not to be deemed absurd that he sometimes admits even
aliens into his school, though for an inferior end. The doctrine which leads to the hope of eternal life belongs to the
Church; while the children of this world are only taught,
incidentally, concerning the state of the present life. If
we observe this distinction, we shall not wonder that some
oracles are common to profane and heathen men, though
the Church possesses the spiritual doctrine of life, as the
treasure of its own inheritance. That another dream succeeded to the former, arose from two causes; for God both
designed to rouse the mind of Pharaoh to more diligent
inquiry, and to add more light to a vision which was obscure. In short, he follows the same course in this dream
which he does in his daily method of procedure; for he
repeats a second time what he has before delivered, and

exclusively Egyptian. . . . . It is scarcely conceivable that a foreign inventor should have confined himself so closely to the peculiar Egyptian symbols. The circumstance that the kine come up out of the Nile, the fat and also the lean, has reference to the fact that Egypt owes all its fertility to this stream, and that famine succeeds as soon as it fails."—*Egypt and the Books of Moses*, p. 28.—*Ed.*

sometimes inculcates still more frequently, not only that the doctrine may penetrate more deeply into men's hearts, and thus affect them the more; but also that he may render it more familiar to their minds. That by the second dream God designed to illustrate more fully what was obscure in the first, appears from this, that the figure used was more appropriate to the subject revealed. At first, Pharaoh saw fat cows devoured by lean ones. This did not so clearly prefigure the seven years' abundance, and as many years of want in corn and other seeds, as the vision of the ears of corn did: for the similitude, in the latter case, better agrees with the thing represented.

8. *In the morning his spirit was troubled.* A sting was left in Pharaoh's heart, that he might know that he had to deal with God; for this anxiety was as an inward seal of the Spirit of God, to give authenticity to the dream; although Pharaoh deserved to be deprived of the advantage of this revelation, when he resorted to magicians and soothsayers, who were wont to turn the truth of God into a lie.[1] He was convinced by a secret impulse that the dream sent by God portended something important; but he seeks out imposters, who would darken, by their fallacies, the light which was divinely kindled; and it is the folly of the human mind to gather to itself leaders and teachers of error. No doubt he believed them to be true prophets; but because he voluntarily closes his eyes, and hastens into the snare, his false opinion forms no sufficient excuse for him; otherwise men, by merely shutting their eyes, might have some plausible pretext for mocking God with impunity: and we see that many seek protection for themselves in that gross ignorance

---

[1] "Pharaoh calls 'all the magicians of Egypt, and all the wise men thereof,' that they might interpret the dream by which he is troubled. . . . . Now, we find in Egyptian antiquity an order of persons, to whom this is entirely appropriate, which is here ascribed to the magicians. The priests had a double office, the practical worship of the gods, and the pursuit of that which in Egypt was accounted as wisdom. The first belonged to the so-called prophets, the second to the holy scribes. These last were the learned men of the nation; as in the *Pentateuch* they are called *wise men*, so the classical writers named them *sages*. . . . . The interpretation of dreams and also divination belonged to the order of the holy scribes."— *Egypt and the Books of Moses*, p. 29.—*Ed.*

in which they knowingly and purposely involve themselves. Pharaoh, therefore, as far as he was able, deprived himself of the benefit of the prophecy, by seeking for magicians as the interpreters of it. So we see it daily happens that many lose hold of the truth, because they either bring a cloud over themselves by their own indolence, or too eagerly catch at false and spurious inventions. But because the Lord would, at that time, succour the kingdom of Egypt, he drew Pharaoh back, as by main force, from his error.

*There was none that could interpret.* By this remedy God provided that the dream should not fail. We know what an inflated and impudent race of men these soothsayers were, and how extravagantly they boasted. How did it then happen that they gave the king no answer, seeing they might have trifled in any way whatever with a credulous man, who willingly suffered himself to be deluded? Therefore, that he might desist from inquiry, he is not allowed to find what he had expected in his magicians: and the Lord so strikes dumb the wicked workers of deceit, that they cannot even find a specious explanation of the dreams. Moreover, by this method, the anxiety of the king is sharpened; because he considers that what has escaped the sagacity of the magicians must be something very serious and secret. By which example we are taught, that the Lord provides the best for us, when he removes the incitements of error from those of us who wish to be deceived; and we must regard it as a singular favour, when either false prophets are silenced, or their fatuity is, in any manner, discovered to us. As for the rest, the king might hence easily gather how frivolous and nugatory was the profession of wisdom, in which the Egyptians gloried above all others; for they boasted that they were possessed of the science of divination which ascended above the very heavens. But now, as far as they are concerned, the king is without counsel, and, being disappointed of his hope, is filled with anguish; nevertheless he does not so awake as to shake off his superstition. Thus we see that men, though admonished, remain still in their torpor. Whence we plainly perceive how inexcusable is the obstinacy of the world, which does not desist from following those delusions which are openly condemned as foolishness, from heaven.

9. *Then spake the chief butler.* Although the Lord took pity on Egypt, yet he did it not for the sake of the king, or of the country, but that Joseph might, at length, be brought out of prison; and further, that, in the time of famine, food might be supplied to the Church: for although the produce was stored with no design beyond that of providing for the kingdom of Egypt; yet God chiefly cared for his Church, which he esteemed more highly than ten worlds. Therefore the butler, who had resolved to be silent respecting Joseph, is constrained to speak for the liberation of the holy man. In saying, *I do remember my faults this day,* he is understood by some as confessing the fault of ingratitude, because he had not kept the promise he had given. But the meaning is different; for he could not speak concerning his imprisonment, without interposing a preface of this kind, through fear, lest suspicion should enter into the mind of the king, that his servant thought himself injured; or, should take offence, as if the butler had not been sensible of the benefit conferred upon him. We know how sensitive are the minds of kings; and the courtier had found this out by long experience: therefore he begins by acknowledging that he had been justly cast into prison. Whence it follows that he was indebted to the clemency of the king for restoration to his former state.

14. *Then Pharaoh sent and called Joseph.* We see in the person of a proud king, as in a glass, what necessity can effect. They whose circumstances are happy and prosperous will scarcely condescend to hear those whom they esteem true prophets, still less will they listen to strangers. Wherefore it was necessary that the obstinacy of Pharaoh should be first subdued, in order that he might send for Joseph, and accept him as his master and instructor. The same kind of preparation is also necessary even for the elect; because they never become docile until the pride of the flesh is laid low. Whenever, therefore, we are cast into grievous troubles, which keep us in perplexity and anxiety, let us know that God, in this manner, is accomplishing his design of render-

ing us obedient to himself. When Moses relates that Joseph, before he came into the presence of the king, changed his garments, we may hence conjecture that his clothing was mean. To the same point, what is added respecting his "shaving himself," ought, in my opinion, to be referred: for since Egypt was a nation of effeminate delicacy, it is probable that they, being studious of neatness and elegance, rather nourished their hair than otherwise.[1] But as Joseph put off his squalid raiment, so, that he might have no remaining cause of shame, he is shaved. Let us know, then, that the servant of God lay in filth even to the day of his deliverance.

15. *And Pharaoh said unto Joseph.* We see that Pharaoh offers himself as a disciple to Joseph, being persuaded, by the statement of the butler, that he is a prophet of God. This is, indeed, a constrained humility; but it is expressly recorded, in order that, when the opportunity of learning[2] is afforded us, we may not refuse reverently to honour the gifts of the Spirit. Now, though Joseph, in referring Pharaoh to God, seems to deny that he himself is about to interpret the dream, yet his answer bears on a different point: for, because he knew that he was conversing with a heathen addicted to superstitions, he wishes, above all things, to ascribe to God the glory due to him; as if he had said, I am able to do nothing in this matter, nor will I offer anything as from myself; but God alone shall be the interpreter of his own secret.[3] Should any one object, that

---

[1] This conjecture of Calvin's is erroneous. "*Herodotus* mentions it among the distinguishing peculiarities of the Egyptians, that they commonly were shaved, but in mourning they allowed the beard to grow. The sculptures also agree with this representation. 'So particular,' says *Wilkinson*, 'were they on this point, that to have neglected it was a subject of reproach and ridicule; and whenever they intended to convey the idea of a man of low condition, or a slovenly person, the artists represented him with a beard.'"—*Egypt and the Books of Moses*, p. 30.—*Ed.*

[2] In the Amsterdam edition, it is "facultas dicendi," but in Hengstenberg's it is "facultas discendi;" and as the French version has it "le moyen d'apprendre," there can be no doubt that the later Latin edition is right. —*Ed.*

[3] The force of Joseph's language is remarkable: "Without me, God will answer to the peace of Pharaoh." He thus entirely renounces, in a single word, all the personal honour which the heathen monarch was dis-

whenever God uses the agency of men, their office ought to be referred to in connection with his command: that indeed I acknowledge, but yet so that the whole glory may remain with God; according to the saying of St. Paul, " Neither is he that planteth anything, neither he that watereth." (1 Cor. iii. 7.) Moreover, Joseph not only desires to embue the mind of Pharaoh with some relish for piety, but, by ascribing the gift of interpreting dreams to God alone, confesses that he is destitute of it, until he obtains it from God. Wherefore, let us also learn, from the example of holy Joseph, to honour the grace of God even among unbelievers; and if they shut the door against the entire and full doctrine of piety; we must, at least, endeavour to instil some drops of it into their minds. Let us also reflect on this, that nothing is less tolerable than for men to arrogate to themselves anything as their own; for this is the first step of wisdom, to ascribe nothing to ourselves; but modestly to confess, that whatever in us is worthy of praise, flows only from the fountain of God's grace. It is especially worthy of notice, that as the Spirit of understanding is given to any one from heaven, he will become a proper and faithful interpreter of God.

16. *God shall give Pharaoh an answer of peace.* Joseph added this from the kindly feeling of his heart; for he did not yet comprehend what the nature of the oracle would be. Therefore he could not, in his character as a prophet, promise a successful and desirable issue; but, as it was his duty sincerely to deliver what he received from the Lord, however sad and severe it might prove; so, on the other hand, this liberty presented no obstacle to his wishing a joyful issue to the king. Therefore, what is here said to the king concerning peace, is a prayer rather than a prophecy.

17. *In my dream.* This whole narration does not need to be explained, for Pharaoh only repeats what we have before considered, with the addition, that the lean cows, having devoured the fat ones, were rendered nothing better. Whereby God designed to testify, that the dearth would be so great, that the people, instead of being nourished by the

posed to pay him, that God alone may have the glory due unto his name. —*Ed.*

abundance of food gathered together, would be famished, and drag on a miserable existence. Joseph, in answering that the two dreams were one, simply means, that one and the same thing was showed unto Pharaoh by two figures. But before he introduces his interpretation, he maintains that this is not a merely vanishing dream, but a divine oracle: for unless the vision had proceeded from God, it would have been foolish to inquire anxiously what it portended. Pharaoh, therefore, does not here labour in vain in inquiring into the counsel of God. The form of speaking, however, requires to be noticed; because Joseph does not barely say that God will declare beforehand what may happen from some other quarter, but what he himself is about to do. We hence infer, that God does not indolently contemplate the fortuitous issue of things, as most philosophers vainly talk; but that he determines, at his own will, what shall happen. Wherefore, in predicting events, he does not give a response from the tables of fate, as the poets feign concerning their Apollo, whom they regard as a prophet of events which are not in his own power, but declares that whatever shall happen will be his own work. So Isaiah, that he may ascribe to God alone the glory due to him, attributes to him, both the revealing of things future, and the government of all his events, by his own authority. (Is. xlv. 7.) For he cries aloud that God is neither deceived, nor deceives, like the idols; and he declares that God alone is the author of good and evil; understanding by *evil*, adversity. Wherefore, unless we would cast God down from his throne, we must leave to him his power of action, as well as his foreknowledge. And this passage is the more worthy of observation; because, in all ages, many foolish persons have endeavoured to rob God of half his glory, and now (as I have said) the same figment pleases many philosophers; because they think it absurd to ascribe to God whatever is done in the world: as if truly the Scripture had in vain declared, that his "judgments are a great deep." (Ps. xxxvi. 7.) But while they would subject the works of God to the judgment of their own brain, having rejected his word, they prefer giving credit to Plato respecting celestial mysteries. "That God," they say, "has foreknowledge of all things, does not involve the necessity of their occurrence:" as if, indeed, we asserted, that bare prescience was the cause of things, instead of maintaining the connection established by Moses, that God foreknows things that are future, because he had determined to do them; but they ignorantly and perversely separate the providence of God from his eternal counsel, and his continual operation. Above all things, it is right to be fully persuaded that, whenever the earth is barren, whether frost, or drought, or hail, or any other thing, may be the cause of it, the whole result is directed by the counsel of God.

32. *And for that the dream was doubled.* Joseph does not mean to say, that what God may have declared but once, is mutable: but he would prevent Pharaoh's confidence respecting the event revealed, from being shaken. For since God pronounces nothing but from his own fixed and steadfast purpose, it is enough that he should have spoken once. But our dulness and inconstancy cause him to repeat the same thing the more frequently, in order that what he has certainly decreed, may be fixed in our hearts; otherwise, as our disposition is variable, so, what we have once heard from his mouth, is tossed up and down by us, until it entirely escapes our memory. Moreover, Joseph not only commemorates the stability of the heavenly decree, but also declares that what God has determined to do, is near at hand, lest Pharaoh himself should slumber in the confident expectation of longer delay. For though we confess that the judgments of God are always hanging over our heads, yet unless we are stimulated by the thought of their speedy approach, we are but slightly affected with anxiety and fear respecting them.

33. *Now therefore let Pharaoh look out a man.* Joseph does more than he had been asked to do; for he is not merely the interpreter of the dream; but, as fulfilling the office of a prophet, he adds instruction and counsel. For we know that the true and lawful prophets of God do not barely predict what will happen in future; but propose remedies for impending evils. Therefore Joseph, after he had uttered a prophecy of the changes which would take

place in fourteen years, now teaches what ought to be done; and exhorts Pharaoh to be vigilant in the discharge of his duty. And one of the marks by which God always distinguished his own prophets from false prognosticators, was to endue them with the power of teaching and exhorting, that they might not uselessly predict future events. Let us grant that the predictions of Apollo, and of all the magicians were true, and were not entangled with ambiguous expressions; yet whither did they tend, but either to drive men headlong in perverse confidence, or to plunge them into despair? A very different method of prophesying was divinely prescribed, which would form men to piety, would lead them to repentance, and would excite them to prayer when oppressed with fear. Moreover, because the prophecy of which mention is here made, was published only for the temporal advantage of this fleeting life, Joseph proceeds no further than to show the king for what purpose the dream had been sent to him; as if he had said, " Be not sorry on account of this revelation; accept this advantage from it, that thou mayest succour the poverty of thy kingdom." However, there is no doubt that God guided his tongue, in order that Pharaoh might entrust him with this office. For he does not craftily insinuate himself into the king's favour, nor abuse the gift of revelation to his private gain: but, what had been divinely ordained was brought to its proper issue without his knowledge; namely, that the famishing house of Jacob should find unexpected sustenance.

35. *Under the hand of Pharaoh.* Whereas prosperity so intoxicates men, that the greater part make no provision for themselves against the future, but absorb the present abundance by intemperance; Joseph advises the king to take care that the country may have its produce laid up in store. Besides, the common people would also form themselves to habits of frugality, when they understood that this great quantity of corn was not collected in vain by the king, but that a remedy was hereby sought for some unwonted calamity. In short, because luxury generally prevails in prosperity, and wastes the blessings of God, the bridle of authority was necessary. This is the reason why Joseph directed that

garners should be established under the power of the king, and that corn should be gathered into them. He concludes at length, that the dream was useful, although at first sight, it would seem sad and inauspicious: because, immediately after the wound had been shown, the means of cure were suggested.

38. *Can we find such a one as this?* We see that necessity is an excellent teacher. If prefects or judges are to be created, some one is advanced to the honour because he is a favourite, without consideration of his desert; whence it happens that they who are most unworthy frequently creep into office. And although we see political order disturbed and mankind involved in many inconveniences, because they who are least suitable, rashly push themselves, by wicked contrivances, into affairs for which they are not able to manage; nevertheless, ambition triumphs, and subverts equity. But necessity extorts a sober judgment. Pharaoh says nothing but what is naturally engraven on the hearts of all men, that honours ought to be conferred on none but competent persons, and such as God has furnished with the necessary qualifications. Experience, however, abundantly teaches, that this law of nature slips from the memory, whenever men are free to offend against it with impunity. Therefore the pride of Pharaoh was wisely so subdued, that he, setting aside ambition, preferred a foreigner just brought out of prison, to all his courtiers, because he excelled them in virtue. The same necessity restrained the nobles of the kingdom, so that they did not each contend, according to their custom, to obtain the priority of rank for themselves. And although it was but a compulsory modesty, inasmuch as they were ashamed to resist the public good; yet there is no doubt, that God inspired them with fear, so that, by the common consent of all, Joseph was made president of the whole kingdom. It is also to be observed that Pharaoh, though he had been infatuated by his soothsayers, nevertheless honours the gifts of the Spirit in Joseph: because God, indeed, never suffers man to become so brutalized, as not to feel his power, even in their darkness. And therefore whatever impious defection may hurry them away, there still abides with them a

remaining sense of Deity. Meanwhile, that knowledge is of little worth, which does not correct a man's former madness; for he despises the God whom with his mouth he proclaims: and has no conception of any other than I know not what confused divinity. This kind of knowledge often enlightens profane men, yet not so as to cause them to repent. Whereby we are admonished to regard any particular principle as of small value, till solid piety springs from it and flourishes.

40. *Thou shalt be over my house.* Not only is Joseph made governor of Egypt, but is adorned also with the insignia of royalty, that all may reverence him, and may obey his command. The royal signet is put upon his finger for the confirmation of decrees. He is clothed in robes of fine linen, which were then a luxury, and were not to be had at any common price. He is placed in the most honourable chariot.[1] It may, however, be asked, whether it was lawful for the holy man to appear with so great pomp? I answer, although such splendour can scarcely ever be free from blame, and therefore frugality in external ornaments is best; yet all kind of splendour in kings and other princes of the world is not to be condemned, provided they neither too earnestly desire it, nor make an ostentatious display of it. Moderation is, indeed, always to be cultivated; but since it was not in Joseph's power to prescribe the mode of investiture, and the royal authority would not have been granted to him without the accustomed pomp of state, he was at liberty to accept more than seemed in itself desirable. If the option be given to the servants of God, nothing is safer for them, than to cut off whatever they can of outward splendour. And where

---

[1] Of the marks of distinction conferred by Pharaoh upon Joseph, mentioned in verses 42 and 43 of this chapter; the first is the signet-ring which was common to the nations of the East as well as to Egypt. The next is the "vesture of fine linen," or *byssus,* which was a peculiarly Egyptian token of honour. The third is the gold chain, or the necklace of gold, "of which the Egyptian monuments afford abundant explanation." Modern objectors to the Mosaic account pretend that all the ornaments here mentioned belong to a later date. But such remarks, as Hengstenberg observes, "have interest only as they show how far the investigations of the rationalists, in reference to the Pentateuch, fall short of the present advanced state of knowledge respecting Egyptian antiquity."—*Ed.*

it is necessary for them to accommodate themselves to public custom, they must beware of all ostentation and vanity. With respect to the explanation of the words; whereas we render them, "At thy mouth all the people shall *kiss*,"[1] others prefer to read, "shall be *armed;*" others, "shall be fed at thy will or commandment;" but as the proper signification of the verb נשק (*nashak*) is to kiss, I do not see why interpreters should twist it to another sense. Yet I do not think that here any special token of reverence is intended; but the phrase rather seems to be metaphorical, to the effect that the people should cordially receive and obediently embrace whatever might proceed from the mouth of Joseph: as if Pharaoh had said, "Whatever he may command, it is my will that the people shall receive with one consent, as if all should kiss him." "The second chariot," is read by the Hebrews in construction, for the chariot of the viceroy, who holds the second place from the king. The sense, however, is clear, that Joseph has the precedence of all the nobles of Egypt.

There are various opinions about the meaning of the word אברך, (*abraik*.) They who explain it by "tender father," because Joseph, being yet in tender years, was endowed with the prudence and gravity of old age, seem to me to bring something from afar to correspond with their own fancy. They who render it "the father of the king," as if the word were compounded of the Hebrew noun אב, (*ab*,) and the Arabic רך, (*rak*,) have little more colour for their interpretation. If, indeed, the word be Hebrew, the meaning preferred by others, "Bow the knee," seems to me more probable. But because I rather suppose that Egyptian terms are referred to by Moses, both in this place and shortly afterwards, I advise the readers not to distort them in vain. And truly those interpreters are ridiculously subtle, who suppose that a Hebrew name was given him by an Egyptian king, which they render either "the Redeemer of the world," or "the Ex-

[1] Osculabitur totus populus ad os tuum. The English version is, "According unto thy word shall all my people be ruled:" which is a free translation, bearing, according to Calvin's explanation, the true sense of the original. The margin of our Bible gives "be armed," or, "kiss,' instead of the words "be ruled."—*Ed.*

pounder of mysteries."[1] I prefer following the Greek interpreters, who, by leaving both words untouched, sufficiently prove that they thought them to be of a foreign language. That the father-in-law of Joseph was, as is commonly believed, a *priest*, is what I cannot refute, though I can scarcely be induced to believe it. Therefore, since כהן (*cohen*) signifies a *prince* as well as a *priest*, it seems to me probable that he was one of the nobles of the court, who might also be the satrap or prefect of the city of On.[2]

46. *And Joseph was thirty years old.* For two reasons Moses records the age at which Joseph was advanced to the government of the kingdom. First, because it is seldom that old men give themselves up to be governed by the young: whence it may be inferred that it was by the singular providence of God that Joseph governed without being envied, and that reverence and majesty were given him beyond his years. For if there was danger lest Timothy's youth should render him contemptible, Joseph would have been equally exposed to contempt, unless authority had been divinely procured for him. And although he could not have obtained this authority by his own industry, yet it is probable that the extraordinary virtues with which God had endowed him,

---

[1] This is the rendering given of the name *Zaphnath-paneah* by Jerome, and by the Chaldee Paraphrast respectively. The reader may consult Rivetus in his Exercitation clviii., Gesenius's Lexicon, and the Commentaries of Bush and Dr. A. Clarke.—*Ed.*

[2] That the word כהן (*cohen*) generally signifies *priest*, is not to be disputed. Gesenius earnestly contends that this is its *invariable* meaning; but to establish his point, he is obliged to regard some as priests who were not of the tribe of Levi. This seems conclusive against him; for there is no room for doubt that none were, or could be, priests who sprang from any other tribe. Yet so much, perhaps, ought to be conceded to the primary meaning of the word, that it should be translated priest, wherever the sense of the passage does not require another interpretation. Such a rule would determine its meaning in this passage. The following remarks of Hengstenberg deserve attention. " According to chapter xli. 45, Pharaoh gives to Joseph, Asenath, the daughter of Potiphera, the priest of On, in marriage. This name (which means he who belongs to the sun) is very common on the Egyptian monuments, and is especially appropriate for the Priest of On, or Heliopolis (the city of the sun). Since Pharaoh evidently intended, by this act, to establish the power bestowed on Joseph upon a firm basis, it is implied in this account; first, that Egyptian High Priests occupied a very important position; and, secondly, that among them the High Priest of On was the most distinguished. Both these points are confirmed by history.."—*See Egypt and the Books of Moses,* p. 32.—*Ed.*

availed not a little to increase and confirm it. A second reason for noting his age is, that the reader may reflect on the long duration of the sufferings with which he had been, in various ways, afflicted. And however humane his treatment might have been; still, thirteen years of exile, which had prevented his return to his father's house, not merely by the bond of servitude, but also by imprisonment, would prove a most grievous trial. Therefore, it was only after he had been proved by long endurance, that he was advanced to a better state. Moses then subjoins, that he discharged his duties with diligence and with most punctual fidelity; for the circuit taken by him, which is here mentioned, was a proof of no common industry. He might, indeed, have appointed messengers, on whose shoulders he could have laid the greater part of the labour and trouble; but because he knew himself to be divinely called to the work, as one who had to render an account to the divine tribunal, he refused no part of the burden. And Moses, in a few words, praises his incredible prudence, in having quickly found out the best method of preserving the corn. For it was an arduous task to erect storehouses in every city, which should contain the entire produce of one year, and a fifth part more.[1] This arrangement was also not less a proof of sagacity, in providing that the inhabitants of any given region should not have to seek food at a distance. Immediately afterwards his integrity is mentioned, which was equally deserving of praise; because in the immense accumulation which was made, he abstained from all self-indulgence, just as if some humble office only, had been assigned to him. But it is to the praise of both these virtues that, after he has collected immense heaps, he remits nothing of his wonted diligence, until he has accomplished all the duties of the office which he had undertaken. The ancient proverb

[1] "The labours of Joseph in building storehouses are placed vividly before us in the paintings upon the monuments, which show how common the storehouse was in ancient Egypt. In a tomb at *Elethya*, a man is represented whose business it evidently was to take account of the number of bushels which another man, acting under him, measures.... Then follows the transportation of the grain. From the measurer, others take it and carry it into the storehouses."—*Egypt and the Books of Moses*, p. 36. —*Ed.*

says, "Satiety produces disgust," and in the same manner abundance is commonly the mother of idleness. Whence, therefore, is it, that the diligence of Joseph holds on its even course, and does not become remiss at the sight of present abundance, except because he prudently considers, that, however great the plenty might be, seven years of famine would swallow it all up? He manifested also his fidelity, and his extraordinary care for the public safety, in this, that he did not become weary by the assiduous labour of seven years, nor did he ever rest till he had made provision for the seven years which still remained.

50. *And unto Joseph were born two sons.* Although the names which Joseph gave his sons in consequence of the issue of his affairs, breathe somewhat of piety, because in them he celebrates the kindness of God: yet the oblivion of his father's house, which, he says, had been brought upon him, can scarcely be altogether excused. It was a pious and holy motive to gratitude, that God had caused him to "forget" all his former miseries; but no honour ought to have been so highly valued, as to displace from his mind the desire and the remembrance of his father's house. Granted that he is Viceroy of Egypt, yet his condition is unhappy, as long as he is an exile from the Church. Some, in order to exculpate the holy man, explain the passage as meaning that he so rejoiced in the present favour of God, as to make him afterwards forgetful of the injuries inflicted upon him by his brethren; but this (in my judgment) is far too forced. And truly, we must not anxiously labour to excuse the sin of Joseph; but rather, I think, we are admonished how greatly we ought to be on our guard against the attractions of the world, lest our minds should be unduly gratified by them. Behold Joseph, although he purely worships God, is yet so captivated by the sweetness of honour, and has his mind so clouded, that he becomes indifferent to his father's house, and pleases himself in Egypt. But this was almost to wander from the fold of God. It was, indeed, a becoming modesty, that from a desire of proclaiming the Divine goodness towards him, he was not ashamed to perpetuate a memorial of his depressed condition in the names of his sons.

They who are raised on high, from an obscure and ignoble position, desire to extinguish the knowledge of their origin, because they deem it disgraceful to themselves. Joseph, however, regarded the commendation of Divine grace more highly than an ostentatious future nobility.

53. *And the seven years.... were ended.* Already the former unwonted fertility, which showed Joseph to have been a true prophet, had procured for him a name and reputation; and in this way the Egyptians had been restrained from raising any tumult against him. Nevertheless, it is wonderful that a people so proud should have borne, in the time of prosperity, the rule of a foreigner. But the famine which followed proved a more sharp and severe curb for the subjugation of their lofty and ferocious spirits, in order that they might be brought into subjection to authority. When, however, Moses says that there was corn in all the land of Egypt, while the neighbouring regions were suffering from hunger, he seems to intimate that wheat had also been laid up by private persons. And, indeed, (as we have said elsewhere,) it was impossible but the rumour of the approaching famine would be spread abroad, and would everywhere infuse fears and solicitude, so that each person would make some provision for himself. Nevertheless, however provident each might be, what they had preserved would, in a short time, be consumed. Whence it appeared with what skill and prudence Joseph had perceived from the beginning, that Egypt would not be safe, unless provisions were publicly gathered together under the hand of the king.

55. *Go unto Joseph.* It is by no means unusual for kings, while their subjects are oppressed by extreme sufferings, to give themselves up to pleasures. But Moses here means something else; for Pharaoh does not exonerate himself from the trouble of distributing corn, because he wishes to enjoy a repose free from all inconvenience; but because he has such confidence in holy Joseph, that he willingly leaves all things to him, and does not allow him to be disturbed in the discharge of the office which he had undertaken.

## CHAPTER XLII.

1. Now when Jacob saw that there was corn in Egypt, Jacob said unto his sons, Why do ye look one upon another?
2. And he said, Behold, I have heard that there is corn in Egypt: get you down thither, and buy for us from thence; that we may live, and not die.
3. And Joseph's ten brethren went down to buy corn in Egypt.
4. But Benjamin, Joseph's brother, Jacob sent not with his brethren: for he said, Lest peradventure mischief befall him.
5. And the sons of Israel came to buy *corn* among those that came: for the famine was in the land of Canaan.
6. And Joseph *was* the governor over the land, *and* he *it was* that sold to all the people of the land: and Joseph's brethren came, and bowed down themselves before him *with* their faces to the earth.
7. And Joseph saw his brethren, and he knew them, but made himself strange unto them, and spake roughly unto them; and he said unto them, Whence come ye? And they said, From the land of Canaan to buy food.
8. And Joseph knew his brethren, but they knew not him.
9. And Joseph remembered the dreams which he dreamed of them, and said unto them, Ye *are* spies; to see the nakedness of the land ye are come.
10. And they said unto him, Nay, my lord; but to buy food are thy servants come.
11. We *are* all one man's sons: we *are* true *men*, thy servants are no spies.
12. And he said unto them, Nay, but to see the nakedness of the land ye are come.
13. And they said, Thy servants

1. Quum autem videret Jahacob quod esset frumentum in Ægypto, dixit Jahacob filiis suis, Utquid aspicitis vos?
2. Et dixit, Ecce, audivi quod est frumentum in Ægypto: descendite illuc, et emite nobis inde, et vivemus, nec moriemur.
3. Descenderunt ergo fratres Joseph decem, ut emerent frumentum in Ægypto.
4. (Nam Benjamin fratrem Joseph non misit Jahacob cum fratribus suis: quia dixit, Ne forte accidat ei mors.)
5. Et venerunt filii Israel, ut emerent in medio venientium: erat enim fames in terra Chenaan.
6. Joseph autem erat dominus super terram: ipse vendebat toti populo terræ: venerunt, inquam, fratres Joseph, et incurvaverunt se ei in faciem super terram.
7. Et vidit Joseph fratres suos, et agnovit eos, et alienum se ostendit eis: locutusque est cum eis dura, et dixit eis, Unde venistis? Et dixerunt, De terra Chenaan ad emendum cibum.
8. Agnovit Joseph fratres suos: ipsi autem non agnoverunt eum.
9. Et recordatus est Joseph somniorum, quæ somniaverat de eis, dixitque, Exploratores estis, ad videndum nuditatem terræ venistis.
10. Et dixerunt ad eum, Nequaquam, domine mi: sed servi tui venerunt ad emendum cibum.
11. Omnes nos filii ejusdem viri sumus: veraces sumus, non sunt servi tui exploratores.
12. Et dixit illis, Nequaquam: sed nuditatem terræ venistis ad videndum.
13. Et dixerunt, Duodecim servi

*are* twelve brethren, the sons of one man in the land of Canaan; and, behold, the youngest *is* this day with our father, and one *is* not.

14. And Joseph said unto them, That *is it* that I spake unto you, saying, Ye *are* spies.

15. Hereby ye shall be proved: By the life of Pharaoh ye shall not go forth hence, except your youngest brother come hither.

16. Send one of you, and let him fetch your brother, and ye shall be kept in prison, that your words may be proved, whether *there be any* truth in you: or else, by the life of Pharaoh, surely ye *are* spies.

17. And he put them all together into ward three days.

18. And Joseph said unto them the third day, This do, and live; *for* I fear God.

19. If ye *be* true *men*, let one of your brethren be bound in the house of your prison: go ye, carry corn for the famine of your houses:

20. But bring your youngest brother unto me; so shall your words be verified, and ye shall not die. And they did so.

21. And they said one to another, We *are* verily guilty concerning our brother, in that we saw the anguish of his soul, when he besought us, and we would not hear; therefore is this distress come upon us.

22. And Reuben answered them, saying, Spake I not unto you, saying, Do not sin against the child? and ye would not hear; therefore, behold, also his blood is required.

23. And they knew not that Joseph understood *them;* for he spake unto them by an interpreter.

24. And he turned himself about from them, and wept; and returned to them again, and communed with them, and took from them Simeon, and bound him before their eyes.

25. Then Joseph commanded to fill their sacks with corn, and to restore every man's money into his

tui fratres sumus, filii viri ejusdem in terra Chenaan: et ecce, minimus est cum patre nostro hodie, et unus non est.

14. Tunc dixit ad eos Joseph, Hoc est quod locutus sum ad vos, dicendo, Exploratores estis.

15. In hoc probabimini: per vitam Pharaonis, si egressi fueritis hinc, nisi quum venerit frater vester minimus huc.

16. Mittite ex vobis unum, et accipiat fratrem vestrum, vos autem vincti eritis, et probabuntur verba vestra, an veritas sit penes vos: sin minus, per vitam Pharaonis certe exploratores estis.

17. Et congregavit eos in custodiam tribus diebus.

18. Dixit autem eis Joseph die tertio, Hoc facite, et vivetis: Deum ego timeo.

19. Si veraces estis, frater vester unus ligetur in domo custodiæ vestræ: vos autem ite, auferte alimentum ad abigendam famem e domibus vestris.

20. Tunc fratrem vestrum minimum adducetis ad me, et vera cognoscentur (*Heb. verificabuntur*) verba vestra, et non moriemini: et fecerunt ita.

21. Dicebat autem alter alteri, Vere deliquimus contra fratrem nostrum: quia vidimus angustiam animæ ejus dum deprecaretur nos, et non audivimus: idcirco venit super nos angustia hæc.

22. Et respondit Reuben ad eos, dicendo, Nonne dixi vobis, dicendo, Ne peccetis in puerum, et non audistis? et etiam sanguis ejus, ecce, requiritur.

23. Ipsi autem ignorabant, quod audiret Joseph: quia interpres erat inter eos.

24. Et vertit se ab eis, et flevit: postea reversus est ad eos, loquutusque est eis: et accepit ab eis Simhon, ligavitque eum in oculis eorum.

25. Tunc præcepit Joseph, et impleverunt vasa eorum frumento: *præcepit* etiam ut restituerent ar-

sack, and to give them provision for the way: and thus did he unto them.

26. And they laded their asses with the corn, and departed thence.

27. And as one of them opened his sack, to give his ass provender in the inn, he espied his money; for, behold, it *was* in his sack's mouth.

28. And he said unto his brethren, My money is restored; and, lo, *it is* even in my sack: and their heart failed *them*, and they were afraid, saying one to another, What *is* this *that* God hath done unto us?

29. And they came unto Jacob their father unto the land of Canaan, and told him all that befell unto them; saying,

30. The man, *who is* the lord of the land, spake roughly to us, and took us for spies of the country.

31. And we said unto him, We *are* true *men;* we are no spies.

32. We *be* twelve brethren, sons of our father: one *is* not, and the youngest *is* this day with our father in the land of Canaan.

33. And the man, the lord of the country, said unto us, Hereby shall I know that ye *are* true *men;* leave one of your brethren *here* with me, and take *food for* the famine of your households, and be gone;

34. And bring your youngest brother unto me: then shall I know that ye *are* no spies, but *that* ye *are* true *men:* so will I deliver you your brother, and ye shall traffick in the land.

35. And it came to pass, as they emptied their sacks, that, behold, every man's bundle of money *was* in his sack: and when *both* they and their father saw the bundles of money, they were afraid.

36. And Jacob their father said unto them, Me have ye bereaved *of my children:* Joseph *is* not, and Simeon *is* not, and ye will take Benjamin *away*. All these things are against me.

37. And Reuben spake unto his

gentum eorum, uniuscujusque in sacco suo, et darent eis escam ad iter : et fecit eis sic.

26. Et tulerunt frumentum suum super asinos suos, et abierunt inde.

27. Aperuit autem unus saccum suum, ut daret pabulum asino suo, in hospitio : et vidit pecuniam suam, et ecce, erat in ore sacci sui.

28. Et dixit fratribus suis, Reddita est pecunia mea, et etiam ecce, est in sacco meo. Et egressum est cor eorum, et obstupuerunt alter ad alterum, dicendo, Utquid hoc fecit Deus nobis?

29. Et venerunt ad Jahacob patrem suum in terram Chenaan, et annuntiaverunt ei omnia quæ acciderant eis, dicendo,

30. Loquutus est vir dominus terræ nobiscum dura, et constituit nos tanquam exploratores terræ.

31. Nos vero diximus ad eum, Veraces sumus, non sumus exploratores.

32. Duodecim sumus fratres filii patris nostri : unus non est, et minimus hodie est cum patre nostro in terra Chenaan.

33. Tunc dixit nobis vir dominus terræ, In hoc cognoscam quod veraces estis, Fratrem vestrum unum relinquite mecum, et *ad expellendam* famem domorum vestrarum capite, et ite :

34. Et adducite fratrem vestrum minimum ad me, tunc cognoscam quod non estis exploratores, sed veraces : fratrem vestrum dabo vobis, et in terra negotiabimini.

35. Porro fuit, ipsis evacuantibus saccos suos, ecce, uniuscujusque ligatura pecuniæ suæ erat in sacco suo : et viderunt ligaturas pecuniarum suarum, ipsi, et pater eorum, et timuerunt.

36. Et dixit ad eos Jahacob pater eorum, Me orbastis, Joseph non est, et Simhon non est, et Benjamin capietis : adversum me sunt omnia hæc.

37. Tunc dixit Reuben ad pa-

father, saying, Slay my two sons, if I bring him not to thee: deliver him into my hand, and I will bring him to thee again.

38. And he said, My son shall not go down with you; for his brother is dead, and he is left alone: if mischief befall him by the way in the which ye go, then shall ye bring down my gray hairs with sorrow to the grave.

trem suum, dicendo, Duos filios meos mori facias, nisi reduxero eum ad te: da eum in manum meam, et ego reducam eum ad te.

38. Et dixit, Non descendet filius meus vobiscum, quia frater ejus mortuus est, et ipse solus remansit: et accidet ei mors in via per quam ibitis: et descendere facietis canitiem meam cum mœrore ad sepulcrum.

1. *Now when Jacob saw.* Moses begins, in this chapter, to treat of the occasion which drew Jacob with his whole family into Egypt; and thus leaves it to us to consider by what hidden and unexpected methods God may perform whatever he has decreed. Though, therefore, the providence of God is in itself a labyrinth; yet when we connect the issue of things with their beginnings, that admirable method of operation shines clearly in our view, which is not generally acknowledged, only because it is far removed from our observation. Also our own indolence hinders us from perceiving God, with the eyes of faith, as holding the government of the world; because we either imagine fortune to be the mistress of events, or else, adhering to near and natural causes, we weave them together, and spread them as veils before our eyes. Whereas, therefore, scarcely any more illustrious representation of Divine Providence is to be found than this history furnishes; let pious readers carefully exercise themselves in meditation upon it, in order that they may acknowledge those things which, in appearance, are fortuitous, to be directed by the hand of God.

*Why do ye look one upon another?* Men are said to look one upon another, when each is waiting for the other, and, for want of counsel, no one dares to attempt anything. Jacob, therefore, censures this inactivity of his sons, because none of them endeavours to provide for the present necessity. Moses also says that they went into Egypt at the command of their father, and even without Benjamin; by which he intimates that filial reverence at that time was great; because envy of their brother did not prevent them from leaving their wives and children, and undertaking a long journey. He also adds, that they came in the midst of a great crowd of people; which enhances the fame of Joseph; who, while supplying food for all Egypt, and dispensing it by measure, till the end of the drought, could also afford assistance to neighbouring nations.

6. *And Joseph was the governor*[1] *over the land.* Moses connects the honour of Joseph with his fidelity and diligence. For although he was possessed of supreme authority, he nevertheless submitted to every possible laborious service, just as if he had been a hired servant. From which example we must learn, that as any one excels in honour, he is bound to be the more fully occupied in business; but that they who desire to combine leisure with dignity, utterly pervert the sacred order of God. Let it be, moreover, understood, that the corn was sold by Joseph, not as if he measured it out with his own hands, or himself received the money for it, seeing that it was set to sale in many parts of the kingdom, and he could scarcely have attended to one single storehouse: but that the whole of the stores were under his power.

7. *He made himself strange unto them.* It may be asked for what purpose Joseph thus tormented his brethren with threats and with terror. For if he was actuated by a sense of the injury received from them, he cannot be acquitted of the desire of revenge. It is, however, probable, that he was impelled neither by anger nor a thirst of vengeance, but that he was induced by two just causes to act as he did. For he both desired to regain his brother Benjamin, and wished to ascertain,—as if by putting them to the torture,—what was in their mind, whether they repented or not; and, in short, what had been their course of life since he had seen them last. For, had he made himself known at the first interview, it was to be feared lest they, keeping their father out of sight, and wishing to cast a vail over the detestable wickedness which they had committed, should only increase it by a new crime. There lurked, also, a not unreasonable suspicion concerning his brother Benjamin, lest they should attempt something perfidious and cruel against him. It

---

[1] השליט (*Hashalit*) " Of the Hebrew Shallet and Shilton, is made in Arabic the name *Sultan,* a title whereby the chief rulers of Egypt and Babylon are still called."—*Ainsworth.*—*Ed.*

was therefore important that they should be more thoroughly sifted; so that Joseph, being fully informed of the state of his father's house, might take his measures according to circumstances; and also, that previous to pardon, some punishment might be inflicted which would lead them more carefully to reflect upon the atrocity of their crime. For whereas he afterwards showed himself to be placable and humane; this did not arise from the fact, that his anger being assuaged, he became, by degrees, inclined to compassion; but rather, as Moses elsewhere subjoins, that he sought retirement, because he could "no longer refrain himself;" herein intimating at the same time, that Joseph had *forcibly* repressed his tears so long as he retained a severe aspect; and, therefore, that he had felt throughout the same affection of pity towards them. And it appears that a special impulse moved him to this whole course of action. For it was no common thing, that Joseph, beholding so many authors of his calamities, was neither angry nor changed in his manner, nor broke out into reproaches; but was composed both in his countenance and his speech, as if he had long meditated at leisure, respecting the course he would pursue. But it may be inquired again, whether his dissimulation, which was joined with a falsehood, is not to be blamed; for we know how pleasing integrity is to God, and how strictly he prohibits his own people from deceit and falsehoods. Whether God governed his servant by some special movement, to depart without fault, from the common rule of action, I know not; seeing that the faithful may sometimes piously do things which cannot lawfully be drawn into a precedent. Of this, however, in considering the acts of the holy fathers, we must always beware; lest they should lead us away from that law which the Lord prescribes to all in common. By the general command of God, we must all cultivate sincerity. That Joseph feigned something different from the truth, affords no pretext to excuse us if we attempt anything of the same kind. For, though a liberty granted by privilege would be pardoned, yet if any one, relying on a private example, does not scruple to subvert the law of God, so as to give himself license to do what is therein forbidden, he shall justly suffer the punishment of his audacity. And yet I do not think that we ought to be very anxious to excuse Joseph, because it is probable that he suffered something from human infirmity, which God forgave him; for by Divine mercy alone could that dissimulation, which in itself was not without fault, escape condemnation.

9. *And Joseph remembered the dreams.* When the boy Joseph had spoken of receiving obeisance, the absurdity of the thing impelled his brethren wickedly to devise his death. Now, although they bow down to him without knowing him, there is yet nothing better for them. Indeed, their only means of safety, is to prostrate themselves at his feet, and to be received by him as suppliants. Meanwhile, their conspiracy, by which they attempted to subvert the celestial decree, lest they should have to bear the yoke, was rendered fruitless. So the Lord forcibly restrains the obstinate, just as wild and refractory horses are wont to be more severely treated, the more they kick and are restive. Wherefore, there is nothing better than meekly to compose the mind to gentleness, that each may take his own lot contentedly, though it be not very splendid. It may, however, seem absurd, that Joseph should, at this time, have recalled his dream to mind, as if it had been forgotten through the lapse of years; which, indeed, could not be, unless he had lost sight of the promises of God. I answer, nothing is here recorded but what frequently happens to ourselves: for although the word of God may be dwelling in our hearts, yet it does not continually occur to us, but rather is sometimes so smothered that it may seem to be extinct, especially when faith is oppressed by the darkness of affliction. Besides, it is nothing wonderful, if a long series of evils should have buried, in a kind of oblivion, his dreams which indicated prosperity. God had exalted him, by these dreams, to the hope of great and distinguished authority. He is, however, cast into a well not unlike a grave. He is taken hence to be sold as a slave; he is carried to a distant land; and, as if slavery would not prove sufficiently severe, he is shut up in prison. And though his misery is in some degree mitigated, when he is released from his iron fetters, yet there was little, if any, pro-

spect of deliverance. I do not, however, think that the hope entertained by him was entirely destroyed, but that a cloud passed over it, which deprived him of the light of comfort. A different kind of temptation followed; because nothing is more common than for great and unexpected felicity to intoxicate its possessors. And thus it happened, as we have recently read, that a forgetfulness of his father's house stole over the mind of the holy man. He was not, therefore, so mindful of his dreams as he ought to have been. Another excuse may probably be alleged; that he, at the moment, compared his dreams with the event. And truly it was no common virtue to apply what was passing, thus immediately for the confirmation of the Divine oracle. For we readily perceive, that those dreams which so quickly recur to the memory, had not been obliterated through length of time. So the disciples remembered the words of the Lord after he had risen from the dead; because, by the sight of the fact predicted, their knowledge became more clear; whereas, before, nothing but transient sparks of it had shined in their hearts.

15. *By the life of Pharaoh.* From this formula of swearing a new question is raised; for that which is commanded in the law, that we should swear only by the name of God, had already been engraven on the hearts of the pious; since nature dictates that this honour is to be given to God alone, that men should defer to his judgment, and should make him the supreme arbiter and vindicator of faith and truth. If we should say that this was not simply an oath, but a kind of obtestation, the holy man will be, in some degree, excusable. He who swears by God wishes him to interpose in order to inflict punishment on perjury. They who swear by their life or by their hand, deposit, as it were, what they deem most valuable, as a pledge of their faithfulness. By this method the majesty of God is not transferred to mortal man; because it is a very different thing to cite him as witness who has the right of taking vengeance, and to assert by something most dear to us, that what we say is true. So Moses, when he calls heaven and earth to witness, does not ascribe deity to them, and thus fabricate a new idol; but, in order that higher authority may be given to the law, he de-

clares that there is no part of the world which will not cry out before the tribunal of God, against the ingratitude of the people, if they reject the doctrine of salvation. Notwithstanding, there is, I confess, in this form of swearing which Joseph uses, something deserving of censure; for it was a profane adulation, among the Egyptians, to swear by the life of the king. Just as the Romans swore by the genius of their prince, after they had been reduced to such bondage that they made their Cæsars equal to gods. Certainly this mode of swearing is abhorrent to true piety. Whence it may be perceived that nothing is more difficult to the holy servants of God than to keep themselves so pure, while conversant with the filth of the world, as to contract no spots of defilement from it. Joseph, indeed, was never so infected with the corruptions of the court, but that he remained a pure worshipper of God: nevertheless we see, that in accommodating himself to this depraved custom of speaking, he had received some stain. His repetition of the expression shows, that when any one has once become accustomed to evil, he becomes exceedingly prone to sin again and again. We observe, that they who have once rashly assumed the license of swearing, pour forth an oath every third word, even when speaking of the most frivolous things. So much the greater caution ought we to use, lest any such indulgence should harden us in this wicked custom.

17. *And he put them altogether into ward.* Here, not by words only, as before, but by the act itself, Joseph shows himself severe towards his brethren, when he shuts them all up in prison, as if about to bring them to punishment: and during three days torments them with fear. We said a little while ago, that from this fact no rule for acting severely and rigidly is to be drawn; because it is doubtful whether he acted rightly or otherwise. Again, it is to be feared lest they who plead his example should be far removed from his mildness, and that they should prove to be rather his apes than his true imitators. Meanwhile, it plainly appears what he was aiming at; for he does not mitigate their punishment, as if at the end of three days he was appeased; but he renders them more anxious about the redemption of their

brother, whom he retains as a hostage. Lest, however, immoderate fear should deter them from returning, he promises to act with good faith towards them : and to convince them of that, he declares that he fears God, which expression is worthy of observation. Doubtless he speaks from the inward feeling of his heart, when he declares that he will deal well and truly with them, because he fears God. Therefore the commencement and the fountain of that good and honest conscience, whereby we cultivate fidelity and justice towards men, is the fear of God. There appears indeed some probity in the despisers of God ; but it soon goes off in smoke, unless the depraved affections of the flesh are restrained as with a bridle, by the thought that God is to be feared, because he will be the Judge of the world. For whoever does not think that he must render an account, will never so cultivate integrity as to refrain from pursuing what he supposes will be useful to himself. Wherefore, if we wish to be free from perfidy, craft, cruelty, and all wicked desire of doing injury, we must labour earnestly that religion may flourish among us. For whenever we act with want of sincerity or humanity towards each other, impiety openly betrays itself. For whatever there is of rectitude or justice in the world, Joseph comprised in this short sentence, when he said, that he feared God.

21. *And they said one to another.* This is a remarkable passage, showing that the sons of Jacob, when reduced to the greatest straits, recall to memory a fratricide committed thirteen years previously. Before affliction pressed upon them, they were in a state of torpor. Moses relates that, even lately, they had spoken without agitation of Joseph's death, as if conscious to themselves of no evil. But now they are compelled (so to speak) to enter into their own consciences. We see then, how in adversity, God searches and tries men ; and how, while dissipating all their flattering illusions, he not only pierces their minds with secret fear, but extorts a confession which they would gladly avoid. And this kind of examination is very necessary for us. Wonderful is the hypocrisy of men in covering their evils ; and if impunity be allowed, their negligence will be increased two-

fold. Wherefore no remedy remains, except that they who give themselves up to slumber when the Lord deals gently with them, should be awakened by afflictions and punishments. Joseph therefore produced some good effect, when he extorted from his brethren the acknowledgment of their sin, in which they had securely pleased themselves. And the Lord had compassion on them, in taking away the covering with which they had been too long deceived. In the same manner, while he daily chastises us by the hand of man, he draws us, as guilty, to his tribunal. Nevertheless it would profit but little to be tried by adversity, unless he inwardly touched the heart; for we see how few reflect on their sins, although admonished by most severe punishments; certainly no one comes to this state of mind but with reluctance. Wherefore, there is no doubt that God, in order to lead the sons of Jacob to repentance, impelled them, as well by the secret instinct of his Spirit as by outward chastisement, to become sensible of that sin which had been too long concealed. Let the reader also observe, that the sons of Jacob did not only fix their minds on something which was close at hand, but considered that divine punishments were inflicted in various ways upon sinners. And doubtless, in order to apprehend the divine judgments, we must extend our views afar. Sometimes indeed God, by inflicting present punishment on sinners, holds them up for observation as on a theatre; but often, as if aiming at another object, he takes vengeance on our sins unexpectedly, and from an unseen quarter. If the sons of Jacob had merely looked for some *present* cause of their sufferings, they could have done nothing but loudly complain that they had been injured; and at length despair would have followed. But while considering how far and wide the providence of God extends, looking beyond the occasion immediately before their eyes, they ascend to a remote cause. It is, however, doubtful, whether they say that they shall be *held guilty* on account of their brother, or for their brother's sake, or that they will themselves *confess* that they have sinned: for the Hebrew noun, אשמים, (*ashaimim,*) is ambiguous, because it sometimes refers to the crime committed, and sometimes to the punishment, as in Latin, *piaculum* signifies both the crime and the expiation. On the whole, it is of little consequence which meaning is preferred, for they acknowledge their sin either in its guilt or its punishment. But the latter sense appears to me the more simple and genuine, that they are deservedly punished because they had been so cruel to their brother.

*In that we saw the anguish of his soul.* They acknowledge that it is by the just judgment of God, that they obtained nothing by their suppliant entreaties, because they themselves had acted so cruelly towards their brother. Christ had not yet uttered the sentence, " With what measure ye mete, it shall be measured unto you again," (Matt. vii. 2,) but it was a dictate of nature, that they who had been cruel to others, were unworthy of commiseration. The more heed ought we to take, that we prove not deaf to so many threatenings of Scripture. Dreadful is that denunciation, " Whoso stoppeth his ears at the cry of the poor, he also shall cry himself, and shall not be heard." (Prov. xxi. 13.) Therefore while we have time, let us learn to exercise humanity, to sympathize with the miserable, and to stretch out our hand for the sake of giving assistance. But if at any time it happens that we are treated roughly by men, and our prayers are proudly rejected; then, at least, let the question occur to us, whether we ourselves have in anything acted unkindly towards others; for although it were better to be wise beforehand; it is, nevertheless, some advantage, whenever others proudly despise us, to reflect whether they with whom we have had to deal, have not experienced similar hardships from us. " Our brother," they say, " entreated us when he was in the last extremity: we rejected his prayers : therefore it is by divine retribution that we can obtain nothing." By these words they bear witness that the hearts of men are so under Divine government, that they can be inclined to equity, or hardened in inflexible rigour. Moreover, their cruelty was hateful to God, because, since his goodness is diffused through heaven and earth, and his beneficence is extended not only to men, but even to brute animals, nothing is more contrary to his nature, than that we should cruelly reject those who implore our protection.

22. *And Reuben answered them.* Because he had attempted to deliver Joseph out of the hands of his brethren, in order to restore him in safety to his father, he magnifies their fault, in not having, at that time, listened to any prudent counsel: and I understand his words as conveying a reproof for their too late repentance. Whereas Joseph was not yet satisfied with this confession, but retained Simeon in bonds,[1] and dismissed the rest in suspense and perplexity, this was not done from malevolence, but because he was not certain about the safety of his brother Benjamin, and the state of his father's house. For he might justly fear lest, when they found that their wicked contrivance of putting their brother to death, was discovered, they might again attempt some horrible crime, as desperate men are wont to do; or, at least, might desert their father, and flee to some other country. Nevertheless the act of Joseph is not to be drawn into a precedent: because it is not always right to be thus austere. We ought also to beware lest the offender be swallowed up by grief, if we are not mild, and disposed to forgiveness. Therefore we must seek the spirit of discretion from heaven, which shall so govern us that we may do nothing by rash impetuosity, or immoderate severity. This, indeed, is to be remembered, that under the stern countenance of Joseph was concealed not only a mild and placid disposition, but the most tender affection.

27. *And as one of them opened his sack.* With what intention Joseph had commanded the price paid for the corn to be secretly deposited in the sacks of his brethren, may easily be conjectured; for he feared lest his father being already impoverished, would not be able again to buy provisions. The brethren, having found their money, knew not where to seek the cause; except that, being terrified, they perceived that the hand of God was against them. That they were greatly astonished appears from their not voluntarily return-

---

[1] Ainsworth says of Simeon, "He seemeth by this, to have been the chief procurer of Joseph's trouble. He was by nature bold and fierce, as his fact against the Shechemites doth manifest." If so, this act of Joseph would appear to him, and perhaps to the rest of the brethren, as a special Divine retribution for his cruelty towards Joseph.—*Ed.*

ing to Joseph, in order to prove their own innocence: for the remedy of the evil was at hand, if they had not been utterly blinded. Wherefore we must ask God to supply us, in doubtful and troubled affairs, not only with fortitude, but also with prudence. We see also how little can be effected even by a great multitude, unless the Lord preside among them. The sons of Jacob ought mutually to have exhorted each other, and to have consulted together what was necessary to be done: but there is an end to all deliberation; no solace nor remedy is suggested. Even while each sees the rest agitated, they mutually increase each other's trepidation. Therefore, the society and countenance of men will profit us nothing, unless the Lord strengthen us from heaven.

28. *What is this that God hath done unto us?* They do not expostulate with God, as if they thought this danger had come upon them without cause: but, perceiving that God was angry with them in many ways, they deplore their wretchedness. But why do they not rather turn their thoughts to Joseph? For the suspicion was natural, that this had been done by fraud, because he wished to lay new snares for them. How does it happen, then, that losing sight of man, they set God as an avenger directly before them? Truly, because this single thought possessed their minds, that a just reward, and such as their sins deserved, would be given them; and, from that time, they referred whatever evils happened to the same cause. Before (as we have said) they were asleep: but from the time that they began to be affected by the lively fear of God's judgment, his providence always presented itself to their view. So David, when, by the inward suggestion of the Spirit, he has learned that the rod with which he was chastised had been sent from heaven, is not distracted or perplexed, though he sees plainly that the evils have proceeded from another quarter; but prays to God to heal the wounds which *He* had made. It is no common act of prudence, and is at the same time profitable, whenever any adversity overtakes us, to accustom ourselves to the consideration of the judgments of God. We see how unbelievers, while they imagine their misfortunes to be accidental, or while they are bent on accusing their enemies,

only exasperate their grief by fretting and raging, and thus cause the anger of God to burn the more against them. But he who, in his affliction, exercises himself in reflecting on his own sins, and sets God before him as his Judge, will humble himself in the divine presence, and will compose his mind to patience by the hope of pardon. Let us, however, remember that the providence of God is not truly acknowledged, except in connection with his justice. For, though the men by whose hand he chastises us are often unjust, yet, in an incomprehensible manner, he executes his judgments through them, against which judgments it is not lawful for us either to reply or to murmur. For sometimes even the reprobate, though they acknowledge themselves to be stricken by the hand of God, yet do not cease to complain against him, as Moses teaches us by the example of Cain. I do not, however, understand that this complaint was made by the sons of Jacob, for the purpose of charging God with tyrannical violence; but because they, being overcome with fear, inferred from this double punishment that God was highly displeased with them.

29. *And they came unto Jacob their father.* Here is a long repetition of the former history, but it is not superfluous; because Moses wished to show how anxiously they made their excuse to their father for having left Simeon in chains, and how strenuously they pleaded with him, that, for the sake of obtaining Simeon's liberty, he should allow them to take their brother Benjamin: for this was greatly to the purpose. We know what a sharp dart is hunger: and yet, though the only method of relieving their want was to fetch corn out of Egypt, Jacob would rather that he and his family should perish, than allow Benjamin to accompany the rest. What can he mean by thus peremptorily refusing what his sons were compelled by necessity to ask, except to show that he was suspicious of them? This also more clearly appears from his own words, when he imputes his bereavement to them. For, though their declaration, that Joseph had been torn by a wild beast, had some colour of probability, there still remained in the heart of the holy patriarch a secret wound, arising from suspicion; because he was fully aware of

their fierce and cruel hatred of the innocent youth. Moreover, it is useful for us to know this; for it appears hence how miserable was the condition of the holy man, whose mind, during thirteen successive years, had been tortured with dire anxiety. Besides, his very silence added greatly to his torment, because he was compelled to conceal the grief he felt. But the chief burden of the evil was the temptation which oppressed him, that the promise of God might prove illusory and vain. For he had no hope except from the promised seed; but he seemed to be bringing up devils at home, from whom a blessing was no more to be expected than life from death. He thought Joseph to be dead, Benjamin alone remained to him uncorrupted: how could the salvation of the world proceed from such a vicious offspring? He must, therefore, have been endowed with great constancy, seeing he did not cease to rely upon God; and being certainly persuaded that he cherished in his house the Church, of which scarcely any appearance was left, he bore with his sons till they should repent. Let the faithful now apply this example to themselves, lest their minds should give way at the horrible devastation which is almost everywhere perceived.

35. *As they emptied their sacks.* Here, again, it appears how greatly they had been alarmed in their journey, seeing that each had not at least examined his sack, after money had been found in one. But these things are written to show that, as soon as men are smitten with fear, they have no particle of wisdom and of soundness of mind, until God tranquillizes them. Moreover, Joseph did not act with sufficient consideration, in that he occasioned very great grief to his father, whose poverty he really intended to relieve. Whence we learn that even the most prudent are not always so careful, but that something may flow from their acts which they do not wish.

36. *Me have ye bereaved.* Jacob does not, indeed, openly accuse his sons of the crime of their brother's murder; yet he is angry as if, two of his sons being already taken away, they were hastening to destroy the third. For he says that all these evils were falling on himself alone; because he does not think that they were affected as they ought to be, nor

shared his grief with him, but were carelessly making light of the destruction of their brethren, as if they had no interest in their lives. It seems, however, exceedingly barbarous that Reuben should offer his two sons to his father to be slain, if he did not bring Benjamin back. Jacob might, indeed, slay his own grandchildren: what comfort, then, could he take in acting cruelly to his own bowels? But this is what I before alluded to, that they were suspected of having dealt perfidiously towards Joseph; for which reason Reuben deemed it necessary to assuage his father's fear, by such a vehement protestation; and to give this pledge, that he and his brethren were designing nothing wicked against Benjamin.

38. *My son shall not go down with you.* Again we see, as in a lively picture, with what sorrow holy Jacob had been oppressed. He sees his whole family famishing: he would rather be torn away from life than from his son: whence we gather that he was not iron-hearted: but his patience is the more deserving of praise, because he contended with the infirmity of the flesh, and did not sink under it. And although Moses does not give a rhetorical amplification to his language, we nevertheless easily perceive that he was overcome with excessive grief, when he thus complained to his sons, "You are too cruel to your father, in taking away from me a third son, after I have been plundered of first one and then another."

## CHAPTER XLIII.

1. AND the famine *was* sore in the land.
2. And it came to pass, when they had eaten up the corn which they had brought out of Egypt, their father said unto them, Go again, buy us a little food.
3. And Judah spake unto him, saying, The man did solemnly protest unto us, saying, Ye shall not see my face, except your brother *be* with you.
4. If thou wilt send our brother with us, we will go down and buy thee food:

1. Porro fames gravis erat in terra.
2. Itaque quum finissent edere alimentum, quod attulerant ex Ægypto, dixit ad eos pater eorum, Revertimini, emite nobis pusillum cibi.
3. Et dixit ad eum Jehudah, dicendo, Contestando contestatus est nos vir, dicendo, Non videbitis faciem meam, nisi fuerit frater vester vobiscum.
4. Si miseris fratrem nostrum nobiscum, descendemus, et ememus tibi cibum.

5. But if thou wilt not send *him*, we will not go down: for the man said unto us, Ye shall not see my face, except your brother *be* with you.

6. And Israel said, Wherefore dealt ye *so* ill with me, *as* to tell the man whether ye had yet a brother?

7. And they said, The man asked us straitly of our state, and of our kindred, saying, *Is* your father yet alive? have ye *another* brother? and we told him according to the tenor of these words. Could we certainly know that he would say, Bring your brother down?

8. And Judah said unto Israel his father, Send the lad with me, and we will arise and go; that we may live, and not die, both we, and thou, *and* also our little ones.

9. I will be surety for him; of my hand shalt thou require him: if I bring him not unto thee, and set him before thee, then let me bear the blame for ever:

10. For except we had lingered, surely now we had returned this second time.

11. And their father Israel said unto them, If *it must be* so now, do this; Take of the best fruits in the land in your vessels, and carry down the man a present, a little balm, and a little honey, spices and myrrh, nuts and almonds.

12. And take double money in your hand: and the money that was brought again in the mouth of your sacks, carry *it* again in your hand; peradventure it *was* an oversight.

13. Take also your brother, and arise, go again unto the man:

14. And God Almighty give you mercy before the man, that he may send away your other brother, and Benjamin. If I be bereaved *of my children*, I am bereaved.

15. And the men took that present, and they took double money in their hand, and Benjamin; and rose up, and went down to Egypt, and stood before Joseph.

16. And when Joseph saw Ben-

5. Quod si non miseris, non descendemus: vir enim ille dixit nobis, Non videbitis faciem meam, nisi fuerit frater vester vobiscum.

6. At dixit Israel, Utquid malefecistis mihi, ut nuntiaretis viro, quod adhuc frater esset vobis.

7. Et dixerunt, Interrogando interrogavit vir ille de nobis et cognatione nostra, dicendo, Num adhuc pater vester vivit? num est vobis frater? et nuntiavimus ei secundum verba ista: numquid sciendo sciebamus, quod dicturus esset, Descendere faciatis fratrem vestrum?

8. Et dixit Jehudah ad Israel patrem suum, Mitte puerum mecum, et surgemus, et proficiscemur, et vivemus, et non moriemur etiam nos, etiam tu, etiam parvuli nostri.

9. Ergo fidejubeo pro illo, de manu mea requiras eum: nisi reduxero eum ad te, et statuero eum ante te, pœnæ obnoxius ero tibi omnibus diebus.

10. Quia nisi tardavissemus, certe nunc reversi fuissemus jam bis.

11. Et dixit illis Israel pater eorum, Si ita nunc *oportet*, hoc facite: tollite de optimis fructibus terræ in vasis vestris, et deferte ad virum munus, pusillum resinæ et pusillum mellis, aromata, et stacten, pineas, et amygdalas.

12. Et pecuniam duplicem capite in manibus vestris: et pecuniam repositam in ore saccorum vestrorum reponetis in manu vestra, si forte error esset.

13. Et fratrem vestrum capite, et surgite, revertemini ad virum.

14. Deus autem omnipotens det vobis misericordias ante virum, et dimittat vobis fratrem vestrum alium, et Benjamin: et ego quemadmodum orbatus sum, orbatus sum.

15. Et ceperunt viri munus hoc, et duplicem pecuniam ceperunt in manu sua, et Benjamin: et surrexerunt, et descenderunt in Ægyptum, et steterunt coram Joseph.

16. Et vidit Joseph cum eis Ben-

jamin with them, he said to the ruler of his house, Bring *these* men home, and slay, and make ready: for *these* men shall dine with me at noon.

17. And the man did as Joseph bade: and the man brought the men into Joseph's house.

18. And the men were afraid, because they were brought into Joseph's house; and they said, Because of the money that was returned in our sacks at the first time are we brought in; that he may seek occasion against us, and fall upon us, and take us for bond-men, and our asses.

19. And they came near to the steward of Joseph's house, and they communed with him at the door of the house,

20. And said, O sir, we came indeed down at the first time to buy food:

21. And it came to pass, when we came to the inn, that we opened our sacks, and, behold, *every* man's money *was* in the mouth of his sack, our money in full weight; and we have brought it again in our hand.

22. And other money have we brought down in our hands to buy food: we cannot tell who put our money in our sacks.

23. And he said, Peace *be* to you, fear not; your God, and the God of your father, hath given you treasure in your sacks: I had your money. And he brought Simeon out unto them.

24. And the man brought the men into Joseph's house, and gave *them* water, and they washed their feet; and he gave their asses provender.

25. And they made ready the present against Joseph came at noon: for they heard that they should eat bread there.

26. And when Joseph came home, they brought him the present which *was* in their hand into the house, and bowed themselves to him to the earth.

27. And he asked them of *their* welfare, and said, *Is* your father

jamin, et dixit præfecto domus suæ, Adduc viros in domum, et macta, et præpara: quia mecum comedent viri in meridie.

17. Et fecit vir, quemadmodum dixit Joseph: et venire fecit vir homines in domum Joseph.

18. Et timuerunt viri, quod adducti essent in domum Joseph, et dixerunt, Propter pecuniam, quæ reddita est in saccis nostris in principio, sumus adducti, ut volvat se contra nos, et jactet se super nos, et capiat nos in servos, et asinos nostros.

19. Et accesserunt ad virum, qui erat super domum Joseph, et loquuti sunt ad eum in ostio domus:

20. Et dixerunt, Quæsumus, domine mi: descendendo descendimus in principio ad emendum escam.

21. Et fuit quum venissemus ad hospitium, et aperuissemus saccos nostros, ecce, pecunia uniuscujusque erat in ore sacci sui: pecunia nostra secundum pondus suum: et retulimus eam in manu nostra.

22. Et pecuniam aliam detulimus in manu nostra ad emendum escam: nescimus, quis posuerit pecuniam nostram in saccis nostris.

23. Et dixit, Pax vobis, ne timeatis, Deus vester, et Deus patris vestri dedit vobis thesaurum in saccis vestris, pecunia vestra venit ad me: et adduxit ad eos Simhon.

24. Et venire fecit vir ille homines in domum Joseph: et dedit aquam, et laverunt pedes suos, et dedit pabulum asinis eorum.

25. Paraverunt autem munus, dum veniret Joseph in meridie: audierunt enim, quod ibi comesturi essent panem.

26. Et venit Joseph ad domum, et attulerunt ei munus, quod erat in manu eorum, in domum: et incurvaverunt se ei super terram.

27. Et interrogavit eos de prosperitate, et dixit, Num sanus est

well, the old man of whom ye spake? *Is* he yet alive?

28. And they answered, Thy servant our father *is* in good health, he *is* yet alive: and they bowed down their heads, and made obeisance.

29. And he lifted up his eyes, and saw his brother Benjamin, his mother's son, and said, *Is* this your younger brother, of whom ye spake unto me? And he said, God be gracious unto thee, my son.

30. And Joseph made haste; for his bowels did yearn upon his brother: and he sought *where* to weep; and he entered into *his* chamber, and wept there.

31. And he washed his face, and went out, and refrained himself, and said, Set on bread.

32. And they set on for him by himself, and for them by themselves, and for the Egyptians, which did eat with him, by themselves: because the Egyptians might not eat bread with the Hebrews; for that *is* an abomination unto the Egyptians.

33. And they sat before him, the first-born according to his birthright, and the youngest according to his youth: and the men marvelled one at another.

34. And he took *and sent* messes unto them from before him: but Benjamin's mess was five times so much as any of theirs. And they drank, and were merry with him.

pater vester senex, quem dixeratis? Num adhuc vivit?

28. Et dixerunt, Prospere est servo tuo patri nostro, adhuc vivit: et prociderunt, et incurvaverunt se.

29. Et levavit oculos suos, et vidit Benjamin fratrem suum, filium matris suæ, et dixit, Num iste est frater vester minimus, quem dixeratis mihi? Et dixit, Deus misereatur tui, fili mi.

30. Et festinavit Joseph, quia incaluerant miserationes ejus super fratrem suum, et quæsivit ut fleret: ingressus est itaque cubiculum, et flevit ibi.

31. Et lavit faciem suam, et egressus est, et vim fecit sibi, et dixit, Apponite panem.

32. Et apposuerunt ei seorsum, illisque seorsum: et Ægyptiis, qui comedebant cum eo, seorsum: non enim poterant Ægyptii comedere cum Hebræis panem: quia abominatio erat Ægyptiis.

33. Et sederunt coram eo primogenitus secundum primogenituram suam, et parvus juxta parvitatem suam: et admirati sunt viri unusquisque ad proximum suum.

34. Et accepit partes a facie sua ad illos, et multiplicavit partem Benjamin plus quam partes omnium illorum, quinque partibus: et biberunt, et inebriaverunt se cum eo.

1. *And the famine was sore in the land.* In this chapter is recorded the second journey of the sons of Jacob into Egypt, when the former supply of provision had been exhausted. It may, however, here be asked, how Jacob could have supported his family, even for a few days, with so small a quantity of corn: for, suppose it to be granted that several asses were conducted by each of the brethren, what was this to sustain three hundred persons?[1] For, since Abraham had a much larger number of servants, and mention has been made above of the servants of Isaac; it is incredible that

---

[1] Dr. A. Clarke supposes the asses to have amounted to several *scores*, if not *hundreds*. The latter supposition seems improbable.—*Ed.*

Jacob was so entirely destitute, as to have no servants left. If we say, that he, being a stranger, had been compelled to sell them all, it is but an uncertain guess. It seems to me more probable that they lived on acorns, herbs, and roots. For we know that the orientals, especially when any necessity urges, are content with slender and dry food, and we shall see presently, that, in this scarcity of wheat, there was a supply of other food. I suppose, therefore, that no more corn had been bought than would suffice to furnish a frugal and restricted measure of food for Jacob himself, and for his children and grandchildren: and that the food of the servants was otherwise provided for. There is, indeed, no doubt that the whole region had been compelled to resort to acorns, and fruits of this kind, for food for the servants, and that wheaten bread was a luxury belonging to the rich. This was, indeed, a severe trial, that holy Jacob, of whom God had engaged to take care, should almost perish, with his family, through hunger, and that the land of which he was constituted the lord, in order that he might there happily enjoy the abundance of all things, should even deny him bread as a stranger. For he might seriously doubt what was the meaning of that remarkable promise, "I am God Almighty, grow and multiply: I will bless thee." It is profitable for us to know these conflicts of the holy fathers, that, fighting with the same arms with which they conquered, we also may stand invincible, although God should withhold present help.

3. *And Judah spake unto him, saying.* Judah seems to feign something, for the purpose of extorting from his father what he knew he would not freely grant; but it is probable that many discourses had been held on both sides, which Moses, according to his custom, has not related. And since Joseph so ardently desired the sight of his brother Benjamin, it is not surprising that he should have laboured, in every possible way, to obtain it. It may also have happened that he had caused some notification or legal summons to be served, by which his brother was cited to make his appearance, as in judicial causes. This however deserves to be noticed, that Moses relates the long disputation which Jacob had with his sons, in order that we may know with what difficulty he

allowed his son Benjamin to be torn away from him. For, though hunger was pressing, he nevertheless contended for retaining him, just as if he were striving for the salvation of his whole family. Whence, again, we may conjecture, that he suspected his sons of a wicked conspiracy; and on this account Judah offers himself as a surety. For he does not promise anything respecting the event, but only, for the sake of clearing himself and his brethren, he takes Benjamin under his care, with this condition, that if any injury should be done to Benjamin, he would bear the punishment and the blame. From the example of Jacob let us learn patient endurance, should the Lord often compel us, by pressure of circumstances, to do many things contrary to the inclination of our own minds; for Jacob sends away his son, as if he were delivering him over unto death.

11. *Take of the best fruits.*[1] Though the fruits which Moses enumerates were, for the most part, not very precious, because the condition of holy Jacob was not such that he could send any royal present; yet, according to his slender ability, he wished to appease Joseph. Besides we know that fruits are not always estimated according to their cost. And now, having commanded his sons to do what he thought necessary, he has recourse to prayer, that God would give them favour with the governor of Egypt. We must attend to both these points whenever we are perplexed in any business; for we must not omit any of those things which are expedient, or which may seem to be of use; and yet we must place our reliance upon God. For the tranquillity of faith has no affinity with indolence: but he who expects a prosperous issue of his affairs from the Lord, will, at the same time, look closely to the means which are in his power, and will apply them to present use. Meanwhile, let the faithful observe this moderation, that when they have tried all means, they still ascribe nothing to their own industry. At the same time, let them be certainly convinced that all their endeavours will be in vain, unless the Lord bless them. It is to be observed, also, in the form of his supplication, that Jacob regards the hearts of men

---

[1] Literally, "Fruits of the song;" alluding to the songs which were sung over the ingathering of harvest.—*Ed.*

as subject to the will of God. When we have to deal with men, we too often neglect to look unto the Lord, because we do not sufficiently acknowledge him as the secret Governor of their hearts. But to whatever extent unruly men may be carried away by violence, it is yet certain that their passions are turned by God in whatever direction he pleases, so that he can mitigate their ferocity as often as he sees good ; or can permit those to become cruel, who before were disposed to mildness. So Jacob, although his sons had found an austere severity in Joseph, yet trusts that his heart will be so in the hand of God, that it shall be suddenly moulded to humanity. Therefore, as we must hope in the Lord, when men deal unjustly with us, and must pray that they may be changed for the better ; so, on the other hand, we must remember that, when they act with severity towards us, it is not done without the counsel of God.

14. *If I be bereaved.* Jacob may seem here to be hardly consistent with himself ; for, if the prayer which Moses has just related, was the effect of faith, he ought to have been more calm ; and, at least, to have given occasion to the manifestation of the grace of God. But he appears to cut himself off from every ground of confidence, when he supposes that nothing is left for him but bereavement. It is like the speech of a man in despair, " I shall remain bereaved as I am." As if truly he had prayed in vain ; or had feignedly professed that the remedy was in the hand of God. If, however, we observe to whom his speech was directed, the solution is easy. It is by no means doubtful that he stood firmly on the promise which had been given to him, and therefore he would hope for some fruit of his prayers ; yet he wished deeply to affect his sons, in order that they might take greater care of their brother. For, it was in no common manner that Benjamin was intrusted to their protection, when they saw their father altogether overcome and almost lifeless with grief, until he should receive his son again in safety. Interpreters, however, expound these words variously. Some think that he complained, because now he was about to be entirely bereaved. To others, the meaning seems to be, that nothing worse could happen ; since he had lost Joseph, whom he had

preferred to all the rest. Others are disposed to mark a double bereavement, as if he had said, "I have lost two sons, and now a third follows them." But what, if we should thus interpret the words, "I see what is my condition; I am a most wretched old man; my house, which lately was filled with people, I find almost deserted." So that, in general terms, he is deploring the loss of all his sons, and is not speaking of a part only. Moreover, it was his design to inspire his sons with a degree of solicitude which should cause them to attend to their duty with greater fidelity and diligence.[1]

16. *And he said to the ruler of his house.* Here we perceive the fraternal disposition of Joseph; though it is uncertain whether he was perfectly reconciled, as I will shortly show, in its proper place. If, however, remembering the injury, he loved his brethren less than before, he was still far from having vindictive feelings towards them. But because it was something suspicious that foreigners and men of ignoble rank should be received in a friendly manner, like known guests, to a banquet, by the chief governor of the kingdom, the sons of Jacob would conceive a new fear; namely, that he wished to cast them all into chains; and that their money had been craftily concealed in their sacks, in order that it might prove the occasion of accusation against them. It is however probable, that the crime which they had committed against Joseph, occurred to their minds, and that this fear had proceeded from a guilty conscience. For, unless the judgment of God had tormented them, there was no cause why they should apprehend such an act of perfidy. It may seem absurd, that unknown men should be received to a feast by a

---

[1] There is, however, another interpretation of the passage which is worthy of attention. In our version, the words are, "If I am bereaved of my children, I am bereaved;" but the expression, *of my children*, is not in the original. The close translation is simply, "If I be bereaved, I am bereaved." And this may be the language of entire resignation to the will of God. Jacob had had a severe struggle in his mind, before he could give up his beloved Benjamin: but having at length succeeded, he seems now freely to surrender himself and his family to the divine will. "If I am bereaved, I am bereaved." I know the worst, and I am prepared to meet it. Ainsworth says, "A like phrase is in Esther iv. 16, 'If I perish, I perish.' Both of them seem to be a committing of themselves, and of the event of their actions, unto God in faith; which, if it fell out otherwise than they wished, they would patiently bear."—*Ed.*

prince of the highest dignity. But why not rather incline to a different conjecture; namely, that the governor of Egypt has done this for the purpose of exhibiting to his friends the new and unwonted spectacle of eleven brethren sitting at one table? It will, indeed, sometimes happen that similar anxiety to that felt by Joseph's brethren, may invade even the best of men; but I would rather ascribe it to the judgment of God, that the sons of Jacob, whose conscience accused them of having inhumanly treated their brother, suspected that they would be dealt with in the same manner. However, they take an early opportunity of vindicating themselves, before inquiry is made respecting the theft. Now, freely to declare that the money had been found in their sacks, and that they had brought it from home to repay it immediately, was a strong mark of their innocence. Moreover, they do this in the very porch of the house, because they suspected that, as soon as they entered, the question would be put to them.

23. *Peace be to you.* Because שלום, (*shalom,*) among the Hebrews, signifies not only peace, but any prosperous and desirable condition, as well as any joyful event, this passage may be expounded in two ways: either that the ruler of Joseph's house commands them to be of a peaceful and secure mind; or that he pronounces it to be well and happy with them. The sum of his answer, however, amounts to this, that there was no reason for fear, because their affairs were in a prosperous state. And since, after the manner of men, it was not possible that they should have paid the money for the corn which was found in their sacks, he ascribes this to the favour of God. For though true religion was then almost extinct in the world, God nevertheless caused some knowledge of his goodness always to remain in the hearts of men, which should render them responsible. Hence it has happened that, following nature as their guide, unbelievers have called every peculiarly excellent gift *Divine*. Moreover, because corruption was so prevalent, that each nation deemed it lawful to worship different gods, the ruler of Joseph's house distinguishes the God worshipped by the sons of Jacob from Egyptian idols. The conjecture, however, is probable, that

this man had been imbued with some sense of religion. We know how great was the arrogance of that nation, and that it supposed the whole world besides, to be deceived in the worship of gods. Therefore, unless he had learned something better, he never would have assigned so great an honour to any other gods than those of his own country. Moreover, he does not ascribe the miracle to the God of the land of Canaan, but to the peculiar God of their father. I, therefore, do not doubt that Joseph, though not permitted openly to correct anything in the received superstitions, endeavoured, at least in his own house, to establish the true worship of the one God, and always held fast the covenant, concerning which, as a boy, he had heard his father speak. This is the more to be observed, because the holy man could not swerve, even in the least degree, from the common practice, without incurring the odium of a nation so proud. Therefore, the excellency of Joseph is commended in the person of his steward; because without fear of public envy, he gives honour, within his own walls, to the true God. If any one should ask, whence he knew that Jacob was a worshipper of the true God; the answer is ready; that Joseph, notwithstanding his assumed severity, had commanded that Simeon should be gently treated in prison. Though he had been left as a hostage, yet, if he had been regarded as a spy, the keeper of the prison would have dealt more harshly with him. There must, therefore, have been some command given respecting the humane or moderate treatment of him. Whence the probable conjecture is elicited, that Joseph had explained the affair to his steward, who was admitted to his secret counsels.

25. *Against Joseph came at noon-day.* It is doubtful whether this was the ordinary hour of dining among the Egyptians, or whether Joseph, on that day, sat down earlier than he was accustomed to do, on account of his guests. It is, however, most likely that the usual custom of dining was observed. Although, among the people of the East, there might be a different manner of living, dinners were in use, not only among the Egyptians, but also in Judea, and in other neighbouring regions. Yet it is probable that this was to them, also, in the place of a supper, both because

they would sit long at table, and our quick method of eating would not have been tolerable to people in those heated climes; especially when they received guests with greater luxury than usual, as it will presently appear, was done at this time. The washing of the feet, (as we have seen before,) was a part of hospitality, and intended to relieve weariness; because, in those parts, the feet might easily become inflamed whenever they journeyed on foot. It was also more honourable, according to ancient custom, that a portion of food should be sent to each from Joseph, rather than that it should be distributed by the cook. But because these things are trivial, and are not conducive to piety, I only slightly touch upon them; and would even omit them entirely, except that, to remove a scruple from the minds of the unskilful, is sometimes useful, if it be but done sparingly and with brevity.

32. *Because the Egyptians might not eat,* &c.[1] Moses says they might not eat with the Hebrews, because they abhorred it, as being unlawful. For seeing that their religion forbade it, they were so bound, that they *could* not do what they did not *dare* to do. This passage teaches us how great was the pride of that nation; for, whence did it arise that they so utterly detested the Hebrews, unless because they thought themselves alone to be pure and holy in the world, and acceptable to God? God, indeed, commands his worshippers to abstain from all the pollutions of the Gentiles. But it behoves any one who separates himself from others, to be himself pure and upright. Therefore superstitious persons vainly attempt to claim this privilege for themselves, seeing they carry their impurity within, and are destitute of sincerity. Superstition, also, is affected with

---

[1] " At the entertainment to which Joseph invited his brethren, they sat apart from the Egyptians, while Joseph was again separated from both. The author [Moses] shows the reason of this in the remark, ' Because the Egyptians might not eat bread with the Hebrews, for that is an abomination to the Egyptians.' *Herodotus* also remarks, that the Egyptians abstained from all familiar intercourse with foreigners, since these were unclean to them, especially because they slew and ate the animals which were sacred among the Egyptians. The circumstance that Joseph eats separately from the other Egyptians is strictly in accordance with the great difference of rank, and the spirit of caste, which prevailed among the Egyptians."— *Egypt and the Books of Moses,* p. 39.—*Ed.*

another disease ; namely, that it is full of pride, so that it despises all men, under the pretext that they are vicious. It is asked, however, whether the Egyptians were separated from Joseph, because they regarded him as polluted: for this the words of Moses seem to intimate. If this interpretation is received, then they esteemed their false religion so highly, that they did not scruple to load their governor with reproaches. I rather conjecture, that Joseph sat apart from them, for the sake of honour ; since it would be absurd that they, who disdained to sit at the same table with him, should be invited as his guests. Therefore it is probable that this distinct order was made by Joseph himself, that he might maintain his own dignity ; and yet that the sons of Jacob were not mixed with the Egyptians, because the former were an abomination to the latter. For though the origin of Joseph was known, yet he had so passed over to the Egyptians, that he had become as one of their body. For which reason, also, the king had given him a name, when he adorned him with the insignia of his office as chief governor. Now, when we see that the church of God was, at that time, so proudly despised by profane men, we need not wonder that we also, at the present day, are subjected to similar reproach. Meanwhile, we must endeavour to keep ourselves pure from the filth of the world, for the Lord's sake ; and yet this desire must be so attempered, that we may be alienated from the vices, rather than from the persons of men. For on this account does God sanctify his children, that they may beware of the vices of the unbelievers among whom they are conversant ; and nevertheless may allure, as many as are curable, to a participation of their piety. Two things are here to be attended to ; first, that we may be fully persuaded of the genuineness of our faith ; secondly, that our excessive and fruitless fastidiousness may not entirely alienate many from the Lord, who otherwise might have been won. For we are not expressly commanded so to abhor the wicked, as not eat with them ; but to avoid such association as may subject us to the same yoke. Besides, this passage confirms what I have before said, that the Hebrews had derived their name, not from their passing over the river, (as some falsely imagine,) but from their ancestor Heber. Nor was the fame of a single small and distantly situated family, sufficiently celebrated in Egypt, to become the cause of public dissension.

33. *The first-born according to his birthright.*[1] Although of the sons of Jacob four were born of bond-women; yet, since they were the elder, they had precedence of their younger brethren, who had descended from free-born mothers; whence it appears that they had been accustomed by their father to keep this order. What, then, some one may say, becomes of the declaration, " the son of the bond-woman shall not be heir with the son of the free-woman?" Truly, I think, since Ishmael was rejected, by the divine oracle proceeding from the mouth of Sarah, as Esau was afterwards, Jacob was fully taught that he had as many heirs as he had sons. Hence arose that equality which caused each to keep his place, first, middle, or last, according to his age. But the design of Moses was to show, that although Benjamin was the youngest, yet he was preferred to all the rest in honour; because Joseph could not refrain from giving him the principal token of his love. It was, indeed, his intention to remain unknown; but affection so far prevails, that, beyond the purpose of his mind, he suddenly breaks out into a declaration of his affection. From the concluding portion of the chapter we gather, what I recently intimated, that the feast was unusually luxurious, and that they were received to it, in a liberal and joyful manner, beyond the daily custom. For the word שכר, (*shakar,*) they "were merry," signifies, either that they were not always accustomed to drink wine, or that there was more than ordinary indulgence at the sumptuous tables spread for them. Here, however, no intemperance is implied, (so that drunkards may not plead the example of the holy fathers as a pretext for their crime,) but an honourable and moderate liberality. I acknowledge, indeed, that the word has a double meaning,

---

[1] " It appears that the brothers of Joseph *sat* before him at the table, while, according to patriarchal practice, they were accustomed to recline. It appears from the sculptures, that the Egyptians also were in the habit of sitting at table, although they had couches."—*Egypt and the Books of Moses,* p. 39.—*Ed.*

and is often taken in an ill sense; as in chap. ix., ver. 21, and in similar places: but in the present instance the design of Moses is clear. Should any one object, that a frugal use of food and drink is simply that which suffices for the nourishing of the body: I answer, although food is properly for the supply of our necessities, yet the legitimate use of it may proceed further. For it is not in vain, that our food has savour as well as vital nutriment; but thus our heavenly Father sweetly delights us with his delicacies. And his benignity is not in vain commended in Psalm civ. 15, where he is said to create " wine that maketh glad the heart of man." Nevertheless, the more kindly he indulges us, the more solicitously ought we to restrict ourselves to a frugal use of his gifts. For we know how unbridled are the appetites of the flesh. Whence it happens that, in abundance, it is almost always lascivious, and in penury, impatient. We must, however, adhere to St. Paul's method, that we know how to abound and to suffer need; that is, we must take great care if we have unusual plenty, that it does not hurry us into luxury; and, on the other hand, we must see to it, that we bear poverty with an equal mind. Some one, perhaps, will say, that the flesh is more than sufficiently ingenious in giving a specious colour to its excesses; and, therefore, nothing more should be allowed to it than necessity demands. And, truly, I confess, we must diligently attend to what Paul prescribes, (Rom. xiii. 14,) " Make not provision for the flesh to fulfil the lusts thereof." But because it greatly concerns all pious people to receive their food from the hand of God, with quiet consciences, it is necessary for them to know to what extent the use of food and wine is lawful.

## CHAPTER XLIV.

1. AND he commanded the steward of his house, saying, Fill the men's sacks *with* food, as much as they can carry, and put every man's money in his sack's mouth.

2. And put my cup, the silver cup, in the sack's mouth of the youngest,

1. Et præcepit præfecto domus suæ, dicendo, Imple saccos virorum esca, quantum potuerint ferre, et pone pecuniam uniuscujusque in ore sacci sui,

2. Et scyphum meum, scyphum argenteum, pone in ore sacci junioris,

and his corn-money. And he did according to the word that Joseph had spoken.

3. As soon as the morning was light, the men were sent away, they and their asses.

4. *And* when they were gone out of the city, *and* not *yet* far off, Joseph said unto his steward, Up, follow after the men; and when thou dost overtake them, say unto them, Wherefore have ye rewarded evil for good?

5. *Is* not this *it* in which my lord drinketh, and whereby indeed he divineth? Ye have done evil in so doing.

6. And he overtook them, and he spake unto them these same words.

7. And they said unto him, Wherefore saith my lord these words? God forbid that thy servants should do according to this thing.

8. Behold, the money which we found in our sacks' mouth we brought again unto thee out of the land of Canaan: how then should we steal out of thy lord's house silver or gold?

9. With whomsoever of thy servants it be found, both let him die, and we also will be my lord's bondmen.

10. And he said, Now also *let it be* according unto your words: he with whom it is found shall be my servant; and ye shall be blameless.

11. Then they speedily took down every man his sack to the ground, and opened every man his sack.

12. And he searched, *and* began at the eldest, and left at the youngest; and the cup was found in Benjamin's sack.

13. Then they rent their clothes, and laded every man his ass, and returned to the city.

14. And Judah and his brethren came to Joseph's house; for he *was* yet there; and they fell before him on the ground.

15. And Joseph said unto them, What deed *is* this that ye have done? wot ye not that such a man as I can certainly divine?

et pecuniam alimenti ejus: et fecit secundum verbum Joseph, quod loquutus fuerat.

3. Mane illuxit, et viri dimissi sunt, ipsi et asini eorum.

4. Ipsi egressi erant urbem, nec longe abierant, quum Joseph dixit præfecto domus suæ, Surge, persequere viros, et apprehende eos, et dices eis, Utquid reddidistis malum pro bono?

5. Nonne hic est, in quo bibit dominus meus: et ipse augurando auguratur in eo? male fecistis quod fecistis.

6. Et apprehendit eos, et loquutus est ad eos verba ista.

7. Et dixerunt ad eum, Utquid loquitur dominus meus secundum verba ista? absit a servis tuis, ut faciant secundum verbum hoc.

8. Ecce: pecuniam, quam invenimus in ore saccorum nostrorum, retulimus ad te e terra Chenaan: et quomodo furati essemus e domo domini tui argentum vel aurum.

9. Is penes quem inventus fuerit e servis tuis, moriatur: et etiam nos erimus domino meo servi.

10. Et dixit, Etiam nunc secundum verba vestra ita sit: is penes quem inventus fuerit, erit mihi servus, et vos eritis innocentes.

11. Et festinaverunt, et deposuerunt unusquisque saccum suum super terram: et aperuerunt singuli saccum suum.

12. Scrutatus est autem: a maximo incepit, et in minimo finivit: et inventus est scyphus in sacco Benjamin.

13. Et sciderunt vestimenta sua, et oneravit unusquisque asinum suum, et reversi sunt in urbem.

14. Veneruntque Jehudah et fratres ejus ad domum Joseph, et erat adhuc ipse ibi: et prostraverunt se coram eo super terram.

15. Et dixit ad eos Joseph, Quod facinus est hoc quod fecistis? nonne nostis quod augurando auguratur vir, qui est sicut ego?

16. And Judah said, What shall we say unto my lord? what shall we speak? or how shall we clear ourselves? God hath found out the iniquity of thy servants: behold, we *are* my lord's servants, both we, and *he* also with whom the cup is found.

17. And he said, God forbid that I should do so: *but* the man in whose hand the cup is found, he shall be my servant; and as for you, get you up in peace unto your father.

18. Then Judah came near unto him, and said, Oh my lord, let thy servant, I pray thee, speak a word in my lord's ears, and let not thine anger burn against thy servant: for thou *art* even as Pharaoh.

19. My lord asked his servants, saying, Have ye a father, or a brother?

20. And we said unto my lord, We have a father, an old man, and a child of his old age, a little one; and his brother is dead, and he alone is left of his mother, and his father loveth him.

21. And thou saidst unto thy servants, Bring him down unto me, that I may set mine eyes upon him.

22. And we said unto my lord, The lad cannot leave his father: for *if* he should leave his father, *his father* would die.

23. And thou saidst unto thy servants, Except your youngest brother come down with you, ye shall see my face no more.

24. And it came to pass, when we came up unto thy servant my father, we told him the words of my lord.

25. And our father said, Go again, *and* buy us a little food.

26. And we said, We cannot go down: if our youngest brother be with us, then will we go down: for we may not see the man's face, except our youngest brother *be* with us.

27. And thy servant my father said unto us, Ye know that my wife bare me two *sons:*

28. And the one went out from

16. Respondit Jehudah, Quid dicemus domino meo? quid loquemur, et in quo justificabimus nos? Deus invenit iniquitatem servorum tuorum: ecce, sumus servi domini mei, etiam nos, etiam ille in cujus manu inventus est scyphus.

17. Ille autem dixit, Absit a me ut faciam hoc: vir in cujus manu inventus est scyphus, ipse erit mihi servus: et vos ascendite in pace ad patrem vestrum.

18. Et accessit ad eum Jehudah, et dixit, Quæso, domine mi: loquatur quæso servus tuus verbum in auribus domini mei, et ne irascatur furor tuus in servum tuum: quia tu sicut Pharao.

19. Dominus meus interrogavit servos suos, dicendo, Numquid est vobis pater vel frater?

20. Et diximus domino meo, Est nobis pater senex, et puer senectutum parvus, frater autem ejus mortuus est: et remansit ipse tantum matri suæ, itaque pater ejus diligit eum.

21. Et dixisti servis tuis, Descendere facite eum ad me, et ponam oculum meum super eum.

22. Respondimus vero domino meo, Non potest puer relinquere patrem suum, et si reliquerit patrem suum, morietur.

23. Tu autem dixisti servis tuis, Nisi descendat frater vester minimus vobiscum, ne addatis ut videatis faciem meam.

24. Fuit igitur, quando ascendimus ad servum tuum patrem meum, et narravimus ei verba domini mei,

25. Dixit pater noster, Revertimini, emite nobis pusillum escæ.

26. Et diximus, non possumus descendere: si fuerit frater noster minimus nobiscum, descendemus: quia non possumus videre faciem viri illius, fratre nostro minimo non existente nobiscum.

27. Tunc dixit servus tuus pater meus nobis, Vos nostis quod duos peperit mihi uxor mea.

28. Egressus est unus a me, et

me, and I said, Surely he is torn in pieces; and I saw him not since :

29. And if ye take this also from me, and mischief befall him, ye shall bring down my gray hairs with sorrow to the grave.

30. Now therefore, when I come to thy servant my father, and the lad *be* not with us; seeing that his life is bound up in the lad's life;

31. It shall come to pass, when he seeth that the lad *is* not *with us*, that he will die: and thy servants shall bring down the gray hairs of thy servant our father with sorrow to the grave.

32. For thy servant became surety for the lad unto my father, saying, If I bring him not unto thee, then I shall bear the blame to my father for ever.

33. Now therefore, I pray thee, let thy servant abide instead of the lad a bondman to my lord; and let the lad go up with his brethren.

34. For how shall I go up to my father, and the lad *be* not with me? lest peradventure I see the evil that shall come on my father.

dixi, Certe rapiendo raptus est: et non vidi eum hactenus.

29. Et capietis etiam hunc a facie mea, et accidet ei mors, descendereque facietis canitiem meam in malo ad sepulcrum.

30. Nunc ergo quum venero ad servum tuum patrem meum, et puer non fuerit nobiscum, (et anima ejus ligata est cum anima ipsius):

31. Erit sane, quum viderit ipse quod non sit puer, morietur, et descendere facient servi tui canitiem servi tui patris nostri cum dolore ad sepulcrum.

32. Servus enim tuus fidejussit pro puero patri meo, dicendo, Si non reduxero eum ad te, obnoxius ero pœnæ patri meo omnibus diebus.

33. Et nunc maneat quæso servus tuus pro puero servus domino meo, puer autem ascendat cum fratribus suis.

34. Quomodo enim ascendam ad patrem meum, si puer non fuerit mecum? ne forte videam malum quod inveniet patrem meum.

1. *And he commanded the steward of his house.* Here Moses relates how skilfully Joseph had contrived to try the dispositions of his brethren. We have said elsewhere that, whereas God has commanded us to cultivate simplicity, we are not to take this, and similar examples, as affording license to turn aside to indirect and crafty arts. For it may have been that Joseph was impelled by a special influence of the Spirit to this course. He had also a reason, of no common kind, for inquiring very strictly in what manner his brethren were affected. Charity is not suspicious. Why, then, does he so distrust his brethren; and why cannot he suppose that they have anything good, unless he shall first have subjected them to the most rigid examination? Truly, since he had found them to be exceedingly cruel and perfidious, it is but an excusable suspicion, if he does not believe them to be changed for the better, until he has obtained a thorough perception and conviction of their penitence. But since, in this respect, it is a rare and very difficult virtue to

observe a proper medium, we must beware of imitating the example of Joseph, in an austere course of acting, unless we have laid all vindictive feelings aside, and are pure and free from all enmity. For love, when it is pure, and exempt from all turbid influence, will best decide how far it is right to proceed. It may, however, be asked, " If the sons of Jacob had been easily induced to betray the safety of Benjamin, what would Joseph himself have done?" We may readily conjecture, that he examined their fidelity, in order that, if he should find them dishonest, he might retain Benjamin, and drive them with shame from his presence. But, by pursuing this method, his father would have been deserted, and the Church of God ruined. And certainly, it is not without hazard to himself that he thus terrifies them: because he could scarcely have avoided the necessity of denouncing some more grievous and severe punishment against them, if they had again relapsed. It was, therefore, due to the special favour of God, that they proved themselves different from what he had feared. In the meantime, the advantage of his examination was twofold; first, because the clearly ascertained integrity of his brethren rendered his mind more placable towards them ; and secondly, because it lightened, at least in some degree, the former infamy, which they had contracted by their wickedness.

2. *And put my cup, the silver cup.* It may seem wonderful that, considering his great opulence, Joseph had not rather drunk out of a golden cup. Doubtless, either the moderation of that age was still greater than has since prevailed, and the splendour of it less sumptuous; or else this conduct must be attributed to the moderation of the man, who, in the midst of universal license, yet was contented with a plain and decent, rather than with a magnificent style of living. Unless, perhaps, on account of the excellence of the workmanship, the silver was more valuable than gold: as it is manifest from secular history, that the workmanship has often been more expensive than the material itself. It is, however, probable, that Joseph was sparing in domestic splendour, for the sake of avoiding envy. For unless he had been prudently on his guard, a contention would

have arisen between him and the courtiers, resulting from a spirit of emulation. Moreover, he commands the cup to be enclosed in Benjamin's sack, in order that he might claim him as his own, when convicted of the theft, and might send the rest away: however, he accuses all alike, as if he knew not who among them had committed the crime. And first, he reproves their ingratitude, because, when they had been so kindly received, they made the worst possible return; next, he contends that the crime was inexpiable, because they had stolen what was most valuable to him; namely, the cup in which he was accustomed both to drink and to divine. And he does this through his steward, whom he had not trained to acts of tyranny and violence. Whence I infer, that the steward was not altogether ignorant of his master's design.

5. *Whereby, indeed, he divineth.*[1] This clause is variously expounded. For some take it as if Joseph pretended that he consulted soothsayers in order to find out the thief. Others translate it, " by which he hath tried you, or searched you out;" others, that the stolen cup had given Joseph an unfavourable omen. The genuine sense seems to me to be this: that he had used the cup for divinations and for magical arts; which, however, we have said, he feigned, for the sake of aggravating the charge brought against them. But the question arises, how does Joseph allow himself to resort to such an expedient? For besides that it was sinful for him to profess augury; he vainly and unworthily transfers to imaginary deities the honour due only to divine grace. On a former occasion, he had declared that he

---

[1] " *Jamblichus*, in his book on Egyptian mysteries, mentions the practice of divining by cups. That this superstition, as well as many others, has continued even to modern times, is shown by a remarkable passage in Norden's Travels. When the author, with his companions, had arrived at Dorri, the most remote extremity of Egypt, or rather in Nubia, where they were able to deliver themselves from a perilous condition, only through great presence of mind, they sent one of their company to a malicious and powerful Arab, to threaten him. He answered them, ' I know what sort of people you are. I have consulted my cup, and found in it, that you are from a people of whom one of our prophets has said, There will come Franks under every kind of pretence to spy out the land. They will bring with them a great multitude of their countrymen, to conquer the country and to destroy all the people.'"—*Egypt and the Books of Moses,* p. 40.—*Ed.*

was unable to interpret dreams, except so far as God should suggest the truth to him; now he obscures this entire ascription of praise to divine grace; and what is worse, by boasting that he is a magician rather than proclaiming himself a prophet of God, he impiously profanes the gift of the Holy Spirit. Doubtless, in this dissimulation, it is not to be denied, that he sinned grievously. Yet I think that, at the first, he had endeavoured, by all means in his power, to give unto God his due honour; and it was not his fault that the whole kingdom of Egypt was ignorant of the fact that he excelled in skill, not by magical arts, but by a celestial gift. But since the Egyptians were accustomed to the illusions of the magicians, this ancient error so prevailed, that they believed Joseph to be one of them; and I do not doubt that this rumour was spread abroad among the people, although contrary to his desire and intention. Now Joseph, in feigning himself to be a stranger to his brethren, combines many falsehoods in one, and takes advantage of the prevailing vulgar opinion that he used auguries. Whence we gather, that when any one swerves from the right line, he is prone to fall into various sins. Wherefore, being warned by this example, let us learn to allow ourselves in nothing except what we know is approved by God. But especially must we avoid all dissimulation, which either produces or confirms mischievous impostures. Besides, we are warned, that it is not sufficient for any one to oppose a prevailing vice for a time; unless he add constancy of resistance, even though the evil may become excessive. For he discharges his duty very defectively, who, having once testified that he is displeased with what is evil, afterwards, by his silence or connivance, gives it a kind of assent.

7. *And they said unto him.* The sons of Jacob boldly excuse themselves, because a good conscience gives them confidence. They also argue from the greater to the less: for they contend, that their having voluntarily brought back the money, which they might with impunity have applied to their own use, was such a proof of their honesty, as to make it incredible that they should have been so blinded by a little gain, as to bring upon themselves the greatest disgrace,

together with immediate danger of their lives. They, therefore, declared themselves ready to submit to any punishment, if they were found guilty of the theft. When the cup was discovered in Benjamin's sack, Moses does not relate any of their complaints; but only declares, that they testified the most bitter grief by rending their garments. I do not doubt that they were struck dumb by the unexpected result; for they were confounded, not only by the magnitude of their grief, but by perceiving themselves to be obnoxious to punishment, for that of which their conscience did not accuse them. Therefore, when they come into the presence of Joseph, they confess the injury, not because they acknowledge that the crime has been committed by them, but because excuse would be of no avail; as if they would say, "It is of no use to deny a thing which is manifest in itself." In this sense, they say that their iniquity has been found out by God; because, although they had some secret suspicion of fraud, thinking that this had been a contrivance for the purpose of bringing an unjust charge against them, they choose rather to trace the cause of their punishment to the secret judgment of God.[1] Some interpreters believe that they here confessed their crime committed against Joseph; but that opinion is easily refuted, because they constantly affirm that he had been torn by a wild beast, or had perished by some accident. Therefore, the more simple meaning is that which I have adduced; that although the truth of the fact is not apparent, yet they are punished by God as guilty persons. They do not, however, speak hypocritically; but being troubled and astonished in their perplexed affairs, there is nothing left for them but the consciousness that this punishment is inflicted by the secret judgment of God. And I wish that they who, when smitten by the rod of God, do not immediately perceive the cause, would adopt the same course; and when they find that men are unjustly incensed against them, would recall to mind the secret judgments of God, by which it becomes us to be humbled. Moreover, whereas Judah speaks in the name of them all, we may hence infer, that he had already obtained precedence among his brethren. And

[1] See verse 16.

Moses exhibits him as their head and chief, when he expressly states that *he* and the rest came. For though the dignity of primogeniture had not yet been conferred upon him, by the solemn judgment of his father, yet it was intended for him. Certainly, in taking the post of speaker for the rest, his authority appears in his language. Again, it is necessary to recall to memory, in reference to the language of Joseph, what I have before said, that although at first he had endeavoured to ascribe the glory to God, he now sins in pretending that he is a soothsayer or diviner. Some, to extenuate the fault, say that the allusion is, not to the art of augury, but to his skill in judging; there is, however, no need to resort to forced expositions for the sake of excusing the man; for he speaks according to the common understanding of the multitude, and thus foolishly countenances the received opinion.

16. *Behold, we are my lord's servants.* They had before called themselves servants through modesty; now they consign themselves over to him as slaves. But in the case of Benjamin they plead for a mitigation of the severity of the punishment; and this is a kind of entreaty, that he might not be capitally punished, as they had agreed to, at the first.[1]

17. *God forbid that I should do so.*[2] If Joseph intended to retain Benjamin alone, and to dismiss the others, he would have done his utmost, to rend the Church of God by the worst possible dissension. But I have previously shown (what may also be elicited from the context) that his design was nothing else than to pierce their hearts more deeply. He must have anticipated great mischief, if he had perceived that they did not care for their brother: but the Lord provided against this danger, by causing the earnest

---

[1] On the whole of this verse, Dr. A. Clarke remarks, "No words can more strongly mark *confusion* and *perturbation* of mind. They no doubt all thought that Benjamin had actually stolen the cup." He also thinks it probable that this very cup had been used by Benjamin at the dinner. —*Ed.*

[2] "God forbid" is an expression frequently used by our translators, both in the Old and New Testament, where the name of God does not occur in the original. The term here used has the same meaning as *Absit* in Latin, and Μὴ γίνοιτο in Greek. Literally this passage would read, "Far be it from me to do so." See also verse 7.—*Ed.*

apology of Judah not only to soften his mind, but even to draw forth tears and weeping in profusion.

18. *Let thy servant, I pray thee, speak a word.* Judah suppliantly asks that leave may be given him to speak, because his narrative was about to be prolix. And whereas nobles are offended, and take it angrily, if any address them with too great familiarity, Judah begins by declaring that he is not ignorant of the great honour which Joseph had received in Egypt, for the purpose of showing that he was becoming bold, not through impertinence, but through necessity. Afterwards he recites in what manner he and his brethren had departed from their father. There are two principal heads of his discourse; first, that they should be the means of bringing a sorrow upon their father which would prove fatal; and secondly, that he had bound himself individually, by covenant, to bring the youth back. With respect to the grief of his father, it is a sign of no common filial piety, that he wished himself to be put in Benjamin's place, and to undergo perpetual exile and servitude, rather than convey to the miserable old man tidings which would be the cause of his destruction. He proves his sincerity by offering himself as a surety, in order that he may liberate his brother. Because חטא (*chatah*) among the Hebrews, sometimes signifies to be in fault, and sometimes to be under penalty; some translate the passage, "I shall have sinned against my father;" or, "I shall be accused of sin;" while others render it, "I shall be deemed guilty, because he will complain of having been deceived by my promise." The latter sense is the more appropriate, because, truly, he would not escape disgrace and censure from his father, as having cruelly betrayed a youth committed to his care.

## CHAPTER XLV.

1. Then Joseph could not refrain himself before all them that stood by him; and he cried, Cause every man to go out from me. And there stood no man with him, while Joseph

1. Tunc non potuit Joseph se comprimere coram omnibus, qui stabant juxta se, et clamavit, Educite omnem virum a me: et non stetit quisquam cum eo, quan-

made himself known unto his brethren.

2. And he wept aloud: and the Egyptians and the house of Pharaoh heard.

3. And Joseph said unto his brethren, I *am* Joseph: doth my father yet live? And his brethren could not answer him; for they were troubled at his presence.

4. And Joseph said unto his brethren, Come near to me, I pray you. And they came near. And he said, I *am* Joseph your brother, whom ye sold into Egypt.

5. Now therefore be not grieved nor angry with yourselves that ye sold me hither; for God did send me before you to preserve life.

6. For these two years *hath* the famine *been* in the land: and yet *there are* five years, in the which *there shall* neither *be* earing nor harvest.

7. And God sent me before you to preserve you a posterity in the earth, and to save your lives by a great deliverance.

8. So now, *it was* not you *that* sent me hither, but God: and he hath made me a father to Pharaoh, and lord of all his house, and a ruler throughout all the land of Egypt.

9. Haste ye, and go up to my father, and say unto him, Thus saith thy son Joseph, God hath made me lord of all Egypt; come down unto me, tarry not:

10. And thou shalt dwell in the land of Goshen, and thou shalt be near unto me, thou, and thy children, and thy children's children, and thy flocks, and thy herds, and all that thou hast:

11. And there will I nourish thee, for yet *there are* five years of famine, lest thou, and thy household, and all that thou hast, come to poverty.

12. And, behold, your eyes see, and the eyes of my brother Benjamin, that *it is* my mouth that speaketh unto you.

do patefecit se Joseph fratribus suis.

2. Et emisit vocem suam cum fletu: et audierunt Ægyptii, audivit et domus Pharaonis.

3. Dixit autem Joseph fratribus suis, Ego sum Joseph, num adhuc vivit pater meus? et non potuerunt fratres ejus respondere ei: quia territi erant a facie ejus.

4. Et dixit Joseph fratribus suis, Accedite quæso ad me. Et accesserunt. Et dixit, Ego sum Joseph frater vester, quem vendidistis in Ægyptum.

5. Et nunc ne dolore afficiamini, et ne sit ira in oculis vestris quod vendideritis me huc: nam propter vitam misit me Deus ante vos.

6. Jam enim duo anni famis fuerunt in medio terræ, et adhuc quinque anni sunt, in quibus non erit aratio et messis.

7. Et misit me Deus ante vos, ut ponam vobis reliquias in terra: et ut vivificem vos evasione magna.

8. Nunc itaque non vos misistis me huc, sed Deus: et posuit me in patrem Pharaoni, et in dominum toti domui ejus, et dominatorem in tota terra Ægypti.

9. Festinate, et ascendite ad patrem meum, et dicite ei, Sic dicit filius tuus Joseph, Posuit me Deus in dominum toti Ægypto, descende ad me, ne stes.

10. Et habitabis in terra Gosen, et eris propinquus mihi, tu et filii tui, et filii filiorum tuorum, et pecudes tuæ, et boves tui, et omnia quæ sunt tibi.

11. Et alam te ibi, quia adhuc quinque anni famis sunt: ne forte inopia vel egestate conficiaris tu et domus tua, et omne quod est tibi.

12. Et ecce, oculi vestri vident et oculi fratris mei Benjamin, quod os meum loquitur ad vos.

13. And ye shall tell my father of all my glory in Egypt, and of all that ye have seen; and ye shall haste and bring down my father hither.

14. And he fell upon his brother Benjamin's neck, and wept; and Benjamin wept upon his neck.

15. Moreover, he kissed all his brethren, and wept upon them: and after that his brethren talked with him.

16. And the fame thereof was heard in Pharaoh's house, saying, Joseph's brethren are come. And it pleased Pharaoh well, and his servants.

17. And Pharaoh said unto Joseph, Say unto thy brethren, This do ye; lade your beasts, and go, get you unto the land of Canaan;

18. And take your father, and your households, and come unto me: and I will give you the good of the land of Egypt, and ye shall eat the fat of the land.

19. Now thou art commanded, this do ye; Take you waggons out of the land of Egypt for your little ones, and for your wives, and bring your father, and come.

20. Also regard not your stuff: for the good of all the land of Egypt *is* yours.

21. And the children of Israel did so, and Joseph gave them waggons, according to the commandment of Pharaoh, and gave them provision for the way.

22. To all of them he gave each man changes of raiment; but to Benjamin he gave three hundred *pieces* of silver, and five changes of raiment.

23. And to his father he sent after this *manner:* ten asses laden with the good things of Egypt, and ten she-asses laden with corn and bread and meat for his father by the way.

24. So he sent his brethren away, and they departed: and he said unto them, See that ye fall not out by the way.

13. Nuntiate autem patri meo omnem gloriam meam in Ægypto, et omnia quæ vidistis: et festinate, et descendere facite patrem meum huc.

14. Et jactavit se super collum Benjamin fratris sui, et flevit: Benjamin quoque flevit super collum ejus.

15. Et osculatus est omnes fratres suos, et flevit super eos, et postea loquuti sunt fratres ejus cum eo.

16. Et vox audita est in domo Pharaonis, dicendo, Venerunt fratres Joseph, et placuit in oculis Pharaonis, et in oculis servorum ejus.

17. Et dixit Pharao ad Joseph, Dic fratribus tuis, Hoc facite, onerate jumenta vestra, et ite, ingredimini terram Chenaan.

18. Et capite patrem vestrum, et familias vestras, et venite ad me: et dabo vobis bonum terræ Ægypti, et comedetis pinguedinem terræ.

19. Et tu jussus es, Hoc facite, capite vobis de terra Ægypti currus pro parvulis vestris, et pro uxoribus vestris: et tollite patrem vestrum, et venite.

20. Et oculus vester ne parcat supellectili vestræ: quia bonum omnis terræ Ægypti vestrum erit.

21. Fecerunt ergo sic filii Israel, et dedit eis Joseph currus juxta sermonem Pharaonis, et dedit eis escam pro itinere.

22. Omnibus ipsis dedit unicuique mutatorias vestes, et ipsi Benjamin dedit trecentos argenteos, et quinque mutatorias vestes.

23. Patri autem suo misit secundum hoc, decem asinos ferentes de bono Ægypti, et decem asinas ferentes frumentum, et panem, et escam patri suo pro itinere.

24. Et dimisit fratres suos, et abierunt, et dixit ad eos, Ne tumultuemini in via.

| | |
|---|---|
| 25. And they went up out of Egypt, and came into the land of Canaan unto Jacob their father, | 25. At ascenderunt ex Ægypto, et venerunt in terram Chenaan, ad Jahacob patrem suum. |
| 26. And told him, saying, Joseph *is* yet alive, and he *is* governor over all the land of Egypt. And Jacob's heart fainted, for he believed them not. | 26. Et nuntiaverunt ei, dicendo, Adhuc Joseph vivit: et quod ipse dominaretur in omni terra Ægypti: et dissolutum est cor ejus, quia non credebat eis. |
| 27. And they told him all the words of Joseph, which he had said unto them: and when he saw the waggons, which Joseph had sent to carry him, the spirit of Jacob their father revived. | 27. Et retulerunt ei omnia verba Joseph, quæ loquutus fuerat ad eos: et vidit currus, quos miserat Joseph ut ferrent eum, et revixit spiritus Jahacob patris eorum. |
| 28. And Israel said, *It is* enough; Joseph my son *is* yet alive: I will go and see him before I die. | 28. Et dixit Israel, Sufficit, adhuc Joseph filius meus vivit: ibo, et videbo eum, antequam moriar. |

1. *Then Joseph could not refrain himself.*[1] Moses relates in this chapter the manner in which Joseph made himself known to his brethren. In the first place, he declares, that Joseph had done violence to his feelings, as long as he presented to them an austere and harsh countenance. At length the strong fraternal affection, which he had suppressed during the time that he was breathing severe threatenings, poured itself forth with more abundant force: whence it appears that nothing severe or cruel had before been harboured in his mind. And whereas it thus bursts forth in tears, this softness or tenderness is more deserving of praise than if he had maintained an equable temper. Therefore the stoics speak foolishly when they say, that it is an heroic virtue not to be touched with compassion. Had Joseph stood inflexible, who would not have pronounced him to be a stupid, or iron-hearted man? But now, by the vehemence of his feelings, he manifests a noble magnanimity, as well as a divine moderation; because he was so superior both to anger and to hatred, that he ardently loved those who had wickedly conspired to effect his ruin, though they had received no

---

[1] The division of chapters in this place is singularly unhappy. It interrupts one of the most touching scenes recorded in the sacred volume, just in the middle. It separates the irresistible appeal of Judah to the feelings of Joseph from its immediate and happy effect. In the Hebrew Bible, the section commences with Judah's address, and no break is made where this chapter commences; so that the whole is given as one continuous narrative. —*Ed.*

injury from him. He commands all men to depart, not because he was ashamed of his kindred, (for he does not afterwards dissemble the fact that they were his brethren, and he freely permits the report of it to be carried to the king's palace,) but because he is considerate for their feelings, that he might not make known their detestable crime to many witnesses. And it was not the smallest part of his clemency, to desire that their disgrace should be wholly buried in oblivion. We see, therefore, that witnesses were removed, for no other reason than that he might more freely comfort his brethren; for he not only spared them, by not exposing their crime; but when shut up alone with them, he abstained from all bitterness of language, and gladly administered to them friendly consolation.

3. *I am Joseph.* Although he had given them the clearest token of his mildness and his love, yet, when he told them his name, they were terrified, as if he had thundered against them: for while they revolve in their minds what they have deserved, the power of Joseph seems so formidable to them, that they anticipate nothing for themselves but death. When, however, he sees them overcome with fear, he utters no reproach, but only labours to calm their perturbation. Nay, he continues gently to soothe them, until he has rendered them composed and cheerful. By this example we are taught to take heed lest sadness should overwhelm those who are truly and seriously humbled under a sense of shame. So long as the offender is deaf to reproofs, or securely flatters himself, or wickedly and obstinately repels admonitions, or excuses himself by hypocrisy, greater severity is to be used towards him. But rigour should have its bounds, and as soon as the offender lies prostrate, and trembles under the sense of his sin, let that moderation immediately follow which may raise him who is cast down, by the hope of pardon. Therefore, in order that our severity may be rightly and duly attempered, we must cultivate this inward affection of Joseph, which will show itself at the proper time.

4. *Come near to me, I pray you.* This is more efficacious than any mere words, that he kindly invites them to his embrace. Yet he also tries to remove their care and fear by

the most courteous language he can use. He so attempers his speech, indeed, that he mildly accuses, and again consoles them; nevertheless, the consolation greatly predominates, because he sees that they are on the point of desperation, unless he affords them timely relief. Moreover, in relating that he had been sold, he does not renew the memory of their guilt, with the intention of expostulating with them; but only because it is always profitable that the sense of sin should remain, provided that immoderate terror does not absorb the unhappy man, after he has acknowledged his fault. And whereas the brethren of Joseph were more than sufficiently terrified, he insists the more fully on the second part of his purpose; namely, that he may heal the wound. This is the reason why he repeats, that God had sent him for their preservation; that by the counsel of God himself he had been sent beforehand into Egypt to preserve them alive; and that, in short, he had not been sent into Egypt by them, but had been led thither by the hand of God.[1]

8. *So now, it was not you that sent me hither.* This is a remarkable passage, in which we are taught that the right course of events is never so disturbed by the depravity and wickedness of men, but that God can direct them to a good end. We are also instructed in what manner and for what purpose we must consider the providence of God. When men of inquisitive minds dispute concerning it, they not only mingle and pervert all things without regard to the end designed, but invent every absurdity in their power, in order to sully the justice of God. And this rashness causes some pious and moderate men to wish this portion of doctrine to be concealed from view; for as soon as it is publicly declared that God holds the government of the whole world, and that nothing is done but by his will and authority, they who think with little reverence of the mysteries of God, break

[1] Only two years of the famine had now elapsed, and there were yet five years in which there should be "neither earing nor harvest," so that this was indeed but the commencement of the grievous suffering to which Jacob's family would have been exposed, but for the extraordinary interposition of Divine providence in their favour. The word *earing* is an obsolete Saxon term by which our translators have rendered the Hebrew word חריש, (*charish,*) which means *ploughing,* or preparing the ground for seed. —*Ed.*

forth into various questions, not only frivolous but injurious. But, as this profane intemperance of mind is to be restrained, so a just measure is to be observed on the other hand, lest we should encourage a gross ignorance of those things which are not only made plain in the word of God, but are exceedingly useful to be known. Good men are ashamed to confess, that what men undertake cannot be accomplished except by the will of God; fearing lest unbridled tongues should cry out immediately, either that God is the author of sin, or that wicked men are not to be accused of crime, seeing they fulfil the counsel of God. But although this sacrilegious fury cannot be effectually rebutted, it may suffice that we hold it in detestation. Meanwhile, it is right to maintain, what is declared by the clear testimonies of Scripture, that whatever men may contrive, yet, amidst all their tumult, God from heaven overrules their counsels and attempts; and, in short, does, by their hands, what he has himself decreed. Good men, who fear to expose the justice of God to the calumnies of the impious, resort to this distinction, that God *wills* some things, but *permits* others to be done. As if, truly, any degree of liberty of action, were he to cease from governing, would be left to men. If he had only *permitted* Joseph to be carried into Egypt, he had not *ordained* him to be the minister of deliverance to his father Jacob and his sons; which he is now expressly declared to have done. Away, then, with that vain figment, that, by the *permission* of God only, and not by his *counsel* or *will*, those evils are committed which he afterwards turns to a good account. I speak of evils with respect to men, who propose nothing else to themselves but to act perversely. And as the vice dwells in them, so ought the whole blame also to be laid upon them. But God works wonderfully through their means, in order that, from their impurity, he may bring forth his perfect righteousness. This method of acting is secret, and far above our understanding. Therefore it is not wonderful that the licentiousness of our flesh should rise against it. But so much the more diligently must we be on our guard, that we do not attempt to reduce this lofty standard to the measure of our own littleness. Let this sentiment remain fixed with us, that while the lust of men exults, and intemperately hurries them hither and thither, God is the ruler, and, by his secret rein, directs their motions whithersoever he pleases. At the same time, however, it must also be maintained, that God acts so far distinctly from them, that no vice can attach itself to his providence, and that his decrees have no affinity with the crimes of men. Of which mode of procedure a most illustrious example is placed before our eyes in this history. Joseph was sold by his brethren; for what reason, but because they wished, by any means whatever, to ruin and annihilate him? The same work is ascribed to God, but for a very different end; namely, that in a time of famine the family of Jacob might have an unexpected supply of food. Therefore he willed that Joseph should be as one dead, for a short time, in order that he might suddenly bring him forth from the grave, as the preserver of life. Whence it appears, that although he seems, at the commencement, to do the same thing as the wicked; yet there is a wide distance between their wickedness and his admirable judgment. Let us now examine the words of Joseph. For the consolation of his brethren he seems to draw the veil of oblivion over their fault. But we know that men are not exempt from guilt, although God may, beyond expectation, bring what they wickedly attempt, to a good and happy issue. For what advantage was it to Judas that the redemption of the world proceeded from his wicked treachery? Joseph, however, though he withdraws, in some degree, the minds of his brethren from a consideration of their own guilt, until they can breathe again after their immoderate terror, neither traces their fault to God as its cause, nor really absolves them from it; as we shall see more clearly in the last chapter. And doubtless, it must be maintained, that the deeds of men are not to be estimated according to the event, but according to the measure in which they may have failed in their duty, or may have attempted something contrary to the Divine command, and may have gone beyond the bounds of their calling. Some one, for instance, has neglected his wife or children, and has not diligently attended to their necessities; and though they do not die, unless God wills it, yet the inhumanity of the father, who wickedly deserted them when he ought to have relieved them, is not screened or excused by this pretext. Therefore, they whose consciences accuse them of evil, derive no advantage from the pretence that the providence of God exonerates them from blame. But on the other hand, whenever the Lord interposes to prevent the evil of those who desire to injure us, and not that only, but turns even their wicked designs to our good; he subdues, by this method, our carnal affections, and renders us more just and placable. Thus we see that Joseph was a skilful interpreter of the providence of God, when he borrowed from it an argument for granting forgiveness to his brethren. The magnitude of the crime committed against him might so have incensed him as to cause him to burn with the desire of revenge: but when he reflects that their wickedness had been overruled by the wonderful and unwonted goodness of God, forgetting the injury received, he kindly embraces the men whose dishonour God had covered with his grace. And truly charity is ingenious in hiding the faults of brethren, and therefore she freely applies to this use anything which may tend to appease anger, and to set enmities at rest. Joseph also is carried forward to another view of the case; namely, that he had been divinely chosen to help his brethren. Whence it happens, that he not only remits their offence, but that, from an earnest desire to discharge the duty enjoined upon him, he delivers them from fear and anxiety as well as from want. This is the reason why he asserts that he was ordained to " put for them a remnant,"[1] that is, to preserve a remaining seed, or rather to preserve them alive, and that by an excellent and wonderful deliverance. In saying that he is a father to Pharaoh, he is not carried away with empty boasting as vain men are wont to be; nor does he make an ostentatious display of his wealth; but he proves, from an event so great and incredible, that he had not obtained the post he occupied by accident, nor by human means; but rather that, by the wonderful counsel of God, a lofty throne had

---

[1] Ver. 7. Ut ponam vobis reliquias in terrâ. " To preserve you a posterity," (or, as in the margin,) " to put for you a remnant" in the earth.—*English translation.—Ed.*

been raised for him, from which he might succour his father and his whole family.

9. *Thus saith thy son Joseph.* In giving this command, he shows that he spoke of his power in order to inspire his father with stronger confidence. We know how dilatory old men are; and, besides, it was difficult to tear holy Jacob away from the inheritance which was divinely promised to him. Therefore Joseph, having pointed out the necessity for the step, declares what a desirable relief the Lord had offered. It may, however, be asked, why the oracle did not occur to their minds, concerning which they had been instructed by their fathers, namely, that they should be strangers and servants in a strange land. (Gen. xv. 13.) For it seems that Joseph here promises nothing but mere pleasures, as if no future adversity was to be apprehended. But though nothing is expressly declared on this point by Moses, yet I am induced, by a probable conjecture, to believe that Jacob was not forgetful of the oracle. For, unless he had been retained by some celestial chain, he never could have remained in Egypt after the expiration of the time of scarcity. For by remaining there voluntarily, he would have appeared to cast away the hope of the inheritance promised him by God. Seeing, then, that he does not provide for his return into the land of Canaan, but only commands his corpse to be carried thither; nor yet exhorts his sons to a speedy return, but suffers them to settle in Egypt; he does this, not from indolence, or because he is allured by the attractions of Egypt, or has become weary of the land of Canaan; but because he is preparing himself and his offspring to bear that tyranny, concerning which he had been forewarned by his father Isaac. Therefore he regards it as an advantage that, at his first coming, he is hospitably received; but, in the meantime, he revolves in his mind what had been spoken to Abraham.

16. *And the fame thereof was heard in Pharaoh's house.* What Moses now relates, was prior in the order of events. For before Joseph sent for his father, the report of the coming of his brethren had reached the palace. And Joseph would not have promised so confidently a home to his brethren in Egypt, except by the king's permission. What,

therefore, Moses had before briefly alluded to, he now more fully explains; namely, that the king, with a ready and cheerful mind, declared his high esteem for Joseph, in freely offering to his father and brethren, the most fertile part of Egypt for their dwelling. And from another statement of Moses it appears that, as long as he lived, the Israelites were treated with clemency and kindness. For, in the first chapter of Exodus, and the eighth verse, the commencement of the tyranny and cruelty is said to have been made by his successor, to whom Joseph was unknown.

22. *And to all of them he gave each man changes of raiment.* That he furnishes his brethren with supplies for their journey is not wonderful: but to what purpose was it that he loaded them with money and garments, seeing they would so soon return? I, indeed, do not doubt that he did it on account of his father and the wives of his brethren, in order that they might have less reluctance to leave the land of Canaan. For he knew that his message would scarcely be believed, unless some manifest tokens of its truth were presented. It might also be, that he not only endeavoured to allure those who were absent, but that he also wished to testify, more and more, his love towards his brethren. But the former consideration has more weight with me, because he took greater care in furnishing Benjamin than the rest. Jerome has translated the expression, "changes of raiment," by "two robes," and other interpreters, following him, expound it as meaning "different kinds of garments." I know not whether this be solid. I rather suppose they were elegant garments, such as were used at nuptials and on festal days; for I think that constant custom was silently opposed to this variety of dress.

24. *See that ye fall not out by the way.* Some explain the passage as meaning, that Joseph asks his brethren to be of tranquil mind, and not to disturb themselves with needless fear; he rather exhorts them, however, to mutual peace. For, since the word רגז, (*ragaz*,) sometimes signifies to tremble or be afraid, and sometimes, to make a tumult, the latter sense is the more appropriate: for we know that the children of God are not only easily appeased, if any one has

injured them, but that they also desire others should live together in concord. Joseph was pacified towards his brethren; but at the same time he admonishes them not to stir up any strife among themselves. For there was reason to fear lest each, in attempting to excuse himself, should try to lay the blame on others, and thus contention would arise. We ought to imitate this kindness of Joseph; that we may prevent, as much as possible, quarrels and strifes of words; for Christ requires of his disciples, not only that they should be lovers of peace, but also that they should be peace-makers. Wherefore, it is our duty to remove, in time, all matter and occasion of strife. Besides, we must know, that what Joseph taught his brethren, is the command of the Spirit of God to us all; namely, that we should not be angry with each other. And because it generally happens that, in faults common to different parties, one maliciously accuses another; let each of us learn to acknowledge and confess his own fault, lest altercations should end in combats.

26. *And Jacob's heart fainted.* We know that some persons have fainted with sudden and unexpected joy. Therefore, certain interpreters suppose that the heart of Jacob was, in a sense, suffocated, as if seized by a kind of ecstatic stupor. But Moses assigns a different cause; namely, that not having confidence in his sons, he was agitated between hope and fear. And we know, that they who are held in suspense, by hearing some incredible message, are struck with torpor, as if they were lifeless. It was not, therefore, a simple affection of joy, but a certain mingled perturbation which shook the mind of Jacob. Therefore, Moses shortly after says, that his spirit revived; when he, having returned to himself, and being composed in mind, believed that which he had heard to be true. And he shows that his love towards Joseph had not languished through length of time, inasmuch as he set no value upon his own life, except so far as it would permit him to enjoy a sight of Joseph. He had before assigned to himself continual sorrow, even to the grave; but now he declares that he shall have a joyful death.

## CHAPTER XLVI.

1. And Israel took his journey with all that he had, and came to Beer-sheba, and offered sacrifices unto the God of his father Isaac.
2. And God spake unto Israel in the visions of the night, and said, Jacob, Jacob. And he said, Here am I.
3. And he said, I *am* God, the God of thy father: fear not to go down into Egypt; for I will there make of thee a great nation.
4. I will go down with thee into Egypt; and I will also surely bring thee up *again*: and Joseph shall put his hand upon thine eyes.

5. And Jacob rose up from Beer-sheba: and the sons of Israel carried Jacob their father, and their little ones, and their wives, in the waggons which Pharaoh had sent to carry him.
6. And they took their cattle, and their goods, which they had gotten in the land of Canaan, and came into Egypt, Jacob, and all his seed with him:
7. His sons, and his sons' sons with him, his daughters, and his sons' daughters, and all his seed, brought he with him into Egypt.
8. And these *are* the names of the children of Israel which came into Egypt, Jacob and his sons: Reuben, Jacob's first-born.
9. And the sons of Reuben; Hanoch, and Phallu, and Hezron, and Carmi.
10. And the sons of Simeon; Jemuel, and Jamin, and Ohad, and Jachin, and Zohar, and Shaul the son of a Canaanitish woman.
11. And the sons of Levi; Gershon, Kohath, and Merari.
12. And the sons of Judah; Er, and Onan, and Shelah, and Pharez, and Zarah: but Er and Onan died in the land of Canaan. And the sons of Pharez were Hezron and Hamul.

1. Itaque profectus est Israel, et quæcunque habebat, et venit in Beer-sebah, et sacrificavit sacrificia Deo patris sui Ishac.
2. Et dixit Deus ad Israel in visionibus noctis, dixit inquam, Jahacob. Ille respondit, Ecce, adsum.
3. Et dixit, Ego sum Deus, Deus patris tui: ne timeas descendere in Ægyptum: quia in gentem magnam ponam te ibi.
4. Ego descendam tecum in Ægyptum, et ego ascendere etiam te faciam ascendendo: Joseph quoque ponet manum suam super oculos tuos.
5. Postea surrexit Jahacob de Beersebah, et sustulerunt filii Israel Jahacob patrem suum, et parvulos suos, et uxores super currus, quos miserat Pharao ad ferendum eum.
6. Et ceperunt pecudes suas, et substantiam quam acquisierant in terra Chenaan: veneruntque in Ægyptum Jahacob, et omne semen ejus cum ipso:
7. Filii ejus, et filii filiorum ejus cum eo, filiæ ejus, et filiæ filiorum ejus: et omne semen suum deduxit secum in Ægyptum.
8. Hæc sunt autem nomina filiorum Israel, qui ingressi sunt in Ægyptum, Jahacob et filii ejus: primogenitus Jahacob, Reuben.
9. Et filii Reuben, Hanoch, et Phallu, et Hesron, et Charmi.
10. Filii vero Simhon, Jemuel, et Jamin, et Ohad, et Jachin, et Sohar, et Saul filius Chenaanitidis.
11. Filii Levi, Gerson, Cehath, et Merari.
12. Filii Jehudah, Her, et Onam, et Selah, et Peres, et Zerah: et mortuus est Her et Onam in terra Chenaan. Fuerunt autem filii Peres, Hesron, et Hamul.

13. And the sons of Issachar; Tola, and Phuvah, and Job, and Shimron.

14. And the sons of Zebulun; Sered, and Elon, and Jahleel.

15. These *be* the sons of Leah, which she bare unto Jacob in Padanaram, with his daughter Dinah: all the souls of his sons and his daughters *were* thirty and three.

16. And the sons of Gad; Ziphion, and Haggi, Shuni, and Ezbon, Eri, and Arodi, and Areli.

17. And the sons of Asher; Jimnah, and Ishuah, and Isui, and Beriah, and Serah their sister. And the sons of Beriah; Heber, and Malchiel.

18. These *are* the sons of Zilpah, whom Laban gave to Leah his daughter; and these she bare unto Jacob, *even* sixteen souls.

19. The sons of Rachel, Jacob's wife; Joseph, and Benjamin.

20. And unto Joseph, in the land of Egypt, were born Manasseh and Ephraim, which Asenath, the daughter of Poti-pherah priest of On, bare unto him.

21. And the sons of Benjamin *were* Belah, and Becher, and Ashbel, Gera, and Naaman, Ehi, and Rosh, Muppim, and Huppim, and Ard.

22. These *are* the sons of Rachel, which were born to Jacob: all the souls *were* fourteen.

23. And the sons of Dan; Hushim.

24. And the sons of Naphtali; Jahzeel, and Guni, and Jezer, and Shillem.

25. These *are* the sons of Bilhah, which Laban gave unto Rachel his daughter; and she bare these unto Jacob: all the souls *were* seven.

26. All the souls that came with Jacob into Egypt, which came out of his loins, besides Jacob's sons' wives, all the souls *were* threescore and six.

27. And the sons of Joseph, which were born him in Egypt, *were* two souls: all the souls of the house of Jacob, which came into Egypt, *were* threescore and ten.

13. Et filii Issachar, Tholah, et Puvah, et Job, et Simron.

14. Filii vero Zebulon, Sered, et Elon, et Jahleel.

15. Isti sunt filii Leah, quos peperit ipsi Jahacob in Padan Aram, et Dinah filiam ejus: omnes animæ filiorum ejus, et filiarum ejus fuerunt triginta et tres.

16. Filii autem Gad, Siphion et Hagghi, Suni et Esbon, Heri et Arodi, et Areli.

17. Et filii Aser, Imnah, et Isvah, et Isvi, et Berihah, et Serah soror eorum. Filii vero Berihah, Heber et Malchiel.

18. Isti sunt filii Zilpah, quam dedit Laban Leah filiæ suæ, et peperit istos ipsi Jahacob, sedecim animas.

19. Filii Rachel uxoris Jahacob, Joseph et Benjamin.

20. Nati sunt autem ipsi Joseph in terra Ægypti, quos peperit ei Asenath filia Poti-pherah principis On, Menasseh et Ephraim.

21. Filii vero Benjamin, fuerunt Belah, et Becher, et Asbel, Gera et Naaman, Ehi et Ros, Muppim, et Huppim, et Arde.

22. Isti sunt filii Rachel qui nati sunt ipsi Jahacob: omnes animæ, quatuordecim.

23. Et filii Dan, Hussim.

24. Filii Nephthali, Jahseel, et Guni, et Jeser, et Sillem.

25. Isti sunt filii Bilhah, quam dedit Laban Rachel filiæ suæ, et peperit istos ipsi Jahacob: omnes animæ septem.

26. Omnes animæ, quæ venerunt cum Jahacob in Ægyptum, quæ egressæ sunt de femore ejus, præter uxores filiorum Jahacob, omnes, inquam, animæ fuerunt sexaginta et sex.

27. Et filii Joseph, qui nati sunt ei in Ægypto, animæ duæ. Omnes animæ domus Jahacob, quæ ingressæ sunt in Ægyptum, fuerunt septuaginta.

28. And he sent Judah before him unto Joseph, to direct his face unto Goshen; and they came into the land of Goshen.

29. And Joseph made ready his chariot, and went up to meet Israel his father, to Goshen, and presented himself unto him; and he fell on his neck, and wept on his neck a good while.

30. And Israel said unto Joseph, Now let me die, since I have seen thy face, because thou *art* yet alive.

31. And Joseph said unto his brethren, and unto his father's house, I will go up, and shew Pharaoh, and say unto him, My brethren, and my father's house, which *were* in the land of Canaan, are come unto me:

32. And the men *are* shepherds, for their trade hath been to feed cattle; and they have brought their flocks, and their herds, and all that they have.

33. And it shall come to pass, when Pharaoh shall call you, and shall say, What *is* your occupation?

34. That ye shall say, Thy servants' trade hath been about cattle from our youth even until now, both we *and* also our fathers; that ye may dwell in the land of Goshen: for every shepherd *is* an abomination unto the Egyptians.

28. Porro Jehudah misit ante se ad Joseph ad præparandum locum ante se in Gosen, et venerunt in terram Gosen.

29. Et ligavit Joseph currum suum, et ascendit in occursum Israel patris sui in Gosen: et conspectus est ei, et jactavit se ad collum ejus, flevitque super collum ejus adhuc.

30. Et dixit Israel ad Joseph, Moriar hac vice, postquam vidi faciem tuam: adhuc enim tu vivis.

31. Et dixit Joseph fratribus suis, et domui patris sui, Ascendam, et nuntiabo Pharaoni: et dicam ei. Fratres mei, et domus patris mei, qui erant in terram Chenaan, venerunt ad me.

32. Atque viri pastores pecudum sunt, quia viri pecuarii sunt: et pecudes eorum, et boves eorum, et omnia quæ erant eis, adduxerunt.

33. Erit ergo quum vocaverit vos Pharao, et dixerit, Quod est opus vestrum?

34. Dicetis, Viri pecuarii fuerunt servi tui a pueritia nostra et usque nunc, etiam nos, etiam patres nostri: ut habitetis in terra Gosen, quia abominatio Ægyptiis est omnis pastor pecudum.

1. *And Israel took his journey.* Because the holy man is compelled to leave the land of Canaan and to go elsewhere, he offers, on his departure, a sacrifice to the Lord, for the purpose of testifying that the covenant which God had made with his fathers was confirmed and ratified to himself. For, though he was accustomed to exercise himself in the external worship of God, there was yet a special reason for this sacrifice. And, doubtless, he had then peculiar need of support, lest his faith should fail: for he was about to be deprived of the inheritance promised to him, and of the sight of that land which was the type and the pledge of the heavenly country. Might it not come into his mind that he had hitherto been deluded with a vain hope? Therefore, by re-

newing the memory of the divine covenant, he applies a suitable remedy against falling from the faith. For this reason, he offers a sacrifice on the very boundaries of that land, as I have just said; that we might know it to be something more than usual. And he presents this worship to the God of his fathers, to testify that, although he is departing from that land, into which Abraham had been called; yet he does not thereby cut himself off from the God in whose worship he had been educated. It was truly a remarkable proof of constancy, that when cast out by famine into another region, so that he might not even be permitted to sojourn in the land of which he was the lawful lord; he yet retains, deeply impressed on his mind, the hope of his hidden right. It was not without subjecting himself to odium that he differed openly from other nations, by worshipping the God of his fathers. But what profit was there in having a religion different from all others? Seeing, then, that he does not repent of having worshipped the God of his fathers, and that he now also perseveres in fear and reverence towards Him; we hence infer how deeply he was rooted in true piety. By offering a sacrifice, he both increases his own strength, and makes profession of his faith; because, although piety is not bound to external symbols, yet he will not neglect those helps, the use of which he has found to be, by no means, superfluous.

2. *And God spake unto Israel.* In this manner, God proves that the sacrifice of Jacob was acceptable to him, and again stretches out his hand to ratify anew his covenant. The vision by night availed for the purpose of giving greater dignity to the oracle. Jacob indeed, inasmuch as he was docile and ready to yield obedience to God, did not need to be impelled by force and terror; yet, because he was a man encompassed with flesh, it was profitable for him that he should be affected as with the glory of a present God, in order that the word might penetrate more effectually into his heart. It is, however, proper to recall to memory what I have said before, that the *word* was joined with it; because a silent vision would have profited little or nothing. We know that superstition eagerly snatches at mere spectres; by which means it presents God in a form of its own. But

since no living image of God can exist without the word, whenever God has *appeared* to his servants, he has also *spoken* to them. Wherefore, in all outward signs, let us be ever attentive to his voice, if we would not be deluded by the wiles of Satan. But if those visions, in which the majesty of God shines, require to be animated by the word, then they who obtrude signs, invented at the will of men, upon the Church, exhibit nothing else than the empty pomps of a profane theatre. Just as in the Papacy, those things which are called sacraments, are lifeless phantoms which draw away deluded souls from the true God. Let this mutual connexion, then, be observed, that the vision which gives greater dignity to the word, precedes it; and that the word follows immediately, as if it were the soul of the vision. And there is no question that this was an appearance of the visible glory of God, which did not leave Jacob in suspense and hesitation; but which, by removing his doubt, firmly sustained him, so that he confidently embraced the oracle.

3. *Jacob, Jacob.* The design of the repetition was to render him more attentive. For, by thus familiarly addressing him, God more gently insinuates himself into his mind: as, in the Scripture, he kindly allures us, that he may prepare us to become his disciples. The docility of the holy man appears hence, that as soon as he is persuaded that God speaks, he replies that he is ready to receive with reverence whatever may be spoken, to follow wheresoever he may be called, and to undertake whatever may be commanded. Afterwards, a promise is added, by which God confirms and revives the faith of his servant. Whereas, the descent into Egypt was to him a sad event, he is bidden to be of good and cheerful mind; inasmuch as the Lord would always be his keeper, and after having increased him there to a great nation, would bring him back again to the place, whence he now compelled him to depart. And, indeed, Jacob's chief consolation turned on this point; that he should not perpetually wander up and down as an exile, but should, at length, enjoy the expected inheritance. For, since the possession of the land of Canaan was the token of the Divine favour, of spiritual blessings, and of eternal felicity; if holy Jacob was

defrauded of this, it would have availed him little or nothing to have riches, and all kinds of wealth and power heaped upon him, in Egypt. The return promised him is not, however, to be understood of his own person, but refers to his posterity. Now, as Jacob, relying on the promise, is commanded boldly to go down into Egypt; so it is the duty of all the pious, after his example, to derive such strength from the grace of God, that they may gird themselves to obey his commands. The title by which God here distinguishes himself, is attached to the former oracles which Jacob had received by tradition from his fathers. For why does he not rather call himself the Creator of heaven and earth, than the God of Isaac or of Abraham, except for this reason, that the dominion over the land of Canaan depends on the previous covenant, which he now ratifies anew? At the same time also, he encourages his servant by examples drawn from his own family, lest he should cease to proceed with constancy in his calling. For, when he had seen that his father Isaac, and had heard that his grandfather Abraham, though long surrounded by great troubles, never gave way to any temptations, it ill became him to be overcome by weariness in the same course; especially since, in the act of dying, they handed their lamp to their posterity, and took diligent care to leave the light of their faith to survive them in their family. In short, Jacob is taught that he must not seek, in crooked and diverse paths, that God whom he had learned, from his childhood, to regard as the Ruler of the family of Abraham; provided it did not degenerate from his piety. Moreover, we have elsewhere stated how far, in this respect, the authority of the Fathers ought to prevail. For it was not the design of God, either that Jacob should subject himself to men, or should approve, without discrimination, whatever was handed down from his ancestors,—seeing that he so often condemns in the Jews, a foolish imitation of their fathers,—but his design was to keep Jacob in the true knowledge of himself.

4. *And Joseph shall put his hand upon thine eyes.* This clause was added for the sake of showing greater indulgence. For though Jacob, in desiring that, when he died, his eyes

should be closed by the hand of Joseph, showed that some infirmity of the flesh was involved in the wish; yet God is willing to comply with it, for the sake of moderating the grief of a fresh banishment. Moreover, we know that the custom of closing the eyes was of the greatest antiquity; and that this office was discharged by one most closely connected with the deceased either by blood or affection.

5. *And Jacob rose up.* By using the words " rose up," Moses seems to denote that Jacob received new vigour from the vision. For although the former promises were not forgotten, yet the addition of the recent memorial came most opportunely, in order that he, bearing the land of Canaan in his heart, might endure his absence from it with equanimity. When it is said that he took with him all that he had acquired, or possessed in the land of Canaan, it is probable that his servants and handmaids came together with his cattle.[1] But, on his departure, no mention is made of them: nay, a little afterwards, when Moses enumerates the separate heads of each tribe, he says that only seventy souls came with him. Should any one say that Jacob had been compelled to liberate his slaves, on account of the famine, or that he lost them through some misfortune to us unknown, the conjecture is unsatisfactory; for it is most incredible that he, who had been an industrious master of a family, and had abounded in the earthly blessings of God, should have become so entirely destitute, that not even one little servant remained to him. It is more probable that, when the children of Israel

---

[1] " A remarkable parallel to the description of the arrival of Jacob's family in Egypt, is furnished by a scene in a tomb at Beni Hassan, representing strangers who arrive in Egypt. They carry their goods with them upon asses. The first figure is an Egyptian scribe, who presents an account of their arrival to a person in a sitting posture, one of the principal officers of the reigning Pharaoh—(compare the phrase, princes of Pharaoh, ver. 15.) The next, likewise an Egyptian, ushers them into his presence, and two of the strangers advance, bringing presents, the wild goat and the gazelle, probably as productions of their country. Four men with bows and clubs follow, leading an ass, on which are two children in panniers, accompanied by a boy and four women. Last, another ass laden and two men, one of whom carries a bow and club, and the other a lyre, on which he plays with the plectrum. All the men have beards, contrary to the custom of the Egyptians," &c.—*Egypt and the Books of Moses*, p. 40. It is supposed by some that this sculpture was intended to represent the arrival of Jacob and his family, recorded in this chapter.—*Ed.*

were themselves employed in servile works, they were then deprived of their servants in Egypt; or, at least, a sufficient number was not left them, to inspire them with confidence in any enterprise. And although, in the account of their deliverance, Moses is silent respecting their servants, yet it may be easily gathered from other passages, that they did not depart without servants.

8. *These are the names of the children of Israel.* He recounts the sons and grandsons of Jacob, till he arrives at their full number. The statement that there were but seventy souls, while Stephen (Acts vii. 14) adds five more, is made, I doubt not, by an error of the transcribers. For the solution of Augustine is weak, that Stephen, by a prolepsis, enumerates also three who afterwards were born in Egypt; for he must then have formed a far longer catalogue. Again, this interpretation is repugnant to the design of the Holy Spirit, as we shall hereafter see: because the subject here treated of, is not respecting the number of children Jacob left behind him at his death, but respecting the number of his family on the day when he went down into Egypt. He is said to have brought with him, or to have found there, seventy souls born unto him, in order that the comparison of this very small number, with that immense multitude which the Lord afterwards led forth, might the more fully illustrate His wonderful benediction. But that the error is to be imputed to the transcribers, is hence apparent, that with the Greek interpreters, it has crept only into one passage, while, elsewhere, they agree with the Hebrew reckoning. And it was easy when numerals were signified by marks, for one passage to be corrupted. I suspect also that this happened from the following cause, that those who had to deal with the Scripture were generally ignorant of the Hebrew language; so that, conceiving the passage in the Acts to be vitiated, they rashly changed the true number. If any one, however, chooses rather to suppose that Luke in this instance accommodated himself to the rude and illiterate, who were accustomed to the Greek version, I do not contend with them.[1] In the

Various methods have been resorted to, for the purpose of accounting for the difference of numbers given in this chapter and in Acts vii. 14. It is true that Luke, after the Septuagint, says there were seventy-five

words of Moses there is, indeed, no ambiguity, nor is there any reason why so small a matter, in which there is no absurdity, should give us any trouble; for it is not wonderful, that, in this mode of notation, one letter should have been put in the place of another. It is more to the purpose, to examine wherefore this small number of persons is recorded by Moses. For, the more improbable it appears, that seventy men, in no lengthened space of time, should have grown to such a multitude; so much the more clearly does the grace of God shine forth. And this is also the reason why he so frequently mentions this number. For it was, by no means, according to human apprehension, a likely method of propagating the Church, that Abraham should live childless even to old age; that, after the death of Isaac, Jacob alone should remain; that he, being increased with a moderate family, should be shut up in a corner of Egypt, and that there an incredible number of people should spring up from this dry fountain.[1] When Moses declares that Shaul, one of the sons of Simeon, was born of a Canaanitish woman, while he does not even mention the mothers of the other sons, his intention, I doubt not, is to fix a mark of dishonour on his race. For the holy Fathers were on their guard, not to mix in marriage with that nation, from which they were separated by the decree of heaven. When Moses, having put down the names of Leah's sons, says there were thirty-three souls, whereas he has only mentioned thirty-two; I understand that Jacob himself is to be reckoned the first in order. The statement that he had so many sons or daughters by Leah does not oppose this conclusion. For although, strictly speaking, his discourse is concerning sons, yet he commences

---

souls, whereas the Hebrew mentions only seventy. The reading of the Septuagint is, "The sons of Joseph, who were with him in Egypt, were nine souls; all the souls of the house of Jacob which came with Jacob into Egypt, were seventy-five souls." Add then *nine* to the sixty-six, mentioned in verse 26, and the number is made up. There is, however, some difficulty to make out the *nine.*—See *Patrick, Poole, Bush,* &c. *in loc.*—ED.

[1] From the date of God's promise of a holy seed to Abraham, unto the birth of Isaac was twenty-five years. Isaac lived sixty years before Jacob was born. Jacob had nearly reached the age of eighty at the time of his marriage. So that about two hundred and forty years elapsed before more than two persons were born of a family which was to be as the stars of heaven, and as the sand on the sea-shore, for multitude!—*See Bush in loc.*—ED.

with the head of the family. I reject the interpretation of the Hebrews, who suppose Jochebed the mother of Moses to be included, as being overstrained. A question suggests itself concerning the daughters, whether there were more than two. If Dinah alone were named, it might be said that express mention was made of her, because of the notorious fact which had happened to her. But since Moses enumerates another female in the progeny of Aser, I rather conjecture that these had remained unmarried, or single; for no mention is made of those who were wives.

28. *And he sent Judah before him unto Joseph.* Because Goshen[1] had been selected by Joseph as the abode of his father and his brethren, Jacob now desires, that, on his coming, he may find the place prepared for him: for the expression which Moses uses, implies, not that he requires a house to be built and furnished for him, but only that he may be permitted there to pitch his tent without molestation. For it was necessary that some unoccupied place should be assigned him; lest, by taking possession of the pastures or fields of the inhabitants, he might give them an occasion for exciting a tumult.

In the meeting of Jacob with his son Joseph, Moses describes their vehement feeling of joy, to show that the holy Fathers were not destitute of natural affection. It must, how-

---

[1] Though Moses does not describe in express terms the position of the land of Goshen; yet the incidental allusions contained in the narrative, are sufficient to fix its locality; and the fact that those allusions are such as could only be made by a writer conversant with its peculiarities, affords decisive evidence of the veracity of Moses as a writer of history..

1. The land of Goshen appears as the eastern border-land of Egypt; for on this side Jacob's family entered, see ver. 28.

2. It appears as lying near the chief city of Egypt, (see xlv. 10.) What that city was, may be inferred from Numbers xiii. 22, which points to Zoan or Tanis. This implies, that Zoan was one of the oldest cities of Egypt, and that it held the first rank. God is said to have performed his "wonders in the field of Zoan," (Ps. lxxviii. 12, 43,) alluding to the plagues of Egypt.

3. The land of Goshen is described as *pasture land*, and,

4. As one of the most *fruitful* regions of Egypt.

" All these circumstances harmonize, and the different points, discrepant as they may seem, find their application, when we fix upon the land of Goshen as the region east of the Tanitic arm of the Nile, as far as the isthmus of Suez, or the border of the Arabian desert."—*See Egypt and the Books of Moses*, pp. 43-45.—*Ed.*

ever, be remembered that, although the affections spring from good principles, yet they always contract some evil, from the corrupt propensity of the flesh; and have chiefly this fault, that they always exceed their bounds: whence it follows, that they do not need to be eradicated, but to be kept within due bounds.

31. *I will go up and show Pharaoh.* After Joseph had gone forth to meet his father for the purpose of doing him honour, he also provides what will be useful for him. On this account, he advises Jacob to declare that he and all his family were keepers of cattle, to the end that he might obtain, from the king, a dwelling-place for them, in the land of Goshen. Now although his moderation deserves commendation on the ground, that he usurps no authority to himself, but that, as one of the common people, he waits the pleasure of the king: he yet may be thought craftily to have devised a pretext, by which he might circumvent the king. We see what he desired. Seeing that the land of Goshen was fertile, and celebrated for its rich pastures; this advantage so allured his mind, that he wished to fix his father there: but then, keeping out of Pharaoh's sight the richness of the land, he puts forth another reason; namely, that Jacob with his sons, were men held in abomination, and that, therefore, he was seeking a place of seclusion, in which they might dwell apart from the Egyptians. It is not, however, very difficult to untie this knot. The fertility of the land of Goshen was so fully known to the king, that no room was left for fraud or cunning, (though kings are often too profuse, and foolishly waste much, because they know not what they grant,) yea, Pharaoh, of his own accord, had offered them, unsolicited, the best and choicest place in the kingdom. Therefore this bounty of his was not elicited from him by stratagem; because he was free to form his own judgment respecting what he would give. And truly Joseph, in order that he might act modestly, felt it necessary to seek a habitation in Goshen, on this pretext. For it would have been absurd, or at least inconsiderate, for men who were obscure and strangers, to desire an abode in the best and most convenient place for themselves, as if they possessed a right to

choose for themselves. Joseph, therefore, having regard to his own modesty and that of his father, adduces another cause, which was yet a true one. For seeing that the Egyptians held the occupation of shepherds in abhorrence,[1] he explains to the king that this would be a suitable retreat for his brethren. Herein was no dissimulation, because, in no other place, was a quiet habitation accessible to them. Nevertheless, though it was hard for the holy Fathers to be thus opprobriously rejected, and, as it were, to be loathed by a whole nation; yet this ignominy with which they were branded, was most profitable to themselves. For, had they been mingled with the Egyptians, they might have been scattered far and wide; but now, seeing that they are objects of detestation, and are thought unworthy to be admitted to common society, they learn, in this state of separation from others, to cherish more fervently mutual union between themselves; and thus the body of the Church, which God had set apart from the whole world, is not dispersed. So the Lord often permits us to be despised or rejected by the world, that being liberated and cleansed from its pollution, we may cultivate holiness. Finally, he does not suffer us to be bound by chains to the earth, in order that we may be borne upward to heaven.

## CHAPTER XLVII.

1. Then Joseph came and told Pharaoh, and said, My father, and my brethren, and their flocks, and their herds, and all that they have, are come out of the land of Canaan; and, behold, they *are* in the land of Goshen.

2. And he took some of his brethren, *even* five men, and presented them unto Pharaoh.

3. And Pharaoh said unto his

1. Et venit Joseph, et nuntiavit Pharaoni, et dixit, Pater meus, et fratres mei, et pecudes eorum, et boves eorum, et omnia quæ erant eis, venerunt e terra Chenaan: et ecce, sunt in terra Gosen.

2. Et de extremis fratribus suis cepit quinque viros, et statuit eos ante Pharaonem.

3. Tunc dixit Pharao ad fratres

---

[1] " The monuments even now furnish abundant evidence of this hatred of the Egyptians to shepherds. The artists of Upper and Lower Egypt vie with each other in caricaturing them. In proportion as the cultivation of the land was the more unconditionally the foundation of the Egyptian state, the idea of coarseness and barbarism was united with the idea of a shepherd among the Egyptians."—*Egypt and the Books of Moses,* p. 42.—*Ed.*

brethren, What *is* your occupation? And they said unto Pharaoh, Thy servants *are* shepherds, both we, *and* also our fathers.

4. They said, moreover, unto Pharaoh, For to sojourn in the land are we come; for thy servants have no pasture for their flocks; for the famine *is* sore in the land of Canaan; now therefore, we pray thee, let thy servants dwell in the land of Goshen.

5. And Pharaoh spake unto Joseph, saying, Thy father and thy brethren are come unto thee:

6. The land of Egypt *is* before thee: in the best of the land make thy father and brethren to dwell; in the land of Goshen let them dwell: and if thou knowest *any* men of activity among them, then make them rulers over my cattle.

7. And Joseph brought in Jacob his father, and set him before Pharaoh: and Jacob blessed Pharaoh.

8. And Pharaoh said unto Jacob, How old *art* thou?

9. And Jacob said unto Pharaoh, The days of the years of my pilgrimage *are* an hundred and thirty years: few and evil have the days of the years of my life been, and have not attained unto the days of the years of the life of my fathers in the days of their pilgrimage.

10. And Jacob blessed Pharaoh, and went out from before Pharaoh.

11. And Joseph placed his father and his brethren, and gave them a possession in the land of Egypt, in the best of the land, in the land of Rameses, as Pharaoh had commanded.

12. And Joseph nourished his father, and his brethren, and all his father's household, with bread, according to *their* families.

13. And *there was* no bread in all the land: for the famine *was* very sore, so that the land of Egypt, and *all* the land of Canaan, fainted by reason of the famine.

14. And Joseph gathered up all

ejus, Quæ sunt opera vestra? Et dixerunt ad Pharaonem, Pastores ovium sunt servi tui, etiam nos, etiam patres nostri.

4. Et dixerunt ad Pharaonem, Ut peregrinaremur in hac terra, venimus, quia non est pascuum pecudibus, quæ sunt servis tuis: gravis enim fames est in terra Chenaan: nunc igitur habitent quæso servi tui in terra Gosen.

5. Et dixit Pharao ad Joseph, dicendo, Pater tuus et fratres tui venerunt ad te.

6. Terra Ægypti coram te est, in optimo terræ hujus habitare fac patrem tuum, et fratres tuos, habitent in terra Gosen. Et si cognoveris quod sint inter eos viri robusti, pones eos præfectos pecorum super ea quæ sunt mihi.

7. Postea adduxit Joseph ipsum Jahacob patrem suum, et statuit eum coram Pharaone, et salutavit Jahacob ipsum Pharaonem.

8. Et dixit Pharao ad Jahacob, Quot sunt dies annorum vitæ tuæ?

9. Et dixit Jahacob ad Pharaonem, Dies annorum peregrinationum mearum sunt triginta et centum anni: pauci et mali fuerunt dies annorum vitæ meæ, et non attigerunt dies annorum vitæ patrum meorum in diebus peregrinationum suarum.

10. Et salutavit Jahacob ipsum Pharaonem, et egressus'est a facie Pharaonis.

11. Et habitare fecit Joseph patrem suum et fratres suos, et dedit eis possessionem in terra Ægypti, in optimo terræ, in terra Rahameses, quemadmodum præceperat Pharao.

12. Et aluit Joseph patrem suum, et fratres suos, et omnem domum patris sui pane, usque ad os parvuli.

13. At panis non erat in omni terra: gravis enim fames erat valde, et elanguit terra Ægypti et terra Chenaan propter famem.

14. Et collegit Joseph omnem pe-

the money that was found in the land of Egypt, and in the land of Canaan, for the corn which they bought: and Joseph brought the money into Pharaoh's house.

15. And when money failed in the land of Egypt, and in the land of Canaan, all the Egyptians came unto Joseph, and said, Give us bread: for why should we die in thy presence? for the money faileth.

16. And Joseph said, Give your cattle; and I will give you for your cattle, if money fail.

17. And they brought their cattle unto Joseph: and Joseph gave them bread *in exchange* for horses, and for the flocks, and for the cattle of the herds, and for the asses; and he fed them with bread for all their cattle for that year.

18. When that year was ended, they came unto him the second year, and said unto him, We will not hide *it* from my lord, how that our money is spent; my lord also hath our herds of cattle: there is not ought left in the sight of my lord, but our bodies and our lands:

19. Wherefore shall we die before thine eyes, both we and our land? buy us and our land for bread, and we and our land will be servants unto Pharaoh; and give *us* seed, that we may live, and not die, that the land be not desolate.

20. And Joseph bought all the land of Egypt for Pharaoh; for the Egyptians sold every man his field, because the famine prevailed over them: so the land became Pharaoh's.

21. And as for the people, he removed them to cities from *one* end of the borders of Egypt even to the *other* end thereof.

22. Only the land of the priests bought he not: for the priests had a portion *assigned them* of Pharaoh, and did eat their portion which Pharaoh gave them; wherefore they sold not their lands.

23. Then Joseph said unto the people, Behold, I have bought you

cuniam, quæ inventa est in terra Chenaan pro alimento quod ipsi emebant; et intulit Joseph pecuniam in domum Pharaonis.

15. Et consumpta est pecunia e terra Ægypti, et e terra Chenaan: et venit omnis Ægyptus ad Joseph, dicendo, Da nobis panem: et utquid moriemur coram te? defecit enim pecunia.

16. Tunc dixit Joseph, Date pecudes vestras, et dabo vobis pro pecudibus vestris, si defecit pecunia.

17. Et adduxerunt pecudes suas ad Joseph, et dedit eis Joseph panem pro equis, et pro grege pecudum, et pro armento boum, et pro asinis: et sustentavit eos pane pro omnibus gregibus illorum anno ipso.

18. Finitus vero est annus ipse, et venerunt ad eum anno secundo, et dixerunt ei, Non abscondemus a domino meo, quod integra pecunia, et grex jumentorum apud dominum meum: non remansit coram domino meo præterquam corpus nostrum, et terra nostra.

19. Utquid moriemur in oculis tuis, etiam nos, etiam terra nostra? eme nos, et terram nostram pro pane, et vivemus nos et terra nostra servi Pharaonis: da semen, et vivemus, et non moriemur, et terra non desolabitur.

20. Et emit Joseph omnem terram Ægypti pro Pharaone: vendiderunt enim Ægyptii unusquisque agrum suum, quia invaluerat super eos fames: et fuit terra ipsi Pharaoni.

21. Et populum transire fecit ad urbes ab extremitate termini Ægypti usque ad extremitatem ejus.

22. Tantummodo terram sacerdotum non emit, quia pars sacerdotibus erat a Pharaone, et comedebant partem suam, quam dederat eis Pharao: idcirco non vendiderunt terram suam.

23. Tunc dixit Joseph ad populum, Ecce, emi vos hodie, et terram

this day, and your land, for Pharaoh: lo, *here is* seed for you, and ye shall sow the land.

24. And it shall come to pass, in the increase, that ye shall give the fifth *part* unto Pharaoh; and four parts shall be your own, for seed of the field, and for your food, and for them of your households, and for food for your little ones.

25. And they said, Thou hast saved our lives: let us find grace in the sight of my lord, and we will be Pharaoh's servants.

26. And Joseph made it a law over the land of Egypt unto this day, *that* Pharaoh should have the fifth *part;* except the land of the priests only, *which* became not Pharaoh's.

27. And Israel dwelt in the land of Egypt, in the country of Goshen; and they had possessions therein, and grew, and multiplied exceedingly.

28. And Jacob lived in the land of Egypt seventeen years: so the whole age of Jacob was an hundred forty and seven years.

29. And the time drew nigh that Israel must die: and he called his son Joseph, and said unto him, If now I have found grace in thy sight, put, I pray thee, thy hand under my thigh, and deal kindly and truly with me: bury me not, I pray thee, in Egypt:

30. But I will lie with my fathers; and thou shalt carry me out of Egypt, and bury me in their burying-place. And he said, I will do as thou hast said.

31. And he said, Swear unto me. And he sware unto him. And Israel bowed himself upon the bed's head.

vestram Pharaoni: ecce, vobis semen, et seretis terram.

24. Et erit, e frugibus dabitis quintam partem Pharaoni, et quatuor partes erunt vobis pro semine agri, et pro cibo vestro, et eorum qui sunt in domibus vestris, et ad comedendum pro parvulis vestris.

25. Et dixerunt, Vivificasti nos: inveniamus gratiam in oculis domini mei, et erimus servi Pharaonis.

26. Et posuit illud Joseph in statutum usque ad diem hanc super terram Ægypti Pharaoni pro quinta *parte:* terra tamen sacerdotum duntaxat non fuit Pharaoni.

27. Et habitavit Israel in terra Ægypti, in terra Gosen: et stationem habuerunt in ea, et creverunt, et multiplicati sunt valde.

28. Et vixit Jahacob in terra Ægypti septendecim annos: et fuerunt dies Jahacob anni vitæ ejus, septem anni et quadraginta et centum anni.

29. Appropinquaverunt autem dies Israel ut moreretur, et vocavit filium suum Joseph, et dixit ei, Si quæso inveni gratiam in oculis tuis, pone quæso manum tuam sub femore meo, et facies mecum misericordiam et veritatem, Ne quæso sepelias me in Ægypto.

30. Et dormiam cum patribus meis; et tolles me ex Ægypto, et sepelies me in sepulcro eorum. Et dixit, Ego faciam secundum verbum tuum.

31. Et dixit, Jura mihi et juravit ei, et incurvavit se Israel ad caput lecti.

1. *Then Joseph came.* Joseph indirectly intimates to the king, his desire to obtain a habitation for his brethren in the land of Goshen. Yet this modesty was (as we have said) free from cunning. For Pharaoh both immediately recognises his wish, and liberally grants it to him; declaring beforehand that the land of Goshen was most

excellent. Whence we gather, that what he gave, he gave in the exercise of his own judgment, not in ignorance; and that he was not unacquainted with the wish of Joseph, who yet did not dare to ask for what was the best. Joseph may be easily excused for having commanded his father, with the greater part of his brethren, to remain in that region. For neither was it possible for them to bring their cattle along with them, nor yet to leave their cattle in order to come and salute the king; until some settled abode was assigned them, where, having pitched their tents, they might arrange their affairs. For it would have shown a want of respect, to take possession of a place, as if it had been granted to them; when they had not yet received the permission of the king. They, therefore, remain in that district, in a state of suspense, until, having ascertained the will of the king, they may, with greater certainty, fix their abode there. That Joseph " brought five from the extreme limits of his brethren,"[1] is commonly thus explained, that they who were of least stature were brought into the presence of the king: because it was to be feared lest he might take the stronger into his army. But since the Hebrew word קצה signifies the two extremities, the beginning and the end; I think they were chosen from the first and the last, in order that the king, by looking at them might form his judgment concerning the age of the whole.

3. *Thy servants are shepherds.* This confession was humiliating to the sons of Jacob, and especially to Joseph himself, whose high, and almost regal dignity, was thus marked with a spot of disgrace: for among the Egyptians (as we have said) this kind of life was disgraceful and infamous. Why, then, did not Joseph adopt the course, which he might easily have done, of describing his brethren as persons engaged in agriculture, or any other honest and creditable

---

[1] Quod Joseph *quinque ex fratrum extremitate adduxit.* In the text Calvin has it, " Et de extremis fratribus suis cepit quinque viros." The English version renders the passage, " *some* of his brethren." Other interpreters, a " definite part." Gesenius, however, translates the term מקצה, " from the whole;" which perhaps gives the best sense. " And he took from the whole number of his brethren, five men, and presented them unto Pharaoh."—*Ed.*

method of living? They were not so addicted to the feeding of cattle as to be altogether ignorant of agriculture, or incapable of accustoming themselves to other modes of gaining a livelihood: and although they would not immediately have found it productive, we see how ready the liberality of the king was to help them. Indeed it would not have been difficult for them to become invested with offices at court. How then does it happen that Joseph, knowingly and purposely, exposes his brethren to an ignominy, which must bring dishonour also on himself, except because he was not very anxious to escape from worldly contempt? To live in splendour among the Egyptians would have had, at first, a plausible appearance; but his family would have been placed in a dangerous position. Now, however, their mean and contemptible mode of life proves a wall of separation between them and the Egyptians: yea, Joseph seems purposely to labour to cast off, in a moment, the nobility he had acquired, that his own posterity might not be swallowed up in the population of Egypt, but might rather merge in the body of his ancestral family. If, however, this consideration did not enter their minds, there is no doubt that the Lord directed their tongues, so as to prevent the noxious admixture, and to keep the body of the Church pure and distinct. This passage also teaches us, how much better it is to possess a remote corner in the courts of the Lord, than to dwell in the midst of palaces, beyond the precincts of the Church. Therefore, let us not think it grievous to secure a sacred union with the sons of God, by enduring the contempt and reproaches of the world; even as Joseph preferred this union to all the luxuries of Egypt. But if any one thinks that he cannot otherwise serve God in purity, than by rendering himself disgusting to the world; away with all this folly! The design of God was this, to keep the sons of Jacob in a degraded position, until he should restore them to the land of Canaan: for the purpose, then, of preserving themselves in unity till the promised deliverance should take place, they did not conceal the fact that they were shepherds. We must beware, therefore, lest the desire of empty honour should elate us: whereas the Lord reveals no other way of salvation, than that of bringing us under discipline. Wherefore let us willingly be without honour, for a time, that, hereafter, angels may receive us to a participation of their eternal glory. By this example also, they who are brought up in humble employments, are taught that they have no need to be ashamed of their lot. It ought to be enough, and more than enough, for them, that the mode of living which they pursue is lawful, and acceptable to God. The remaining confession of the brethren (verse 4) was not unattended with a sense of shame; in which they say, that they had come to sojourn there, compelled by hunger; but hence arose advantage not to be despised. For as they came down few, and perishing with hunger, and so branded with infamy that scarcely any one would deign to speak with them; the glory of God afterwards shone so much the more illustriously out of this darkness, when, in the third century from that time, he wonderfully led them forth, a mighty nation.

5. *And Pharaoh spake unto Joseph.* It is to be ascribed to the favour of God that Pharaoh was not offended when they desired that a separate dwelling-place might be granted to them; for we know that nothing is more indignantly borne by kings, than that their favours should be rejected. Pharaoh offers them a perpetual home, but they rather wish to depart from him. Should any one ascribe this to modesty, on the ground that it would have been proud to ask for the right of citizenship, in order that they might enjoy the same privilege as natives; the suggestion is indeed plausible. It is, however, fallacious, for in asking to be admitted as guests and strangers, they took timely precaution that Pharaoh should not hold them bound in the chains of servitude. The passage of Sophocles is known:—

"Ὅς τις δὲ πρὸς τύραννον ἐμπορεύεται,
Κείνου 'στὶ δοῦλος, κἂν ἐλεύθερος μόλῃ.[1]

---

[1] The passage does not occur in any of the tragedies of Sophocles extant; but it is found among the fragments of lost plays, selected from different authors of antiquity by whom they had been quoted. The words here introduced are taken from Plutarch's Life of Pompey. It may be observed, that the word τύραννος is not necessarily to be understood in a bad sense. It sometimes merely means a king; but the idea of *arbitrary* power, whe-

"Who refuge seeks within a tyrant's door,
When once he enters there, is free no more."
*Langhorne's Plutarch.*

It was therefore of importance to the sons of Jacob to declare, *in limine,* on what condition they wished to live in Egypt. And so much the more inexcusable was the cruelty exercised towards them, when, in violation of this compact, they were most severely oppressed, and were denied that opportunity of departure, for which they had stipulated. Isaiah indeed says that the king of Egypt had some pretext for his conduct, because the sons of Jacob had voluntarily placed themselves under his authority, (Is. lii. 4;) but he is speaking comparatively, in order that he may the more grievously accuse the Assyrians, who had invaded the posterity of Jacob, when they were quiet in their own country, and expelled them thence by unjust violence. Therefore the law of hospitality was wickedly violated when the Israelites were oppressed as slaves, and when the return into their own country, for which they had silently covenanted, was denied them; though they had professed that they had come thither as guests; for fidelity and humanity ought to have been exercised towards them, by the king, when once they were received under his protection. It appears, therefore, that the children of Israel so guarded themselves, as in the presence of God, that they had just ground of complaint against the Egyptians. But seeing that the pledge given them by the king proved of no advantage to them according to the flesh; let the faithful learn, from their example, to train themselves to patience. For it commonly happens, that he who enters the court of a tyrant, is under the necessity of laying down his liberty at the door.

6. *The land of Egypt.* This is recorded not only to show that Jacob was courteously received, but also, that nothing was given him by Joseph but at the command of the king. For the greater was his power, the more strictly was he bound to take care, lest, being liberal with the king's property, he might defraud both him and his people. And I

ther well or ill used, is always involved in it. For the passage itself, see "Sophoclis Tragædiæ Septem." Tom. ii. Fragmenta, p. 95. *Oxon.,* 1826.—*Ed.*

would that this moderation so prevailed among the nobles of the world, that they would conduct themselves, in their private affairs, no otherwise than if they were plebeians : but now, they seem to themselves to have no power, unless they may prove it by their license to sin. And although Joseph, by the king's permission, places his family amidst the best pastures; yet he does not avail himself of the other portion of the royal beneficence, to make his brethren keepers of the king's cattle; not only because this privilege would have excited the envy of many against them, but because he was unwilling to be entangled in such a snare.

7. *And Joseph brought in Jacob his father.* Although Moses relates, in a continuous narrative, that Jacob was brought to the king, yet I do not doubt that some time had intervened ; at least, till he had obtained a place wherein he might dwell; and where he might leave his family more safely, and with a more tranquil mind ; and also, where he might refresh himself, for a little while, after the fatigue of his journey. And whereas he is said to have blessed Pharaoh, by this term Moses does not mean a common and profane salutation, but the pious and holy prayer of a servant of God. For the children of this world salute kings and princes for the sake of honour, but, by no means, raise their thoughts to God. Jacob acts otherwise ; for he adjoins to civil reverence that pious affection which causes him to commend the safety of the king to God. And Jeremiah prescribes this rule to the Jews, that they should pray for the peace of Babylon as long as they were to live in exile ; because in the peace of that land and empire their own peace would be involved. (Jer. xxix. 7.) If this duty was enjoined on miserable captives, forcibly deprived of their liberty, and torn from their own country ; how much more did Jacob owe it to a king so humane and beneficent? But of whatever character they may be who rule over us, we are commanded to offer up public prayers for them. (1 Tim. ii. 1.) Therefore the same subjection to authority is required severally from each of us.

8. *How old art thou ?* This familiar question proves that Jacob was received courteously and without ceremony. But the answer is of far greater moment, in which Jacob declares

that the time of his pilgrimage was a hundred and thirty years. For the Apostle, in his epistle to the Hebrews, (xi. 13-16,) gathers hence the memorable doctrine, that God was not ashamed to be called the God of the patriarchs, because they had confessed themselves to be strangers and pilgrims on the earth. Of one man only this is mentioned; but because he had been instructed by his forefathers, and had handed down the same instruction to his son, the Apostle honours them all with the same eulogy. Therefore, as they were not ashamed to wander during the whole course of their life, and to be opprobriously called foreigners and strangers wherever they came; so God vouchsafed to them the incomparable dignity, that they should be heirs of heaven. But (as it has been said before) no persons ever had a more peculiar and hereditary possession in the world, than the holy fathers had in the land of Canaan. The Lord is said to have cast his line, in order that he might assign to each nation its bounds: but an eternal possession, through a continual succession of ages, was never promised to any nation, as it was to the posterity of Abraham. In what spirit, then, ought we to dwell in a world, where no certain repose, or fixed abode is promised us? Moreover, this is described by Paul as the common condition of all pious persons under the reign of Christ, that they should "have no certain dwelling-place;" (1 Cor. iv. 11;) not that all should be alike cast out as exiles, but because the Lord calls all his people, as by the sound of the trumpet, to be wanderers, lest they should become fixed in their nests on earth. Therefore, whether any one remains in his own country, or is compelled continually to change his place, let him diligently exercise himself in the meditation, that he is sojourning, for a short time, upon earth, till, having completed his course, he shall depart to the heavenly country.

9. *Few and evil have the days of the years of my life been.* Jacob may here seem to complain that he had lived but a little while, and that, in this short space of time, he had endured many and grievous afflictions. Why does he not rather recount the great and manifold favours of God which formed an abundant compensation for every kind of evil? Besides, his complaint respecting the shortness of life seems unworthy

of him; for why did he not deem a whole century and a third part of another sufficient for him? But if any one will rightly weigh his words, he rather expresses his own gratitude, in celebrating the goodness of God towards his fathers. For he does not so much deplore his own decrepitude, as he extols the vigour divinely afforded to his fathers. Certainly it was no new and unwonted thing to see a man, at his age, broken down and failing, and already near to the grave. Wherefore, this comparison (as I have said) was only intended to ascribe glory to God, whose blessing towards Abraham and Isaac had been greater than to himself. But he does not compare himself with his fathers in sufferings, as if they had been treated with greater indulgence; for we know that they had been tried to the utmost with all kinds of temptations: he merely states that he had not attained their age; as if he had said, " I, indeed, have arrived at those years which, by others, is deemed a mature old age, and which complete the proper term of life; but the Lord so prolonged the life of my fathers, that they far exceeded this limit." He makes mention of *evil* days, in order to show that he was not so much broken down and consumed by years, as by labours and troubles; as if he had said, " My senses might yet have flourished in their vigour, if my strength had not been exhausted by continual labours, by excessive cares, and by most grievous sufferings." We now see that nothing was less in the mind of the holy man than to expostulate with God. Yet it may seem absurd that he speaks of his life as being shorter than that of his fathers. For, whence does he conjecture that so little time should still remain for him, as to prevent him from attaining their age? Should any one answer, that he formed this conjecture from the weakness of his body, which was half dead; the solution will not prove satisfactory. For Isaac had dimness of sight and trembling limbs thirty years before his death. But it is not absurd to suppose that Jacob was every moment giving himself over to death, as if the sepulchre were before his eyes. He was, however, uncertain what length of time was decreed for him in the secret counsel of God. Wherefore, being unconcerned about the remainder of his life, he speaks just as if he were about to die on the next day.

12. *And Joseph nourished his father, &c., according to their families.*¹ Some explain the expression, " the mouth of the little one," as if Joseph nourished his father and his whole family, in the manner in which food is conveyed to the mouths of children. These interpreters regard the form of speech as emphatical, because, during the famine, Jacob and his family had no more anxiety about the providing of food than children, who cannot even stretch out their hand to receive it. Others translate it " youth," but I know not with what meaning.² Others take it, simply, according to the proportion and number of the little children. To me the genuine sense seems to be that he fed all, from the greatest to the least. Therefore, there was sufficient bread for the whole family of Jacob, because, by the care of Joseph, provision was made to supply nourishment even to the little ones. In this manner Moses commemorates both the clemency of God, and the piety of Joseph; for it was an instance of uncommon attention, that these hungry husbandmen, who had not a grain of corn, were entirely fed at his expense.

13. *And all the land of Canaan fainted.* It was a memorable judgment of God, that the most fertile regions, which were accustomed to supply provisions for distant and transmarine nations, were reduced to such poverty that they were almost consumed. The word להה, (*lahah,*) which Moses uses, is explained in two ways. Some say that they were driven to madness on account of the famine; others, that they were so destitute of food that they fainted; but whichever method of interpretation be approved, we see that they who had been accustomed to supply others with food, were themselves famishing. Therefore it is not for those who cultivate fertile lands to trust in their abundance; rather let them acknowledge that a large supply of provision does not so much spring from the bowels of the earth, as it distils, or rather flows down from heaven, by the secret blessing of God. For there is no luxuriance so great, that it is not soon exchanged for barrenness, when God sprinkles it with

---

¹ Usque ad os parvuli. Even to the mouth of the little one. לפי חטף, (*Lephi chataph.*)

² Alii vertunt pubem; sed nescio quo sensu.

salt instead of rain. Meanwhile, it is right to turn our eyes to that special kindness of God by which he nourishes his own people in the midst of famine, as it is said in the thirty-seventh Psalm and the nineteenth verse. If, however, God is pleased to try us with famine, we must pray that he would prepare us to endure hunger with a meek and equal mind, lest we should rage, like fierce, and even ravenous wild beasts. And although it is possible that grievous commotions were raised during the protracted scarcity, (as it is said in the old proverb that the belly has no ears,) yet the more simple sense of the passage seems to me to be, that the Egyptians and Canaanites had sunk under the famine, and were lying prostrate, as if at the point of death. Moreover, Moses pursues the history of the famine, with the intention of showing that the prediction of Joseph was verified by the event; and that, by his skill and industry, the greatest dangers were so well and dexterously provided against, that Egypt ought justly to acknowledge him as the author of its deliverance.

14. *And Joseph gathered up all the money.* Moses first declares that the Egyptian king had acted well and wisely, in committing the work of providing corn to the sole care and authority of Joseph. He then commends the sincere and faithful administration of Joseph himself. We know how few persons can touch the money of kings without defiling themselves by peculation. Amid such vast heaps of money, the opportunity of plundering was not less than the difficulty of self-restraint. But Moses says, that whatever money Joseph collected, he brought into the house of the king. It was a rare and unparalleled integrity, to keep the hands pure amidst such heaps of gold. And he would not have been able to conduct himself with such moderation, unless his divine calling had proved as a bridle to hold him in; for they who are restrained from thefts and rapaciousness by worldly motives alone, would immediately put forth their hand to the prey, unless they feared the eyes and the judgments of men. But inasmuch as Joseph might have sinned without a witness of his fault; it follows that the true fear of God flourished in his breast. Plausible and well coloured

pretexts, in excuse of the theft, would doubtless present themselves. "When you are serving a tyrant, why may it not be lawful for you to apply some part of the gain to your own advantage?" So much the more does it appear that he was fortified by downright honesty; since he repelled all temptations, lest he should desire fraudulently to enrich himself at the expense of another.

15. *And when money failed.* Moses does not mean that all the money in Egypt had been brought into the royal treasury; for there were many of the nobles of the court free from the effects of the famine; but the simple meaning of the expression is that nearly all had been exhausted; that now the common people had not money enough to buy corn; and that, at length, extreme necessity had driven the Egyptians to the second remedy of which he is about to speak. Moreover, although, like persons driven to desperation, they might seem arrogantly to rise up against Joseph; yet the context shows that nothing was farther from their minds than to terrify, by their boldness, the man whose compassion they suppliantly implore. Wherefore the question, *Why should we die in thy presence?* has no other signification than that they felt themselves ruined, unless his clemency should afford them relief. But it may be asked how the Canaanites supported their lives. There is indeed no doubt that a grievous pestilence, the attendant on famine, would carry off many, unless they received assistance from other regions, or were miserably fed on herbs and roots. And perhaps the barrenness was not there so great, but that they might gather half, or a third part of their food, from the fields.

16. *Give your cattle.* It was a miserable spectacle, and one which might have softened hearts of iron, to see rich farmers, who previously had kept provision stored in their granaries for others, now begging food. Therefore, Joseph might be deemed cruel, because he does not give bread gratuitously to those who are poor and exhausted, but robs them of all their cattle, sheep, and asses. Seeing, however, that Joseph is transacting the business of another, I dare not charge his strictness with cruelty. If, during the seven

fruitful years, he had extorted corn by force from an unwilling people, he would now have acted tyrannically in seizing their flocks and herds. But seeing that they had been at liberty to lay up, in their private stores, what they had sold to the king, they now pay the just penalty of their negligence. Joseph also perceived that they were deprived of their possessions by a divine interposition, in order that the king alone might be enriched by the spoils of all. Besides, since it was lawful for him to offer corn for sale, it was also lawful for him to exchange it for cattle. Truly, the corn belonged to the king; why then should he not demand a price from the purchasers? But they were poor, and therefore it was but just to succour them in their want. Were this rule to prevail, the greater part of sales would be unlawful. For no one freely parts with what he possesses. Wherefore, if his valuation of the cattle was fair, I do not see what was deserving of reprehension in the conduct of Joseph; especially as he was not dealing with his own property, but had been appointed prefect over the corn, with this condition, that he should acquire gain, not for himself, but for the king. If any one should object that he ought at least to have exhorted the king to content himself with the abundant pecuniary wealth which he had obtained; I answer, that Moses relates, by the way, but a few things out of many. Any one, therefore, may easily conjecture, that a business of such great consequence, was not transacted by Joseph, without the cognizance and judgment of the king. But what, if it appeared to the king's counsellors, an equitable arrangement, that the farmers should receive, in return for their cattle, food for the whole year? Lastly, seeing that we stand or fall by the judgment of God alone, it is not for us to condemn what his law has left undecided.

18. *They came to him the second year.* Moses does not reckon the second year from the date of the famine, but from the time when the money had failed. But since they knew, from the oracle, that the termination of the dearth was drawing near, they desired not only that corn should be given them for food, but also for seed. Whence it appears that they had become wise too late, and had neglected

the useful admonition of God, at the time when they ought to have made provision for the future. Moreover, when they declare that their money and cattle had failed, they do it, not for the purpose of expostulating with Joseph, as if they had been unjustly deprived of these things by him; but for the purpose of showing that the only thing remaining for them was to purchase food and seed at the price of their lands, and that they could not otherwise be preserved, unless Joseph would enter into this compact. For it would have been the part of impudence to offer no price or compensation. They begin by saying, that they had nothing at hand, and that, therefore, their lives would be lost, unless Joseph were willing to buy their lands; and in order to excite his compassion, they ask again, why he would suffer them to die, and their very land to perish? For this is the death of the earth, when the cultivation of it is neglected, and when, being reduced to a desert, it can bring forth nothing more.

20. *And Joseph bought all the land.* Any one might suppose it to be the height of cruel and inexplicable avarice, that Joseph should take away from the miserable husbandmen, the very fields, by the produce of which they nourished the kingdom. But I have before showed, that unless every kind of purchase is to be condemned, there is no reason why Joseph should be blamed. If any one should say that he abused their penury; this alone would suffice for his excuse, that no wiles of his, no circumvention, no force, no threats, had reduced the Egyptians to this necessity. He transacted the king's business with equal fidelity and industry; and fulfilled the duties of his office, without resorting to violent edicts. When the famine became urgent, it was lawful to expose wheat to sale, as well to the rich as to the poor: afterwards it was not less lawful to buy the cattle; and now, at last, why should it not be lawful to acquire the land for the king, at a just price? To this may be added, that he extorted nothing, but entered into treaty with them, at their own request. I confess, indeed, that it is not right to take whatever may be offered without discrimination: for if severe necessity presses, then he who wishes, by all means,

to escape it, will submit to hard conditions. Therefore, when any one thus invites us, to defraud him, we are not, by his necessities, rendered excusable. But I do not defend Joseph, on this sole ground, that the Egyptians voluntarily offered him their lands, as men who were ready to purchase life, at any price; but I say, this ought also to be considered, that he acted with equity, even though he left them nothing. The terms would have been more severe, if they themselves had been consigned to perpetual slavery; but he now concedes to them personal liberty, and only covenants for their fields, which, perhaps, the greater part of the people had bought from the poor. If he had stripped of their clothing those whom he was feeding with corn, this would have been to put them indirectly and slowly to death. For what difference does it make, whether I compel a man to die by hunger or by cold? But Joseph so succours the Egyptians, that in future they should be free, and should be able to obtain a moderate subsistence by their labour. For though they might have to change their abode, yet they are all made stewards of the king: and Joseph restores to them, not only the lands, but the implements which he had bought. Whence it appears that he had used what clemency he was able, in order to relieve them. Meanwhile, let those who are too intent on wealth beware lest they should falsely employ Joseph's example as a pretext: because it is certain that all contracts, which are not formed according to the rule of charity, are vicious in the sight of God; and that we ought, according to that equity which is inwardly dictated to us by a secret instinct of nature, so to act towards others, as we wish to be dealt with ourselves.

21. *And as for the people, he removed them to cities.* This removal was, indeed, severe; but if we reflect how much better it was to depart to another place, in order that they might be free cultivators of the land, than to be attached to the soil, and employed as slaves in servile work; no one will deny that this was a tolerable, and even a humane exercise of authority. Had each person cultivated his field, as he had been accustomed to do, the exaction of tribute would have seemed to be grievous. Joseph, there-

fore, contrived a middle course, which might mitigate the
new and unwonted burden, by assigning new lands to each,
with a tribute attached to them. The passage may, however,
be differently expounded; namely, that Joseph caused all the
farmers to go to the cities to receive the provisions, and to
settle their public accounts. If this sense is approved, the
fact that Egypt was divided into provinces, afterwards called
*nomes*, (νομοὶ,) may probably hence have received its origin.
This removing from place to place would, however, have been
alike injurious to the king and to the people at large, because
they would not be able to make their skill and practice applicable to new situations. Yet, since the matter is not of
great moment, and the signification of the word is ambiguous, I leave the question undecided.

22. *Only the land of the priests.* The priests were exempted from the common law, because the king granted
them a maintenance. It is, indeed, doubtful, whether this
was a supply for their present necessity, or whether he was
accustomed to nourish them at his own expense. But seeing that Moses makes mention of their lands, I rather
incline to the conjecture, that, whereas they had before
been rich, and this dearth had deprived them of their income, the king conferred this privilege upon them; and
hence it arose that their lands remained unto them free.[1]
The ancient historians, however, injudiciously invent many
fables concerning the state of that land. I know not whether
the statement that the farmers, content with small wages,
sow and reap for the king and the priests, is to be traced
to this regulation of Joseph or not. But, passing by
these things, it is more to the purpose to observe, what

[1] The following passage from Sir J. G. Wilkinson's Manners and
Customs of the Ancient Egyptians, will be read with interest. The
priests " enjoyed important privileges, which extended to their whole
family. They were exempt from taxes; they consumed no part of their
own income in any of their necessary expenses; and they had one of the
three portions into which the land of Egypt was divided, free from all
duties. They were provided for, from the public stores, out of which they
received a stated allowance of corn, and all the other necessaries of life;
and we find that when Pharaoh, by the advice of Joseph, took all the
land of the Egyptians in lieu of corn, the priests were not obliged to make
the same sacrifice of their landed property, nor was the tax of the fifth
part entailed upon it, as on that of other people."—Vol. i. p. 262.—*Ed.*

Moses wished distinctly to testify; namely, that a heathen king paid particular attention to Divine worship, in supporting the priests gratuitously, for the purpose of sparing their lands and their property. Truly this is placed before our eyes, as a mirror, in which we may discern that a sentiment of piety which they cannot wholly efface, is implanted in the minds of men. It was the part of foolish, as well as of wicked superstition, that Pharaoh nourished such priests as these, who infatuated the people by their impostures: yet this was, in itself, a design worthy of commendation, that he did not suffer the worship of God to fall into decay; which, in a short time, must have happened, if the priests had perished in the famine. Whence we infer how sedulously we ought to be on our guard, that we undertake nothing with an indiscreet zeal; because nothing is more easy, in so great a corruption of human nature, than for religion to degenerate into frivolous trifles. Nevertheless, because this inconsiderate devotion (as it may be called) flowed from a right principle, what should be the conduct of our princes, who desire to be deemed Christians? If Pharaoh was so solicitous about his priests, that he nourished them to his own destruction, and that of his whole kingdom, in order that he might not be guilty of impiety against false gods; what sacrilege is it, in Christian princes, that the lawful and sincere ministers of holy things should be neglected, whose work they know to be approved by God, and salutary to themselves? But it may be asked, whether it was lawful for holy Joseph to undertake this office, for by so doing, he employed his labour in cherishing impious superstitions? But though I can readily grant that in such great, and arduous, and manifold offices of trust, it was easy for him to slide into various faults; yet I dare not absolutely condemn this act; nor can I, however, deny that he may have erred, in not resisting these superstitions with sufficient boldness. But since he was required by no law, to destroy the priests by hunger, and was not altogether allowed to dispense the king's corn at his own pleasure; if the king wished that food should be gratuitously supplied to the priests, he was no more at liberty to deny it to them than to the nobles at court. Therefore, though he did not willingly take charge of such dependents, yet when the king imposed the duty upon him, he could not refuse it, though he knew them to be unworthy to be fed on the dirt of oxen.

23. *Then Joseph said unto the people.* Here Moses describes the singular humanity of Joseph, which, as it then repressed all complaints, so, at this time, it justly dispels and refutes the calumnies with which he is assailed. The men, who were entirely destitute, and, in a sense, exiles, he reinstates in their possessions, on the most equitable condition, that they should pay a fifth part of the produce to the king. It is well known that formerly, in various places, kings have demanded by law the payment of tenths; but that, in the time of war, they doubled this tax. Therefore, what injury, can we say, was done to the Egyptians, when Joseph burdened the land, bought for the king, with a fifth part of its income; especially seeing that country is so much richer than others, that with less labour than elsewhere, it brings forth fruit for the maintenance of its cultivators? Should any one object that the king would have acted more frankly had he taken the fifth part of the land; the answer is obvious, that this was useful not only as an example, but also, for the purpose of quieting the people, by shutting the mouths of the captious. And certainly this indirect method, by which Joseph introduced the tax of a fifth part, had no other object than that of inducing the Egyptians to cultivate their lands with more alacrity, when they were convinced that, by such a compact, they were treated with clemency. And to this effect was their confession, which is recorded by Moses, expressed. For, first, they acknowledge that they owe their lives to him; secondly, they do not refuse to be the servants of the king. Whence we gather, that the holy man so conducted himself between the two parties, as greatly to enrich the king, without oppressing the people by tyranny. And I wish that all governors would practise this moderation, that they would only so far study the advantage of kings, as could be done without injury to the people. There is a celebrated saying of Tiberius Cæsar, which savoured little of tyranny, though

he appears to have been a sanguinary and insatiable tyrant, that it is the part of a shepherd to shear the flock, but not to tear off the skin. At this day, however, kings do not believe that they rule freely, unless they not only flay their subjects, but entirely devour them. For they do not generally invest any with authority, except those who are sworn to the practice of slaughter. So much the more does the clemency of Joseph deserve praise, who so administered the affairs of Egypt, as to render the immense gains of the king compatible with a tolerable condition of the people.

27. *And Israel dwelt in the land.* Moses does not mean that Jacob and his sons were proprietors of that land which Pharaoh had granted them as a dwelling-place, in the same manner in which the other parts of Egypt were given to the inhabitants for a perpetual possession : but that they dwelt there commodiously for a time, and thus were in possession by favour, provided they continued to be peaceable. Hence the cause that they so greatly increased, in a very short space of time. Therefore, what is here related by Moses belongs to the history of the following period ; and he now returns to the proper thread of his narrative, in which he purposed to show how God protected his Church from many deaths ; and not that only, but wonderfully exalted it by his own secret power.

28. *And Jacob lived.* It was no common source of temptation to the holy old man, to be an exile from the land of Canaan, for so many years. Be it so, that on account of the famine, he was compelled to go to Egypt ; why could he not return when the fifth year was passed ? For he did not stupidly lie there in a state of torpor, but he remained quiet, because free egress was not allowed him. Wherefore, also, in this respect, God did not lightly exercise his patience. For, however sweet might be the delights of Egypt, yet he was more than miserable to be deprived of the sight of that land which was the lively figure of his celestial country. With the men of this world, indeed, earthly advantage would have prevailed : but such was the piety of the holy man, that the profit of the flesh weighed nothing against the loss of spiritual good. But he was more deeply wounded, when he saw his death approaching : because, not only was

he himself deprived of the inheritance promised to him, but he was leaving his sons, of doubtful, or at least of feeble, faith, buried in Egypt as in a sepulchre. Moreover, his example is proposed to us, that our minds may not languish or become enfeebled by the weariness of a protracted warfare: yea, the more Satan attempts to depress them to the earth, the more fervently let them look and soar towards heaven.

29. *And he called his son Joseph.* Hence we infer, not only the anxiety of Jacob, but his invincible magnanimity. It is a proof of great courage, that none of the wealth or the pleasures of Egypt could so allure him, as to prevent him from sighing for the land of Canaan, in which he had always passed a painful and laborious life. But the constancy of his faith appeared still more excellent, when he, commanding his dead body to be carried back to Canaan, encouraged his sons to hope for deliverance. Thus it happened that he, being dead, animated those who were alive and remained, as with the sound of a trumpet. For, to what purpose was this great care respecting his sepulture, except that the promise of God might be confirmed to his posterity? Therefore, though his faith was tossed as upon the waves, yet it was so far from suffering shipwreck, that it conducted others into the haven. Moreover, he demands an oath from his son Joseph, not so much on account of distrust, as to show that a matter of the greatest consequence was in hand. Certainly he would not, by lightly swearing, profane the name of God: but the more sacred and solemn the promise was, the more ought all his sons to remember, that it was of great importance that his body should be carried to the sepulchre of his fathers. It is also probable that he prudently thought of alleviating any enmity which might be excited against his son Joseph. For he knew that this choice of his sepulchre would be, by no means, gratifying to the Egyptians; seeing it seemed like casting a reproach on their whole kingdom. This stranger, forsooth, as if he could find no fit place for his body in this splendid and noble country, wishes to be buried in the land of Canaan. Therefore, in order that Joseph might more freely dare to ask, and might more easily obtain, this favour from the king, Jacob binds him by an oath. And

certainly Joseph afterwards makes use of this pretext, to avoid giving offence. This also was the reason why he required Joseph to do for him that last office, which was a duty devolving on the brothers in common; for such a favour would scarcely have been granted to the rest; and they would not have ventured on the act, unless permission had been obtained. But, as strangers and mean men, they had neither favour nor authority. Besides, it was especially necessary for Joseph to be on his guard, lest becoming ensnared by the allurements of Egypt, he should gradually forsake his own kindred. It must, however, be known, that the solemnity of an oath was designedly interposed by Jacob, to show that he did not, in vain, desire for himself, a sepulchre in the land where he had met with an unfavourable reception; where he had endured many sufferings; and from which, at length, being expelled by hunger, he had become an exile. As to his commanding the hand to be put under his thigh, we have explained what this symbol means in chapter xxiv. ver. 2.

30. *But I will lie with my fathers.*[1] It appears from this passage, that the word "sleep," whenever it is put for "die," does not refer to the soul, but to the body. For, what did it concern him, to be buried with his fathers in the double cave,[2] unless to testify that he was associated with them after death? And by what bond were he and they joined together, except this, that not even death itself could extinguish the power of their faith; which would seem to utter this voice from the same sepulchre, "Now also we have a common inheritance."

31. *And Israel bowed himself upon the bed's head.* By this expression, Moses again affirms that Jacob esteemed it a singular kindness, that his son should have promised to do what he had required respecting his burial. For he exerts his weak body as much as he is able, in order to give thanks unto God, as if he had obtained something most desirable. He is said to have worshipped towards the head of his bed: because, seeing he was quite unable to rise from the bed on which he lay, he yet composed himself with a solemn air

[1] Dormiam, "I will sleep."
[2] The cave of Machpelah. See above, on Gen. xxiii. 9.—*Ed.*

in the attitude of one who was praying. The same is recorded of David (1 Kings i. 47) when, having obtained his last wish, he celebrates the grace of God. The Greeks have translated it, "at the top of his staff:" which the Apostle has followed in the Epistle to the Hebrews, (xi. 21.) And though the interpreters seem to have been deceived by the similitude of words; because, with the Hebrews, מִטָּה signifies "bed," מוֹטָה, "a staff;" yet the Apostle allows himself to cite the passage as it was then commonly used, lest he might offend unskilful readers, without necessity.[1] Moreover, they who expound the words to mean that Jacob worshipped the sceptre of his son, absurdly trifle. The exposition of others, that he bowed his head, leaning on the top of his staff, is, to say the least, tolerable. But since there is no ambiguity in the words of Moses, let it suffice to keep in memory what I have said, that, by this ceremony, he openly manifested the greatness of his joy.

## CHAPTER XLVIII.

1. AND it came to pass after these things, that *one* told Joseph, Behold, thy father *is* sick: and he took with him his two sons, Manasseh and Ephraim.

2. And *one* told Jacob, and said, Behold, thy son Joseph cometh unto thee: and Israel strengthened himself, and sat upon the bed.

3. And Jacob said unto Joseph,

1. Et fuit post hæc dictum fuit ipsi Joseph, Ecce, pater tuus ægrotat: tunc accepit duos filios suos secum, Menasseh et Ephraim.

2. Et nuntiavit ipsi Jahacob, et dixit, Ecce, filius tuus Joseph venit ad te. Et roboravit se Israel, et sedit super lectum.

3. Et dixit Jahacob ipsi Joseph,

---

[1] The reasoning of Calvin, besides being in every respect unsatisfactory, is founded on a misquotation of the original. He appears to have put down the words from memory, or else his transcriber has made the mistake for him. The only difference between the words rendered "a bed" and a "staff" lies in the Masoretic punctuation; of which, it is well known, the authority is disputed. Perhaps one of the strongest arguments on the side of those opposed to the *points*, is derived from this passage and the Apostle's interpretation of it. If the word is not pointed, then it may mean either a bed or a staff; if, on the other hand, the present points are of equal authority with the text, the Apostle has quoted it wrong. The latter supposition is not to be endured. It seems to follow, then, that the original was either not pointed, or the copy used by St. Paul was pointed differently from the present text, or he knew that the points were not to be relied upon, for giving the precise meaning of the Holy Spirit in the word.—*Ed.*

God Almighty appeared unto me at Luz in the land of Canaan, and blessed me,

4. And said unto me, Behold, I will make thee fruitful, and multiply thee, and I will make of thee a multitude of people; and will give this land to thy seed after thee *for* an everlasting possession.

5. And now thy two sons, Ephraim and Manasseh, which were born unto thee in the land of Egypt, before I came unto thee into Egypt, *are* mine; as Reuben and Simeon, they shall be mine.

6. And thy issue, which thou begettest after them, shall be thine, *and* shall be called after the name of their brethren in their inheritance.

7. And as for me, when I came from Padan, Rachel died by me in the land of Canaan in the way, when yet *there was* but a little way to come unto Ephrath: and I buried her there in the way of Ephrath; the same *is* Beth-lehem.

8. And Israel beheld Joseph's sons, and said, Who *are* these?

9. And Joseph said unto his father, They *are* my sons, whom God hath given me in this *place*. And he said, Bring them, I pray thee, unto me, and I will bless them.

10. Now the eyes of Israel were dim for age, *so that* he could not see. And he brought them near unto him; and he kissed them, and embraced them.

11. And Israel said unto Joseph, I had not thought to see thy face; and, lo, God hath shewed me also thy seed.

12. And Joseph brought them out from between his knees, and he bowed himself with his face to the earth.

13. And Joseph took them both, Ephraim in his right hand toward Israel's left hand, and Manasseh in his left hand toward Israel's right hand, and brought *them* near unto him.

14. And Israel stretched out his right hand, and laid *it* upon Ephraim's head, who *was* the younger, and his

Deus omnipotens apparuit mihi in Luz in terra Chenaan, et benedixit mihi.

4. Et dixit ad me, Ecce, ego crescere facio te, et multiplicabo te, et ponam te in cœtum populorum, et dabo terram hanc semini tuo post te in hæreditatem perpetuam.

5. Et nunc duo filii tui, qui nati sunt tibi in terra Ægypti, antequam venirem ad te in Ægyptum, mei sunt, Ephraim et Menasseh, sicut Reuben et Simhon erunt mei.

6. Verum liberi tui, quos generabis post eos, tui erunt: secundum nomen fratrum suorum vocabuntur in hæreditate sua.

7. Porro me veniente e Padan, mortua est mihi Rachel in terra Chenaan in via, quum adhuc esset milliare terræ ad veniendum in Ephrath: et sepelivi eam in via Ephrath, ipsa est Bethlehem.

8. Et vidit Israel filios Joseph, et dixit, Cujus sunt isti?

9. Et dixit Joseph patri suo, Filii mei sunt quos dedit mihi Deus hic. Et dixit, Duc eos quæso ad me, et benedicam eis.

10. (Oculi enim Israel graves erant propter senectutem, nec poterat videre) et accedere fecit eos ad illum, et osculatus est eos, et amplexatus est eos.

11. Et dixit Israel ad Joseph, Videre faciem tuam non putabam, et ecce, videre fecit me Deus etiam semen tuum.

12. Eduxit itaque Joseph eos a genibus suis, et incurvavit se in faciem suam super terram.

13. Et tulit Joseph ambos ipsos, Ephraim ad dexteram suam, a sinistra Israel, et Menasseh ad sinistram suam, a dextra Israel: accedere inquam fecit ad eum.

14. Et extendit Israel dexteram suam, et posuit super caput Ephraim, qui erat minor: et sinistram

left hand upon Manasseh's head, guiding his hands wittingly; for Manasseh *was* the first-born.

15. And he blessed Joseph, and said, God, before whom my fathers Abraham and Isaac did walk, the God which fed me all my life long unto this day,

16. The Angel which redeemed me from all evil, bless the lads; and let my name be named on them, and the name of my fathers Abraham and Isaac; and let them grow into a multitude in the midst of the earth.

17. And when Joseph saw that his father laid his right hand upon the head of Ephraim, it displeased him: and he held up his father's hand, to remove it from Ephraim's head unto Manasseh's head.

18. And Joseph said unto his father, Not so, my father: for this *is* the first-born; put thy right hand upon his head.

19. And his father refused, and said, I know *it*, my son, I know *it*: he also shall become a people, and he also shall be great; but truly his younger brother shall be greater than he, and his seed shall become a multitude of nations.

20. And he blessed them that day, saying, In thee shall Israel bless, saying, God make thee as Ephraim, and as Manasseh. And he set Ephraim before Manasseh.

21. And Israel said unto Joseph, Behold, I die; but God shall be with you, and bring you again unto the land of your fathers.

22. Moreover, I have given to thee one portion above thy brethren, which I took out of the hand of the Amorite with my sword and with my bow.

suam super caput Menasseh: consulto dirigens manus suas, quum Menasseh esset primogenitus.

15. Et benedixit ipsi Joseph, et dixit, Deus, in cujus conspectu ambulaverunt patres mei Abraham et Ishac, Deus qui pascit me ab ætate mea usque ad diem hanc,

16. Angelus qui redemit me ab omni malo, benedicat pueris: et vocetur in eis nomen meum, et nomen patrum meorum Abraham et Ishac, et instar piscium sint in multitudinem in medio terræ.

17. Vidit autem Joseph, quod poneret pater suus manum dexteram suam super caput Ephraim, et displicuit in oculis ejus, et sustentavit manum patris sui, ut removeret eam a capite Ephraim, super caput Menasseh.

18. Et dixit Joseph patri suo, Non sic, pater mi: quia iste est primogenitus, pone dexteram tuam super caput ejus.

19. Verum renuit pater ejus, et dixit, Novi, fili mi, novi, etiam ipse erit in populum, et etiam ipse crescet: et tamen frater ejus minor crescet magis quam ipse, et semen ejus erit plenitudo Gentium.

20. Et benedixit eis in die ipsa, dicendo, In te benedicet Israel, dicendo, Ponat te Deus sicut Ephraim et Menasseh: et posuit Ephraim ante Menasseh.

21. Et dixit Israel ad Joseph, Ecce, ego morior: et erit Deus vobiscum, et redire faciet vos ad terram patrum vestrorum.

22. Ego autem dedi tibi partem unam super fratres tuos, quam cepi e manu Emoræi gladio meo, et arcu meo.

1. *After these things.* Moses now passes to the last act of Jacob's life, which, as we shall see, was especially worthy of remembrance. For, since he knew that he was invested by God with no common character, in being made the father of the fathers of the Church, he fulfilled, in the immediate

prospect of death, the prophetic office, respecting the future state of the Church, which had been enjoined upon him. Private persons arrange their domestic affairs by their last wills; but very different was the method pursued by this holy man, with whom God had established his covenant, with this annexed condition, that the succession of grace should flow down to his posterity. But before I enter fully on the consideration of this subject, these two things are to be observed, to which Moses briefly alludes: first, that Joseph, being informed of his father's sickness, immediately went to see him; and, secondly, that Jacob, having heard of his arrival, attempted to raise his feeble and trembling body, for the sake of doing him honour. Certainly, the reason why Joseph was so desirous of seeing his father, and so prompt to discharge all the other duties of filial piety, was, that he regarded it as a greater privilege to be a son of Jacob, than to preside over a hundred kingdoms. For, in bringing his sons with him, he acted as if he would emancipate them from the country in which they had been born, and restore them to their own stock. For they could not be reckoned among the progeny of Abraham, without rendering themselves detested by the Egyptians. Nevertheless, Joseph prefers that reproach for them, to every kind of wealth and glory, if they may but become one with the sacred body of the Church. His father, however, rising before him, pays him becoming honour, for the kindness received at his hand. Meanwhile, by so doing, he fulfils his part in the prediction, which before had inflamed his sons with rage; lest his constituting Ephraim and Manasseh the heads of two tribes, should seem grievous and offensive to his sons.

3. *And Jacob said unto Joseph.* The design of the holy man was to withdraw his son from the wealth and honours of Egypt, and to reunite him to the holy race, from which he had been, for a little while, separated. Moreover, he neither proudly boasts of his own excellence, nor of his present riches, nor of his power, for the sake of inducing his son to comply with his wishes; but simply sets before him the covenant of God. So also it is right, that the grace of adoption, as soon as it is offered to us, should, by filling our thoughts, extinguish

our desire for everything splendid and costly in the world. This passage is, doubtless, remarkable. Joseph was possessed of the most exalted dignity; he foresees that the most excellent nobility would pass, through the memory of his name, to his posterity: he is able to leave them an ample patrimony: nor would it be difficult so to advance them in royal favour, that they might obtain rank among the nobles of the kingdom. Too many examples show how easy it is not only to be caught, but altogether fascinated, by such allurements. Yea, the greater part know, by their own experience, that, as soon as the least ray of hope beams upon us, from the world, we are torn away from the Lord, and alienated from the pursuit of the heavenly life. If a very few drops thus inebriate our flesh, how dangerous is it to drink from the full bowl? But to all the riches and honours of Egypt, Jacob opposes the vision in which God had adopted himself and his race, as his own people. Whenever, therefore, Satan shall try to entangle us with the allurements of the world, that he may draw us away from heaven, let us remember for what end we are called; in order that, in comparison with the inestimable treasure of eternal life, all that the flesh would otherwise prefer, may become loathsome. For, if holy Joseph formerly held an obscure vision in such esteem, that, for this sole object, forgetting Egypt, he gladly passed over to the despised flock of the Church; how shameful, at this day, is our folly, how vile our stupor, how detestable our ingratitude, if, at least, we are not equally affected, when our heavenly Father, having opened the gate of his kingdom, with unutterable sweetness invites us to himself? At the same time, however, we must observe, that holy Jacob does not obtrude vain imaginations, for the purpose of alluring his son; but places before him the sure promise of God, on which he may safely rely. Whence we are taught, that our faith is not rightly founded on anything except the sole word of God; and also, that this is a sufficiently firm support of faith, to prevent it from ever being shaken or overthrown by any devices whatever. Wherefore, whenever Satan attempts to draw us hither and thither by his enticements, let us learn to turn our minds to the word of God, and so firmly to rely upon its hidden blessings, that, with a lofty spirit, we may spurn those things which the flesh now sees and touches. Jacob says that God appeared to him in the land of Canaan, in order that Joseph, aspiring after that land, might become alienated in the affection of his heart from the kingdom of Egypt.

*And blessed me.* In this place the word " blessed" does not signify the present effect or manifestation of a happy life, in the way in which the Lord is sometimes said to bless his people, when he indeed declares, by the favour with which he follows them, that he openly makes them happy, because they are received under his protection. But Jacob regards himself as blessed, because he, having embraced the grace promised to him, does not doubt of its effect. And, therefore, I take what immediately follows; namely, *I will make thee fruitful*, &c., as explanatory of what precedes. Now the Lord promised that he would cause an assembly of nations to descend from him: because thirteen tribes, of which the whole body of the nation consisted, were, in a sense, so many nations. But since this was nothing more than a prelude to that greatness which should afterwards follow, when God, having scattered seed over the whole world, should gather together a church for himself, out of all nations; we may, while we recognise the accomplishment of the benediction under the old dispensation, yet allow that it refers to something greater. When therefore the people increased to so great a multitude, and thirteen populous tribes flowed from the twelve patriarchs, Jacob began already to grow to an assembly of nations. But from the time that the spiritual Israel was diffused through all quarters of the world, and various nations were congregated into one Church, this multiplication tended towards its completion. Wherefore, it is no wonder that holy Jacob should so highly estimate this most distinguished mark of divine favour, though, indeed, it was deeply hidden from carnal perception. But inasmuch as the Lord had held him long in suspense, profane men have said, that the old man was in his dotage. Few indeed are to be found, in this age, like Joseph, who disregarding the enjoyment of pleasures which are at hand, yield entire submission to the plain declaration of God's word. But as Jacob, relying in confidence on invisible grace, had overcome every kind of temptation: so now his son, and the true heir of his faith, regards with reverence the oracles of the Lord; esteeming more highly the promise which he was persuaded had come down from heaven, though it was in the form of a dream, than all the riches of Egypt which he enjoyed.

*For an everlasting possession.* We have elsewhere shown the meaning of this expression: namely, that the Israelites should be perpetual heirs of the land until the coming of Christ, by which the world was renewed. The Hebrew word עולם (*olam*) is by some taken merely for *a long time*, by others for *eternity*: but seeing that Christ prolongs, to the end of time, the grace which was previously shadowed forth to the patriarchs; the phrase, in my judgment, refers to eternity. For that portion of land was promised to the ancient people of God, until the renovation introduced by Christ: and now, ever since the Lord has assigned the whole world to his people, a fuller fruition of the inheritance belongs to us.

5. *And now thy two sons.* Jacob confers on his son the special privilege, that he, being one, should constitute two chiefs; that is, that his two sons should succeed to an equal right with their uncles, as if they had been heirs in the first degree. But what is this! that a decrepid old man assigns to his grandchildren, as a royal patrimony, a sixth part of the land in which he had wandered as a stranger, and from which now again he is an exile! Who would not have said that he was dealing in fables? It is a common proverb, that no one can give what he has not. What, therefore, did it profit Joseph to be constituted, by an imaginary title, lord of that land, in which the donor of it was scarcely permitted to drink the very water he had dug for with great labour, and from which, at length, famine expelled him? But it hence appears with what firm faith the holy fathers relied upon the word of the Lord, seeing they chose rather to depend upon his lips, than to possess a fixed habitation in the land. Jacob is dying an exile in Egypt; and meanwhile, calls away the governor of Egypt from his dignity into exile, that he may be well and happy. Joseph, because he acknowledges his

father as a prophet of God, who utters no inventions of his own, esteems as highly the dominion offered to him, which has never yet become apparent, as if it were already in his possession. Moreover, that Jacob commands the other sons of Joseph, (if there should be any,) to be reckoned in the families of these two brothers, is as if he directed them to be adopted by the two whom he adopts to himself.

7. *And as for me, when I came from Padan.* He mentions the death and burial of his wife Rachel, in order that the name of his mother might prove a stimulus to the mind of Joseph. For since all the sons of Jacob had sprung from Syria, it was not a little to the purpose, that they should be thoroughly acquainted with the history which we have before considered; namely, that their father, returning into the land of Canaan, by the command and under the protection of God, brought his wives with him. For if it was not grievous to women, to leave their father, and to journey into a distant land, their example ought to be no slight inducement to their sons to bid farewell to Egypt; and at the command of the same God, strenuously prepare themselves for taking possession of the land of Canaan.

8. *And Israel beheld Joseph's sons.* I have no doubt that he had inquired concerning the youths, before he called them his heirs. But in the narration of Moses there is a *hysteron proteron.* And in the answer of Joseph we observe, what we have elsewhere alluded to, that the fruit of the womb is not born by chance, but is to be reckoned among the precious gifts of God. This confession indeed finds a ready utterance from the tongues of all; but there are few who heartily acknowledge that their seed has been given them by God. And hence a large proportion of man's offspring becomes continually more and more degenerate: because the ingratitude of the world renders it unable to perceive the effect of the blessings of God. We must now briefly consider the design of Moses: which was to show that a solemn symbol was interposed, by which the adoption might be ratified. Jacob puts his hands upon his grandsons; for what end? Truly to prove that he gave them a place among his sons: and thus constitutes Joseph who was *one*, into two *chiefs*. For

this was not his wish as a private person; according to the manner in which fathers and grandfathers are wont to pray for prosperity to their descendents: but a divine authority suggested it, as was afterwards proved by the event. Therefore he commands them to be brought near to him, that he might confer on them a new honour, as if he had been appointed the dispenser of it by the Lord; and Joseph, on the other hand, begins with adoration, giving thanks to God.

12. *And Joseph brought them out.* Moses explains more fully what he had touched upon in a single word. Joseph brings forth his sons from his own lap to his father's knees, not only for the sake of honour, but that he may present them to receive a blessing from the prophet of God; for he was certainly persuaded, that holy Jacob did not desire to embrace his grandsons after the common manner of men; but inasmuch as he was the interpreter of God, he wished to impart to them the blessing deposited with himself. And although, in dividing the land of Canaan, he assigned them equal portions with his sons, yet the imposition of his hands had respect to something higher; namely, that they should be two of the patriarchs of the Church, and should hold an honourable pre-eminence in the spiritual kingdom of God.

14. *And Israel stretched out his right hand.* Seeing his eyes were dim with age, so that he could not, by looking, discern which was the elder, he yet intentionally placed his hands across. And therefore Moses says that he *guided his hands wittingly,* because he did not rashly put them forth, nor transfer them from one youth to the other for the sake of feeling them: but using judgment, he purposely directed his right hand to Ephraim who was the younger: but placed his left hand on the first-born. Whence we gather that the Holy Spirit was the director of this act, who irradiated the mind of the holy man, and caused him to see more correctly, than those who were the most clear-sighted, into the nature of this symbolical act. I shall avoid saying more, because we shall be able to inquire into it from other passages.

15. *God before whom.* Although Jacob knew that a dispensation of the grace of God was committed to him, in order that he might effectually bless his grandchildren; yet he arro-

gates nothing to himself, but suppliantly resorts to prayer, lest he should, in the least degree, detract from the glory of God. For as he was the legitimate administrator of the blessing, so it behoved him to acknowledge God as its sole Author. And hence a common rule is to be deduced for all the ministers and pastors of the Church. For though they are not only called witnesses of celestial grace, but are also entrusted with the dispensation of spiritual gifts; yet when they are compared with God, they are nothing; because he alone contains all things within himself. Wherefore let them learn willingly to keep their own place, lest they should obscure the name of God. And truly, since the Lord, by no means, appoints his ministers, with the intention of derogating from his own power; therefore, mortal man cannot, without sacrilege, desire to seem anything separate from God. In the words of Jacob we must note, first, that he invokes God, in whose sight his fathers Abraham and Isaac had walked: for since the blessing depended upon the covenant entered into with them, it was necessary that their faith should be an intervening link between them and their descendants. God had chosen them and their posterity for a people unto himself: but the promise was efficacious for this reason, because, being apprehended by faith, it had taken a lively root. And thus it came to pass, that they transmitted the right of succession to Jacob himself. We now see that he does not bring forward, in vain, or unseasonably, that faith of the fathers, without which he would not have been a legitimate successor of grace, by the covenant of God: not that Abraham and Isaac had acquired so great an honour for themselves, and their posterity; or were, in themselves, so excellent; but because the Lord seals and sanctions by faith, those benefits which he promises us, so that they shall not fail.

*The God which fed me.* Jacob now descends to his own feelings, and states that from his youth he had constantly experienced, in various ways, the divine favour towards him. He had before made the knowledge of God received through his word, and the faith of his fathers, the basis of the blessing he pronounces; he now adds another confirmation from experience itself; as if he would say, that he was not pronouncing a blessing which consisted in an empty sound of words, but one of which he had himself enjoyed the fruit, all his life long. Now though God causes his sun to shine indiscriminately on the good and evil, and feeds unbelievers as well as believers: yet because he affords, only to the latter, the peculiar sense of his paternal love in the use of his gifts, Jacob rightly uses this as a reason for the confirmation of his faith, that he had always been protected by the help of God. Unbelievers are fed, even to the full, by the liberality of God: but they gorge themselves, like swine, which, while acorns are falling for them from the trees, yet have their snouts fixed to the earth. But in God's benefits this is the principal thing, that they are pledges or tokens of his paternal love towards us. Jacob, therefore, from the sense of piety, with which the children of God are endued, rightly adduces, as proof of the promised grace, whatever good things God had bestowed upon him; as if he would say, that he himself was a decisive example to show how truly and faithfully the Lord had engaged by covenant to be a father to the children of Abraham. Let us also learn hence, carefully to consider and meditate upon whatever benefits we receive from the hand of God, that they may prove so many supports for the confirmation of our faith. The best method of seeking God is to begin at his word; after this, (if I may so speak,) experimental knowledge is added. Now whereas, in this place, the singular gratitude of the holy man is conspicuous; yet this circumstance adds to his honour, that, while involved in manifold sufferings, by which he was almost borne down, he celebrates the continual goodness of God. For although, by the rare and wonderful power of God, he had been, in an extraordinary manner, delivered from many dangers; yet it was a mark of an exalted and courageous mind, to be able to surmount so many and so great obstacles, to fly on the wings of faith to the goodness of God, and instead of being overwhelmed by a mass of evils, to perceive the same goodness in the thickest darkness.

16. *The Angel which redeemed me.* He so joins the Angel to God as to make him his equal. Truly he offers him divine worship, and asks the same things from him as from God. If this be understood indifferently of any angel what-

ever, the sentence is absurd. Nay, rather, as Jacob himself sustains the name and character of God, in blessing his son,[1] he is superior, in this respect, to the angels. Wherefore it is necessary that Christ should be here meant, who does not bear in vain the title of Angel, because he had become the perpetual Mediator. And Paul testifies that he was the Leader and Guide of the journey of his ancient people. (1 Cor. x. 4.) He had not yet indeed been sent by the Father, to approach more nearly to us by taking our flesh, but because he was always the bond of connection between God and man, and because God formally manifested himself in no other way than through him, he is properly called the Angel. To which may be added, that the faith of the fathers was always fixed on his future mission. He was therefore the Angel, because even then he poured forth his rays, that the saints might approach God, through him, as Mediator. For there was always so wide a distance between God and men, that, without a mediator, there could be no communication. Nevertheless though Christ appeared in the form of an angel, we must remember what the Apostle says to the Hebrews, (ii. 16,) that " he took not on him the nature of angels," so as to become one of *them*, in the manner in which he truly became *man;* for even when angels put on human bodies, they did not, on that account, become men. Now since we are taught, in these words, that the peculiar office of Christ is to defend us and to deliver us from all evil, let us take heed not to bury this grace in impious oblivion: yea, seeing that now it is more clearly exhibited to us, than formerly to the saints under the law, since Christ openly declares that the faithful are committed to his care, that not one of them might perish, (John xvii. 12,) so much the more ought it to flourish in our hearts, both that it may be highly celebrated by us with suitable praise, and that it may stir us up to seek this guardianship of our best Protector. And this is exceedingly necessary for us; for if we reflect how many dangers surround us, that we scarcely pass a day without being delivered from a thousand deaths; whence does this

---

[1] In benedicendo filio. It appears that though the singular number is used, yet reference is made to the two grandsons of Jacob.—*Ed.*

arise, except from that care which is taken of us, by the Son of God, who has received us under his protection, from the hand of his Father.

*And let my name be named on them.* This is a mark of the adoption before mentioned: for he puts his name upon them, that they may obtain a place among the patriarchs. Indeed the Hebrew phrase signifies nothing else than to be reckoned among the family of Jacob. Thus the name of the husband is said to be called upon the wife, (Is. iv. 1,) because the wife borrows the name from the head to which she is subject. So much the more ridiculous is the ignorance of the Papists, who would prove hence that the dead are to be invoked in prayers. Jacob, say they, desired after his death to be invoked by his posterity. What! that being prayed to, he might bring them succour; and not—according to the plain intention of the speaker—that Ephraim and Manasseh might be added to the society of the patriarchs, to constitute two tribes of the holy people! Moreover it is wonderful, that the Papists, having under this pretext framed for themselves innumerable patrons, should have passed over Abraham, Isaac, and Jacob, as unworthy of the office. But the Lord, by this brutish stupor, has avenged their impious profanation of his name. What Jacob adds in the next clause, namely, that they should *grow into a multitude*,[1] refers also to the same promise. The sum amounts to this, that the Lord would complete in them, what he had promised to the patriarchs.

17. *And when Joseph saw.* Because by crossing his arms, Jacob had so placed his hands as to put his left hand upon the head of the first-born, Joseph wished to correct this proceeding, as if it had been a mistake. He thought that the error arose from dimness of vision; but his father followed the Spirit of God as his secret guide, in order that he might transfer the title of honour, which nature had conferred upon

---

[1] ידגו, (*yedegu*,) Ainsworth translates the passage, "let them increase like fish into a multitude." The Hebrew word for fish is from the above root, because of their prolific property; and consequently the use of such a term naturally suggests the notion of an extraordinary increase. Thus the Chaldee paraphrase adds, "like the fishes of the sea." Hence, in the time of Moses there were 85,200 men of war descended from Joseph, a greater number than from any other of Jacob's sons. *See Ainsworth.—Ed.*

the elder to the younger. For, as he did not rashly assume to himself the office of conveying the blessing; so was it not lawful for him to attempt anything according to his own will. And at length it was evident by the event, that whatever he had done had been dictated to him from heaven. Whereas Joseph took it amiss, that Manasseh, who by the right of nature was first, should be cast down to the second place, this feeling arose from faith and from holy reverence for the prophetic office. For he would easily have borne to see him make a mistake in the order of embracing the youths; if he had not known that his father, as a minister of divine grace, so far from acting a futile part, was but pronouncing on earth what God would ratify in heaven. Yet he errs in binding the grace of God to the accustomed order of nature: as if the Lord did not often purposely change the law of nature, to teach us that what he freely confers upon us, is entirely the result of his own will. If God were rendering to every one his due, a certain rule might properly be applied to the distribution of his favours; but since he owes no one anything, he is free to confer gifts at his own pleasure. More especially, lest any one should glory in the flesh, he designedly illustrates his own free mercy, in choosing those who had no worthiness of their own. What shall we say was the cause, why he raised Ephraim above his own brother, to whom, according to usage, he was inferior? If any one should suppose that Ephraim had some hidden seed of excellence, he not only vainly trifles, but impiously perverts the counsel of God. For since God derives from himself and from his own liberality, the cause, why he prefers one of the two to the other: he confers the honour upon the younger, for the purpose of showing that he is bound by no claims of human merit; but that he distributes his gifts freely, as it seems good unto him. And while this liberty of God is extended to every kind of good, it yet shines the most clearly in the first adoption, whereby he predestinates to himself, those whom he sees fit, out of the ruined mass. Wherefore, be it our part to leave to God his whole power untouched, and if at any time, our carnal sense rebels, let us know that none are more truly wise than they who are willing to account themselves blind, when contemplating the wonderful dealings of God, in order that they may trace the cause of any difference he makes, to *himself* alone. We have seen above, that the eyes of Jacob were dim: but in crossing his arms, with apparent negligence, in order to comply with God's purpose of election, he is more clear-sighted than his son Joseph, who, according to the sense of the flesh, inquires with too much acuteness. They who insanely imagine that this judgment was formed from a view of their works, sufficiently declare, by this one thing, that they do not hold the first rudiments of faith. For either the adoption common both to Manasseh and to Ephraim, was a free gift, or a reward of debt. Concerning this second supposition all ambiguity is removed, by many passages of Scripture, in which the Lord makes known his goodness, in having freely loved and chosen his people. Now no one is so ignorant, as not to perceive that the first place is not assigned to one or the other, according to merit; but is given gratuitously, since it so pleases the Lord. With regard to the posture of the hands, the subtlety of certain persons, who conjecture that the mystery of the cross was included in it, is absurd; for the Lord intended nothing more than that the crossing of the right hand and the left should indicate a change in the accustomed order of nature.

19. *He also shall become a people.* Jacob does not dispute which of the youths shall be the more worthy; but only pronounces what God had decreed with himself, concerning each, and, what would take place after a long succession of time. He seeks, therefore, no causes elsewhere; but contents himself with this one statement, that Ephraim will be more greatly multiplied than Manasseh. And truly our dignity is hidden in the counsel of God alone, until, by his vocation, he makes it manifest what he wills to do with us. Meanwhile, sinful emulation is forbidden, when he commands Manasseh to be contented with his lot. They are therefore altogether insane, who hew out dry and perforated cisterns, in seeking causes of divine adoption; whereas, everywhere, the Scripture defines in one word, that they are called to salvation whom God has chosen, (Rom. viii. 29,) and that the primary source of election is his free good pleasure. The form of the benediction,

which is shortly afterwards related, more fully confirms what I have alluded to, that the grace of God towards both is commended, in order that Manasseh, considering that more was given to him than he deserved, might not envy his brother. Moreover, this blessing pronounced on Ephraim and Manasseh is not to be taken in the same sense as the former, in which it is said, *In thy seed shall all nations be blessed:* but the simple meaning is, that the grace of God should be so conspicuous towards the two sons of Joseph, as to furnish the people of Israel with a form by which to express their good wishes.

21. *And Israel said unto Joseph.* Jacob repeats what he had said. And truly all his sons, and especially Joseph and his sons, required something more than one simple confirmation, in order that they might not fix their abode in Egypt, but might dwell, in their minds, in the land of Canaan. He mentions his own death, for the purpose of teaching them that the eternal truth of God by no means depended on the life of men: as if he had said, my life, seeing it is short and fading, passes away; but the promise of God, which has no limit, will flourish when I also am dead. No vision had appeared unto his sons, but God had ordained the holy old man as the intermediate sponsor of his covenant. He therefore sedulously fulfils the office enjoined upon him, taking timely precaution that their faith should not be shaken by his death. So when the Lord delivers his word to the world by mortal men, although they die, having finished their course of life according to the flesh; yet the voice of God is not extinguished with them, but quickens us even at the present day. Therefore Peter writes, that he will endeavour, that after his decease, the Church may be mindful of the doctrine committed unto him. (2 Pet. i. 15.)

*Unto the land of your fathers.* It is not without reason that he claims for himself and his fathers, the dominion over that land in which they had always wandered as strangers; for whereas it might seem that the promise of God had failed, he excites his sons to a good hope, and pronounces, with a courageous spirit, that land to be his own, in which, at length, he scarcely obtained a sepulchre, and that only by favour. Whence then was this great confidence, except that he would accustom his sons, by his example, to have faith in the word of God? Now this doctrine is also common to us; because we never rely with sufficient firmness on the word of God, so long as we are led by our own feelings. Nay, until our faith rises to lay hold on those things which are removed afar off, we know not what it is to set our seal to the word of God.

22. *I have given to thee one portion.* In order to increase the confidence of his son Joseph, Jacob here assigns him a portion beyond his proper lot. Some expound the passage otherwise; as if he called him a double heir in his two sons, thus honouring him with one portion more than the rest. But there is no doubt that he means a certain territory. And John, (chap. iv. 5,) removes all controversy; for, speaking of the field adjoining Sychar, which before was called Shechem, says, it was that which Jacob gave to his son Joseph. And, in the last chapter of Joshua, (ver. 32,) it is said to have come into the possession of the sons of Joseph. But in the word שכם, (*shechem*,) which among the Hebrews signifies a *part*, allusion is made to the proper name of the place. But here a question arises; how can he say that he had obtained the field by his sword and by his bow, which he had purchased with money, as is stated before, (chap. xxxiii. 19,) and is again recorded in the above mentioned chapter of Joshua? Seeing, however, that only a small portion of the field, where he might pitch his tents, was bought, I do not doubt that here he comprised a much greater space. For we may easily calculate, from the price, how small a portion of land he possessed, before the destruction of the city. He gives, therefore, now to his son Joseph, not only the place of his tent, which had cost a hundred pieces of silver, but the field which had been the common of the city of Sychar. But it remains to inquire how he may be said to have obtained it by his sword, whereas the inhabitants had been wickedly and cruelly slain by Simeon and Levi. How then could it be acquired by the right of conquest, from those against whom war had been unjustly brought; or rather, against whom, without any war, the most cruel perfidy had been practised?

Jerome resorts to allegory, saying that the field was obtained by money, which is called strength, or justice. Others suppose a prolepsis, as if Jacob was speaking of a future acquisition of the land : a meaning which, though I do not reject, seems yet somewhat forced. I rather incline to this interpretation : first, that he wished to testify that he had taken nothing by means of his two sons Simeon and Levi; who, having raged like robbers, were not lawful conquerors, and had never obtained a single foot of land, after the perpetration of the slaughter. For, so far were they from gaining anything, that they compelled their father to fly ; nor would escape have been possible, unless they had been delivered by miracle. When, however, Jacob strips them of their empty title, he transfers the right of victory to himself, as being divinely granted to him. For though he always held their wickedness in abhorrence, and will show his detestation of it in the next chapter ; yet, because they had armed his whole household, they fought as under his auspices. Gladly would he have preserved the citizens of Shechem, a design which he was not able to accomplish ; yet he appropriates to himself the land left empty and deserted by their destruction, because, for his sake, God had spared the murderers.[1]

## CHAPTER XLIX.

1. AND Jacob called unto his sons, and said, Gather yourselves together, that I may tell you *that* which shall befall you in the last days.

2. Gather yourselves together, and hear, ye sons of Jacob; and hearken unto Israel your father.

1. Postea vocavit Jahacob filios suos, et dixit, Congregate vos, et annuntiabo vobis quod eventurum est vobis in novissimo dierum.

2. Congregate vos, et audite filii Jahacob, audite inquam Israel patrem vestrum.

[1] Perhaps this interpretation of a confessedly obscure passage, will be deemed rather ingenious than solid. It is supposed by many, that Jacob refers to some transaction of which no record is preserved. He may, like Abraham, on some occasion, have armed his household to recover from the hands of the Amorites the field of Shechem, which he had previously purchased. But the whole must be left in hopeless obscurity. Ainsworth thinks that Jacob is speaking proleptically, and representing the future conduct of his children under Joshua, whose sword and bow he here calls his own. But this seems far-fetched. The Chaldee interpretation, that the sword and bow are figuratively used for *prayer* and *supplication*, is still more improbable.—*Ed.*.

3. Reuben, thou *art* my first-born, my might, and the beginning of my strength, the excellency of dignity, and the excellency of power:

4. Unstable as water, thou shalt not excel; because thou wentest up to thy father's bed; then defiledst thou *it*: he went up to my couch.

5. Simeon and Levi *are* brethren; instruments of cruelty *are in* their habitations.

6. O my soul, come not thou into their secret; unto their assembly, mine honour, be not thou united! for in their anger they slew a man, and in their self-will they digged down a wall.

7. Cursed *be* their anger, for *it was* fierce; and their wrath, for it was cruel: I will divide them in Jacob, and scatter them in Israel.

8. Judah, thou *art he* whom thy brethren shall praise: thy hand *shall be* in the neck of thine enemies; thy father's children shall bow down before thee.

9. Judah *is* a lion's whelp: from the prey, my son, thou art gone up: he stooped down, he couched as a lion, and as an old lion; who shall rouse him up?

10. The sceptre shall not depart from Judah, nor a lawgiver from between his feet, until Shiloh come; and unto him *shall* the gathering of the people *be:*

11. Binding his fole unto the vine, and his ass's colt unto the choice vine; he washed his garments in wine, and his clothes in the blood of grapes:

12. His eyes *shall be* red with wine, and his teeth white with milk.

13. Zebulun shall dwell at the haven of the sea; and he *shall be* for an haven of ships: and his border *shall be* unto Zidon.

14. Issachar *is* a strong ass couching down between two burdens:

15. And he saw that rest *was* good, and the land that *it was* pleasant; and bowed his shoulder to bear, and became a servant unto tribute.

3. Reuben primogenitus meus, tu fortitudo mea, et principium roboris mei: excellentia dignitatis et excellentia roboris.

4. Velocitas *fuit tibi* instar aquæ, non excelles: quia ascendisti cubile patris tui, tunc polluisti stratum meum, evanuit.

5. Simhon et Levi fratres, arma iniquitatis in habitationibus eorum.

6. In secretum eorum non veniat anima mea, in cœtu eorum non uniaris lingua mea: quia in furore suo occiderunt virum, et voluntate sua eradicaverunt murum.

7. Maledictus furor eorum, quia robustus, et ira eorum, quia dura est: dividam eos in Jahacob et dispergam eos in Israel.

8. Jehudah *es* tu, laudabunt te fratres tui: manus tua erit in cervice inimicorum tuorum, incurvabunt se tibi filii patris tui.

9. Ut catulus leonis Jehudah: e præda, fili mi, ascendisti: incurvavit se, cubuit sicut leo, sicut leo major, quis suscitabit eum?

10. Non recedet sceptrum ex Jehudah, et Legislator e medio pedum ejus, donec veniat Messias: et ei erit aggregatio populorum.

11. Ligans ad vitem pullum suum, et ad ramum filium asinæ suæ: lavit in vino vestimentum suum, et in sanguine uvarum operimentum suum.

12. Rubicundus oculis a vino, et candidus dentibus a lacte.

13. Zebulon in portu marium habitabit, et erit in portum navium, et terminus ejus usque ad Sidon.

14. Issachar *ut* asinus osseus, cubans inter duas sarcinas.

15. Et vidit requiem, quod esset bonum: et terram quod esset pulchra, et inclinavit humerum suum ad portandum, et fuit tributo serviens.

16. Dan shall judge his people, as one of the tribes of Israel.

17. Dan shall be a serpent by the way, an adder in the path, that biteth the horse heels, so that his rider shall fall backward.

18. I have waited for thy salvation, O Lord.

19. Gad, a troop shall overcome him: but he shall overcome at the last.

20. Out of Asher his bread *shall be* fat, and he shall yield royal dainties.

21. Naphtali *is* a hind let loose: he giveth goodly words.

22. Joseph *is* a fruitful bough, *even* a fruitful bough by a well, *whose* branches run over the wall.

23. The archers have sorely grieved him, and shot *at him*, and hated him:

24. But his bow abode in strength, and the arms of his hands were made strong by the hands of the mighty *God* of Jacob: (from thence *is* the Shepherd, the stone of Israel:)

25. *Even* by the God of thy father, who shall help thee; and by the Almighty, who shall bless thee with blessings of heaven above, blessings of the deep that lieth under, blessings of the breasts, and of the womb:

26. The blessings of thy father have prevailed above the blessings of thy progenitors unto the utmost bound of the everlasting hills: they shall be on the head of Joseph, and on the crown of the head of him that was separate from his brethren.

27. Benjamin shall ravin *as* a wolf: in the morning he shall devour the prey, and at night he shall divide the spoil.

28. All these *are* the twelve tribes of Israel: and this *is it* that their father spake unto them, and blessed them; every one according to his blessing he blessed them.

29. And he charged them, and said unto them, I am to be gathered unto my people: bury me with my

16. Dan judicabit populum suum sicut unus e tribubus Israel.

17. Erit Dan *ut* serpens juxta viam, *ut* cerastes juxta semitam, mordens calcaneos equi, et cecidit equitans retrorsum.

18. Salutem tuam exspectavi Jehova.

19. Gad, exercitus succidet eum, et ipse succidet ad extremum.

20. Aser, erit pinguis panis ejus, et ipse dabit delicias regis.

21. Naphthali *ut* cerva dimissa, dans eloquia pulchritudinis.

22. *Ut* arbor fructificans Joseph, ut ramus crescens juxta fontem, rami incedent super murum.

23. Et amaritudine affecerunt eum, et jaculati sunt, et odio habuerunt eum sagittarii.

24. Et mansit in fortitudine arcus ejus, et roboraverunt se brachia manuum ejus a manibus potentis Jahacob, inde pastor lapidis Israel.

25. A Deo patris tui, et adjuvabit te: et ab Omnipotente, et benedicet tibi benedictionibus cœli sursum, benedictionibus abyssi cubantis deorsum, benedictionibus uberum et vulvæ.

26. Benedictiones patris tui fortiores fuerunt benedictionibus genitorum meorum, usque ad terminum collium perpetuorum erunt super caput Joseph, et super verticem Nazaræi inter fratres suos.

27. Benjamin *ut* lupus rapiet, mane comedet prædam, et vesperi dividet spolia.

28. Omnes istæ tribus Israel duodecim. Et hoc est quod loquutus est eis pater eorum, et benedixit eis, unicuique secundum benedictionem suam, benedixit eis.

29. Et præcepit eis, et dixit ad eos, Ego congregor ad populum meum: sepelite me cum patribus

| | |
|---|---|
| fathers in the cave that *is* in the field of Ephron the Hittite, | meis in spelunca, quæ est in agro Hephron Hittæi. |
| 30. In the cave that *is* in the field of Machpelah, which *is* before Mamre, in the land of Canaan, which Abraham bought with the field of Ephron the Hittite, for a possession of a burying-place. | 30. In spelunca, quæ est in agro duplici, quæ est ante Mamre: in terra Chenaan, quam emit Abraham cum agro ab Hephron Hittæo in possessionem sepulcri. |
| 31. There they buried Abraham and Sarah his wife; there they buried Isaac and Rebekah his wife; and there I buried Leah. | 31. Ibi sepelierunt Abraham et Sarah uxorem ejus: ibi sepelierunt Ishac et Ribcah uxorem ejus, et ibi sepelivi Leah. |
| 32. The purchase of the field, and of the cave that *is* therein, *was* from the children of Heth. | 32. Emptio agri et speluncæ, quæ est in eo, *fuit* a filiis Heth. |
| 33. And when Jacob had made an end of commanding his sons, he gathered up his feet into the bed, and yielded up the ghost, and was gathered unto his people. | 33. Et finem fecit Iahacob præcipiendi filiis suis: et collegit pedes suos in lecto et obiit, et aggregatus est ad populos suos. |

1. *And Jacob called.* In the former chapter, the blessing on Ephraim and Manasseh was related, because, before Jacob should treat of the state of the whole nation about to spring from him, it was right that these two grandsons should be inserted into the body of his sons. Now, as if carried above the heavens, he announces, not in the character of a man, but as from the mouth of God, what shall be the condition of them all, for a long time to come. And it will be proper first to remark, that as he had then thirteen sons, he sets before his view, in each of their persons, the same number of nations or tribes: in which act the admirable lustre of his faith is conspicuous. For since he had often heard from the Lord, that his seed should be increased to a multitude of people, this oracle is to him like a sublime mirror, in which he may perceive things deeply hidden from human sense. Moreover, this is not a simple confession of faith, by which Jacob testifies that he hopes for whatever had been promised him by the Lord; but he rises superior to men, as the interpreter and ambassador of God, to regulate the future state of the Church. Now, since some interpreters perceived this prophecy to be noble and magnificent, they have thought that it would not be adorned with its proper dignity, unless they should extract from it certain new mysteries. Thus it has happened, that in striving earnestly to elicit profound alle-

gories, they have departed from the genuine sense of the
words, and have corrupted, by their own inventions, what
is here delivered for the solid edification of the pious.
But lest we should depreciate the literal sense, as if it did
not contain speculations sufficiently profound, let us mark
the design of the Holy Spirit. In the first place, the sons
of Jacob are informed beforehand, of their future fortune,
that they may know themselves to be objects of the special
care of God; and that, although the whole world is governed
by his providence, they, notwithstanding, are preferred to
other nations, as members of his own household. It seems
apparently a mean and contemptible thing, that a region
productive of vines, which should yield abundance of choice
wine, and one rich in pastures, which should supply milk, is
promised to the tribe of Judah. But if any one will consider that the Lord is hereby giving an illustrious proof
of his own election, in descending, like the father of a
family, to the care of food, and also showing, in minute
things, that he is united by the sacred bond of a covenant
to the children of Abraham, he will look for no deeper mystery. In the second place; the hope of the promised inheritance is again renewed unto them. And, therefore, Jacob,
as if he would put them in possession of the land by his
own hand, expounds familiarly, and as in an affair actually
present, what kind of habitation should belong to each of
them. Can the confirmation of a matter so serious, appear
contemptible to sane and prudent readers? It is, however, the principal design of Jacob more correctly to point
out from whence a king should arise among them, who
should bring them complete felicity. And in this manner
he explains what had been promised obscurely, concerning
the blessed seed. In these things there is so great weight,
that the simple treating of them, if only we were skilful interpreters, ought justly to transport us with admiration.
But (omitting all things else) an advantage of no common
kind consists in this single point, that the mouth of impure
and profane men, who freely detract from the credibility of
Moses, is shut, so that they no longer dare to contend that
he did not speak by a celestial impulse. Let us imagine

that Moses does not relate what Jacob had before prophesied, but speaks in his own person; whence, then, could he divine what did not happen till many ages afterwards? Such, for instance, is the prophecy concerning the kingdom of David. And there is no doubt that God commanded the land to be divided by lot, lest any suspicion should arise that Joshua had divided it among the tribes, by compact, and as he had been instructed by his master. After the Israelites had obtained possession of the land, the division of it was not made by the will of men. Whence was it that a dwelling near the sea-shore was given to the tribe of Zebulun; a fruitful plain to the tribe of Asher; and to the others, by lot, what is here recorded; except that the Lord would ratify his oracles by the result, and would show openly, that nothing then occurred which he had not, a long time before, declared should take place? I now return to the words of Moses, in which holy Jacob is introduced, relating what he had been taught by the Holy Spirit concerning events still very remote. But some, with canine rage, demand,[1] Whence did Moses derive his knowledge of a conversation, held in an obscure hut, two hundred years before his time? I ask in return, before I give an answer, Whence had he his knowledge of the places in the land of Canaan, which he assigns, like a skilful surveyor, to each tribe? If this was a knowledge derived from heaven, (which must be granted,) why will these impious babblers deny that the things which Jacob had predicted, were divinely revealed to Moses? Besides, among many other things which the holy fathers had handed down by tradition, this prediction might then be generally known. Whence was it that the people, when tyrannically oppressed, implored the assistance of God as their deliverer? Whence was it, that at the simple hearing of a promise formerly given, they raised their minds to a good hope, unless that some remembrance of the divine adoption still flourished among them? If there was a general acquaintance with the covenant of the Lord among the people; what impudence will it be to deny that the heavenly servants of God more accurately investigated whatever was important to be known

---

[1] Sed oblatrant quidam protervi canes.

respecting the promised inheritance ? For the Lord did not utter oracles by the mouth of Jacob which, after his death, a sudden oblivion should destroy ; as if he had breathed, I know not what sounds, into the air. But rather he delivered instruction common to many ages ; that his posterity might know from what source their redemption, as well as the hereditary title of the land, flowed down to them. We know how tardily, and even timidly, Moses undertook the province assigned him, when he was called to deliver his own people: because he was aware that he should have to deal with an intractable and perverse nation. It was, therefore, necessary, that he should come prepared with certain credentials which might give proof of his vocation. And, hence, he put forth these predictions, as public documents from the sacred archives of God, that no one might suppose him to have intruded rashly into his office.

*Gather yourselves together.*[1] Jacob begins with inviting their attention. For he gravely enters on his subject, and claims for himself the authority of a prophet, in order to teach his sons that he is by no means making a private testamentary disposition of his domestic affairs ; but that he is expressing in words, those oracles which are deposited with him, until the event shall follow in due time. For he does not command them simply to listen to his wishes, but gathers them into an assembly by a solemn rite, that they may hear what shall occur to them in the succession of time. Moreover, I do not doubt, that he places this future period of which he speaks, in opposition to their exile in Egypt, that, when their minds were in suspense, they might look forward to that promised state. Now, from the above re-

---

[1] The reader will observe, that the entire structure of these predictions is poetical. The prophecies of the Old Testament are generally delivered in this form ; and God has thus chosen the most natural method of conveying prophetic intelligence, through the medium of that elevated strain of diction, which suggests itself to imaginative minds, which is peculiarly fitted to deal with sublime and invisible realities, and which best serves to stir up animated feelings, and to fix important truths in the memory of the reader. They who wish to examine more minutely the poetical character of the chapter, are referred to Dr. Adam Clarke's Commentary, and to Caunter's Poetry of the Pentateuch. A few observations, in passing, will be made in the notes to such passages as derive elucidation from their poetical structure.—*Ed.*

marks, it may be easily inferred, that, in this prophecy is comprised the whole period from the departure out of Egypt to the reign of Christ: not that Jacob enumerates every event, but that, in the summary of things on which he briefly touches, he arranges a settled order and course, until Christ should appear.

3. *Reuben, thou art my first-born.* He begins with the first-born, not for the sake of honour, to confirm him in his rank; but that he may the more completely cover him with shame, and humble him by just reproaches. For Reuben is here cast down from his primogeniture; because he had polluted his father's bed by incestuous intercourse with his mother-in-law. The meaning of his words is this: " Thou, indeed, by nature the first-born, oughtest to have excelled, seeing thou art my strength, and the beginning of my manly vigour; but since thou hast flowed away like water, there is no more any ground for arrogating anything to thyself. For, from the day of thy incest, that dignity which thou receivedst on thy birth-day, from thy mother's womb, is gone and vanished away. The noun אוֹן, some translate *seed*, others *grief;* and turn the passage thus: " Thou, my strength, and the beginning of my grief or seed." They who prefer the word *grief*, assign as a reason, that children bring care and anxiety to their parents. But if this were the true meaning, there would rather have been an antithesis between strength and sorrow. Since, however, Jacob is reciting, in continuity, the declaration of the dignity which belongs to the first-born, I doubt not that he here mentions the beginning of his manhood. For as men, in a certain sense, live again in their children, the first-born is properly called the " beginning of strength." To the same point belongs what immediately follows, that he had been the excellency of dignity and of strength, until he had deservedly deprived himself of both. For Jacob places before the eyes of his son Reuben his former honour, because it was for his profit to be made thoroughly conscious whence he had fallen. So Paul says, that he set before the Corinthians the sins by which they were defiled, in order to make them ashamed. (1 Cor. vi. 5.) For whereas we are disposed

to flatter ourselves in our vices, scarcely any one of us is brought back to a sane mind, after he has fallen, unless he is touched with a sense of his vileness. Moreover, nothing is better adapted to wound us, than when a comparison is made between those favours which God bestows upon us, and the punishments we bring upon ourselves by our own fault. After Adam had been stripped of all good things, God reproaches him sharply, and not without ridicule, " Behold Adam is as one of us." What end is this designed to answer, except that Adam, reflecting with himself how far he is changed from that man, who had lately been created according to the image of God, and had been endowed with so many excellent gifts, might be confounded and fall prostrate, deploring his present misery? We see, then, that reproofs are necessary for us, in order that we may be touched to the quick by the anger of the Lord. For so it happens, not only that we become displeased with the sins of which we are now bearing the punishment, but also, that we take greater care diligently to guard those gifts of God which dwell within us, lest they perish through our negligence. They who refer the " excellency of dignity" to the priesthood, and the " excellency of power" to the kingly office, are, in my judgment, too subtle interpreters. I take the more simple meaning of the passage to be; that if Reuben had stood firmly in his own rank, the chief place of all excellency would have belonged to him.

4. *Unstable as water.* He shows that the honour which had not a good conscience for its keeper, was not firm but evanescent; and thus he rejects Reuben from the primogeniture. He declares the cause, lest Reuben should complain that he was punished when innocent: for it was also of great consequence, in this affair, that he should be convinced of his fault, lest his punishment should not be attended with profit. We now see Jacob, having laid carnal affection aside, executing the office of a prophet with vigour and magnanimity. For this judgment is not to be ascribed to anger, as if the father desired to take private vengeance of his son: but it proceeded from the Spirit of God; because Jacob kept fully in mind the burden imposed upon

him. The word עלה (*alach*) at the close of the sentence signifies to depart, or to be blown away like the ascending smoke, which is dispersed.[1] Therefore the sense is, that the excellency of Reuben, from the time that he had defiled his father's bed, had flowed away and become extinct. For to expound the expression concerning the bed, to mean that it ceased to be Jacob's conjugal bed, because Bilhah had been divorced, is too frigid.

5. *Simeon and Levi are brethren.* He condemns the massacre of the city of Shechem by his two sons Simeon and Levi, and denounces the punishment of so great a crime. Whence we learn how hateful cruelty is to God, seeing that the blood of man is precious in his sight. For it is as if he would cite to his own tribunal those two men, and would demand vengeance on them, when they thought they had already escaped. It may, however, be asked, whether pardon had not been granted to them long ago; and if God had already forgiven them, why does he recall them again to punishment? I answer, it was both privately useful to themselves, and was also necessary as an example, that this slaughter should not remain unpunished, although they might have obtain l previous forgiveness. For we have seen before, when they were admonished by their father, how far they were from that sorrow which is the commencement of true repentance; and it may be believed that afterwards they became stupified more and more, with a kind of brutish torpor, in their wickedness; or at least, that they

---

[1] The literal translation of Calvin's version is, "Thy velocity was like that of water, thou shalt not excel: because thou wentest up into thy father's couch, then thou pollutedst my bed, he has *vanished.*" This gives the patriarch's expression a different turn from that supposed by our translators; who understand the last word in the sentence to be a repetition of what had been said before, only putting it in the third person, as expressive of indignation; as if he had turned round from Reuben to his other children and said—" Yes, I declare he went up into my bed!" Another view is given in the margin of our Bible, "My couch is gone;" which means that, by this defilement, the marriage bond was broken. To this version Calvin objects at the close of the paragraph. But both these constructions seem forced. Calvin's appears the most natural. He represents Reuben as having lost all, by his criminal conduct. Honour, excellence, priority, virtue, and consequently character and influence, had all *gone up* as the dew from the face of the earth, and had *vanished away.* —*Ed.*

had not been seriously affected with bitter grief for their sin. It was also to be feared lest their posterity might become addicted to the same brutality, unless divinely impressed with horror at the deed. Therefore the Lord, partly for the purpose of humbling them, partly for that of making them an example to all ages, inflicted on them the punishment of perpetual ignominy. Moreover, by thus acting, he did not retain the punishment while remitting the guilt, as the Papists foolishly dream: but though truly and perfectly appeased, he administered a correction suitable for future times. The Papists imagine that sins are only half remitted by God; because he is not willing to absolve sinners gratuitously. But Scripture speaks far otherwise. It teaches us that God does not exact punishments which shall compensate for offences; but such as shall purge hearts from hypocrisy, and shall invite the elect—the allurements of the world being gradually shaken off—to repentance, shall stir them up to vigilant solicitude, and shall keep them under restraint by the bridle of fear and reverence. Whence it follows that nothing is more preposterous, than that the punishments which we have deserved, should be redeemed by satisfactions, as if God, after the manner of men, would have what was owing paid to him; nay, rather there is the best possible agreement between the gratuitous remission of punishments and those chastenings of the rod, which rather prevent future evils, than follow such as have been already committed.

To return to Simeon and Levi. How is it that God, by inflicting a punishment which had been long deferred, should drag them back as guilty fugitives to judgment; unless because impunity would have been hurtful to them? And yet he fulfils the office of a physician rather than of a judge, who refuses to *spare*, because he intends to *heal ;* and who not only heals two who are sick, but, by an antidote, anticipates the diseases of others, in order that they may beware of cruelty. This also is highly worthy to be remembered, that Moses, in publishing the infamy of his own people, acts as the herald of God: and not only does he proclaim a disgrace common to the whole nation, but brands with infamy, the special tribe from which he sprung. Whence it plainly appears, that he paid no respect to his own flesh and blood; nor was he to be induced, by favour or hatred, to give a false colour to anything, or to decline from historical fidelity: but, as a chosen minister and witness of the Lord, he was mindful of his calling, which was that he should declare the truth of God sincerely and confidently. A comparison is here made not only between the sons of Jacob personally; but also between the tribes which descended from them. This certainly was a specially opportune occasion for Moses to defend the nobility of his own people. But so far is he from heaping encomiums upon them, that he frankly stamps the progenitor of his own tribe with an everlasting dishonour, which should redound to his whole family. Those Lucianist dogs, who carp at the doctrine of Moses, pretend that he was a vain man who wished to acquire for himself the command over the rude common people. But had this been his project, why did he not also make provision for his own family? Those sons whom ambition would have persuaded him to endeavour to place in the highest rank, he puts aside from the honour of the priesthood, and consigns them to a lowly and common service. Who does not see that these impious calumnies have been anticipated by a divine counsel rather than by merely human prudence, and that the heirs of this great and extraordinary man were deprived of honour, for this reason, that no sinister suspicion might adhere to him? But to say nothing of his children and grandchildren, we may perceive that, by censuring his whole tribe in the person of Levi, he acted not as a man, but as an angel speaking under the impulse of the Holy Spirit, and free from all carnal affection. Moreover, in the former clause, he announces the crime: afterwards, he subjoins the punishment. The crime is, that the arms of violence are in their tabernacles; and therefore he declares, both by his tongue and in his heart, that he holds their counsel in abhorrence,[1] because, in their desire of revenge, they cut off a city with its inhabitants. Respecting the meaning of the words commentators differ. For some take the

---

[1] If this interpretation were admitted, the passage would read thus: "Simeon and Levi are brethren, instruments of cruelty are their swords."

word מכרות (*makroth*) to mean *swords*; as if Jacob had said, that their *swords* had been wickedly polluted with innocent blood. But they think more correctly, who translate the word *habitations;* as if he had said, that unjust violence dwelt among them, because they had been so sanguinary. I do not doubt that the word כבד (*chabod*) is put for the *tongue,* as in other places;[1] and thus the sense is clear, that Jacob, from his heart, so detests the crime perpetrated by his sons, that his tongue shall not give any assent to it whatever. Which he does, for this end, that they may begin to be dissatisfied with themselves, and that all others may learn to abhor perfidy combined with cruelty. *Fury,* beyond doubt, signifies a perverse and blind impulse of anger:[2] and *lust* is opposed to rational moderation;[3] because they are governed by no law. Interpreters also differ respecting the meaning of the word שׁור (*shor*).[4] Some translate it "bullock," and think that the Shechemites are allegorically denoted by it, seeing they were sufficiently robust and powerful to defend their lives, had not Simeon and Levi enervated them by fraud and perfidy. But a different exposition is far preferable, namely, that they "overturned a wall." For Jacob magnifies the atrociousness of their crime, from the fact, that they did not even spare *buildings* in their rage.

[1] In cœtu eorum non uniaris lingua mea. This is Calvin's version; and it may perhaps be vindicated by the use made of the word כבד in other passages, where the tongue is metaphorically called the *glory* of man. Yet the passage plainly admits of another and perhaps a more simple signification.—*Ed.*

[2] Quia in furore suâ, &c. Because in their fury they killed a man.—*Ed.*

[3] *Libido* is not the word used in Calvin's version, though his commentary proceeds on that supposition. His words are "voluntate suâ eradicaverunt murum." In their will, or pleasure, they uprooted a wall.—*Ed.*

[4] The marginal reading of our Bible for "they digged down a wall," is "they houghed oxen." Some translators who think that the word ought to be rendered "ox," and not "wall," regard the word *ox* as a metaphorical term for a brave and powerful man. Thus Herder, in Caunter's Poetry of the Pentateuch, gives the following version:—

"My heart was not joined in their company,
When in anger they slew a hero,
And in revenge destroyed a noble ox."

Dr. A. Clarke suggests an alteration in the word, which gives the passage another sense:

"In their anger they slew a man,
And in their pleasure they murdered a *prince.*"—*Ed.*

7. *Cursed be their anger.* What I have said must be kept in mind; namely, that we are divinely admonished by the mouth of the holy prophet, to keep at a distance from all wicked counsels. Jacob pronounces a woe upon their fury. Why is this, unless that others may learn to put a restraint upon themselves, and to be on their guard against such cruelty? However, (as I have already observed,) it will not suffice to preserve our hands pure, unless we are far removed from all association with crime. For though it may not always be in our power to repress unjust violence; yet that concealment of it is culpable, which approaches to the appearance of consent. Here even the ties of kindred, and whatever else would bias a sound judgment, must be dismissed from the mind: since we see a holy father, at the command of God, so severely thundering against his own sons. He pronounces the anger of Simeon and Levi to be so much the more hateful, because, in its commencement, it was violent, and even to the end, it was implacable.

*I will divide them in Jacob.* It may seem a strange method of proceeding, that Jacob, while designating his sons patriarchs of the Church, and calling them heirs of the divine covenant, should pronounce a malediction upon them instead of a blessing. Nevertheless it was necessary for him to begin with the chastisement, which should prepare the way for the manifestation of God's grace, as will be made to appear at the close of the chapter: but God mitigates the punishment, by giving them an honourable name in the Church, and leaving them their right unimpaired: yea, his incredible goodness unexpectedly shone forth, when that which was the punishment of Levi, became changed into the reward of the priesthood. The dispersion of the Levitical tribe had its origin in the crime of their father, lest he should congratulate himself on account of his perverse and lawless spirit of revenge. But God, who in the beginning had produced light out of darkness, found another reason why the Levites should be dispersed abroad among the people,—a reason not only free from disgrace, but highly honourable,—namely, that no corner of the land might be destitute of competent instructors. Lastly, he constituted them overseers and governors, in his name, over every part of the land, as if he would scatter everywhere the seed of eternal salvation, or would send forth ministers of his grace. Whence we conclude, how much better it was for Levi to be chastised at the time, for his own good, than to be left to perish, in consequence of present impunity in sin. And it is not to be deemed strange, that, when the land was distributed, and cities were given to the Levites, far apart from each other, this reason was suppressed,[1] and one entirely different was adduced; namely, that the Lord was their inheritance. For this, as I have lately said, is one of the miracles of God, to bring light out of darkness. Had Levi been sentenced to distant exile, he would have been most worthy of the punishment: but now, God in a measure spares him, by assigning him a wandering life in his paternal inheritance. Afterwards, the mark of infamy being removed, God sends his posterity into different parts, under the title of a distinguished embassy. In Simeon there remained a certain, though obscure trace of the curse: because a distinct territory did not fall to his sons by lot; but they were mixed with the tribe of Judah, as is stated in Joshua xix. 1. Afterwards they went to Mount Seir, having expelled the Amalekites and taken possession of their land, as it is written, 1 Chron. iv. 40-43. Here, also, we perceive the manly fortitude of holy Jacob's breast, who, though a decrepit old man and an exile, lying on his private and lowly couch, nevertheless assigns provinces to his sons, as from the lofty throne of a great king. He also does this in his own right, knowing that the covenant of God was deposited with him, by which he had been called the heir and lord of the land: and at the same time he claims for himself authority as sustaining the character of a prophet of God. For it greatly concerns us, when the word of God sounds in our ears, to apprehend by faith the thing proclaimed, as if his ministers had been commanded to carry into effect what they pronounce. Therefore it was said to Jeremiah, " See I have this day set

---

[1] As being no longer applicable to the case, because it was purely personal and belonged to Levi, only as an individual, and not to his descendents.—*Ed.*

thee over the nations and over the kingdoms, to root out, and to pull down, and to destroy, and to throw down, and to build, and to plant." (Jer. i. 10.) And the prophets are generally commanded to set their faces against the countries which they threaten, as if they were furnished with a large army to make the attack.

8. *Judah, thou art he whom thy brethren shall praise.* In the word *praise* there is an allusion to the name of Judah; for so he had been called by his mother, because his birth had given occasion for praising God. The father adduces a new etymology, because his name shall be so celebrated and illustrious among his brethren, that he should be honoured by them all equally with the first-born.[1] The *double portion*, indeed, which he recently assigned to his son Joseph, depended on the right of primogeniture: but because the *kingdom* was transferred to the tribe of Judah, Jacob properly pronounces that his name should be held worthy of praise. For the honour of Joseph was temporary; but here a stable and durable kingdom is treated of, which should be under the authority of the sons of Judah. Hence we gather, that when God would institute a perfect state of government among his people, the monarchical form was chosen by him. And whereas the appointment of a king under the law, was partly to be attributed to the will of man, and partly to the divine decree; this combination of human with divine agency must be referred to the commencement of the monarchy, which was inauspicious, because the people had tumultuously desired a king to be given them, before the proper time had arrived. Hence their unseemly haste was the cause why the kingdom was not immediately set up in the tribe of Judah, but was brought forth, as an abortive offspring, in the person of Saul. Yet at length, by the favour and in the legitimate order of God, the pre-eminence of the tribe of Judah was established in the person of David.

*Thy hand shall be in the neck of thine enemies.* In these

[1] The original privilege of the birthright, taken from Reuben, was divided between Joseph and Judah; Joseph receiving the *double portion* belonging to the eldest son; Judah the regal distinction.—*Ed.*

words he shows that Judah should not be free from enemies; but although many would give him trouble, and would endeavour to deprive him of his right, Jacob promises him victory; not that the sons of David should always prevail against their enemies, (for their ingratitude interfered with the constant and equable course of the grace of God,) but in this respect, at least, Judah had the superiority, that in his tribe stood the royal throne which God approved, and which was founded on his word. For though the kingdom of Israel was more flourishing in wealth and in number of inhabitants, yet because it was spurious, it was not the object of God's favour: nor indeed was it right, that, by its tinselled splendour, it should eclipse the glory of the Divine election which was engraven upon the tribe of Judah. In David, therefore, the force and effect of this prophecy plainly appeared; then again in Solomon; afterwards, although the kingdom was mutilated, yet was it wonderfully preserved by the hand of God; otherwise, in a short space, it would have perished a hundred times. Thus it came to pass, that the children of Judah imposed their yoke upon their enemies. Whereas defection carried away ten tribes, which would not bow their knees to the sons of David; the legitimate government was in this way disturbed, and lawless confusion introduced; yet nothing could violate the decree of God, by which the right to govern remained with the tribe of Judah.

9. *Judah is a lion's whelp.* This similitude confirms the preceding sentence, that Judah would be formidable to his enemies. Yet Jacob seems to allude to that diminution which took place, when the greater part of the people revolted to Jeroboam. For then the king of Judah began to be like a sleeping lion, for he did not shake his mane to diffuse his terror far and wide, but, as it were, laid him down in his den. Yet a certain secret power of God lay hidden under that torpor, and they who most desired his destruction, and who were most able to do him injury, did not dare to disturb him. Therefore, after Jacob has transferred the supreme authority over his brethren to Judah alone; he now adds, by way of correction, that, though his power should happen

to be diminished, he would nevertheless remain terrible to his enemies, like a lion who lies down in his lair.[1]

10. *The sceptre shall not depart.* Though this passage is obscure, it would not have been very difficult to elicit its genuine sense, if the Jews, with their accustomed malignity, had not endeavoured to envelop it in clouds. It is certain that the Messiah, who was to spring from the tribe of Judah, is here promised. But whereas they ought willingly to run to embrace him, they purposely catch at every possible subterfuge, by which they may lead themselves and others far astray in tortuous by-paths. It is no wonder, then, if the spirit of bitterness and obstinacy, and the lust of contention have so blinded them, that, in the clearest light, they should have perpetually stumbled. Christians, also, with a pious diligence to set forth the glory of Christ, have, nevertheless, betrayed some excess of fervour. For while they lay too much stress on certain words, they produce no other effect than that of giving an occasion of ridicule to the Jews, whom it is necessary to surround with firm and powerful barriers, from which they shall be unable to escape. Admonished, therefore, by such examples, let us seek, without contention, the true meaning of the passage. In the first place, we must keep in mind the true design of the Holy Spirit, which, hitherto, has not been sufficiently considered or expounded with sufficient distinctness. After he has invested the tribe of Judah with supreme authority, he immediately declares that God would show his care for the people, by preserving the state of the kingdom, till the promised felicity should attain its highest point. For the dignity of Judah is so maintained as to show that its proposed end was the common salvation of the whole people. The bless-

---

[1] Bishop Lowth's translation is this:—
"Judah is a lion's whelp.
From the prey, my son, thou art gone up—
He stoopeth down, he coucheth as a lion,
And as a lioness; who shall rouse him?"

It is to be observed that three different words are here used in the original to express the metaphor, which illustrates the character of the tribe of Judah. First, גור, (*gur*,) the lion's cub; secondly, אריה, (*aryah*,) the full-grown lion; and, thirdly, לביא, (*labi*,) the old lioness. These different terms are supposed to represent the tribe of Judah in its earliest period, in the age of David, and in subsequent times.

ing promised to the seed of Abraham (as we have before seen) could not be firm, unless it flowed from one head. Jacob now testifies the same thing, namely, that a King should come, under whom that promised happiness should be complete in all its parts. Even the Jews will not deny, that while a lower blessing rested on the tribe of Judah, the hope of a better and more excellent condition was herein held forth. They also freely grant another point, that the Messiah is the sole Author of full and solid happiness and glory. We now add a third point, which we may also do, without any opposition from them; namely, that the kingdom which began from David, was a kind of prelude, and shadowy representation of that greater grace which was delayed, and held in suspense, until the advent of the Messiah. They have indeed no relish for a spiritual kingdom; and therefore they rather imagine for themselves wealth and power, and propose to themselves sweet repose and earthly pleasures, than righteousness, and newness of life, with free forgiveness of sins. They acknowledge, nevertheless, that the felicity which was to be expected under the Messiah, was adumbrated by their ancient kingdom. I now return to the words of Jacob.

*Until Shiloh come,* he says, the sceptre, or the dominion, *shall remain in Judah.* We must first see what the word שׁילוֹה (*shiloh*) signifies. Because Jerome interprets it, "He who is to be sent," some think that the place has been fraudulently corrupted, by the letter ה substituted for the letter ח; which objection, though not firm, is plausible. That which some of the Jews suppose, namely, that it denotes the place (Shiloh) where the ark of the covenant had been long deposited, because, a little before the commencement of David's reign, it had been laid waste, is entirely destitute of reason. For Jacob does not here predict the time when David was to be appointed king; but declares that the kingdom should be established in his family, until God should fulfil what he had promised concerning the special benediction of the seed of Abraham. Besides the form of speech, "until Shiloh come," for "until Shiloh come to an end," would be harsh and constrained. Far more correctly and consistently do other interpreters take this expression to mean " his son," for among the Hebrews a son is called שׁיל, (*shil.*) They say also that ה is put in the place of the relative ו; and the greater part assent to this signification.[1] But again, the Jews dissent entirely from the meaning of the patriarch, by referring this to David. For (as I have just hinted) the origin of the kingdom in David is not here promised, but its absolute perfection in the Messiah. And truly an absurdity so gross, does not require a lengthened refutation. For what can this mean, that the kingdom should not come to an end in the tribe of Judah, till it should have been erected? Certainly the word *depart* means nothing else than to *cease*. Further, Jacob points to a continued series, when he says the scribe[2] shall not depart from between his feet. For it behoves a king so to be placed upon his throne that a lawgiver may sit between his feet. A kingdom is therefore described to us, which after it has been constituted, will not cease to exist till a more perfect state shall succeed; or, which comes to the same point; Jacob honours the future kingdom of David with this title, because it was to be the token and pledge of that happy glory which had been before ordained for the race of Abraham. In short, the kingdom which he transfers to the tribe of Judah, he declares shall be no common kingdom, because from it, at length, shall proceed the fulness of the promised benediction. But here the Jews haughtily object, that the event convicts us of error. For it appears that the kingdom by no means endured until the coming of Christ; but rather that the sceptre was broken, from the time

[1] Calvin seems to assent to this interpretation, which is by no means generally accepted. Gesenius renders שׁילה, *tranquillity*—" until tranquillity shall come;" but the more approved rendering is " the Peaceable One," or " the Pacifier." He who made peace for us, by the sacrifice of Himself.—*Ed.*

[2] Scribam recessurum negat ex pedibus. But in the text, Calvin uses the word *Legislator;* the French version translates it *Legislateur;* and the English translation is lawgiver. It is evident that Calvin had a reason for using the term *Scribe;* for the original מחקק, (*mechokaik,*) rather means a scribe or lawyer, than a *lawgiver;* and rather describes one who aids in the administration of laws, than one who frames them. In this sense, he supposes, and probably with truth, that the term is here applied. The expression " from between his feet," has been the subject of much criticism; but perhaps no view of it is so satisfactory as that maintained by Calvin.—*Ed.*

that the people were carried into captivity. But if they give credit to the prophecies, I wish, before I solve their objection, that they would tell me in what manner Jacob here assigns the kingdom to his son Judah. For we know, that when it had scarcely become his fixed possession, it was suddenly rent asunder, and nearly its whole power was possessed by the tribe of Ephraim. Has God, according to these men, here promised, by the mouth of Jacob, some evanescent kingdom? If they reply, the sceptre was not then broken, though Rehoboam was deprived of a great part of his people; they can by no means escape by this cavil; because the authority of Judah is expressly extended over all the tribes, by these words, " Thy mother's sons shall bow their knee before thee." They bring, therefore, nothing against *us*, which we cannot immediately, in turn, retort upon *themselves*.

Yet I confess the question is not yet solved; but I wished to premise this, in order that the Jews, laying aside their disposition to calumniate, may learn calmly to examine the matter itself, with us. Christians are commonly wont to connect perpetual government with the tribe of Judah, in the following manner. When the people returned from banishment, they say, that, in the place of the royal sceptre, was the government which lasted to the time of the Maccabees. That afterwards, a third mode of government succeeded, because the chief power of judging rested with the SEVENTY, who, it appears by history, were chosen out of the regal race. Now, so far was this authority of the royal race from having fallen into decay, that Herod, having been cited before it, with difficulty escaped capital punishment, because he contumaciously withdrew from it. Our commentators, therefore, conclude that, although the royal majesty did not shine brightly from David until Christ, yet some pre-eminence remained in the tribe of Judah, and thus the oracle was fulfilled. Although these things are true, still more skill must be used in rightly discussing this passage. And, in the first place, it must be kept in mind, that the tribe of Judah was already constituted chief among the rest, as pre-eminent in dignity, though it had not yet obtained the dominion. And, truly, Moses elsewhere testifies, that supremacy was voluntarily conceded to it by the remaining tribes, from the time that the people were redeemed out of Egypt. In the second place, we must remember, that a more illustrious example of this dignity was set forth in that kingdom which God had commenced in David. And although defection followed soon after, so that but a small portion of authority remained in the tribe of Judah; yet the right divinely conferred upon it, could by no means be taken away. Therefore, at the time when the kingdom of Israel was replenished with abundant opulence, and was swelling with lofty pride, it was said, that the lamp of the Lord was lighted in Jerusalem. Let us proceed further: when Ezekiel predicts the destruction of the kingdom, (chap. xxi. 26,) he clearly shows how the sceptre was to be preserved by the Lord, until it should come into the hands of Christ: "Remove the diadem, and take off the crown; this shall not be the same: I will overturn, overturn, overturn it, until he come whose right it is." It may seem at first sight that the prophecy of Jacob had failed when the tribe of Judah was stripped of its royal ornament. But we conclude hence, that God was not bound always to exhibit the visible glory of the kingdom on high. Otherwise, those other promises which predict the restoration of the throne, which was cast down and broken, were false. Behold the days come in which I will "raise up the tabernacle of David that is fallen, and close up the breaches thereof, and I will raise up his ruins." (Amos ix. 11.) It would be absurd, however, to cite more passages, seeing this doctrine occurs frequently in the prophets. Whence we infer, that the kingdom was not so confirmed as always to shine with equal brightness; but that, though, for a time, it might lie fallen and defaced, it should afterwards recover its lost splendour. The prophets, indeed, seem to make the return from the Babylonian exile the termination of that ruin; but since they predict the restoration of the kingdom no otherwise than they do that of the temple and the priesthood, it is necessary that the whole period, from that liberation to the advent of Christ, should be comprehended. The crown, therefore, was cast down, not for one day only, or from one single head, but for a long time, and in various methods, until God placed it on Christ, his own lawful king. And truly Isaiah describes the origin of Christ, as being very remote from all regal splendour: " There shall come forth a rod out of the stem of Jesse, and a branch shall grow out of his roots." (Isaiah xi. 1.) Why does he mention Jesse rather than David, except because Messiah was about to proceed from the rustic hut of a private man, rather than from a splendid palace? Why from a tree cut down, having nothing left but the root and the trunk, except because the majesty of the kingdom was to be almost trodden under foot till the manifestation of Christ? If any one object, that the words of Jacob seem to have a different signification; I answer, that whatever God has promised at any time concerning the external condition of the Church, was so to be restricted, that, in the mean time, he might execute his judgments in punishing men, and might try the faith of his own people. It was, indeed, no light trial, that the tribe of Judah, in its third successor to the throne, should be deprived of the greater portion of the kingdom. Even a still more severe trial followed, when the sons of the king were put to death in the sight of their father, when he, with his eyes thrust out, was dragged to Babylon, and the whole royal family was at length given over to slavery and captivity. But this was the most grievous trial of all; that when the people returned to their own land, they could in no way perceive the accomplishment of their hope, but were compelled to lie in sorrowful dejection. Nevertheless, even then, the saints, contemplating, with the eyes of faith, the sceptre hidden under the earth, did not fail, or become broken in spirit, so as to desist from their course. I shall, perhaps, seem to grant too much to the Jews, because I do not assign what they call a real dominion, in uninterrupted succession, to the tribe of Judah. For our interpreters, to prove that the Jews are still kept bound by a foolish expectation of the Messiah, insist on this point, that the dominion of which Jacob had prophesied, ceased from the time of Herod; as if, indeed, they had not been tributaries five hundred years previously; as if, also, the dignity of the royal race had not been extinct as long as the tyranny of Antiochus prevailed; as if, lastly, the Asmonean race had not usurped to itself both the rank and power of princes, until the Jews became subject to the Romans. And that is not a sufficient solution which is proposed; namely, that either the regal dominion, or some lower kind of government, are disjunctively promised; and that from the time when the kingdom was destroyed, the scribes remained in authority. For I, in order to mark the distinction between a lawful government and tyranny, acknowledge that counsellors were joined with the king, who should administer public affairs rightly and in order. Whereas some of the Jews explain, that the *right* of government was given to the tribe of Judah, because it was unlawful for it to be transferred elsewhere, but that it was not necessary that the *glory* of the crown once given should be perpetuated, I deem it right to subscribe in part to this opinion. I say, in part, because the Jews gain nothing by this cavil, who, in order to support their fiction of a Messiah yet to come, postpone that subversion of the regal dignity which, in fact, long ago occurred.[1] For we must keep in memory what I have said before, that while Jacob wished to sustain the minds of his descendents until the coming of the Messiah; lest they should faint through the weariness of long delay, he set before them an example in their temporal kingdom: as if he had said, that there was no reason why the Israelites, when the kingdom of David fell, should allow their hope to waver; seeing that no other change should follow, which could answer to the blessing promised by God, until the Redeemer should appear. That the nation was grievously harassed, and was under servile oppression some years before the coming of Christ happened, through the wonderful

---

[1] Quia nihil hoc cavilla proficiunt Judæi, ad figmentum venturi sui Messiæ trahentes vetustum regni excidium. Literally translated, the sense of the passage would not be obvious to the English reader. It is hoped that the true meaning of the passage is given above. The original, however, is given, that the learned reader may form his own judgment. It is well known that modern Jews regard their present depression as a proof that the Messiah has not yet come, and therefore they draw out (trahentes) or postpone the execution of God's threatened judgments, which we regard as having taken place under Titus and the Romans, to a period still future. This seems to be Calvin's meaning.—*Ed.*

counsel of God, in order that they might be urged by continual chastisements to wish for redemption. Meanwhile, it was necessary that some collective body of the nation should remain, in which the promise might receive its fulfilment. But now, when, through nearly fifteen centuries, they have been scattered and banished from their country, having no polity, by what pretext can they fancy, from the prophecy of Jacob, that a Redeemer will come to them? Truly, as I would not willingly glory over their calamity; so, unless they, being subdued by it, open their eyes, I freely pronounce that they are worthy to perish a thousand times without remedy. It was also a most suitable method for retaining them in the faith, that the Lord would have the sons of Jacob turn their eyes upon one particular tribe, that they might not seek salvation elsewhere; and that no vague imagination might mislead them. For which end, also, the election of this family is celebrated, when it is frequently compared with, and preferred to Ephraim and the rest, in the Psalms. To us, also, it is not less useful, for the confirmation of our faith, to know that Christ had been not only promised, but that his origin had been pointed out, as with a finger, two thousand years before he appeared.[1]

*And unto him shall the gathering of the people be.* Here truly he declares that Christ should be a king, not over one people only, but that under his authority various nations shall be gathered, that they might coalesce together. I know, indeed, that the word rendered "gathering" is differently expounded by different commentators; but they who derive it from the root קהה, to make it signify the *weakening* of the people, rashly and absurdly misapply what is said of the

---

[1] On this passage, which has given so much trouble to commentators, and which Calvin has considered at such length, it may be observed, that the term rendered *sceptre* means also *rod*, and sometimes is translated *tribe;* perhaps because each of the twelve tribes had its *rod* laid up in the tabernacle and temple. Hence it may be inferred that the expression, "The sceptre shall not depart from Judah," means that Judah alone should continue in its integrity, as a tribe, till the coming of the Messiah. This renders it unnecessary to attempt any proof of the retention of regal power and authority in the tribe. See Ainsworth and Bush *in loc.* The reader may also refer to an elaborate investigation of the subject in Rivetus, Exercitations 178 and 179.—*Ed.*

saving dominion of Christ, to the sanguinary pride with which they puffed up. If the word *obedience* is preferred, (as it is by others,) the sense will remain the same with that which I have followed. For this is the mode in which the gathering together will be effected; namely, that they who before were carried away to different objects of pursuit, will consent together in obedience to one common Head. Now, although Jacob had previously called the tribes about to spring from him by the name of *peoples*, for the sake of amplification, yet this gathering is of still wider extent. For, whereas he had included the whole body of the nation by their families, when he spoke of the ordinary dominion of Judah, he now extends the boundaries of a new king : as if he would say, "There shall be kings of the tribe of Judah, who shall be pre-eminent among their brethren, and to whom the sons of the same mother shall bow down : but at length He shall follow in succession, who shall subject other *peoples* unto himself." But this, we know, is fulfilled in Christ; to whom was promised the inheritance of the world; under whose yoke the nations are brought; and at whose will they, who before were scattered, are gathered together. Moreover, a memorable testimony is here borne to the vocation of the Gentiles, because they were to be introduced into the joint participation of the covenant, in order that they might become one people with the natural descendents of Abraham, under one Head.

11. *Binding his fole unto the vine, and his ass's colt*, &c. He now speaks of the situation of the territory which fell by lot to the sons of Judah; and intimates, that so great would be the abundance of vines there, that they would everywhere present themselves as readily as brambles, or unfruitful shrubs, in other places. For since asses are wont to be bound to the hedges, he here reduces vines to this contemptible use. The hyperbolical forms of speech which follow are to be applied to the same purpose; namely, that Judah shall wash his garments in wine, and his eyes be red therewith. He means that the abundance of wine shall be so great, that it may be poured out to wash with, like water, at no great expense; but that, by constant copious drinking, the eyes would contract redness. But it seems by no means

proper, that a profuse intemperance or extravagance should be accounted a blessing. I answer, although fertility and affluence are here described, still the abuse of them is not sanctioned. If the Lord deals very bountifully with us, yet he frequently prescribes the rule of using his gifts with purity and frugality, lest they should stimulate the incontinence of the flesh. But in this place Jacob, omitting to state what is lawful, extols that abundance which would suffice for luxury, and even for vicious and perverse excesses, unless the sons of Judah should voluntarily use self-government. I abstain from those allegories which to some appear plausible; because, as I said at the beginning of the chapter, I do not choose to sport with such great mysteries of God. To these lofty speculators the partition of the land which God prescribed, for the purpose of accrediting his servant Moses, seems a mean and abject thing. But unless our ingratitude has attained a senseless stupor, we ought to be wholly transported with admiration at the thought, that Moses, who had never seen the land of Canaan, should treat of its separate parts as correctly as he could have done, of a few acres cultivated by his own hand. Now, supposing he had heard a general report of the existence of vines in the land; yet he could not have assigned to Judah abundant vineyards, nor could he have assigned to him rich pastures, by saying that his teeth should be white with drinking milk, unless he had been guided by the Spirit.

13. *Zebulun shall dwell at the haven of the sea.* Although this blessing contains nothing rare or precious, (as neither do some of those which follow,) yet we ought to deem this fact as sufficiently worthy of notice, that it was just as if God was stretching out his hand from heaven, for the deliverance of the children of Israel, and for the purpose of distributing to each his own dwelling-place. Before mention is made of the lot itself, a maritime region is given to the tribe of Zebulun, which it obtained by lot two hundred years afterwards. And we know of how great importance that hereditary gift was, which, like an earnest, rendered the adoption of the ancient people secure. Therefore, by this prophecy, not only one tribe, but the whole people, ought to have been encouraged

to lay hold, with alacrity, of the offered blessing which was certainly in store for them. But it is said that the portion of Zebulun should not only be on the sea-shore, but should also have havens; for Jacob joins its boundary with the country of Zidon; in which tract, we know, there were commodious and noble havens. For God, by this prophecy, would not only excite the sons of Zebulun more strenuously to prepare themselves to enter upon the land; but would also assure them, when they obtained possession of the desired portion, that it was the home which had been distinctly proposed and ordained for them by the will of God.

14. *Issachar.* Here mention is partly made of the inheritance, and an indication is partly given of the future condition of this tribe. Although he is called a *bony* ass on account of his strength,[1] which would enable him to endure labours, especially such as were rustic, yet at the same time his sloth is indicated: for it is added a little afterwards, that he should be of servile disposition. Wherefore the meaning is, that the sons of Issachar, though possessed of strength, were yet quiet rather than courageous, and were as ready to bear the burden of servitude as mules are to submit their backs to the packsaddle and the load. The reason given is, that, being content with their fertile and pleasant country, they do not refuse to pay tribute to their neighbours, provided they may enjoy repose. And although this submissiveness is not publicly mentioned either to their praise or their condemnation, it is yet probable that their indolence is censured, because their want of energy hindered them from remaining in possession of that liberty which had been divinely granted unto them.

16. *Dan shall judge his people.* In the word *judge* there is an allusion to his name: for since, among the Hebrews, דין signifies to judge, Rachel, when she returned thanks to God, gave this name to the son born to her by her handmaid, as if God had been the vindicator of her cause and right. Jacob now gives a new turn to the meaning of the name; namely, that the sons of Dan shall have no mean part in the government of the people. For the Jews foolishly restrict it to Samson, because he alone presided over the whole

[1] Asinus osseus.

people, whereas the language rather applies to the perpetual condition of the tribe. Jacob therefore means, that though Dan was born from a concubine, he shall still be one of the judges of Israel : because not only shall his offspring possess a share of the government and command, in the common polity, so that this tribe may constitute one head ; but it shall be appointed the bearer of a standard to lead the fourth division of the camp of Israel.[1] In the second place, his subtle disposition is described. For Jacob compares this people to serpents, who rise out of their lurking-places, by stealth, against the unwary whom they wish to injure. The sense then is, that he shall not be so courageous as earnestly and boldly to engage in open conflict ; but that he will fight with cunning, and will make use of snares. Yet, in the meantime, he shows that he will be superior to his enemies, whom he does not dare to approach with collected forces, just as serpents who, by their secret bite, cast down the horse and his rider. In this place also no judgment is expressly passed, whether this subtlety of Dan is to be deemed worthy of praise or of censure : but conjecture rather inclines us to place it among his faults, or at least his disadvantages, that instead of opposing himself in open conflict with his enemies, he will fight them only with secret frauds.[2]

18. *I have waited for thy salvation, O Lord.* It may be asked, in the first place, what occasion induced the holy man to break the connection of his discourse, and suddenly to burst forth in this expression ; for whereas he had recently predicted the coming of the Messiah, the mention of salvation would have been more appropriate in that place. I think, indeed, that when he perceived, as from a lofty watch-

---

[1] See Numbers ii., where the order of the tribes in their encampment is given. Judah had the standard for the three tribes on the east, Reuben for the three tribes on the south, Ephraim for the three tribes on the west, and Dan for the remaining three tribes on the north of the tabernacle.—*Ed.*

[2] The word שְׁפִיפֹן, (*sheppiphon,*) translated " adder," occurs only in this place. It is supposed by Bochart to be the *cerastes,* " a serpent so called," says Calmet, " because it has horns on its forehead." Dr. A. Clarke gives this translation :—

" Dan shall be a serpent on the way,
A cerastes upon the track,
Biting the heels of the horse,
And his rider shall fall backwards."—*Ed.*

tower, the condition of his offspring continually exposed to various changes, and even to be tossed by storms which would almost overwhelm them, he was moved with solicitude and fear; for he had not so put off all paternal affection, as to be entirely without care for those who were of his own blood. He, therefore, foreseeing many troubles, many dangers, many assaults, and even many slaughters, which threatened his seed with as many destructions, could not but condole with them, and, as a man, be troubled at the sight. But in order that he might rise against every kind of temptation with victorious constancy of mind, he commits himself unto the Lord, who had promised that he would be the guardian of his people. Unless this circumstance be observed, I do not see why Jacob exclaims here, rather than at the beginning or the end of his discourse, that he waited for the salvation of the Lord. But when this sad confusion of things presented itself to him, which was not only sufficiently violent to shake his faith, but was more than sufficiently burdensome entirely to overwhelm his mind, his best remedy was to oppose to it this shield. I doubt not also, that he would advise his sons to rise with him to the exercise of the same confidence. Moreover, because he could not be the author of his own salvation, it was necessary for him to repose upon the promise of God. In the same manner, also, must we, at this day, hope for the salvation of the Church: for although it seems to be tossed on a turbulent sea, and almost sunk in the waves, and though still greater storms are to be feared in future; yet amidst manifold destructions, salvation is to be hoped for, in that deliverance which the Lord has promised. It is even possible that Jacob, foreseeing by the Spirit, how great would be the ingratitude, perfidy, and wickedness of his posterity, by which the grace of God might be smothered, was contending against these temptations. But although he expected salvation not for himself alone, but for all his posterity, this, however, deserves to be specially noted, that he exhibits the life-giving covenant of God to many generations, so as to prove his own confidence that, after his death, God would be faithful to his promise. Whence also it follows, that, with his last breath, and as if in the midst of death, he laid hold on eternal life. But if he, amidst obscure shadows, relying on a redemption seen afar off, boldly went forth to meet death; what ought we to do, on whom the clear day has shined; or what excuse remains for us, if our minds fail amidst similar agitations?[1]

19. *Gad, a troop.* Jacob also makes allusion to the name of Gad. He had been so called, because Jacob had obtained a numerous offspring by his mother Leah. His father now admonishes him, that though his name implied a *multitude*, he should yet have to do with a great number of enemies, by whom, for a time, he would be oppressed: and he predicts this event, not that his posterity might confide in their own strength, and become proud; but that they might prepare themselves to endure the suffering by which the Lord intended, and now decreed to humble them. Yet, as he here exhorts them to patient endurance, so he presently raises and animates them by the superadded consolation, that, at length, they should emerge from oppression, and should triumph over those enemies by whom they had been vanquished and routed; but this only at the last. Moreover, this prophecy may be applied to the whole Church, which is assailed not for one day only, but is perpetually crushed by fresh attacks, until at length God shall exalt it to honour.

20. *Out of Asher.* The inheritance of Asher is but just alluded to, which he declares shall be fruitful in the best and finest wheat, so that it shall need no foreign supply of food, having abundance at home. By *royal dainties*, he means such as are exquisite. Should any one object, that it is no great thing to be fed with nutritious and pleasant bread; I answer; we must consider the end designed; namely, that they

---

[1] Jewish commentators suppose the patriarch's exclamation to have been suggested in this place, by a prospective view of the temporal deliverances wrought for Israel, by warriors of the tribe of Dan. So the Chaldee Paraphrast represents him as saying, "I look not for the salvation of Gideon, because it is a temporal salvation; nor for the salvation of Sampson the son of Manoah, because it is transitory; but I look for the redemption of Christ the Son of David, who is to come to call to himself the children, whose salvation my soul desireth." *See Bush and Dr. A. Clarke.* Yet there is something affecting in the thought, that the exclamation might be a sudden burst of holy desire for the immediate fruition of the glory which the dying patriarch now saw so near at hand.— *Ed.*

might hereby know that they were fed by the paternal care of God.

21. *Naphtali.* Some think that in the tribe of Naphtali fleetness is commended; I rather approve another meaning, namely, that it will guard and defend itself by eloquence and suavity of words, rather than by force of arms. It is, however, no despicable virtue to soothe ferocious minds, and to appease excited anger, by bland and gentle discourse; or if any offence has been stirred up, to allay it by a similar artifice. He therefore assigns this praise to the sons of Naphtali, that they shall rather study to fortify themselves by humanity, by sweet words, and by the arts of peace, than by the defence of arms. He compares them to a hind let loose, which having been taken in hunting, is not put to death, but is rather cherished with delicacies.[1]

22. *Joseph is a fruitful bough.* Others translate it, "a son of honour,"[2] and both are suitable; but I rather incline to the former sense, because it seems to me that it refers to the name Joseph, by which *addition* or *increase* is signified; although I have no objection to the similitude taken from a tree, which, being planted near a fountain, draws from the watered earth the moisture and sap by which it grows the faster. The sum of the figure is, that he is born to grow like a tree situated near a fountain, so that, by its beauty and lofty stature, it may surmount the obstacles around it. For I do not interpret the words which follow to mean that there will be an assemblage of *virgins* upon the walls, whom

---

[1] As the word אילה, rendered *hind*, sometimes means a tree, it is supposed by some, that it should be so translated here. Bochart suggests this translation:—

"Naphtali is a spreading oak,
Producing beautiful branches."

Dr. A. Clarke strenuously defends this version, and says, "perhaps no man who understands the genius of the Hebrew language will attempt to dispute its propriety." Yet perhaps the received translation is not to be so easily disposed of. It may be granted that Bochart's figure is more beautiful; but it will be difficult to show that his translation is equally literal and correct. Caunter suggests another rendering:—

"Naphtali is a deer roaming at liberty,
He shooteth forth noble branches,"—or antlers.—*Ed.*

[2] "Filium decoris." The original is בן פרת, (*Ben porath*,) literally, "the son of fruitfulness." The name of Joseph's son, Ephraim, is derived from this word.—*Ed.*

the sight of the tree shall have attracted; but, by a continued metaphor, I suppose the tender and smaller branches to be called daughters.[1] And they are said "to run over the wall" when they spread themselves far and wide. Besides, Jacob's discourse does not relate simply to the whole tribe, nor is it a mere prophecy of future times; but the personal history of Joseph is blended with that of his descendents. Thus some things are peculiar to himself, and others belong to the two tribes of Ephraim and Manasseh. So when Joseph is said to have been "grieved," this is wont to be referred especially to himself. And whereas Jacob has compared him to a tree; so he calls both his brethren and Potiphar, with his wife, "archers."[2] Afterwards, however, he changes the figure by making Joseph himself like a strenuous archer, whose bow abides in strength, and whose arms are not relaxed, nor have lost, in any degree, their vigour; by which expressions he predicts the invincible fortitude of Joseph, because he has yielded to no blows however hard and severe. At the same time we are taught that he stood, not by the power of his own arm, but as being strengthened by the hand of God, whom he distinguishes by the peculiar title of "the mighty God of Jacob," because he designed his power to be chiefly conspicuous, and to shine most brightly in the Church. Meanwhile, he declares that the help by which Joseph was assisted, arose from hence, that God had chosen that family for himself. For the holy fathers were extremely solicitous that the gratuitous covenant of God should be remembered by themselves and by their children, whenever any benefit was granted unto them. And truly it is a mark of shameful negligence, not to inquire from what fountain we drink water. In the mean time he tacitly censures the impious and ungodly fury of his ten sons; because, by attempting the murder of their brother, they, like the giants, had carried on

[1] בנות, (*Banoth*,) literally, "the *daughters* went over the wall." But Calvin, with our translators, wisely interprets the expression as a poetical one, meaning the branches, (which are the daughters of the tree,) according to a very usual phraseology of the Hebrew Scriptures.— *Ed.*

[2] Archers, literally, "Lords of the arrows."
"The archers shot at him with poisoned arrows,
They have pursued him with hatred."
*Waterland in Caunter's Poetry of the Pentateuch*, vol. i., p. 223.—*Ed.*

war against God. He also admonishes them for the future, that they should rather choose to be protected by the guardianship of God, than to make him their enemy, seeing that he is alike willing to give help to all. And hence arises a consideration consolatory to all the pious, when they hear that the power of God resides in the midst of the Church, if they do but glory in him alone; as the Psalm teaches, "Some trust in chariots, and some in horses; but we will invoke the name of the Lord our God." (Psal. xx. 7.) The sons of Jacob, therefore, must take care lest they, by confiding in their own strength, precipitate themselves into ruin; but must rather bear themselves nobly and triumphantly in the Lord.

What follows admits of various interpretations. Some translate it, "From thence is the shepherd, the stone of Israel;" as if Jacob would say, that Joseph had been the nourisher and rock, or stay of his house. Others read, "the shepherd of the stone," in the genitive case, which I approve, except that they mistake the sense, by taking "stone" to mean family. I refer it to God, who assigned the office of shepherd to his servant Joseph, in the manner in which any one uses the service of a hireling to feed his flock. For whence did it arise that he nourished his own people, except that he was the dispenser of the Divine beneficence? Moreover, under this type, the image of Christ is depicted to us, who, before he should come forth as the conqueror of death and the author of life, was set as a mark of contradiction, (Heb. xii. 3,) against whom all cast their darts; as now also, after his example, the Church also must be transfixed with many arrows, that she may be kept by the wonderful help of God. Moreover, lest the brethren should maliciously envy Joseph, Jacob sets his victory in an amiable point of view to them, by saying that he had been liberated in order that he might become their nourisher or shepherd.

25. *Even by the God of thy father.* Again, he more fully affirms that Joseph had been delivered from death, and exalted to such great dignity, not by his own industry, but by the favour of God: and there is not the least doubt that he commends to all the pious, the mere goodness of God, lest

they should arrogate anything to themselves, whether they may have escaped from dangers, or whether they may have risen to any rank of honour. *By the God of thy father.* In designating God by this title, he again traces whatever good Joseph has received, to the covenant, and to the fountain of gratuitous adoption; as if he had said, " Whereas thou hast proved the paternal care of God in helping thee, I desire that thou wouldst ascribe this to the covenant which God has made with me." Meanwhile, (as we have said before,) he separates from all fictitious idols the God whom he transmits to his descendents to worship.

After he has declared, that Joseph should be blessed in every way, both as it respects his own life, and the number and preservation of his posterity; he affirms that the effect of this benediction is near and almost present, by saying, that he blessed Joseph more efficaciously than he himself had been blessed by his fathers. For although, from the beginning, God had been true to his promises, yet he frequently postponed the effect of them, as if he had been feeding Abraham, Isaac, and Jacob with nothing but words. For, to what extent were the patriarchs multiplied in Egypt? Where was that immense seed which should equal the sands of the sea shore and the stars of heaven? Therefore, not without reason, Jacob declares that the full time had arrived in which the result of his benediction, which had lain concealed, should emerge as from the deep. Now, this comparison ought to inspire us with much greater alacrity at the present time; for the abundant riches of the grace of God which have flowed to us in Christ, exceeds a hundredfold, any blessings which Joseph received and felt.

What is added respecting *the utmost bound of the everlasting hills,* some wish to refer to distance of place, some to perpetuity of time. Both senses suit very well; either that the felicity of Joseph should diffuse itself far and wide to the farthest mountains of the world; or that it should endure as long as the everlasting hills, which are the firmest portions of the earth, shall stand. The more certain and genuine sense, however, is to be gathered from the other passage, where Moses repeats this benediction; namely, that the fertility of the land would extend to the tops of the mountains; and these mountains are called perpetual, because they are most celebrated. He also declares that this blessing should be *upon his head*, lest Joseph might think that his good wishes were scattered to the winds; for by this word he intends to show, if I may so speak, that the blessing was substantial. At length he calls Joseph נזיר, (*nazir*,) among his brethren, either because he was their *crown*, on account of the common glory which redounds from him to them all, or because, on account of the dignity by which he excels, he was *separated* from them all.[1] It may be understood in both senses. Yet we must know that this excellency was temporal, because Joseph, together with the others, was required to take his proper place, and to submit himself to the sceptre of Judah.

27. *Benjamin shall ravin as a wolf.* Some of the Jews think the Benjamites are here condemned; because, when they had suffered lusts to prevail, like lawless robbers, among them, they were at length cut down and almost destroyed by a terrible slaughter, for having defiled the Levite's wife. Others regard it as an honourable encomium, by which Saul, or Mordecai was adorned, who were both of the tribe of Benjamin. The interpreters of our own age most inaptly apply it to the apostle Paul, who was changed from a wolf into a preacher of the Gospel. Nothing seems to me more probable than that the disposition and habits of the whole tribe is here delineated; namely, that they would live by plunder. *In the morning they would seize and devour the prey, in the evening they would divide the spoil;* by which words he describes their diligence in plundering.

28. *All these are the twelve tribes of Israel.* Moses would teach us by these words, that his predictions did not apply only to the sons of Jacob, but extended to their whole race. We have, indeed, shown already, with sufficient clearness,

---

[1] " The blessings of thy father have prevailed over the blessings of the eternal mountains,
And the desirable things of the everlasting hills.
These shall be on the head of Joseph,
And on his crown who was separated from his brethren."
*Dr. A. Clarke.*

that the expressions relate not to their persons only; but this verse was to be added, in order that the readers might more clearly perceive the celestial majesty of the Spirit. Jacob beholds his twelve sons. Let us grant that, at that time, the number of his offspring, down to his great grandchildren, had increased a hundredfold. He does not, however, merely declare what is to be the condition of six hundred or a thousand men, but subjects regions and nations to his sentence; nor does he put himself rashly forward, since it is found afterwards, by the event, that God had certainly made known to him, what he had himself decreed to execute. Moreover, seeing that Jacob beheld, with the eyes of faith, things which were not only very remote, but altogether hidden from human sense; woe be unto our depravity, if we shut our eyes against the very accomplishment of the prediction in which the truth conspicuously appears.

But it may seem little consonant to reason, that Jacob is said to have blessed his posterity. For, in deposing Reuben from the primogeniture, he pronounced nothing joyous or prosperous respecting him; he also declared his abhorrence of Simeon and Levi. It cannot be alleged that there is an *antiphrasis* in the word of benediction, as if it were used in a sense contrary to what is usual; because it plainly appears to be applied by Moses in a *good*, and not an *evil* sense. I therefore reconcile these things with each other thus; that the temporal punishments with which Jacob mildly and paternally corrected his sons, would not subvert the covenant of grace on which the benediction was founded; but rather, by obliterating their stains, would restore them to the original degree of honour from which they had fallen, so that, at least, they should be patriarchs among the people of God. And the Lord daily proves, in his own people, that the punishments he lays upon them, although they occasion shame and disgrace, are so far from opposing their happiness, that they rather promote it. Unless they were purified in this manner, it were to be feared lest they should become more and more hardened in their vices, and lest the hidden *virus* should produce corruption, which at length would penetrate to the vitals. We see how freely the flesh indulges it-

self, even when God rouses us by the tokens of his anger.
What then do we suppose would take place if he should always connive at transgression? But when we, after having been reproved for our sins, repent, this result not only absorbs the curse which was felt at the beginning, but also proves that the Lord blesses us more by punishing us, than he would have done by sparing us. Hence it follows, that diseases, poverty, famine, nakedness, and even death itself, so far as they promote our salvation, may deservedly be reckoned blessings, as if their very nature were changed; just as the letting of blood may be not less conducive to health than food. When it is added at the close, *every one according to his blessing*, Moses again affirms, that Jacob not only implored a blessing on his sons, from a paternal desire for their welfare, but that he pronounced what God had put into his mouth; because at length the event proved that the prophecies were efficacious.

29. *And he charged them.* We have seen before, that Jacob especially commanded his son Joseph to take care that his body should be buried in the land of Canaan. Moses now repeats that the same command was given to all his sons, in order that they might go to that country with one consent; and might mutually assist each other in performing this office. We have stated elsewhere why he made such a point of conscience of his sepulture; which we must always remember, lest the example of the holy man should be drawn injudiciously into a precedent for superstition. Truly he did not wish to be carried into the land of Canaan, as if he would be the nearer heaven for being buried there: but that, being dead, he might claim possession of a land which he had held during his life, only by a precarious tenure. Not that any advantage would hence accrue to him privately, seeing he had already fulfilled his course; but because it was profitable that the memory of the promise should be renewed, by this symbol, among his surviving sons, in order that they might aspire to it. Meanwhile, we gather that his mind did not cleave to the earth; because, unless he had been an heir of heaven, he would never have hoped that God, for the sake of one who was dead, would

prove so bountiful towards his children. Now, to give the greater weight to his command, Jacob declares that this thing had not come first into his own mind, but that he had been thus taught by his forefathers. " Abraham," he says, " bought that sepulchre for himself and his family: hitherto, we have sacredly kept the law delivered to us by him. You must therefore take care not to violate it, in order that after my death also, some token of the favour of God may continue with us."

33. *He gathered up his feet.* The expression is not superfluous: because Moses wished thereby to describe the placid death of the holy man: as if he had said, that the aged saint gave directions respecting the disposal of his body, as easily as healthy and vigorous men are wont to compose themselves to sleep. And truly a wonderful vigour and presence of mind was necessary for him, when, while death was in his countenance, he thus courageously fulfilled the prophetic office enjoined upon him. And it is not to be doubted that such efficacy of the Holy Spirit manifested itself in him, as served to produce, in his sons, confidence in, and reverence for his prophecies. At the same time, however, it is proper to observe, that it is the effect of a good conscience, to be able to depart out of the world without terror. For since death is by nature formidable, wonderful torments agitate the wicked, when they perceive that they are summoned to the tribunal of God. Moreover, in order that a good conscience may lead us peacefully and quietly to the grave, it is necessary to rely upon the resurrection of Christ; for we then go willingly to God, when we have confidence respecting a better life. We shall not deem it grievous to leave this failing tabernacle, when we reflect on the everlasting abode which is prepared for us.

## CHAPTER L.

1. And Joseph fell upon his father's face, and wept upon him, and kissed him.

2. And Joseph commanded his servants the physicians to embalm

1. Et jactavit se Joseph super faciem patris sui, et flevit super eum, et osculatus est eum.

2. Et præcepit Joseph servis suis medicis, ut aromatibus condirent

his father: and the physicians embalmed Israel.

3. And forty days were fulfilled for him; for so are fulfilled the days of those which are embalmed: and the Egyptians mourned for him threescore and ten days.

4. And when the days of his mourning were past, Joseph spake unto the house of Pharaoh, saying, If now I have found grace in your eyes, speak, I pray you, in the ears of Pharaoh, saying,

5. My father made me swear, saying, Lo, I die: in my grave which I have digged for me in the land of Canaan, there shalt thou bury me. Now therefore let me go up, I pray thee, and bury my father, and I will come again.

6. And Pharaoh said, Go up and bury thy father, according as he made thee swear.

7. And Joseph went up to bury his father: and with him went up all the servants of Pharaoh, the elders of his house, and all the elders of the land of Egypt,

8. And all the house of Joseph, and his brethren, and his father's house: only their little ones, and their flocks, and their herds, they left in the land of Goshen.

9. And there went up with him both chariots and horsemen: and it was a very great company.

10. And they came to the threshing-floor of Atad, which *is* beyond Jordan; and there they mourned with a great and very sore lamentation: and he made a mourning for his father seven days.

11. And when the inhabitants of the land, the Canaanites, saw the mourning in the floor of Atad, they said, This *is* a grievous mourning to the Egyptians: wherefore the name of it was called Abel-mizraim, which *is* beyond Jordan.

12. And his sons did unto him according as he commanded them:

13. For his sons carried him into the land of Canaan, and buried him in the cave of the field of Machpelah,

patrem suum, et aromatibus condiverunt medici ipsum Israel.

3. Completi autem sunt ei quadraginta dies: sic enim complentur dies *eorum* qui condiuntur aromatibus: et fleverunt eum Ægyptii septuaginta diebus.

4. Transierunt itaque dies luctus ejus: et loquutus est Joseph ad domum Pharaonis dicendo, Si quæso inveni gratiam in oculis vestris, loquimini quæso in auribus Pharaonis, dicendo,

5. Pater meus adjuravit me, dicendo, Ecce, ego morior: in sepulcro meo, quod fodi mihi in terra Chenaan, sepelies me: nunc igitur ascendam, obsecro, et sepeliam patrem meum, et revertar.

6. Et dixit Pharao, Ascende, et sepeli patrem tuum, quemadmodum adjuravit te.

7. Ascendit ergo Joseph ut sepeliret patrem suum: ascenderuntque cum eo omnes servi Pharaonis seniores domus ejus, et omnes seniores terræ Ægypti,

8. Et omnis domus Joseph, et fratres ejus, et domus patris ejus: tantummodo parvulos suos, et pecudes suas, et boves suos reliquerent in terra Gosen.

9. Et ascenderunt cum eo etiam currus, etiam equites: et fuit turma gravis valde.

10. Porro venerunt usque ad aream Atad, quæ est trans Jordanem: et planxerunt ibi planctu magno et gravi valde: et fecit patri suo luctum septem diebus.

11. Et viderunt habitatores terræ Chenaanæi luctum in area Atad, et dixerunt, Luctus gravis est iste Ægyptiis: idcirco vocatum fuit nomen ejus Abel-Misraim, (*id est luctus Ægyptiorum,*) qui est trans Jordanem.

12. Fecerunt ergo filii ejus ei sic, quemadmodum præceperat eis.

13. Quia tulerunt eum filii ejus in terra Chenaan, sepelieruntque eum in spelunca agri duplici, quam

which Abraham bought with the field, for a possession of a burying-place of Ephron the Hittite, before Mamre.

14. And Joseph returned into Egypt, he, and his brethren, and all that went up with him to bury his father, after he had buried his father.

15. And when Joseph's brethren saw that their father was dead, they said, Joseph will peradventure hate us, and will certainly requite us all the evil which we did unto him.

16. And they sent a messenger unto Joseph, saying, Thy father did command before he died, saying,

17. So shall ye say unto Joseph, Forgive, I pray thee now, the trespass of thy brethren, and their sin; for they did unto thee evil: and now, we pray thee, forgive the trespass of the servants of the God of thy father. And Joseph wept when they spake unto him.

18. And his brethren also went and fell down before his face; and they said, Behold, we *be* thy servants.

19. And Joseph said unto them, Fear not; for *am* I in the place of God?

20. But as for you, ye thought evil against me; *but* God meant it unto good, to bring to pass, as *it is* this day, to save much people alive.

21. Now therefore fear ye not: I will nourish you, and your little ones. And he comforted them, and spake kindly unto them.

22. And Joseph dwelt in Egypt, he and his father's house: and Joseph lived an hundred and ten years.

23. And Joseph saw Ephraim's children of the third *generation:* the children also of Machir, the son of Manasseh, were brought up upon Joseph's knees.

24. And Joseph said unto his brethren, I die: and God will surely visit you, and bring you out of this land unto the land which he sware to Abraham, to Isaac, and to Jacob.

25. And Joseph took an oath of the children of Israel, saying, God

emit Abraham cum agro in possessionem sepulcri, ab Hephron Hittæo, ante Mamre.

14. Et reversus est Joseph in Ægyptum, ipse et fratres ejus, et omnes qui ascenderant cum eo ad sepeliendum patrem ejus, postquam sepelivit patrem suum.

15. Videntes autem fratres Joseph, quod mortuus esset pater eorum, dixerunt, Fortasse odio habebit nos Joseph, et reddendo reddet nobis omne malum, quo affecimus eum.

16. Propterea mandarunt ad Joseph, dicendo, Pater tuus præcepit, antequam moreretur, dicendo,

17. Sic dicetis Joseph, Obsecro, parce nunc sceleri fratrum tuorum, et peccato eorum: quia malum intulerunt tibi, nunc igitur parce quæso sceleri servorum Dei patris tui. Flevit autem Joseph, dum illi loquerentur cum eo.

18. Nam profecti sunt etiam fratres ejus, et prostraverunt se coram eo, et dixerunt, Ecce, sumus tibi servi.

19. Et dixit ad eos Joseph, Ne timeatis: numquid enim loco Dei sum?

20. Vos quidem cogitastis adversum me malum: Deus *autem* cogitavit illud in bonum, ut faceret secundum diem hanc, ut vivificaret populum multum.

21. Nunc itaque ne timeatis, ego alam vos, et parvulos vestros. Et consolatus est eos, et loquutus est ad cor eorum.

22. Et habitavit Joseph in Ægypto, ipse et domus patris ejus: et vixit Joseph centum et decem annos.

23. Et vidit Joseph ipsi Ephraim filios tertiæ generationis: etiam filii Machir filii Menasseh educati sunt super genua Joseph.

24. Et dixit Joseph fratribus suis, Ego morior, et Deus visitando visitabit vos, et ascendere faciet vos e terra hac ad terram, quam juravit Abraham, Ishac et Jahacob.

25. Et adjuravit Joseph filios Israel, dicendo, Visitando visitabit

will surely visit you, and ye shall carry up my bones from hence.

26. So Joseph died, *being* an hundred and ten years old: and they embalmed him, and he was put in a coffin in Egypt.

Deus vos, et tolletis ossa mea hinc.

26. Itaque mortuus est Joseph filius centum et decem annorum: et aromatibus condierunt eum, et positus est in arca in Ægypto.

1. *And Joseph fell upon his father's face.* In this chapter, what happened after the death of Jacob, is briefly related. Moses, however, states that Jacob's death was honoured with a double mourning—natural (so to speak) and ceremonial. That Joseph falls upon his father's face and sheds tears, flows from true and pure affection; that the Egyptians mourn for him seventy days, since it is done for the sake of honour, and in compliance with custom, is more from ostentation and vain pomp, than from true grief: and yet the dead are generally mourned over in this manner, that the last debt due to them may be discharged. Whence also the proverb has originated, that the mourning of the heir is laughter under a mask. And although sometimes minds are penetrated with real grief; yet something is added to it, by the affectation of making a show of pious sorrow, so that they indulge largely in tears in the presence of others, who would weep more sparingly if there were no witnesses of their grief. Hence those friends who meet together, under the pretext of administering consolation, often pursue a course so different, that they call forth more abundant weeping. And although the ceremony of mourning over the dead arose from a good principle; namely, that the living should meditate on the curse entailed by sin upon the human race, yet it has always been tarnished by many evils; because it has been neither directed to its true end, nor regulated by due moderation. With respect to the genuine grief which is not unnaturally excited, but which breaks forth from the depth of our hearts, it is not, in itself, to be censured, if it be kept within due bounds. For Joseph is not here reproved because he manifests his grief by weeping; but his filial piety is rather commended. We have, however, need of the rein, and of self-government, lest, through intemperate grief, we are hurried, by a blind impulse, to murmur against God:

for excessive grief always precipitates us into rebellion. Moreover, the mitigation of sorrow is chiefly to be sought for, in the hope of a future life, according to the doctrine of Paul.

2. *And Joseph commanded his servants.* Although formerly more labour was expended on funerals, and that even without superstition, than has been deemed right subsequently to the proof given of the resurrection exhibited by Christ:[1] yet we know that among the Egyptians there was greater expense and pomp than among the Jews. Even the ancient historians record this among the most memorable customs of that nation. Indeed it is not to be doubted (as we have said elsewhere) that the sacred rite of burial descended from the holy fathers, to be a kind of mirror of the future resurrection: but as hypocrites are always more diligent in the performance of ceremonies, than they are, who possess the solid substance of things; it happens that they who have declined from the true faith, assume a far more ostentatious appearance than the faithful, to whom pertain the truth and the right use of the symbol. If we compare the Jews with ourselves, those shadowy ceremonies, in which God required them to be occupied, would, at this time, appear intolerable; though compared with those of other nations, they were moderate and easily to be borne. But the heathen scarcely knew why they incurred so much labour and expense. Hence we infer how empty and trivial a matter it is, to attend only to external signs, when the pure doctrine which exhibits their true origin and their legitimate end, does not flourish. It is an act of piety to bury the dead. To embalm corpses with aromatic spices, was, in former times, no fault; inasmuch as it was done as a public symbol of future incorruption. For it is not possible but that the sight of a dead man should grievously affect us; as if one common end, without distinction, awaited both us and the beasts that perish. At this day the resurrection of Christ is a sufficient support for us against yielding to this temptation. But the an-

---

[1] Que depuis que Jesus Christ nous a baillé claire demonstrance de la resurrection des morts—than since the time that Jesus Christ has given us a clear demonstration of the resurrection of the dead.—*French Translation.*

cients, on whom the full light of day had not yet shone, were aided by figures : they, however, whose minds were not raised to the hope of a better life, did nothing else than trifle, and foolishly imitate the holy fathers. Finally, where faith has not so breathed its odour, as to make men know that something remains for them after death, all embalming will be vapid. Yea, if death is to them the eternal destruction of the body, it would be an impious profanation of a sacred and useful ceremony, to attempt to place what had perished under such costly custody. It is probable that Joseph, in conforming himself to the Egyptians, whose superfluous care was not free from absurdity; acted rather from fear than from judgment, or from approval of their method. Perhaps he improperly imitated the Egyptians, lest the condition of his father might be worse than that of other men. But it would have been better, had he confined himself to the frugal practice of his fathers. Nevertheless though *he* might be excusable, the same practice is not now lawful for *us*. For unless we wish to subvert the glory of Christ, we must cultivate greater sobriety.

3. *And forty days were fulfilled for him.* We have shown already that Moses is speaking of a ceremonial mourning; and therefore he does not prescribe it as a law, or produce it as an example which it is right for us to follow. For, by the laws, certain days were appointed, in order that time might be given for the moderating of grief in some degree; yet something also was conceded to ambition. Another rule, however, for restraining grief is given to us by the Lord. And Joseph stooped, more than he ought, to the perverted manners of the Egyptians ; for the world affects to believe that whatever is customary is lawful ; so that what generally prevails, carries along everything it meets, like a violent inundation. The seventy days which Moses sets apart to solemn mourning, Herodotus, in his second book, assigns to the embalming. But Diodorus writes that the seasoning of the body was completed in thirty days. Both authors diligently describe the method of embalming. And though I will not deny that, in the course of time, the skill and industry in practising this art increased, yet it appears to me

probable that this method of proceeding was handed down from the fathers.[1]

4. *Joseph spake unto the house of Pharaoh.* A brief narration is here inserted of the permission obtained for Joseph, that, with the goodwill and leave of the king, he might convey his father's remains to the sepulchre of "the double cave." Now, though he himself enjoyed no common degree of favour, he yet makes use of the courtiers as his intercessors. Why did he act thus, unless on the ground that the affair was in itself odious to the people? For nothing (as we have said before) was less tolerable to the Egyptians, than that their land, of the sanctity of which they made their especial boast, should be despised. Therefore Joseph, in order to transfer the offence from himself to another, pleads necessity: as if he would say, that the burying of his father was not left to his own choice, because Jacob had laid him under obligation as to the mode of doing it, by the imposition of an oath. Wherefore, we see that he was oppressed by servile fear, so that he did not dare frankly and boldly to profess his own faith; since he is compelled to act a part, in order to transfer to the deceased whatever odium might attend the transaction. Now, whereas a more simple and upright confession of faith is required of the sons of God, let none of us seek refuge under such pretexts: but rather let us learn to ask of the Lord the spirit of fortitude and constancy which shall direct us to bear our testimony to true religion. Yet if men allow us the free profession of religion, let us give thanks for it. Now, seeing that Joseph did not dare to move his foot, except by permission of the king, we infer hence, that he was bound by his splendid fortune, as by golden fetters. And truly, such is the condition of all who are advanced to honour and favour in royal courts; so that there is nothing better for men of sane mind, than to be content with a private condition. Joseph also mitigates the offence which he feared he was giving, by another circum-

[1] It would appear that the mourning for Jacob was a kind of royal mourning. "On the death of every Egyptian king, a general mourning was instituted throughout the country for seventy-two days."—*Manners and Customs of the Ancient Egyptians, by Sir J. G. Wilkinson,* vol. i. p. 255.—*Ed.*

stance, when he says, that the desire to be buried in the land of Canaan was not one which had recently entered into his father's mind, because he had dug his grave there long before; whence it follows that he had not been induced to do so by any disgust taken against the land of Egypt.

5. *And Pharaoh said.* We have seen that Joseph adopts a middle course. For he was not willing utterly to fail in his duty; yet, by catching at a pretext founded on the command of his father, he did not conduct himself with sufficient firmness. It is possible that Pharaoh was inclined, by the modesty of his manner, more easily to assent to his requests. Yet this cowardice is not, on that account, so sanctioned that the sons of God are at liberty to indulge themselves in it: for if they intrepidly follow where duty calls, the Lord will give the issue which is desired, beyond all expectation. For, although, humanly speaking, Joseph's bland submission succeeded prosperously, it is nevertheless certain that the proud mind of the king was influenced by God to concede thus benignantly what had been desired. It is also to be observed, what great respect for an oath prevailed among blind unbelievers. For, though Pharaoh himself had not sworn, he still deemed it unlawful for him to violate, by his own authority, the pledge given by another. But at this day, reverence for God has become so far extinct, that men commonly regard it as a mere trifle to deceive, on one side or another, under the name of God. But such unbridled license, which even Pharaoh himself denounces, shall not escape the judgment of God with impunity.

7. *And Joseph went up.* Moses gives a full account of the burial. What he relates concerning the renewed mourning of Joseph and his brethren, as well as of the Egyptians, ought by no means to be established as a rule among ourselves. For we know, that since our flesh has no self-government, men commonly exceed bounds both in sorrowing and in rejoicing. The tumultuous clamour, which the inhabitants of the place admired, cannot be excused. And although Joseph had a right end in view, when he fixed the mourning to last through seven successive days, yet this excess was not free from blame. Nevertheless, it was not

without reason that the Lord caused this funeral to be thus honourably celebrated: for it was of great consequence that a kind of sublime trophy should be raised, which might transmit to posterity the memory of Jacob's faith. If he had been buried privately, and in a common manner, his fame would soon have been extinguished; but now, unless men wilfully blind themselves, they have continually before their eyes a noble example, which may cherish the hope of the promised inheritance: they perceive, as it were, the standard of that deliverance erected, which shall take place in the fulness of time. Wherefore, we are not here to consider the honour of the deceased so much as the benefit of the living. Even the Egyptians, not knowing what they do, bear a torch before the Israelites, to teach them to keep the course of their divine calling: the Canaanites do the same, when they distinguish the place by a new name; for hence it came to pass that the knowledge of the covenant of the Lord flourished afresh.[1]

14. *And Joseph returned.* Although Joseph and the rest had left so many pledges in Egypt, that it would be necessary for them to return; it is yet probable that they were rather drawn back thither by the oracle of God. For God never permitted them to choose an abode at their own will; but as he had before led Abraham, Isaac, and Jacob in their journeyings, so he held their sons shut up in the land of Goshen, as within barriers. And there is no doubt that the holy fathers left that oracle which we have in the fifteenth chapter and the thirteenth verse, to their sons, to be kept in faithful custody as a precious treasure.[2] They return, therefore, into Egypt, not only because they were compelled by present necessity, but because it was not lawful for them to

---

[1] Calvin, in his criticism on Joseph's conduct with reference to his father's funeral, seems to bear hard upon the motives of the patriarch. As there is nothing in Joseph's previous history which is derogatory either to his moral courage or his integrity, it is scarcely justifiable to impute a want of firmness and of straightforwardness to him on this occasion. Is not the concluding portion of Calvin's remarks a sufficient answer to all that has gone before? And may we not conclude, that the whole of the circumstances of Jacob's funeral were divinely ordered to perpetuate his memory?—*Ed.*

[2] "And he said unto Abram, Know of a surety that thy seed shall be a stranger in a land that is not theirs, and shall serve them; and they shall afflict them four hundred years."

shake off with the hand, the yoke which God had put upon their necks. But if the Lord does not hold all men bound by voluntary obedience to himself, he nevertheless holds their minds by his secret rein, that they may not withdraw themselves from his government; nor can we form any other conjecture than that they were restrained by his fear, so that even when admonished of the tyrannical oppression which was coming upon them, they did not attempt to make their escape. We know that their disposition was not so mild as to prevent them from rebelling against lighter burdens. Wherefore, on this point, a special sense of religious obligation subdued them, so that they prepared themselves quietly and silently to endure the hardest servitude.

15. *And when Joseph's brethren saw that their father was dead.* Moses here relates, that the sons of Jacob, after the death of their father, were apprehensive lest Joseph should take vengeance for the injury they had done him. And whence this fear, but because they form their judgment of him according to their own disposition? That they had found him so placable they do not attribute to true piety towards God, nor do they account it a special gift of the Spirit: but rather, they imagine that, out of respect to his father alone, he had hitherto been so far restrained, as barely to postpone his revenge. But, by such perverse judgment, they do a great injury to one who, by the liberality of his treatment, had borne them witness that his mind was free from all hatred and malevolence. Part of the injurious surmise reflected even upon God, whose special grace had shone forth in the moderation of Joseph. Hence, however, we gather, that guilty consciences are so disturbed by blind and unreasonable fears, that they stumble in broad day-light. Joseph had absolved his brethren from the crime they had committed against him; but they are so agitated by guilty compunctions, that they voluntarily become their own tormentors. And they have not themselves to thank, that they did not bring down upon themselves the very punishment which had been remitted; because the mind of Joseph might well have been wounded by their distrust. For, what could they mean by still malignantly suspecting him to whose compassion they had again

and again owed their lives? Yet I do not doubt, that long ago they had repented of their wickedness; but, perhaps, because they had not yet been sufficiently purified, the Lord suffered them to be tortured with anxiety and trouble: first, to make them a proof to others, that an evil conscience is its own tormentor, and, then, to humble them under a renewed sense of their own guilt; for, when they regard themselves as obnoxious to their brother's judgment, they cannot forget, unless they are worse than senseless, the celestial tribunal of God. What Solomon says, we see daily fulfilled, that "the wicked flee when no man pursueth;" (Prov. xxviii. 1;) but, in this way, God compels the fugitives to give up their account. They would desire, in their supine torpor, to deceive both God and men; and they bring upon their minds, as far as they are able, the callousness of obstinacy: in the mean time, whether they will or no, they are made to tremble at the sound of a falling leaf, lest their carnal security should obliterate their sense of the judgment of God. (Lev. xxvi. 36.) Nothing is more desirable than a tranquil mind. While God deprives the wicked of this singular benefit, which is desired by all, he invites us to cultivate integrity. But especially, seeing that the patriarchs, who were already affected with penitence for their wickedness, are yet thus severely awakened, a long time afterwards, let none of us yield to self-indulgence; but let each diligently examine himself, lest hypocrisy should inwardly cherish the secret stings of the wrath of God; and may that happy peace, which can find no place in a double heart, shine within our thoroughly purified breasts. For this due reward of their neglect remains for all those who do not draw nigh to God sincerely and with all their heart, that they are compelled to stand before the judgment-seat of mortal man. Wherefore, there is no other method which can free us from disquietude, but that of returning into favour with God. Whosoever shall despise this remedy, shall be afraid not only of man, but also of a shadow, or a breath of wind.

16. *And they sent a messenger.* Because they are ashamed themselves to speak, they engage messengers of peace, in whom Joseph might have greater confidence. But here also

we perceive that they who have an accusing conscience are destitute of counsel and of reason. For if Jacob had been solicitous on this point, why did he not effect reconciliation between the son who was so obedient unto himself, and his brethren? Besides, for what reason should they attempt to do that through mediators, which they could do so much better in their own persons? The Lord, therefore, suffers them to act like children; that we, being instructed by their example, may look for no advantage from the use of frivolous inventions. But it may be asked, where the sons of Jacob found men to whom they could venture to commit such a message; for it was no light thing to make known their execrable crime to strangers? And it would have been folly to subject themselves to this infamy among the Egyptians. The most probable conjecture is, that some domestic witnesses were chosen from the number of their own servants; for though Moses makes no mention of such, when he relates that Jacob departed into Egypt; yet that some were brought with him, may easily be gathered from certain considerations.

17. *Forgive, I pray thee now.* They do not dissemble the fact that they had grievously sinned; and they are so far from extenuating their fault, that they freely heap up words in charging themselves with guilt. They do not, therefore, ask that pardon should be granted them as if the offence were light: but they place in opposition to the atrocity of their crime, first, the authority of their father, and then the sacred name of God. Their confession would have been worthy of commendation, had they proceeded directly, and without tortuous contrivances, to appease their brother. Now, since they have drawn from the fountain of piety the instruction that it is right for sin to be remitted to the servants of God; we may receive it as a common exhortation, that if we have been injured by the members of the Church, we must not be too rigid and immoveable in pardoning the offence. This humanity indeed is generally enjoined upon us towards all men: but when the bond of religion is superadded, we are harder than iron, if we are not inclined to the exercise of compassion. And we must observe, that they

expressly mention the God of Jacob: because the peculiar faith and worship by which they were distinguished from the rest of the nations, ought to unite them with each other in a closer bond: as if God, who had adopted that family, stood forth in the midst of them as engaged to produce reconciliation.

*And Joseph wept when they spake unto him.* It cannot be ascertained with certainty from the words of Moses, whether the brethren of Joseph were present, and were speaking, at the time he wept. Some interpreters imagine that a part was here acted designedly; so that when the mind of Joseph had been sounded by others, the brethren, soon afterwards, came in, during the discourse. I rather incline to a different opinion; namely, that, when he knew, from the messengers, that their minds were tormented, and they were troubling themselves in vain, he was moved with sympathy towards them. Then, having sent for them, he set them free from all care and fear; and their speech, when they themselves were deprecating his anger, drew forth his tears. Moreover, by thus affectionately weeping over the sorrow and anxiety of his brethren, he affords us a remarkable example of compassion. But if we have an arduous conflict with the impetuosity of an angry temper, or the obstinacy of a disposition to hatred, we must pray to the Lord for a spirit of meekness, the force of which manifests itself not less effectually, at this day, in the members of Christ, than formerly in Joseph.

19. *Am I in the place of God?* Some think that, in these words, he was rejecting the honour paid him: as if he would say, that it was unjustly offered to him, because it was due to God alone. But this interpretation is destitute of probability, since he often permitted himself to be addressed in this manner, and knew that the minds of his brethren were utterly averse to transfer the worship of God to mortal man. And I equally disapprove another meaning given to the passage, which makes Joseph refuse to exact punishment, because he is not God: for he does not restrain himself from retaliating the injury, in the hope that God will prove his avenger. Others adduce a third signification; namely, that the whole affair was conducted by the counsel of God, and

not by his own : which though I do not entirely reject, because it approaches the truth, yet I do not embrace the interpretation as true. For the word תחת (*tachat*) sometimes signifies *instead of*, sometimes it means *subjection*. Therefore if the note of interrogation were not in the way, it might well be rendered, "Because I am *under* God;" and then the sense would be, "Fear not, for I am under God;" so that Joseph would teach them, that because he is subject to the authority of God, it is not his business to lead the way, but to follow. But, whereas ה, the note of interrogation, is prefixed to the word, it cannot be otherwise expounded than to mean that it would be wrong for him, a mortal man, to presume to thwart the counsel of God. But as to the sum of the matter, there is no ambiguity. For seeing that Joseph considers the design of divine providence, he restrains his feelings as with a bridle, lest they should carry him to excess. He was indeed of a mild and humane disposition; but nothing is better or more suitable to assuage his anger, than to submit himself to be governed by God. When, therefore, the desire of revenge urges us, let all our feelings be subjected to the same authority. Moreover, since he desires his brethren to be tranquil and secure, from the consideration, that he, ascribing due honour to God, willingly submits to obey the Divine command; let us learn, hence, that it is most to our advantage to deal with men of moderation, who set God before them as their leader, and who not only submit to his will, but also cheerfully obey him. For if any one is impotently carried away by the lust of the flesh, we must fear a thousand deaths from him, unless God should forcibly break his fury. Now as it is the one remedy for assuaging our anger, to acknowledge what we ourselves are, and what right God has over us; so, on the other hand, when this thought has taken full possession of our minds, there is no ardour, however furious, which it will not suffice to mitigate.

20. *Ye thought evil against me.* Joseph well considers (as we have said) the providence of God; so that he imposes it on himself as a compulsory law, not only to grant pardon, but also to exercise beneficence. And although we have treated at large on this subject, in the forty-fifth chapter,

yet it will be useful also to repeat something on it now. In the first place, we must notice this difference in his language: for whereas, in the former passage, Joseph, desiring to soothe the grief, and to alleviate the fear of his brethren, would cover their wickedness by every means which ingenuity could suggest; he now corrects them a little more openly and freely; perhaps because he is offended with their disingenuousness. Yet he holds to the same principle as before. Seeing that, by the secret counsel of God, he was led into Egypt, for the purpose of preserving the life of his brethren, he must devote himself to this object, lest he should resist God. He says, in fact, by his action, " Since God has deposited your life with me, I should be engaged in war against him, if I were not to be the faithful dispenser of the grace which he had committed to my hands." Meanwhile, he skilfully distinguishes between the wicked counsels of men, and the admirable justice of God, by so ascribing the government of all things to God, as to preserve the divine administration free from contracting any stain from the vices of men. The selling of Joseph was a crime detestable for its cruelty and perfidy; yet he was not sold except by the decree of heaven. For neither did God merely remain at rest, and by conniving for a time, let loose the reins of human malice, in order that afterwards he might make use of this occasion; but, at his own will, he appointed the order of acting which he intended to be fixed and certain. Thus we may say with truth and propriety, that Joseph was sold by the wicked consent of his brethren, and by the secret providence of God. Yet it was not a work common to both, in such a sense that God sanctioned anything connected with or relating to their wicked cupidity: because while they are contriving the destruction of their brother, God is effecting their deliverance from on high. Whence also we conclude, that there are various methods of governing the world. This truly must be generally agreed, that nothing is done without his will; because he both governs the counsels of men, and sways their wills and turns their efforts at his pleasure, and regulates all events: but if men undertake anything right and just, he so actuates and moves them inwardly by his Spirit, that whatever is good in them, may justly be said to be received from him : but if Satan and ungodly men rage, he acts by their hands in such an inexpressible manner, that the wickedness of the deed belongs to them, and the blame of it is imputed to them. For they are not induced to sin, as the faithful are to act aright, by the impulse of the Spirit, but they are the authors of their own evil, and follow Satan as their leader. Thus we see that the justice of God shines brightly in the midst of the darkness of our iniquity. For as God is never without a just cause for his actions, so men are held in the chains of guilt by their own perverse will. When we hear that God frustrates the wicked expectations, and the injurious desires of men, we derive hence no common consolation. Let the impious busy themselves as they please, let them rage, let them mingle heaven and earth ; yet they shall gain nothing by their ardour; and not only shall their impetuosity prove ineffectual, but shall be turned to an issue the reverse of that which they intended, so that they shall promote our salvation, though they do it reluctantly. So that whatever poison Satan produces, God turns it into medicine for his elect. And although in this place God is said to have " meant it unto good," because contrary to expectation, he had educed a joyful issue out of beginnings fraught with death : yet, with perfect rectitude and justice, he turns the food of reprobates into poison, their light into darkness, their table into a snare, and, in short, their life into death. If human minds cannot reach these depths, let them rather suppliantly adore the mysteries they do not comprehend, than, as vessels of clay, proudly exalt themselves against their Maker.

*To save much people alive.* Joseph renders his office subservient to the design of God's providence ; and this sobriety is always to be cultivated, that every one may behold, by faith, God from on high holding the helm of the government of the world, and may keep himself within the bounds of his vocation ; and even, being admonished by the secret judgments of God, may descend into himself, and exhort himself to the discharge of his duty : and if the reason of this does not immediately appear, we must still take care that we do not fly in confused and erratic circuits, as fanatical men are wont to do. What Joseph says respecting his being divinely chosen "to save much people alive," some extend to the Egyptians. Without condemning such an extension, I would rather restrict the application of the words to the family of Jacob; for Joseph amplifies the goodness of God by this circumstance, that the seed of the Church would be rescued from destruction by his labour. And truly, from these few men, whose seed would otherwise have been extinct before their descendents had been multiplied, that vast multitude sprang into being, which God soon afterwards raised up.

21. *I will nourish you.* It was a token of a solid and not a feigned reconciliation, not only to abstain from malice and injury, but also to "overcome evil with good," as Paul teaches, (Rom. xii. 21 :) and truly, he who fails in his duty, when he possesses the power of giving help, and when the occasion demands his assistance, shows, by this very course, that he is not forgetful of injury. This requires to be the more diligently observed, because, commonly, the greater part weakly conclude that they forgive offences if they do not retaliate them; as if indeed we were not taking revenge when we withdraw our hands from giving help. You would assist your brother if you thought him worthy : he implores your aid in necessity; you desert him because he has done you some unkindness; what hinders you from helping him but hatred? Therefore, we shall then only prove our minds to be free from malevolence, when we follow with kindness those enemies by whom we have been ill treated. Joseph is said to have spoken "to the heart of his brethren," because, by addressing them with suavity and kindness, he removed all their scruples; as we have before seen, that Shechem spoke to the heart of Dinah, when he attempted to console her with allurements, in order that, forgetting the dishonour he had done her, she might consent to marry him.

22. *And Joseph dwelt in Egypt.* It is not without reason that Moses relates how long Joseph lived, because the length of the time shows the more clearly his unfailing constancy: for although he is raised to great honour and power among the Egyptians, he still is closely united with his father's

house. Hence it is easy to conjecture, that he gradually took his leave of the treasures of the court, because he thought there was nothing better for him to do than to hold them in contempt, lest earthly dignity should separate him from the kingdom of God. He had before spurned all the allurements which might have occupied his mind in Egypt: he now counts it necessary to proceed further, that, laying aside his honour, he may descend to an ignoble condition, and wean his own sons from the hope of succeeding to his worldly rank. We know how anxiously others labour, both that they themselves may not be reduced in circumstances, and that they may leave their fortune entire to their posterity: but Joseph, during sixty years, employed all his efforts to bring himself and his children into a state of submission, lest his earthly greatness should alienate them from the little flock of the Lord. In short, he imitated the serpents, who cast off their *exuviæ*, that, being stripped of their old age, they may gather new strength. He sees the children of his own grandchildren; why does not his solicitude to provide for them increase, as his children increase? Yet he has so little regard for worldly rank or opulence, that he would rather see them devoted to a pastoral life, and be despised by the Egyptians, if only they might be reckoned in the family of Israel. Besides, in a numerous offspring during his own life, the Lord afforded him some taste of his benediction, from which he might conceive the hope of future deliverance: for, among so many temptations, it was necessary for him to be encouraged and sustained, lest he should sink under them.

24. *And Joseph said unto his brethren.* It is uncertain whether Joseph died the first or the last of the brethren, or whether a part of them survived him. Here indeed Moses includes, under the name of brethren, not only those who were really so, but other relations. I think, however, that certain of the chiefs of each family were called at his command, from whom the whole of the people might receive information: and although it is probable that the other patriarchs also gave the same command respecting themselves, since the bones of them all were, in like manner, conveyed

into the land of Canaan; yet special mention is made of Joseph alone, for two reasons. First, since the eyes of them all were fixed upon him, on account of his high authority, it was his duty to lead their way, and cautiously to beware lest the splendour of his dignity should cast a stumblingblock before any of them. Secondly, it was of great consequence, as an example, that it should be known to all the people, that he who held the second place in the kingdom of Egypt, regardless of so great an honour, was contented with his own condition, which was only that of the heir of a bare promise.

*I die.* This expression has the force of a command to his brethren to be of good courage after his death, because the truth of God is immortal; for he does not wish them to depend upon his life or that of another man, so as to cause them to prescribe a limit to the power of God; but he would have them patiently to rest till the suitable time should arrive. But whence had he this great certainty, that he should be a witness and a surety of future redemption, except from his having been so taught by his father? For we do not read that God had appeared unto him, or that an oracle had been brought to him by an angel from heaven; but because he was certainly persuaded that Jacob was a divinely appointed teacher and prophet, who should transmit to his sons the covenant of salvation deposited with him; Joseph relies upon his testimony not less securely than if some vision had been presented to him, or he had seen angels descending to him from heaven: for unless the hearing of the word is sufficient for our faith, we deserve not that God, whom we then defraud of his honour, should condescend to deal with us: not that faith relies on human authority, but because it hears God speaking through the mouth of men, and by their external voice is drawn upwards; for what God pronounces through men, he seals on our hearts by his Spirit. Thus faith is built on no other foundation than God himself; and yet the preaching of men is not wanting in its claim of authority and reverence. This restraint is put upon the rash curiosity of those men, who, eagerly desiring visions, despise the ordinary ministry of the Church; as if it were absurd that God, who formerly showed himself to the fathers out of heaven, should send forth his voice out of the earth. But if they would reflect how gloriously he once descended to us in the person of his only-begotten Son, they would not so importunately desire that heaven should daily be opened unto them. But, not to insist upon these things; when the brethren saw that Joseph,—who in this respect was inferior to his fathers, as having been partaker of no oracle,—had been imbued by them with the doctrine of piety, so that he contended with a faith similar to theirs; they would at once be most ungrateful and malignant, if they rejected the participation of his grace.

25. *God will surely visit you.* By these words he intimates that they would be buried as in oblivion, so long as they remained in Egypt: and truly that exile was as if God had turned his back on them for a season. Nevertheless, Joseph does not cease to fix the eyes of his mind on God; as it is written in the Prophet, "I will wait upon the Lord that hideth his face from the house of Jacob." (Is. viii. 17.) This passage also clearly teaches what was the design of this anxious choice of his sepulchre, namely, that it might be a seal of redemption: for after he has asserted that God was faithful, and would, in his own time, grant what he had promised, he immediately adjures his brethren to carry away his bones. These were useful relics, the sight of which plainly signified that, by the death of men, the eternal covenant in which Joseph commands his posterity safely to rest, had by no means become extinct; for he deems it sufficient to adduce the oath of God, to remove all their doubts respecting their deliverance.

END OF THE COMMENTARIES ON THE FIRST BOOK OF MOSES
CALLED GENESIS.

# INDEX

## OF HEBREW WORDS EXPLAINED.

| א | | ב | Vol. Page | ז | Vol. Page |
|---|---|---|---|---|---|
| | Vol. Page | בֶּן | { i. 425 | זֹאת | { i. 135, 164 |
| אָב | ii. 329 | | { ii. 142 | | { ii. 134 |
| אֲבִימֶלֶךְ | ii. 58 | בנה | i. 133 | זֶבַע | i. 193 |
| אֲבָל | i. 461 | בנים | ii. 193 | | |
| אֲבָנָה | i. 425 | בֶּן־עַמִּי | i. 518 | ח | |
| אֲבַק | ii. 195 | ברא | i. 70, 107 | | |
| אָברֵךְ | ii. 329 | בקע | ii. 22 | חוה | i. 181 |
| אָדָם | i. 128 | בְּשַׁגַּם | i. 243 | חיה | i. 576 |
| אֲדֹנָי | { i. 72, 109, 401 | בְּתוֹךְ | i. 161 | חטא | ii. 372 |
| | | | | חטאת | i. 202 |
| אָוֶן | ii. 442 | ג | | חטף | ii. 406 |
| אוֹר | { i. 83, 337 | גד | ii. 145 | חנִיכִים | i. 385 |
| אֲחָדִים | ii. 102 | גּוֹי | i. 346 | חסד | i. 553 |
| אָחוּ | ii. 317 | גוּר | ii. 452 | חרש | ii. 377 |
| אַיָּלָה | ii. 446 | גַּם | { i. 245 | חשׁב | i. 405 |
| אִישׁ | i. 135 | | { ii. 167 | | |
| אֵל | { i. 442 | גרשׁ | i. 184 | ט | |
| | { ii. 172, 239 | | | | |
| אֱלֹהִים | { i. 71, 72, 107, 108, 531 | ד | | טוּרִי | i. 278 |
| | | דּוֹד | ii. 146 | | |
| | (ii. 239 | דּוּדָאִים | ii. 146 | י | |
| אַלּוֹן | i. 352 | דֻן | i. 241 | יָאבָק | ii. 195 |
| אַךְ | i. 294 | דוּר | i. 251 | יַבֵּק | ii. 195 |
| אַף־כִּי | i. 146 | | | ידגו | ii. 430 |
| אַרְבַּע | i. 577 | ה | | יהו | { i. 108, 109, 190, 401 |
| אֲרוּיִם | i. 337 | הֶבֶל | i. 191 | | |
| אֲרוֹם | i. 140 | הגן | i. 161 | | ii. 114 |
| אַרְיֵה | ii. 452 | הַחֶרֶב | i. 185 | יוֹסֵף | ii. 149 |
| אִשָּׁה | i. 135 | הִדֶּקֶל | i. 118 | ימים | ii. 102, 254 |
| אַשְׁמִים | ii. 344 | היה־הוה | i. 109 | יַעֲקֹב | ii. 49 |
| אֲשֶׁר | i. 107 | היום | i. 160 | יפת | i. 308 |
| אֶת | i. 190 | הִקּוּם | i. 268 | יצבון | i. 174 |
| | | הַמַּכְפֵּלָה | i. 582 | יצוא | i. 297 |
| ב | | הפעם | i. 135 | יצר | i. 70 |
| בָּא | ii. 145 | הקרה | ii. 19 | יקרא | i. 438 |
| בבי | i. 332 | השׁלִיט | ii. 338 | ירא | i. 566 |
| בגד | ii. 145 | | | ירה | i. 566 |
| בֶּהֱמָה | i. 91 | ו | | ישׂא | ii. 127 |
| בוהו | i. 73 | וגם | i. 245 | ישׁופך | i. 170 |
| בִּי | ii. 153 | ויאהל | i. 376 | | |
| בלל | i. 332 | ויבן | i. 133 | כ | |
| | | ויצא | i. 279 | כבד | ii. 447 |
| | | ושׁוב | i. 279 | כוֹהֵן | ii. 330 |

# INDEX OF HEBREW WORDS EXPLAINED.

| | Vol. Page | | Vol. Page | | Vol. Page |
|---|---|---|---|---|---|
| כלה | i. 485 | נחש | i. 168 / ii. 151 | ראשך | ii. 310 |
| כנגדו | i. 130 | | | רבי | i. 186 |
| כרוב | i. 186 | נע | i. 210 | רגז | ii. 382 |
| | | נפלים | i. 244 / ii. 39 | רגליו | ii. 127 |
| **ל** | | | | רהבת | ii. 68 |
| לביא | ii. 452 | נפש | i. 112 | רוח | i. 160 |
| להה | ii. 406 | נפש־חיה | i. 88 | רחף | i. 74 |
| להט | i. 185 | נשא | i. 200, 211 | ריק | i. 385 |
| להשכיל | i. 151 | נשק | ii. 329 | רך | ii. 329 |
| לח | ii. 120 | | | רמש | i. 91 |
| לי | ii. 153 | **ע** | | רקיע | i. 79 |
| לכן | i. 214 | ערן | i. 115 | | |
| למקום | ii. 239 | עון | i. 506 | **ש** | |
| לעשת | i. 107 | עולם | i. 245, 375 / ii. 424 | שאת | i. 200 |
| לפי | ii. 406 | עוף | i. 211, 420 | שבע | i. 556 / ii. 134 |
| לפני | ii. 152 | על | i. 278 / ii. 113, 193 | שדי | i. 442, 443 |
| לקה | i. 231 | עלח | ii. 444 | שוח | ii. 28 |
| לרוח | i. 160 | עלם | i. 245 | שור | ii. 200, 447 |
| לשני | ii. 189 | עמה | i. 152 | שוף | i. 168 |
| | | ענה | i. 429 | שוק | i. 402 |
| **מ** | | עץ | i. 161 | שיח | i. 110 |
| מאד | i. 100 | עצבון | i. 174 | שיל | ii. 454 |
| מארות | i. 83 | ערום | i. 140 | שילה | ii. 454 |
| מה | i. 164 | עשית | i. 164 | שילוה | ii. 453 |
| מואב | i. 518 | | | שכם | ii. 434 |
| מועדים | i. 85 | **פ** | | שכר | ii. 362 |
| מוטה | ii. 418 | פלא | i. 475 | שלום | ii. 358 |
| מחנות | ii. 189 | פלג | i. 325 | שלם | ii. 212 |
| מחקק | ii. 454 | פן | i. 149 | שער | ii. 49 |
| מיטה | ii. 418 | פניאל | ii. 201 | שפה | i. 168 |
| מכרות | ii. 447 | פרא | i. 434 | שפיפון | i. 168 / ii. 463 |
| מלא | ii. 134 | פרדס־ים | i. 113 | שקק | i. 402 |
| מנחה | i. 193 | פתח | i. 308 | שרה | i. 459 / ii. 200 |
| מערת | i. 582 | פתל | ii. 143 | | |
| מצבה | ii. 118 | | | שרץ | i. 88, 91 |
| מצחק | i. 542 | **צ** | | שר־הטבחים | ii. 275 |
| מקצה | ii. 399 | ציד | i. 317 | | |
| מרחפת | i. 73 | צבאם | i. 103 | **ת** | |
| משק | i. 402 | | | תוהו | i. 73 |
| | | **ק** | | תולדות | i. 108, 251 / ii. 258 |
| **נ** | | קדש | i. 105 | | |
| נד | i. 210 | קהה | ii. 460 | תחת | ii. 486 |
| נדד | i. 210 | קנה | ii. 64 | תם | ii. 49 |
| נדן | i. 240 | קניתי | i. 191 | תמים | i. 251 |
| נוד | i. 215 | קצה | ii. 399 | תנינם | i. 89 |
| נוח | i. 233 | קרדו | i. 278 | תרפים | ii. 169, 174 |
| נוע | i. 210 | קשיטה | ii. 213 | תשופך | i. 170 |
| נזיר | ii. 470 | **ר** | | תשופנה | i. 170 |
| נחם | i. 233 | ראה | i. 566 | תשופנו | i. 170 |
| | | ראי | i. 436 | | |

# INDEX

## OF PASSAGES OF HOLY SCRIPTURE QUOTED OR REFERRED TO IN THE COMMENTARY AND NOTES ON THE BOOK OF GENESIS.

**GENESIS.**

| Chap. | Ver. | Vol. | Page |
|---|---|---|---|
| i. | 28 | i. | 132 |
| iv. | 7 | i. | 173 |
| v. | 1 | i. | 94 |
|  |  |  | 103 |
|  |  |  | 244 |
| vii. | 11 | i. | 244 |
| ix. | 24 | i. | 235 |
| x. | 21 | i. | 235 |
| xi. | 31 | i. | 15 |
| xv. | 7 | i. | 342 |
|  | 18 | ii. | 381 |
|  |  |  | 481 |
|  | 30 | ii. | 481 |
| xx. | 1 | i. | 363 |
| xxi. | 5 | ii. | 11 |
|  | 15 | i. | 110 |
| xxii. | 18 | i. | 348 |
|  |  | ii. | 60 |
| xxiii. | 9 | ii. | 417 |
| xxiv. | 2 | ii. | 417 |
| xxv. | 2 | ii. | 11 |
|  | 13-16 | i. | 124 |
| xxvii. | 3 | ii. | 268 |
| xxix. | 3 | ii. | 111 |
|  | 4 | ii. | 15 |
| xxxiii. | 19 | ii. | 484 |
| xxxiv. | 12 | ii. | 130 |
| xxxv. | 7 | i. | 531 |
| xxxvii. | 36 | ii. | 301 |
| xlv. | 10 | ii. | 393 |
| xlvii. | 29 | ii. | 12 |
| xlix. | 19 | ii. | 145 |

**EXODUS.**

| iii. 13-16 | i. | 110 |
| vi. 3 | i. | 109 |
| xii. 40 | i. | 415 |
| xxxii. 20 | ii. | 236 |

**LEVITICUS.**

| vii. 18 | i. | 405 |
| xvii. 4 | i. | 405 |
| xviii. 25 | i. | 488 |
| xxvi. 1 | ii. | 118 |
|  36 | ii. | 483 |

**NUMBERS.**

| vi. 23 | i. | 391 |
|  24 | ii. | 82 |

| Chap. | Ver. | Vol. | Page |
|---|---|---|---|
| xii. | 6 | i. | 399 |
|  |  |  | 414 |
|  |  | ii. | 112 |
| xiii. | 22 | ii. | 393 |
| xxii. | 12 | ii. | 88 |
| xxiii. | 10 | i. | 418 |

**DEUTERONOMY.**

| vi. | 13 | ii. | 76 |
| x. | 8 | i. | 349 |
|  | 17 | i. | 72 |
| xxxii. | 11 | i. | 74 |
|  | 35 | i. | 416 |

**JOSHUA.**

| xiii. | 34 | i. | 244 |
| xv. | 54 | i. | 576 |
| xix. | 1 | ii. | 449 |
| xxii. | 22 | i. | 72 |
| xxiv. | 2 | i. | 333 |
|  | 32 | ii. | 434 |

**JUDGES.**

| xiii. 18 | ii. | 201 |

**1 SAMUEL.**

| xiv. 44 | i. | 395 |
| xv. 22 | i. | 193 |
|  |  | 350 |
| xvi. 7 | i. | 194 |

**2 SAMUEL.**

| xix. 19 | i. | 405 |
| xxiv. 16 | i. | 505 |

**1 KINGS.**

| i. 47 | ii. | 418 |

**2 KINGS.**

| xii. 15 | i. | 405 |
| xviii. 4 | ii. | 236 |
| xix. 35 | i. | 505 |

**1 CHRONICLES.**

| i. 32 | ii. | 33 |
| iv. 4-43 | ii. | 449 |

**JOB.**

| Chap. | Ver. | Vol. | Page |
|---|---|---|---|
| xxi. | 13 | ii. | 37 |
| xxxviii. | 8 | i. | 82 |

**PSALMS.**

| v. | 10 | i. | 248 |
| xiv. | 3 | i. | 248 |
| xvi. | 6 | i. | 400 |
| xix. | 1 | i. | 60 |
| xx. | 7 | ii. | 468 |
| xxxiii. | 5 | i. | 173 |
|  | 6 | i. | 82 |
|  | 7 | i. | 81 |
|  | 7 | ii. | 185 |
| xxxiv. | 14 | ii. | 179 |
|  | 16 | i. | 330 |
| xxxvi. | 7 | ii. | 324 |
| xxxvii. | 6 | ii. | 173 |
| l. | 14 | i. | 223 |
|  | 23 | i. | 354 |
| li. | 5 | i. | 155 |
|  | 19 | i. | 354 |
| lv. | 25 | i. | 295 |
| lxviii. | 13 | i. | 81 |
| lxxviii. | 12, 43 | ii. | 393 |
| lxxxviii. | 49 | i. | 504 |
| xci. | 11 | i. | 504 |
| cii. | 28 | ii. | 254 |
| civ. | 2 | i. | 79 |
|  | 3 | i. | 161 |
|  | 4 | i. | 277 |
|  | 15 | ii. | 363 |
|  | 29 | i. | 74 |
|  |  |  | 105 |
|  | 30 | i. | 74 |
|  | 31 | i. | 80 |
| cv. | 12-15 | i. | 364 |
|  | 14 | i. | 523 |
|  | 18 | ii. | 301 |
| cvi. | 31 | i. | 405 |
| cx. | 4 | i. | 388 |
| cxiii. | 9 | ii. | 41 |
| cxv. | 17 | i. | 208 |
| cxvi. | 12 | i. | 283 |
| cxxi. | 28 | ii. | 39 |
| cxxvii. | 2 | i. | 176 |
|  |  | ii. | 64 |
|  | 3 | i. | 190 |
|  |  |  | 537 |
|  |  | ii. | 141 |

| Chap. | Ver. | Vol. | Page |
|---|---|---|---|
| cxxxii. | 14 | i. | 456 |
| cxxxvii. | 3 | i. | 587 |
| cxxxix. | 7 | i. | 161 |
| cxlviii. | 4 | i. | 80 |

**PROVERBS.**

| x. | 12 | ii. | 74 |
| xxi. | 2 | i. | 525 |
|  | 12 | ii. | 74 |
|  | 13 | ii. | 345 |
|  | 30 | i. | 331 |
| xxviii. | 1 | ii. | 488 |

**CANTICLES.**

| iv. | 6 | i. | 566 |
| vii. | 13 | ii. | 146 |

**ISAIAH.**

| i. | 3 | ii. | 63 |
|  | 15 | i. | 194 |
| ii. | 2 | i. | 346 |
|  | 4 | i. | 347 |
| vi. | 3 | i. | 72 |
| viii. | 13 | ii. | 177 |
|  | 17 | ii. | 492 |
| xi. | 1 | ii. | 457 |
| xix. | 18 | i. | 331 |
| xxiii. | 18 | i. | 319 |
| xxiv. | 11 | i. | 73 |
| xxx. | 1 | i. | 517 |
| xxxiv. | 11 | i. | 73 |
| xxxvii. | 12 | i. | 122 |
| xl. | 5 | i. | 253 |
| xliv. | 25 | i. | 84 |
| xlv. | 7 | ii. | 324 |
|  | 11 | ii. | 145 |
| lii. | 4 | ii. | 402 |
| liv. | 9 | i. | 283 |
| lv. | 6 | ii. | 95 |
|  | 25 | i. | 167 |
| lxv. | 11 | ii. | 145 |
|  | 16 | i. | 349 |
|  | 24 | ii. | 20 |
|  | 25 | i. | 167 |

**JEREMIAH.**

| i. | 10 | ii. | 450 |
| ii. | 10, 11 | ii. | 225 |

# INDEX OF PASSAGES OF SCRIPTURE.

| Chap. | Ver. | Vol. | Page |
|---|---|---|---|
| v. | 22 | i. | 81 |
| x. | 2 | i. | 84 |
| xxix. | 7 | ii. | 403 |
| xxxiv. | 18 | i. | 413 |
| xxxviii. | 9 | ii. | 311 |
| xlix. | 32 | i. | 160 |
| lii. | 23 | i. | 160 |

### EZEKIEL.

| xvi. | 48, 49 | i. | 491 |
|---|---|---|---|
|  | 49 | i. | 374 |
|  |  |  | 497 |
| xx. | 12 | i. | 107 |
| xxi. | 26 | ii. | 456 |
| xxiii. | 21 | ii. | 95 |
| xxvii. | 23 | i. | 122 |
| xxviii. | 14, 17 | i. | 187 |

### DANIEL.

| ii. | 28 | ii. | 308 |
|---|---|---|---|
| ix. | 21 | ii. | 19 |

### AMOS.

| iii. | 7 | i. | 479 |
|---|---|---|---|
| vi. | 2 | i. | 318 |
| ix. | 11 | ii. | 456 |

### JONAH.

| iii. | 4 | i. | 526 |
|---|---|---|---|

### MICAH.

| ii. | 15 | i. | 97 |
|---|---|---|---|

### ZECHARIAH.

| ii. | 13 | i. | 253 |
|---|---|---|---|

### MALACHI.

| i. | 3 | ii. | 98 |
|---|---|---|---|
|  |  |  | 187 |
| ii. | 14 | ii. | 133 |
|  | 15 | i. | 97 |
|  |  |  | 187 |

### MATTHEW.

| v. | 45 | i. | 210 |
|---|---|---|---|
| vii. | 2 | ii. | 345 |
| viii. | 12 | i. | 448 |
| x. | 16 | i. | 140 |
| xi. | 24 | i. | 488 |
| xviii. | 22 | i. | 222 |
| xix. | 5 | i. | 136 |
| xxvi. | 41 | i. | 507 |

### LUKE.

| Chap. | Ver. | Vol. | Page |
|---|---|---|---|
| i. | 9 | i. | 477 |
| xvii. | 26 | i. | 255 |
|  |  |  | 264 |
|  | 32 | i. | 514 |
| xxiv. | 51 | i. | 391 |

### JOHN.

| i. | 14 | i. | 310 |
|---|---|---|---|
|  | 51 | ii. | 113 |
| iv. | 5 | ii. | 434 |
| v. | 17 | i. | 103 |
| viii. | 11 | ii. | 287 |
| xi. | 51 | i. | 307 |
| xii. | 31 | i. | 171 |
| xvii. | 12 | ii. | 429 |

### ACTS.

| vii. | 14 | ii. | 391 |
|---|---|---|---|
|  | 16 | ii. | 213 |
| xiv. | 17 | i. | 60 |
| xv. | 9 | i. | 195 |
|  | 16 | i. | 309 |

### ROMANS.

| i. | 18 | i. | 497 |
|---|---|---|---|
|  | 20 | i. | 59 |
| ii. | 4 | i. | 419 |
|  | 15 | i. | 160 |
| iii. | 5, 6 | i. | 489 |
|  | 10 | i. | 155 |
|  | 12 | i. | 248 |
| iv. | 3 | i. | 404 |
|  | 4 | i. | 407 |
|  | 11 | i. | 454 |
|  | 19 | i. | 460 |
|  |  |  | 476 |
|  | ii. |  | 33 |
|  | 21 | i. | 476 |
| v. | 12 | i. | 152 |
|  |  |  | 155 |
|  |  |  | 177 |
| vii. | 6 | i. | 162 |
| viii. | 20 | i. | 105 |
|  | 28 | ii. | 167 |
| ix. | 5 | ii. | 146 |
|  | 7, 8, 12 | ii. | 46 |
|  | 8 | i. | 449 |
|  |  |  | 544 |
| xi. | 16 | i. | 447 |
| xii. | 21 | ii. | 155 |
|  |  |  | 498 |
| xiii. | 1 | i. | 382 |
|  | 14 | ii. | 363 |
| xiv. | 14 | i. | 292 |
|  | 16 | ii. | 85 |

| Chap. | Ver. | Vol. | Page |
|---|---|---|---|
| xiv. | 23 | i. | 99 |
| xv. | 8 | i. | 447 |
| xvi. | 20 | i. | 171 |

### 1 CORINTHIANS.

| i. | 21 | i. | 63 |
|---|---|---|---|
| ii. | 14 | i. | 242 |
| iii. | 7 | ii. | 151 |
|  |  |  | 323 |
| iv. | 11 | i. | 210 |
|  |  |  | 356 |
|  | ii. |  | 404 |
| v. | 9 | i. | 528 |
| vi. | 5 | ii. | 442 |
| x. | 4 | ii. | 429 |
|  | 13 | ii. | 59 |
| xi. | 10 | i. | 533 |
| xv. | 22 | i. | 180 |
|  | 45 | i. | 112 |

### 2 CORINTHIANS.

| i. | 20 | i. | 563 |
|---|---|---|---|
| iii. | 7 | i. | 126 |
| v. | 17 | ii. | 95 |

### GALATIANS.

| ii. | 15 | i. | 448 |
|---|---|---|---|
| iii. | 17 | i. | 348 |
|  |  |  | 415 |
| iv. | 3 | i. | 186 |
|  | 21 | i. | 541 |
|  | 29 | i. | 543 |

### EPHESIANS.

| ii. | 3 | i. | 155 |
|---|---|---|---|
|  | 6 | i. | 63 |
|  | 14 | i. | 449 |
|  | 18 | i. | 448 |
|  | 23 | i. | 94 |
| v. | 6 | i. | 528 |
| vi. | 4 | i. | 431 |

### PHILIPPIANS.

| ii. | 3 | ii. | 141 |
|---|---|---|---|
|  | 7 | ii. | 278 |

### COLOSSIANS.

| i. | 5 | i. | 258 |
|---|---|---|---|
| ii. | 11 | i. | 456 |
| iii. | 10 | i. | 94 |

### 1 TIMOTHY.

| Chap. | Ver. | Vol. | Page |
|---|---|---|---|
| i. | 9 | i. | 126 |
| ii. | 1 | ii. | 403 |
|  | 14 | i. | 152 |
| iv. | 5 | i. | 292 |

### 2 TIMOTHY.

| ii. | 12 | i. | 410 |
|---|---|---|---|

### HEBREWS.

| i. | 3 | i. | 326 |
|---|---|---|---|
|  | 14 | i. | 504 |
| ii. | 16 | ii. | 429 |
| vii. | 3 | i. | 388 |
|  | 7 | ii. | 82 |
|  | 9 | i. | 892 |
| ix. | 27 | i. | 232 |
| xi. | 1 | i. | 376 |
|  | 3 | i. | 59 |
|  |  |  | 63 |
|  | 4 | i. | 193 |
|  | 5 | i. | 232 |
|  | 7 | i. | 254 |
|  |  |  | 259 |
|  | 13-16 | ii. | 404 |
|  | 19 | i. | 563 |
|  | 21 | ii. | 418 |
| xii. | 3 | ii. | 468 |
|  | 16 | ii. | 53 |
|  | 17 | ii. | 95 |
| xiii. | 2 | i. | 469 |
|  | 3 | i. | 523 |

### JAMES.

| i. | 13 | i. | 561 |
|---|---|---|---|
|  | 14 | i. | 164 |
| ii. | 11 | i. | 268 |
| v. | 16 | i. | 526 |

### 1 PETER.

| i. | 12, 13 | ii. | 201 |
|---|---|---|---|
| iii. | 6 | i. | 474 |
|  |  |  | 543 |
| iii. | 21 | i. | 258 |
|  |  |  | 273 |

### 2 PETER.

| i. | 15 | ii. | 433 |
|---|---|---|---|
|  | 20, 21 | i. | 171 |
| iii. | 6 | i. | 286 |

### REVELATION.

| xxii. | 2 | i. | 116 |
|---|---|---|---|

# GENERAL INDEX.

## A

ABEL, was probably Cain's twin brother, i. 189, 191; his profession a keeper of sheep, 192; respect which God had to him and to his sacrifice, 194-196; is murdered by Cain, 204, 205.

Abimelech, king of Gerar, in the time of Abraham, takes Sarah, Abraham's wife, to his house, i. 522; is warned by God in a dream not to injure her, 523; asserts his innocence, 524; is compassionated by God, 525; is commanded to restore Sarah to Abraham, 525, 526; obeys the command, 527; his kindness to Abraham, 532; Abraham's prayer in his behalf, 533; covenant between him and Abraham, 551-556.

Abimelech, king of the Philistines in the time of Isaac, reproves Isaac for having given out that Rebekah was his sister, ii. 58, 61, 62; denounces capital punishment against such as should injure Isaac, 63, 65, 66, 72; desires to enter into covenant with Isaac, 72-75; the covenant between them, 76.

Abram, or Abraham, son of Terah, means of determining the period between the deluge and the calling of, i. 332; his calling to be accounted the renovation of the Church, 333; his father and grandfather apostates from the true worship of God, 333, 334; was not his father's eldest son, 335; his wife Sarah's sterility, 338; leaves his native soil and proceeds to Canaan in obedience to the command of God, 338, 340-346; was, previous to this, plunged in idolatry, 343, 387; the divine promises made to him, 346-349, 410, 411, 414-420, 444-459, 571, 572; the strength of his faith, 346, 350, 352, 353, 357, 358, 376, 386, 411, 412, 459, 460, 464, 547, 560, 561, 563, 564, 567, 568; builds an altar to God in token of his gratitude, 353, 356, 368, 377; his faith directed to the blood of Christ, 355; his continual wanderings, 356, 357; goes down to Egypt, 358; persuades his wife to use dissimulation, 359; his sin in this, 360, 362, 365; his departure from Egypt, 367; his wealth, ib.; strife between his herdsmen and those of Lot, 370, 371; his endeavours to restore peace, 371, 372; is treated unjustly by Lot, 372, 373; this loss made up to him by God, 374, 375; rescues Lot from the four kings, 383; entered into covenants of friendship with the princes of Canaan, 384; is called an Hebrew from his ancestor Eber, ib.; undertakes war by the direction of God's Spirit, 383-386; is entertained and blessed by Melchizedek, 386, 387, 391, 392; gives tithes to Melchizedek, 392; his freedom from avarice, 394, 395; his complaint of being childless, 401, 402; his faith of having a numerous seed strengthened by the sight of the stars, 403, 404; was justified by faith alone, 404-406; the time when he was thus justified, 408, 409; offers sacrifice at the command of God, 412, 413; is promised a placid and quiet death, 418; the nations enumerated whose land was to be given to his offspring, 421; is prevailed upon by Sarah to take Hagar as a concubine, 424; long believed Ishmael to be the promised seed, 442; his name changed from Abram to Abraham, 447; the covenant made with him a spiritual one, 450; is promised a legitimate seed by Sarah, 459; his prayer in behalf of Ishmael, 461;

ii. 98 ; circumcises himself and his family, i. 464; angels appear to him, and his hospitality towards them, 469-471 ; is forewarned of the destruction of Sodom and Gomorrah, 478-480, 483; his intercession in behalf of Sodom, 486-491; witnesses the destruction of Sodom and the other cities of the plain, 515, 516; leaves the neighbourhood of these cities, 520; an additional instance of his infirmity, 521, 530; why he did not become a father till advanced in age, 537 ; circumcises Isaac, 539 ; his age at the birth of Isaac, ib. ; ejects Ishmael and his mother from his family, 541, 545, 547, 548 ; the thought of this painful to him, 544 ; his house a lively image of the Church, 545; is commanded for the trial of his faith to slay his son Isaac with his own hand, 559-566; prepares to obey the divine command, 567, 568; is prevented from slaying Isaac, and his piety approved, 569, 570 ; his wife's death, 575, 576 ; his grief for her, 578 ; his desire to have a family burying-place in Canaan, 579; purchases for this purpose the cave of Machpelah, 581, 584 ; why he would not allow his son to marry a Canaanitish woman, ii. 12; whether he was married to Keturah during the lifetime of Sarah, 32-35; his sons by Keturah, 35 ; constitutes Isaac his sole heir, ib. ; his incomparable patience, 36 ; his death, 36, 37, 60.

Abraham, children of, twofold, i. 545 ; ii. 573.

Abundance, the mother of idleness, ii. 332.

Accusations, unjust, ii. 173.

Adam, was well instructed as to his origin and the creation of the world, i. 58; was created in the image of God, 91-96, 227, 228 ; contrast between him and Christ, 112 ; the positive law imposed upon him, 125, 126 ; inducements he had to obey this law, 126 ; the kind of death threatened to his disobedience, ib. ; woman necessary to him even in innocency, 130, 131; gave names to every living creature, 131; how he knew that Eve was formed from his side, 134, 135; did not fall except by the permission and ordination of God, 143, 144 ; is prevailed upon by the woman to eat the forbidden fruit, 151, 152 ; in what his first sin consisted, 152-154 ; his defection the ruin of all his posterity, 154 ; whether the souls of men are propagated by descent from him, 156 ; the time of the fall, ib. ; his sense of shame after it, 158, 159 ; his attempts at self-defence, 163, 164 ; sentence pronounced upon him, 172-180 ; his death dates immediately from his transgression, 179 ; ironical reproof addressed by God to him, 182 ; is debarred from the fruit of the tree of life, 183 ; is driven from the garden of Eden, 184 ; his return to the garden of Eden prevented by angels, 185; his family in various ways corrupt themselves, 223; he himself, his wife, and others of his children, true worshippers of God, 224; transmitted his fallen nature to his children, 228 ; his age at his death, 231. See *Eve. Man. Satan. Serpent.*

Adoration, falling on the face the ancient rite of, i. 445.

Adoration, put for the civil respect shewn to men, i. 581.

Adoption, degrees of, i. 447-449 ; is founded in the good pleasure of God alone, ii. 49.

Adultery, its criminality and hatefulness in the sight of God, i. 523, 528; ii. 63, 296, 297 ; why Christ did not punish it, 287 ; the adulteress burnt to death in the Patriarchal ages, 286 ; why the adulterer was less severely punished, ib.

Affections, human, in what sense ascribed to God, i. 247, 249.

Afflictions, are to be traced to sin, i. 178; ii. 282; utility of, i. 438 ; ii. 162, 195, 321, 344 ; are sent by God, 196 ; their power in awakening the conscience, 343, 357, 358, 370; our duty under them to accustom ourselves to the consideration of God's judgments, 347, 349 ; are common to the good and the bad, 383.

Africans, the, Ham, the progenitor of, i. 313.

Age, commonly signifies antiquity, i. 245 ; is put for a long period of time, 375.

Alexander the Great, i. 121.

Allegories not to be too much indulged in interpreting the Scriptures, i. 257, 279, 545 ; ii. 438, 439, 461.

## GENERAL INDEX.                                499

Allurements of the world to be guarded against, ii. 332.
Ambition, its baneful effects, i. 319, 380; ii. 141; prompted men to build the Tower of Babel, i. 323, 327, 328; is the mother of all contentions, 372.
Ambrose quoted, i. 578; ii. 91.
Amorites, the, God's longsuffering towards, i. 418, 419.
Anabaptists, their error in denying that God's covenant includes infants, i. 297, 298.
Anagogy, meaning of, i. 168.
Anah, the first who produced mules, ii. 254.
Angels, ridiculous opinion of the Jewish writers as to God's holding communication with them and the earth when about to create man, i. 92; are confirmed, 158; appointed to prevent Adam from re-entering the garden of Eden after his expulsion, 185; why called cherubim, 186; that sometimes ascribed to them which belongs peculiarly to God, 432, 475; three of them appear to Abraham, 468-471; on appearing to the fathers bodies were given them for a time, 472, 478; were called "men" from the form they assumed, 478; are ministers of God's wrath as well as of his grace, 504, 505; are not to be prayed to or worshipped, ii. 25; are ministers to the faithful, 113, 185, 186; Christ the head of, 113.
Angelical perfection erroneously placed in poverty, i. 367.
Anger, its blindness, i. 427; lengths to which it will hurry men, 428; ii. 228.
Anger, Holy, ii. 141.
Anger of God proceeds with a slow step to avenge itself, i. 419.
Animals, were created on the sixth day of the creation, i. 90; the skins of, the first clothing of our first parents, 181, 182; why they perished in the deluge, 250; distinction between clean and unclean, in the days of Noah, 266, 282; some remains of man's original dominion over them survived the fall, 290; the promise of this dominion renewed to Noah, ib.; grant of them for food to man, 291, 292; the eating of their blood forbidden, 293; the unclean not to be eaten by the Jews, ib.

Antediluvian world, the, God's longsuffering towards, i. 240, 241, 243, 247; universality and inveteracy of the wickedness of, 247, 248, 253, 255. See *Giants.*
Anthropomorphites, the, their error, i. 94.
Antiphrasis, a rhetorical figure, ii. 471.
Apocrypha quoted, i. 78.
Apostasy of mankind, early and extensive, after the deluge, ii. 166-170, 237.
Ararat, the mount on which the ark rested, i. 278.
Arians referred to, i. 71, 95.
Aristotle maintained the eternity of the world, i. xlix; quoted, 318; dwells on second causes, and overlooks God, 512, 532.
Ark, the, in which Noah and his family were preserved from the deluge, its structure, i. 255, 256; was more than sufficient to contain all the creatures God commanded Noah to take into it, 257; was an image of the Church, 257, 273; the number of animals to be taken into it, 266, 269; was made secure from the deluge not by human artifice, but by divine miracle, 272; raven sent forth by Noah, i. 279. See *Noah.*
Ark, cavil of Porphyry in reference to the, refuted, i. 257.
Armenia, mountains of, their great height, i. 278.
Arrian quoted, i. 121.
Arts, the invention of, i. 217, 218.
Asher, future condition of the tribe of, predicted by Jacob on his deathbed, ii. 465.
Asiatics, Shem was their progenitor, i. 313.
Astrology condemned, i. 84.
Astronomy, imperfect state of, in Calvin's time, i. 86; is to be studied, ib.; was first cultivated among the heathen, 218.
Asphaltites, the lake, or the Dead Sea, i. 381.
Assyrians, the, Chaldea founded by, i. 370.
Athenians, the, i. xlix.
Augustine quoted, i. 61, 93, 117, 152, 156, 204, 256, 257, 266, 368, 455, 541, 570; ii. 34, 241, 391.
Authority of God should regulate us in every thing, i. 350, 351.
Avarice, its blindness, i. 372, 373; the root of all evil, ii. 163.

## B

BABEL the seat of Nimrod's empire, i. 317, 318.

Babel, the building of the tower of, i. 323; wherein consisted the criminality of, 323, 324, 327, 328; the period from the deluge to, 324; grief with which it would affect Noah, 325; confusion of tongues at, 325, 326, 329-331; brick used in, 326; meaning of the term Babel, 332.

Balaam, his wicked device for seducing the Israelites to defection, i. 240.

Baptism, Noah's deliverance from the universal deluge, a figure of, i. 273; is now substituted for circumcision, 456; is not to be despised, 458; not necessary to salvation, ib.; sin of parents in its neglect, ib.; is a mark of separation from the profane, ii. 223.

Barnes, Rev. Albert, of Philadelphia, his testimony in favour of our authorized version of the Scriptures, i. xiv.

Bdellium, i. 124.

Beauty, personal, is the gift of God, i. 361, 522; dangers to which it exposes one, ii. 295.

Beer-sheba, origin of the name, i. 556.

Beginning of strength, the, why first-born so called, ii. 442.

Believers, true, are the legitimate sons of Abraham, ii. 45. See *People of God.*

Benefits, temporal, bestowed upon God's people and upon unbelievers in a different way, ii. 428.

Benjamin, son of Jacob by Rachel, his birth, ii. 244, 338, 346, 348; is greatly beloved by his father, 350; is with difficulty allowed by his father to go down to Egypt, 355; Joseph's affection for him, 362, 368; future disposition and habits of the tribe of, predicted by Jacob on his death-bed, 470.

Bernard quoted, i. 157.

Berosus quoted, i. 324.

Bethel, ii. 120, 233.

Bethuel, father of Rebekah, ii. 26, 169.

Bible, the, Tyndale's version of, i. xvii; the Geneva version of, its author, xvii.

Bilhah, the maid-servant of Rachel, ii. 142.

Birds and fishes, were created on the fifth day of the creation, i. 88.

Birthday, the celebration of it common, ii. 312.

Birthright. See *Primogeniture.*

Bless, what it is to do so, i. 90, 105, 347.

Blessing an ancient custom, ii. 82; whence the custom arose, 182.

Blessing the people, a duty of the Levitical priests, i. 391; ii. 199.

Blessing, God's, its efficacy, i. 289, 300, 381; ii. 106, 150; is the ordinary attendant on good faith and equity, 154; is put for his promise, 240.

Blessings, earthly, mingled with troubles, ii. 65.

Blood, the eating of, for a time forbidden, i. 293.

Bowing towards the ground, a token of reverence common among oriental nations, i. 470.

Bricks, employed in building the tower of Babel, i. 326.

Brides, an ancient custom in the East to give them veiled to their husbands, ii. 29.

Briers and thorns, their production a consequence of sin of man, i. 104.

Burial of the dead, religiously observed in all ages and among all people, i. 578, 579; is a symbol of the future resurrection, ii. 245, 477. See *Dead. Funeral.*

## C

CAIN, was probably Abel's twin brother, i. 189; Eve's words on his birth, 190, 191; his life in appearance well regulated, 192; why he and his offering were not accepted of God, 196; how he came to know that his offering was rejected and Abel's accepted, 196, 197; his wrath thereby excited against Abel, 197, 198; is reprimanded by God, 198, 199, 201; disguises his hatred of Abel under the colour of fraternal regard, 204; his malignant feelings break forth in accusation against his brother, and he murders him, 204, 205; is summoned to God's tribunal, 205, 206; is convicted, 206-208; judgment pronounced upon him, 208-211; complains of being too severely punished, 212; his dread of violence from men, 213; a mark set on him by God to keep others from doing him violence, 214, 222; what is meant

GENERAL INDEX. 501

by his departing from the presence of the Lord, 214 ; all his children not named by Moses, 215 ; builds a city, and his motives for doing so, 216.
Calendar, Jewish, i. 264, 286.
Calling upon the name of God. See *Invoking the name of God.*
Calvin, comparison between him and Luther as reformers and commentators, i. viii; his impartiality as an interpreter of Scripture, ix ; animadversions on Bishop Horsley's opinion of him as an expositor of the Prophecies, xi, xii; the Latin version of Leo Juda, the basis of his version of the Scriptures, xv ; assists Robert Peter Olivetan in the publication of the first French Protestant Bible, xvi ; order in which his commentaries succeeded each other, xviii; medals of Calvin, xxiii ; he denounces the schismatics of his own day, lii ; why he avoided prolixity in his commentaries on the books of Moses, liii ; incorrect views of the planetary system in his time of which he partook, 61, 173 ; his references to the Reformation, 224 ; and to the corruptions of his own time, i. 334, 376, 530, 547 ; ii. 29, 127, 128, 209, 219, 361, 464.
Camarina, a city of Sicily, ii. 110.
Canaan, son of Ham, i. 301 ; why the judgment of God was pronounced on him for the sin of his father, i. 305-307.
Canaan, the land of, promised to Abraham and his seed, i. 346 ; Abraham enters into covenant with the princes of, 384 ; was a mirror or pledge to the fathers of the heavenly inheritance, 448 ; ii. 91, 92, 115, 386 ; famine in, 353, 408 ; was not divided among the Israelites by the will of man, 440.
Canaanites, the, were doomed to destruction on account of their wickedness, i. 345, 352, 353; their cruelty and pride, 356 ; their idolatry, 369, 377 ; the patriarchs on their guard not to form marriages with, ii. 392.
Canonists, the, 584.
Carnal counsels, are cursed by God, i. 517.
Carnal security, to be guarded against, ii. 234.
Cato quoted, i. liv.

Cause, the first, independent of second causes, i. 82, 83.
Causes, second, our proneness to conceive of them as necessary to God, i. 82.
Celibacy condemned, i. 128 ; ii. 121.
Celebrity of name gained by crimes, evils of, i. 246.
Chaldea founded by the Assyrians, i. 320 ; its fertility, 357.
Chaldean paraphrast quoted, i. 147, 238, 278.
Charity does not forbid the exercise of caution as to unknown persons, i. 362 ; is ingenious in hiding the faults of brethren, ii. 380.
Charran in Mesopotamia, i. 339.
Chastisements, God's, i. 178.
Chastity, to be religiously cultivated, ii. 220.
Chedorlaomer, i. 381.
Cherubim, why angels are so called, i. 186 ; why God is said to sit between the cherubim which overshadowed the ark of the covenant, ib.
Childbirth, pains of, traceable to the first transgression of Eve, i. 171.
Children, of Abraham, twofold, i. 545 ; ii. 573 ; ought to be subject to their parents in contracting marriage, i. 551, ii. 14, 219 ; are not the offspring of chance, 141 ; are the gift of God, 135, 141, 208 ; are bonds to unite their parents, 148. See *Parents.*
Christ, contrast between him and Adam, i. 112 ; is God, 75, 475; was typified by Melchizedek, 388, 389 ; his priesthood, 389; is an eternal king, ib. ; was present in all the ancient oracles, 433 ; was the end of the Levitical law, 456 ; often appeared under a human form to the fathers in company with angels, 470, 472, 475, 495; ii. 165, 429 ; is the head of angels, 113 ; was symbolized by Jacob's vision of the ladder, 113 ; all nations to be blessed in him, 116 ; is the living image of God, 202 ; was typified by Joseph, 261, 266 ; sprang from the tribe of Judah, 277 ; derived no glory from that descent, 278 ; why he did not punish adultery, 287 ; the name "angel" applied to him, 429; his peculiar office to deliver his people from all evil, 429 ; his coming announced by Jacob on his death-bed under the name Shiloh,

452-459; opposition to be made to him predicted, 468.
Chronological difficulties, i. 243, 244.
Chrysostom, incorrectly refers the image of God in which man was created, to the dominion with which man was invested over the inferior creation, i. 94.
Church, her seed however small preserved from the creation to the deluge, i. 227; her enemies exposed to God's vengeance, 416; her state shadowed forth in the ejection of Ishmael and his mother from the family of Abraham, 541, 545; two kinds of persons born in her, 546; the true church to be distinguished from the hypocritical, 547; small in her beginnings, ii. 40, 41; preserved in the person of one man, 110; is an object of derision to the wicked, 209; disgraceful examples often steal into her, 246; privilege of having a place in her, 400; her salvation to be hoped for in her lowest condition, 464, 468; is constantly assailed by enemies, 465.
Chus, put for Ethiopia, i. 124.
Circumcision, a solemn memorial of God's adoption of the family of Abraham, i. 451; reasons why it was enjoined, 453; why called "a seal of the righteousness of faith," 454; why to be performed on the eighth day after the birth of the man-child, 454, 456; was to be performed on the servants or slaves of the Jews, 455; was abolished by the coming of Christ, 456; baptism substituted in its place, ib.; the doom of the uncircumcised, 457, 458.
Cities, were originated by Cain, i. 216; why fortified, ib.
Clothing of our first parents, was at first the skins of slain beasts, i. 181; why they were so clothed, 182.
Command of God, is to be obeyed even when the reason of it is not apparent, i. 147.
Compassion, not to be touched with, held by the Stoics to be a heroic virtue, ii. 375.
Concord to be cultivated, i. 348, 372; ii. 130, 382. See *Peace*.
Concubine, to whom the term was applied among the Hebrews, ii. 35.
Confession of sin, to be made from the heart, i. 288, 477.
Confession, Popish, ii. 101.

Conflict of God with his people, ii. 196, 197.
Confusion of tongues at Babel, i. 325 326, 329-331.
Conscience, power of, i. 201, 206, 525; ii. 52, 75, 174, 178, 299, 343, 357, 358, 369, 370; the approbation of, more to be valued than the plaudits of the whole world, ii. 298, 299.
Conscience, a good, is called a brazen wall, i. 211; the fear of God the fountain of, ii. 343; a peaceful death the effect of, 473.
Conscience, a guilty, is a cruel executioner, i. 202; its secret compunctions the voice of God, 205, 206; is disturbed by unreasonable fears, ii. 482, 483.
Consecration by oil, an ancient custom, ii. 119.
Contention, warned against, i. 370-372, 428; ambition the mother of, 372; ii. 174, 189; our duty to endeavour to prevent, 383.
Contracts, are to be equitably formed, ii. 411.
Convivial feasts, not forbidden, i. 542.
Copernicus, his discoveries respecting the planetary system, i. 61.
Corruption of human nature in consequence of Adam's fall, i. 154, 248, 284; its transmission from Adam, 156. See *Adam*.
Counsels, carnal, cursed by God, i. 517.
Covenant, God's, error of the Anabaptists in denying that it includes infants, i. 297, 298; is eternal, i. 450.
Covenant between Isaac and Abimelech, ii. 76.
Covenants, were anciently confirmed by sacrifices, i. 413; and by raising a heap of stones, ii. 179; were engraven in brass or sculptured in stone, i. 451.
Crates, the Theban, i. 368.
Create, meaning of the word, i. 89.
Creation of the world, the memory of it obliterated shortly after the building of Babel and the dispersion of mankind, i. xlviii; the facts connected with it known by the tradition of the fathers before Moses committed them to writing, 58, 59; the credibility of his narrative of it confirmed, 58; the cavil why so short a space of time has elapsed since the creation of the world refuted, 61; the agency of the Holy Spirit in creating the world, 73; the error that God cre-

ated the world in a moment refuted, 78, 103; the history of the creation the book of the unlearned, 80; philosophical accuracy of language not studied by Moses in his history of it, 85-87; was distributed over six days for our sake, 92; after its completion the work approved of God, 100.
Crime and fault, great difference between, i. 524.
Crimes, celebrity of name gained by, evils of, i. 246.
Cross, the, to be borne patiently, ii. 102.
Cruelty, its hatefulness to God, ii. 444.
Cupidity condemned, ii. 509.
Cups, divining by, prevalent among the Egyptians, ii. 368.
Curse pronounced on the serpent, i. 166-168; and on Adam, after his apostasy, 172-180; and on the earth for his sin, 173, 174.
Curtius, Quintus quoted, i. 123.

## D

DAN, character and future condition of the tribe of, predicted by Jacob on his death-bed, ii. 462, 463.
Day of salvation to be improved without delay, ii. 95.
Dead, the, mourning for, if duly moderated, lawful, i. 578; closing their eyes an ancient custom, ii. 390; principle in which the embalming of them originated, 477. See *Burial*.
Dead Sea, or the lake Asphaltites, i. 381.
D'Albret, Jeanne, Queen of Navarre, Calvin's encomium on her as a friend of the Reformation, i. xlvi, xlvii.
Death, the effect of sin, i. 127, 179, 180; is fitted to correct the pride of man, 328; peace in, the great distinction between the reprobate and the children of God, 417; is not the destruction of the whole man, ii. 38; peace in, the effect of a good conscience, 473.
Deborah, Rebekah's nurse, her great age and death, ii. 239.
Decrees of God, in vain for men to strive to defeat them, ii. 90; have no affinity with the crimes of men, 379.
Deluge, the, reasons unknown to us why the Spirit of God has left so imperfect an account of the state of the world between it and the creation, i. 227; was caused by the wickedness of man, 240, 247, 253, 255; the divine forbearance previously long exercised toward mankind, 241, 247, 249; why it involved the inferior animals in destruction, 250; its approach foretold to Noah, 254; probably commenced in spring, 264, 280; was brought on gradually, 270, 271; is not to be ascribed to chance, 272, 273, 278; Noah's deliverance from it a figure of baptism, 273; its waters abated by the instrumentality of the winds, 277, 278; is never again to be repeated, 283; complete restoration of the world subsequent to it, 286; fabulous account of it by the heathen poets, 313; rapid multiplication of mankind after it, 314, 380, 381.
Depravity of man, is total and universal, i. 248, 284, 285; manifested in the early and rapid corruption of the descendents of Shem, 333, 334. See *Corruption of human nature*.
Devils, their enmity against God, i. 212; are his executioners, 505.
Diligence commended, ii. 24, 338.
Dinah, probably the only daughter of Jacob, ii. 148, 170; her vain curiosity, 218; her chastity violated by Shechem, 218; is desired by Shechem in marriage, 219, 393.
Dinners in use among the Egyptians, ii. 359.
Dionysius impiously boasted that the gods favour the sacrilegious, i. 222.
Dissimulation, to be guarded against, ii. 273, 369.
Distinction between the godly and ungodly, i. 411, 417, 418; ii. 347, 348.
Distinction between the true and hypocritical Church, i. 547.
Distinctions of rank advantageous, i. 246.
Divining by cups, prevalent among the Egyptians, ii. 368.
Divorce, not to be rashly allowed, i. 136; more tolerable than polygamy, ii. 133.
Dominion, the lust of, prevalent among men in all ages, i. 386.
Dove, sent forth by Noah from the ark after the water of the deluge began to abate, i. 279.
Dreams, a means by which God was wont to reveal his secrets, i. 414, 526; ii. 112, 261, 306, 307, 387.

Drunkenness, its criminality, i. 301; drunkenness of Noah, ib.; and of Lot, 518; its punishment, ib.

Dulia and Latria of Papists, i. 582.

E

EARTH, the, its germinating principle derived from God, i. 82, 83; is cursed for the sin of man, 173, 174, 283.

Earth, the, put for its inhabitants, i. 253.

Eastern customs, the knowledge of, important for illustrating the Scriptures, ii. 22.

Eber, a descendent of Shem, his offspring chosen to be God's peculiar people, i. 320; the Hebrews derive their name from, 320, 384; ii. 361.

Eden, where situated, i. 115, 119-122, 185. See *Angels*. *Paradise*.

Edomites. See *Idumeans*.

Egypt, seven years of famine in, ii. 323-326, 408; probable origin of its division into provinces, 412; its priests enjoyed important privileges, ib.

Egyptians, the, boasted of an antiquity far before the Mosaic date of the creation, i. xlix; maintained a vigorous commerce with other nations from the most ancient times, 316; were proud and cruel, 365; the vengeance God would inflict on them for oppressing the Israelites revealed to Abraham, 416; corruption of the marriage relation prevalent among, ii. 296; their women under less restraint than those of the East or of Greece, 301; their insignia of supreme authority, 328; dinners in use among, 359; were forbidden by their religion to eat with foreigners, 360; were in the habit of sitting at table, 362; practised divining by cups, 368; were accustomed to the illusions of magicians, 369; their abhorrence of the occupation of shepherds, 395, 399; violated the law of hospitality in oppressing the Israelites, 402; their custom of mourning for the dead, 476, 479; expense and pomp of their funerals, 477.

Egyptian antiquities, confirm the authority of the Pentateuch, i. 360; ii. 310, 318, 319, 322, 328, 330, 331, 360, 362, 368, 390, 395, 479.

Egyptian ladies, their personal appearance, i. 360; origin of the custom of their being veiled, 362.

Egyptian magicians, ii. 319, 369.

Elect, the, are renewed by the Spirit of God, ii. 52.

Election, distinguishes the true from the bastard children of Abraham, i. 447, 448; national and individual, ii. 45-47; is to be traced to the sovereignty of God, 48; is the origin of holiness, ib.; did not originate in the foreseen good works of the elected, 51, 93; is immutable, 49, 84, 246.

Elohim, the plural of the noun for God, whether an argument for a plurality of persons in the Godhead, i. 71; Dr. Hengstenberg's explanation of the word, 72, 108, 110.

Embalming the dead, principle in which it originated, ii. 477, 478.

Enoch, his singular piety, i. 230, 253; was taken out of the world in an unusual way, 231; his age when thus removed, ib.; his translation an example of immortality for the encouragement of the godly, 231, 232.

Envy, to be guarded against, ii. 141.

Ephraim, son of Joseph, is blessed by Jacob, ii. 426, 430-432; character and condition of the tribe of, predicted by Jacob on his death-bed, 467.

Ephron, Abraham purchases a sepulchre from, i. 583.

Equity, God's blessing the ordinary attendant on, ii. 154.

Er, the son of Judah, his wickedness, ii. 279; is prematurely cut off by God, 280.

Erasmus, his services to the Reformation, i. vi.

Esau, struggle between him and his brother Jacob in their mother's womb, ii. 42; covenant of salvation did not belong to his posterity, 44; his birth, and reason of the name given him, 48; was addicted to hunting in his youth, 49; is preferred by his father to Jacob, 49, 50, 77, 83, 84, 90; was a representation of the reprobate, 52; sells his birthright, 53, 54; his marriage with strangers, 77; is deprived of his father's blessing, 93; his distress on that account, 94, 95; felt no genuine penitence, 96, 97, 108,

109; is blessed by his father, 98, 99; becomes an exile from the kingdom of God, 98, 99; purposes to murder Jacob, 100; attempts reconciliation with his father, but not careful about pleasing God, 108; marries a third wife, 109; his impious and ferocious character, 187; meets Jacob with unexpected benevolence and kindness, 207; interview between him and Jacob, 208; his descendents, 252. See *Judas.*

Eternity of the world maintained by Aristotle, i. xlix.

Eucherius held the tree of life to be a figure of Christ, i. 117.

Eunuch, a term applied to satraps and princes of the courts of oriental kings, ii. 274, 301, 306.

Euphrates, the, i. 118, 119, 121, 122.

Europeans, Japheth, the progenitor of, i. 313.

Eve, her formation, i. 128, 129, 131, 132, 135; objection against the manner of her formation answered, 133; is tempted and overcome by Satan, 146-151; prevails on Adam to eat the forbidden fruit, 151, 152; in what her first sin consisted, 152-154; her sense of shame after her fall, 158, 159; her attempt at self-defence before God, 164, 165; sentence pronounced upon her, 171; her name given her by Adam, 181; was a true worshipper of God, 224. See *Adam. Cain. Abel.*

Events, future, not now revealed by God, ii. 43.

Evils, sin the cause of all, i. 177.

Example of the saints not to be imitated, unless agreeable to the word of God, i. 253, 412; ii. 21, 71, 120, 134, 339, 389.

Examples, evil, the worst contagion, i. 230, 252.

Eye, the, an inlet to sin, ii. 295.

Eyes of the dead, closing them an ancient custom, ii. 390.

## F

FABLES, Jewish, i. 337, 495, 540, 570, 576.

Face of God, what is meant by one's being hidden from, i. 212.

Fair complexion, anciently deemed a recommendation in Egypt, i. 360.

Faith, our knowledge that the worlds were created by the word of God to be traced to, i. 63; how it produces purity, 195; is an active principle, 258, 346, 353; is supported by external symbols, 298, 412, 451; ii. 387; should remain unshaken, amidst the greatest outward distresses, i. 353, 376; ii. 107; in what sense it justifies, i. 407; good men not justified first by faith and afterwards by works, 408, 409; cannot be disjoined from a pure conscience, 445; its only foundation the word of God, 446; ii. 422; springs from election, i. 449; its property to take encouragement for the future from the experience of the past, 510; secures victory over temptations, 562; is often mixed with anxious care, ii. 20; distinguishes the spiritual from the carnal seed of Abraham, 45; is not exempt from all fear, 189.

Faith of Abraham. See *Abraham.*

Faith of Isaac. See *Isaac.*

Faith of Lot. See *Lot.*

Faith of Noah. See *Noah.*

Faithful, the, are justified by faith alone, like Abraham, i. 407; are liable to be assailed on every side, 414; their prayers are heard by God, 434, 516, 526; ii. 19, 42; are useful to others, 106; are the true Israelites, 242. See *People of God.*

Faithfulness of God, i. 538; ii. 23.

Fall of man. See *Adam. Eve. Satan. Serpent.*

Falling on the face, the ancient rite of adoration, i. 445.

Falsehood, God's truth not to be aided by, ii. 88.

Fathers, the patriarchal, were animated by the hope of a better life, i. 576; are not to be imitated in opposition to the law of God, 253, 412; ii. 21, 71, 120, 134, 339, 389.

Fault and crime, great difference between, i. 524.

Faults of good men, the, why many studiously pry into, i. 303.

Fear, the fruit of iniquity, i. 216.

Fear of God, may, from the corruption of our nature, degenerate into a fault, i. 476; is not inconsistent with faith, 481, 482; ii. 117, 118; the want of it leads to all kinds of wickedness and cruelty, i. 529; ii. 180; actuates all the pious, 177; is the source of integrity, 343.

Feasts, convivial, not forbidden, i. 542.
Feet, washing of the, a custom in the East, i. 471.
Felicity, God the source of, to his people, i. 400.
First-born, why called " the beginning of strength," ii. 442; advantages of primogeniture, ii. 53, 208, 248.
Fishes and birds, created on the fifth day of the creation, i. 88.
Flatterers of kings, i. 362.
Flesh, a name applied by God to man as a mark of ignominy, i. 242; and also without any mark of censure, 253; "all flesh," a name given to animals of every kind, 259.
Forbearance of God, i. 329, 374, 418, 419, 484, 485, 526.
Forgiveness, duty of, ii. 376, 484, 489; men more ready to forgive themselves than others, 288.
Fortune, the Deluge not to be ascribed to, i. 272, 273, 278.
Fratricide, abhorrence of the crime of, among the heathen, ii. 265.
Fraud of Laban. See *Laban*.
French Protestant Bible, the first, Calvin's share in it, i. xvi.
Frugality commended, i. 491.
Funerals, pride displayed in, i. 328; were conducted with greater expense and pomp among the Egyptians than among the Jews, ii. 477. See *Burial*.
Future events, not now revealed by God, ii. 43.
Future life, a, known to the patriarchs, ii. 38, 91, 92, 115, 417, 477; consolation of, the chief mitigation of sorrow, 274.

G

GAD, son of Jacob, his birth, ii. 145; future condition of the tribe of, predicted by Jacob on his death-bed, 465.
Ganges, the river, incorrectly supposed to be Pison, i. 119, 123.
Garden of Eden. See *Eden*.
Genesis, the great object of the book of, i. 64, 65.
Geneva version of the Bible, its author, i. xvii.
Gentiles, their calling to the faith of the gospel predicted, i. 309, 446, 447, 449, 450; ii. 460.
Gerundensis, ii. 306.
Giants, the antediluvian, why so called, i. 244; were proud and ferocious tyrants, 246; were the first nobility, ib.; fables invented by the heathen poets concerning, 246, 324.
Gihon, incorrectly thought by many to be the Nile, i. 119, 124.
God, curious inquiries into his *essence* condemned, i. 60; nature of his rest on the seventh day after the creation of the world, 103; works constantly in the government of the world, 103; is not the author of evil, 142, 144; his care of his own people, 208, 276, 400, 416, 430, 517, 523, 550; ii. 26, 61, 136, 150, 171, 208, 233; what is implied in one's being hidden from his face, i. 212; human affections ascribed to him, 247, 249; has no need of new counsel, after the manner of men, 250, 478; uses the language of irony, 330: his authority should regulate us in everything, 350, 351; is the source of his people's felicity, 400; allows them to question him, 411; two ways in which he looks down upon men for the purpose of helping them, 433; what is meant by living before him, 461; stretches forth his hand to save his people at the critical moment, 502; different ways in which he is said to be present with men, 551; in what sense he is said to tempt men, 561; ii. 196; sometimes speedily answers prayer and sometimes delays the answer, ii. 19, 80; how the name "man" is applied to him, 197; what is meant by seeing him face to face, 202; he restrains the cruelty of the wicked, 207; sense in which ascending and descending are ascribed to him, 242; distinction between his *willing* and *permitting* certain things condemned, 378, 487; makes use of the wickedness of men for accomplishing his purposes, 379, 488; his sovereignty in distributing his gifts, 431. See *Faithfulness of God. Forbearance of God. Grace of God. Judge of the World. Power of God. Providence of God. Truth of God.*
Godly and ungodly, distinction between them, i. 411, 417, 418; ii. 347, 348.
Gomorrah, wickedness of its inhabitants, i. 483, 484, 491; is destroyed by fire and brimstone from heaven, 512; why infants were involved in that destruction, 513. See *Sodom*.

# GENERAL INDEX.

Good, the. See *People of God.*
Goshen, position of the land of, ii. 393, 394, 398.
Gospel, impediments to the preaching of it through the whole world, i. 465; is to be offered indiscriminately to all, 503; the preaching of it called "the kingdom of heaven," ii. 118; the pride of man opposed to it, 264.
Government of God. See *Providence of God.*
Government, civil, is not to be violated, i. 431.
Government, monarchical, chosen by God for his ancient people as the most perfect form, ii. 450.
Grace of God, is not bound to the accustomed order of nature, i. 431; is what makes one man excel another, ii. 52.
Grass, the earth on the third day of the creation commanded to bring it forth, i. 82.
Gratitude to God. See *Thanksgiving.*
Gratitude to man, duty of, i. 386, 393.
Greek interpreters or Septuagint. See *Septuagint.*
Greek translations of the Pentateuch, were procured by Ptolemy, king of Egypt, i. xlviii.
Gregory I., Pope, argument by which he defends statues and pictures in churches, i. 80.
Grief at the wickedness of men, in what sense it is ascribed to God, i. 249.
Grief, immoderate, on the death of friends to be restrained, ii. 273; if duly moderated is not to be censured, 476; the consolation of a future life the chief mitigation of, 274.

## H

Hagar, Sarah's handmaid, i. 425, 426; begins to hold her mistress in contempt, 427; is met in the wilderness in her flight from the house of her mistress by an angel, 430; is reproved by him for her flight, 432; is encouraged by him, 432-434; betakes herself to prayer, 435; her previous character, 435, 438; her penitential spirit, 437, 438; is ejected with her son Ishmael from the family of Abraham, 541, 547, 548; her distress after her ejection, 549; is met by an angel, 550; ii. 36.
Ham, the youngest son of Noah, i. 235; mocks his father, 301; his wicked character, 302; why the judgment of God for his mockery of his father is pronounced on his son Canaan and not on himself, 305-307; was the progenitor of the Africans, 313.
Hamor, the father of Shechem, endeavours to obtain Dinah, Jacob's daughter, for his son in marriage, ii. 222; perfidy and cruelty of Jacob's sons towards, 222-228.
Haran, son of Terah, and brother of Abraham, his death, i. 337.
Harp and organ invented by Jubal, i. 218.
Harvest and seed time secured so long as the earth endures, i. 286; songs sung at the ingathering of harvest, ii. 355.
Havila, the land of, i. 123.
Head, to lift up one's head, what it denotes, ii. 309; to lift up the head from off one, its meaning, 311.
Heart, integrity of, proceeds from God, ii. 343.
Hearts of men are in the hand of God, ii. 73, 207, 237, 345, 355.
Heathen, the, were the first cultivators of astronomy and medicine, i. 218.
Heathen philosophers, their ignorance of the creation and origin of the world and of the human race, i. xlviii, xlix.
Heathen poets, their fables concerning the antediluvian giants, i. 246, 324; their fabulous account of the deluge, 313; and of the rapid multiplication of men after it, 381, 513.
Heathen sacrifices, their origin, i. 193.
Heavens and earth, God exhibited in, i. 59; our eyes not sufficiently clearsighted to discern what they represent, 62; the knowledge to be thence derived not sufficient for salvation, ib.
Hebrews, the, derived their name from Eber, a descendant of Shem, i. 320; ii. 361; the Egyptians forbidden by their religion to eat with, ii. 360. See *Israelites. Jews.*
Hebrew Doctors. See *Jewish Writers.*
Hebrew language has no neuter gender, i. 533.
Hebrew points, i. 189; ii. 418.
Hebron, was anciently called Kirjath-arba, i. 576.
Hengstenberg, Dr., his explanation of the word Elohim, i. 72, 108, 110.
Henry IV. of France, Calvin's Commentary on Genesis dedicated to

him when a boy, i. xlv; Calvin's advices to him, liii, liv.

Herbs and trees, why created before the sun and moon, i. 82.

Hiddekel, a name applied to the Tigris, i. 118, 121-123.

History, advantages of the study of, i. 480.

Historians, heathen, are fabulous in treating of a remote antiquity, i. xlix.

Holy life, a, is inseparable from true faith, i. 445.

Homicide, frivolous distinction of, into four kinds by the Jews, i. 249.

Honour due to parents, i. 302; ii. 14, 264.

Honours to be conferred only on the deserving, ii. 327.

Horace quoted, i. 177, 327.

Hospitality, is practised by Abraham, i. 468; the duty of, 469; Lot distinguished for, 495, 496, 498; the oppression of the Israelites in Egypt a violation of the law of, ii. 402.

Human nature, corruption of, the consequence of Adam's fall, i. 154, 248, 284; its transmission from Adam, 156. See *Adam*.

Human race, why God willed that they should proceed from one source, i. 97.

Humanity commended and enjoined, i. 294, 348, 428, 469; ii. 128, 345; humanity of Reuben, ii. 267.

Husbands, duty of wives to obey their, i. 474, 533; brides in the East given veiled to their, ii. 29; are not to be too obsequious to their wives, 301.

Hypocrisy, God's hatred of, i. 196; is to be guarded against, 443; ii. 143; is deeply rooted in the human mind, 224, 266, 343; hypocrisy of Jacob's sons, 267.

Hypocrites, nothing sincere in their religious worship, i. 196, 197; their pretended friendship to be dreaded, 204; distinguished from the genuine worshippers of God, 354; always seek excuses, 476; mingle in the Church with the people of God, and despise them, 546, 547; ii. 48; a lively picture of them exhibited in Esau, ii. 100, 109; never truly repent, 109; ascribe their prosperity to God's favour for them, 143, 172; heap false complaints upon the good, 172; disguise one sin by another, 272.

Hypotyposis, a rhetorical figure, its meaning, i. 330.

I

IDLENESS condemned, i. 125; ii. 238, 332.

Idolatry, propensity of the human mind to, ii. 169, 170, 358; madness of, 173, 174, 234, 235.

Idumeans, the, are descended from Abraham, i. 446; were cut off from the body of the Church, ii. 44, 98, 99; Isaac's prediction concerning, 99, 253, 254.

Image of God in which man was created, Augustine's refined speculations concerning, i. 93; is erroneously referred by Anthropomorphites to the human body, 94; in what it consists, 94, 95; image of God and likeness of God phrases of synonymous import, 93, 94; why Paul denies the woman to be the image of God, 96; Christ the living image of God, ii. 202.

Images, popish, worship of, ii. 174.

Immortality, not to be sought on earth, i. 327.

Impatience, to be guarded against, i. 427.

Impunity of the wicked is sometimes an occasion of alluring even the good to sin, i. 254.

Incest, is abhorrent to nature, ii. 246, 288.

Infants, error of the Anabaptists in denying that God's covenant is common to, i. 297, 298; cruel superstition of consigning them to perdition when a sudden death has prevented their being baptized, 458; why involved in the destruction of Sodom and Gomorrah, 513; unnatural for mothers not to nurse their own, 540.

Ingratitude, entered into the first sin of Adam and Eve, i. 153; is to be guarded against, 438, 521, 549; ii. 26, 54, 74, 201.

Inheritance, or felicity, reward put for, i. 400.

Iniquity, fear, the fruit of, i. 216.

Injuries, duty in reference to, ii. 172, 177, 489.

Insects, noxious, are to be traced to the sin of man, i. 104.

Integrity of heart particularly required by God, i. 443; integrity of life proceeds from the fear of God, ii. 343.

GENERAL INDEX.  509

Invoking the name of God, often put for the whole of divine worship, i. 223, 354, 368, 377, 557 ; ii. 71.

Iphigenia, painter's representation of the sacrifice of, ii. 246.

Irony, used by God in reproving Adam, i. 182 ; and in speaking of the builders of the tower of Babel, 330.

Isaac, the divine promise concerning, i. 462, 468 ; his birth, 537, 538 ; is circumcised, 539 ; is openly contemned when an infant by Ishmael, 542 ; the Mediator promised in his person, 565 ; voluntarily surrenders himself when his father, for the trial of his faith, is commanded by God to slay him with his own hand, 569 ; his father prevented from slaying him, 569, 570 ; his veneration for his father, ii. 14 ; his father's servant providentially directed to Rebekah, in choosing a wife for him, 20-23 ; Rebekah's parents are induced to give her to him in marriage, 24, 25 ; his piety, 28 ; is met by Rebekah, 29 ; is married to her, ib.; his bitter grief on the death of his mother, ib.; is constituted by his father his sole heir, 35 ; had no children long after his marriage, 41 ; the constancy of his faith, 41, 42 ; loves Esau more than Jacob, 49, 50, 77, 83, 84, 90 ; is forbidden to go to Egypt, 59 ; is commanded to settle in the promised land, ib.; is incited by God to follow his father's example, 60 ; inferior to his father in patience, 62 ; his dissimulation in giving out to the men of Gerar that Rebekah was only his sister, 60, 61 ; is reproved for this by King Abimelech, 58, 61, 62 ; his prosperity, 64, 66 ; is envied by the Philistines, 65 ; the wrongs he suffered in Gerar, 67 ; his patience and composure, 68 ; removes to Beer-sheba, ib.; is favoured with a vision, 69 ; builds an altar, 71 ; compact between him and Abimelech, 72-76 ; his old age, 83 ; is led by Jacob's artifice to pronounce on him the blessing of primogeniture, 84, 88, 89 ; did so by a secret providence, 90, 91 ; is afterwards convinced of this, 94, 96 ; his blessing on Esau, 98, 99 ; pronounces anew the benediction on Jacob, 105, 106 ; his death, 247, 248.

Ishmael, son of Abraham, i. 433 ; the warlike and formidable character of himself and his descendents, 434, 435 ; was long believed by his father to be the promised seed, 442 ; his father's prayer in his behalf, 461 ; is commanded by God to be circumcised, 462 ; his father's prayer for him heard, 462, 463 ; ii. 98 ; his open contempt for his infant brother Isaac, i. 542 ; the impiety involved in this, 543 ; is ejected with his mother from his father's house, 541, 547, 548 ; his distress after his ejection, 549 ; his earthly prosperity connected with his relationship to Abraham, 551 ; was subject to his mother in contracting marriage, ib.; celebrates with Isaac the obsequies of his deceased father, ii. 38 ; his sons, 39 ; his degeneracy and that of his descendents, 109.

Ishmaelites, boundaries of their country, i. 124.

Israel. See *Jacob*.

Israelites, their long captivity and slavery revealed to Abraham, i. 414 ; their adoption by God, 448 ; ii. 45-47 ; were not all his regenerated children, i. 449 ; circumcision a solemn memorial of their adoption, 451, 453 ; their servants or slaves were to be circumcised, 455 ; their oppression in Egypt a violation of the laws of hospitality, ii. 402 ; the land of Canaan not divided among them by the will of man, 440 ; their future condition predicted by Jacob on his deathbed, 420-472. See *Hebrews. Jews*.

Issachar, future condition of the tribe of, predicted by Jacob on his deathbed, ii. 462.

J

JABAL, a descendent of Cain, was the inventor of tents, i. 217, 218.

Jabbok, the brook so called, ii. 195.

Jacob, struggle between him and his brother Esau in their mother's womb, ii. 42 ; his being preferred by God to Esau the effect of sovereign grace, 44, 45, 51, 93 ; his birth, and reason of the name given him, 48 ; his mild disposition in his youth, 49 ; is less beloved by his father than Esau, 49 ; is more beloved by his mother than Esau, 50 ; obtains from Esau the birthright for a mess of pottage, 53, 54 ;

surreptitiously obtains his father's blessing, 84, 86, 87, 88; his death resolved on by Esau, 100; is forced in consequence to become a wanderer from his father's house, 101, 102; has pronounced on him anew, previous to his departure, the blessing by his father, 105, 106; trial of his faith, 108; the arduousness of his journey, 111; his vision of the ladder, 112, 114-116; how he was the fountain of blessedness to all nations, 116; extols the goodness of God, 117; erects a stone as a memorial of gratitude for the vision, 118; his vows to God, 120-123; pours a libation on the stone he had erected, 123; arrives in Mesopotamia at the house of his uncle Laban, 127; informs his uncle of his circumstances, 128; employs himself in honest labours, 129; is hardly dealt with by his uncle, 130, 150, 151, 154, 165, 176; his affection for Rachel, his uncle's daughter, 131; is deceived by Laban, and marries Leah, 132; also marries Rachel, 134; fails in kindness to Leah, 135; his polygamy punished by domestic strife, 140, 147; is hurried by Rachel into a third marriage, 142; desires to leave Laban and return to his parents, 149; his treaty with Laban, by which he was to receive the spotted offspring of the sheep and goats, 152; his device for making the sheep and goats bring forth a spotted offspring, 155, 156; is treated inhumanely by Laban's sons, 162, 163; returns to his own country under the special guidance of God, 163; his wives consent to go with him, 164, 165, 167, 168; dream in which an angel of the Lord appeared to him, 165; is pursued by Laban, who accuses him of robbery, 171-173; his defence, 174-178; his placable character, 179; covenant between him and Laban, 178-180; his alarm at the prospect of meeting his brother Esau, 185, 205; the means he adopts for appeasing his brother, 188; betakes himself to prayer, 190; acknowledges his own want of merit, 191, 192; his rich present to his brother, 194; wrestles with God, who appeared to him in the form of a man, 195-197; prevails, 198, 199; his name changed from Jacob to Israel, 200, 240; his reverence towards his brother, 206; is met by Esau with unexpected kindness, 207, 211; interview between the two brothers, 208, 210; his suspicion of Esau, 211; erects an altar, 213; his grief on hearing of the violation of his daughter Dinah's chastity, 220; the perfidy and cruelty of his sons to the Shechemites, 222-228; expostulates with them, 228; is commanded by God to go up to Bethel, 233; purifies his house from idols, ib.; his infirmity in burying the idols under an oak and not rather destroying them, 236; builds an altar at Bethel, 237; his numerous trials, 243; loses Rachel by death, 244; his grief for Joseph, when sold by his brethren, 272, 273; his ten sons go down to Egypt to buy corn, 337, 346; his suspicion of his sons, 348; their second journey into Egypt, 353; allows with difficulty his son Benjamin to go down with them, 355-357; his feelings on hearing that Joseph was alive and governor of Egypt, 383; his deep rooted piety, 387; his vision in which God ratifies his former covenant with him, 387-389; goes down to Egypt with his family, 390; Goshen selected as an abode for him and his sons by Joseph, 393, 394, 398; his descendants providentially kept from intermarrying with the Egyptians, 395, 400; condition on which his sons wished to live in Egypt, 402; is introduced to Pharaoh by Joseph, 403; binds Joseph by an oath to bury him in Canaan, 416, 417; his address to his sons on his death-bed, and his predictions concerning the future fortunes of their families, 420-472; charges his sons to bury him in Canaan, 472; his placid death, 473; mourning for him by his sons and the Egyptians, 476; is buried in Canaan, 480; his funeral honourably celebrated, 481.

Japheth, the eldest son of Noah, i. 235, 320; his filial piety and modesty, 302, 303; the benediction his father pronounces on him, 308; was the progenitor of the Europeans, 313.

Jehovah, a name of God, place where it first occurs in Scripture, and its meaning, i. 109.

Jerome, i. 113; his petulant reproaches

against the married state, 128; quoted, 131, 160, 200, 245, 278, 280, 294, 317, 388, 437, 473, 485, 566, 583, 584; ii. 19, 22, 435, 453.

Jerusalem was anciently called Salem, i. 388.

Jews, the, began the day with the evening, i. 77; divide their year into six parts, 286; their forming one church with the Gentiles predicted, 309, 446, 447; their error in holding circumcision to be still in force, 456; their foolish gloriation in the origin of their nation, ii. 50, 146, 226; their superstition, 203. See *Hebrews. Israelites.*

Jewish Calendar, i. 264, 286.

Jewish Writers, their ridiculous opinion respecting God's holding communication with the earth and angels at the creation of man, i. 92, 107; imagine Abel's sacrifice was consumed by fire from heaven, 196, 200, 213; their fable respecting Lamech, 219, 228; and concerning Abraham, 337, 349, 436; and concerning the angels who appeared to Lot, 495; and concerning Sarah's giving milk, 540; and concerning the ram which appeared on Mount Moriah when Abraham was about to sacrifice his son, 570; and concerning Sarah's beauty in her old age, 576; their frivolous distinction of four kinds of homicide, 294.

Job, his unbecoming language under the pressure of affliction, ii. 273.

Joseph, son of Jacob by Rachel, his birth, ii. 149; is wickedly conspired against by his brethren, 258; the cause of this his father's partiality for him, 259; his future eminence revealed to him in dreams, 260-262, 340; was a type of Christ, 261, 266; his brethren's envy and hatred of him increased by their knowledge of his dreams, 262, 263; his death cruelly contrived by them, 264-266; his murder prevented by the humanity of Reuben, 267, 268; is sold by them to a company of Midianites, 270, 271; his brethren's false report to his father that he had been torn in pieces by wild beasts, 271-273; is sold by the Midianites to Potiphar, the Egyptian, 274; gains the favour of Potiphar, 293; is placed by Potiphar over his house and over all his substance, 294; was distinguished for the graces of his person, 295; is tempted by the wife of Potiphar, 296; his fidelity and integrity, 296-298; is falsely accused by her, 300; is cast into prison by Potiphar, 300, 301; conciliates the goodwill of the keeper of the prison, 302, 303; interprets the dream of Pharaoh's chief butler, and chief baker, 307-310; is forgotten by the chief butler after his restoration to office, 312; interprets Pharaoh's dreams, 324, 325; is made governor of Egypt, 328; and has the precedence of all its nobles, 329; his marriage to the daughter of the Prefect of the city On, 330; his labours in erecting storehouses, 331; his ten brethren come down to Egypt to buy corn, 337; his apparent harshness towards them, 338; his swearing by the life of Pharaoh censurable, 341, 342; shuts his brethren up in prison, 342; endeavoured to establish the worship of the true God in his own family, 359; his affection for Benjamin, 362; entertains his brethren, 359-362; was sparing in domestic splendour, 367; his dissimulation towards his brethren, 368, 369; makes himself known to them, 375, 376; borrows from the providence of God an argument for exercising forgiveness towards them, 380, 382; selects Goshen as an abode for them and his father, 393, 394, 398; his faithful administration, 407, 410; his singular humanity, 414; his father binds him by an oath to bury him in Canaan, 416, 417; his faith, 422; his two sons Ephraim and Manasseh are blessed by Jacob, 426, 430-432; his grief on his father's death, 476; buries his father in Canaan, 480; his affection for his brethren, 485, 486, 488; his death-bed scene, ii. 490-492.

Josephus quoted, i. 278, 583.

Jovinian, Jerome's book against, i. 128.

Jubal, a descendent of Cain, the inventor of the harp and organ, i. 218.

Judas, character of his repentance, i. 211. See *Esau.*

Judah, son of Jacob, his sin in marrying a Canaanitish woman, ii. 278, 279; his perfidy and cruelty to Tamar, his daughter-in-law, 282-286; his incest with her, 283, his purpose of bringing her to punishment, 286, 287; acknowledges his sin, 288; undertakes to his father to secure the safety of Benjamin in going down to Egypt, 355; his precedence among his brethren, 370-372; the blessing pronounced on his descendents by Jacob on his death-bed, 450; the Messiah to spring from the tribe of, 452.

Judge of the world, God proved to be so by his punishing the wicked, i. 479; as such he always does right, 489.

Judgment, A future, proof of, from the instances of the punishment of sin in the present state, i. 210.

Judgments of God, design of the record of, their infliction of, in Scripture, i. 482; often involve the righteous with the wicked, 487, 488; are often delayed, 484.

Justice between man and man to be cultivated, ii. 62, 129.

Justin quoted, i. 316.

Juvenal quoted, i. 202, 328.

## K

KETURAH, whether Abraham took her to wife during the lifetime of Sarah, ii. 32, 35, 36.

Kimchi, David, quoted, i. 147.

Kindness to relations, duty of, ii. 128; and to all men, 128, 135.

Kingdom of heaven, the preaching of the Gospel so called, ii. 118.

King, the term put for the superior magistrates of towns, i. 381.

Kings, corruption of the courts of, i. 362; flatterers of, 362; moderation enjoined upon, 364; were forbidden by the Levitical law to intrude into the priestly office, 388, 415; splendour not to be altogether condemned in, ii. 328.

Kirjath-arba, the ancient name of Hebron, i. 576.

Kiss, the friendly, abuse of, ii. 128.

## L

LABAN, the Syrian, the brother of Rebekah, ii. 40, 111, 127, 128; his injustice to Jacob, 129, 130, 132, 133, 150, 151, 154, 165, 176; betrothes Rachel to Jacob and then fraudulently substitutes Leah in her place, 132; inhumanity of his sons to Jacob, 162, 163; his idolatry, 169, 173, 174, 181, 182; pursues Jacob, 172; is mollified towards him, 177, 178; covenant between them, 173-180.

Labour, wearisome and exhausting, the fruit of Adam's apostasy, i. 175, 176; manual, not enjoined on all men, i. 175.

Lactantius quoted, i. 243.

Ladder seen by Jacob in his dream, a representation of Christ as Mediator, ii. 113.

Lamech, a descendent of Cain, the first who was guilty of polygamy, i. 217; his sanguinary and obdurate character, 219, 220, 222.

Languages. See *Tongues*.

Latria and Dulia of the Papists, i. 582.

Law of God, the, in what sense it is the minister of death, i. 126; what is denoted by the life or power of, 162; is a perfect rule, 252; the second table of, sometimes put for the whole of our duty, 482.

Lawsuits, whence they arise, ii. 130.

Leah, daughter of Laban, ii. 131; becomes the wife of Jacob by the fraud of her father, 132; her children, 136; her pious feeling manifested in the names she gave them, ib.; gives her maid-servant to Jacob, 144; her son Reuben brings mandrakes out of the field to her, 146; contention between her and her sister Rachel, 147, 148; is willing to leave her father's house and to accompany Jacob to his own country, 167, 168; was a holy woman, 244.

Leo Juda, his Latin version of the Hebrew Scriptures, the basis of Calvin's version, i. xv.

Levi, son of Jacob, his cruelty to the Shechemites, ii. 226, 229; his cruelty denounced by Jacob on his deathbed, 444, 448; origin of the dispersion of the tribe of, among the other tribes of Israel, 448.

Levitical economy, use of the symbols of, i. 186; was abolished by the coming of Christ, 456.

Levitical priesthood subordinate to the priesthood of Christ, i. 393.

Life, human, reason why God accounts it so sacred, i. 295; long life the gift of God, ii. 280; yet no evidence of his favour, ib.; integrity of, proceeds from fear of God, 343.

Lifting the hand put for swearing, i. 394.

Lifting up one's head, what it denotes, ii. 309; lifting the head from off one, its meaning, 311.

Light, its creation, i. 76.

"Likeness of God," and "grace of God," phrases of synonymous import, i. 93, 94.

Living before God, what it implies, i. 461.

Lot, accompanies Abraham, his uncle, to Canaan, i. 350; strife between his herdsmen and those of Abraham, 370-372; his avarice, and injustice to Abraham, 372, 373; what he suffered by separating from Abraham, 375; is taken prisoner by four kings, 383; is rescued by Abraham, ib.; two angels appear to him, 495; his hospitality towards them, 495, 496, 498; risks his life for their defence, 499; his sin in offering his daughters to be polluted, 499, 500; is informed by the angels of their mission to destroy Sodom, 503, 504; invites his sons-in-law to join him in leaving Sodom, and they despise his warning, 505; his tardiness in leaving Sodom 506; is hastened out of it with apparent violence by the angels, 507; is forbidden in his escape to look behind him, 508; defects in his faith, 508-510; he prays for the preservation of Zoar, 510, 511; his wife transformed into a statue of salt, 513; the sin for which she was thus punished, 514, 515; his deliverance from the ruin of Sodom was for Abraham's sake, 516; he departs from Zoar, 517; his intemperance and judicial infatuation, 518.

Love to our neighbour, duty of, ii. 135.

Lucan quoted, i. 339.

Lucianists, the, ii. 226, 446.

Lust, God's abhorrence of, ii. 227.

Luther, his qualifications as a reformer, i. vii; comparison between him and Calvin as commentators, viii; quoted, 241, 334, 335, 375.

Luz, ii. 120.

Lying, its hatefulness in the sight of God, ii. 212.

## M

MACHPELAH, the cave of, purchased by Abraham for a burying-ground, i. 583; ii. 417.

Magicians of Egypt, ii. 319, 369.

Magistrates. See *Rulers*.

Man, created on the sixth day, i. 90; consultation of God when about to create him, 91; this intended to commend to us the dignity of our nature, 92; is invested with authority over the inferior living creatures, 96, 98; created male and female, 97; date of the permission of animal food to, 99; his humble origin, 111; his dignity, ib.; three gradations to be noted in his creation, 112; was created for useful employment, 125; was formed to be a social being, 128, 213; woman created for his good, 128-130; his duty to the woman, 130; ferocity of the brute animals against him a consequence of the fall, 132; why not created without a possibility of sinning, 158; his total and universal depravity, 154, 248, 284. See *Adam*. *Mankind*.

Man, a name applied to God, ii. 197.

Manasseh, son of Joseph, is blessed by Jacob, ii. 426, 430-432; future character and condition of the tribe of, predicted by Jacob on his death-bed, 467.

Mandrakes, ii. 146.

Manes, the founder of Manichæism, his fundamental error, i. 143.

Manichæism, does injustice to God by demanding a cause superior to his will, i. 61; its heresy of the existence of two principles, i. 143, 144; and that the soul of man is a portion of the Divine Spirit, 241.

Mankind, their universal wickedness the cause of the deluge, i. 240; their rapid multiplication after the deluge, 314, 380, 381.

Manoah, ii. 201.

Marriage, original institution of, i. 98, 134, 136; was designed for the good of man, 128-131; twofold artifice of Satan in attempting the defamation of, 134; ought to be formed between one man and one woman only, 136, 137; the degeneracy that resulted from the descendants of Seth marrying the daughters of Cain, 237-240; the law of, sanctioned anew after the deluge, 289; sacredness of, 228, 523, 528; ii. 11, 29, 63, 181, 297; children ought to be subject to their parents in contracting it, i. 551; ii. 14; religious observances connected with it in the patriarchal age, 132; not the custom then to give the younger daughters in marriage before the elder, 132.

Married state, temperance to be used in, i. 239; inconveniences of, 428.

Marry, how the Latin verb *nubo*, " to

marry," came to have that signification, ii. 29.

Mass, the Popish, sacrifice of, not supported by Melchizedek's offering bread and wine to Abraham, i. 390, 391.

Masters, their duty to their servants, i. 431.

Means are not to be neglected, ii. 355.

Medals of Calvin, i. xxiii.

Mediator between God and man, an office which always belonged exclusively to Christ, ii. 495.

Medicine was first cultivated among the heathen, i. 218.

Melchizedek, is preferred to Abraham, i. 386; entertains Abraham and his servants, 386, 387; was not Shem, 345, 387; was a king and priest, 387; mystery of his origin, 388; was a figure of Christ, ib.; his presenting bread and wine to Abraham no argument for the Popish mass, 390, 391; blesses Abraham, 391; and receives tithes from him, 392.

Merit, man destitute of all, i. 265, 479, 572; ii. 51, 191, 221, 302.

Mind, tranquillity of, how best secured, ii. 483.

Ministers of the Gospel, that is sometimes ascribed to them which belongs only to God, i. 267; do not speak in the exercise of their office as private men, ii. 94, 427; are to denounce the vengeance of God, 311.

Miracles not unreasonable, i. 514.

Miseries of men, the, God said to listen to, i. 433, 434.

Moderation to be observed in adorning the person, ii. 21, 328; and in feasting, 362, 363, 461.

Monarchy, the form of government chosen by God for his ancient people as the most perfect, ii. 450.

Money in use in the time of Jacob, ii. 213.

Moon, the, made on the fourth day of the creation, i. 83; a twofold advantage from the course of the sun and moon, 84, 85.

Moriah, the mount on which Abraham was commanded to sacrifice his son Isaac, i. 565; reason of its name, 566.

Moses writes popularly and not philosophically, i. 120, 256, 381; his slaying the Egyptian, 383; in what sense he is said to have seen God face to face, ii. 201; his impartiality in branding with infamy even the tribe from which he sprung, 445, 446.

Moses, the books of, Ptolemy, king of Egypt, procured translations of them into Greek, i. xlviii.

Mothers, unnatural for them not to nurse their own children, i. 540.

Mountains of Armenia, their great height, i. 278.

Mourning for the dead, lawful if duly moderated, i. 578; ceremony of, good principle from which it arose, and its abuse, ii. 476. See *Burial. Funeral.*

Mules were first produced by Anah, ii. 254.

Multitude, the, not to be heedlessly followed, i. 230, 252, 273, 501.

Munster, Sebastian, his Latin version of the Hebrew Scriptures, i. xv.

Murder, forbidden, i. 294; God the avenger of, 294, 295; reason why he is determined to avenge it, 295; ii. 103.

Murderers and robbers, their remorse of conscience, i. 210, 211.

Music adapted to the services of religion, i. 218.

Musical instruments, the invention of, i. 218.

N

NAKEDNESS, a sense of shame of, whence it originated, i. 137, 303.

Name of God, the, is not to be profaned, ii. 143, 222. See *Invoking the name of God.*

Naphtali, the tribe of, its future character and condition predicted by Jacob on his death-bed, ii. 466.

Nations, first settlement of, after the confusion of tongues at the building of the Tower of Babel, i. 313, 315.

Natural philosophy, defective state of, in Calvin's time, i. 86.

Navarre, Jeanne d'Albret, Queen of, Calvin's encomium on her as a friend of the Reformation, i. xlvi, xlvii.

Nearchus quoted, i. 121.

Nebatheans, the, i. 124.

Neighbour, love to our, duty of, ii. 135.

Nile, the, Gihon incorrectly thought by many to be, i. 119, 124; value of the aquatic plants of, ii. 317.

Nimrod, his eminence, ambition, and tyranny, i. 316-319, 326; Babel, the seat of his empire, 317.

# GENERAL INDEX. 515

Noah, his birth and reason of the name given him, i. 233, 234; the time when he was warned of the general deluge, 235; his children, 235, 300; his upright character, 251; his virtue the more remarkable from the corruption of the age in which he lived, 252; is admonished by God of the coming deluge, 254; is commanded to build an ark and promised miraculous preservation, 254, 258, 267; his faith in the promise, 254; obstacles to the building of the ark over which his faith triumphed, 259-261; his faith confirmed by repeated oracles, 264; why his righteousness is assigned as the cause of his being preserved, 265; his obedience, 268; his deliverance from the deluge a figure of baptism, 273; his supposed feelings when floating for months on the waters of the deluge, 276; sends forth a raven from the ark, 279; afterwards sends forth a dove, ib.; goes forth from the ark, at the divine command, 280; builds an altar unto the Lord, and offers sacrifices, 281, 282; his sacrifices are accepted, 282; dominion over the inferior animals promised to him, 290; grant to him and his posterity of the inferior animals for food, 291; this only a restoration of the original grant, 291, 292; God's covenant with him giving security against a second deluge, 296-299; he renews the culture of the fields, 300; his drunkenness, 300, 301; is mocked by his son Ham, 301; is treated with filial piety and modesty by his sons Shem and Japheth, 303; pronounces the judgment of God upon Ham's sin, 304-307; blesses Shem, 308; and Japheth, 308; predicts the union of Jews and Gentiles into one Church, 309; the rapid increase of his descendants and their corruption previous to his death, 310; his grief at the building of the Tower of Babel, 325, 334.

Nobility, origin of, i. 244; the Jews boast in vain of the nobility of their origin, ii. 226.

Nod, land of, origin of the name, i. 215.

Nose jewels used for ornamenting the person in the patriarchal ages, ii. 22.

Novatians, their error in cutting off the lapsed from the hope of pardon, ii. 247.

Nubo, the Latin verb for "to marry," how it came to have this signification, ii. 29.

Nurses, to whom the name was applied in ancient times, ii. 27.

## O

OATH, an, force and nature of, i. 394; ii. 341; elliptical forms of making oath among the Hebrews, i. 395, 553; may be demanded in a lawful cause, 394, 554; ii. 13, 76, 180; is not to be rashly made, i. 395; ii. 13, 76, 341.

Obedience to God's law, its value in the sight of God, i. 163, 193, 350; ought to be universal, 262; is the offspring of faith, 346; is commended, 351, 445, 506, 527, 539, 548, 562; ii. 25, 60, 233; our tardiness in yielding it, i. 506.

Obedience to magistrates, duty of, i. 431.

Obedience to parents, duty of, ii. 264.

Obstinacy in sin, is too common, i. 206, 241, 323, 496, 502; ii. 100; often increases, the nearer God's judgments approach, i. 505.

Offspring, a special gift of God, ii. 135, 141, 208.

Oil, consecration by, an ancient custom, ii. 119.

Old age, hope of the virtuous in, i. 417, 418; ii. 37.

Olivetan, Robert Peter, publishes with the assistance of Calvin, the first French Protestant Bible, i. xvi.

On, the name of a city, ii. 330.

Onan, his wickedness, ii. 281.

Onyx-stone, the, i. 124.

Oracles, God manifested himself to the fathers through, i. 198, 205; some of them common to profane and heathen men, ii. 318.

Organ and harp invented by Jubal, i. 218.

Orientals, the, bowing towards the ground a token of reverence among, i. 470; their custom of washing the feet, 471; were immoderate in the use of ceremonies, 582; ii. 29, 206; were addicted to polygamy, 133; in cases of scarcity were content with slender food, 354.

Origen, his allegories, i. 114, 256, 257, 545.

Origin of the human race, disgraceful ignorance prevalent in the heathen world respecting, i. xlviii.

Original sin, why denied by Pelagius, i. 154; pervades the whole soul, 155, 162, 284.
Ornaments, external, moderation to be observed in, i. 182; ii. 21, 328.
Over-curiosity and captiousness to be guarded against, i. 306, 314.
Ovid quoted, i. 381, 513.

P

PAPISTS, claim the title of the Church, i. 1; though divided among themselves combine against the Gospel, lii; their foolish clamour about following the fathers, 253, 273; their doctrine of transubstantiation, 298, 391; their attempts to cover the abominations of their clergy, 303; their inventions in the worship of God, 355, 446; their sacrifice of the mass not supported from Melchizedek's offering bread and wine to Abraham, 390, 391; have virtually abolished the sacraments, 452; their disputes concerning God's absolute power, 476; how they stigmatized the Reformers, 501; their praying to the dead, 526; their seven sacraments, 539; ii. 388; their glorying in their long succession, i. 547; maintain the merit of good works, 572; their dulia and latria, 582; their traffic in sepulchres, 584; ii. 430; hold that the efficacy of the sacraments depends on him who consecrates them; ii. 89, 101, 118; their confession, 101; pollution of their temples, 118; their confused farago of vows, 121; their celibacy, 121, 134; their worship of images, 174; their superstitions, 235, 238; their absurd doctrine as to God's retaining the punishment while remitting the guilt of sin, 445.
Paradise, in which our first parents were originally placed, i. 113; the most fertile and pleasant part of the earth, 114; its situation, 115, 119-122; was richly replenished with every kind of fruitful trees, 115.
Parents, our first, their apostasy the ruin of the whole human race, i. 154; the skins of slain animals their first clothing, 181; why they were so clothed, 182. See *Adam. Eve.*
Parents, impious contempt of, abominable in the sight of God, i. 304; when God punishes their sins in their children, 305, 306; honour due to, 302; ii. 14, 264; are to transmit the knowledge of God's works to their children, i. 481; and to instruct them in the fear of God, 483; ii. 110; have ground to expect the grace of God to their children, i. 517; honour God has conferred on, ii. 146; are to purge their families from every stain of evil, 170; their sin in the excessive indulgence of their children, 223; duty of obedience to, 264. See *Children.*
Patience, duty of exercising, i. 432, 520; ii. 42, 67, 144, 161, 177; the cross to be borne with, ii. 102.
Patriarchs, antediluvian, their long lives, i. 229; deplored the miserable condition of mankind through Adam's fall, and the increasing wickedness of the world, 233.
Patriarchs, postdiluvian, were not men of savage manners and iron hardness of heart, ii. 30; were severely tried, 58; the land of Canaan a mirror and pledge to them of the heavenly inheritance, 91, 92; their faith in God's promise in the midst of their wanderings, 107; their imperfect knowledge of God, 201; were in the habit of reclining at table, 362; their faith always fixed on the coming of Christ, 429.
Patriarchal age, simplicity of, ii. 22, 127; chastity of, 62, 128, 131.
Peace, our just rights in some degree to be sacrificed for the sake of, i. 372, 373; the great blessing of, 434; suits for to be kindly met, ii. 75, 179. See *Concord.*
Pelagius, denied original sin, i. 154; maintained that sin proceeded from Adam by imitation, 155.
Peniel, ii. 201.
Pentateuch, the, Ptolemy king of Egypt procured translations of, into Greek, i. xlviii; authenticity of, confirmed by Egyptian antiquities. See *Egyptian Antiquities.*
People of God, the, never want enemies, i. 348; efficacy of the prayers of, 434, 516, 526; God's almighty power a ground of confidence to, 443; are often involved in the same divine judgments with the wicked, 487, 488; imperfection of the faith of, 500; ii. 206; are delivered by God at the critical moment, i. 502, 524; are in danger of disregarding the divine threatenings, 507; their

# GENERAL INDEX. 517

preciousness in the sight of God, 523; are tried according to the measure of their faith, 564; have no reason for languishing when their outward man is perishing, ii. 37; may lawfully complain of their enemies, 73; are not always governed in their actions by the Spirit of God, 85; are for the most part despised by the world, 136; in what sense God wrestles with them, 196; their deliverance delayed for the trial of their faith, 312; are strangers and pilgrims in this world, 404; difference in the way in which temporal benefits are bestowed on them and on unbelievers, 428; are purified by the divine chastisements, 471, 472. See *Faithful*.

Perfection, angelical, erroneously placed in poverty, i. 367.

Pharaoh, king of Egypt when Abraham sojourned in that country, i. 362-365.

Pharaoh, king of Egypt in Joseph's time, casts his chief butler and chief baker into prison, ii. 305; restores the chief butler to his office, 310; beheads the chief baker, 311; celebrates his birth-day, 312; his dreams, 318, 319; and their interpretation by Joseph, 324, 325; makes Joseph governor of Egypt, 328; gratuitously maintains the Egyptian priests during the famine, ii. 412.

Philistines, the, their cruelty, ii. 65.

Philosophers condemned, who in studying the works of creation are forgetful of the Creator, i. 60. See *Heathen philosophers*.

Piety, how its genuineness is proved, i. 482; a sense of, implanted in the minds of men, ii. 413.

Pious, the. See *People of God*.

Pison, the, incorrectly thought by many to be the Ganges, i. 119, 123.

Plato, character of his writings, i. xlix; ascribes reason and intelligence to the stars, 87; defends the sacredness of the marriage tie, 128, 388; his remarks on the hope of the virtuous in old age, 417; ii. 37, 324.

Pliny quoted, i. 121-123.

Plurality of persons in the Godhead, proved from the Mosaic account of the creation of man, i. 92, 183; farther proof of, 331; is not proved from the history of the destruction of Sodom and Gomorrah, 513, 531.

Poets, heathen. See *Heathen poets*.

Polygamy condemned, i. 97; inconsistent with the original divine institution of marriage, 136, 137, 424, 573; ii. 33, 142; was introduced by Lamech, a descendant of Cain, i. 217; began at an early period to prevail in every direction, ii. 77, 181, 252.

Pomponius Mela quoted, i. 121.

Poor, the, admonished, i. 369.

Pope, the, i. 307; his barbarity in imposing celibacy on the clergy, i. 551; ii. 14, 219.

Popish religion, its character, i. 446. See *Papists*.

Porphyry, his cavil in reference to the ark refuted, i. 257.

Posterity of Adam. See *Adam. Corruption of Human nature. Man. Mankind.*

Potiphar, an officer of the court of Pharaoh, king of Egypt, buys Joseph from the Midianites, ii. 274; his favour for him, 293; places him over his house and over all his substance, 294; his wife tempts Joseph, 296-298; and falsely accuses him, 300; he casts Joseph into prison, 300, 301; his anger towards Joseph is mitigated, 306.

Poverty, angelical perfection erroneously placed in, i. 367; does not want its advantages, ii. 65.

Power of God, the, is not to be estimated by human reason, i. 475; by doubting the divine promises, we sinfully detract from, 476; is not limited because he is unable to destroy the reprobate without saving the elect, 511.

Prayer, ought to be regulated by the will of God, i. 509; ii. 17, 190, 191; its answer sometimes speedily granted, and at other times delayed, ii. 19, 20; manner in which it ought to be performed, 17, 190, 191; encouragement to perseverance in, 42; ought to be accompanied with the use of means, 193; is the armour which renders us invincible in affliction, 302.

Prayers of the faithful, are heard by God, i. 434, 516, 526; ii. 19, 42; are useful to others, ii. 106.

Pride, betrayed itself in the first sin of Adam and Eve, i. 153; is with difficulty corrected, 328; its punishment, 548; is natural to the human heart, ii. 144; is the companion of

unbelief, 173; is opposed to the Gospel, 264.
Pride of the Egyptians, ii. 360, 361.
Pride of the Sodomites, i. 501.
Priesthood, Levitical, subordinate to the priesthood of Christ, i. 303.
Priests, Egyptian, were gratuitously maintained by Pharaoh during the famine, ii. 412.
Priests, Levitical, were to bless the people, i. 391; ii. 199.
Primogeniture, or birthright, advantages of, ii. 53, 208, 248.
Profession of religion. See *Religion*.
Prolepsis, a rhetorical figure, its meaning, i. 344, 356, 553; ii. 180, 187, 212, 391, 435.
Promises of God, the faith of his people established by their being repeated, i. 265; by doubting them we sinfully detract from God's power, 476; the fulfilment of them sometimes long deferred, ii. 116.
Prophecies of Scripture, are nearly all written in verse, i. 305; ii. 441.
Prophets, the ancient, excited hatred by uttering the divine threatenings, ii. 311; the true distinguished from the false, 326.
Prosperity, is to be ascribed to God, ii. 74, 151, 193, 211, 293; intoxicates men, ii. 326, 341.
Proud, the, fight against God, i. 327, 328, 331. See *Pride*.
Providence of God, is to be reposed on when God seems to be most forgetful of us, i. 276; human affairs under, 436; success in our affairs to be ascribed to, ii. 23, 112, 127; its secret influence keeps men from destroying each other, 208; watches for the salvation of the righteous when it most seems to sleep, 232; Joseph's history a beautiful example of, 260, 307, 330, 378-380; is inseparable from God's eternal counsel, 325; admirable method of the operation of, 337, 376.
Ptolemy, king of Egypt, procured the translation of the books of Moses into Greek, i. xlviii.
Punishment, a dread of, not true repentance, i. 211; its inefficacy to bring the wicked to true repentance, ii. 98; while remitting the guilt of sin, God does not retain the punishment, 445.
Purity, how it is the effect of faith, i. 195.

R

Rabbins, Jewish, referred to, i. 85, 130.
Race, a, resemblance of human life to, i. 402.
Rachel, daughter of Laban, ii. 127; is greatly beloved by Jacob, 131, 205; becomes his wife, 134; envies her sister Leah, 141; hurries Jacob into a third marriage, 142; her pride, 144; contention between her and her sister Leah, 140, 147, 148; birth of her son Joseph, 149; is willing to leave her father's house, and accompany Jacob to his own country, 167, 168; carries off her father's household gods, 169; her superstition, 170; manner in which she concealed her theft, 175; her death, 244; her burial, 245, 425, 462.
Rain, is in the hand of God, i. 80, 111, 512.
Rainbow, the, existed before the deluge, i. 299; was consecrated into a sign or pledge giving security against a second deluge, 290.
Rank, distinctions of, advantageous, i. 246.
Raven sent forth by Noah from the ark, i. 279.
Rebekah, is providentially selected by Abraham's servant as a wife for Isaac, ii. 20-23; her parents are induced to give her to Isaac in marriage, 24, 25; her departure from her father's house, 27; she meets Isaac, 29; is married to him, ib.; her sterility during the first twenty years of her married state, 40; asks counsel of God, 43; loves Jacob more than Esau, 50; her sinful stratagem to procure for Jacob his father's blessing, 84, 85, 87; her trial from Esau's purpose to murder Jacob, 101-103.
Reclining at table, a patriarchal custom, ii. 362.
Reformation. See *Calvin*. *Erasmus*.
Religion, a, is not to be rashly changed, ii. 225.
Religion, Popish, its character, i. 446. See *Papists*.
Religion, an external profession of, requisite, i. 354; ii. 71, 213, 214, 238; a sense of religion is engraven on the hearts of all men, 358.
Remission of the *fault* and of the *punishment*, a distinction unfounded, i. 178.

GENERAL INDEX. 519

Repentance, true, is not a dread of punishment, 211; a sign of, 532; never too late in this world, ii. 95; inefficacy of punishment to bring the wicked to, 98; men seldom drawn to it except by the fear of punishment, 229, 236.

Repentance of the reprobate, its character, i. 211; ii. 95. See *Esau. Judas.*

Repentance, in what sense it is ascribed to God, i. 248, 526.

Reprobate, the, represented in the person of Esau, ii. 52. See *Wicked.*

Reproofs, necessity of, ii. 443.

Rest of God on the seventh day after the creation, i. 103.

Resurrection, burial the symbol or mirror of, ii. 245, 477.

Reuben, son of Jacob and Leah, his birth, ii. 135; brings mandrakes out of the field to his mother, 146; his incest with Bilhah, his father's wife, 245; his humanity towards Joseph, 267, 350; is deprived of the rights of primogeniture by his father on his death-bed, 442, 443.

Revenge forbidden, i. 416; ii. 73, 155, 486.

Reward put for inheritance or felicity, ii. 400.

Reward of works, is a free gift of God, and not merited, i. 265, 572; ii. 302.

Rich, the, are admonished, i. 369; are prone to oppress others, ii. 66.

Riches, do not render it impossible for men to cultivate religion, i. 367; disadvantages of, 369; ii. 28, 65, 194.

Rising up put for deliberating, ii. 272; and for receiving new vigour, 390.

Robbers and murderers, their remorse of conscience, i. 210, 211.

Rulers, subjection to, not to be rashly shaken off, i. 382, 431; are not to govern proudly and tyrannically, 414, 431; our duty to them when unduly severe, 432.

S

SABBATH, original institution of, i. 105; the precept in the decalogue respecting it peculiar to the Jews, 106, 456; in what sense it was abrogated by the coming of Christ, 107.

Sabellius, his error on the doctrine of the Trinity, i. 71.

Sacrifices, their divine institution, i. 192-194, 281, 291; ii. 71, 213, 214; whence the heathen derived the custom of offering them, i. 193; the right of washing before them common among all nations, 194; were intended to teach that there is no access to God but through a Mediator, 281, 355; mode in which covenants were ratified by sacrifices, 413.

Sacrament, what it is, i. 451.

Sacraments, the end and use of, i. 298, 452; are not to be severed from God's word, 298; ii. 180; are lifeless phantoms in the Papacy, i. 452; ii. 114, 388; seven sacraments of the Papists, i. 539.

Said, put for decreed, i. 250.

Saints in heaven confirmed, i. 158.

Salem, the ancient name of Jerusalem, i. 388; another city of that name, ii. 212.

Salvation, day of, to be improved without delay, ii. 95.

Sarai, the wife of Abraham, her sterility, i. 337; is persuaded by her husband to use dissimulation, 359; her beauty, 360-362, 522; her chastity preserved by the guardianship of God, 363, 364; her criminal method for obtaining offspring by her husband, 422, 423, 425, 426; is held in contempt by Hagar, her handmaid, 427; her anger thereby excited, 227, 428, 430; seed is promised to Abraham by her, 459; her name changed from Sarai to Sarah, ib.; her unbelief, 474, 475; her falsehood, 476; is reproved by the angel, 477; was Abraham's sister in the second degree, 530; why she did not become a mother till at an advanced age, 537; her joy on the birth of Isaac, 539, 540; urges Abraham to eject Ishmael and his mother from the family, 541; was governed in this by a secret impulse of the Spirit, 543; her death, 575-577; Abraham's grief for her, 578.

Satan, made use of the serpent in seducing our first parents, i. 140, 145, 165; why his name is omitted in the Mosaic account of their fall, 141; was not created evil and wicked, 142; his craft in seducing Adam not directly but through the person of his wife, 145; what impelled him to plot the destruction of the human family, 146; his artifice in tempting the woman, 146-151; overcomes her, 151; sentence pronounced on him, 168-171 ; has set himself from the beginning to corrupt the worship of God, 223; is an ingenious contriver of falsehoods, 246, 569; is a wonderful adept at deceiving, 401 ; his wiles to be guarded against, 425 ; is God's executioner, 504 ; is the ape of God, ii. 69 ; in what way he tempts, i. 169; ii. 191, 192, 196, 246, 295.

Satiety produces ferocity, ii. 66 ; and disgust, 332.

Saturn, the planet, reference to, 86, 87.

Schismatics denounced, i. lii.

Scriptures, the, are not to be tortured to an allegorical sense, i. 257, 279, 545 ; ii. 438, 439, 461.

Scripture, the prophecies of, are nearly all written in verse, i. 305 ; ii. 441.

Security of the wicked, i. 505; ii. 54, 111; carnal, to be guarded against, ii. 234.

Seed of the woman, means her posterity generally, i. 170.

Seed of Abraham, meaning of the words, i. 171.

Seed-time and harvest secured as long as the earth endures, i. 28.

Seeking God, best method of, ii. 428.

Self-love blinds us in judging of what is right, ii. 129, 178, 224.

Self-renunciation enjoined, ii. 351.

Semiramis, i. 121 ; is said to have founded Babylon, i. 318.

Senses, the, inlets to sin, ii. 295.

Septuagint, the, greatly neglected by the heathen, i. xlviii; quoted, 131, 136, 160, 199, 242, 279, 498 ; ii. 330, 391, 418.

Sepulchre purchased by Abraham, i. 583; ii. 417.

Serpent, made use of by Satan for seducing our first parents, i. 140, 145 ; how it is called subtle, 140 ; is to be understood literally and not allegorically, 142; is said to have done what Satan did by its instrumentality, 166 ; the sentence pronounced upon it, 166-168.

Servants, male and female, termed "souls," i. 351 ; their duty when harshly treated by their masters, 431.

Servetus, maintained that Christ was the son of God, only as to his human nature, i. 75.

Seth, his birth and the piety of himself and his family, i. 223, 224 ; the offspring of Adam traced only in the Mosaic narrative through the line of Seth, because the Church was confined to his family, 227, 228, 234 ; was born, like others of Adam's children, in sin, 228, 229 ; the corruption of his descendants by intermarrying with the daughters of Cain, 237-240, 245; why his descendants are called " the sons of God," 238, 239.

Seven, the number, designates in Scripture a multitude, i. 222.

Shechem, or Sichem, i. 352 ; ii. 212, 434.

Shechem, violates the chastity of Dinah, Jacob's daughter, ii. 218 ; desires to obtain her in marriage, 219, 222; perfidy and cruelty of the sons of Jacob towards, 222-228.

Shechemites, the, their idolatry, ii. 214; facility with which they submit to be circumcised, 225 ; the perfidy and cruelty of Jacob's sons towards, 222-228, 447.

Shekel of the sanctuary, its value, i. 583.

Shem, the second son of Noah, i. 235 ; his filial piety and modesty, 302, 303; blessing pronounced on him by his father, 308; was the progenitor of the Asiatics, 313 ; the Mosaic history principally relates to his race, 314; the benediction pronounced on him did not descend to all his offspring indiscriminately, but only to the sons of Eber, 320 ; a great part of his posterity apostatized from the true worship of God, 333.

Shepherds, the occupation of, held in abomination by the Egyptians, ii. 395, 399.

Shield, God ascribes to himself the office and property of, i. 400.

Shiloh, meaning and reference of the term, ii. 453.

Sichem. See *Shechem.*

Siddim, battle fought in the vale of, i. 381.

Signs, their use, i. 298, 453 ; are not to be severed from God's word, 298 ; 420, 451; ii. 388; the faithful ascend from them to heaven, 215.

Simeon, son of Jacob, his cruelty to the Shechemites, ii. 226, 229 ; is retained in prison by his brother Joseph, 346, 348, 359 ; his cruelty

GENERAL INDEX. 521

denounced by his father on his death-bed, 444, 448.
Sin, the cause of death, i. 180; we are not compelled to its commission, 561; confession of, to be made from the heart, ii. 288, 477; its existence not only *permitted* but *ordained* by God, 378; and yet he is not the author of it, 379, 487, 488. See *Affliction*.
Sister, a term of wide signification among the Hebrews, i. 530.
Slavery, its origin, i. 351, 431, 455.
Sobriety of mind recommended, i. 151, 412; ii. 114.
Socrates referred to, i. lii.
Sodom, fertility of the plain of, i. 373; wickedness of its inhabitants, 373, 374, 483, 484, 491, 496-501; their ingratitude, 394; their cruelty, 499; their pride, 501; it did not perish by chance, 480; its approaching destruction revealed to Abraham, 479, 486-491; and to Lot, 503, 504; is destroyed by fire and brimstone from heaven, 512; why infants were involved in its destruction, 513; God's design in recording its destruction, 482. See *Gomorrah*.
Son of God, the, all things created by, i. 74, 75; Christ, according to Servetus, only the son of God as to his human nature, 75.
Songs sung at the ingathering of the harvest, ii. 355.
Sons of God, why Seth's descendants are so designated, i. 238, 239; a twofold class of, exist in the Church, 449.
Sophocles quoted, ii. 401.
Souls put for male and female servants, i. 351.
Souls of men, whether they are propagated by descent, i. 156.
Sovereignty of God in distributing his gifts, ii. 431. See *Election*.
Speaking to the heart put for addressing courteously, ii. 249.
Speculations, erratic, to be avoided in interpreting the Scriptures, i. 198.
Spirit of God, the, his agency in the creation of the world, i. 73; his grace necessary for the mortification of sin, 204.
Splendour in kings and princes not to be altogether condemned, ii. 328.
Stapulensis, Jacobus Faber, translator of the first printed French version of the Scriptures, i. xvi.

Stars, the, made to shine by night on the fourth day of the creation, i. 83; reason and intelligence ascribed to them by Plato, 87.
Steuchus, Augustinus, quoted, i. 70.
Stoics, their opinion that it is a heroic virtue not to be touched with compassion, condemned, ii. 375.
Stones, covenants anciently confirmed by raising a heap of, ii. 179.
Strabo quoted, i. 121.
Subjection to magistrates, not to be rashly shaken off, i. 382; is enjoined, ii. 403.
Subterfuges to which sinners resort, i. 164.
Succoth, two cities of this name, ii. 212.
Sun, the, why herbs and trees were created before, i. 82, 83; advantages derived from the course of the sun and moon, 84, 85.
Superstition, is natural to the human mind, ii. 170; infatuates men, 175; confounds things sacred and profane, 181; is pertinacious and rebellious, 236; pride of, 361.
Suspicion, is sometimes excusable, ii. 366.
Swearing, form of, by lifting the hand, i. 394; and by putting the hand under the thigh of the imposer of the oath, ii. 12, 417.
Sychar, formerly called Shechem, ii. 434.
Symbols of the Levitical economy, their design, i. 186.
Sympathy produced by common sufferings, ii. 309.

T

TABLE, reclining at, a patriarchal custom, ii. 362.
Tamar, the wife of Er, the son of Judah, ii. 281; is treated perfidiously and cruelly by Judah, 282-286; is guilty of incest with him, 283; gives birth to twins, 289.
Temperance to be exercised in the conjugal state, i. 239; and in eating and drinking, 491, 542.
Temples, Popish, their pollution, ii. 118.
Temporal judgments were more commonly inflicted under the former than under the present dispensation, ii. 280.
Tempting, in what sense applied to God, i. 561; ii. 196.
Temptations, faith secures the victory

over, i. 562; are not to be rushed into, ii. 59.

Ten, the number, put for many, ii. 165.

Terah, the father of Abraham, leaves his native soil and proceeds to Canaan in company with his son, i. 338, 340-346.

Terror of God which the reprobates have, ii. 118, 177.

Tertullian quoted, i. 293.

Thanksgiving commended, i. 281, 308, 353, 556, 571; ii. 23, 26, 68, 118, 135, 186, 201, 243, 332.

"That," in Scripture, oftener denotes the consequence than the cause, i. 483.

Thorns and briers, their production from the earth, a consequence of the sin of man, i. 104.

Threatenings of God, the, are intended for the elect as well as for the reprobate, i. 254; are despised by the latter, 505; are sometimes disregarded by the faithful, 507; design of, 526.

Tiberius Cæsar, a celebrated saying of, ii. 414.

Tigris, the, is called Hiddekel, i. 118, 121-123.

Tithes, were given by Abraham to Melchizedek, i. 392; right of the tribe of Levi to, under the law, 393; Jacob vows them to God, ii. 124; were exacted by kings in various places, 414.

Tongues, confusion of, at the building of the Tower of Babel, i. 325, 326, 329-331.

Tranquillity of mind, how best secured, ii. 483.

Translation of Enoch, i. 231, 232.

Transubstantiation, i. 391.

Tree of knowledge of good and evil, why so called, and why forbidden to our first parents, i. 118, 125, 126; inducements they had to obedience, 127.

Tree of life, its sacramental character, i. 116; was held by Augustine and Eucherius to be a figure of Christ, 117; supposed by some to have had the power of perpetuating the life of the body, ib.; our first parents after the fall debarred from the fruit of, 183.

Trees and herbs, why created before the sun and moon, i. 82.

Trent, Council of, ii. 109.

Tribes of Israel. See under each name.

Trinity, the, error of Sabellius on the doctrine of, i. 71. See *Plurality of persons in the Godhead.*

Troubles mixed with the blessings of this earthly life, ii. 65.

True Church of God, distinction between it and hypocritical church, i. 547.

Truth of God is not to be aided by falsehood, ii. 88.

Tyrants, on submission to the authority of, i. 382.

Tyndale's version of the Bible, i. xvii.

Tyre, the king of, compared to a chief angel, i. 187.

UNBELIEF, the root of the first sin of Adam and Eve, i. 152, 153; is sometimes borne with and sometimes severely punished by God, 477; pride the companion of, ii. 173.

Uncircumcised. See *Circumcision.*

Ur of the Chaldeans, origin of the name, i. 337.

V

VEILS, origin of the Egyptian ladies wearing, i. 362; brides in the East given veiled to their husbands, ii. 29.

Vengeance of God, is to be denounced by the ministers of the Gospel, ii. 311.

Verse, the prophecies of Scripture nearly all written in, i. 305; ii. 441.

Vision, one of the ways in which God manifested himself to the prophets, i. 399, 526; ii. 69, 70, 112, 166, 240, 387; a special mark of the divine glory stamped on the vision, i. 401; ii. 69.

Vowing is not to be indiscriminately condemned, ii. 121; the abominable vows of Papists, ib.

Vulgate quoted, i. 135, 136, 147, 163, 164, 170, 173, 279, 284, 381.

W

WALKING with God, what it means, i. 230, 253.

Walking before God, its meaning, i. 443; ii. 426.

Washing before sacrifices common among all nations, i. 194.

Washing of feet a custom in the East, i. 471.

GENERAL INDEX.     523

Way of the Lord, what it denotes, i. 482.
Wealth. See *Riches*.
Wealthy, the. See *Rich*.
Whittingham, William, brother-in-law to Calvin, was the author of the Geneva version of the Bible, i. xvii.
Wicked, the, character of their repentance, i. 211; ii. 95, 108, 109; make the offences of others a pretext for indulgence in sin, i. 302; their trouble in death, 418; their obstinacy in sin, 552; ii. 299; despise God's threatenings, i. 505; their security, ib.; ii. 54, 111; are forgetful of God, 101; are not able altogether to despise his grace, 108; their terror of God, 118, 177; judge of others by their own dispositions, 179; their cruelty restrained by God, 207; often do good to the faithful contrary to their intention, 253; are devoted to destruction, 305. See *Reprobate*.
Wickedness of man is not excused because God may overrule it for good, ii. 379.
Will of God, why manifested to us, i. 481; nothing done without it, ii. 378, 487.
Winds, the, are governed by God, i. 277.
Wine, introduction of its use, i. 300; may be used in moderation, ii. 362, 363.
Wisdom, first step of, to ascribe nothing to ourselves, ii. 323.
Wives, their duty to obey their husbands, i. 474, 533; ii. 300, 301.
Woman, a contraction for womb-man, i. 135.
Woman, the, why denied by Paul to be the image of God, i. 96; was created to be the help-meet of man, 128, 129; was necessary to man even in a state of innocency, 130, 131; her subjection to her husband, 172; effects of Eve's first transgression upon her, ib.
Woman, seed of the, meaning of, i. 171.
Women, rarely mentioned in Scripture genealogies, i. 573; ii. 148.
Word, or promise of God, to be trusted in, 267, 276; is better than external signs, 299; is conjoined with symbols, 421, 451; ought not to be separated from his power, 476; tranquillizes the mind, ii. 70; is sometimes forgotten in affliction, 340; faith founded upon, 422.
Word of God, or the Scriptures, the most certain rule of our life, i. 539; ii. 87, 134; ought not to be adulterated, 311. See *Scriptures*.
Works, good, what is necessary to their being so, i. 194, 195, 409; do not justify, 265, 407, 572; the grace of Christ alone gives them worth, 266; the rewards of them are the rewards of grace, 265, 572; ii. 302.
World, the, its eternity maintained by Aristotle, i. xlix; not eternal, 70, 109; the error that God created it in a moment refuted, 78, 103; why God took the space of six days in creating it, 78; its continual preservation to be ascribed to him, 103, 104; the physical disorders in it the fruit of sin, 104, 177. See *Creation*, &c.
World, the allurements of, to be guarded against, ii. 332.
Worldly advantages are not to be suffered to draw us aside from the path of duty, ii. 112.
Worship of God, faith necessary in order to its being acceptable, i. 282; use of, ii. 71; early and extensive apostasy of mankind from it after the deluge, 166-170, 237.
Worshippers of God, the true, distinguished from hypocrites, i. 344.

Y

YEAR, the, began, according to the Jewish calendar, in March, i. 264; was divided by the Jews into six parts, 286.

Z

ZEAL, preposterous, ii. 87.
Zebulon, character of the tribe of, predicted by Jacob on his death-bed, ii. 461.